RE-VISIONING FAMILY THERAPY

Re-Visioning Family Therapy

Race, Culture, and Gender in Clinical Practice

SECOND EDITION

edited by **Monica McGoldrick**
Kenneth V. Hardy

THE GUILFORD PRESS
New York   London

616.89156
R327
2008

©2008 The Guilford Press
A Division of Guilford Publications, Inc.
72 Spring Street, New York, NY 10012
www.guilford.com

Printed in the United States of America

This book is printed on acid-free paper.

Last digit is print number: 9   8   7   6   5   4   3   2   1

Library of Congress Cataloging-in-Publication Data

Re-visioning family therapy : race, culture, and gender in clinical practice /
[edited by] Monica McGoldrick, Kenneth V. Hardy.—2nd ed.
    p. ; cm.
  Includes bibliographical references and index.
  ISBN 978-1-59385-427-0 (hardcover : alk. paper)
  1. Family psychotherapy—United States. 2. Minorities—Mental health—
United States. 3. Sexual minorities—Mental health—United States. 4. Cultural
psychiatry—United States. I. McGoldrick, Monica. II. Hardy, Kenneth V.
  [DNLM: 1. Family Therapy. 2. Cultural Diversity. 3. Minority Groups—
psychology. WM 430.5.F2 R453 2008]
  RC488.5.R497 2008
  616.89′156—dc22

                                                            2008010076

As we were putting the finishing touches on this book,
we learned of the tragic and untimely death
of our brother in spirit, teacher, innovator,
and, most importantly, friend, Michael White.
We would like to dedicate this book
to Michael and Cheryl for sharing your lives with us
and for all that you have given to us
during our decades of friendship. We will never forget.
—M. M. and K. V. H.

To Margaret Pfeiffer Bush and Aunt Mamie Cahalane,
and all those like them,
whose invisibility was a hidden shame
and who bravely transformed the constraints of their lives
into a love that inspires and carries us through life.
—M. M.

To my family . . .
both those with whom I share blood and ancestry
as well as those with whom I share
only a common ancestry
. . . for teaching me the life-transcending lessons of survival,
humility, and perseverance. Your quiet dignity, sacrifice, and
grace have been a source of strength and have provided clarity
of vision and purpose to my life.
—K. V. H.

About the Editors

Monica McGoldrick, LCSW, PhD (h.c.), Director of the Multicultural Family Institute in Highland Park, New Jersey, is also Associate Professor of Clinical Psychiatry at the University of Medicine and Dentistry of New Jersey–Robert Wood Johnson Medical School. Her videotape of clinical work with a multicultural family around issues of loss is one of the most widely respected in the field. Several of her books have become best-selling classics, including *Ethnicity and Family Therapy*; *The Expanded Family Life Cycle*; *Genograms: Assessment and Intervention*; *Women in Families*; *Living Beyond Loss: Death in the Family*; and this text, *Re-Visioning Family Therapy: Race, Culture, and Gender in Clinical Practice*. Her book *You Can Go Home Again: Reconnecting with Your Family* translates her ideas about family relationships for a popular audience, using examples such as Beethoven, Groucho Marx, Sigmund Freud, and the Kennedys. Ms. McGoldrick has received the American Family Therapy Academy's award for Distinguished Contribution to Family Therapy Theory and Practice. An internationally known author, she speaks widely on culture, class, gender, the family life cycle, and other topics.

Kenneth V. Hardy, PhD, is Professor of Family Therapy at Drexel University in Philadelphia and Director of the Eikenberg Institute for Relationships in New York City. He is a former Professor of Family Therapy at Syracuse University, where he also served as the Director of Clinical Training and Research and Chairperson of the Department of Child and Family Studies. Dr. Hardy is also the former Director of the Center for Children, Families, and Trauma at the internationally renowned Ackerman Institute for the Family in New York City. He maintains a private practice in New York City, specializing in family therapy. His work has received considerable public acclaim in both the electronic and print media, with appearances on *The Oprah Winfrey Show*, *Dateline NBC*, ABC's *20/20*, and PBS.

Contributors

Nuha Abudabbeh, PhD, World Bank, Washington, DC

Norma Akamatsu, MSW, Northampton Institute for Family Therapy, Northampton, Massachusetts

Makungu M. Akinyela, PhD, LMFT, Family Center of South Dekalb, Decatur, Georgia, and Department of African American Studies, Georgia State University, Atlanta, Georgia

Lisa Berndt, LCSW, Center for the Vulnerable Child, Children's Hospital and Research Center, Oakland, California

Nancy Boyd-Franklin, PhD, Graduate School of Applied and Professional Psychology, Rutgers, The State University of New Jersey, Piscataway, New Jersey

Nollaig O'Reilly Byrne, MD, Department of Child and Family Psychiatry, Mater Misericordia Hospital, Dublin, Ireland

Chloe Carmichael, MA, Department of Clinical Psychology, Long Island University, Brooklyn, New York

Ken Dolan-Del Vecchio, LMFT, LCSW, SPHR, private practice, Morristown, New Jersey

Celia Jaes Falicov, PhD, private practice and Department of Psychiatry, University of California at San Diego, San Diego, California

Linda Stone Fish, PhD, Department of Marriage and Family Therapy, Syracuse University, Syracuse, New York

John Folwarski, MSW, Raritan Bay Mental Health Center, Perth Amboy, New Jersey

Peter Fraenkel, PhD, Center for Work and Family, Ackerman Institute for the Family, and Department of Clinical Psychology, The City College of the City University of New York, New York, New York

Nydia Garcia-Preto, LCSW, Multicultural Family Institute, Highland Park, New Jersey

Robert-Jay Green, PhD, Rockway Institute for LGBT Research and Public Policy, and California School of Professional Psychology, Alliant International University, San Francisco, California

MaryAnna Domokos-Cheng Ham, EdD, Family Therapy Program, University of Massachusetts Boston, Boston, Massachusetts

Kenneth V. Hardy, PhD, Eikenberg Institute for Relationships, New York, New York, and Department of Family Therapy, Drexel University, Philadelphia, Pennsylvania

Paulette Moore Hines, PhD, Office of Prevention Services and Research, University Behavioral HealthCare, University of Medicine and Dentistry of New Jersey, Piscataway, New Jersey

Hugo Kamya, PhD, School of Social Work, Simmons College, Boston, Massachusetts

Jodie Kliman, PhD, Massachusetts School of Professional Psychology and the Boston Institute for Culturally Accountable Practices, Boston, Massachusetts

Robin LaDue, PhD, private practice, Renton, Washington

Tracey A. Laszloffy, PhD, private practice, Norwich, Connecticut

John J. Lawless, PhD, Utica Unit, Empire State College, Utica, New York

Fernando López-Colón, PhD, Ann Arbor Center for the Family, Ann Arbor, Michigan

Jayne Mahboubi, PsyD, LCSW, ACSW, private practice and Impaired Professionals Program, Ridgeview Institute, Smyrna, Georgia

Nasim Mahboubi, BA, volunteer service, Bahá'í World Centre, Haifa, Israel

Vanessa McAdams-Mahmoud, LCSW, private practice, Decatur, Georgia

Imelda Colgan McCarthy, MSW, PhD, private practice, and PhD Programmes, University College Dublin, Dublin, Ireland

Monica McGoldrick, LCSW, PhD (h.c.), Multicultural Family Institute, Highland Park, New Jersey

Peggy McIntosh, PhD, Wellesley College Centers for Research on Women, Wellesley, Massachusetts

Marsha Pravder Mirkin, PhD, Department of Psychology, Lasell College, Newton, Massachusetts

Matthew R. Mock, PhD, Center for Multicultural Development, California Institute for Mental Health, Sacramento, California; Department of Psychology, John F. Kennedy University, Pleasant Hill, California; Alliant International University, California School of Professional Psychology, San Francisco, California; and private clinical and consulting practice, Berkeley, California

Elijah C. Nealy, MDiv, LCSW, Lesbian, Gay, Bisexual and Transgender Community Center, New York, New York

Elaine Pinderhughes, MSW, Graduate School of Social Work, Boston College, Boston, Massachusetts

Tazuko Shibusawa, PhD, LCSW, Silver School of Social Work, New York University, New York, New York

Carlos E. Sluzki, MD, College of Health and Human Services and Institute for Conflict Analysis and Resolution, George Mason University, Fairfax, Virginia, and Department of Psychiatry and Behavioral Sciences, School of Medicine and Health Sciences, George Washington University, Washington, DC

David Trimble, PhD, Department of Psychiatry, Boston University School of Medicine, and Center for Multicultural Training in Psychology and the Boston Institute for Culturally Accountable Practices, Boston, Massachusetts

Froma Walsh, MSW, PhD, Chicago Center for Family Health and Department of Psychiatry, Pritzker School of Medicine, University of Chicago, Chicago, Illinois

Marlene F. Watson, PhD, Programs in Couple and Family Therapy, College of Nursing and Health Professions, Drexel University, Philadelphia, Pennsylvania

Preface

This book's goal is to transform the focus of our work beyond the interior of the family, so that we can begin to see how our clients' lives are constrained by larger societal structures and develop new ways of working based on a more contextual understanding of ourselves, our society, our history, and our clients' lives.

We have been struggling to envision theory and practice that would be a part of transforming our field to see our clients and ourselves more clearly and to provide services that are more healing—that offer a sense of hope and belonging for all who seek our help. While our companion volume *Ethnicity and Family Therapy*, now in its third edition, begins with the lens of ethnicity in its exploration of culture, *Re-Visioning Family Therapy: Race, Culture, and Gender in Clinical Practice* explores the intersections of different cultural perspectives (ethnicity, class, race, gender, sexual orientation, and religion) in viewing families and family therapy from more inclusive cultural perspectives.

The aim of this book has been to provide in one relatively short, accessible volume a broad range of brief contributions by many of those who have been working to "re-vision" the family therapy field through a cultural lens. The chapters in this volume are reflective of the paradigmatic shift that we hope will take place in our field. We have worked assiduously to include chapters that expand our definition of knowledge from an exclusive reliance on evidence-based, scientifically tested practice to one that also includes subjective knowledge. Creating space for the inclusion of personal stories of suffering, subjugation, and strife born out of experiences with oppression honors a different kind of knowledge. There is great wisdom in learning from the experiences of those relegated to the margins of our society. The book includes many personal stories, a few of them known over the years to some of us, but now available for a wider audience, which help us pay attention to those who have been hidden from history. We consider it important to create space for personal stories and experiences because of how our history may both enrich and hinder our work as therapists, and this is central to our view of re-visioning family therapy.

We hope that this new edition will be another step toward finding ways to contain opposites, contradictions, and ambiguities—not oversimplifying the issues and at the same time not obfuscating the prejudices and oppression that are defining and destroying us.

Each author was given frustratingly little space and asked to present a few key ideas of clinical relevance in a reader-friendly format to contextualize the oppressions that are its focus and to suggest re-visions for our clinical work. We applaud the authors for their courage to contend with these difficult issues and rejoice in them as our cohorts, going through life with us, knowing we are not yet clear about how these power dimensions operate on us, but striving with each other's help to see the road more clearly.

Re-Visioning Family Therapy is intended to be exciting and suggestive rather than comprehensive in its articulation of where we need to go in our work. Most of the material is intentionally personal. We want to make clear how hidden aspects of our history have influenced our need to change the future. Our ideas have evolved from our frustrations with the traditional boundaries of the field and our wish to expand our vision to see more clearly where we may go. This book has been an opportunity to push our own and each other's boundaries in hopes of helping to transform our field to more contextual work with clients. We trust the reader will give us the benefit of the doubt, realizing that many of these ideas are still in progress, awaiting the leavening of future conversations to better see the issues. We know we have inadvertently left out or marginalized some in this book and will continue to push ourselves to learn from our "sins of omission" in the future. We hope this second edition will soon be out of date again, as the ideas expressed become commonplace and accepted practice. When this re-visioning occurs we will be in the fortunate position of once more trying to reformulate the ideas to accommodate the evolving process. We hope this book will provide a small window into the new world of possibilities.

PART I. THEORETICAL PERSPECTIVES

Like the other institutions of our society, family therapy has been structured in ways to support the dominant value system and keep invisible certain hidden organizing principles of our lives, including class, race, gender, and sexual orientation. The chapters in the first section, indeed in the book as a whole, evolved out of the work many in our field are doing to incorporate those hidden dimensions and to transform our definitions of "home" and "family" so that all of us may feel safe and included. Together these chapters offer a framework for the possibilities of re-visioning family therapy from a contextual point of view.

In the opening chapter we locate this re-visioning in the history of the family therapy field in general. Following the path established by Peggy McIntosh in the field of education, we try to contextualize the history and possible future of our field. McIntosh's framework provides a useful tool for assessing where our field is as well as where it is that we ultimately must get to during this re-visioning process.

The next two chapters, by Celia Jaes Falicov and Carlos Sluzki, address the complexity of culture and cultural identity in relation to migration, the complexities of transnational families, and issues of loss, adaptation, and network reconstruction. As we pulled together our ideas for this book, issues of immigration dominated the national news and raised an array of thorny clinical issues regarding family therapy with populations who are increasingly non-U.S. born, non-English speaking, and from countries often considered "third world" or whose citizenry is believed to have little to offer this country. We believe that the ideas discussed by both Falicov and Sluzki will be enormously helpful to all who work with immigrant families, both documented and nondocumented.

Next, Tracey Laszloffy lays out the dimension of class, one of the essential and until now most invisible elements of re-visioning family therapy from a cultural perspective. It goes unacknowledged that many groups in society are not represented in our institutions and do not have the same entitlements to participate even in our world of family therapy. It goes unsaid that where you come from does matter; that you cannot shed your past, become whatever you want, or move up classwise just through hard work and desire. This chapter addresses directly the therapeutic implications of class relations and invites us as therapists to consider the ways in which our work is shaded by the nuances of class.

Froma Walsh and Kenneth Hardy, in their respective chapters, provide very provocative and thoughtful discussions of two of the most poignant, volatile, and sensitive issues integral to the process of re-visioning: religion/ spirituality and race. Religion and spirituality play a powerfully influential role in virtually all areas of family life. Yet having a critical discussion about religion is not only difficult to do, it is often considered inappropriate, sacrilegious, and taboo. We believe religion is a salient variable because it influences many of the more controversial issues that we, as a society, seem to grapple with passionately on a daily basis. Family-related issues such as same-gender marriages, abortion, masturbation, premarital sex, mother employment, and childrearing practices ignite strong feelings, even seemingly irreconcilable acrimony, because they are all connected to religion. Just a few days prior to writing this preface, Republican presidential candidate and former Governor of Massachusetts Mitt Romney, a practicing Mormon, delivered a major speech addressing religion and faith to quiet rising concerns regarding his religious beliefs and whether he could be trusted as an elected leader. Similarly, Democratic presidential candidate Barack Obama was forced to claim and reclaim his Christian identity amid numerous allegations that he was really a Muslim. Although it is seldom acknowledged overtly, religion is a major organizing principle in our society. Walsh's chapter is a firm but gentle reminder of the role that religion and spirituality play in our everyday lives. Race, like religion, is also an important factor that must be placed at the forefront of the agenda for re-visioning family therapy. The 2008 presidential campaign was a poignant reminder of the subtleties and complexities associated with race in the United States. While Obama's nomination for President was, on the one hand, heralded as a measurable sign of colorblindness in our society, it also demonstrated just how much we are still organized by race. Throughout the 2008 presidential campaign, we were amazed how much Obama had to project a nonracial identity in order to be regarded as a a serious candidate who would represent all Americans, not just African Americans. He seldom talked about race unless he was coerced to do so in respoonse to a personal attack. Even though Obama made concerted efforts to avoid the mentioning of race, it was still an integral part of the discourse, sometimes overtly but mostly by innuendo and the use of code words. As race slipped into the campaign, it highlighted the sharp differences that often exist between the racially based perceptions of whites and African Americans. Michele Obama made a reference to "feeling proud to be an American for the first time." Most Blacks understood her position, agreed, and identified with her statement, while many whites considered her statement to be indicative of her and her husband's lack of patriotism. Hardy reminds us that race always influences our perceptions and ultimately our relationships both in and outside of the family. We must not fail to see race. Vanessa McAdams-Mahmoud's chapter supports this thesis regarding the omnipresence of race, as she provides an incisive analysis of the types of adaptations that couples and families make in response to racial and other forms of oppression. McAdams-Mahmoud's chapter, like all of the others in this text, reminds us once again of the importance of using a cultural lens to help us see that family behavior is tightly interwoven with the sociocultural context in which it occurs.

PART II. CULTURAL LEGACIES AND STORIES: THERAPISTS' EXPERIENCES

This book's attempt to re-vision families and family therapy has led us to seek new, more inclusive ways to discuss our work. Personal narratives are a major part of this attempt to shift our paradigm. From Murray Bowen's first account of his own family at a 1967 research meeting, which stunned the field by breaking the rules of academic and professional discourse, we have gradually been stretching and transforming the boundaries of our dialogues to create more inclusive ways of thinking about our work. Clearly, the individualistic models of "scientific" discourse about therapy have proven inadequate to the realm of healing. These models are of limited relevance in a world where our lives are so profoundly interconnected. It is often through personal narratives that we may learn most about those aspects of our experience that have not fit into our theoretical and clinical models. These stories may be key to liberating us toward new visions of our work.

The authors of this section have focused on giving voice to experiences that have generally been marginalized in the main cultural stories of our society. My (M. M.) chapter, "Finding a Place Called 'Home,' " offers reflections of a lifelong journey to develop a deeper and more complex understanding of myself as a cultural being. In a sense this section is devoted to all of our respective journeys to find home. In so doing we share our triumphs and our tribulations. Interestingly, the process of finding home involves each of us, as a fundamental part of the existential search, identifying and claiming disavowed parts of our selves that we have to make peace with as part of the journey.

Elaine Pinderhughes's classic chapter on her research on her own family explores the silenced history of white exploitation and internalized racism in her own Black and white ancestors. Her story is a remarkable unpacking of the multigenerational traumatic impact of racism on a family. Fernando López-Colón's story of his search for his past and his identity in his lost mother's story is a remarkable example of the hidden oppressions of colonized groups and of the power of uncovering the submerged cultural dimensions of one's history. It is also a striking example of the interface of racial and cultural oppression and mental illness. Marlene Watson provides a gripping and heartfelt account of what it means to grow up as an African American female in an oppressive society where societal messages regarding race, class, and gender often collide. As Watson enlightens us, the messages that women receive, particularly Black women, are crazy-making and often laced with painful issues of loss.

Jayne and Nasim Mahboubi offer an interesting intergenerational (mother–daughter) description of their perspectives on their biracial African American–Iranian family. We believe this chapter will be particularly elucidating as the international tensions of the Middle East intensify. With the government of the United States increasing focus on terrorism and the "axis of evil," xenophobia and widespread Islamophobia and misinformation about the Middle East are rampant. The Mahboubis' story offers a personal and humanistic look at what it means to transcend racial, religious, and national boundaries to make a meaningful connection with a feared "other."

John Folwarski's personal recollection of a childhood in a Polish orphanage turns out to be a profound reflection of the effects of Polish subordination in European history as well as a story of the impact of immigrant cultural disruption. Folwarski's story is also an indirect testimonial to other salient themes that are replete in many of the stories told in this volume: stories of belonging and disconnection, stories of home and homelessness, as well as stories of suffering and survival.

The other authors in this section—Lisa Berndt, Jodie Kliman, David Trimble, Linda Stone Fish, MaryAnna Domokos-Cheng Ham, Nuha Abudabbeh, and John Lawless—all share stories of cultural legacies and their recurring efforts to integrate the frayed threads of their histories into their contemporary lives. Berndt's pathway to finding home required her to come to terms with the rabid manifestations of racism that she was exposed to as a child growing up in Texas. Acknowledging and claiming this ugly part of her past was in many ways a necessary precursor to the modern-day clarity that she brings to her anti-racism work. Her story, along with John Lawless's account of what it meant to grow up in a racist family, should provide inspiration to other White and majority-group therapists regarding how the process of embracing disavowed parts of our cultural legacies can liberate and motivate us as advocates for social justice.

Linda Stone Fish, a gifted teacher and therapist, provides an in-depth look at how issues associated with her Jewish identity and that of a Palestinian graduate student manage to creep into the sacred space of the classroom and graduate education. Her chapter provides a poignant discussion of the importance of being able to see the world through the eyes of those we consider "other." Abudabbeh's chapter offers a rare but important overview of her Muslim Arab identity and how all of the parts of her world are integrated.

Jodie Kliman and David Trimble's chapter is not a story about their efforts to integrate parts of their ethnic/racial or religious heritage. Instead, they share the grief of parents who have endured one of the most painful losses imaginable, the untimely loss of a child. Kliman and Trimble discuss how they, as loving and dedicated Jewish parents, coped with the loss of their beloved son, Jacob, who had become a fundamentalist Christian, and how they use his death as an inspiration for transformation. We are grateful to David and Jodie for the model they have provided to all of us of what it really means to build bridges across religious and other cultural divides.

And, finally, MaryAnna Domokos-Cheng Ham's chapter offers a critical and insightful examination of the life experiences of a multiracial person searching for a sense of belonging. In a society that is obsessed with binary notions of race, this chapter brings a much needed visibility and attention to the challenges and triumphs of what it means to be a person of mixed-race heritage.

I (M. M.) have told aspects of my own story, trying to separate out some of the threads of privilege from those of oppression in a journey to find the meaning of the concept "home." In sharing aspects of my own story I tried to dissect the complexities of racial and class privilege in relation to a history of gender and ethnic oppression. All of the chapters in Part II highlight a reconnection with history, personal and cultural, and provide an impressive model of the power to challenge those who would deny us access to our history.

PART III. RACIAL IDENTITY AND RACISM: IMPLICATIONS FOR THERAPY

Typically, discussions of culture and racism focus on the marginalized group as the "other." Often, whiteness, and the multitudinous ways in which it shapes interactions, both inside and outside of families, remains invisible. Re-visioning our field will require that we explore instead those who see themselves as the norm or who have established the norms. The chapters included in this section are attempts to deconstruct the dominant group.

This section begins with Hardy and Laszloffy's examination of pro-racist ideology, which exposes all of the subtle, unintentional, but harmful ways in which our attitudes, beliefs, and behaviors support racism and the oppression of those who are targeted. We have then included Peggy McIntosh's classic challenge to our "invisible knapsack of White privilege," part of her crucial series of articles that have helped us to begin re-visioning race as well as gender in the field of education. McIntosh's chapter takes the lofty, virtually abstract concept of white privilege and simplifies it in a way that makes its impact visible in the most mundane everyday experiences. Ken Dolan-Del Vecchio offers a critique of white male dominance, and considers what must change so that white men can be collaborative partners with everyone else in families and communities in the 21st century.

In her chapter Nydia Garcia-Preto takes a new and fresh look at the ever-challenging issues of multiracial identity and the complexities, pitfalls, and strategies associated with bridging two or more worlds.

Tracey Laszloffy builds on the ideas discussed by Garcia-Preto and invites the reader behind a metaphorical, one-way mirror to witness and consider the array of thorny clinical issues that must be considered when providing therapy to mixed-race couples. With its focus on deconstructing whiteness, challenging white privilege, and working toward collaboration, Part III highlights a significant facet in the transformation of family therapy.

PART IV. IMPLICATIONS FOR CLINICAL PRACTICE

The chapters in this section each attempt to focus on specific clinical issues for particular cultural groups. They are meant to be suggestive rather than comprehensive, indicating the subtlety and complexity of our cases, when considered through a cultural filter. Each of the chapters in this section offers a re-visioning perspective by moving the subject under consideration "from margin to center," in bell hooks's phrase. They use the group's own frame of reference for assessment and intervention, challenging our field's dominant notions of clinical practice. We believe the process of locating oneself and using one's personal story as a frame of reference for our clinical work is essential to the re-visioning process.

Elijah Nealy examines the much-neglected area of lesbian and family life and the need for therapists to understand the particular challenges facing those who live within a novel or marginalized family configuration. Nealy invites the reader to see how critical it is for us as a field and for society to rethink our traditional notions of family with questions of who is included in such definitions and who remains invisible and marginalized.

The chapter by Marsha Pravder Mirkin and Hugo Kamya addresses the profound disruptions of migration, when families belong to more than one culture as most families in the United States do, and suggests some of the larger implications of considering the complexity of biculturality, difference, and acculturation. If we read them carefully, they can help us rethink the very nature of our identity. Instead of measuring immigrants as "others," we will use their experience to re-vision our very notions of assessment and intervention.

Paulette Moore Hines discusses hope as an effective tool of assessment and intervention. She examines issues of transcendence, spirituality, hope, and resilience, which have long been eschewed in our theory and practice. For thousands of years such ideas have been the primary resources for people in emotional distress. It is high time we reintegrate this dimension into our conceptual formulations. The belief in something beyond our individuality and our personal self-interest is our only hope to have a future. We trust that in the next few years this area will begin to receive the attention it deserves, as more therapy incorporates transcendent ideas into our clinical assessment of families under stress and in our approaches to healing.

Nancy Boyd-Franklin explores the complex interaction of racial identity issues, racism, and trauma through the example of the U.S. response to Hurricane Katrina as it affected the lives of African Americans.

We must also develop transformative intervention models based on a re-visioning of families from a contextual perspective. Imelda Colgan McCarthy and Nollaig O'Reilly Byrne have been developing their Fifth Province model for many years. They illustrate their Fifth Province model, the creativity of their thinking, and work with a complex and tragic case example.

Makungu Akinyela's chapter highlights both his creativity and his cultural sensitivity in the treatment of African American couples. He introduces an African-centered model, Testament Therapy, to our readers as a therapeutic approach to working effectively with African American couples while honoring their racial and cultural traditions and legacies.

Tazuko Shibusawa's chapter, along with several others in this section, encourage us to think more broadly about race as an integral part of the re-visioning process. Her examination of biracial couples moves the discussion of race beyond the normal binary notions of Black and white and provides an in-depth discussion of the salient factors to consider and to challenge when providing couple treatment across racial boundaries. Her discussion of biracial couples of Asian descent sheds light on a group that is often invisible in the many conversations regarding race as well as raising important issues about couple therapy in general. Bringing light to the invisible has to be a hallmark of the re-visioning of family therapy.

The chapters by Fraenkel, Carmichael, LaDue, and Green all redirect our attention to those prone to being forgotten or overlooked in discussions of family therapy. Fraenkel and Carmichael offer the reader a window into the world of families who are homeless. The compassion and creativity that they bring to the work is refreshing and instructive and pricks our consciousness. Homelessness is rarely discussed in family therapy circles, yet countless numbers of families are affected.

LaDue's chapter is an informative and provocative overview of Native American families and culture. Her chapter serves as a salient reminder of how easy it is to "forget" and why we should all be dedicated to remembering. She offers invaluable insight to a host of critical factors that underpin working with Native American families. Robert-Jay Green's chapter on gay and lesbian couples provides an array of practical information that will be helpful for working more effectively with lesbian and gay couples.

PART V. IMPLICATIONS FOR TRAINING

The chapters in this section are devoted to providing cutting-edge ideas for what graduate programs and training institutes must do to prepare the next generation of family therapists, with an eye toward cultural competency. The re-visioning of family therapy requires programs, faculty, and supervisors to reject long-held objectives of training that is ostensibly color blind, gender free, classless, and oblivious to sexual orientation.

The chapters by Norma Akamatsu and Matthew Mock both provide state-of-the-art strategies to invite trainees to think critically about issues of social justice, power, and multiculturalism. My (K. V. H.) chapter, "On Becoming a GEMM Therapist: Work Harder, Be Smarter, and *Never* Discuss Race," is a satirical account of the powerful but unclaimed messages that students of color have to adhere to in order to be accepted in the field. GEMM is an acronym for Good Effective Mainstream Minority, a status that can best be achieved by denying one's race and the meanings attached to it, to be considered acceptable in mainstream society. It is our hope that the re-visioning of family therapy will eliminate the pressure on therapists of color to try to fit into a white standard and allow instead for honoring multiple pathways to participation and achievement.

Our chapter in this section provides an overview of the program/ institutional domains that must be considered and altered when making the transition from training approaches that ignore or minimize contextual issues to those approaches that are guided by multicultural perspectives. If our vision for the field is ever to be actualized, the training of the next generation of family therapists will be crucial.

In many respects, this book represents our concerted effort to practice what we preach. Critical to the re-visioning process that we envision is paying acute attention to who gets included and who doesn't. It is our belief that as human beings we appeal to the bigger parts of ourselves when we are mindful and respectful of who is at the metaphorical table and how we pay attention to what is needed to keep us all actively engaged once we are there. Both our hope and our renewed vision for the field rest on our robust assumption that each of us will actively resist the "business as usual" mentality that has guided our thinking and our field. This book is very much about such resistance. It is dedicated to a recognition of our unique, culturally based stories of suffering and survival as well as our common humanity. How we manage to make peace with and hold such seemingly disparate aspects of our experience is exactly what the re-visioning of family therapy is ultimately about. We hope that you will read, reflect, and receive our call to join us in the struggle to re-vision family therapy.

Acknowledgments

My deepest thanks go to my coeditor and coauthor, Ken Hardy, for his wisdom, dedication, creativity, and humor in working on this book. We have had great conversations going back more than 25 years. This collaboration has given us the chance to push our thinking forward in ways I hope we can keep expanding. His ideas and moral compass have been a profound inspiration to me for many years. I thank him for wonderful times we have had (not as many as I had hoped!) working through the ideas and details and laughing together over the problems along the way. I am in awe of his brilliance, creativity, and deep commitment to the endeavor of re-visioning family therapy.

I am also in awe of the contributors to this volume who have found the courage to write about their most painful life experiences and deepest ideas with trust that the readers will bring empathy to their reading. For the pain and courage of so many whose experiences are acknowledged in this book I am profoundly grateful.

I thank also my mentor and companion Scott Joplin, whose music saw me through the work on this book and through so many other endeavors in my life. His magnificent music and the effort of his life to voice his intuitions, love, and hope in his compositions have been an ongoing inspiration to me for many years.

Seymour Weingarten supported this book from its first inception, and Jim Nageotte offered good counsel and support throughout the development of this second edition.

I thank Fran Snyder, who supports me every day in concentrating on the issues we are trying to address in this book. Her support makes my work possible, and I am deeply grateful to her for that. Laura Benton entered my life at a crucial time when we were in the thick of work on this book. With a quiet creativity and support, Laura was a great help in researching, editing, and creating genograms. And my life-mates Nydia Garcia-Preto, Paulette Moore Hines, Jayne Mahboubi, Nollaig and Henry Byrne, John Folwarski, Fernando López-Colón, Robert-Jay Green, Froma Walsh, Carol Anderson, Elaine Pinderhughes, Barbara Petkov, Charlee and Alex Sutton, Sueli Petry, Eliana Gil, Nancy Boyd-Franklin, A. J. Franklin, and Debra Chatman Finley have all offered help and inspiration when needed. Their support is an ongoing richness to me every day.

My sisters, Morna Livingston and Neale McGoldrick, have been throughout my life a major source of support and inspiration, both creative teachers and authors in their own right. I feel I am never alone when I connect with their belief in me and their efforts to promote the same kinds of cultural transformation in their own lives and work.

My husband, another creative teacher and writer, supports me every day in more ways than he realizes. I am very grateful. I thank him for the many wonderful days we worked in parallel on our books. And I thank my son for doing his thing, which leaves me free to do mine, and hope that now that he is embarking on his career, he will have many life endeavors as gratifying as I have had. My nephews, Guy and Hugh Livingston, have also inspired me with their efforts to build cultural bridges in their music and artistic creativity, and I thank them for their support and for what they are doing along similar lines in their worlds to promote cultural understanding and transformation.

Thanks also to Dan Morin for his creativity and dedication to developing genograms, including the pictures in this edition. Ken and I were committed to having genograms included wherever possible in the text to illustrate our basic idea that mapping out the cultural context, best done with genograms, is essential for the work we believe in. Dan's program is making this mapping possible.

I thank my parents, Margaret Bush and Aunt Mamie Cahalane, for giving me the courage to face truths about our family and about myself, which their strength helped me to acknowledge. They live in my heart and have made this book possible. And I thank the associates and fellows of the Multicultural Family Institute as well as all my students and clients, who challenge and inspire me every day.

—MONICA MCGOLDRICK

My involvement in this important body of work would not have been possible without the generosity, commitment, and dedication of my beloved friend, colleague, and soul sister Monica McGoldrick. Whether on the streets of Amsterdam, New York City, or Anaheim, I have appreciated immensely the intense, vein-protruding conversations that we have had over the years about matters of human indignities and social justice. As we both are well aware, we have not always agreed with each other's positions, yet we have always genuinely respected each other. Thank you in the most heartfelt way for inviting me to work with you on the second edition of *Re-Visioning Family Therapy*. Our many conversations, collaborations, and brainstorming sessions regarding this issue have been inspirational and life transforming. Thank you for believing in me and for your foresight in using the collaborative spirit of our relationship to demonstrate that working across vast cultural divides is possible.

I would also like to thank Jim Nageotte of The Guilford Press for his guidance, support, and sage advice throughout every phase of this project. A special thanks is also extended to our many friends, colleagues, and brothers and sisters of the struggle who have contributed to the book. We thank you for your tireless efforts, patience with short turnaround times, and willingness to "go there with and for us" in the telling of your stories for the book. Obviously, without your contributions we have no book.

And, finally but not insignificantly, I would also like to thank my family for their unrelenting support and for being a tremendous source of inspiration, motivation, and resolve in my life. I am so painfully aware virtually every day of my life that every single accomplishment, accolade, and particle of privilege that I enjoy has been achieved by standing firmly on your tired, weary, but omnipresent shoulders. Please know that it is permanently etched in the walls of my psyche and soul that your individual and collective sacrifices and suffering have provided the pathway to my opportunities. I will never forget . . . and I am eternally grateful. One of the reasons why this book has been so important to me personally is because of the possibility that it promises for the emergence of a new world order—an invitation for us to think differently about each other, and because we think differently, we are able to act differently with each other. It is my hope and desire that the next generation of Hardys and McGoldricks, as well as the descendants of the many others who have contributed to this book, will inherit a different world where skin color, the shape of one's eyes, whom one loves romantically, or where one's ancestral roots are buried will not determine access to opportunity, dignity, and respect. This is the re-visioning that we envision with this book.

—Kenneth V. Hardy

Contents

PART IV. IMPLICATIONS FOR CLINICAL PRACTICE

PART V. IMPLICATIONS FOR TRAINING

PART I

Theoretical Perspectives

CHAPTER 1

Introduction

Re-Visioning Family Therapy
from a Multicultural Perspective

Monica McGoldrick
Kenneth V. Hardy

Treasure ways of thinking more than the facts you have accumulated.
Facts will be presented to you in such a way as to veil the ways of thinking
embedded in them. To reveal these hidden ways of thinking, to suggest
alternative frameworks, to imagine better ways of living in evolving
worlds, to imagine new human relations that are freed from persisting
hierarchies, whether they be racial or sexual or geopolitical—this is the
work of educated human beings. Education is the practice of freedom.
                          —ANGELA DAVIS, Grinnell College Graduation
                                    (*New York Times*, June 10, 2007, p. 34)

Please call me by my true names,
so I can wake up
and so the door of my heart can be left open.
                              —THICH NHAT HANH, "Please Call Me
                               by My True Names" (1991, pp. 123–124)

The recent dramatic increase in immigrants in the United States is forcing
us to come to terms with our multiculturality. At no time in our nation's
history have so many people who were born abroad been residents of the
United States (Roberts, 2004). And never before, despite previous waves

of immigration, has our nation been so diverse. This situation is forcing us to challenge our unquestioned assumptions about who we are and what our values should be. The cultural richness and complexity of the immigrant generation, especially those whose cultures are most different from the dominant European American values of our society, offer us the greatest possibilities for re-visioning who we are and who we can be. Our diversity can become our greatest strength. When we instead fear our diversity, our prejudices and rigidities as a nation are highlighted. Our fears give rise to our pernicious ability to exclude others and to dehumanize those who are not considered to belong.

Immigrants and people of color more than any other people experience our society from a multicultural perspective. Their bicultural lens could be a model for the cultural flexibility we require as family therapists in the most culturally diverse nation that has ever existed.

Coming to terms with our diversity as a nation transforms our awareness of what it means to be quintessentially American. As Sanford Ungar (1997) writes of becoming conscious of the meaning of his family's migration for him, a third-generation grandchild of Eastern European Jewish immigrant ancestors:

> I was no less American than ever before, of course, but now, in middle age, I had discovered my own immigrant consciousness. Indeed, in that sense, I could now feel more authentically American. (p. 18)

Only by attending to the multiplicitous voices that have until now been silenced in the dominant story of who we are as a nation can we become "more authentically American." Although African Americans, Hmong refugees, and recent immigrants from Sri Lanka have their own culture of origin and particular experiences of migration and/or dislocation, they need equally to feel themselves included in the definition of "American."

Family therapy has ignored this multicultural dimension of our society. We have proceeded to develop models without regard for their cultural limitations. We have failed to notice that families from many cultural groups never come to our therapy or find our techniques helpful. It is we who must change—to include them.

The failure of societies to embrace and respect diversity is the greatest single threat to the survival of our civilization. We must break the constraints of our traditional monocular vision of families as white,[1] heterosexual, and middle class. We need to redefine the boundaries of our field to a cultural viewpoint that takes into account the diversity of our society and the way that societal oppression has silenced the voices and constrained the lives of individuals, families, and whole communities since our nation was founded. Racial, sexist, cultural, classist, and heterosexist power hierarchies constrain our clients' lives and determine what gets defined as a problem and what services our society will set up to respond to these problems.

Family therapy, which, like any set of ideas and practices, is always evolving, originally developed mostly in reaction to Freudian psychology, which had focused primarily on intrapsychic processes as the core of human psychology. Family therapy provided a kind of corrective perspective, focusing attention on interpersonal processes among family members as central to understanding psychological functioning. Although some family therapists eschewed any other level of analysis than the interpersonal–family level, most came to think in terms of multiple systemic levels, from the biological to the familial to the cultural. However, it has been very hard to shift our thinking about therapy beyond the family to consider the therapeutic implications of the cultural context in which families are embedded.

To re-vision the dominant discourses within family therapy, we must examine the ways in which we have organized our theory and practice and analyze how this arrangement replicates the dominant value systems of our society. Such re-visioning will be a slow and difficult evolution and will not take place without a backlash. In this chapter we want to map out a series of phases that describe both the past and the possible future of family therapy, a framework we hope will contribute to the transformation of theory and practice.

Our entire society is organized to accommodate a type of family structure that represents less than 6% of U.S. households—nuclear family units with employed fathers and homemaker mothers who devote themselves to the care of husbands and children. Family therapy, like our dominant social ideology in general, has tended to be oriented toward a view of families as self-sufficient, nuclear units. However, our definition of a two-parent family as being critical for child development has always been a euphemism for a structure that includes a mother who is perpetually on call for everyone emotionally and physically and a distant, money-providing father. Families with such a structure cannot help being problematic. Although poor families are the only ones seen as deficient, because of their obvious and critical dependence on systems beyond themselves for their survival, the reality is that all families are dependent for their survival on systems beyond themselves. But those of us who are of the dominant groups fail to realize this, because of the ways the government and others support us. Our needs are met and taken for granted and so rendered invisible to us (Coontz, 1992). Schools, courts, the police, and all other societal institutions operate for the protection and benefit of the dominant groups. Thus those of us who make the rules and definitions are kept blind to our privilege (see McIntosh, Chapter 21, this volume) and to our dependence on those who take care of us. The problem is not the dependence of certain people on the society but the delusion of autonomy. The dominant groups are using up the world's resources with no awareness or accountability (Gore, 2006; Ehrlich, 1995; Ehrenreich, 1990). The economic system, the prison system, the drug reha-bilitation industry, the gun industry, and the legal and governmental systems make money for the dominant groups of our society on the backs of the poor and the disenfranchised, who serve us in our homes, hotels, hospitals, and factories, making our clothing and supplies, while we remain blind to our connection to them, not seeing our exploitation or the bias in our behavior. We seldom see the poor or the working class, who are an invisible workforce toiling tirelessly for our comfort. They come at night to hospitals, hotels, and the halls of academia. They are commissioned essentially to "keep America clean." It never seems to matter that they, like us, are parents, grandparents, beloved children, aunts, uncles, nieces, and nephews; they remain objectified, invisible, and known only by the services that they provide for us, such as "the trash lady" or " the maid."

Paradoxically, the ideals stated, but not meant, in our Constitution could be the foundation of a truly egalitarian society, perhaps the first in human history, but only if we acknowledge the pernicious, unspoken exclu-sions on which it was founded. To do this, we must admit that our founders built slavery and the disenfranchisement of people of color and women into the system and that these inequities remain in place to this day. Our history books still brag about the foundation of our nation, minimizing the slaugh-ter, slavery, and forced invisibility of more than half of the population. This is hard to see, because what we espouse overtly mystifies the underlying facts of exclusion. But our society makes it very difficult to notice the intersection between the spoken and the unspoken. So we continue to invest in the ideal that we are the land of the free, yet some of us are and have always been freer than others. We continue to believe that escaping the walls of poverty is simply a matter of personal will and hard work, denying that wealth and class privilege are well-elaborated systems that negate the individual efforts of the poor while inflating the opportunities of the economically and racially privileged.

Therapists need to revise our books to make room for the unspoken structures, the cultural, racial, class- and gender-biased hierarchies that are the underpinnings of our society. It goes unacknowledged that African Americans, Latinos, Asians, and other racially oppressed people do not have the same entitlements to participate in our institutions, even in our world of family therapy.

Therapists must begin to think of families in terms of the communi-ties they live in. We have ignored community, focusing on the interior of the nuclear family in the present time—ignoring all that came before. We remain convinced that it is impossible to understand or treat poor families without a comprehensive understanding of how stigma and limited access to resources affect their symptoms and presentation. We continually turn a blind eye to the pervasive impact of oppression on the poor, the racially oppressed, and other marginalized groups who behave in predictable ways, not because of who they are but because of the context of devaluation and discrimination they live in. Delivering more culturally competent services will require our field to consider the broader ecology of families. Widening our lens to take history, context, and community into account will require us to reconsider many of our assumptions.

Children need more than one or even two adults to raise them, and adults need more than one or two close relationships to get them through life. As family therapists we need to encourage our clients to go beyond the dominant culture's definitions of family, to pay attention to relationships with siblings, nieces and nephews, grandchildren, aunts, and uncles. And beyond this we must attend to friendships and to the health, safety, and community contexts in which families live. We need to consider the role of housekeepers, maids, and nannies, as well as godparents, teachers, and other mentors, in the rearing of children.

THE PROBLEMS OF NAMING AND THE DSM

In family therapy, we get paid by the names we give to the problems our clients present to us. An early 19th-century physician in the United States, Samuel Cartwright, described two mental disorders prevalent among slaves (Tavris, 1992; DeGruy Leary, 2005):

1. *Drapetomania*, characterized by a single symptom: the uncontrollable urge to escape slavery. This was literally a "flight-from-home mania."
2. *Dysathesia aethiopia*, for which many symptoms were described: destroying property on the plantation, being disobedient, talking back, fighting with their masters, and refusing to work.

These diagnoses turned the desire for liberty into a sickness that was the problem of the slave, not the slave owner. And there was no corresponding disorder characterized by the irresistible urge to possess slaves. The brutal acts of inhumanity that slavery involved were not considered reflections of mental illness. Cartwright instead focused on the *mental disorders* of the slave for wanting to escape slavery. He, incidentally, believed that these disorders were almost completely treatable by whipping or amputation of toes. The slave owner became completely invisible in this nomenclature and, of course, was viewed as needing no intervention. Using labels to control others continues fairly unabated. Homosexuality was considered a mental illness until it was voted out of existence in 1973, but those who promote hatred and violence against homosexuals receive no labeling to this day. We are much more likely to diagnose the victims of abuse than the perpetrators. We define practically the whole life course of those who have experienced trauma but leave out of our descriptions and nomenclature those who traumatize others, just as we did with slavery. Racism is not only not a diagnosis, it is not even listed in the index for the 800-page DSM-IV. The perpetrators of violence against others are still not named in the DSM. We further obscure who does what to whom by labels, such as "alcoholic family" and "violent family," which obscure the agents and victims of abuse. And even when homosexuality was removed from the DSM as a mental disorder, the decision masqueraded as a scientific decision, as do all decisions about the manual (Spiegel, 2002; Tomm, 1990; Caplan & Cosgrove, 2004; Kutchins & Kirk, 1997). The chief architect of the DSM, Robert Spitzer, played a key role in removing homosexuality from the category of mental illness, but he did not want to give it the stamp of normalcy, viewing it as "suboptimal" behavior. He argued that if the DSM were to include suboptimal behaviors as mental disorders, it would have to include such phenomena as "celibacy, religious fanaticism, racism, vegetarianism, and male chauvinism" as diagnostic categories (Kutchins & Kirk, 1997, p. 76). He assumed the other American Psychiatric Association members would not want to make such a list of disorders to be diagnosed and treated, and the organization went along with his wishes.

The DSM-IV claims that its naming is based on "scientific evidence," but a significant part of this "research" has been funded by drug companies (Kupers, 1995). The voting process by American Psychiatric Association committees is disguised as science. This diagnostic manual includes diagnosis number 301.6, dependent personality disorder, for the person who "has difficulty expressing disagreement with others because of fear of loss of support or approval." The description adds a note that this is not to include "realistic fears of retribution" but gives no guidelines as to how one would assess whether a person's fears are realistic—the obvious decisive factor for such a label. The DSM has no comparable diagnosis for those who use their power to control and intimidate others. Nor is there a diagnosis for those who are pathologically fearful of intimacy or unable to develop friendships, nor for those who have a need for sexual conquests or who react to their fear of aging by leaving their age-mate partners and establishing sexual relationships with women the age of their children (Kupers, 1995). The DSM has failed to provide diagnoses for those who are racist, misogynist, or homophobic.

Indeed, it is not sufficient, according to the DSM-IV, to have been physically or sexually violent to receive a diagnosis of conduct disorder or antisocial personality disorder. The most one can give is a V-code, number 61, which mentions, with not one sentence of description or explanation, "sexual or physical abuse of child or adult." And this situation exists in a society in which a woman is beaten on the average every 18 seconds and in which physical abuse is the most common cause of injury for women, more widespread than breast cancer or car accidents (U.S. Dept. of Justice, 1994).

Similarly, families of color, families of the poor, and immigrant families, whose norms and values are different from the dominant norm, remain marginalized, invalidated, and pathologized as deficient, dysfunctional, or, worse, invisible. The DSM editors specifically rejected the suggestions of their cultural advisors to make any reference whatsoever in the manual to the need to consider cultural context in understanding mental disorders. They included only a glossary that makes reference to "culture-bound" disorders, that is, disorders recognized only within a particular culture (Mezzich et al., 1999). And even that glossary omitted reference to any European American culture-bound syndromes, such as anorexia, including only non-European American syndromes in what the cultural consultants called "a museum of exotica" (Mezzich et al., 1999, p. 460).

I (K. V. H.) have suggested, only partly in jest (2007), the development of a DSM-M (marginalization version), which would bring attention to the role that the oppressor plays in the life of the oppressed. The DSM-M would, for example, contain diagnostic categories such as the following:

1. *Addiction to domination disorder (ADD)*: This category would be reserved for those who cannot resist subjugating others through use of force, domination, and a reliance on the establishment of rigid hierarchical boundaries.

2. *Privilege disorder*: This category would be for those who enjoy the unearned benefits afforded to them by virtue of living in a patriarchal, sexist, heterosexist, racist, Christian-oriented society. One of the major features of this disorder is to have privilege but claim not to know or feel it.

3. *Oppositional cop disorder (OCD)*: This would be reserved for police and other individuals or groups who use excessive force, particularly toward the disadvantaged, without discernible provocation. A generalized, overly aggressive demeanor toward people of color, gays, and the poor often characterizes the disorder.

4. *Clinical oppression disorder (COD)*: This condition is often manifested in marginalized people who have lived their lives in the midst of sociocultural oppression. The major symptoms associated with COD are learned voicelessness, learned helplessness, suppressed anger and rage, and a generalized sense of suspicion, with ideas of persecution.

Karl Tomm has suggested another diagnosis—"DSM Syndrome"—characterized by a compulsive desire to objectify and label people according to predetermined psychiatric categories (Tomm, 1990).

Such a satirical DSM-M nosology highlights the invisibility of the systems of domination and oppression that wreak havoc on the lives of oppressed people while remaining firmly unnamed.

LABELS: MAKING ROOM FOR BOTH GROUP CONNECTIONS AND UNIQUENESS

Labels can be both reassuring and dangerous. They define boundaries—who is in and who is out. Labels of self-definition may be reassuring because they define a group to which we belong, thus overcoming our sense of isolation. But they also define the limits of that belonging. Coming to define myself (MM) as Irish American, for example, has been an affirmation at the deepest level of my identity (see my discussion in Chapter 8). It gave me a profound sense that neither I nor my family were alone in our ways of experiencing the world—that much of what I thought was strange or eccentric made sense in the light of Irish history. At a certain point, however, when I define myself as "Irish American" or by any other fixed group identity, the boundary becomes exclusionary and distances me from others who are not Irish, although I may be better served by emphasizing my connections to them.

As a society, we need to transform the way we think about sameness and difference. Our survival as human beings depends on whether we can remove the blinders of denial that prevent our seeing our human connectedness to each other. At the same time, we must make more room for tolerance of our differences.

If we look carefully enough, each of us is a hodgepodge. Developing "cultural competence" requires us to go beyond the dominant values and explore the complexity of culture and cultural identity, not without values and judgments about what is adaptive, healthy, or "normal" but without accepting unquestioningly our society's definitions of these culturally determined categories. We need to develop a perspective on our identity that allows for at least three levels:

1. Our uniqueness as individuals.
2. Our various group identities that give us a sense of home—of defining our relatedness to others.
3. Our common partnership with every other human being, without a sense of which we will surely perish.

The goal is to create a world that we can each call home, a place in which we each have a voice, in which our flowing sense of group identities gives us more a sense of boundaries that include than of divisions that exclude. The notion of culture is almost a mystical sense of connection with all the threads of which our human community is woven.

Dealing with the subject of cultural diversity is, therefore, a matter of balance between validating the differences among us and appreciating the forces of our common humanity. Group boundaries may prevent people from defining themselves in all their complexity. They may emphasize exclusion of others over affiliation with group members. This reflects a negative way of defining group boundaries and usually also incorporates covert power hierarchies. It is the unacknowledged aspect of power that creates a harmful effect, as when ethnic differences are described in such a way that the status differences between groups go unnamed. As family therapists, we need to help our clients develop multiple affiliative group identities, which increase the flexibility of their lives, to fit their ever-evolving circumstances. To do this we must expand our psychological theories of development to describe our identities with all their multiplicity (McGoldrick & Carter, 2005).

We believe in helping clients understand their cultural selves as fluid, ever-changing aspects of who they are. The narrator, Vivian Twostar, in *The Crown of Columbus* (Erdrich & Dorris, 1991), described brilliantly the complexity of her multicultural identity:

> I belong to the lost tribe of mixed bloods, that hodgepodge amalgam of hue and cry that defies easy placement. When the DNA of my various ancestors— Irish and Coeur d'Alene and Spanish and Navajo and God knows what else— combined to form me, the result was not some genteel indecipherable puree that comes from a Cuisinart. You know what they say on the side of the Bisquick box? ... Mix with fork. Leave lumps. That was me. (p. 123)

Her amusing analogy to Bisquick is very apt, because our cultural identities do not involve some clearly measured parts, but rather an ever-changing mixture of identities, some of which may have particular prominence in a given context, while a different aspect comes to the fore under other circumstances. The narrator articulates extremely well the way we may identify ourselves in different contexts and the advantages of a multilayered identity:

> There are advantages to not being this or that. You have a million stories, one for every occasion, and in a way they're all lies and in another way they're all true. When Indians say to me, "What are you? I know exactly what they're asking, and answer Coeur d'Alene. I don't add, "Between a quarter and a half," because that's information they don't require, first off—though it may come

later if I screw up and they're looking for reasons why. If one of my Dartmouth colleagues wonders, "Where did you study?" I pick the best place, the hardest one to get into, in order to establish that I belong. If a stranger on the street questions where [my daughter] gets her light brown hair and dark skin, I say the Olde Sodde and let them figure it out. (pp. 123–124)

The narrator conveys beautifully the complexity of how a multiracial person handles the "lumps" of the various parts of a complex identity in different social contexts. She goes on to describe the special perspective of people at the margins, which is a primary insight regarding the re-visioning of our field—valuing the perspectives of those at the margins. They can see things people at the center do not see.

My roots spread in every direction, and if I water one set of them more often than others, it's because they need it more. ... I've read anthropological papers written about people like me. We're called marginal, as if we exist anywhere but on the center of the page ... But there are bonuses to peripheral vision. Out beyond the normal bounds, you at least know where you're not. You escape the claustrophobia of belonging, and what you lack in security you gain by realizing—as those insiders never do—that security is an illusion ... "Caught between two worlds," is the way we're often characterized, but I'd put it differently. We are the catch. (p. 124)

This brilliant expression of a multifaceted cultural identity, composed of complex heritages, highlights the impact of one's social location and the need to underline one or another aspect of culture in a given context in response to others' projections. Recently, we've been experiencing the poignancy of what those who belong have to learn from those who are at the margins with presidential candidate Barack Obama's multicultural identity. His awareness of the importance or understanding our "lumps" and embracing our multicultural identities offers promise for the future of family therapy as well as for our society.

I am the son of a black man from Kenya and a white woman from Kansas. I was raised with the help of a white grandfather who survived a Depression to serve in Patton's Army during World War II and a white grandmother who worked on a bomber assembly line at Fort Leavenworth while he was overseas. I've gone to some of the best schools in America and lived in one of the world's poorest nations. I am married to a black American who carries within her the blood of slaves and slaveowners—an inheritance we pass on to our two precious daughters. I have brothers, sisters, nieces, nephews, uncles, and cousins of every race and every hue. Scattered across three continents and for as long as I live, I will never forget that in no other country on Earth is my story even possible. (Obama Speech, Available at *www.nytimes.com2008/03/18/us/politics/18text-obam.html*)

It is possibly Obama's very mixed identity that makes him able to connect with different groups, and to see more clearly than most what is possible in this country. We must, as family therapists who are necessarily always crossing cultural borders, amplify our understanding of these different cultural territories between and among people.

Clinically, we must find ways of working that hold each person accountable for his or her behavior, including intentional or unintentional sexism, racism, or other unjust behavior, at the same time that we must convey a message of respect, care, belonging, and empathy for the painful history that has involved all of us in both trauma and denial. This requires that we move beyond our denial that we are all connected to each other, the abuser, the victim of abuse, and the one who stands by in silence.

CLASS

Whatever we keep secret about class—about how much or how little money we have, about class contempt and class elitism, about the pain of unacknowledged class distance from our family members—costs us. It keeps us from being free and from learning about the experiences of those from different classes than our own. We should dare to put our prejudices on the table, to examine them, and to determine what they cost us. We believe we must radically change our family therapy training to help trainees have the courage to discuss these issues, as well as those pertaining to race, gender, ethnicity, religion, and sexual orientation. A first step is to acknowledge our prejudices and to know that we will make mistakes. We will blurt out comments or express microaggressions that are indicators of our prejudice without realizing it. If we are lucky, someone will draw this to our attention, and we will move along in overcoming our silences about class privilege and oppression.

BACKLASH WITHIN FAMILY THERAPY

In family therapy, as in every other structure of our society, we see repeated efforts to silence the marginalized voices that would speak up. For years the field stayed in a reactive stance to the feminist critique of the 1980s. Many men withdrew from professional meetings. More recently, as the issues of culture and race have begun to be asserted, people say that we must go slowly or whites will retreat from our organizations. But we will not have a future if we have only a white future. We cannot go on the way we were going. And the field's dilemma is the same as that of the whole society.

One aspect of the backlash is the accusation that those who advocate attention to oppression, culture, and diversity are stultifying us with a straitjacket of "political correctness" (Tataki, 1994) The first *Psychotherapy Networker* magazine on cultural diversity was titled "Multiculturalism: Has It Got Us All Walking on Eggshells?" (*Family Therapy Networker*, 1994). This drew our attention to the discomfort of the privileged rather than to the pain of the oppressed. Such discussion implicitly blames those who attempt to discuss their oppression for making the privileged uncomfortable—thus blocking discussion of privilege. The truth is that those who draw our attention to such social phenomena as the absence of people of color in our professional organizations or inequities in the status of women or minorities in salary, power, and visibility make us uncomfortable. Asserting that we do not feel "safe" in an atmosphere that values "political correctness" is an expression of the privilege of feeling safe, as those who are marginalized are never safe.

Tamasese and Waldegrave (1993) have described how claims of injustice are often overtly acknowledged in "liberal therapeutic environments" but then subtly avoided. They describe three techniques by which accountability for injustice is undermined. In *paralysis*, people become so overwhelmed by their own pain that, fearing the possibility that they might offend again in the future, they do nothing and feel impotent. A response of overwhelming guilt can end up entrenching the status quo. Others respond in a *patronizing* way, taking on the issues of the oppressed to the extent that they inappropriately become self-appointed spokespeople for them. A third response is <u>*individualizing*</u>, through which a person denies the relevance of group norms and behaviors, making it impossible to discuss issues of power, privilege, and accountability:

> [This] cleverly sidesteps the institutional and collective reality of discrimination. It is the collective of men and the history of patriarchy, which has created the environment that privileges the decisions and actions of men over women. No matter how committed to women a man may be, he may still continue to benefit at every level in a patriarchal society, at their expense. (Tamasese & Waldegrave, 1993, p. 32)

Denial that one belongs to the category of privilege, such as denying that one is "white," for example, keeps one from having to be accountable for the privileges of whiteness and makes discussion of the problems of racism, sexism, and other discrimination impossible.

There are many signs of backlash within our organizations. People of color are often blamed for not wanting to join our associations. Faculty members may say, "We would love to hire a faculty person of color but we can't find any" or "We invited so-and-so, but she is a prima donna and didn't respond." Most do not question their standards for defining a "senior family therapist." Requirements such as having the "right" credentials, being in the field for a long time, or having trained with the field's leaders set up a conundrum, because the very problem to be solved is that family therapy, like the society at large, has excluded and marginalized people of color. In the rare instances in which a person of color is recruited, it is often difficult for him or her to feel included and fully appreciated. Many institutions are oblivious to the subtle but persistent pressures that they apply to people of color to fit into the prevailing racial norms of the setting. Too often people of color are required to relinquish who they genuinely are racially in order to be "mainstreamed," which often translates into to being white-like, near-white, neo-white ... anything but person-of-color-identified. To survive and be fully accepted within the field, many therapists of color have to become what I (K. V. H.) have referred to as GEMMs (Good Effective Mainstream Minority family therapists; see Hardy, Chapter 38, this volume).

It is not surprising that many clinicians of color have not defined themselves as family therapists, because they have not felt at home in our context. We have not realized that we have to change both our context and our requirements in order to welcome them. Dominant-culture therapists sometimes say that they would gladly mentor someone of color but that their offers have not been accepted; they fail to consider the reasons that a person from a marginalized group might not want to join with us. Our institutions themselves have to change. Would a white person feel comfortable as the only white person included in a group, expected to represent all others of his or her race? Probably not.

Some members of the dominant group make subtly disqualifying comments: "These issues just aren't relevant to my work. This topic doesn't interest me. I think we need to talk about trauma and evidence-based practice instead." Or they may say "We did cultural diversity last year; we need something new this year." These attitudes assume that we can continue our old routines without changing our institutional structures, allowing those who experience oppression to speak out only every so often and then going back to business as usual.

Others in power try to promote conflicts among those without social power. The 1 million people in the United States at the highest income level make as much money as the next 100 million put together. As African American law professor Derrick Bell (1993) has pointed out, if people realized their commonalities and shared interests across racial lines, it would create a revolution. It is much safer for the dominant group to promulgate myths that it is "angry" Black men, "controlling" women, or "perverse" homosexuals we really have to fear rather than the power structure that holds our dominant group in place. The government has long pitted Native American tribes against each other, defining what quantum of blood was necessary to belong and pressing people to belong to only one group. An example of this type of mythologizing within family therapy was the blame placed on working mothers (Coyne, 1992) for keeping "invisible" child care workers of color in their families without considering that the men in these families leave all home and child responsibilities to their wives while they define the laws of the society and control employment and family structures.

THE EVOLUTION OF FAMILY THERAPY

Peggy McIntosh (1983, 1990) has described five phases of educational and personal "re-vision" with regard to both gender and race. Using these different lenses, we might broaden our perspective as family therapists to include the categories of culture, class, race, and gender in our thinking.

Starting with *Phase 1*, in which women and minorities were absent from academic discussion, McIntosh describes several evolutionary stages of re-visioning curricula to include a shifting consciousness of these dimensions. For example, she takes the discipline of history and explores how it might change at each phase of re-visioning. In the first phase, history is about ordering of events of privileged white men's achievement, accomplishment, and success; wars, rulers, and so forth. An English course might be organized around "Man's Quest for Knowledge."

As notions of history first expand (*Phase 2*), the lens may be widened to include some women and minorities in the discussion of history: Elizabeth Cady Stanton, Mary Cassatt, Frederick Douglass, Clara Barton, and Sacagawea, might be included, but the focus of interest remains the same—an ordering of events and accomplishments of certain individuals. The principle difference is that by broadening our focus to include some "second stringers" who have also had an impact on history, science, or the arts, we do begin to include some women and some minorities in our discussion.

As consciousness evolves (*Phase 3*), there begins to be a rethinking of the place of women and minorities in society. History courses may begin to focus on them as "a problem," discussing how women struggled to get the vote, the history of the antislavery movement, and so forth. In this phase there is a consciousness that prior curricula have ignored them. The question is asked, for example, "Did women have a 'Renaissance'?" The answer is: "No, and neither did people of color, at least not during the Renaissance." Efforts to modify the exclusion of women or people of color now focus on social forces that have kept them invisible.

In *Phase 4*, conceptions of history undergo a more radical transformation. The historian is now included in the notion of history. Instead of being an "objective" ordering of the "facts" of the past, history becomes an interactive process, in which the historian influences the stories and there is an interactive fluidity in perspectives about history.

In *Phase 5*, a phase that McIntosh says she herself cannot clearly envision, history will itself be reconceived to include us all.

Following McIntosh, we propose several perspectives through which we might imagine the field of family therapy could evolve.

Traditional Universalist Perspective

This was the primary perspective in family therapy in the 1960s and 1970s and continues in some quarters as we have entered the 21st century. The primary definers of families and family therapy in this era were such people as Bowen, Minuchin, Ackerman, Whitaker, Jackson, Watzlawick, Weakland, Bateson, Framo, Boszormenyi-Nagy, Lidz, Fleck, and Haley. There was one prominent woman in the field in this early era, Virginia Satir, who played a major role until a quadrannial meeting of the Family Process Advisory Editors in 1972, which set up a confrontation entitled "Is Virginia Satir Dangerous for Family Therapy?" In this meeting Satir and her "second," Kitty LaPerriere, were pitted against Sal Minuchin and his "second," Frank Pittman. The very idea of setting up a discussion of ideas as a duel with seconds obviously comes from a very patriarchal and linear worldview. Beyond that, it is hard to conceive that the field would have tolerated a plenary titled "Is Murray Bowen Dangerous for Family Therapy?" or "Is Sal Minuchin Dangerous for Family Therapy?" Satir never attended another major family therapy meeting and devoted more and more time after that to working abroad.

Within its traditional framework, family therapy was white male family therapy—invented by white men, whose theories implicitly defined "family" to mean intact, middle-class, heterosexual, white families, organized with the man as head of the household and the woman as primary caretaker of all family relationships. The theoretical focus was on family members interacting as systemic units, with no acknowledgment of their unequal power to influence interactions. Common concepts taught about the understanding of family relationships concerned complementarity, homeostasis, triangles, pursuer–distancer, recursive feedback loops, cognitive behavioral exchanges, enmeshment and disengagement, and overfunctioning and underfunctioning. One prime theoretician, Bowen, emphasized a scale of "differentiation" as the measure of human maturity, according to which those who define themselves primarily by the standards of others would be lower on the scale. The fact that this has been required of women and people of color was not mentioned. Similarly, the structural approach, another leading approach to family therapy in this era, tended to hold women responsible for family problems without reference to their unequal power within the family and to explicitly promote men to take the role of "head" of the family. Men were expected to control their families, and women were expected to take care of the needs of all family members.

Within this traditionalist lens neither racism nor sexism was considered as relevant in understanding systems. Problems were formulated and assessed according to unquestioned white male definitions, which were discussed as universal truths (the DSM categories). No reference was made to race, gender, or sexual orientation as categories requiring specific attention in the family therapy field. No one pointed out that there were no people of color in the field as either leaders or followers. Groups and individuals fitting into this perspective might include Ackerman, Boszormenyi-Nagy, Bowen, Haley, Mental Research Institute–Palo Alto strategic (Jackson, Watzlawick, Weakland, Fisch); systemic (Milan group); Whitaker, Bateson, Erickson, deShazer, and O'Hanlon. The structural group did train many people of color and focused a lot of their work around families of color; their training was, however, one of the most conservative in advocating patriarchal gender arrangements.

Gender Perspective

In the late 1970s and early 1980s a new gender perspective emerged, spurred by articles by Rachel Hare-Mustin (1978) and by Kerrie James and Deborah MacIntyre (1983) in Australia and by the establishment in 1977 of the Women's Project (Marianne Walters, Betty Carter, Peggy Papp, and Olga Silverstein). Women began to notice that the field was defined primarily or exclusively by men. A few women had risen to prominence before the feminist critique of the field: Peggy Papp, Mara Selvini, Kitty LaPerriere, and others. However, the majority of presenters at conferences were white men, the leading texts were authored by white men, and the primary research in the field was led by white men, who still assumed that a family was white, middle class, and intact unless otherwise noted. Women's lack of power in families was still overlooked.

At the beginning of the 1980s, the journals and professional organizations had a predominance of white heterosexual men at the helm. *Family Process* had only one women on its board, and only 10% of its advisory editors were women. Almost all presenters at every quadrennial meeting were men. By the 1982 meeting, "Epistemology, Efficacy, and Ethics," a few "junior" women had become advisory editors, but the program was still very much in the hands of the men who ran the organization. One woman, Olga Silverstein, was invited by these men to critique Mara Selvini's ideas, and Selvini responded hotly. This conflict between the only two women on the program seemed to be constructed into it. The discussants for all the male presenters at the event were colleagues who were their supporters. Bell (1993) and others have written of how those without a voice in our society are pitted against each other in order to keep invisible the role of the dominant group in maintaining the status quo.

Although the ratio of male to female presenters was still about 14:1 at the next *Family Process* meeting in 1986, a panel of all women was arranged on gender issues, scheduled on the last morning of the conference—a Sunday. One person of color presented at the meeting—an African American epidemiologist, who was not a family therapist. "Women's issues" were still seen as a domain exclusive to women and separate from "regular" family theory and practice. There was almost no notice taken that all the participants remained white, so the feminist critique, without being acknowledged as such, was only a white feminist critique.

Two pivotal networking meetings of women family therapists in 1984 and 1986, called "Stonehenge," solidified a collaboration among women therapists that had been missing until then. A third international meeting of women family therapists in 1990 in Denmark expanded the networking of women family therapists with those in other countries. The consciousness raising of women's networking related initially more to gender than to race and culture, which took almost 10 more years to get on the table. A critique of the organization of the field began to evolve. But the primary ideas and readings in most family training programs were still those of white heterosexual men. In 1990 *Family Process*, under pressure from junior advisory editors, committed itself to having at least one-third women and 10% people of color on its advisory editorial board.

As the Women's Project and others began to write about and to present on feminist family therapy, the absence of women and minorities in many discussions was increasingly recognized as a problem. New areas of research emerged, bringing into focus the inequality of gender roles in families, the oppression of women, violence against women in families, and mother blaming in family therapy theory and writings. Still, the first-ever plenary presentation on male violence, which laid out the most basic dimensions of the problem in society and called for the development of therapeutic models to address them, was criticized as an appallingly unjust, unbalanced attack on men because the issue of women's violence was not addressed. This issue has still not become a topic of mention by mainstream men in our field.

By the late 1980s the American Family Therapy Academy (AFTA) for the first time had a predominance of white women in leadership positions. At the annual conference the majority of presenters were women. White male leaders reacted with outrage. They had not noticed that during the first decades of family therapy most presentations had been made by and virtually all the key awards had been given to white men. In the mid-1980s, four women (the Women's Project) had to share one award, and the awards committee proposed that two others (Goldner and Hare-Mustin) share another, because neither had "quite done enough" to deserve a full award for their contribution to the field. By the 1990s AFTA had a president and a vice president who were both women. The organization's programs dealt with cultural diversity for 3 years in a row, but its leadership worried that the emphasis on the concerns of women and culture were causing men to leave the organization. By the mid-1990s, some of the major texts began to include sections on feminist family therapy but still made no reference to gender inequities in couples or families. It was not until this time that there was any public acknowledgment of the heterosexist bias of the field, and books and articles began to appear then about gay, lesbian, bisexual, and transgender families.

Cultural Perspectives

During the later 1980s an expanded cultural perspective emerged, although one strong thread had developed from the 1960s with the work of a small minority of theoreticians and clinicians whose work focused on the poor. This group included the authors of *Families of the Slums* (Minuchin, Montalvo, Guerney, Rosman, & Schumer, 1967) and others, including Auerswald, Minuchin, and Montalvo. Through the 1970s Harry Aponte, Braulio Montalvo, Salvador Minuchin, Carlos Sluzki, and a very few others spoke and wrote about multiproblem, poor minority families. Others, such as Nancy Boyd-Franklin and Elaine Pinderhughes, wrote about African American families, racism, and the poor, but these were seen as special topics, not pertaining to family therapy itself. Similarly, writers on couples therapy, child abuse, the family life cycle, and other issues pertinent to family therapy continued to use white families as the norm and neglected to consider cultural differences and social inequalities. As time went on, family therapy conferences began to include one or two presenters of color to present on issues of "minority families" as opposed to "families." By 1985 the Family Therapy Academy had given about 75 awards, but not one had gone to a man or woman of color. The two most well-known men of color in the early family therapy movement, Harry Aponte and Braulio Montalvo, did not receive awards until the 1990s.

The American Association for Marriage and Family Therapy (AAMFT), while claiming to represent family therapists throughout the United States and Canada, was equally as remiss as AFTA in its recognition of women and people of color. Although founded in 1942, the AAMFT did not elect its first woman president until the 1990s, and the first president of color was not elected until the 2000s. The organization moved from California to Washington, D.C., but did not have a person of color on its national staff until 1982, despite its location in two of the most culturally diverse regions in the country. The AAMFT guidelines and standards for practice did not mention a single word about "culture" or "diversity" until the early 1990s. Fortunately, from that time on there was a gradual shift toward an emerging cultural perspective in family therapy.

However, notions of culture and class were still applied primarily to people of color, immigrants, or those with specific diagnoses. One could still discuss "couples," "child-focused families," "genograms," or "the family life cycle" without specific mention of gender, class, culture, or race. The term "family," unless otherwise qualified, still generally meant intact, once-married, heterosexual, white, middle-class couples and their children. Even a family's third generation was often referred to as an "extended family," as if "family" included only those living together in the present.

The emerging cultural perspectives did expand the ways in which families and family therapy were thought about to include the dimensions of gender and culture, although these dimensions were for a long time viewed as "special" features of certain families rather than as basic dimensions for understanding all families. Gradually perspectives began to expand beyond just asking that more minorities be included in leadership positions. Some family institutes offered workshops, usually by visiting presenters of color, on poor Black families, although, again, these discussions were still generally marginalized rather than integrated into the main body of family therapy.

Gradually, beginning in the 1990s, cultural diversity workshops became more common at major family therapy meetings. African Americans appeared on panels and more books and articles began to appear on Black families and other cultural minorities; there was some acknowledgement that researchers had ignored the experience of families of color. Accepted definitions in the field of family therapy now began to be questioned; these definitions had labeled both people of color and women as deficient—undifferentiated, enmeshed, or having high expressed emotionality.

A few institutions, to encourage change in the balance of white therapists, awarded a small number of minority scholarships in modest amounts. However, when minorities did not sign up for family therapy training, it was seen as their problem. By the early 1990s the AAMFT, with much fanfare, gave out a mere $5,000 in minority scholarships.

The annual American Family Therapy Academy had a plenary on culture, in which it was intended that people of privilege would begin to take some responsibility for their own part in cultural problems. Three white therapists presented three white cases and had a panel of discussants, including one African American (myself, K. V. H.). I said that if I had been the therapist in these cases, race would have been an issue, because I rarely have the luxury of working with a case in which race is not an issue. This issue was not picked up by the other discussants, who moved on to other issues of more interest.

Transforming Our Vision

A fourth perspective, requiring second-order change, began developing later in the 1990s. From this perspective all families, not just "minorities," are seen as embedded in and bounded by class, culture, gender, and race. Using this perspective, how a society defines gender, race, culture, and class relationships is critical to understanding how *all* family processes are structured.

This phase of family therapy, which has not yet become mainstream, aims to meet the needs of people of all cultural backgrounds. Courses on couples therapy use theory developed on families beyond European American couples and include Black[1] couples, Chinese couples, interracial couples, and gay couples, not just occasionally but as a core of the course. Theorists whose work has developed primarily in a context of work with nondominant-culture families become core faculty in training programs. The faculty and students of training programs become more culturally diverse. It will require second-order change for the leaders of the field to make room for the inclusion of knowledge and teaching other than that of the dominant groups. Faculties of training programs will need to be reconstituted to reflect diversity, and subject matter will need to be rethought from more inclusive perspectives. Emphasis will shift from the teachings of a few highly valued leaders to experiential and reciprocal learning. The wisdom and strengths of American Indian, African American, and other nondominant cultures will become an integral component of family therapy theories.

Student training will include home visits and studies of the cultural values and healing customs of Muslim families, Asian Indian families, and Latino families. Students will be encouraged to collaborate with indigenous cultural leaders in the community to help families. Questions about how families are located in their communities will become routine in assessment. Training will involve exploration of the assumptions of the theorists in the field as well as of faculty, students, and clients. The field will expand to include study of healing in cultures around the world. Spiritual, physical, psychological, and biological solutions to problems will be increasingly employed in an integrated way.

FAMILY THERAPY REDEFINED AND RECONSTRUCTED TO INCLUDE US ALL

This final phase is hard to envision, just as it has been for Peggy McIntosh in the field of education. Its description must await our learning to see around the next corner. Surely in this phase family intervention will occur in more flexible contexts with a more diverse array of helpers and a more flexibly defined "family." Intervention strategies will draw from cultural healing the world over. Family therapy training may focus on how we understand those who are different from ourselves. It is so difficult even to picture a world not divided by our current hierarchical structures that it is hard to imagine what healthy families or therapy may come to look like. One thing seems sure: As we expand the boundaries of our field, we open up enormous possibilities of helping families in multiple contexts and with a great variety of healing tools, from music, meditation, prayer, and poetry to community meetings and empowerment.

NOTE

1. In this chapter we have capitalized "Black" and lower-cased "white" in spite of the convention to do the reverse, because it seems to us that "Black" is a word which at least to some extent was chosen by African Americans to refer to themselves, while "white" does not deserve the "specialness" of capitalization as an honor to the distinction.

REFERENCES

Bell, D. (1993). *Faces at the bottom of the well: The permanence of racism.* New York: Basic Books.

Caplan, P. J., & Cosgrove, L. (Eds.). (2004). *Bias in psychiatric diagnosis.* New York: Aronson.

Coontz, S. (1992). *The way we never were: American families and the nostalgia trap.* New York: Basic Books.

Coyne, J. (1992, May–June). Stonewalling feminism [Letter to the editor]. *Family Therapy Networker.*

DeGruy Leary, J. (2005). *Posttraumatic slave syndrome: America's legacy of enduring injury and healing.* Milwaukie, OR: Uptone Press.

Ehrenreich, B. (1990). *Fear of falling: The inner life of the middle class.* New York: Harper.

Ehrlich, P. (1995). *The population bomb.* Cutchogue, NY: Buccaneer Books.

Erdrich, L., & Dorris, M. (1999). *The crown of Columbus.* New York: Harper Perennial.

Family Therapy Networker. (1994, July/August). *Multiculturalism: Has it got us all walking on eggshells?*

Gore, A. (2006). *An inconvenient truth.* New York: Viking.

Hanh, T. N. (1991). Please call me by my true names. In *Peace is every step.* New York: Boston.

Hardy, K. V. (1991). For minorities only: Tips for becoming a GEMM family therapist. *Family Therapy News, 22*(5), 5.

Hardy, K. V. (2007, March 16). *Towards a new vision of psychotherapy.* Keynote address presented at the Psychotherapy Networker Symposium, Washington, DC.

Hare-Mustin, R. (1978). A feminist approach to family therapy. *Family Process, 17,* 181–194.

James, K., & McIntyre, D. (1983). The reproduction of families: The social role of family therapy? *Journal of Marital and Family Therapy, 9,* 119–129.

Kupers, T. A. (1995). The politics of psychiatry: Gender and sexual preference in DSM IV. *Masculinities, 3*(2), 67–78.

Kutchins, H., & Kirk, S. A. (1997). *Making us crazy: DSM: The psychiatric bible and the creation of mental disorders.* New York: Free Press.

THEORETICAL PERSPECTIVES

McGoldrick, M., & Carter, B. (2005). Self in context: The individual life cycle in systemic perspective. In B. Carter & M. McGoldrick (Eds.), *Expanding the family life cycle: Individual, family, community* (pp. 27–46). Boston: Allyn & Bacon.

McIntosh, P. (1983). *Interactive phases of curricular re-vision: A feminist perspective* (Working Paper No. 124). Wellesley, MA: Center for Research on Women.

McIntosh, P. (1990). *Interactive phases of curricular and personal re-vision with regard to race* (Working Paper No. 219). Wellesley, MA: Center for Research on Women.

Mezzich, J. E., Kirmayer, L. J. Kleinman, A., Fabrega, H., Parson, D. L., Good, B., et al. (1999). The place of culture in the DSM-IV. *Journal of Nervous and Mental Disease, 187*(8), 457–464.

Minuchin, S., Montalvo, B., Guernay, B. G., Rosman, B. L., & Schumer, F. (1967). *Families of the slums: An exploration of their structure and treatment*. New York: Basic Books.

Obama, B. (2008). Speech 3/18. Available at *www.nytimes.com2008/03/18/us/politics/18text-obam.html*.

Roberts, S. (2004). *Who we are now: The changing face of America in the 21st century*. New York: Times Books.

Spiegel, A. (2002). *Eight-one words: The story of how the American Psychiatric Association decided in 1973 that homosexuality was no longer a mental illness* [Radio broadcast]. Chicago: Chicago Public. Retrieved from *www.thisamericanlife.org/Radio_Episode.aspx?sched=1188*.

Tamasese, K., & Waldegrave, C. (1993). Culture and gender accountability in the "just therapy" approach. *Journal of Feminist Family Therapy, 5*(2), 29–45.

Tataki, R. (Ed.). (1994). *From different shores: Perspectives on race and ethnicity in America* (2nd ed.). New York: Oxford University Press.

Tavris, C. (1992). *The mismeasure of Women*. New York: Simon & Schuster.

Tomm, K. (1990). A critique of the DSM. *Dulwich Centre Newsletter, 3*, 5–8.

Ungar, S. (1995). *Fresh blood: The new American immigrants*. New York: Simon and Schuster.

U.S. Department of Justice. (1994, January). *Violence against women: A national crime victimization survey report*.

CHAPTER 2

Transnational Journeys

Celia Jaes Falicov

A Chilean woman, wearing a head scarf and quite emaciated, sits with her husband and their 2-year-old child in my office. This mother lost all of her hair very soon after leaving her 7-year-old son from a previous marriage in the care of her own mother in Chile. Since then, she says, "I have been suffering from a cancer of the soul." She has her son's framed photo face down in a drawer and cannot bear to make a phone call to him, her emotional suffering is so intense.

A 12-year-old boy has just arrived from Tlaxcala, Mexico, to be reunited with his mother, a laundry worker, from whom he has been separated since age 6. He is rebellious and defies her, arguing that she has no right to discipline him because she "abandoned" him to become a "a woman of ill repute," an idea his rural Mexican grandmother has repeated often in disapproval of the mother having migrated alone to look for a job in the United States.

A 31-year-old Czech woman sits sobbing in my office. She wonders whether her migration 8 years ago to California to marry her African American husband was too much of a sacrifice. Her educated, successful husband does not understand her. It seems absurd to him that her parents' imminent divorce in Prague could cause her such great consternation. After all, he can pay for her to visit her country anytime she wants or even for her parents to visit.

A South Korean mother married to a wealthy American investor brings to therapy her 10-year-old daughter, who is underachieving in private school. The child is very quiet and listless, almost morose. The mother worries that if this goes on, her daughter will not be able to go to Harvard University. She complains that the girl is also falling behind in her practice of piano, ballet, and sports. Mother and daughter spend long summers in South Korea, where the girl's achievements are rejoiced over by the extended family. Part of this mother's distress is precipitated by her fear of her family's judgment of her as a mother who is doing a poor job raising her daughter and squandering American opportunities.

A Puerto Rican middle-aged woman is brought to therapy by her husband and daughters following manic and paranoid-like episodes. She and her husband have managed, after 20 years of extreme hard work, to gradually bring to San Diego 36 members of their original community in Puerto Rico. The couple had become the advisors and economic helpers for this network. Recently, however, a change in attitude within this network may have precipitated the client crises. She had been told by several members in this network that they had grown tired of her "meddling and controlling" everybody, shattering her hopes of recreating her community.

The people in the preceding vignettes are from different countries, different class backgrounds, races, languages, genders, and generations. Yet they have one ailment in common: They deeply feel the disruption of their attachments to family, country, and culture. They strive to keep alive old connections while they shape new lives for themselves far from their birthplaces. Like many immigrants before them, with great determination and daring, they left their countries because they imagined that their lives would be better. The families they formed have been transformed by their migration, as have been the families they left.

In the past, immigrants to the United States handled their long-distance attachments in a variety of ways: Some cut off their ties completely, some maintained tenuous connections, and still others returned to their families and countries. The outcomes depended on the geographic distances, the economic resources, the legal status, and the emotional makeup of the people involved. Although these factors operate today as well, ease of transportation and new technologies of communication and information are constructing a scenario that allows the emergence of transnational lives. Immigrants are understood to be *transnationals* or *transmigrants* when they maintain multiple relations (familial, economic, social, religious) that span geographic, cultural, and political borders. As Schiller, Basch, and Blanc-Szanton (1992, p. ix) state: "Transmigrants take actions, make decisions and feel concerns within a field of social relations that links together their country of origin and their country or countries of settlement."

Transnational families are able to keep up their economic and emotional ties by staying in touch via monetary remittances, phone calls, e-mails, audiotapes, videotapes, and occasional visits for family events, special holidays, and vacations. They can also keep abreast of the latest cultural, economic, and political news and cultural changes in their countries through radio, television, and the Internet. Because lives and relationships are linked across borders, transnationalism offers the attractive, albeit ambiguous, possibility of living with two hearts instead of a broken heart (Falicov, 2007). Family and social connections have a greater chance to remain alive, sometimes throughout the immigrant's lifetime, and even to become an important part of his or her children's cultural legacies (Stone, Gomez, Hotzoglou, & Lipnitsky, 2005). The nostalgic lament "There is no place like home" may still be reserved for a native land that remains vibrant. Yet, when immigrants have children in the new country, have jobs, buy property, and develop communities, they acquire another vibrant new "home" as well.

Proximity to the United States, such as Mexican immigrants have, facilitates decisions to migrate that involve the separation of spouses and also separation of father and children or mother and children. But for the past 10 years, families from faraway places, such as China, Taiwan, or the Philippines, have begun similar lifestyles. Engineers from China or Taiwan may take jobs in Silicon Valley and maintain long-distance relationships with their families for several years. They manage to reunite their families in this country and settle them in schools and communities. Yet they may also seize the opportunity to return to their countries several years later, when a stable future for the family can be envisioned in a familiar environment in which cultural and social status dissonance will not be suffered. These types of temporary immigrants, who have variously been called "astronauts" or "modern nomads" (Wong, 2007), rely on extended households that have not atrophied or disappeared but, rather, are used as tools by many transnationals to adapt to economic globalization.

Although the term "transnational" has been around for the past 30 years, it has now fully captured the attention of a wide variety of migration scholars. Like immigration, transnationalism can be best understood by using an interdisciplinary approach that gathers the insights of several disciplines subsumed under the rubric of migration studies. For family therapists, transnational families are one form of the "brave new families" of this century that present theoretical and therapeutic challenges and demand a new analytical frame for issues of migration, social location, and acculturation. Transnational family arrangements affect community and trigenerational relationships. Even more critically, separations and reunifications between spouses or between parents and children strike at the core of the basic family unit.

TRANSNATIONAL LIVES AND IMPLICATIONS FOR FAMILY INTERVENTION

Transnationalism involves processes of migration that encompass a very large relationship system. Migration is not an experience that belongs solely to those who leave their countries. The protagonists include those who leave, those who stay, and those who come and go for generations to come. Children of transnationals also develop objective and subjective ties to their ancestral homes. Spouses of immigrants also develop a variety of connections and reactions to the language, values, and countries of their mates. The vignettes at the beginning of this chapter illustrate some of these connections, how they persist, and how they are reactivated by various life transitions. Because of fast and accessible communications and frequent contacts, all these players together form a richly interconnected system that continues to evolve over time.

A family's migration narrative, stimulated by a therapist's questions, must include attention to the past and the current complex interactions among all the migration players, whether real or imagined. Answers to questions about the degree of involvement with language, visits to and from the country of origin, sending remittances, frequency of communication via phone or e-mail, and the practice of listening to the country's news, TV programs, or movies may give a measure of the extent to which clients are involved in transnational social fields (Stone et al., 2005).

Answers to questions about the state of mind and heart of those whose stayed behind and their reactions to the migration, initially and over time, are very important. This information sheds light on internal states, interpersonal conflicts, or personal decisions for an individual or family. Therefore, it is central for family therapy theory and practice to delve further into the nature of the interactions maintained at long distance and the weight these have on the presenting concerns of clients.

Separations and Reunifications

Transnationalism may incur many sacrifices in family life. Poor immigrants have always been separated from their families, lured by the promise of an eventual better economic future for all. Separation from extended family and separation of father and children have been common, and economic globalization, by opening up labor opportunities for women, has affected core relationships of care. There are now an unprecedented number of women who separate from their mates and from children of all ages. This sacrifice may have grave consequences, such as husbands and wives and parents and children who reunite after years of separation only to find themselves to be strangers to each other (Nazario, 2007).

Spousal Relationships

Men often leave their families to search for better economic conditions and better futures for their children, and their families become temporarily matrifocal. Sometimes wives have more skills or more promising job opportunities, and they leave their children with their husbands in a patrifocal household. In addition to poverty, other injustices may plague the lives of women who take on the migration journey on their own. They may come to the United States to escape spousal abuse or other types of maltreatment tied to alcoholism, economic exploitation, or infidelity.

In many instances, a reunion between husbands and wives, separated for years, is a very difficult adaptation. A Mexican meat packer who manages to bring his wife and four children to the United States after 12 years of separation finds his wife, in spite of occasional visits and frequent long distance contacts, to have difficulties with closeness and to be resentful of his demands. A Filipino husband, who migrates with his children to reunite with his wife after several years of separation, faces a wife who is furious at her not-unfounded suspicion that he had been carrying on an extramarital affair while she was very far away from home seeking a better future for the whole family.

Spouses grow apart and fall out of love, become jealous, feel envy, and may become depressed at both the decision to separate and the decision to reunite. Of course, there are many couples who rejoice to live with each other again and reconnect easily, but they are most likely not seen in the psychotherapy office.

Changes in values affecting gender relationships often take place in the sending and the receiving countries as part of these transnational journeys. Returning, or come-and-go immigrants, may negatively alter their towns' customs and moral values. These processes appear to weaken family and spousal ties due to an increase in liberal ideas and drug use and a decrease in religiosity (Cornelius & Lewis, 2007).

Relationships between Parents and Children

Separations between parents and children have a host of consequences—some temporary, others long term. Sometimes the sibling group gets separated, as the migrating parent or parents take some children with them and leave others in the care of relatives. The siblings who have accompanied the parents may later incur the envy of the other siblings, who felt rejected or abandoned. Adjustment problems at reunification with a father or a mother range from anger and rebelliousness to excessive clinging, dependency, and fears, depending on the age of the child.[1]

In the first vignette at the beginning of this chapter, we see a mother in unbearable emotional pain, with her heart divided and unable to connect with her child at long distance. The separation debilitates her to the point of psychosomatic symptoms. Her collaboration with her own mother, who takes care of her child back home, is poor and full of tension. The task of therapy is to deal with her depression in a systemic way. In the second vignette, we see a preadolescent child, who hides his hurt at having felt abandoned, in rebellious and offensive confrontation with the mother.

Both of these mothers were very responsible, obtained the full child-rearing support of the grandmothers as caretakers, and sent economic remittances to them. Yet they lacked their emotional approval for the migration. The eventual continuation of their maternal function is jeopardized by this situation. Family therapy needs to undertake transnational thinking and action whenever possible and help empower the mother to become a long-distance partner in raising her child. Furthermore, it is important, if possible, to work with the three generations at the time of reunification, transnationally if necessary. wow.

THE NATURE OF CONNECTIONS AT LONG DISTANCE

To theorize about transnational families demands an exploration of the differences between relationships maintained at long distance and relationships in the intimacy of intensely shared family life. Although transnationalism may assuage the pain of separation and longing for loved ones by allowing connection, one might ask to what extent transnationalism creates connections experienced as "real" and viable in their immediacy as opposed to connections that rely primarily on memory and imagination and, at best, occasional renewal. If transnational relationships provide instrumental and affective support, these are necessarily limited to extraordinary or occasional circumstances, as opposed to daily interactions. Thus the experience of absence may still override the presence obtained via long-distance communications.

In a previous chapter, I referred to the value of several types of rituals that immigrants seem to develop spontaneously (Falicov, 2003). These rituals assume various forms: connection rituals, memory rituals, recreation of spaces, and preserving cultural rituals. Among these, probably the most significant in terms of transnational lives are connection rituals. Exploring the presence or absence of these rituals is very helpful in evaluating the degree of cultural immersion of the transmigrant in the sending culture.

Forms of Connection Rituals

Remittances

The practice of sending money and other resources regularly to families of origin and hometowns is widespread among immigrants of many countries. In these sending towns, once a week, twice or once a month, or less frequently, many women, men over 50, and youths wait for their money orders to buy food, pay rent, handle a medical or dental emergency, or continue to pay for the materials to build a home. These monetary remittances have tremendous importance as economic resources in situations of poverty and also make the absent person present psychologically (Falicov, 2002a). Symbolically, the immigrant is doing his or her part at long distance and still is part of the family. Amounts of money sent are often commensurate with salaries earned but also with length of time in the United States. The longer the person has been in the United States (Cornelius & Lewis, 2007), the less money may be sent over time, for a variety of reasons—such as finding a new spouse in this country who objects to the sharing of resources.

In the countries of origin, packing and mailing services to the United States have proliferated, many in the same places at which the relatives pick up their remittances. Through these local services, relatives do their part to maintain the connection with those who left by sending photos, music CDs, videos, postcards, stamps of local religious figures or saints, candles, holy waters, and favorite regional foods, including some unauthorized ones.[2]

Family therapists will learn about these exchanges mostly by asking, because most clients would consider them natural or unimportant and would not necessarily speak about the possible meanings they have. These exchanges could symbolize strong continuity of family ties and of cultural habits and a new definition of the present as including what used to be considered the immigrant's past. With immigrant clients, therapists can explore whether relationships would be enhanced or conflicts decreased by utilizing remittances of various sorts. Care must be exerted to include a discussion of the meanings invested by all involved, as ambiguities could arise, for example, if remittances unwittingly contribute to deepening the social inequalities between those who are there and those who are here.

Communications

Just as economic connections acquire various emotional meanings, more direct emotional contacts, such as are possible via phone calls, e-mails, or special messages through cards or letters, are equally important in maintaining connections. The ease of these communications has vastly improved. For less than $10 today's immigrants can purchase a telephone company service that lets them receive an unlimited number of phone calls from their relatives in many Latin American, Asian, and other countries. Phone cards that can be purchased in many street stands in major American cities also make long phone conversations very inexpensive. Families of limited means may not have computers in their homes, but they sometimes use Internet cafés in their countries. However, telephones may still be the preferred way to connect for the vast majority of immigrants. These technologies open up many possibilities for sharing concerns, informal chatting, and so forth.

Therapists could inquire about or suggest the possibility of making use of these communication devices for therapeutic purposes. However, it is important to consider that these suggestions may be received with considerable ambivalence. Parents separated from their children may cope with the distress and sorrow by blocking affect and choosing not to open themselves to the intense emotions of hearing the voices of their children, knowing the details of their lives, or having to answer their questions.

Daily routines are not shared, and often truths are not, either. The flow of information between those who have left and those who have stayed may be selective and superficially positive. Each side may be being protective of the other. Economic transmigrants, in particular, may be invested in making the migration appear worthwhile by not sharing problematic aspects of what they have encountered. The South Korean mother mentioned in the early vignette wanted to make sure that her family of origin would believe that her migration was worthwhile in the sense of what matters to them— the education of her child. Having to face a less successful outcome was painful.

Speaking of suffering may worry relatives. Speaking too positively may give rise to resentments or envy in the family of origin. It is hard to hit the right mark, because ambiguous, evasive, or distorted communications have the effects of disrupting family intimacy. It may behoove therapists to explore possibilities for specific communications between a client and members of his or her family for specific purposes of clarification, of sharing a difficult situation, of seeking advice, or of sharing remorse for a past deed.

Virtual Communities

Remittances extend well beyond the family. Many transnationals continue to have a presence, virtual or real, in their communities of origin through participation in a variety of causes and social projects. At the psychological level, these connections probably help to deal with losses of social and cultural capital while assuaging feelings of guilt for leaving to acquire more resources. Transnationals can support projects that are symbolically connected with issues that have been the cause of suffering or joy by donating money for services related to hunger, health, education, or religion. It may mean that their sacrifices have not been in vain. They can attempt to repair old regrets or look forward to a better future for their communities or themselves, such as fulfilling the dream of home ownership. Sometimes the attempts to remain connected to the community move from the virtual to the realized, as when an immigrant fulfills the dream of community reunification by helping the migration of members of their original communities. However, problems sometimes arise in these attempts, as in the case of the Puerto Rican woman whose breakdown was precipitated by the rejection of the community that she had helped to reconstitute and who was now embroiled in a negative gossip system.

Original communities can be imagined as home extensions, with their physical and human resources. Therapists must capitalize on these resources the way families do. If resources permit, it may be desirable to send at-risk adolescents to school in their parents' countries in order to get them away from the undesirable influences in this country, such as gang involvement. Unfortunately, this social phenomenon can also be exported, resulting in the appearance of U.S.-like gangs in such places as Ecuador, Guatemala, and El Salvador.

LEGACIES IN MOTION:
THE SECOND GENERATION AND TRANSNATIONALISM

Transnationalism has important consequences for the second generation. Attachments to country and culture in the children of immigrants could be, at least in part, the outcome of either unconscious or purposeful induction on the parents' part. Telling stories to share the past, to create bridges with the present, and to caution against excessive Americanization is one of the rituals of immigrant family life that lend a sense of narrative coherence and family continuity (Falicov, 2003).

Through these interactions, children of immigrants may become *emotional transmigrants* (Wolf, 2002). Some children of Cuban or Greek immigrants are mesmerized by the beauty of the beaches in Cuba or in Greece, although these beaches may be conjured in their imaginations only (Stone et al., 2005). The voices of their parents may populate these idealized accounts, perhaps because of the magnetic power of the immigrant story within their families (Falicov, 2005).

Rather than feeling " lost in translation," as the second generation presumably became in the past, the new second generations may attempt to "grow in translation." Yet positive transnationalism may not be sufficient to overcome the negative experiences of immigrant children who face racism and discrimination in school. Suarez-Orozco and Suarez-Orozco (2001) observed that immigrant children develop a keen eye for the negative reception they suffer because of their ethnicity. These authors conclude that parents' positive mirroring of their ethnic group may not fully compensate for the distorted reflections that their children encounter outside the home, which, of course, affects their own ethnic identity formation and even their view of their parents' culture or status. In the face of discrimination, psychological defenses such as idealization may be used, but denigration and self-destructiveness may also occur. For example, in the movie *My Family* (Nava, 1995), Chucho, the son who has been selling marijuana in the barrios of Los Angeles, says that he engaged in this business to avoid undergoing the oppression his father endured as a poor immigrant, in spite of the fact that both parents instilled in him a great deal of love for Mexican culture.

The exploration of transnational affiliation may be significant for the second generation, even though they may not make reference to immigration per se or experience the same poignancy of ambiguous loss that their parents have (Falicov, 2005). The second generation may travel, learn language and traditions, and accept or reject cultural values. Exploration of language spoken in the household is important, as bilingual households are more ndicative of transnationalism. The second generation and the one-and-a-half generation—that is, those who migrated before age 12—may have knowledge about their birth stories or about how their first names were chosen and passed on by their parents, as these names often contain cultural meanings and symbols (Stone et al., 2005). Likewise, cultural theories of illness and home remedies, including for concerns presented in therapy, may coexist with mainstream use of services and cures.

A man's attachment to his father's cultural legacy could lead him to search for a wife in the father's country, as in the case of a Lebanese American young man who went to Lebanon and paid a dowry to secure a Lebanese wife and bring her to the United States. In therapy for marital conflict, it was discovered that this client had attributed the failure of his parents' marriage to his Lebanese American mother's lack of tolerance for his Lebanese father's infidelities. This client believed that his mother had defended her rights as a result of her Americanization and that a nonacculturated Lebanese wife would be insurance against women's modern entitlements. Ironically, he did not take into account the possibility that a native-born young Lebanese woman had grown up in a environment of rapidly changing gender roles. Indeed, his wife came from a family in which the father was nurturing and involved and did not fit the patriarchal stereotype. Paradoxically, for this young wife, her first encounter with overt family patriarchy occurred with her young American husband.

THEORIES OF ACCULTURATION AND TRANSNATIONALISM

Acculturation theory was based on the idea that there is only one place that a person can call "home." By and large the assumption has been that eventual assimilation by changing their language and culture was a good outcome for immigrants in a pluralistic society. Clinicians interested in cultural values have used acculturation theory to judge how far along immigrants are on the continuum of adaptation to the new society.

Transnationalism upsets the applecart of traditional linear ideas about the gradual assimilation of immigrants. The crossings of geographic, political, and cultural borders creates a bidirectional flow whereby changes and adjustments occur in the sending and receiving countries. New relationships are created and old ones maintained, and both undergo cultural negotiations and hybridizations.

The liveliness of these cultural connections between homes could be interpreted as working against assimilation to the host country. It appears more likely, however, that new immigrants and their children combine transnational and assimilative practices inside and outside their homes at different stages of their lives and that they use these various combinations to construct their flexible bicultural identities. Furthermore, gender, race, and social class, along with experiences of discrimination and xenophobia, interact with transnational identities and create great diversity in family stories. Several of my Latina clients, in spite of strong family and cultural attachments, are leery of endogamy because they are critical of aspects of Latino male socialization that could make men in their cultural group questionable candidates for marriage. They may prefer to marry American men, whom they perceive to be more egalitarian. At the individual level, what seems to occur is a selective biculturalism that requires exploration for each client.

The level of acculturation of today's immigrant is unpredictable. Or perhaps it always was. In most families, continuity and change are happening side by side in creative, nonlinear ways. Some family members may adhere to certain customs, such as home remedies or foods; but the same members or others may oppose vigorously the arranged marriages favored in their culture. Some preferences may have remained unchanged, such as the insistence on modest attire for a daughter. But other aspects of the same patriarchal ideology may have been transformed—for example, an insistence on higher education for young women so that they may be economically independent from domineering men if need be. In short, rather than predicting inevitable assimilation, it is possible to imagine transnationalism and assimilation as coexisting, particularly for the first and the second generations.

BINATIONAL COMPARATIVE STUDIES

Transnationalism has also affected how migration studies are conceived and conducted. New studies involve comparing people who are culturally similar but who live in different places—for example, immigrants to the United States and people who have remained in the same original localities. These studies hold promise for a more thorough and grounded understanding of the processes involved in migration at many levels. Their findings hold promise of useful clinical applications. Only a few examples of these binational studies can be mentioned here.

The SALUD Mexican Immigrant Project (Farley, 2002) compared the health status of those who stayed in their hometown of Guanajuato, Mexico, with that of immigrants to Colorado who originated from the same areas. The findings indicated that emotional problems such as depression, anxiety, substance abuse, and posttraumatic stress caused greater disability than physical problems among the immigrant population as opposed to their Mexican counterparts. Based on these findings, an array of collaborative transnational health projects has been undertaken between the two locations, origin and destination, designed to improve the mental health status of this population of clients (see Falicov, 2002b).

Many contemporary comparative ethnographies collect data in two or more communities. Noteworthy for this chapter are studies that compare life situations in Mexican locations with the changes taking place in the United States for immigrants from those same locations.

A comparison of sexuality and love in couples who have migrated to Atlanta, Georgia, with similar couples who have remained in their small Mexican towns in Jalisco makes a compelling case for changes in cultural ideals about types of marriages preferred. In her sophisticated analysis of interviews, anthropologist Jennifer Hirsch (2003) describes how women and men in both places are attempting to create modern marriages based on sexual love and trust (*confianza*) while striving to maintain the strengths of traditional marital bonds based on respect and commitment.

Another important study illustrates how immigrants and their children move back and forth between New York and their home village in Puebla, Mexico, borrowing from and contributing to both communities as they forge new gender relationships, new parental practices, new conceptions of adolescence, and even new strategies for social mobility in both places while also maintaining many continuities of values and traditions (Smith, 2006).

An interesting example of a transnational type of study in family therapy is offered by Gomez de Leon del Rio and Vicencio Guzman (2006). Clinical interviews in Ocotepec and Cuernavaca in Mexico revealed a large number of cases in which the family's requests for therapy were strongly connected with the departure of family members to the United States, as the stress and anxieties of these families begin with the trip itself and with waiting for a report of safe arrival at the United States destination. In addition to the information about the effects of family fragmentation, these studies have the potential for developing models for professional collaboration and transnational therapeutic interventions.

Binational studies hold the most promise for elucidating issues related to globalization, migration, and culture change. They also hold promise for developing collaborative relationships among anthropologists, sociologists, service providers, and policymakers.

CONCLUSION

The themes of loss and discontinuity that dominated the clinical literature on immigrants are revised in this chapter with a stress on contact and continuity with the sending societies made possible by global communication advances. Families separated across countries may be able to maintain greater connections than in the past but may also suffer separations that affect core relationships between spouses and between parents and children. The processes precipitated by migration, here and in the immigrants' countries, create personal and cultural complexities through disconnections, renewals, and transformations that affect the first and the second generations. Therapists need to take into account the nature of long-distance relationships in terms of theory, practice, and policy to ensure services to families that enhance their opportunities for resilient adaptations. Binational studies have the potential to supply useful comparative information about health, mental health, and changing values and practices. Therapists must also become transnational in their thinking and practices by making use of the various new technologies of communication to include the clients' families and communities in their places of origin in the processes of maintaining and renewing family life at long distance.

NOTES

1. Current policies that intend to restrict nondocumented immigration separate families even more dramatically by impeding visits or reunification, since traveling between the hometown and the United States has become even more terribly dangerous (Cornelius et al., 2005)
2. The need for these social and cultural remittances, particularly in the Mexico–United States circuit, is so extensive that businesses have seized the opportunity. They obtain transportation permits across borders that facilitate robust exchanges of goods and resources between separated family members (Rivera-Sanchez, 2007).

REFERENCES

Cornelius, W. (2005, April). *Immigration patterns changing with new border security*. Los Angeles: Associated Press Wire Service.

Cornelius, W., & Lewis, J. (Eds.). (2007). *Impacts of border enforcement on Mexican migration*. San Diego: University of California Center for Migration Studies.

Falicov, C. J. (2002a). Ambiguous loss: Risk and resilience in Latino families. In M. Suarez-Orozco & M. Paez (Eds.), *Latinos: Remaking America* (pp. 274–288). Berkeley: University of California Press.

Falicov, C. J. (2002b). Commentary on "The Salud Mexican Immigrant Project." *The Family Psychobiologist, 18*(1), 1, 7–8.

Falicov, C. J. (2003.). Immigrant family processes. In F. Walsh (Ed.), *Normal family processes* (pp. 280–300). New York: Guilford Press.

Falicov, C. J. (2005). Emotional transnationalism and family identities. *Family Process, 44*(4), 399–406.

Falicov, C. J. (2007). Working with transnational immigrants: Expanding meanings of family, community on culture. *Family Process, 46*(2), 157–172.

Farley, T. (2002). Cultural transition and integrated health care: The SALUD Mexican immigrant projects. *The Family Psychologist, 18*(1), 1, 6–8.

Gomez de Leon del Rio, J., & Vicencio Guzman, J. (2006). The impact of absence: Families, migration, and family therapy in Ocotepec, Mexico. *American Family Therapy Academy* [Monograph Series], *2*(1), 34–43.

Hirsch, J. (2003). *A courtship after marriage: Sexuality and love in Mexican transnational families*. Los Angeles: University of California Press.

Nava, G. (Director). (1995). *My family* [Motion picture]. U.S. New Line Cinema.

Rivera-Sanchez, M. (2007, February). *El valor de las remisas socioculturales*. Paper presented at conference "Educar a Migrantes," Culiacán, Sinaloa, Mexico.

Nazario, S. (2007). *Enrique's journey: The story of a boy's dangerous odyssey to reunite with his mother*. New York: Random House.

Schiller, N. G., Basch, L., & Blanc-Szanton, C. (1992). Towards a definition of transnationalism: Introductory remarks and research questions. In N. G. Schiller, L. Basch, & C. Blanc-Szanton (Eds.), *Towards a transnational perspective on migration: Race, class, ethnicity and nationalism reconsidered* (pp. ix–xv). New York: New York Academy of Sciences.

Smith, R. C. (2006). *Mexican New York: Transnational lives of new immigrants*. Berkeley: University of California Press.

Stone, E., Gomez, E., Hotzoglou, D., & Lipnitsky, J. (2005). Transnationalism as a motif in family stories. *Family Process, 44*, 381–398.

Suarez-Orozco, C., & Suarez-Orozco, M. (2001). *Children of immigration*. Cambridge, MA: Harvard University Press.

Wolf, D. L. (2002). There is no place like "home": Emotional transnationalism and the struggles of second-generation Filipinos. In P. Levitt & M. C. Waters (Eds.), *The changing face of home: The transnational lives of the second generation* (pp. 255–294). New York: Sage.

Wong, B. P. (2007). Immigration, globalization, and the Chinese American family. In J. E. Lansford, K. Deater-Deakard, & M. H. Bornstein (Eds.), *Immigrant families in contemporary society* (pp. 212–230). New York: Guilford Press.

CHAPTER 3

Migration and the Disruption of the Social Network

Carlos E. Sluzki

Our personal social networks—that rather stable but continually evolving interpersonal fabric woven of close and distant family members, friends, work and study connections, and relationships that result from informal and formal participation in community organizations (religious, social, political, health-related, etc.)—constitute a key depository of our identities, our histories, and our well-being (Sluzki, 1996). Countless research projects have evidenced the tight correlation between quality of the personal social support system and the individual's health and chances of survival (Berkman, 1984; Berkman & Kawachi, 2000; House, Robbins, & Metzner, 1982; Schoenbach, Kaplan, Friedman, & Kleinbach, 1986). This correlation extends to a varied array of factors, such as frequency of myocardial infarctions (Orth-Gomer, Rosengren, & Wilhelmsen, 1993) and recovery from that disorder (Medalie, Snyder, Groen, Neufeld, Goldbourt, et al., 1973), tuberculosis (Holmes, 1956), accidents (Tillman & Hobbes, 1949), likelihood of rehospitalization after being discharged from a psychiatric hospital (Dozier, Harris, & Bergman, 1987), and even the common cold (Cohen, Doyle, Skoner, Rabin, & Gwaltney, 1997).

The personal social network is a dynamic, evolving system. It affects and is affected by each of the normative stages in a person's life. In fact, most of the rituals that recognize life passages, from birth to marriage to death, include active network participation. It is also extremely sensitive to cultural and gender variables: Different cultures have different norms and expectations in terms of network involvement in people's everyday lives, and females and males show marked differences in network development and maintenance and utilization skills.

In the increasingly mobile society that characterizes our industrial and postindustrial eras, relocation (within countries) and migration (between countries) constitute an almost normative phenomenon that unavoidably entails a major disruption in the social niche of the individual (Sluzki, 1979, 1992). Normativity notwithstanding, this disruption and its effects are seldom explicitly recognized by either the public or mental health professionals. As a result, people who migrate can do little to manage these processes (and, when they suffer the consequences of that disruption, they experience it as *their own* failure).

This chapter illustrates the severe effects of the disruption of the personal social network during migration with a poignant clinical case and underlines some therapeutic stances that may ameliorate their effect.

CASE BACKGROUND AND INITIAL INTERVIEW

A family of Filipino origin came to a family medicine clinic to seek treatment for a 14-year-old boy who had begun 2 months earlier to exhibit striking symptoms: body tics, such as moving his arms as if to shoo flies away, and voicing clicking sounds as well as profanities uttered in the course of conversations or out of the blue, alternating with otherwise pleasant and appropriate behavior and speech. The youngster acted oblivious to those behaviors and, when confronted about them, could not explain them. Their disruptive interference with the young man's daily social behavior had recently increased to the point that he had been suspended from school. Further, he could no longer use public transportation, as fellow passengers would take the insults he was muttering personally and occasionally confronted him. The clinically astute reader will have already recognized in this description the traits of Tourette syndrome, which many specialists attribute to a neurological base, although others define it as an independent diagnostic category.

During the interview, this slender, properly dressed, shy, and pleasant youngster participated moderately. His utterances as well as his silences, were punctuated by occasional noises, insults, and abrupt movements that occurred, so to speak, on a channel parallel to that of the conversation but crisscrossing it rather frequently. The boy seemed almost indifferent to the symptoms and their effects. When, after one of these bizarre behaviors, I would ask him "What was that?" he would either deny those enactments or define them as puzzling for himself (his typical answers were "Nothing" or "I don't know"). The content of his contribution to the conversation was, otherwise, totally appropriate for his age, without any hint of additional "pathology." Until he was suspended from the school, his academic performance had been satisfactory.

His parents—a young, educated, elegant, and socially gracious couple fluent in English—expressed their preoccupation and puzzlement about their son. A younger daughter, 10 years old, participated appropriately in the interview. She "normalized" her brother's unusual behavior except in public situations, in which it made her laugh or feel ashamed.

As the interview progressed, I explored everybody's theories about the boy's symptoms. The parents informed me that their family physician had made a provisional diagnosis of schizophrenia, but they did not understand very clearly what it meant. Neither the youngster himself nor his sister offered any theory or insight into the matter. In turn, I stated that I had not yet been able to produce a cogent explanation for the youngster's behavior, but that I supposed that, as frequently is the case with tics, it had to do with stress. This vague, tension-reducing statement seemed to satisfy the parents, at least at that point in the session. I informed them that I would recommend temporarily a medication for the boy—more specifically haloperidol, which is recommended for this syndrome in the psychopharmacological literature. I also proposed to follow this consultation with a few meetings with the parents alone, to explore with them additional elements of their family history, so that I could better understand their predicament.

The decision to medicate (and in general terms my wish to keep myself up-to-date with clinical psychopharmacology) reflected my commitment to maintaining a balanced biopsychosocial perspective in clinical practice and my desire to avoid the risk of depriving patients under my care of the possible benefit of psychotropic medications. However, this eclectic position contains an unavoidable drawback: Once I have added the medication, I lose the possibility of discriminating the relative contribution of the psychosocial interventions and the neurobiological interventions to any improvement. In turn, my decision to interview the parental couple alone derived from my impression during the first interview that they kept a stance of "model parents" in front of their children—and, indeed, in front of me, if not of each other. This fits also with what I understand is a dominant value in people heavily influenced by Asian-Oriental cultures: saving face at all expense.

INTERVIEWS WITH THE PARENTS ALONE

In the course of the two interviews with the parents that followed—scheduled 2 weeks apart—the family history unfolded. They both belonged to upper-middle-class traditional Filipino families and had been raised in tightly knit, extended family, and a protected environment. He was a lawyer, and his father, also an attorney, had been a senator representing an opposition party. She, in turn, had a private college education. They had known each other since childhood, as their parents shared social circles and clubs. Almost predictably, they had begun their courtship as adolescents and married young with everybody's blessing. Their two children had been embraced by the welcoming web of their two extended families. Their social life evolved in a sheltered and stable fashion, following class- and culture-outlined social pathways. However, 5 years before this interview, after a military *coup d'état* that unleashed a political persecution of those opposed to the new de facto regime, his family of origin and, by extension, this couple became potential targets for political victimization. Responding to the encouragement of their families and to protect themselves, as well as their children, the couple moved to the United States. While receiving economic support from both families, the husband started working full time. Because his credentials as an attorney were not valid in the United States, he accepted a position as coordinator of a local social center for the Filipino community. The wife decided to complete training as dental hygienist and started working part time during the hours their children were in school. Both mentioned with a smile that the adaptation to the new circumstances hadn't been easy, but, in what I understood was an effort to keep up the proper appearances, both affirmed that it had been a positive experience.

In turn, through my own interventions I introduced progressively the "shadow" of their story, responding to their descriptions with occasional comments—even illustrated by some personal anecdotes—about the difficulties inherent in the experience of immigration, about normative situations of cross-cultural misunderstanding and dissonance, and about the family difficulties triggered by the unavoidable interpersonal overload of migration. In this fashion I generated an empathetic echo about untold aspects of their recent history. This had the progressive effect of normalizing their difficulties and legitimizing their experiences. Their pain ceased being a sign of weakness or incompetence and became a common, if not unavoidable, effect of inherently difficult circumstances. My comments also modeled for them a stance of openness about one's own pain that contributed to defining the context of therapy as a safe one.

They became progressively more expressive and less defensive with me. Even more important, they opened up to each other. Once and over again, when one of them would describe (almost confess) some specific area of difficulties, the other would respond with surprise: "You never told me that! I did not realize that you were having such a bad time." I eventually remarked: "Each one of you seems to have tried to take care of the other through minimizing comments about your own difficulties. But that may have the unavoidable aftereffect of reducing your alertness to the other's signals." They found this comment very helpful and relieving. At one point the wife began to sob while expressing her isolation and feelings of loneliness, and the husband exclaimed with astonishment and tenderness that those were the first tears he had seen her weep since they arrived in the United States.

This rich unfolding of the spouses' individual and joint histories also allowed me to glance at the vicissitudes of their social network in the course of this difficult transition. Each of them had grown up in an extended family, with a broad and dense net of relatives and acquaintances, including many stable, long-lasting friendships with classmates and playmates from childhood, adolescent friends and teammates, workmates turned friends, and conjoint (couple) friends. Even after their marriage, despite getting along very well and loving each other, each spouse kept his or her own personal network of close friends, in addition to the shared friends with whom they socialized. The wife could confide her emotional problems to her female cousins and friends, her parents, and her brothers and could ask for and provide advice and emotional nourishment. And so could her husband within his own old and stable network. In fact, the couple simply *did not need* to develop a broad range of areas of intimacy, nor had they acquired the skills to do so, as many of these interpersonal functions were consistently and nonconflictually covered by other members of their network. In addition, such intimacy was not prescribed by their culture (including the culture of their class), within which men and women kept many separate social relations, activities, and encounters.

Once the family migrated, the couple's interpersonal net collapsed dramatically. They now lived surrounded by people with whom they had little in common. They were not skilled in developing new relationships quickly (a skill that is often developed, for instance, by members of military families, who have to move frequently from base to base). There was also a class difference between them and many people of their community; their upper-class bias made it harder for them to reach out to these others. This substantial social vacuum was, of course, within their awareness, but the extent of its effect on them was not. One of these effects was that each one of them began to expect that the other would fulfill interpersonal roles and functions previously covered by others, as well as provide newly needed reciprocal support. Each spouse expected the other to become an unconditional soother, lover, confidant, companion, and sounding board, despite the fact that some of these roles were totally new for them within the couple relationship. And this was happening precisely during a period in which each of the spouses was overloaded and needy and, therefore, less open and accessible to the needs of the other. Besides, both were trapped by certain added constraints inherent in their culture in regard to behaviors that are considered acceptable and expected for a couple. It was difficult for them to lower the drawbridge of intimacy when some of the potential exchanges would lessen the face-saving quality of merely formal exchanges.

We gently explored these difficulties, overloads, and pains of loneliness. An added step was reached when I introduced an idea that was rather novel for them: that perhaps their children were experiencing these same types of emotions and difficulties. Moreover, I suggested that perhaps their son's strange behavior was a way of demanding attention, despite the inconveniences brought about by his method. The spouses stated that a good part of their effort had been dedicated to easing the transition for their children, but they acknowledged that their efforts had been focused more on practical matters than on providing emotional support. The husband worried that he had distanced himself from the youngsters, particularly from his son. The wife told him gently that since the move, he had been less expressive of his affection in general (thus gently implying that she had also been affected by this), although she quickly justified it on the basis of his work overload and the other family responsibilities he had assumed. The husband accepted her observation at face value and reassured her that he would do his best to express his affection for all three of them. In general terms, both partners acknowledged self-critically that they had been stingy in their support of each other; they vowed to increase their sensitivity toward each other's needs, as well as to be more open about their own needs, following relational pathways explored and experienced as safe in the course of both sessions.

Despite my curiosity, because I did not wish to sidetrack our focus from the interpersonal processes, I explored only minimally how the son's symptoms were evolving. When I did ask, they mentioned that he was improving markedly. Indeed, in the course of the second session with the couple, they let me know that the boy had returned to school and no longer had difficulties in social situations or on public transportation. Also, as we were finishing the session, and as if it were an afterthought, the father mentioned that there were signals of improvement in the political climate in the Philippines that might open up the possibility of the family's return there. He confessed that one of his few areas of trepidation was his sense that to return home without having "conquered America" would be tantamount to failure. His wife told him that she had already feared that such a sense of failure would trouble him and that she hadn't mentioned the issue before for fear of offending him, because she knew how important success was for him. She then showered him with praises for, and evidences of, his success, especially considering the many difficulties entailed by their abrupt migration. The spouses also took advantage of this atmosphere of openness and intimacy to reveal to each other that they had kept private contact through mail with friends and relatives in their country and acknowledged that their until-then unspoken desire to return had conspired against developing a fulfilling social network in the United States: "Why should we make the effort to establish social contacts if we were thinking of returning to our country soon?" Both laughed, relieved that this topic could now be discussed. I suggested to them that, once they felt totally comfortable with this topic, they might discuss it with their children, who might also bear some secret hopes similar to or different from theirs. This last comment worried the parents: What would happen if they wanted to return but their children did not? This second session with the parents alone closed with their expressions of gratitude, which I reciprocated by stating that I had also learned a lot from their openness.

FOLLOW-UP MEETING

I scheduled a follow-up interview 1 month later with the whole family, in which the parents described changes in the family climate—specifically, more closeness and warmth. They also mentioned that they were discussing openly the pros and cons of a return to the Philippines. They were planning for their son to be the first one to leave, as he needed to prepare for the examinations for admission into an elite private secondary school. He would live temporarily with his grandparents until the return of the rest of the family. I commented that there was something epic in sending the son as a scout to explore the territory and prepare the locals for the family's reentry. Smiling at the metaphor, they praised their son for his new potential role. The boy—who was continuing to take the prescribed medication and to function well in school—did not present any symptomatic behavior during the session.

I had one last interview with them 4 months later, in which they commented that the son—who was remaining free of symptoms—had already returned and that everybody was excited about their own return. The couple, as well as their daughter, appear happy and well connected. They left with expressions of extreme appreciation. Some 8 months after that session, I received a postcard from the family, signed by all, sending me season's greetings from the Philippines.

DISCUSSION

Even though the network disruption that follows a relocation is more readily explicit and salient as a theme for families belonging to cultures that favor close-knit, extended family ties and that are characterized by low geographic mobility, the active exploration of those variables with any family that has migrated or relocated, regardless of the culture of origin of the family, will show that these vicissitudes constitute a theme of almost universal appeal. This theme constitutes one of those "strange attractors" (Sluzki, 1998) that will organize the collective conversation in a meaningful way, with powerful transformative potentials of the collective experience.

In the rich tapestry of processes characterizing therapy with a family such as this one, I would like to highlight the following points:

- The vicissitudes of the experience of migration constitute a narrative that is readily accepted by all the participants—family and therapist alike—as a legitimate and meaningful subject of the therapeutic conversation. It allows all the characters of the story to be placed in dignifying loci; it permits the therapist to define areas of conflict that do not hinge negatively on the intentions or competence of all the participants; and it generates a background against which actions acquire a positive meaning, difficulties are legitimized, problems are redefined, and alternative solutions are developed. From that perspective, the theme of migration expands and reorganizes the description of the problems and the range of potential solutions.
- Migration unavoidably overloads any family, and especially the parents. Many functions previously fulfilled by the members of the extended network—relatives as well as friends—remain unfulfilled; each member of the family, experiencing that void, expects the other to fill in, regardless of the fact that the other may never have done so before. As these needs go unsatisfied, complaints and resentment often ensue, which only contribute to escalating both partners' needs and lack of availability.
- This increase in needs and reciprocal expectations takes place precisely when the partners are most overloaded and less able to fulfill each other's needs.
- The dedication to fulfilling children's needs is frequently a smoke screen to hide the needs of the adults. At the same time, the parents' need to concentrate on everyday survival may make them miss clues to the pain and difficulties in their children, especially if those mimic the parents' problems.
- A key component for functioning as both cultural broker and legitimizer of the experiences of dissonance requires that the therapist maintain an empathetic, contextualizing, and normalizing stance, with assumptions of competence and good intent about the participants' behaviors.

The explicit focus of the therapist on the vicissitudes of the process of migration is readily understood by the consulting families and has the powerful effect of both demystifying and depathologizing the therapeutic process. Symptoms and conflicts are thus not an expression of pathology or of incompetence but the by-product of an intrinsically and unavoidably complex and painful process for which people are seldom prepared and for which they have to develop new skills and awareness.

REFERENCES

Berkman, L. F. (1984). Assessing the physical health effects of social networks and social support. *Annual Review of Public Health, 5*, 413–432.

Berkman, L. F., & Kawachi, I. (2000). *Social epidemiology*. New York: Oxford University Press.

Cohen, S., Doyle, W. J., Skoner, D. P., Rabin, B. S., & Gwaltney, J. M., Jr. (1997). Social ties and susceptibility to the common cold. *Journal of the American Medical Association, 277*(24), 1940–1944.

Dozier, M., Harris, M., & Bergman, H. (1987). Social network density and rehospitalization among young adult patients. *Hospital and Community Psychiatry, 38*(1), 61–65.

Holmes, T. H. (1956). Multidiscipline studies of tuberculosis. In P. J. Soarer (Ed.), *Personality, stress and tuberculosis* (pp. 92–102). New York: International Universities Press.

House, J., Robbins, C., & Metzner H. (1982). The association of social relations with mortality: Prospective evidence from the Tecumseh Community Health Study. *American Journal of Epidemiology, 116*, 123–140.

Medalie, J. H., Snyder, M., Groen, J. J., Neufeld, H. N., Goldbourt, U., & Riss, E. (1973). Angina pectoris among 10,000 men: 5-year incidence and multivariate analysis. *American Journal of Medicine, 55*, 583–594.

Orth-Gomer, K., Rosengren, A., & Wilhelmsen, L. (1993). Lack of support and incidence of coronary heart disease in middle-aged Swedish men. *Psychosomatic Medicine, 55*, 37–43.

Schoenbach, V., Kaplan, H., Friedman, L., & Kleinbach, D. (1986). Social ties and mortality in Evans County, Georgia. *American Journal of Epidemiology, 123*, 577–591.

Sluzki, C. E. (1979). Migration and Family conflict. *Family Process, 18*(1), 379–392.

Sluzki, C. E. (1992). Network disruption and network reconstruction in the process of migration/relocation. *Family Systems Medicine, 10*(4), 359–364.

Sluzki, C. E. (1996). *La red social: Frontera de la terapia sistemica* [*The social network: Frontier of systemic therapy*]. Barcelona, Spain: Gedisa.

Sluzki, C. E. (1998). Strange attractors and the transformation of narratives in therapy. In M. F. Hoyt (Ed.), *The handbook of constructive therapies* (pp. 159–179). San Francisco: Jossey-Bass.

Tillman, W., & Hobbes, G. (1949). The accident-prone automobile driver: A study of psychiatric and social background. *American Journal of Psychiatry, 106*, 321–330.

CHAPTER 4

Social Class

Implications for Family Therapy

Tracey A. Laszloffy

The United States is a society divided along class lines, although rarely, if ever, is this reality acknowledged. Preferring to live in a state of collective denial about our class segregation, we cling to idealized notions that we are a classless society. Although it is obvious that some people have a lot of money and some have very little, as a society we resist public acknowledgment or discourse about class stratification and inequality. This is ironic given that another one of our popular myths is that we all have an equal opportunity for upward mobility, raising the question, "if we are a classless society, how can there be an upper place to move to?" Yet both notions, although contradictory, are firmly rooted in America. Hence, although we are a nation wedded to the myth that we are class-free, the vast majority aspire to the ranks of the elite, convinced by the myth of equal opportunity that their aspirations are within their reach.

The myth of equal opportunity has as its logical extension another deeply rooted myth, which is the conclusion that what each person has or does not have is the direct result of her or his effort and perseverance. The danger of this myth is that it leads those with economic privilege to feel self-righteous and deserving and to defend what they have on the grounds that their hard work alone produced their success. Conversely, for the economically disadvantaged, what they do not have is regarded as the result of their failure to exercise a comparable level of effort, ingenuity, and persistence. In short, what they lack is considered their fault and their fault alone.

MYTHS AND REALITIES

The three aforementioned myths—(1) that we are a classless society, (2) yet we all have an equal chance of upward mobility, and (3) therefore we are all individually responsible for what we have or do not have—obscure our understanding of the realities of how class shapes our society. Moreover, the misconceptions generated by these myths lead to additional myths that further undermine our ability to clearly recognize how class organizes our lives. Hence, this chapter begins by identifying and debunking several key myths that contaminate our perception of and ability to address class issues both in our lives and in therapy.

"Blessed Are the Poor"

The role that Judeo–Christian roots play in shaping American values contributes to a long-standing myth that poverty is synonymous with virtue. According to this myth, the poor are valued because their material deprivation underpins spiritual abundance. Hence poverty is regarded as a pathway to spiritual purity. Although this is a noble sentiment, in truth very few Americans, of all class levels, genuinely believe this. If they did, most would be striving to live with less instead of madly pursuing more. To the contrary, to be poor in America is to be degraded and dismissed, scorned and shamed. To be poor is to be loathed and treated with such disdain by the privileged classes that at some point, the poor come to loathe themselves. Bombarded with an endless barrage of messages that to be poor is a mark of inferiority and an indicator that one is defective, the poor internalize these beliefs and learn to devalue themselves just as the broader society devalues them. Far from the myth of being blessed, the reality is that the poor are viewed, treated, and therefore experience themselves, as cursed.

"I'm Middle-Class"

Most Americans identify themselves as belonging to the amorphous "middle class." This was the case even during the Great Depression. The factors that lead most people to claim that they are middle class differ depending on one's actual class location. The wealthy fall prey to the myth of middle-classness because they evaluate their class standing by looking upward. They compare themselves with those who have more, not less; hence they see their "deprivation" rather than their great abundance (hooks, 2000). Among the poor, the myth of middle-classness often is a response to the shame of poverty and the desire to distance oneself from this shame. Because poverty is devalued, many of the poor prefer to avoid this association, opting instead for the safety of the all-encompassing "middle-class" label. Hence, whether barely surviving at the poverty line or possessing a vast portfolio of blue-chip stocks, both the poor and the rich advance the myth that they are middle class.

Most Americans are located somewhere in the "middle" to the extent that they are neither poor nor rich. However, the concept of middle class really is a myth because, in reality, tremendous diversity characterizes the wide span of area that is the "middle" of the extremes. Consider two "middle-class" families who each refer to themselves as middle class but, as the details of their lifestyles reveal, their levels of economic privilege differ greatly. The first family lives on a tight budget. They have limited disposable income after paying their bills and are beginning to accumulate credit card debt that could hurt them down the road. The second family perceives themselves as having to be cautious about their finances, yet their disposable income and wise investments enable them to live a very comfortable lifestyle and to enjoy a multitude of luxuries. Consequently, the claim of being middle class is part of a mythology that obscures the reality of class diversity and complexity in America.

"All Black People Are Poor and All White People Are Rich"

In the minds of most Whites, the face of poverty is Black, and for most Blacks, all White faces are wealthy. In reality, although a disproportionate number of Black people are indeed poor (as a function of racism), the vast majority of poor people in America are White. The myth that most Blacks are poor and Whites are wealthy is fueled by the mass media that portray reality in these terms. Despite the growing numbers of economically privileged Blacks, including elites whose names are known the world over (e.g., Oprah Winfrey, Bill Cosby, Will Smith, Colin Powell, Condoleeza Rice), most White people view these individuals as exceptions, and the rule that poverty is Black remains unchanged. Moreover, racial solidarity among Whites, irrespective of class status, fuels the perception that Whites are a single monolithic group, and because the system of power is White, for Black people especially, this fuels the erroneous perception that all Whites are financially well off.

"Only the Poor Receive Welfare"

The concept of welfare instantly conjures up associations with government-funded social programs for the poor (e.g., Aid to Families with Dependent

Children [AFDC], Women, Infants, and Children [WIC], Medicare/Medicaid, food stamps). Although this does constitute a real aspect of welfare, the idea that only the poor receive welfare in the United States is a commonly held myth. In reality, an array of government programs exist that provide financial support to Americans of all socioeconomic levels.

In 2005, in spite of the fact that farm profits were at a near-record high of $72 billion, over $25 billion in federal aid was paid out in farm subsidies, which was nearly double what was paid to families living below the poverty line (Morgan, Gaul, & Cohen, 2006). Farm subsidy payments began in the 1930s to provide a limited safety net to working farmers. Since then, they have ballooned into a massive infrastructure of entitlements that have cost taxpayers $172 billion over the past decade alone. Although some of these funds benefit small, working farmers, in reality, most farmers (60%) receive no subsidies whatsoever. Instead, the overwhelming beneficiaries are millionaire landowners, foreign speculators, and absentee landlords—which explains why over 80% of farm subsidies are paid to farmers with a net worth of more than half a million dollars (Zinsmeister, 2006).

Corporate welfare (e.g., tax breaks, government grants, contracts, cut rate insurance, loans, loan guarantees) costs taxpayers about $100 billion annually, and the direct costs are only a small part of the picture. Taxpayers pay the highest percentage of corporate subsidies indirectly by absorbing the hardships and expenses associated with health and safety problems for workers and consumers, toxic waste cleanup and other pollution costs, and so forth (Korten, 1999). Whereas U.S. corporate profits total approximately $500 billion per year, a conservative estimate indicates that the indirect, externalized costs of industry to consumers comes to about $2.5 trillion annually (Estes, 1996). Moreover, there are no time limits to corporate welfare benefits. In the mid-1990s major reforms in social welfare programs were enacted, which included imposing time limits on welfare benefits and requiring work, training, or education in exchange for benefits. Yet no similar ethic of reform has been applied to the corporate welfare system. When it comes to handing out subsidies to corporations, there is no "2 years and off" time limit. Hence, the notion that it is only the poor who receive welfare is truly a myth.

IMPLICATIONS FOR FAMILY THERAPY

Given the lack of critical consciousness about class in society and the extent of our misconceptions and misunderstandings about how class shapes our lives, it is hardly surprising that the field of family therapy has devoted marginal substantive attention to addressing class issues. Yet, as this chapter has argued, class matters. Class is like the air that we breathe. We cannot see it or touch it, but it is all around us, influencing our lives and relationships at all times. Many factors are shaped by class, including parenting styles, political affiliations, approaches to finances, temporal orientation (e.g., emphasis on "here and now" vs. future orientation), and perceived locus of control (e.g., external vs. internal). Consequently, therapists must be tuned into seeing and understanding how class shapes their lives and their clients' lives.

Exploring Class Stories

We all have a class story. All of us were born into a class status, and we all grew up in one or more class status locations. Our early experiences with our class locations shaped the development of our class identity. For some, our class status and class identity are synonymous, yet this is not the case for everyone. Class status is an external construct that reflects where we are located within the system overall. Although our class status often is assumed to be a product of our income level, it reflects instead a complex interaction between several factors, including income, education, occupation, and wealth (e.g., assets that result from an accumulation of income). Class identity is an internal construct that reflects our psychological social class orientation. Whereas our class status is not fixed and can change throughout our lives, our class identities tend to remain more constant. For most of us, our class identity is heavily influenced by our primary class status while growing up.

It is important for therapists to explore their own class stories to identify the class locations they occupied during their lives and to examine how these experiences formed their class identities. Particular attention should be devoted to considering current class status and class identity, with an eye toward recognizing areas of divergence between each of these. An example follows.

> Celina is a family therapist who grew up in a working-class family and then shifted into an upper-middle-class lifestyle as an adult. Despite the outward change in her class status, inwardly the way Celina perceived and functioned in the world was heavily reflective of her working-class roots. One of the benefits of the divergence between her current class status and class identity was that low-income clients were often amazed by how naturally she connected with them and related to their life experiences, in spite of her solidly upper-middle-class lifestyle. At the same time, she explained that a disadvantage she routinely encountered was that when she interacted with colleagues, "I usually feel like an imposter. There's a certain way that upper-middle-class people think and do things, and they expect me to fit in with that, but I don't. I often feel out of place and afraid of being 'found out.'"
>
> Exploring her class story and, in particular, recognizing the gaps in her class status and identity enhanced Celina's awareness of the signifi-

cance of class. It also helped her to see how her perceptions and reactions were affected by her class experience. This self-knowledge was a powerful tool in her work with clients of all class backgrounds.

Naming Class

Once therapists are tuned into class dynamics in therapy, it is necessary to find ways to bring that awareness forth and to integrate it into the therapeutic process. In other words, therapists need to find ways to talk with their clients about class. These conversations can begin with questions that ask clients to identity their class status, to describe their class history growing up, and/or to articulate their class identity. Any of these lines of inquiry bring class issues to the forefront, so they can be addressed directly and explicitly. Once class has been named outright and addressed up front, therapists can then work to connect class issues with the problems that clients present with in therapy.

Confronting Class Biases and Prejudices

It is not enough to be aware that class matters and that our class experiences shape our views, behaviors, and relationships in specific ways. It also is necessary to be mindful of our class-based biases and prejudices. Although it is possible to have biased and prejudicial views against members of any socioeconomic group, by virtue of living within a society that systematically devalues the poor, all of us, irrespective of our class stories, are likely to harbor negative attributions toward low-income people.

The mass media combine with market forces to promote obsessive materialism and hedonistic consumerism that brainwash us into believing that our worth is reflected in the clothes we wear, the cars we drive, how we decorate our living spaces, the technology we use, and so forth. Poor people, by virtue of having little materially, are treated as if they have little in terms of human value. As suggested by Aponte (1994), what the poor lack in bread often obscures an appreciation for what they possess in spirit.

The pervasive devaluation of the poor makes all of us, clients and therapists alike and irrespective of our socioeconomic level, prone to making devaluing assumptions and comments about the poor. When this occurs, it is incumbent on therapists to challenge this devaluation, whether that means looking within to challenge ourselves, each other, our family and friends, or our clients. Such challenging may or may not change the view of the person expressing the devaluation, but the critical point is not to remain silent when biases and prejudices are communicated. Following are two examples of how devaluation of the poor was expressed by clients in therapy, one implicitly and the other explicitly, and how therapists challenged these views.

Implied Devaluation

Trevor, a 43-year-old male, was dating Wilma, a 45-year-old female. In the third session he was speaking about his relationship with Wilma's 23-year-old daughter, Shayla, from her first marriage. He explained, "I want so much to like her and to have a meaningful relationship with her because I love Wilma, but to be honest, I just cannot find a way to connect with Shayla. I could never say this to Wilma, but Shayla seems to lack basic intellect and depth. Frankly, I don't understand why, because she was raised in a stable, solidly upper-middle-class family."

The therapist quickly picked up on the classism reflected in Trevor's comment. She challenged his implied devaluation of the poor by asking him to explain the connection between being upper middle class and intellectual development and depth. Trevor was stunned by the question because it quickly exposed his classist associations, which he was dismayed to realize.

Explicit Devaluation

Laurel, a 23-year-old woman, and Gerald, a 27-year-old male, had been dating for 5 months when Gerald suggested they get a place together. During a session with her therapist, Laurel was exploring her feelings about living with Gerald. Although she was excited about the possibility, she expressed concern about the apartment Gerald wanted them to move into, saying, "I just don't think I could be comfortable there." When probed by the therapist about why, Laurel said, "It's in a poor neighborhood, and even though the actual apartment looks nice, I wouldn't be surprised if there are cockroaches. Poor people usually are not very clean. I also don't think I'd feel safe walking in that neighborhood at night because of the crime."

In this case, the client's classism was overt. She made no secret of her devaluing attitudes about the poor. Although the therapist could have ignored the client's classism, instead she challenged it by asking Laurel how she knew with such certainty that poor people were dirty and that the neighborhood, simply because it was low income, was unsafe. She asked, "Have you had many experiences hanging out in poor neighborhoods?" Laurel responded that she had not, but she defended her views by saying that they were common knowledge. To that the therapist explained that there were many views that were assumed to be common knowledge but that were based on little more than stereotypes. To make her point, she referred to a gender stereotype that she knew would register with the client about men being smarter than women. Laurel acknowledged that she could see the therapist's point, although this did not actually change her position.

The goal in questioning the client's devaluing attitudes toward the poor was not to change her view but rather to introduce questions that challenged unexamined stereotypes. The therapist sought to introduce the possibility of another way of seeing things in addition to the client's view. In this case, initially the challenge did not change the client's view, but by introducing an alternative perspective, a seed was planted that started to grow. Over time this seed cracked the foundation of the client's dominant story about poor people.

Clinical Example

Saul and Maria had been married for 5 years and had a 4-year-old daughter, Theresa. An upper-middle-class family, Maria was an attorney, and Saul was a senior executive at a computer software company. Their presenting complaint was lack of intimacy and closeness. Saul explained, "We disagree about almost everything, and that's led to a lot of frustration and distance. We can't even agree on how to use the paper towels. I use a lot of them because they're there to be used. She can't stand this. She skimps on every little piece, which makes no sense because we have an entire garage full of rolls since she stocks up at Sam's Club. It just makes no sense."

Maria agreed, saying, "It's amazing how different we are. I mean Saul is very passive. He is just so laid back. If something isn't done the right way, he shrugs his shoulders and says not to worry because it will all somehow work out. That drives me crazy. Things don't just 'work out' in life. That's why I have to take charge of everything." Saul agreed with this, adding that he experienced Maria as very controlling and critical, with a tendency to erupt into anger over even small things, which made him want to avoid her.

To better understand the roots of their ways of being, the therapist asked many questions about each partner's family of origin. Moreover, because he was attuned to contextual issues, the therapist sensed that class played a key role in their dynamics. Hence, he specifically asked questions about their class stories. He learned that Saul grew up in an upper-middle-class family. His father was a successful banker who, Saul said, worked long hours. "He loved us but he just wasn't around much." He described his mother as a stay-at-home mom who was "devoted to her family." In contrast, Maria grew up in a poor family. Her mother worked in the housekeeping department of a local motel, and her father vacillated between bouts of unemployment and low-paying jobs that offered no benefits or security. Maria explained, "my father was an alcoholic, and while he never hit us kids, he did hit my mother. He was an angry, critical man." She described her mother as "kind and loving but powerless with my father."

The information that the therapist had gathered about their class stories affirmed for him that some of the differences that were straining the couple's relationship were rooted in their differing class identities. Growing up in a poor family, Maria felt constantly fearful that there would never be enough of the basics. She admitted to feeling intense shame and rage while growing up about many things, including her family's poverty. "I was humiliated to live in such a destitute condition. I never had decent clothes to wear to school. I never had friends over to our house because it was embarrassing. Sometimes we barely had enough to eat. I survived by learning how to scrimp and hoard whatever I could get my hands on."

Because Saul grew up in an upper-middle-class family, much like the one he enjoyed currently, he had the benefit of a basic level of comfort and security that he never had to question. In material terms, he had been conditioned to trust that he would always have enough. Once their respective class stories became overt, the therapist supported the clients in seeing the connections between their backgrounds and their current approaches to life.

By virtue of growing up poor, Maria had learned to "scrimp and hoard." Even though her adult life was such that she could afford a garage full of paper towels, her behavior continued to be guided by her childhood class identification. Because Saul never had to worry about having enough of the basics while growing up, he had a far greater trust that he would always have what he needed materially; hence, he could not relate to Maria's conservation. Moreover, Maria struggled with a deeply rooted sense of shame about not being good enough, and, in numerous ways, she had organized her adult life to compensate for this childhood wound. Her need for control and her perfectionism were expressions of her battle with feeling devalued. Because Saul did not have this sense of class-based shame, he did not feel a relentless pressure to prove his worth. He did not know what economic hardship and shame felt like, so he did not fear these things. To an extent, his laid-back approach to life was an expression of the privilege he had enjoyed while growing up that allowed him to feel secure that somehow he would always have what he needed and he did not have to worry.

Therapy was the beginning of each partner's realizing how their respective class experiences had influenced their personalities and their marriage. Saul explained, "I'm seeing for the first time how our class backgrounds affected us. It helps me because instead of feeling perplexed and irritated by how Maria does things, I understand better, and that helps me feel more compassionate and tolerant." Maria agreed with Saul and stated, "It helps me as well to realize some of why we each are the way we are. It also helps me understand part of my anger and resentment toward him. I resent that he never had to worry and suffer the way I did growing up, and even now, he doesn't worry like I do. I think it's part of why his laid-back approach pisses me off. Not only does it make me feel unsafe because he is too chilled out, but I also sense where this comes from, and it's like a knife in my side reminding me of security he had while growing up that I never had and that I can't even enjoy now that I have more than I ever dreamed possible."

wow!

Prior to therapy, Saul and Maria were largely unaware of the influence of their class histories on their present lives. Had the therapist not been open to considering class and exploring each partner's class story, the clients most likely never would have realized how their class experiences growing up had shaped their personalities and relational dynamics. With their expanding insight, they were able to talk explicitly about experiences and feelings that had remained unrecognized, unnamed, and therefore unaddressed throughout their lives. Talking openly about issues that were hidden in the shadows for so long diffused feelings of confusion, frustration, and anger and paved the way for understanding and compassion, all of which were critical to repairing the relational strains that had become calcified between the couple.

RE-VISIONING CLASS IN FAMILY THERAPY

Acknowledging that class matters is an essential first step. It paves the way for seeing and addressing class issues in therapy. But this is not enough. If we are committed to more than "business as usual," and if we care about transforming the ever-widening gap between the haves and the have-nots, we need to re-vision class in family therapy.

Economist David Korten (2000) identified two reality systems that are defined by opposing values and divergent patterns of behavior. The first is the life reality system that values the living world and is characterized by balance, synergy, cooperation, restraint, and a respect for both the parts and the whole. The second is the money reality system that values wealth and is characterized by unchecked growth, accumulation of material goods and capital, competition, extreme individualism, and the pursuit of self-interest with little concern for the well-being of others. The field of family therapy, although rhetorically committed to the life reality system, is politically and pragmatically complicit with the money reality system. Consequently, re-visioning class in family therapy requires that we confront the ways that we conspire with a money reality system. What follows are a list of issues we might consider in the spirit of re-visioning class in family therapy.

1. One of the most fundamental ways of re-visioning family therapy in terms of class is by going "back to the future" ... by rediscovering and reaffirming our commitment to systemic thinking and practice. Systems theory affirms life by recognizing that a dynamic balance must exist between individuals and the collective, or between the parts and the whole. Although systems theory forms the root of family therapy, increasingly the field has abandoned its systemic focus in favor of the individualistic orientation that dominates the mainstream mental health industry. The life reality that is cen-

tral to family therapy through systems theory has been increasingly replaced with the money reality rooted in individualistic approaches to treatment that dominate mainstream mental health. Practically speaking, re-visioning class in family therapy through reaffirming a systemic orientation would include such things as (a) insisting on working with relationship systems and not just individuals; (b) refusing to use individual diagnostic categories to define problems; and (c) cautiously resisting interventions that locate problems and hence their solutions solely within individuals (e.g., drug therapy).

2. The degree to which we are driven by the money-reality system versus the life-reality system is reflected in the extent to which our services are made available on a sliding scale to noninsured, low-income clients. As part of re-visioning class in family therapy, those of us who are in private practice might consider what percentage of our services are now and could be in the near future made available to those without insurance and who cannot afford to pay out of pocket for therapy.

3. Even more radical than making our services available to those without insurance is abandoning our reliance on insurance companies altogether. The insurance industry has taken totalitarian-like control over our clinical practice and, because they prioritize profits over people, as long as we sustain our unholy alliance with them the care that we provide is ultimately determined by the financial bottom line. Practicing outside of the mandates of insurance companies allows us to dictate the type, duration, and quality of care we offer. Without insurance companies, we would earn less money because we would have to reduce our fees for clients who could not otherwise afford our full rates. Our resistance to this idea only speaks to how much we are controlled by a money reality versus a life reality. To re-vision class in family therapy, it is imperative that we confront our attachment to a money reality by pushing ourselves to make the shift in values that would free us to reject our reliance on the insurance industry.

4. Pharmaceutical companies are the other corporate entity that has taken virtual control over the field of family therapy. The lure of a "quick fix" seduces many of us to sell out healing, which takes time, for the speedier results of "getting high." According to the money reality, time is money, and, hence, to the extent that our reality system is defined by money rather than life, we are tempted to medicate pain rather than doing the more time consuming and less cost-effective work of healing it. Re-visioning class in family therapy calls us to resist the money-motivated appeal of drugs in favor of life-centered approaches to healing.

5. Many of the operating practices that guide our clinical work and that we accept as a given expose our complicity with a reality system dedicated to money and not life. The rarely questioned practice of limiting therapy sessions to a 50-minute hour is one such example. This artificially constructed time frame is driven by money, not clients' needs. It allows

therapists to squeeze in a maximum number of clients within a therapy day, thereby maximizing financial gain. Relatedly, the practice of scheduling clients back-to-back in assembly-line fashion is another example of how money dictates therapeutic practice. One has to question the extent to which therapists can give clients their optimal attention and care when they are booked so tightly day after day and week after week. As part of re-visioning class in family therapy, it is critical that we question the ways ← that we allow financial motivators to define clinical decisions such as session length and scheduling.

6. An inevitable consequence of a money reality is that it leads us to equate human value and worth with material worth and, hence, to devalue the poor. Our devaluation of the poor leads many of us to act like agents of social control with poor versus middle- or upper-income families. Because ← we have less respect for poor clients, we are more likely to intrude into their private lives, to impose restraints and conditions on them, to assume the worst of them, and to interact with them in ways that are subtly demeaning and disrespectful. As part of re-visioning class in family therapy, we would confront our underlying assumption that human worth is defined by material worth, and, as a result, we would challenge our devaluing attitudes toward and treatment of poor clients.

7. Re-visioning class in family therapy demands that we rethink our relationship with materialism and explore voluntary simplicity as an alternative. Many of us are driven to accumulate wealth and material goods and to hoard what we have. We are enslaved to jobs that require long hours so that we can support materially saturated lifestyles. Not only are we burdened by the pressure to work for money and not for joy, but also there is an inverse relationship between our material wealth and the poverty that is endured by most of the world's population. In the interests of shifting from a money reality to a life reality, each of us has to be willing to give something up so that all human beings can live with a basic standard of well-being and decency. Voluntary simplicity benefits all of us. For those with economic privilege, it frees us to work more for joy than to accumulate things, and for those who are economically disadvantaged, it contributes to a world in which resources are used and distributed more equitably.

8. Because the earth is a system, what happens in one part affects the whole. Obsessed with unchecked expansion and material accumulation, the global economic machine ravages the environment like a cancer. In the short term, the most vulnerable among us are most directly assaulted by ecological destruction, but in time these practices will be the end for all of us. To re-vision class in family therapy we must embrace environmental activism and ecojustice as a fundamental part of challenging a money reality and shifting toward a life reality. Doing this means adopting a lifestyle that is rooted in sustainable living. In conjunction with such groups as Global Action Plan

(GAP), each of us has the power to improve the quality of life for all by reducing our individual and collective burden on the planet.

SUMMARY

Hampered as we are by a variety of myths and misconceptions about class issues, including the myth that we are a class-free society, minimal acknowledgement of and discourse about class takes place in the United States. The lack of critical consciousness about class is also reflected in family therapy, in which minimal attention has been devoted to recognizing and exploring how class dynamics influence our lives and relationships. This chapter identified several common myths and realities about class in the United States, followed by a discussion of implications for family therapy, including how to "see" and address class dynamics in therapy. In the spirit of this book, which is dedicated to re-visioning family therapy, this chapter proposes specific steps we can take individually and collectively to transform class in our lives and in relationship to our work as therapists.

REFERENCES

Aponte, H. (1994). *Bread and spirit: Therapy with the new poor: Diversity of race, culture, and values*. New York: Norton.

Estes, R. (1996). *Tyranny of the bottom line: Why corporations make good people do bad things*. New York: Berrett-Koehler.

hooks, b. (2000). *Where we stand: Class matters*. New York: Routledge.

Korten, D. (2000). *The post-corporate world: Life after capitalism*. New York: Berrett-Koehler.

Morgan, D., Gaul, G. M., & Cohen, S. (2006, July 2). Farm program pays $1.3 billion to people who don't farm. *Washington Post*, p. A01

Zinsmeister, K. (2006, January/February). Respect the limits that made the U.S. *The American Enterprise*, 54–58.

CHAPTER 5

Spirituality, Healing, and Resilience

Froma Walsh

Spirituality is not simply a special topic. Rather, like culture and ethnicity, it involves streams of experience that flow through all aspects of life, from family heritage to personal belief systems, rituals and practices, and shared faith communities. Indeed, a systemic approach to practice needs to encompass a holistic biopsychosocial–spiritual orientation. This chapter briefly surveys the growing diversity and significance of spiritual beliefs and practices and their powerful influence in healing and resilience.

Spiritual beliefs influence ways of dealing with adversity, the experience of suffering, and the meaning of symptoms, their cause, and their future course. They also influence how people communicate about their pain, their approach toward health and mental health professionals, and their preferred pathways in recovery. Many who seek help for physical, emotional, or interpersonal problems are also in spiritual distress. It is therefore important for clinicians to address the spiritual dimension as a source of understanding distress, as well as a potential resource for healing and resilience.

RELIGION

The terms "religion" and "spirituality" are commonly interchanged. *Religion* can be defined as an organized, institutionalized belief system, set of practices, and faith community. It includes shared moral values and beliefs about God or a Higher Power and a spiritual afterlife. Sacred scriptures, teachings, and rituals provide guidelines for living out core beliefs and marking major life transitions. Involvement in a community of shared faith offers fellowship, pastoral guidance, and support in times of need. Religious belief systems provide faith explanations of past history and present experiences; they predict the future and offer pathways toward understanding the meaning of life (Campbell & Moyers, 1988). In all religions, the family is central in rites marking the birth of a new member, entry into the adult community, marriage vows, and the death of a loved one. Rituals and ceremonies carry profound significance, connecting family members with their larger community, its history, and its survival over adversity.

Americans are significantly more religious than others in industrialized Western nations in spiritual beliefs and practices: 96% believe in God or a universal spirit; 80% believe in an afterlife; 72% believe in Heaven, and 56% believe in Hell. Most believe in angels, and half believe in the devil (Gallup & Lindsey, 1999).

The vast majority of Americans are Christian. However, the religious landscape has been changing dramatically, with a surge in Evangelical Christian denominations and growing numbers in Buddhist, Muslim, Hindu, and other faiths (Pew Forum on Religion and Public Life, 2008). Over one-quarter have left the faith they were raised in for another denomination. Organized religion is flourishing in many forms, yet growing numbers of people who consider religion or spirituality important are unaffiliated.

African Americans are the most religious group: They participate actively in their congregations and look to their faith for strength in dealing with adversity (Boyd-Franklin & Lockwood, in press). Alongside advanced medical and mental health services, those from Eastern and indigenous cultures may also turn to traditional healing methods for physical or emotional problems (Comas-Diaz, 1981; Falicov, in press).

We must be cautious not to assume that particular individuals adhere to doctrines of their religion. For instance, Catholics are among the most devout worshippers, yet 78% disagree with the Church's refusal to sanction remarriage after divorce (Gallup & Lindsey, 1999). Over 60% believe that those who have abortions are still good Catholics. Personal attitudes about euthanasia are strongly polarized within and across religions: over 60% approve of assisted dying in some or most situations, but fundamentalists tend to be strongly opposed. Younger people tend to be more liberal in their beliefs than their elders are, often generating intergenerational tensions in families.

Interfaith marriage, traditionally prohibited by many religions, is now widespread and accepted, with the support of interfaith movements and blurring of racial and ethnic barriers. However, the high rate of intermarriage by Jews (53%) is of deep concern to their community.

Spirituality: Transcendent Beliefs and Practices

Spirituality, an overarching construct, refers more generally to transcendent beliefs and practices. Spirituality can be experienced either within or outside formal religious structures. It involves an active investment in internal values and fosters a deep sense of meaning, wholeness, harmony, and connectedness within oneself and with all others (Griffith & Griffith, 2002). Such unity with all life, nature, and the universe is at the core of many religions and indigenous faith traditions. Universally, the spirit is seen as our vital essence, the source of life and power. In many languages the word for "spirit" and "breath" are the same.

Spirituality invites an expansion of awareness and personal responsibility for and beyond oneself, from local to global concerns. Morality involves the activity of informed conscience: judging right and wrong based on principles of justice, decency, and compassion (Doherty, in press). Moral or ethical values spur actions that go beyond repairing conditions to improving them; to responding to the suffering of others; to dedicating efforts to help others; and to alleviating injustice (Perry & Rolland, in press).

Most Americans (85%) say that religion or spirituality is important in their lives. One-third view it as the most important part of their lives, fostering closeness in their families, fulfillment in jobs, and hopefulness about the future. Spiritual beliefs and practices foster strong family functioning, especially in times of crisis (Beavers & Hampson, 2003). A system of values that transcends the limits of experience enables family members to better accept the inevitable risks and losses in living and loving fully. In surveys (Gallup & Lindsay, 1999), over 80% say that religion was important in their family of origin, and 75% report that their current family relationships have been strengthened by religion in the home. "Family ties, loyalty, and traditions" were ranked highest in strengthening the family. Next, were "moral and spiritual values," which far outranked "family counseling" or "parent training classes."

Congruence between religious or spiritual beliefs and practices yields a sense of well-being and wholeness. Some adhere to religious practices but do not find spiritual meaning in them. Many are strong believers but do not actively participate in congregational life, viewing their faith as a matter between themselves and God. Many who do not follow formal religion live out their secular humanistic values.

Many who do not consider themselves religious do find spiritual meaning through communion with nature, the arts, or activism. The author Alice Walker (1997) combined all three in her spiritual journey. Her beloved mother was devoted to her rural church and active in bringing children in need into her home and looking out for the welfare of others in their struggling African American community. Walker dropped out of the church at age 13, feeling that the structure, preacher, and teachings reinforced gender inequality. She found that nature nourished her soul, as through long country walks. She became what she calls a "born-again pagan," experiencing spirituality through the land. Her nature-derived and activist spirit found powerful expression in her writing and work in movements for social justice. Following in her mother's footsteps, she believes that if you just accept conditions and do nothing, nothing changes, and you become shut down. Instead, she found activism transformative, believing that it is almost impossible to stay depressed about anything if you act to change it.

In our rapidly changing world, religion is less often a given that people are born into and accept unquestioningly. Instead, individuals, couples, and families commonly choose among spiritual beliefs and practices to fit their lives. The combining of varied elements has been likened to a platter of "religious linguini" (Deloria, 1994). As spiritual diversity within families increases, many are creating their own recipes for spiritual nourishment.

In the midst of global socioeconomic transformations, some are alarmed by a seeming collapse of moral values and seek spiritual moorings. Accelerated pressures of daily life, consumerism, and pop culture foster a widespread yearning for coherence and meaningful connections in fragmented lives. The rise in religious fundamentalism in many parts of the world expresses, in part, a desire to return to traditions that provide clear structure, values, and absolute certainties in the face of rapid social change. Natural and human-caused disasters shatter illusions of invulnerability and heighten awareness of the precariousness of life and the interconnection of all on our planet. For recovery and resilience in facing an uncertain future, people turn above all else to their loved ones and to their faith (Koenig, 2006; Walsh, 2007).

Intertwining of Spiritual and Cultural Influences

Religion and culture are interwoven in all aspects of spiritual experience. Frank McCourt (1998) experienced his Irish Catholic upbringing as a faith that seemed "mean, scrimped, and life-denying." He formed the image of an angry, vengeful God: "a God who'd let you have it upside your head if you strayed, transgressed, coveted. ... He had His priests preaching hellfire and damnation from the pulpit and scaring us to death." In traveling to Italy, McCourt was struck by the contrasts: "Statues and pictures of the Virgin Mary in the Irish churches seemed disembodied and she seemed to be saying, 'Who is this kid?' In contrast, Italian art portrayed a voluptuous, maternal Mary with a happy infant Jesus at her bosom." McCourt wondered: "Was it the weather? Did God change His aspect as He moved from the chilly north to the vineyards of Italy?" (p. 64). He thought that, all in all, he'd prefer the Italian expression of Catholicism to the Irish one.

Differences are also found between families from rural, traditional backgrounds and those from urban, educated, and middle-class settings. Religion is further intertwined with such influences as race, recent immigration, and fit with the dominant culture. Prejudice or discrimination may suppress religious identification and expression.

In contrast to the individualism in American culture, most spiritual orientations worldwide see human experience as embedded within the family and larger community. As the African theologian John Mbiti (1970) describes this sociocentric view: "I am because we are." These bonds continue beyond death, over the generations. In Asian Hindu and Buddhist cultures, for instance, prayers may be said daily in front of portraits of grandparents or home shrines in the belief that the spirits of ancestors can be communicated with directly; if honored appropriately, they will confer their blessings and protection from harm.

In a predominantly Christian nation of Western European origins, we must be cautious not to superimpose that template of values on other beliefs and practices. It is crucial not to judge diverse spiritual traditions, particularly those of indigenous cultures, as inferior by European Christian standards. Early European American conquerors viewed Native Americans as primitive heathens, regarding their spiritual beliefs and practices as pagan witchcraft. Government programs and religious missionary boarding schools acculturated Indian children in Christianity and Western ways, eradicating their own tribal language, cultural identity, and spiritual heritage. Today, many native youths are returning to the spiritual roots of their ancestors, seeking identity and worth in their spiritual community (Deloria, 1994).

Prayer, Meditative Practices, and Rituals

Every spiritual orientation values some form of prayer or meditation. It may involve chanting or reading scriptures or rituals such as lighting candles or incense. Prayer has strong meaning for Americans: 90% say they pray at least weekly; 75% pray daily (Gallup & Lindsay, 1999). For most, prayer originates in the family and is centered in the home. Almost all pray for their family's health and happiness. Prayer may serve varied functions: to connect with God; to express praise and gratitude; to gain perspective; to sustain strength and courage; to find solace and comfort; to request help or guidance; or to appeal for a miracle. Some (30%) have stopped praying, most because they lost the habit; a few (10%) because they had lost their faith.

Meditation facilitates clarity and tranquility; it eases tension, pain, and suffering (Kabat-Zinn, 2003). Mindfulness in still, focused concentration can lead to more deliberate action (Nhat Hanh, 1991). A contemplative state can be experienced in communion with nature, art, or music. Shared meditative experiences foster genuine and empathic communication, reduce defensive reactivity, and deepen couple and family bonds (Gale, in press).

Rituals serve valuable functions in every faith tradition, connecting individuals with their families and communities and guiding them in life-cycle passage through rites such as communion, baptism, bar and bat mitzvahs, weddings, and funerals (Imber-Black, in press). Ceremonies provide continuity with the past and into the future, with those before and after us. They facilitate difficult transitions and comfort the dying and the bereaved (Walsh, 2004). In these ways, painful or disruptive transitions can catalyze growth and transformation. Rituals also transcend a particular suffering or tragedy, connecting it with the human condition.

When Religion Harms

Religious beliefs or experiences may fuel guilt, shame, or worthlessness, contributing to addictions, destructive behavior, or social isolation. Some religious doctrines and harsh, narrow, or judgmental convictions can wound the spirit. Patriarchy, sexism, and heterosexism are cultural patterns embedded in most religious traditions.

Patriarchal values have been used to sanction the subordination, abuse, and killing of women and girls. Many have turned to faiths such as Baha'i and to reform movements within religions that promote the equality of men and women in family life and society. Some have found nontraditional expressions of spirituality and interest in ancient goddess-centered or Wicca traditions.

Religious beliefs may underlie harmful patterns in couple and family relationships, such as abusive and demeaning treatment. One fundamentalist Christian woman supported her husband's right to beat her because she had challenged his authority; she believed that to be "a woman of God," a good wife was required to be submissive. As family therapists, we have an ethical responsibility to challenge beliefs that are harmful to any member, whether based in family, ethnic, or religious traditions. Above all, every religion upholds the core values of respect for others and the dignity and worth of all human beings.

The condemnation of homosexuality in religious doctrine has been a source of deep anguish for individuals and couples of diverse sexual orientation. Many have felt exiled from traditional faith communities. Some denominations preach the immorality of homosexual practice alongside a loving acceptance of the person as a human being created by God. Such a dualistic attitude nevertheless perpetuates stigma and shame, pathologizing "unnatural" and "immoral" sexual behavior and bonds. Gay men and lesbians have increasingly been forging their own spiritual pathways (O'Neill & Ritter, 1992). Long-standing religious opposition to same-sex unions is being challenged by a growing number of clergy and congregations. Despite deep schisms over these issues in many denominations, most parishioners are far more tolerant in their personal lives.

Religious extremist groups have posed a growing threat of violence worldwide. Although Muslim fundamentalist terrorists view themselves as adherents of Islam, the Quran does not condone suicide or the killing of innocent people, and the vast majority of Muslims abhor such acts. In the United States, violence has also, at times, been associated with extremist Christian groups espousing creeds of racism and religious intolerance. Imposition of the dogmatic belief that there is only one "true religion" has led to catastrophic consequences throughout human times, as in holy wars to convert, subjugate, or annihilate nonbelievers.

TAPPING SPIRITUAL RESOURCES FOR HEALING AND RESILIENCE

Resilience is the ability to rebound from life crises and overcome the challenges of prolonged adversity. Belying the American dominant cultural myth of the "rugged individual," resilience is relational: nurtured by family, community, cultural, and spiritual connections. A resilience-oriented approach to practice identifies and strengthens resources that enable families to rally and support optimal adaptation (Walsh, 2003, 2006).

A growing body of research finds that health, healing, and resilience are strengthened by a personal spirituality that is lived out in daily life, relationships, and service to others in need (Koenig, McCullough, & Larson, 2001; Pargament, 2007). Those with deep faith cope better with stress, have fewer alcohol or drug problems, less depression, and lower rates of suicide. Prayer, meditation, and spiritual rituals can strengthen health and healing by influencing neurological, immune, and cardiovascular systems. Those with a deep and integrated spirituality are more likely to be tolerant, giving, and forgiving in their personal relationships.

Numerous studies of resilience have noted the importance of strong faith and involvement in a religious community. In their longitudinal study of resilience in at-risk youths in poor multiethnic families on the island of Kauai, Werner and Smith (2001) found that religion was an important protective factor from childhood throughout adulthood. Personal faith and varied religious affiliation strengthened individuals and their families through times of adversity by providing a sense of hope, mission, and salvation. One woman described her deep church involvement since adolescence and her abiding faith in God: When she felt like life wasn't worth living, there was a God who loved her and would help her come through. Follow-up studies found that resilience could be forged and lives transformed throughout the life cycle. A crisis could become an epiphany, opening lives to a spiritual dimension previously untapped.

Suffering, and often the injustice or senselessness of it, are ultimately spiritual issues (Wright, Watson, & Bell, 1996). Emerging research in the trauma field finds that spirituality is a significant influence in resilience and posttraumatic growth (Walsh, 2007). Beyond coping or surviving trauma, loss, or hardship, transformation and positive growth can be forged out of adversity. By tapping resources for resilience, those who have been struggling can emerge stronger and more resourceful in meeting future challenges. This is particularly important in work with refugees, who often draw on traditional beliefs and practices alongside formal religion (Kamya, in press).

The Power of Belief Systems

In the empirically based Western world, it is said that "seeing is believing." Native Americans might say instead that we need to believe it in order to see it (Deloria, 1994). Shared belief systems are at the very heart of resilience—for individuals, families, and communities. We respond to adversity by making meaning of our experience—by linking it to our social world, to our cultural and faith beliefs, to our multigenerational past, and to our hopes and dreams for the future. How families view their problems and their options can make all the difference between coping, healing, and growth or dysfunction and despair.

Spiritual teachings in major faith traditions (Wolin, Wolin, Raganathan, Saymeh, & Zeyada, in press) offer facilitative beliefs to foster problem solving, healing, and growth. Affirming beliefs that we are valued and have potential to succeed help us to rally in times of crisis. Belief that a loving God or guardian angels watch over us can bolster strength and courage, particularly when struggling alone. However, some religious doctrines and harsh, narrow, or judgmental convictions can wound the spirit and block adaptation. Beliefs that we are unworthy can fuel self-loathing, destructive behavior, or social isolation. Spiritual beliefs and practices can support three key processes in resilience: meaning making, hope, and transcendence (Walsh, 2003, 2006, in press).

Meaning Making

The ability to clarify and give meaning to adversity makes it easier to bear. Spiritual beliefs offer meaning, purpose, and connection beyond ourselves, our families, and our troubles. They bring clarity about our lives and render unexpected events less threatening.

In adversity, religious beliefs about causality come to the fore. Western faith traditions emphasize personal responsibility: We are masters of our fate. Misfortune may be taken as a sign that some are sinful and deserve to suffer or be punished by God. Those who are leading good lives often struggle with questions of "Why me?" and may agonize over personal failings or feel a sense of injustice. Spirituality offers comfort and meaning beyond comprehension. The Biblical Book of Job is a story of resilience in which persistent adversity holds meaning in testing both faith and endurance.

In many faith traditions, such as Islam, adversity is more likely ascribed to fate or God's will. For Hindus, misfortune may result from bad karma due to conduct or circumstances in a previous life. In many indigenous traditions, when things go wrong in a family, blame is commonly externalized onto others who are envious, spiteful, or wish them harm; they may turn to shamans or to faith healers, potions, and practices to restore health or good fortune (Falicov, in press). Some view mental illness as a form of spiritual unrest through the agency of a "ghost" or vengeful spirit or as a punishment for transgressions.

Hope: A Positive Outlook

Hope is like oxygen for the spirit, enabling us to carry on our best efforts in the face of overwhelming challenges. Spirituality plays a vital role in sustaining hope. Hope is a future-oriented belief; no matter how bleak the present, a better future can be envisioned. Martin Luther King, Jr., avowed that although we must accept finite disappointment we must never lose infinite hope. The Reverend King has been a guiding spirit to many oppressed people through his abiding faith that social justice would prevail. Yet his was not a passive faith in waiting for God's deliverance or hope for better times to come. Rather, it was a rallying call to collective action to bring about change, emphasizing personal responsibility, initiative, and perseverance—all hallmarks of resilience.

Resilience involves both active mastery and acceptance, as expressed in the serenity prayer at the heart of recovery movements. Energy and efforts are channeled to "master the possible," accepting what cannot be changed. Those of Eastern traditions, less focused on mastery, are more attuned to living in harmony with nature. Those with a European American orientation often have more difficulty accepting situations beyond their control. Yet, even when a traumatic experience or terminal illness cannot be reversed, families can be helped to heal psychosocially and spiritually.

Transcendence

Through religion, many satisfy a deep need to be connected to a set of values, a larger community, and a shared heritage. Stories, scripture, music, and rituals preserve and transmit these vital connections. Such linkages are especially valuable for immigrant families, whose members can lose their sense of identity and community in pressures for assimilation to the dominant culture (Falicov, in press).

A value system, whether religious or secular humanist, provides a moral compass to guide actions and ethical relationships. It transcends the limits of our experience, enabling us to view our own situations, which may be painful, uncertain, and frightening, from a broader perspective. Without this larger view, we are more vulnerable to suffering and despair.

Spirituality can also catalyze positive transformation from adversity. In the wake of trauma, harm, or injustice, major faith traditions encourage forgiveness instead of holding onto grievances, feelings of rage, or thoughts of revenge (Hargrave, 1994; Worthington, Berry, & Parrott, 2001). One mother, whose son was killed in neighborhood violence, turned to her childhood religious teachings to ease her grief and to better attend to her family's deep suffering (Walsh, 2007). Recalling Bible teachings that unforgiveness destroys the mind, body, and spirit, she decided she needed to forgive the youth who had shot her son, while holding him accountable for his actions. Supported by a priest and the parish, her journey of forgiveness was healing for her and led to a positive transformation in the young offender. Her husband found his own healing pathway through activism, taking leadership in community action for gun control.

The paradox of resilience is that the worst of times can also bring out our best. A crisis can yield growth in unforeseen directions. It can be an epiphany, awakening family members to the importance of loved ones, healing old wounds, and reordering priorities for more meaningful relationships and life pursuits. Resilient individuals and families commonly emerge from shattering crises with a heightened sense of purpose in their lives and compassion for the plight of others. Their experience of adversity and suffering may inspire advocacy on behalf of others, for social justice, and for the environment (Perry & Rolland, in press).

A core conviction of the potential for human resilience must be joined with compassion for those unable to overcome their life challenges. We must be cautious not to attribute lack of success or of recovery from illness to insufficient spiritual purity. Moreover, as we encourage families to have faith and hope and to strive to overcome the odds, we must also change the odds against them. We must work with larger systems to transform policies and practices to better enable families to thrive and to bring their best hopes and dreams to fruition.

INTEGRATING SPIRITUALITY IN FAMILY THERAPY

The powerful influence of spirituality has only recently begun to be addressed in clinical training and practice. The general public has expressed a need for mental health and health care professionals to attend to this dimension. Surveys (Gallup & Lindsay, 1999) find that 81% of respondents want their own spiritual practices and beliefs integrated into any counseling; 75% want physicians and other helping professionals to address their spiritual concerns as part of their care. Half of elderly people want their doctors to pray with them as they face death. While clinicians must guard against imposing their own convictions, in general, clients are less interested in their therapist's spiritual orientation and more interested in sharing their own spiritual concerns. Clinicians should not presume that spiritual matters are unimportant if they are not voiced. When clients are not asked about their spiritual beliefs and practices, they are likely to edit out this dimension of their lives.

Just as family therapists inquire about ethnicity and other aspects of culture, assessment should routinely explore the significance of spirituality in clients' lives and note spiritual and religious orientations and issues on family genograms (McGoldrick, Gerson, & Petry, 2008). How might clients draw on past, current, or potential spiritual resources to ease distress, heal suffering, and strengthen resilience? Might clients who are not "religious" explore a broader or more personal approach to seeking spiritual nourishment? Rituals are encouraged in family therapy to mark important milestones, to restore continuities with family heritage, to create new patterns, and to foster healing (Imber-Black, Roberts, & Whiting, 2003).

Spiritual distress, or an inability to invest life with meaning, impedes coping and mastery in the face of life challenges. It is crucial to learn whether spiritual issues contribute to current concerns, conflicts, or cutoffs; to suffering, shame, and guilt; or to spiritual malaise. Even when presenting problems do not ostensibly involve spirituality, a spiritual source of distress may emerge. One woman was referred for therapy with inconsolable grief many months after the stillbirth of her second child. Raised in a devout Catholic family, she "fell away" from the church and married a nonobservant Jewish man. Religion didn't seem important to them when their first child, a son, was born. Now she believed that the stillbirth of the second child was God's punishment for not having baptized her son. Reluctant to reveal this belief to her Jewish in-laws, she had withdrawn in her grief and guilt. Individual and couple sessions were combined for mutual support, open communication, and decision making. Consultation with a priest and rabbi were also helpful to them.

Where religious ideas or experiences may have contributed to guilt or shame, we can help clients invest in spiritual practices or communities that link them in more positive ways to offer a larger vision of humanity and connection. A wide range of spiritual resources can be encouraged as they fit clients' belief systems and preferences—from prayer or meditative practices, creative rituals, faith communities, and clergy guidance to communion with nature, expression through the arts, social advocacy, or service to others.

Facing Death and Loss

The end of life offers gifts when faced openly with courage and compassion. More than any other human experience, death and loss can be transformative, teaching us about the meaning of life, what matters most, and the significance of relational bonds. These are spiritual issues. Therapists can encourage family members' full presence and involvement in the dying process, drawing on their spiritual beliefs and practices to assist them (Kamya, 2000).

People of many faiths find comfort in the belief that the spirit lives on after death (Walsh, 2004). Some believe the soul resides in a spirit world for eternity; others believe in reincarnation in new life forms. Many believe that they can be in contact with spirits, particularly in times of need, for reassurance to the bereft or when a serious wrong has not been attended to. The spirits of the deceased live on in the minds, hearts, deeds, and stories of loved ones. They can haunt as ghosts or become guardian angels and guiding spirits, inspiring best efforts and actions, especially in troubled times.

Recovery from Abuse and Addictions

An emphasis on spirituality has been a key component in 12-step recovery programs, which can be a valuable adjunct to couple or family therapy (Minnick, 1997). These programs address such spiritual matters as identity, integrity, an inner life, and interdependence. The connection with a Higher Power through prayer and meditation facilitates reflection and sustains positive efforts. The steps promote a spiritual awakening, preparing family members to practice principles for abstinence and greater well-being and often sparking life-altering transformations.

Overcoming Barriers of Poverty and Racism

Aponte (1994) urges therapists to attend to spiritual as well as practical needs of poor and marginalized families who have lost hope in their chances for a better life. They suffer a wounding of the soul in a pervasive sense of injustice, helplessness, and rage at inequalities. He encourages therapists to go beyond theory and technique to reach for meaning and purpose in people's lives and revitalize family and community spirit:

> Therapy can be an enemy or a friend to spirit. The technology of therapy has attempted to replace tradition, ritual, and customs. ... However, just as medi-

cation can only succeed when it cooperates with the healing powers of the body, therapy only works when it joins with the indigenous forces of culture and faith in people's lives. (p. 8)

Social Activism as an Expression of Spirituality

People gain resilience in overcoming adversity and healing from trauma through collaborative efforts to right a wrong or to bring about needed change in larger systems. Following his daughter's death caused by a drunk driver, one father was consumed by rage and helplessness, not wanting to go on living. At his therapist's encouragement, he visited his daughter's grave to seek inspiration for the path ahead. That night he slept deeply for the first time and awoke from a dream of his beautiful, smiling daughter, "knowing" that her loving spirit would want him to forge a larger purpose and benefit to others out of the tragedy. Therapists can invite such openings toward activism and its healing potential (Perry & Rolland, in press).

Responsiveness to Spiritual Diversity

As societies become increasingly diverse, clinicians need to develop a spiritual pluralism, with knowledge and respect for varied beliefs and practices. Therapeutic approaches need to be sensitive to learn how each family, from its own distinct sociocultural background, blends core principles of their faith with varied aspects of their lives. With growing spiritual diversity within families, therapists can facilitate communication, mutual understanding, tolerance, and respect. Therapists can help members shift from a stance of "moral superiority" to an acceptance of different spiritual pathways.

If therapist and clients are of the same religion, it can be easier to form a natural rapport. However, one may overidentify with or be hesitant to question beliefs that one assumes to be shared. Clinicians, especially when they come from dominant cultural groups, must be cautious not to take their own values as the norm nor to be judgmental toward faith differences. We must seek understanding of the meaning and function of spirituality for each family and its members.

Therapists and trainees are encouraged to explore their own family religious traditions and reflect on their own spiritual journeys. It is also important to develop linkages for referral and consultation with pastoral counselors, chaplains, and community clergy for spiritual matters beyond the therapist's role or expertise. Above all, we deepen our therapeutic relationship and effectiveness when we open our work to the spiritual dimension of our clients' experience, explore their concerns, and tap spiritual wellsprings for healing and resilience.

REFERENCES

Aponte, H. (1994). *Breed and spirit: Therapy with the new poor.* New York: Norton.

Beavers, W. R., & Hampson, R. B. (2003). Measuring family competence: The Beavers Systems model. In F. Walsh (Ed.), *Normal family processes* (3rd ed., pp. 549–580). New York: Guilford Press.

Boyd-Franklin, N., & Lockwood, T. (in press). Spirituality and religion: Implications for psychotherapy with African American clients and families. In F. Walsh (Ed.), *Spiritual resources in family therapy* (2nd ed.). New York: Guilford Press.

Campbell, J., & Moyers, W. (1988). *The power of myth.* New York: Doubleday.

Comas-Díaz, L. (1981). Puerto Rican Espiritismo and psychotherapy. *American Journal of Orthopsychiatry, 51,* 636–645.

Deloria, V., Jr. (1994). *God is red: A native view of religion* (2nd ed.). Golden, CO: Fulcrum.

Doherty, W. (in press). Morality and spirituality in therapy. In F. Walsh (Ed.), *Spiritual resources in family therapy* (2nd ed.). New York: Guilford Press.

Falicov, C. (in press). Religion and spiritual traditions in immigrant families: A Latino example. In F. Walsh (Ed.), *Spiritual resources in family therapy* (2nd ed.). New York: Guilford Press.

Gale, J. (in press). Meditation and relational connectedness. In F. Walsh (Ed.), *Spiritual resources in family therapy* (2nd ed.). New York: Guilford Press.

Gallup, G., Jr., & Lindsay, D. M. (1999). *Surveying the religious landscape: Trends in U.S. beliefs.* Harrisburg, PA: Morehouse.

Griffith, J., & Griffith, M. (2002). *Encountering the sacred in psychotherapy.* New York: Guilford Press.

Hargrave, T. (1994). *Families and forgiveness.* New York: Brunner/Mazel.

Imber-Black, E. (in press). Rituals and spirituality. In F. Walsh (Ed.), *Spiritual resources in family therapy* (2nd ed.). New York: Guilford Press.

Imber-Black, E., Roberts, J., & Whiting, R. (Eds.). (2003). *Rituals in families and family therapy* (2nd ed.). New York: Norton.

Kabat-Zinn, J. (2003). Mindfulness-based interventions in context: Past, present, and future. *Clinical Psychology: Science and Practice, 10*(2), 144–156.

Kamya, H. (2000). Bereavement issues and spirituality. In V. J. Lynch (Ed.), *HIV/AIDS at year 2000* (pp. 242–256). Boston: Allyn & Bacon.

Kamya, H. (in press). The significance of faith in healing from refugee trauma. In F. Walsh (Ed.), *Spiritual resources in family therapy* (2nd ed.). New York: Guilford Press.

Koenig, H., McCullough, M. E., & Larson, D. (Eds.). (2001). *Handbook of religion and health.* New York: Oxford University Press.

Koenig, H. G. (2006). *In the wake of disaster: Religious responses to terrorism and catastrophe.* Philadelphia: Templeton Foundation Press.

Mbiti, J. (1970). *African religions and philosophy.* Garden City, NY: Anchor Books.

McCourt, P. (1998, December). God in America: When you think of God, What do you see? *Life, 21*(13), 60–74.

McGoldrick, M., Gerson, R., & Petry, S. (2008). *Genograms: Assessment and intervention.* New York: Norton.

Minnick, A. M. (1997). *Twelve step programs: Contemporary American quest for meaning and spiritual renewal.* New York: Praeger.

Nhat Hanh, T. (1992). *Peace is every step: The path of mindfulness in everyday life.* New York: Bantam Books.

O'Neill, C., & Ritter, K. (1992). *Coming out within: Stages of spiritual awakening for lesbians and gay men*. New York: HarperCollins.

Pargament, K. (2007). *The psychology of religion and coping* (2nd ed.). New York: Guilford Press.

Perry, A. D. V., & Rolland, J. S. (in press). Spirituality expressed in community action and social justice: A therapeutic means to liberation and hope. In F. Walsh (Ed.), *Spiritual resources in family therapy* (2nd ed.). New York: Guilford Press.

Pew Forum on Religion and Public Life (2008). *U.S. Religious landscape survey*. Retrieved from *http://www.PewForum, org/ReligiousLandscape*.

Walker, A. (1997). *Anything we love can be saved: A writer's activism*. New York: Random House.

Walsh, F. (2003). Family resilience: Framework for clinical practice. *Family Process, 42*(1), 1–18.

Walsh, F. (2004). Spirituality, death, and loss. In F. Walsh & M. McGoldrick (Eds.), *Living beyond loss: Death in the family* (2nd ed., pp. 182–210). New York: Norton.

Walsh, F. (2006). *Strengthening family resilience* (2nd ed.). New York: Guilford Press.

Walsh, F. (2007). Traumatic loss and major disaster: Strengthening family and community resilience. *Family Process, 46*, 207–247.

Walsh, F. (Ed.). (in press). *Spiritual resources in family therapy* (2nd ed.). New York: Guilford Press.

Werner, E. E., & Smith, R. S. (2001). *Journeys from childhood to midlife: Risk, resilience, and recovery*. Ithaca, NY: Cornell University Press.

Wolin, S. J., Wolin, S., Raganathan, S., Saymeh, D., & Zeyada, H. (in press). Five spiritual perspectives on resilience: Buddhist, Christian, Jewish, Hindu, Muslim. In F. Walsh (Ed.), *Spiritual resources in family therapy* (2nd ed.). New York: Guilford Press.

Worthington, E. L., Jr., Berry, J. W., & Parrott, L. (2001). Unforgiveness, forgiveness, religion, and health. In T. G. Plante & A. C. Sherman (Eds.), *Faith and health: Psychological perspectives* (pp. 107–138). New York: Guilford Press.

Wright, L., Watson, W. L., & Bell, J. M. (1996). *Beliefs: The heart of healing in families and illness*. New York: Basic Books.

CHAPTER 6

Race, Reality, and Relationships

Implications for the Re-Visioning of Family Therapy

Kenneth V. Hardy

Race, reality, and relationships are often complexly entangled in ways that are difficult to discern. The volatility of race as a phenomenon, the acute silence that often accompanies racial interactions, and the general lack of attention devoted to the intricacies of relationship development and maintenance all contribute to the difficulty in deconstructing this entanglement. In both our personal lives and our clinical practices, the entanglement of race, realities, and relationships is a powerful and pervasive force.

THE PHENOMENON OF RACE: AN INVISIBLE FENCE

Race is a major organizing principle in everyday life. It is a basic construct that shapes one's attitudes, beliefs, and behaviors (Hardy & Laszloffy, 2000). In this regard, it is my assumption that virtually every act, deed, behavior, or interaction that one engages in is shaped by the nuances of race in some way. Although seldom explicitly acknowledged, race is one of the key factors that determines who participates in certain interactions and how. This is in part why countless numbers of children of color, for example, live lives trapped behind the walls of an invisible prison. They often see no way out of the deplorable conditions they have to contend with because they under-

stand the implicit rules of racial participation. There are no physical structures restricting their movement or overt messages designed to discourage
them from aiming their hopes and dreams high. Yet too many of them strive
for little and settle for even less because they understand the rules. They are
acutely aware, even in the face of incessant public denials and disclaimers,
that there are two sets of rules regarding opportunities, one for Whites and
another for them. Even for children of color who remain determined to beats
the odds, some sense of hopelessness is common. For many of these young
people, race is not only an organizing principle but also a major boundary
marker. For them, race is like the invisible fences that pet owners use to keep
their dogs contained within a circumscribed space. After a very short while,
dogs learn where the boundaries are that should not be crossed unless they
are willing to be shocked. Race, perhaps more often than we can imagine,
operates as a kind of invisible fence. For those who are oppressed by virtue
of their racial identities, the boundaries are tightly restrictive, whereas for
those who are privileged, the boundaries are far more fluid and expansive.

THE SIGNIFICANCE OF RACE

Race is integral to our beings, in much the same way that the concept of
personality is, for example. It would be inconceivable that one could exist
without a personality or that one's personality could somehow be totally
bifurcated from one's core being. Because of the pervasive impact of racist
structures on our lives, skin color and hair texture, which in and of themselves have virtually no bearing on the differences among human beings,
have taken on profound implications for every member of our society, defining what their options are, influencing where they can go, how they are
viewed, and what part they can play in the "American Dream." In other
words, each of us is located racially and contains a racial self. Whether
acknowledged or not, who we are racially and/or who we are perceived
to be racially shapes our attitudes, beliefs, and behaviors. Race is not only
significant in terms of how we see ourselves, but it is also a powerful prism
through which we are "seen" and perceived by others. The denial or lack of
awareness and sensitivity to race does not negate or diminish its pervasive
significance in our lives.

THE VOLATILITY OF RACE

In U.S. culture,[1] race is a volatile, poignant, often denied but ubiquitous
phenomenon. In many ways, the long arms and checkered history of poor
race relationships contaminate most relationships, especially those occur-

ring interracially. Popular declarations such as "I don't see color"; "What is race?; "Race doesn't really exist"; "Race is nothing more than a social construction"; or "there are diversities other than race" do very little to invite critical inquiry, analysis, or much-needed dialogue about race. As such, the ways in which race is inextricably intertwined with clients' and therapists' real-life experiences and ultimately with the relationships we cultivate (or fail to) with each other, both in and outside of the consulting room, remain unexplored. Unfortunately, the significance of race as an organizing principle in our lives is often marginalized or denied. Consequently, it remains a highly charged, often avoided, divisive experience that shapes our lives in far-reaching ways that we cannot talk about constructively. The dilemmas in addressing race are precipitated and supported by a recursive dynamic. The more silence there is regarding race, the more volatile the subject is to broach; the more volatile conversations about race are, the more silence is recruited as a remedy. This dynamic perpetuates a no-change position and impedes a comprehensive understanding of race, realities, and relationships

NOTIONS ABOUT REALITY

Outside of academic and clinical circles, the notion of *reality* is probably not a much-talked-about phenomenon. Even within some academic circles, conversations about reality are often considered ridiculously abstract and esoteric. Yet it is my belief that notions of reality play a significant role in human relationships. Even without consideration of race, the notion of reality is a salient factor warranting careful scrutiny and discussion.

I believe the notion of what is real is at the core of most conflicts in human relationships. Whether it is conflict between intimate partners, cultural groups, small communities, or nations, clashes regarding what we perceive as real are usually central. These conflicts are often compounded and magnified by the unexamined belief that reality is a fixed universal phenomenon. In this regard, it becomes rather easy for warring sides to stand firmly in the righteousness of their rightness. Both the impetus for and the perceived solutions to these types of conflicts revolve around the issue of "right" and "wrong." The assumption, of course, is that "the solution" to "the problem" is to determine who or what is right or wrong, and whose view of reality is "correct."

Although this is a rather simplistic ideal to subscribe to, putting it into actual practice is often infinitely more complicated, especially when race is factored into the equation. When race and reality are entangled, most interactions tend to become even more rigidified and polarized. Consider the following vignette.

Between Black and White

During conducting a racial sensitivity training session for social workers in a large, diverse human services agency, a White participant became quickly baffled by and frustrated with a vocal, enraged African American member of the group. The White worker, overcome with exasperation, angrily stated to Ishmir, "why are you so angry? Nobody here had a damn thing to do with slavery or the oppression of your people. ... Get over the past, let it go! ... 'Cause I am a little sick and tired of hearing you whine, complain, make excuses, and not take responsibility. ... You have the same opportunities that everyone else here has. ... What do you want from me? ... Tell me, what do you want?" There was an intense and eerie silence that followed this exchange. All eyes were uncomfortably but inquisitively placed on Ishmir. He sat silently stoic for several minutes. When he spoke, he did so in an uncharacteristically slow, methodical, and gentle voice. With unwelcomed tears in his dazed eyes, he said in a Martin Luther King-type cadence, "What I want from you ... what I want from you, ... and all other White people here is to remember ... that those who were the perpetrators can NEVER REMEMBER WHAT WAS DONE but to those to whom it was done ... WE CAN NEVER FORGET."

Karen appeared confused by Ishmir's intense response and his affect. "I don't know what you are talking about," she replied with a tinge of disdain in her voice.

He shouted back: "You don't want to know. ... It benefits you to claim you don't know ... that's your White privilege."

It was difficult for Karen to acknowledge any form of racial privilege that she possessed. To the best of her recollection, she and her family had worked hard to earn everything that she and they had. She could not understand why this simple *fact* was difficult for Ishmir to grasp. To Ishmir, Karen was nothing more than another arrogant racist White woman who didn't want to understand. His persistent pursuit of this point with Karen only angered her more. As she expressed more anger, Ishmir responded with increased anger and a barrage of accusations. The interaction culminated with Karen abruptly leaving the room stating, "I don't need this bullshit," and with Ishmir declaring: "This is why you can't talk to White people about this stuff. ... I will never do it again."

The exchange between Ismir and Karen was typical. Like so many other attempts to talk openly about race, this interaction escalated rapidly and ended even more quickly. Serious attempts to discuss race openly seldom extend beyond two- to three-exchange interactions before they are stifled by volatility, silence, or a combination of the two. Conversations about race usually are avoided altogether, characterized by a tense and façade-like silence, or there is engagement that quickly escalates and ends before closure. The interaction between Karen and Ishmir illustrated all of the complexities associated with addressing race. There was no common language between them, no tools within their reach to quickly employ to circumvent the inevitable impasse, and not enough space created to encourage constructive engagement in a more expansive conversation. Their conversation, despite the intense rhetoric, was ultimately about "right" and "wrong." Both Karen and Ishmir were convinced that their respective points of view were irrefutably right, and thus the impasse.

Ishmir's comment regarding those who "do" and those who are "done to" was profound in one sense. It hinted at the possibility that he had some awareness of a potential clash between experience of and definition of "reality" and of the possible coexistence of multiple realities—that of "the oppressor" and the "the oppressed." Unfortunately, both Karen and Ishmir's respective notions of reality became more calcified as their emotions intensified. Their interaction offered a perfect portrait of the difficulty involved in sustaining meaningful engagement when race and reality become rigidly entangled. The *basic race-related truths* that both Karen and Ishmir held about themselves and each other contaminated their interaction and significantly reduced any chances of a viable relationship existing between them. Race and the strongly held race-related realities that we possess have an enduring impact on our relationships.

I assume that all of us have some (subjective) notions of reality that are informed by race. Hence it is inevitable that race will have a profound impact on our subjective realities and ultimately our relationships. Interestingly, this is a point to which many people often take exception. I was amused that, subsequent to my making a similar point in an undergraduate class at Syracuse University, many students sternly and vehemently disagreed that race had anything to do with their relationships, while they sat in racially segregated clusters in the classroom.

THE CENTRALITY OF RELATIONSHIPS

We are relational beings and live our lives in a relational context. Relationships are integral to our beings, and the same case could be made for race. I believe that it is virtually impossible to exorcise race from relationships. For example, rigidly segregated racial relationships, as well as those with more flexible boundaries, are both similarly intertwined with race. Largely because of its visual qualities, race is introduced into most relationships long before a formal introduction or acknowledgment occurs. Though it is seldom acknowledged overtly, just as race is introduced, so are a host of race-related realities that may have to be negotiated before a viable relationship can exist. Although there are certainly relationships in which race is openly and effectively addressed as an ongoing process, it remains, in most instances, a stain and/or strain for most.

Racial Stains

The gulf that has divided the races historically remains a backdrop to most social interactions between and among the various races. Race relationships, especially cross-race, are stained with invisible remnants from a contentious and tumultuous history. It is very difficult for individuals from different racial groups to interact on face value. Often, these relationships are tainted with suspicion, prejudice, and guardedness before a single word is ever spoken. These are the stains. They have to be acknowledged and negotiated before meaningful trustworthy interaction can occur. Karen and Ishmir's relationship, for example, had little chance of developing largely because it was severely stained, unbeknownst to them. Racial stains are often a precursor to strained (racial) relationships.

Racial Strains

I believe that most cross-race relationships are strained to some degree. Strained race relationships refer to the polite, cautious, conflict- and intimacy-avoidant, nontrusting but semifunctional interactions that take place among members of diverse racial groups. There is functional engagement that is usually utilitarian; however, the core of the relationship is fragile. When race is discussed or acknowledged, it is usually done so in a cautious and cursory manner. At least three critical factors both contribute to and reinforce strained racial relationships: context differences, lack of tools for engagement, and silence.

Context Differences

Race, as a powerful organizing principle, imbues some with power and privilege while assigning others to positions of subjugation. The sociocultural contexts of the privileged and the subjugated are often worlds apart. In essence, they live in different contexts and thus in different worlds. When one's context is different, so is one's reality. This is precisely what Ishmir was referring to when he admonished Karen that "remembering and forgetting" were experiences tied to one's context and ultimately to one's privilege and/or the absence thereof. When members of different racial groups occupy the same physical space but are separated by divergent existential realities that are neither acknowledged nor negotiated, a strained relationship is the best that can be hoped for and achieved.

Lack of Tools for Constructive Engagement

One of the major detrimental consequences of not acknowledging differences in context and reality is that there has been a dearth of attention devoted to developing effective skills for facilitating constructive engagement. Strained racial relationships are failed attempts at (constructive) engagement. When the tools necessary for traversing and negotiating differences are nonexistent, constructive engagement is virtually impossible. As a result, differences are tolerated rather than negotiated, becoming the essence of a strained relationship.

Silence

The vehicle that is most often used to facilitate the toleration of differences is silence. When it comes to race, the implicit but widely understood rules are "Don't ask—don't tell" and "It is better to not ever say what you mean." In either case, the message is clear: The less you say about race the better. In this regard, silence is golden.

Race is a very difficult and sensitive issue to address regardless of the situation or circumstance. Both in and outside of therapy, interactions involving race are often awkward, contaminated by racial stains, and ultimately strained. As concerted efforts are made to integrate issues of social justice and diversity into the therapeutic process, more concentrated attention to the subtleties and complexities of race are of paramount significance. Although the major emphasis of this chapter is on an examination of race, reality, and relationships in a generic sense, the implications for family therapists should be clear and compelling.

IMPLICATIONS FOR FAMILY THERAPISTS

In my view, family therapists are ultimately relationship experts and should have a viable role wherever relationships exists, which is essentially everywhere. As such, our roles and responsibilities should extend beyond the traditional scope of couple and family work. I believe that we have an ethical imperative to assume an active role in transforming the human condition both within and beyond the walls of therapy. In other words, it is within our purview to promote hope and healing for the world (Hardy, 2001). It is incumbent on us to see our commitment to systemic change as a much broader mandate.

As relationship experts, we have a responsibility to disentangle and deconstruct the entangled web of race, reality, and relationships as a way of offering new and inspired possibilities for our collective being. In our quest to promote more harmonious relationships within and outside of the consulting room, acknowledging, treating, and healing strained relationships must be a priority. Here are a few suggestions that we as a community can employ to jump-start this process.

1. *Become catalytic agents in breaking the silence.* As relationship experts, we must be more vigilant in leading by example. We can do so by taking risks to "name" race and actively and proactively promote dialogue. I am highlighting race here because it is the focus of this chapter; however, I believe this issue needs to be considered much more broadly to include a host of other social justice and diversity-related issues on which our voices are often muted. Dialogues must occur within our communities, our networks of personal relationships, and our work settings before we attempt to fully address these issues in clinical practice.

2. *Recognize the healing potential of dialogues.* Dialogue provides an effective pathway to bridging differences. It is only through dialogue that stained and strained relationships can move from polarization to engagement. Even a dialogue that is mired in repetition and self-indulgence offers the potential for healing; however. it must be guided in this direction. When breaking the silence and promoting the healing potential of dialogue, it is imperative to move the interaction from "talk for talk's sake" to dialogue designed to bridge differences. Critical to this process is ensuring that space is allocated for all voices to be expressed and that authentic possibilities exist for the coexistence of multiple realities.

3. *Promote critical racial introspection.* It is difficult to effectively address the interconnectedness of race, reality, and relationships without engaging in critical introspection. Too often conversations about race become hopelessly stifled because they become too sharply focused around *other*. As relationship experts, it is important for us to facilitate meaningful conversations about race both in and outside of therapy. Our task is to promote self-reflection, starting with ourselves and encouraging our clients to do so, as well. The following questions may be useful in this process:

- How do I define myself racially?
- What meaning(s) do I attach to who I am racially?
- What meaning(s) do I imagine others attach to who I am racially?
- What realities/perceptions do I have that are informed by race?
- How does race inform my intimate relationships?
- How does race inform my nonintimate relationships?
- How do my relationships inform my views about race?
- How does my race facilitate interactions with members of another race?

- How is my race a detriment to my interactions with members of another race?
- What has my experience been in having others witness my answers to these questions?

SUMMARY

In some ways, as therapists we live in the same racial context as do our clients. Thus we are prone to the same racially based biases, misconceptions, and trepidations that are true of the general population. Although I believe our roles as relationship experts uniquely position us to address the intricacies of race, realities, and relationships, this feat is a difficult one to achieve unless we start with *ourselves*. Perhaps our grandest challenge is for each of us to dare challenge *ourselves* to examine the ways in which our lives are shaped by the intersection of race, reality, and relationships.

NOTE

1. Historically at least, this has been true of the United States.

REFERENCES

Hardy, K. V. (2001). Healing the world in 50-minute intervals: A response to family therapy saves the planet. *Journal of Marital and Family Therapy, 27*(1), 19–22.

Hardy, K. V., & Laszloffy, T. A. (2000). The development of children and families of color: A supplemental framework. In W. Nichols, D. Becvar, & A. Napier (Eds.), *Clinical handbook of individual and family development* (pp. 109–128). New York: John Wiley.

CHAPTER 7

Understanding Families in the Context of Cultural Adaptations to Oppression

Vanessa McAdams-Mahmoud

Many therapists work with people who have experienced oppression, overtly and/or covertly. In this chapter, oppression is defined as the systematic suppression and denial of a targeted group's human and/or civil rights, such as the right to speak freely, to assemble peaceably, to be treated equally in employment, housing, and under the law, and to exercise the right to vote and to practice the religion of their choice.

It is easy to see that if these rights are violated, the effects can be devastating and have long-term effects on the family system or the partner relationship of that individual. In working with couples of color, accounts are common of racial abuse, unjust imprisonment, police brutality, employment discrimination, racial harassment, sexual and financial victimization, religious and housing discrimination, and the subversion of the right to vote.

For some couples, the damage is overt and distinct, and they are able to articulate and fight against the violation without damaging the relationship and by mutually supporting one another. In other couples, the damage may be covert and hidden or, if overt, the couple may not be able to effectively communicate about the hurt and the damage done to them. They may end up blaming or being alienated from their partners as a result.

Samia was a young African American nurse practitioner who had difficulty finding a job in the small rural community in which she and her
husband of 1 year were living after she graduated. She was a gentle,
soft-spoken young woman. She interviewed with several of the all-
White medical groups in the area and was not hired by any, although
she graduated near the top of her class and was highly recommended.
The only job she could get was one at the local prison. For 2 years, she
was subjected to rude, abusive behavior at the hands of the inmates
and guards. The majority of the prisoners were Black, and the prison
administrators were mostly White. The administrators had no sympa-
thy for the way Samia was treated and refused to intervene in the situation.

Samia became very depressed and would often cry on her way
to work and while she was at work in the middle of the day. She felt
she could not quit because her extended family was depending on her
income to assist them.

Her husband, Barry, an engineer, seemed to see her depression
as a character defect rather than an illness. He became alienated and
angry with her depressive symptoms, for example, sleeping all the time
when she was home, irritability, lack of pride in self and appearance,
neglect of the sexual and intimate side of their relationship, and so
forth. He began staying away from home and eventually moved out of
their apartment.

By the time that this couple came to treatment, they were well on their
way to divorce. Within the boundaries of the therapeutic relationship, we
began to deconstruct the conflict back to the time when they had "lost" one
another, when Samia was working in the prison. They became able to talk
about and name the racism that she had encountered while seeking employment and the dehumanizing experience of the prison work.

Barry, with education about depression, was better able to see the
effects of the oppression that his wife had suffered and more prepared to be
supportive. Once Samia felt that the pain she had suffered was better understood by her husband, she became aware of ways in which she had pushed
him away during the height of her depression. They were able, over time, to
begin the reconciliation process and the saving of their marriage.

With no discussion of the historical, racial, and social context of the
community in which they live, this couple's struggle with one another would
be seen as problems with their communication patterns, her depression, or
his distancing within the marriage. They might be stuck in blaming one
another rather than learning to face together a social reality that was hostile
to the survival of their marriage.

The United States has 5% of the world's population and 25% of the
world's incarcerated population. More people have been jailed for drug law

violations in the United States than have been incarcerated for all offenses in all of Western Europe. There are more than 7 million people incarcerated, on parole, or probation in the United States. One-third of this population is African American. Young Black men in their 20s and 30s constitute 2% of the national population and are incarcerated at a rate 17 times greater than the national rate. Thirteen percent of Black men are disenfranchised because of felony convictions (Human Rights Watch, 2006, p. 1). In many states a felony conviction may result in the loss of the right to vote. The chances of receiving a prison term following a drug offense arrest increased 447% between 1980 and 1992, during the height of the "crack" cocaine epidemic, and 20–25% of African American men were unemployed, the highest in two decades. Children who were born during this time began to reach the age of majority in 2001 and will continue to enter the adult phase of their lives through 2013. The U.N. Commission on Human Rights stated that

> the racially disparate impact of current drug control efforts prioritizing criminal prosecution and harsh mandatory sentences raises serious questions about the willingness of the United States to meet its international human rights obligations. ... In choosing to prioritize arrests and imprisonment of drug offenders, the United States opted for policies that have had a devastating effect on Black communities. (Human Rights Watch, 2000, p. 2)

The effects of the removal of African American men from their communities through incarceration during these years are being felt in families all over the United States and will continue to be felt for years to come.

As a therapist, I encounter these effects in the hunger for a father's presence in the lives of his daughters and sons. I see the results in the difficult struggle for financial survival waged by wives, girlfriends, children, and mothers without the income, love, and presence that these men could have contributed to their families. I see the results in women's settling for a less viable or compatible partner than the one who was lost or in their decisions to be alone rather than settle for less.

Has this type of oppression contributed to a permanent change in the way in which families are created and maintained in the African American community and in other communities similarly affected? Has the combination of unemployment, the flooding of communities with highly addictive drugs, and the imprisonment of those who seek solace in drug use or economic survival in drug selling helped to speed the development of the unitary family to mother and children rather than mother, father, and children? Along with the economic ability of women to support their children, the decrease in stigma of out-of-wedlock births, and widespread divorce, it is clear that the traditional nuclear family is not viable or achievable for many people. Is this the permanent norm for the foreseeable future?

AFRICAN AMERICAN FAMILY CONSTRUCTION

In response to these shifting realities, within the African American community I frequently encounter in my practice many different ways in which people have begun to construct family. It is interesting to me that some of these ways parallel ways in which family has been constructed in West Africa within different ethnic groups. The family, after all, is formed in order to raise and nurture young human beings to maturity, to educate and to protect them from danger until they can care for themselves. In Africa, monogamous marriage and various forms of plural marriage have coexisted for thousands of years. The forms of marriage vary according to the ethnic group and class and seem to transform over time in response to the changing social, geographical, and economic realities of the community in which they are contracted.

In the African American community, monogamous marriage remains a desirable ideal. However, whether the couple or each individual feels "ready" for marriage or capable of creating and sustaining a successful marriage seems to be a more and more difficult question. Marriage becomes, for some, something that they may achieve at some distant point in the future.

Until that day comes, however, many partners choose to create family by having children together, whether or not they may end up marrying one another. The families that are created in this process do not all resemble the Western nuclear family ideal of mother, father, and children.

The forms of family construction I encounter most often are monogamous/married; monogamous/married with blended family; monogamous/married with parallel family; unmarried partners; single-parent family with unmarried partner; single-parent family with married partner; religiously polygamous family.

Monogamous/Married Family

The families that I see who have constructed this family style are typically stable financially, with both partners having marketable skills and education. They often come from families whose parents were married for at least a portion of their lives. The stress on these families sometimes come from the expectations of the extended family who are not doing well financially or who have experienced the effects of addiction, encounters with the criminal justice system, or death due to chronic illness or homicide. In addition to the complex task of maintaining a healthy marriage, this family may be expected to take in or assist relatives or the children of relatives because of the success they have achieved. The experience of oppression may be felt by people they love, and therefore they feel obligated to help in some way. Employment discrimination, the lack of a promotion due to racism, the loss of a job because of racial harassment can destabilize not only this nuclear family but also the extended family that depends on it.

Monogamous Blended Family

These families are composed of a husband, a wife, and their children from previous relationships. These families are also typically stable financially, with both partners having marketable skills and education. They often come from families whose parents were married for at least a portion of their lives. The partners in this family have the added stress of maintaining harmonious relationships with the other biological parent of the children and gaining the respect and love of the children of their partner. Families often seek treatment and support in negotiating these relationships. Oppression that is experienced by the biological mothers or fathers of their children can directly affect the functioning of these families. Socioeconomic differences in lifestyles and in the neighborhoods in which their children may live or go to school when not with them can cause difficulties in the blended family that may have developed a different lifestyle and cultural style.

Monogamous/Married with Parallel Family

These families are composed of a husband and a wife with children who are officially married and recognized by the extended family, their church, and community. Usually sometime in the life cycle of the family the husband establishes a relationship with another woman (the "outside woman"), has children with her, and supports both families. The second family may not be acknowledged by the wife or extended family. However, at some point the children may be recognized by the extended family and, at times, eventually by the wife. Sometimes the recognition does not happen until the death of the husband or the death or illness of the "outside" woman. I have worked with families who have absorbed the children from the other, unofficial family into the official family at these times. This dramatic moment of official recognition often becomes pivotal in the lives of the children who are "recognized," the official wife who must struggle with ambivalent feelings of betrayal and duty, the half-siblings who must get used to the idea of their father's other life, and so forth. This pattern might seem very dysfunctional compared with Western models, but it becomes more understandable when compared with West African models of family life. I think it is useful to contrast West African and African American models of family life. Often African American families retain customs, cultural attitudes, even language styles that are easily traced to West African ethnic groups.

In Nigeria, there is a similarly constructed family that is composed of the "inside" wife, or official wife, and her children and the "outside" wife and her children. They often live in different areas. Most often the official wife is better educated, with a higher status than the outside wife, and will reside in the city. The marriage will have been contracted publicly, with some official religious ceremony. The outside wife and her children will reside in a more rural area, and the marriage may have been contracted without much ceremony, if any. The husband acknowledges all of his children and feels responsibility for being a formal father figure for them all (Parkin & Nyamawaya, 1987). The role of father is often a formal one in African families. The relationship will be one in which children treat their father with respect but emotional distance and he recognizes them as his own and provides for their support and expects them to abide by his wishes for them.

Unmarried Partners

This family pattern may occur with couples with their own biological children or prior to having children. In many ways, this is a trial relationship without full legalized commitment. The partners usually share a household. The primary issue with these couples, spoken or unspoken, is, Are you "the one" for me, the one I will eventually marry?

If not, why not? How do I handle these feelings of attachment if this arrangement is only temporary? What keeps me from wanting to make the final commitment with you? Often the obstacle to marriage is financial and practical. In many couples I have worked with, either one or both partners are having difficulty maintaining a stable income, are involved in getting an education, or are having difficulty extricating themselves from the family of origin. Barriers to employment, difficulty in funding education, addiction in the family, or criminal justice involvement can often complicate and delay the decision. In addition, maturational, developmental, and psychodynamic issues can make the decision to marry can seem like a Herculean task.

Single-Parent Family with Unmarried Partner

This particular family pattern is the source of much sociological angst: the single mother with children. In their book *Promises I Can Keep*, Kathryn Edin and Maria Kefalas (2005) discuss the reasons that poor women put motherhood before marriage. What is unique about their work is that they actually asked the women why they made the choice they made despite the challenges they knew would lie ahead. The authors state that

> poor women realize that marriage is fragile and so they make their primary emotional investments in their relationships with their children, which are not subject to the threats that so often destroy relationships between men and

women. Sonia, a twenty-three-year-old Puerto Rican mother of a four-year-old son, puts it this way: "My son is my heart. When I have hard times I always tell myself I wanted him. Even if I get that rock on my finger, that white picket fence and that deed that says the house is mine, [I'll still have my son] just in case anything goes sour. I'll say to my husband, "You leave! This boy is *mine*." (p. 211)

The authors also found that despite cultural differences in family-related behavior, the worldviews as to what constituted the right conditions for marriage were more universal. African Americans seem to value and aspire to marriage more than Whites or Puerto Ricans do, but they are less likely than Whites to achieve it. Whites were most likely to reject marriage outright but most likely to be married. Among African American women, men's earnings and employment are more important for predicting marriage than among Whites and Hispanics (Edin & Kefalas, 2005, pp. 212–213).

Anything that impedes African American men being fully employed will directly affect the rate of marriage in the African American community. High rates of incarceration, unemployment, lack of funding for education and training, and substance use or dependence will often determine whether a single mother chooses to marry her partner or whether her partner feels stable enough to offer marriage. Working with these couples in therapy often involves these issues, as well as issues of power and mutual respect.

Single-Parent Family with Married Partner

This particular family pattern is often based on mutual attraction and economic convenience. It is incumbent on the married male partner to provide substantive support for the woman who has decided to accept this arrangement, or she may tire of it and seek a marriageable partner. It is also a question whether the man can negotiate both relationships in a "fair "manner to both partners. In my practice, I usually see the woman and/or her children in therapy.

This arrangement may go on for many years and evolve into the parallel family if she also has children with this partner. But most often the woman has had all of the children she wants and is looking for companionship and economic help, as well as a father figure for her children. Her male partner may become well known to her circle of friends and family. Often, she has some problems with guilt or with her religious beliefs and struggles with loneliness. However, she does not see a way to handle her responsibilities to her children by herself.

The Religiously/Culturally Polygynous Family

As African Americans became more conscious of positively identifying with their African heritage, more individuals began to consciously experiment with and hold viable the creation of polygynous families (Kilbride, 1994). Those African Americans who have converted to Islam and those African Americans who practice the Yoruba religion are most likely to create polygynous families. This practice in these communities is seen as a solution to the removal of large numbers of marriageable men from the community and a way in which all women with whom a man has children will enjoy an equal level of respectability and support. It is seen as a way in which all children can be publicly acknowledged by their fathers and by their community. In the case of Islam, there are clearly defined rights and limits on numbers of wives, on ways in which wives and children should be treated, on property inheritance, and so forth.

The problem with this is that there is no religious court that enforces the *sharia* (religious law) in the community when it is unjustly and incorrectly used or violated. In the Yoruba community, there is an even more confusing dilemma, as there is no codified practice of how polygyny should be conducted and practiced.

In working with these families, I have seen problems with the ways in which the marriages are contracted and conducted. Some seem more like affairs and have the same effect as affairs on the first marriage. Some, although contracted according to *sharia*, are unstable because the husband has inadequate means to support both families. Some work relatively well. However, second and third wives have no protection under the law of the United States and cannot share in the husband's social security benefits, insurance, and so forth.

CONCLUSION

In response to oppression, the shape of African American families is changing. One of the constant cultural principles and values of African American life is the value of improvisation. This value can be seen in music, dance, cuisine, hairstyles, clothing, and so forth. It is also seen in family life. We construct families as arks for survival through difficult waters, through floods, across oceans. The families we left in Africa, the families that we constructed during 400 years of slavery, the families that we constructed post-Reconstruction, and the families we constructed post-Civil Rights and post-"crack" have been improvised with one overriding purpose. That overriding purpose has been to survive and to thrive until better times come, as we struggle for empowerment and the ending of the oppression of our hopes and dreams. Any therapist who works with families who live daily with oppression should struggle against value judgments about the way in which oppressed people have chosen to survive and construct family. Rather, seek to help ease the pain, name racism and oppression for what it is, and become an ally with that family, whatever its shape.

Hopefully, its members can move beyond survival into flourishing and thriving with your help.

REFERENCES

Edin, K., & Kefalas, M. (2005). *Promises I can keep*. Berkeley: University of California Press.

Human Rights Watch. (2000). *Racism, racial discrimination, xenophobia, and all forms of discrimination*. U.N. Commission on Human Rights, 56th session. Retrieved from daccess-ods.un.org/access.Asf/Get?Open&DS=E/CN.4/2000/NGO/18&Lang=E.

Karanja wa Wambui. (1987). "Outside wives" and "inside wives" in Nigeria: A study of changing perceptions in marriage. In D. Parkin & D. Nyamawaya (Eds.), *Transformations of African Marriage* (International African Seminars). Manchester, UK: Manchester University Press.

Kilbride, P. (1994). *Plural marriage for our times: A reinvented option?* Westport, CT: Bergin & Harvey.

PART II

Cultural Legacies and Stories

Therapists' Experiences

CHAPTER 8

Finding a Place Called "Home"

Monica McGoldrick

What potential is lost when we are not able to know or come to terms
with our cultural heritage? What price do we pay when those who
pull the curtains of history allow us to know our history only dimly or
with shame? The story of many in our society is one of identity forever
blurred by the winds of silence and the sands of amnesia. It is a story of
being rooted in uprootedness. The themes that reverberate in each story
are those of near destruction and survival, shame and guilt, the long
fuse of unresolved anger, the recovery of pride and identity. Many have
had to live with their deepest stories denied. We now endeavor toward
a time when hope and history will rhyme and everyone may receive the
world's respect for who they truly are.
—PARAPHRASE OF TOM HAYDEN (1998, pp. 8–9)

The 1960s radical, Tom Hayden, like myself, grew up knowing nothing
about his Irish heritage. Yet, without realizing his connection to his starving
ancestors who were in the United States because of the Irish Famine of the
1840s, his first political act after leaving college was to bring food to share-
croppers. Many years later, having learned much about his history, he wrote
a book called *Irish on the Inside* about those who have had to live with their
deepest stories denied.

Growing up in my family there were many things about my privilege,
as well as about my oppression, that I did not know or did not know that I
knew—many issues that were mystified, obscured, or kept invisible by my
community, my family, and my education, and later in my social work and

family therapy training. Susan Griffin (1992) writes profoundly about this experience in her memoir *A Chorus of Stones*:

> We forget that we are history. . . . We are not used to associating our private lives with public events. Yet the histories of families cannot be separated from the histories of nations. To divide them is part of our denial. All that I was taught at home or in school was colored by denial and thus it became so familiar to me that I did not see it. We keep secrets from ourselves that all along we know. . . . I do not see my life as separate from history. In my mind my family secrets mingle with the secrets of statesmen and bombers. My life [is not] divided from the lives of others. I who am woman, have my father's face. And he, I suspect, had his mother's face. (pp. 7–8)

For myself, I started way back when it comes to understanding my cultural and family legacies. I grew up with no sense whatsoever of my cultural or family history. In fact, I had no real personal connection to culture prior to going to Ireland in 1975 at age 32, even though I am 100% Irish by heritage (fourth-generation American). Without realizing it, I grew up with race at the center of my family's existence, because the person who raised us was Margaret Pfeifer Bush, an African American, descended from slaves in North Carolina, who lived with or near our family from the time I was born until she died, the year after I left home for college. But we had no conscious awareness of our racial arrangements any more than we did of our cultural arrangements.

I did have deep feelings about the two places I grew up: Brooklyn, home of Ebbets Field and the Brooklyn Dodgers, and Solebury, Pennsylvania, where from age 6 I grew up on a little farm in Bucks County. The person with whom I share some of the deepest connections regarding my childhood is Jim Michener, my best friend in early childhood, who has basically never returned to the United States since the Vietnam War and still lives in Southeast Asia. We have reminisced a great deal about detailed memories of the barn, the playhouse, the scary places in the basement, the sheep, where the clothes line was, and the bridge over the brook that led into the woods. It is odd that he and I should still need to share so many memories of these details from our childhood.

In spite of this concern for memories, I am puzzled that I grew up with virtually no sense of my cultural heritage. It seems we were definitely trying to "pass" for the dominant group—and because of our skin color and opportunities we could. What we lost in the process was the sense of who we really were.

In this generation, almost everyone in my family seems to be seeking better perspective through continually trying to build cultural bridges. Is this why I decided on pursuing Russian "culture" from the time I was in high school, trying to teach myself the language and pursuing it in college and graduate school? Of course, I thought culture referred only to others and that I myself was "regular." Is this why I decided to live in the International House in graduate school? Is this why I chose to marry my husband, an immigrant from Greece, who left home for education as did all the males in his family? My husband's relatives were themselves immigrants to Greece, arriving there in 1922 after hundreds of years in Turkey.

Perhaps it is all part of the globalization of our world in our times. One of my nephews moved to Europe after college, and is now an immigrant to Paris, where he lives with his wife, another immigrant, from South Africa. Her parents were themselves immigrants from Germany and the Netherlands. My other nephew has migrated to California, and has traveled often to Japan and China, creating musical connections between Asian and European/U.S. music. My older sister, an architectural photographer, has written books about they Stepwells in India, the gardens in Italy, and is now completing a book about the water systems of Yemen. My younger sister, a high school teacher, has taught and lived the past 3 years in Shanghai.

Somehow I am part of a family that is always trying to cross cultural bridges. Is it just globalization that has led to our family's interest in culture? I don't know. I have wondered why I grew up knowing nothing about my cultural history. Was it, as Nuala O'Faolain put it, because "something that had happened more than a hundred years ago and that was almost forgotten, was so terrible that it knocked the happiness out of people and they tried to forget?" (2001, p. 5).

I was born in 1943. There were people still alive at that time who had lived through the Irish Famine years. It is surely true, as O'Faolain puts it:

> The trauma must be deep in the genetic material of which I was made. I cannot forget it, yet I have no memory of it. It is not mine, but who else can own it. Our own forebears must have been part of the system too. If you and I are sitting here today, we have to ask ourselves how our people survived? What did our people do at the time, that you and I came to be born? Anyone who had a field of cabbages or turnips put a guard to keep off the starving. We were those guards. (pp. 73–74)

My Irish ancestors came to the United States in the 1840s and 1850s at the time of the Famine. I never heard about this traumatic immigration experience from their children (my grandparents) or their grandchildren (my parents). I also never heard about the Irish who didn't get away, or about the bodies my family must have walked past in order to escape.

There were many things about my privilege and about my oppression that I grew up not knowing or not knowing that I knew, many issues that were mystified, obscured, or kept invisible by my community, my family, my teachers, and even my professional training. As I think about my family two generations later passing for the dominant group, I am reminded of the memoir of Beryl Fletcher (2003), an Australian of British ancestry, who writes:

> I suffer from a deep form of homelessness that I believe to be common to whites[1] of my generation whose parents and grandparents came as colonizers and invaders to already inhabited lands. Our stories and myths came from the Northern Hemisphere. Our books, our rituals, our moral universe were forcibly imposed upon the original inhabitants. But we could not keep ourselves apart from the mythologized landscapes of the conquered people. We absorbed them through our senses. Our bodies grew into the shape of the land. At the same time we were taught that everything of importance, of good quality, came from the North. Especially England. ... In the small dark hours of night, the mattress and pillow that cradles your body at that particular time is home. ... I know this intellectually, but I am still mired emotionally with the restless legacy of the colonial mind ... Deep in the bone is the certainty that real life is taking place elsewhere. (pp. 32–33)

Fletcher's comments about home remind me of how complex that concept is. Giamatti in a marvelous essay about baseball, described its associations in ways which convey its relationship to culture:

> Home is an English word virtually impossible to translate ... No translation catches the associations, the mixture of memory and longing ... the aroma of inclusiveness, of freedom from wariness, that cling to the word home ... Home is a concept, not a place; it is a state of mind where self-definition starts; it is origins—the mix of time and place and smell and weather wherein one first realizes one is an original, perhaps like others, especially those one loves, but discrete, distinct, not to be copied. Home ... remains in the mind as the place where reunion, if it ever were to occur, would happen ... It is about restoration of the right relations among things—and going home is where that restoration occurs, because that is where it matters most. (Halberstam & Robson, 1998, pp. 99–101)

Home is a place where we could own our cultural heritage and not have our deepest stories denied. It is about the right relations among things. But society's invisible structuring of class, culture, race, gender, and sexual orientation limits relationships, as they were limited in my family, my schooling, and in the communities in which I have lived. None of these issues was ever mentioned in my childhood, my adolescence, my college or graduate experience, or in my study of family therapy. Historically, some of us have found our safety at the expense of others. We seek safety that jeopardizes others or denies them their own sense of belonging and spiritual connection. For the most part, we do this unwittingly.

The McGoldrick side of my family settled in Brooklyn—my beloved Brooklyn, where the highlight of my childhood was going to see my Dodger hero Jackie Robinson play at Ebbets Field. But I had no idea of what Jackie Robinson had really done or had had to contend with to integrate baseball. I never thought about what my ancestors, who came here as members of another race, did to become white. Were they in the draft riots in New York City in 1863, just a few years after they came to the United States? Many Irish, after being drafted, turned against African Americans, blaming them for the Civil War, and staging lynchings and burnings around the city, including the burning of a Black orphan asylum of young children. Were my ancestors part of this? Did they speak up? Did they remain silent?

Growing up, I never thought (except in the superficial sense that we often went looking for arrowheads) about the fact that the land we lived on both in Brooklyn and in Pennsylvania had been Lenape land. I never thought about the treaties that had been made and broken with the Lenape for the land we called our own—that we were really standing on their land. I didn't know that many of the streets I knew—Flatbush Avenue, Kings Highway—were originally Native trails, and that in 1655 a law was passed that no Indian could pow wow or worship within any town in the colony. This law was hardly necessary, as the Indian population in New York had mostly been massacred already. And I didn't know that in 1776 nearly one third of the population of Brooklyn (3,700) was Black, all but a handful of whom were slaves. Indeed, Brooklyn had the highest slave population of any city north of the Mason-Dixon line! Two-thirds of all white families in Brooklyn at that time owned slaves!

Nor did I know that almost 100 years later, in 1860, just after my family had settled there, Abraham Lincoln did not carry Brooklyn. Abolition was not popular anywhere in New York City, and without an upstate landslide, New York could have lost them the election. Brooklyn was pro-slavery, in spite of our Brooklyn hero Walt Whitman. Where did my relatives stand? I did not know that New York City had the highest population of slaves after Charleston, and as a city built on commerce, benefited from slavery more than any northern city.

What did my family do later when they rose in status, education, and positions within the city? How did my grandfather relate to African Americans when he was a police inspector and had responsibility for riots in Harlem? What did my father do when he was New York City Comptroller and then City Rent Commissioner in relation to the segregation and inequalities in New York City real estate? All my life my family lived in effectively segregated communities, though they believed in justice and equality and spoke of it often. Did that bother them? My preschool, grade school, and high schools never had more than one or two people of color.

I then went to Brown University, in Rhode Island, where there were probably not 10 African Americans in the entire university. Now, Brown has Ruth Simmons, the first ever African American President of an Ivy League school, and she has been supporting research on the slave history of Brown, which of course I also never knew about. Rhode Island was developed on the slave trade and had more slaves per capita than any other New England colony, though slavery also played a major role in the development of New York City, which as a financial center thrived on the sale of the products of slavery. John Brown, for whom my University was named, was one of the biggest slave traders, although his own brother Moses was an outspoken abolitionist and a true hero of the era. Why didn't I ever know the slave heritage of my school, my cities, or the wealth of so much of the north, or even about the heroism of men like Moses Brown and other abolitionists who should have been like Jackie Robinson, my role models for social justice?

I have been wondering what will help us realize that as Susan Griffin says, our personal stories and the history of the world are all one story? How can we recognize that somewhere within ourselves we know the secrets we keep from ourselves and from each other? And what does it cost us to keep these secrets and wear these blinders? T. S. Eliot said humankind can bear very little reality and maybe that is true. But it costs us a lot to deaden ourselves to avoid the cognitive dissonance that would occur if we allowed ourselves to see the pain that our silence and denial leave others to bear. How can we realize that somewhere within ourselves we know the secrets we keep from ourselves and from each other? *Yes, it is built on some else back.*

"Home" is about much more than where we live physically. It is not just where we sleep, and it is not just the nostalgic home of our childhood or our wished-for childhood. It is a spiritual and psychological place of liberation. Home is a space, where we could all belong—with each other—strengthened by what we take from those who have come before us, creating a safe haven for those who are with us in our time, and insuring that we leave a safe space for all those who will come after us. My notions of "going home" have been radically challenged as I have become aware of the constraints of class, culture, gender, and race on the structure of who I am. I have been coming to realize that "going home" means going to a place most of us have never been, since home in our society has not been a safe place for most people in our country—not for women, children, people of color, or gays and lesbians, given the pervasiveness of corporal punishment, child sexual abuse, the mistreatment and devaluing of women, and the appalling racism and homophobia of our society.

UNACKNOWLEDGED ASPECTS OF MY GROWING UP

Although we never mentioned gender in my family, my father was a visiting dignitary, while two women—one the servant of the other, my mother and Margaret—raised three girls in what was most of the time an all-female household. There were clearly different and preferential rules regarding men, but these rules were kept invisible. While the influence of my Irish background would have been obvious to anyone who could recognize Irish behavior, looks, or names, I never knew that I was Irish. Moreover, we were taught that class did not matter, though we learned implicitly who was above us and who was below us in class, and had a complete set of hierarchical prescriptions for our behavior (acceptable schools to attend, people whom we could date or befriend, etc.). Though we were dimly aware of social stratification, class was never mentioned in my family, and we were led to believe that we lived in a class-blind as well as a color-blind family, community, and society. At the same time we organized our relationships completely according to prescribed and biased rules of gender, class, culture, race, and sexual orientation.

I think now that I could grow up not knowing that I had a cultural background probably only because I could "pass" for a member of the dominant group. Had I been Black or Latino, I would have known that I had a culture. As my mother put it when I began asking questions, "We're Americans now, Monica. Our ancestors were just peasants. What difference does it make where we came from?" It was not until the mid-1970s that I realized I was Irish. Through my interest in Murray Bowen's theory, I had begun to explore my own roots and inspired a family trip to Ireland, where I had the overwhelming feeling that I had come home. Everywhere I seemed to see my relatives, people who related in the same way my family did—using humor, teasing, and ridicule to keep others in line or to maintain distance in male–female relationships; failing to talk about the most important things that were happening; giving someone the "silent treatment." Patterns I had experienced all my life suddenly had a context: my family wasn't "crazy," I was just Irish! It was a transformative experience that has never left me. I still think of Ireland as home in some deep way, and defining myself as Irish American has been an affirmation at the deepest level of my belonging. Much that I thought was strange or eccentric I now see has meaning because of our cultural history. It has been very reassuring to give a name to these cultural aspects of my life that were unacknowledged as I grew up.

UNSUNG SHEROES: MY MOTHER

I grew up hearing my mother and everyone else tell me how special my father was. My mother, on the other hand, I experienced as intimidating, unaffectionate, and difficult. Had my father had the same inhibition about expressing his warmth that my mother did, I am sure I would have been less judgmental of that failing. I now realize that nothing in my experience led me to have empathy for my mother's life or for the difficulties of her position in raising us. She was a city person, extremely energetic, intelligent, and social, who for 8 years raised us in a country house to live out a dream of my father's, while he remained in the city—"the good provider" who was "making our dreams come true." My mother spent her life serving as our chauffeur and trying to invent things to do with her life, isolated from everything she had ever known. This life was not *her* dream by a very long shot. Much later, she admitted that she nearly went crazy there, wishing desperately to be with my father and to have a career of her own again in New York City. Instead, she had to make the most of her enormous energy and ability in an extremely confining situation. She developed many home-related skills: rewiring lamps, painting, plumbing, and buying and fixing antiques.

My mother was also a great storyteller. I regret that I spent so many years not listening to her. Her family stories were primarily about the men in our family—her admired uncle, her beloved husband, and her beloved father. She did not talk about her mother, whom she hated for all of her life. Her mother had had an affair with a local priest (not the thing for an Irish matron to do!) and had no patience for her three daughters, especially the youngest, my mother. Indeed, when my mother was small, her mother used to tell her not to come home from school because Father Egan would be there. My mother did not tell me that her mother was also the first woman on Staten Island to drive a car, that she had an amazing eye for beautiful objects, or that, as my cousin put it, she was one of the early liberated women of her era.

Late in life my mother told me she had always been "somebody's something," first "Inspector Cahalane's daughter," then "Joe McGoldrick's wife," and now, she added, "I'm Monica's mother. Just once I'd like first to be known as Helen McGoldrick, who stands on her own two feet. But that's never going to happen, Monica."

The pain of always having to be "somebody's something" is a problem I have come to realize is mine as well as hers. Her history, fears, inadequacies, and struggles continue through me. Because of the time in which she lived, she was not able to be all that she could be. She, her two sisters, and their classmates at Barnard College in the 1930s were a privileged and exceptionally talented group of women who, for the most part, had to submerge their identities into those of the men and children in their lives. My mother had a successful career in public relations before she met my father, but she gave up her career and even her name to be Mrs. Joseph McGoldrick.

For years I resented her for what I saw as bragging and covering up who we really were by coloring stories to impress others with our accomplishments—where we went to school and so forth. When I switched from Russian studies to social work, my mother was embarrassed. She could not even bring herself to use the term "social work." It probably indicated to her a loss in her own precariously gained class status. She would introduce me by saying, "This is my daughter Monica, who is doing psychiatric ... at Yale." Now I feel shame about the anger and contempt I subtly conveyed toward her; I realize that she did it because she was unsure of her own status, and had been made to feel invisible and inadequate all her life. I have come to see it as my business that my mother was not free to be all she could be, and that we judged her so harshly for not being good at certain aspects of mothering. We did not validate or accept her for the great strengths she possessed. Her invisibility made our lives visible. I have come to realize it was not my mother who was inadequate but the yardstick by which I measured her. As Ruth Bader Ginsburg said on her swearing in as a U.S. Supreme Court justice, "I would like to be the kind of woman my mother would have been had she lived in different times."

UNSUNG SHEROES: MARY GERTRUDE CAHALANE

There were other unsung "sheroes" in my family. Aunt Mamie Cahalane, my grandfather's sister, was the only sister of seven brothers and a widowed father. The men in her family, fearing the loss of their caretaker, discouraged all suitors who came to call. So Aunt Mamie took care of her father and all seven brothers until they died or left home. She became the Santa Claus for five generations of our family, as well as for her whole court at 90 St. Marks Place on Staten Island. Yet she lived in poverty all her life, "on relief," as it was called then. Not having the education for work that our culture sanctions with remuneration, she could not make ends meet. She taught me a great deal about what you can give others beyond your pocketbook—about humor and generosity and beauty that has nothing to do with physical assets or great accomplishments of the sort that get rewarded in our individualistic, competitive, materialistic society. She was another invisible "shero" of my life.

UNSUNG SHEROES: MARGARET BUSH

My third invisible shero was Margaret Bush, descended from slaves in Asheville, North Carolina. She was the person to whom I was closest both emotionally and physically all my life until her death the year after I left for college. It was to her that I confided my problems—about boyfriends, about teachers, and about my mother. She was always there for me and loved me unconditionally. She had lost her twin sons and her first husband. She gave up living with her second husband, Joe, much of the time to live with us—a common story for many African Americans, who were forced to sacrifice their own families for the white families they served. I miss her every day, and she, too, lives in my heart and makes me who I am. And I know I have an ongoing responsibility to her to seek the right relations among people and to speak for those who have given me a chance.

But how do I find the right relation? How do I deal with the shadow side of my relationship with Margaret, who, like so many others, worked in the home of a white family, and gave to them love and care that deprived their own families? This is the story of racism. What I received is the complement to what my African American friends were denied when their mothers or fathers had to serve white families at their own expense. And this is part of the unacknowledged benefit I have gotten from racism. It is painful to realize that my love and benefit have meant someone else's loss and deprivation and that the two are intertwined.

I grew up thinking that I was innocent—that I had nothing to do with racism and certainly not with slavery. I did not recognize Margaret's white uniform as a symbol of her status within our family. Nor did I grasp the significance of the fact that she did not learn how to read until after I did—when she was 50 years old. This, too, goes back to the history of slavery, when slaves could be killed for learning to read, as could anyone who taught them. How ignorant of me not to know or sense anything of her dilemma. Her invisible life made mine visible. I realize that I am a part of all that came before, that I have benefited from racism and benefit from it every day in the unearned white privilege I experience in terms of my safety and status in many contexts. These include the fact that most books are written for me as a white person, so even when Margaret did learn to read, she was forced to read about white middle-class families with Dick and Jane, leaving invisible, yet again, her history and her ancestors' courage to survive, which she would have found more gratifying and affirming to read.

I am coming slowly and painfully to realize what it means to say that we who are white carry around, in Peggy MacIntosh's terms (Chapter 21, this volume), a kind of invisible knapsack of privilege—which contains special provisions, maps, passports, and visas, blank checks, and emergency gear. We cannot see it, but those who don't have one can. And we need to listen to their experience and think about the meaning of our privilege rather than focusing on how we are exceptions and do not have as much privilege as others may think.

BECOMING AWARE OF GENDER, RACE, AND CLASS: PROFESSIONAL AND PERSONAL STRUGGLES

Until I was over 40, I never noticed how my professional education was structured in terms of gender, class, race, and other characteristics. As a young family therapist, I never noticed that the leaders of the field were virtually all men, and I certainly never noticed that they were all white heterosexuals and that a high percentage were psychiatrists, whereas the followers were largely women social workers. The major gurus—Ackerman, Haley, Minuchin, Bowen, and Whitaker—were all intimidating to me, but part of the gender problem was also, in Betty Friedan's (1963) phrase, a "problem that had no name." I remember being especially intimidated and put off by Nat Ackerman, whose objectifying and sexualizing of women and whose manner of confronting and discounting others were frankly scary. Salvador Minuchin also often seemed to disqualify or embarrass trainees, and Murray Bowen had an offensive way of responding to a question he did not like by saying: "Next question."

I admired the leaders' intelligence and ability, but they left me feeling inadequate. I felt I could never do what they did, but the idea never crossed my mind that this might have to do with my being a woman. I noticed how men on panels were insulting to Virginia Satir, but I focused on how, amazingly, she never let herself respond with humiliation, aggression, or defensiveness. Satir became the one I followed most closely; I never missed one of her workshops, no matter what. She had a way of validating each comment, finding something useful in each question.

I did not notice that gays and lesbians were never mentioned. Nor did I have any awareness of the absence of people of color in the field or in my life. I knew no African American family therapists. I admired Harry Aponte and Braulio Montalvo but had no contact with them. It was years before this myopia was challenged and I began to be uncomfortable with the whiteness of the field, the maleness of the leadership, and the heterosexism embodied in it.

Gender

It was not until years after realizing that I was Irish that I first became aware of gender as an issue in my life and in our field—not until the 1980s. And when I began to become aware of it, it created more than a transformation; it created great turmoil in my personal, as well as my professional, life. With my Irishness, I could maintain a distance. I was Irish, yes, but that was a limited part of my identity. And I could "pass" for "regular" in most contexts. I had also married a Greek, and my friends came from many different backgrounds. In most contexts it was not salient. I could get away from it. With gender, however, I could not escape it. Wherever I went, the rules for gender inequality applied. When I left work, I went back to what I was coming to realize was a family pervaded by sexism, with a husband who thought he was helping me if he did any chores around the house. But then I realized I, too, was sexist because I felt grateful for his "help." Soon thereafter we had our son, an event that put me even further in touch with the patriarchal arrangements of my life, as I saw that all aspects of child rearing in our society—from the structure of childcare to children's TV, literature, clothing, and education—are pervaded by sexism and inequality. I could not get away from it. My mother felt sorry for my husband when I went away on business. My husband thought of me as "abandoning" him and going "on vacation" when I went to a professional meeting. I myself had to prepare days ahead of time for my absence and make up for it for days afterward. This was so different from my father's traveling when I was a child. Our whole family organized itself for his return, which was always a special occasion.

As I became aware of the inequities of my relationship with my husband, I struggled with how to address them. I tried to be very patient, carefully judging just when I could bring up an issue, so as not to overload the circuits—not when he'd had a hard day or was in a bad mood. By the time I did raise an issue, I had usually been troubled by it for a very long time; yet my husband would see me as "ruining" our relationship by starting the conversation. And a part of me believed this also. If I were just more generous or more worthy or knew better how to express myself, I would be able to work things out with him without conflict.

In my work as well, once I began to notice the gender inequities, I became aware (as my closest women colleagues were realizing at the same time) that they pervaded our field, as well as every other aspect of our society. Commenting on these issues at family therapy meetings brought about powerful reactions. I remember the first panel on gender at a meeting of the American Family Therapy Academy, when Virginia Goldner gave an amazing presentation on gender and generation. She pointed out that of these two fundamental categories of human relations, family therapists had been raised to notice generation but to keep gender invisible (Goldner, 1989). I marveled at her clarity. What she said was so true. How had I not seen it? But afterward, many men disparaged her; one of the leaders in the field even described her as "Darth Vader." Another time, the first occasion of a national family therapy conference program with a strong predominance of women, many men within the organization were outraged. They felt betrayed and thought this represented the desire of the women to "kill off" the men. In the same year, many of the same men organized a major quadrennial meeting of the senior family therapy journal and were unfazed that they had included almost no women or minorities. Years later I read somewhere that white people tend to think people of color are "taking over" when their percentages reach something like 14% of a group. I thought back to these experiences and sensed the same discomfort and fear of changing the balance, however unequal it may be to start with.

I have been mystified over the years by the reactivity of men to these issues. No matter how carefully we tried to express ourselves—to say that feminism was about a new structuring of gender relationships as partnerships, not about women winning a competition against men—it was often virtually impossible to have conversations. People spoke of the possibility that the men would withdraw from the field if the women didn't get off "this kick." One close male friend asked me after a year or so whether I wasn't ready to move on from "that fad." As cautious or careful as I tried to be, the feedback I got was blaming, disparaging, and self-justifying:

> "Monica, you used to be so nice. What happened to you? Why are you so angry at men? Did you hate your father? Are you getting divorced? You are ruining our relationship. And anyway, I'm not sexist, I didn't do anything. I loved my mother, I respect my wife, I've never abused a woman— why are you blaming me for this? And why are you saying we have power? I don't have any power. I feel quite powerless. What you're saying doesn't relate to me. We men have problems, too. We're not allowed to feel. We've lost our fathers. We're walled off." (And so on.)

Of course, it is the nature of patriarchy that men do not realize their power, because in a society where everyone is measured hierarchically there is always someone ahead of you or just at your heels to take your place. But it seemed impossible to get men to envision a way of being that wasn't about winning or losing. This changing consciousness in the family therapy field began a very difficult time when distrust increased between men and women: Women feared that they would be sandbagged, while men feared that women were out to get them.

Race and Racism

After a few years, the issue shifted. We began to be confronted by colleagues of color about race and racism. Here I fell on the other side of the power imbalance, so I heard the issues very differently. Suddenly I was the one who was defensive, blaming, disparaging, and self-justifying. I felt like saying to others the same things I had heard men saying about feminism:

> "You used to be so nice. Why are you so angry? You're being divisive. This will ruin our relationship. I had nothing to do with racism, slavery, or segregation. My ancestors were oppressed like yours were. I would love to change things, but I don't have the power either. We have to deal with sexism first; then we'll get to racism. You must be talking about someone else. I'm not prejudiced. We have our problems, too—let me tell you about them."

I was trying to exclude myself from the category of oppressor, just as I had heard men do so many times—defending their behavior by reference to their good intentions, their own victimization or powerlessness, or their kindness to women at a personal level. And as I heard my own reactivity, I gradually began to think that I must be part of the problem or I would not be getting so defensive. Again, I remembered all the times I had heard men say, "We can't listen when you speak in that angry tone of voice. It makes us feel unsafe. If you would say it nicely, we would listen." And I realized that I had to start listening differently. I needed to really listen, and to believe what others described as their experience.

One day I got an insight about how to do this from my friend Paulette Hines during a school consultation. The principal was trying to get us to understand what he was up against with "those people" who just accuse you of being a racist "no matter how hard you try." He described a mother who was upset about the school's ways of handling lateness and absenteeism, finally blurting out, "I see this school is just as racist as it was when I went here 30 years ago!" The principal saw this as proof that "those people are difficult and have an 'attitude.'" Paulette quietly stopped him in his tracks, saying, "Do you have any idea what she was referring to?" He had no idea. Her comment struck me deeply. We tend to react almost viscerally against being labeled "racist." But how can we not be racist, living in a racist society for all of our lives? What if we were to move toward comments about racism instead of running away by defending ourselves? What if we were really to try to understand what people mean when they say that to us? That is what we as women were saying to men for so long:

> "Just listen. Try to take in the pain of what we are saying, instead of thinking of the exceptions. When we speak of men's violence, for example, give some acknowledgment, rather than getting irate that we have not mentioned women's violence."

That is what we had wanted. But with racism the accusation is so painful. Most white people's image of racism extends only to lynching or the Ku Klux Klan, whereas when people of color use the word, they are often referring to being treated as invisible, to being ignored in a store, or to the everyday microaggressions and insults that we who are white make through our ignorance of their history and experience. For years, when I gave a presentation about culture, I prefaced my comments by talking about my fear that others would hear my comments as prejudiced or racist, and I appealed to my audience not to think in those terms. That was when I still thought I was not a racist. Now I realize that the point is more to urge the listener to be kind enough to call it to my attention when I do make a racist comment so that I can learn to do better.

What I did was put the burden on the other to make me feel "OK." Subtly, if the subject of racism did come up, I wanted the other person somehow to make peace with the issue by the end of the discussion, just as men often wanted gender problems to be resolved by the end of the conversation. They hoped that their comments would somehow resolve the issue so that women would no longer be upset. Such wishes assume that the issues are small, can be resolved within the course of a conversation, and will not require transforming our entire societal arrangements. I have noticed at family therapy meetings that when African Americans or other people of color experience frustration, anger, or pain, white people want to get them feeling "OK" within a single conversation. I have done this myself, but I am coming to see the arrogance of this idea. What they are upset about will not be taken care of in the space of one conversation. How can we demand that their pain or anger cease if the problems remain? I have realized that my invisible knapsack of privilege must disappear before such issues are resolved. To men who said they were not sexist, I used to reply, "Until you are actively working against gender inequality, you are part of the problem." Unless my own life is about overcoming racism, I am also part of the problem. My privilege will not disappear of its own accord. I must work so that everyone is entitled to those privileges, which we all deserve. Then we will all have a home.

Many white people say that they cannot let themselves be very conscious of racism or they get overwhelmed by guilt and shame. They feel that they will have to give up everything before their lives will become congruent with notions of "liberty and justice for all." And so denial becomes an easier approach. They move away from the issues, which is very easy for us whites to do, because our society is so very segregated that we can generally live our lives quite oblivious to our connectedness to people of color. We can walk away and pretend these issues do not relate to us. We can do this as long as we do not think about who cares for us when we are sick, needy, old, or on vacation or who makes our shoes, our clothes, and the home products that keep us comfortable. But our denial will surely kill us in the long run.

I have been trying to think differently about these issues—to listen, to attempt to learn about my ignorance, so that gradually I can overcome it. I am beginning to see the racism in a lot of my work. I spoke about couples or families and didn't really mean Black couples or families. I spoke about women and didn't really include women of color. In fact, in the mid-1980s, when I co-organized conferences for women family therapists and almost no women of color came, I kept trying to figure out how to include them—how to get them to recognize the importance of the issues. One who did attend questioned how little reference there was to issues concerning women of color. I felt irritated with her, because I thought it was so hard to think about the gender inequality that if we added race, we'd never "get it straight." Now I realize I had it wrong. The truth is that if we don't include race in the discussion of gender, we will never get it straight. Women of color have been saying and showing clearly for a long time that they prioritize gender differently. They have been saying and showing by their absence and silence that the field of family therapy often has not related to them. And we have thought it was their problem. We have thought we could go on with family therapy as usual, even though it was really white family therapy.

I also realize that telling only the stories of the positive values and actions of my family or my culture keeps me part of the problem. Our family members may include Nazis, as well as victims of the Holocaust; members of the Ku Klux Klan and slave owners or people who have through history benefited from the slave trade. This would include all who have been educated in the Ivy League, which grew wealthy on money from slavery and created affirmative action for their descendents that is still in place, even as affirmative action for descendents of slaves is being dismantled. Any time I try to distinguish my family or my ancestors from the oppressors, I may be standing next to a person whose ancestors were slave owners, making this person's acknowledgment of that legacy even more difficult. I believe we need to create a crucible that can contain the history of us all. If we notice our connections to each other and help each other to acknowledge all of our history, then together we can all work to change our future.

Class

When first challenged to think about class, I thought the issue did not pertain to me. I was just "regular." I am learning that this is a common reaction among people of privilege such as myself. We consider ourselves "regular" only because the people we see around us in our schools, on vacation, and in the media tend be like ourselves. I had no appreciation of the complex ways my whole life has always been organized by class hierarchies. My clothes, my home, the pictures on my wall, the music I listen to, the restaurants in which I feel comfortable eating or the places where I would feel comfortable going for vacation, and, of course, even the fact that I can go to a restaurant or on vacation are all about class (and race and gender). Yet it was never mentioned at home or in my training. I had somehow learned the class code for all the degrees in our field—MD, PhD, EdD, DSW, MSW, MA, and so forth—the hierarchy for rating colleges and universities, professions, and neighborhoods, although these things were never discussed directly in my family and are rarely acknowledged directly in our profession.

The entire structure of our lives is organized by these dimensions. How we celebrate life-cycle rituals such as death or marriage is a matter of class (as well as gender, race, culture, and sexual orientation). In my family (at least since the early 1960s), it would be considered inappropriate to have a fancy wedding, with prescribed outfits, food, drink, and music. But for the classes just above and just below that of our family, these rituals were an absolute necessity, and somehow I learned the rules for all this without it being discussed directly. My family had an invisible judgmental attitude that I find very difficult to challenge in myself or even to become aware of about the values of those who do things differently because they have a different social location.

I am trying to make myself aware of how pervasively and insidiously the rules of class influence feelings of "otherness," of not being "OK" in one situation or another. I am trying to pay attention to the pressure to hide who we are in social situations— whether it is to hide Anglo roots or money that would distance us socially in the mental health field or to hide our family's poverty or working-class origins. My parents were the upper-middle-class Ivy League-educated children of working-class parents, whose own parents were poor, uneducated immigrants. In my generation, my sisters and I moved down in class from my parents' social standing, which had resulted from my father's being well known in academia and reform politics. My family included various members who were in different classes, but the social distance this created was almost never dealt with directly. I think now that my mother was always fearful of losing her social status, which depended entirely on my father's career, and this anxiety led her to try continuously to impress people with our credentials and accomplishments. I never even thought about the possibility that this behavior reflected her insecurities about her position as a woman and as a descendent of poor immigrants, but it led her to be judgmental about the friends we chose and many times made it hard for her to just be herself. I had no awareness of the contextual factors that undoubtedly contributed to this. I want to create a sense of home where all can be appreciated for who they truly are and judged not by the color of their skin, their gender, sexual orientation, or social location, but, as Martin Luther King put it, by the content of their character. Then we will truly be home.

NOTE

1. In this chapter I have capitalized "Black" and lowercased "white" in spite of the convention to do the reverse, because it seems to me that "Black" is a word which at least to some extent was chosen by African Americans to refer to themselves, while "white" does not deserve the specialness of capitalization as an honor to the distinction.

REFERENCES

Fletcher, B. (2003). *The house at Karamu*. Melbourne, Australia: Spinefex.

Friedan, B. (1963). *The feminist mystique*. New York: Norton.

Goldner, V. (1989). *Generation and gender: Normative and covert hierarchies*. In M. McGoldrick, C. M. Anderson, & F. Walsh (Eds.), *Women in families: A framework for family therapy*. New York: Norton.

Griffin, S. (1992). *A chorus of stones: The private life of war*. New York: Doubleday.

Halberstam, D., & Robson, K. S. (Eds.). (1998). *A great and glorious game: Baseball writings of A. Bartlett Giamatti*. Chapel Hill, NC: Algonquin Books.

Hayden, T. (1998). *Irish hunger: Personal reflections on the legacy of the famine*. Boulder, CO: Roberts Rinehart Publishers.

O'Faolain, N. (2001). *My dream of you*. New York: Riverhead Books.

CHAPTER 9

Black Genealogy Revisited

Restorying an African American Family

Elaine Pinderhughes

The invisibility of African Americans in the recorded history of the United States has led to a pervasive ignorance for everyone, Black or White, about African Americans and their contributions to the building of our country. African Americans themselves have colluded in maintaining secrecy about their history. With no power to affect the writing of American history and few resources to disseminate our story, it has remained invisible or distorted by negative stereotypes, and we have until recently remained unable or unwilling to challenge the distortions, untruths, and omissions that have been accepted about our past. Sealing off the past has been a way of dealing with the pain, hardship, humiliation, and degradation that have marked African American history from slave times to the present. But we are coming to realize that knowledge of the past, even if painful, can nourish a people's strength. This realization has stimulated us to unseal these memories and reclaim the truth, no matter how cruel and shocking, so that the festering wound can begin to heal and so that we can better cope with the present and build the future. Only by exploring this painful history can we learn of the ingenious survival practices developed during and after slavery, which may guide us toward our own salvation as a nation. Many individuals have joined in the movement to search out their family odysseys in order to see more clearly the struggle of our people to live with dignity and to find some sense of meaning and value, even as they have been dehumanized.

This chapter is part of my contribution to this effort. Discovering pride and love for my extended family which I had repressed has become an expansive experience for me. I value greatly what I have learned about my relatives' legacy of strength and endurance. This new learning has enabled me to achieve a greater sense of integration and personal clarity within my family, along with a more fundamental sense of authenticity, rootedness, and continuity with history and time.

THE BEGINNINGS OF MY RESEARCH: GAPS IN MY KNOWLEDGE

I began to research my family in 1977 and was able to trace two branches of my mother's family back to the 18th century. Growing up in a segregated, protected, and very supportive middle-class African American community, I had thought very little about my family origins. Apart from some stories about my two grandmothers, there was minimal mention of our history by the family. All of my grandparents had died before my birth, and since my parents had left the other members of their extended families behind in Louisiana in their search for a better life in Washington, D.C., I had had little contact with them. My mother died when I was only 16, and it was not until my father died at age 88, when I myself was well into middle age, that my curiosity about my origins led to action.

I had always wondered how a family as impoverished as my father's had been—toiling in the bayous, harvesting rice, and battling snakes in the swamps—could produce such a bevy of high achievers. He became a dentist, and his siblings included a physician, a pharmacist, a nurse, and an undercover agent. (The agent was seen by the family as a "stool pigeon"; I later became aware that he had been the family scapegoat. We have learned recently of his heroic acts, as he was recognized for bravery in the line of duty.)

I was secretly more curious about my mother's family, but I could not let myself admit this, for reasons that will become clear shortly. As I began my search, I ran into barriers in researching my father's family prior to 1880. However, the search for my mother's family produced knowledge that has had a profound influence on my life.

Prior to my research, I knew only a few facts about my mother's family (see Figure 9.1 for a genogram reflecting my knowledge at this stage). I knew that my mother, Ollie Bourgeois, was the granddaughter of Lettie Bibbs Roberson, who had been born a slave. I had met Great-Grandma Lettie on several occasions when we visited Louisiana in my childhood. I also knew my mother's brother, Henry, and one of her sisters, Coralee. My grandmother, Cecelia, for whom my sister was named, had died when

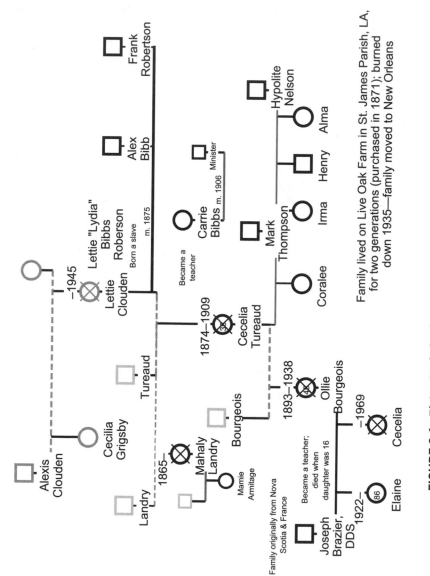

FIGURE 9.1. Elaine Pinderhughes's genogram: Knowledge at start of research.

my mother was 16, just as my mother had died when I was 16. Whenever my mother had mentioned her mother's death, it was with great sadness. Although I knew my mother carried her father's name, Bourgeois (which I often wrote on documents when asked to give her maiden name), I knew nothing else about him and never dared to ask, although I was curious.

This side of the family was shrouded in shame for me as a girl. I knew that this was somehow connected with my mother's name and her appearance, which I suspected was related to her father's being a White man and not being married to her mother. Mother had always refused to discuss her father. I did not learn his first name, Adolphe, until I procured a copy of my mother's death certificate. I also learned from my research that my maternal grandmother's last name had been Tureaud, and that she too had been fathered by a White man, whose name she bore.

As a child, I had known my great-grandmother Lettie's second husband, Frank Roberson. I had also heard stories about the warmth and caring of her first husband, Alec Bibbs, who, along with many other family members, had helped to raise my mother. Lettie had two other daughters besides my grandmother: Mahaly Landry, whom I learned had been named for her White father, and Carrie Bibbs, Alec's daughter. Mahaly, like my grandmother, also had a daughter, Mamie Armitage, by a White man.

When I was a girl, my mother had taken my sister and me to visit Live Oak, the farm in St. James Parish, Louisiana, where Lettie's family had lived for two generations. In 1935, Live Oak burned down in a tragic fire, and the family members living there were forced to move to New Orleans to live with friends and relatives. Just before I began the research I learned that Great-Grandma Lettie had also had a sister, Cecelia Grigsby. I was astounded to learn that the name of my sister and grandmother went even further back. Cecelia Grigsby's grandchildren turned out to have information about her and Lettie when they were children and slaves!

This was all I knew about my mother's family when I began, though I knew my father's family well. They often traveled from Louisiana to D.C., perhaps because they were more affluent, and we had many visits with them. I remember now a certain pride and even arrogance among my father's relatives about the family and their achievements. When my father's two brothers visited, there was pride that *three* Drs. Brazier were together. My mother's family and their history were far less familiar to me.

THE RESEARCH

I began my search by trying to locate Great-Grandmother Lettie Roberson and her family in the census records. I started with the censuses of 1900 and

1880, preparing myself for the likelihood that I would not be able to trace her further back; census records before emancipation did not record slaves as people but only by number as property of the owner, and I would have to find her owner (which wasn't very likely). Because slaves had no identity except as property, they could rarely be traced by name except through slave sale deeds and owners' wills. Legal documents of all other kinds were connected with the owner, not with the individual slave (Blockson, 1977; Herbert, 1976). To trace a Black family before 1870, one has to identify the slave owner. Thus, unless I could locate Great-Grandma Lettie's owner, my search would end before it even began. If I could find this information, I might trace the family through slave sales and probate records as far back as possible. If this worked, I could deduce from the information I gathered something about the family's values, roles, and behavioral interactions that might shed some light on my family's current lives.

The search for Great-Grandma Lettie's owner took 5 weeks of work. I hypothesized that her maiden name might be a clue to her owner. So I sought her marriage license, death certificate, baptismal record, and information from persons in St. James Parish who knew her. I spent over 50 hours just reading census records in the National Archives. I read books about slavery in Louisiana in general and in St. James Parish in particular. I studied the records and private papers of White members of the Tureaud, Landry, and Bourgeois families, hoping to find her owner. My search took me to the New Orleans Public Library, Dillard University, the Louisiana State Library at Baton Rouge, and Louisiana State University. I did title searches of property and slaves in courthouses in St. James Parish, as well as in Natchez, Mississippi, and Woodville, Mississippi.

At first, most of my activity directed at finding Lettie's owner was unsuccessful. I traveled to cemeteries, only to find records burned up. I fought with clerks, who denied the existence of death certificates that I knew were on file. After two skirmishes with the Louisiana Vital Statistics Office, I finally located Lettie's death certificate, when the librarian at the New Orleans Public Library found in a basement archive an undertaker's record book that listed a Lettie "Robinson" as age 74. Because I knew Lettie was close to 100 years old when she died, I almost discounted this information. However, on a hunch, I sent for the record. It turned out that Lettie had been "passing" for 74 because of insurance regulations. The 5 weeks it took to trace one generation into slavery may be compared with the 1 hour it took to track the White Bourgeois line back five generations to 1719!

Among the documents I eventually found were the following (see Figure 9.2 for a genogram reflecting the information provided in these documents):

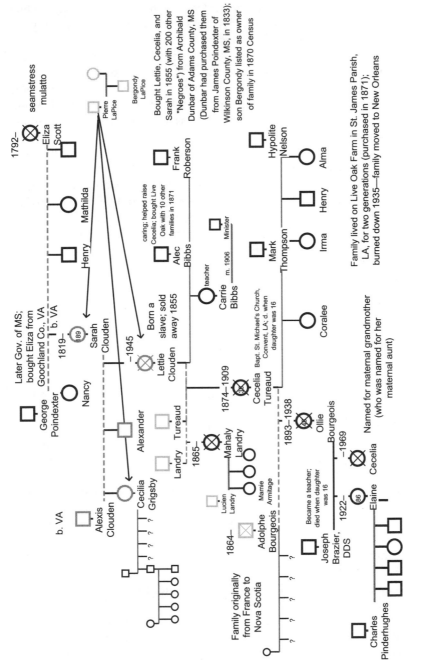

FIGURE 9.2. Elaine Pinderhughes's genogram with information from research.

- *My mother's death certificate, signed by her sister, Coralee,* which stated her father's name as Adolphe. I remember well the anxiety and pain I experienced on first viewing this document.
- *The census records of 1880,* which listed Lettie, her husband, Alec Bibbs (then called "Alexander Bebe"), and her daughters, Mahaly and Cecelia. The records indicated that Lettie's parents were born in Maryland. Also listed in the household was a "Sara Clanton," who was identified as "mother." I assumed this to be Alec Bibbs's mother.
- *The census of 1900,* which listed Lettie (now calling herself "Lydia") and Alec with Cecelia Tureaud's children, Ollie, Eddie, and Coralee.
- *The deed to the Live Oak property,* which revealed that the property, acquired in 1871, is still owned by the family. Lettie's marriage certificate, dated 1875, which showed her maiden name as Clouden. I began to suspect that the "Sara Clanton" listed as "mother" in the 1880 census might actually be my great-great-grandmother, and that her name had been misspelled in the census record.
- *Lettie's death certificate,* which stated her father's name as Alexis Clouden.
- *Cecelia Tureaud's baptismal record,* located in St. Michael's Church, Convent, Louisians, which listed her as born in 1874 and named her godparents but not her father. It read: "Marie Cecilia, de Hattie Clouden. Le 27 September, j'ai baptise Marie Cecilia, nee le 9 Mai de Hattie Clouden. Parrain Camille Melancon; Marraine Coralie Lanoue." The birth record of my mother, who was also baptized there, was missing.
- *The census of 1870,* which listed Lettie with her mother, Sarah Clouden, and her daughter, Mahaly. Listed adjacent to Lettie was Bergondy LaPice, a planter, who I soon discovered was the son of the owner of the family.
- *Conveyance records in St. James Parish,* which revealed that Lettie's owner was Pierre LaPice, the father of Bergondy LaPice. These records listed the property of the LaPice family and recorded the sale of over 200 Negroes in 1855, among whom were Lettie, Cecelia, and Sarah, all the right ages.
- *Records of slave sales involving Sarah Clouden, Lettie's mother.* These sales occurred in 1852, 1837, and 1833. The sale of 1837 listed Lettie's mother, Sarah, with a family group including her brothers, sisters, and mother, Eliza Scott, a mulatto seamstress. Eliza was sold for $1,000, and it was noted that she could pick 140 bales of cotton. Sarah, who was sold for $1,200, could pick 160 bales. Pierre LaPice had purchased Sarah, Eliza, and her family from Archibald Dunbar of Adams County, Mississippi. Dunbar, in turn, had pur-

chased them from James Poindexter of Wilkinson County, Mississippi, in 1833. Poindexter had come to Mississippi in 1808 from Goochland County, Virginia, bringing his family and chattel ("chattel" included animals and slaves).

I also received information from neighbors and friends who had known the Bourgeois family and Great-Grandma Lettie's family when they lived in St. James Parish. I was able to trace the ancestry of my grandfather, Adolphe Bourgeois, back to 1719 in Nova Scotia and was told that there are data tracing the family from there back to France.

RE-VISIONING THE HISTORICAL CONTEXT

My research has shown how racism has operated in the lives of African American families. The domination and exploitation of African Americans have created conditions that have caused ignorance, gaps, and confusion about the realities of Black people's presence and existence—effects reflected not only in the difficulties of tracing Black people's lineage but also in psychological consequences that persist to this day.

Again, the sheer scarcity and inadequacy of information are remarkable in themselves. Although Blacks greatly outnumbered Whites in St. James Parish, far fewer data are available on Blacks. Lillian Bourgeois (1976), in her history of the parish, notes that "four thousand Whites owned eight thousand Blacks." She says that the wealth of antebellum St. James was exclusively in land and slaves, but she devotes a mere four pages to slavery.

As noted earlier, the census records and other official/legal documents are also incomplete and confusing. I found that my family members, like others, were listed in pre-Civil War census records as numbers under their slave owners' names. It is often assumed that slaves took their owners' last names, but I discovered that this happened less often than has been assumed. The few slavery-era documents that did give names indicated that none of my family members took their owners' names or were related to them by blood or affection. I also found in the census records of 1870, 1880, and 1900 that many Black families had children with different last names, in contrast to White families, in which the children usually had the same last name.

The confusion and ambivalence so typical of racism were seen also in the Catholic Church, which owned slaves and supported slavery but at the same time mandated that slaves be well cared for and that "accurate" records be kept (Herbert, 1976). However, there were glaring omissions in these records as well. During slavery, slave children were listed as born of the mothers and belonging to the owners of the mothers. There was no mention of the fathers, or even of the fathers' owners. After slavery, fathers were listed only when the parents were married.

Black children's having many last names and the omission of fathers from all slavery-era and many postslavery church records are simply the most prominent evidence of the widespread exploitation visited on Black families, reflected in the fact that children had many different fathers. Slave owners frequently forced slave women into cohabitation and pregnancy (Franklin, 1966). The cohabitor might be the master himself or a White overseer or a Black other than the husband—whomever the owner deemed suitable for fathering the babies he intended to sell. Whether the fathers were White or Black, fathers' names in cases of cohabitation were simply omitted from birth records, both during slavery and after. Obviously, there were several such omissions in my family. As I have noted earlier, my grandmother's birth record did not list her father's name, and my mother's birth record was missing from the records at the church where she was baptized. I do not know whether these omissions occurred because of the need to hide White paternity, but this would be a reasonable surmise. In any case, this practice predicted the long-standing tendency in this country to nullify and neglect maleness in Black families. For all intents and purposes, the Black male was a zero; he did not exist.

As I pondered these findings—the absence of White fathers as well as Black fathers in the records—I came to the conclusion that the White man was the original abandoning father in this country. Throughout history, lower-caste women have been exploited by upper-caste men, who became the absent fathers of their children. These men were the models for the absent Black men in Black families. They persisted in having sexual relationships with Black women while being protected by their society from acknowledging their paternity or taking responsibility for their behavior, though the society knew of it.

I found this fact to be all the more ironic when I learned during a research project we conducted in Nigeria in 1974 that among the Yoruba tribe—the group from which probably the largest number of slaves was taken—there was *no* illegitimacy (Pinderhughes, 1978). Whenever a man impregnated a woman, he married her. Although this custom was facilitated by the practice of polygamy, it meant also that at the time the slaves were taken from Africa, every mother had a husband and every child had a legal father. I also pondered the fact that under polygamy the children in one family had several mothers and one father, whereas under slavery and the conditions that have since prevailed in the United States, children in one family may have one mother but several fathers.

This precedent of abandonment is illustrated in my own family, in which the absent and abandoning fathers were all Whites. The irresponsibility of such abandonment is compounded by the confusion, deception,

and hysteria that have been and are still connected with the reality of miscegenation. According to a White librarian I spoke with, New Orleans "is
very nervous about birth certificates" because of the large number of Whites
who have Black blood, and their extensive records proving Black ancestry
are kept under lock and key. It is estimated that 80% of the Whites of
French descent in New Orleans have Black relatives and that 30% have
Black blood of which they are unaware. Stories abound in the area about
White politicians and well-known figures who have Black ancestors. During
Reconstruction, many light-skinned Blacks in New Orleans altered records
in order to identify themselves as White; however, copies of these records
still exist unaltered. Exposure of the records validating the Black ancestry
of one prospective bride led her to have a psychotic break. Another fled the
country. The appalling fact is that in Louisiana until 1982, a person could
only be considered legally White if he had no more than 1/64th "Negro"
blood.

Thus the pervasive domination, exploitation, and abandonment of
Blacks by Whites massively influenced the psychology, personality development, and interracial behavior of all involved. A major effect for Blacks has
been the fragmentation of identity. My research has sought to address and
correct this in my own life.

RESTORYING THE FAMILY:
SEEING THE FAMILY IN CONTEXT

Restorying the family and placing it in the context of the times in which my
ancestors lived facilitated my awareness of the cutoffs, secrets, fusion, and
confusion caused by racism. I now understand that the abandonment by
her White father, plus the poverty and desperation that followed the 1935
fire at Live Oak, were so painful to my mother that she could not mention
them—and I did not dare ask.

I have learned via this research that there is much to be proud of in
my mother's family. They were hard-working people with a strong sense
of responsibility. I discovered that Alec Bibbs and members of 10 other
families bought Live Oak in 1871. Live Oak was thus owned by a cooperative of families, and our family still has a legal claim to the property.
Neighbors recollected the sharing that had characterized family and community interaction. The support among neighbors and extended family is
well documented, especially in relation to the children. Although the White
fathers were irresponsible and abandoned their children, other family members loved and cared for them. The household was well organized, and the
farm flourished. Although life was harsh, these resourceful and competent
people also had much love, abundance, and pleasure. I heard many stories

of the efficiency of the farm, with its variety of crops and livestock; I also heard much about the warmth and good times, as well as hard times, that the family shared in the big old house with its encircling verandah. Neighbors still remember the wedding of Lettie's daughter Carrie in 1906 to a young minister, as they remember the hardworking and competent Lettie, my great grandma.

When Cecelia, my grandmother, died, leaving my mother a young teenager, others in the family provided nurturance and protection. After the fire in 1935, everyone rallied and worked to keep the extended family together. Families showed courage in naming their children after their fathers, no matter who they were. And they had pride, courage to survive, zest for life, and strong religious beliefs.

I found myself remembering many things I had forgotten: pleasant gatherings in the evenings at Live Oak on the few occasions when my mother, my sister, and I visited; being taken for horseback and buggy rides; being loved and cared about by these gentle, caring people; and their togetherness and enjoyment of one another. I see this now in great contrast to the more lonely, isolated existence of our nuclear family in D.C. And I understand better my mother's eternal depression and longing for home, which she frequently shared with me. She greatly missed her family's humor, loyalty, and sense of working together. Also, the family showed dedication to improving the quality of life for its members. Whereas Lettie and Mahaly were laborers (they farmed, cut sugar cane, etc.), Carrie and Ollie were educated to be teachers.

In exposing the family secrets and confronting the shame that entrapped the family, I have come to understand why they went to such lengths not to discuss the pain and humiliation of slavery and the sexual exploitation of women. But I have also come to understand that in trying to build a better life and attempting desperately to forget the past, their defensive behavior only reinforced the secrets—rigidifying costly emotional cutoffs, fragmenting personal and group identity, and creating for individuals within the family a nonauthentic sense of self. Undoing the secrets and facing the shame have opened up the emotional cutoffs, freeing family members from their negative consequences. And recognizing the family's positive achievements has contributed to the healing, as well.

HOW MY FAMILY ADAPTED TO RACISM

"Racism" is behavior, both individual and institutional, that is based on the belief in the superiority of one group of people and the inferiority of another because of national and ethnic origins (Pinderhughes, 1973). Family research can document some of the ways in which Black people have responded to the racism that has so dominated their environment in the United States. The slaves, when brought to this country from Africa, were forced to deal with Whites' definitions of them as lazy, dumb, evil, sexual, dirty, and so on. Although some slaves simply adopted these behaviors in the course of playing a role (to "trick" or placate the slave owners), others internalized these definitions. Probably those slaves who felt the most powerless assumed these behaviors in the most exaggerated form in an effort to turn their painful sense of powerlessness into some sense of power and initiative. (In many ways, this behavior has continued into the present: For example, some individuals assume the pose of "superstud" or use manipulative, resistant, or oppositional behaviors to convey some sense of control and counteract their sense of powerlessness; see Pinderhughes, 1983, 1990). Others reacted to their slave roles by identifying with the aggressor—by mimicking the values of the slave master as superior, entitled, and supercompetent. It was paradoxical (and also somewhat "crazy-making") for individuals who belonged to a group relegated to inferior status to perceive themselves as superior. This solution evidenced itself in a kind of elitism in my family, spanning generations right down to me.

The tendency toward elitism among African Americans caused me pain more than once, when my family and I have been seen by others as "stuck up." I have always been uncomfortable with an elitist stance within myself, which I realized distanced me from certain people. Since I was young, I have found that, when I least expected it, I had unintentionally offended someone. I was always disturbed by this, and I worked hard to cope with this tendency in myself. Until I researched my family history, I had attributed it entirely to growing up in Washington, D.C., being the daughter of a well-known dentist, and attending Dunbar High School (that breeding ground of the old "Black elite"). However, understanding my family history has put me in touch with a more fundamental basis of elitism as a response to racism.

The story has an ironic twist, as my mother's family was the part of the family of which I was ashamed. It is true that, as discussed earlier, I have come to view this family connection as a source of pride. However, it has also become clear that these strong, courageous, loving people were themselves racist and elitist—sometimes hating their Blackness, loving Whiteness, and feeling superior to other Blacks.

1. The first clue that turned up in my research was the fact that Great-Grandma Lettie had been a "house nigger" and a "mammy." As her sister Cecelia's grandchildren said, their mother and Lettie were well treated. They told me that after her master's family ate, the "house niggers," almost all of whom were light-skinned, were allowed to have the pickings, whereas the dark-skinned ones were not. Cecelia was remembered as very loyal and pro-

tective of her White employers, to whom she once claimed to be related. She protected their secrets, ran to them when angered by her own family, and seemed "to love them more than she did us," as one of her grandchildren sadly stated. It was not rare that a Black child whose parents' job it was to care for the children of White employers would possess such a perception. I can recall two clients whose memories of maternal deprivation were connected with feelings that their mothers were more loving and accepting of their White charges than of their own children.

2. The second clue concerns the issue of skin color: Lettie, I was told, had definite preferences based on skin color. My aunt Mahaly's grandchildren, who knew her well, told of how Lettie discouraged them from playing with dark-skinned children; the lessons of the "big house" had indeed remained with her. Regardless of the circumstances surrounding the origins of Mahaly and Cecelia, as well as Lettie's two biracial granddaughters, it appears that she highly valued their skin color.

3. The third clue was the discovery that Eliza Scott, Lettie's grandmother, had been identified in the slave sale record of 1837 as a mulatto and a seamstress—two characteristics that may have caused the family to regard themselves as special in those days. Indeed, on my visit back to St. James Parish, Miss Lavinia, who had been Coralee's childhood playmate and who knew the family well, remarked on what she perceived as the arrogance of the family.

4. I found a final source of such a response in attributes of the slave owners themselves. In my readings on plantation life in St. James Parish during and immediately following slavery, I became aware of the sense of connection, both in history and in attitude, that many people entertained in relation to French royalty and privilege. Pierre LaPice—owner of Lettie, Cecelia, and their mother, Sarah—was actually the son of a nobleman in the court of Louis XIV ("Sword's Plunge," 1963). Archibald Dunbar, from whom LaPice purchased Sarah, her siblings, and their mother, Eliza Scott, was the son of a titled English gentleman, Sir William Dunbar. James Poindexter, Eliza's former owner (who, I believe, brought her to Mississippi from Virginia), had been the governor of Mississippi. Here is ample evidence for such expectations of entitlement. Historians and others have pointed out how the identities and self-worth of slaves were often tied up with those of their masters: Those belonging to the wealthiest slave owners felt the most superior.

Embracing such "identification with the aggressor," which embodies self-negation and self-hatred, is only one example of the contradictions that characterized the lives of slaves as they attempted to cope. This identification was a consequence of the fused master–slave relationship that slave masters forged in the attempt to stamp out African identity, to create a slave identity, and thus to facilitate bonding to the masters. A dramatic example from *Roots* (Haley, 1976) was the slave master's attempt to force Kunta Kinte to accept the name of "Toby."

During our research sojourn in Nigeria, we had found people whose identity and sense of themselves constituted the very antithesis of such a slave mentality. We met the Oba of Ekeri-Iketi, who knew his lineage for 30 generations. Our research colleague, Dr. Akinsola Akiwowo, told us that when he was disobedient as a boy, his mother chastised him by reading his *oriki*, which was a recitation of his relationship to his ancestors back through time. The contrast here is extreme indeed between the clear and positive African identity and the situation in which slaves came to be known as "Mr. Henry's gal" or "Miss Sophie's boy."

As I pondered these interrelated issues, I wondered: Did my family adopt an orientation of identification with the aggressor? As I drove through Mississippi and saw the elaborate antebellum houses and Christian academies, I remembered my family's passion for large houses, including the one in which I was reared (and, I thought with irony, the one in which I now reside).

Another issue related to the family's sense of entitlement was my mother's outstanding beauty. No one ever mentioned her without reference to her beauty. Her beauty had been a major issue in my battle for self-esteem. I also knew the pain it had brought her, for she had often shared with me ugly incidents of rejection by others who envied her beauty and her fair color. I learned one source of her pain when her brother, Henry, told me this story: When their mother, Cecelia, married his father, Hypolite Nelson, a dark-skinned man, his relatives so abused my mother, Ollie, that she was sent away from her beloved family to stay with an aunt in a distant city. I had known that my mother, despite her unusual beauty, was often sad and depressed. I knew this well, for she was my first client, as she shared much of her sadness and depression with me. (I have often wondered whether, through my becoming a "parentified child," as the family therapists label it, and listening to her pain and perpetual mourning, I may have saved her from a breakdown.) Clearly, Ollie's fair skin had led to the loss of her mother, stepfather, friends, and family.

I have also discovered that my grandfather, Adolphe Bourgeois, lived in the community and had a family, including other daughters, and that everyone knew him as Ollie's father. Ever since, I have tried to imagine how Ollie must have felt and been pained by the destructiveness of racism as it touched her life. Abandoned by her father because she was not White enough (or at least not White), and abused by her stepfather, in-laws, and others because she was not dark enough, she was in a poignantly tragic situation. She appeared to be the circuit breaker for the anxiety, hostility, and resentment of many others in the systems in which she was trapped.

My mother's full reality, however, was that, though envied and rejected by some, she was also admired and adored by many others. Her unusual beauty was both a curse and a blessing. Though they sent her away, she still remained special to her mother, grandmother, aunts, uncle, and siblings. Reared by her Aunt Carrie and Carrie's husband, the Reverend David Price, a district superintendent of the Methodist Church, my mother lived a fairly privileged life—such as privilege was in those days. Never the parental oldest child (as is usual in a large family), my mother was rather the special, idealized one, playing a role that stabilizes a family just as the role of scapegoat can. It is not surprising that she loved fairy tales, "Cinderella" being her favorite. Only now do I understand why. And she sent me messages that I should achieve for her, so she could live through me at the same time that I would be her therapist. This elitism and specialness—basic values in determining behavior in the family for five generations—entrapped me also and further reinforced the partially nonseparate relationship I had with my mother. I worked hard to live up to her expectations.

Another of Mother's favorite stories was Longfellow's *Evangeline*, the story of French lovers in Nova Scotia who were tragically separated and, after the banishment of the French to Louisiana, doomed to search for one another in vain. Only after learning that the Bourgeois family was Acadian, having emigrated from France to Nova Scotia and then (involuntary) to Louisiana, did I understand the appeal of this story for her. She never mentioned why this story of loss and sadness meant so much to her; nor did she ever speak of how it felt to see her father often, knowing who he was but being unacknowledged by him.

The family expectation of entitlement may have had other sources as well. Many in St. James Parish confirmed for me that Lettie was the family matriarch. As a child, I both respected and feared her. As the initiator, decision maker, and authority, she held the power in the family; others were dependent on her and less able to exercise initiative. When all the power in any group is invested in one person, the power relationship is not very different from that between master and slave. Understandably, relationships in the families of former slaves, who identified strongly with their masters, were characterized by authoritarianism, unequal power, and imbalanced interactions. Nevertheless, Lettie's superior power held the family together, keeping it functioning in support of its members. When Live Oak burned down and forced the family to move to New Orleans, living on friends, other relatives, and the state, Lettie suffered great humiliation, and the family became disorganized.

Finally, the authoritarian nature of the relationships within the family can be viewed in terms of the male–female dyads in Lettie's generation. Lettie had two children by White men who took no responsibility. Her Black husband, Alec Bibbs, helped her rear these White men's children and, later, the granddaughters as well. How did Bibbs feel about this? Did he feel exploited, overwhelmed, and undermined as a man, or was he loving and protective of his wife's children and grandchildren? Perhaps both. Whatever his feelings, the power and the sense of entitlement had belonged to his wife.

THE IMPLICATIONS OF MY RESEARCH FOR THERAPY

Understanding my family's struggle to survive and thrive in a societal context of domination, oppression, mystification, and exploitation has been an act of liberation. It has enabled me to understand the residual effects of the past, which have reinforced the fragmented, often negative identity that has plagued African Americans. Through this experience, I was able to replace the shame, ignorance, and confusion that surrounded my heritage with pride, knowledge, and understanding—truly a transformative process.

As I have shared my experience with other therapists, many have had strong and immediate responses. They identify with different aspects—the sadness, the pain, the anger, or the guilt. My work both in my personal research and as a therapist has centered on the importance of being clear about who we are culturally. Whenever we find ourselves in the presence of the unfamiliar cultural adaptations and realities of persons who are different—whether that difference is one of race, ethnicity, gender, sexual orientation, or socioeconomic background—we need to try to understand and manage our responses so that they will not interfere with our work (Pinderhughes, 1989; Pinderhughes, Hopps, & Shankar, 1995).

I have found two concepts especially helpful in this process. The first is the telling of one's story as a way of restorying the past (Laird, 1989; Griffin, 1992) and constructing a coherent narrative (Lifton, 1993). This highlights the significance of the meaning that people assign to their experience, both the past and the present, as reflected in their beliefs and perceptions. It can point the way to solving problems that have been created by the societal projection process. As Susan Griffin (1992) has put it, the restorying of our history involves

> moving beyond one's own family and explicitly merging our story with the larger themes of connectedness between the personal and the political, the private and the public, the individual and all of history. Through telling seemingly unrelated story fragments and brief scenes from history, we can overcome the bifurcating, reductionistic process that dominates Western thinking and alienates us from each other and from an intimate relationship with our surround. (p. 5)

Another idea I have found very useful is Murray Bowen's (1976) concept of the "societal projection process"—an expansion of his concept of the family projection process to the level of society. According to this concept, the dominant group in society may stabilize itself, relieving tension and anxiety for itself through the presence of a victim group, which it views as weak and less competent. Among the "victim groups" Bowen has identified are minorities and the poor. He says:

> These groups fit the best criteria for long-term anxiety relieving projection. They are vulnerable to become the pitiful objects of the benevolent, oversympathetic segment of society that improves its functioning at the expense of the pitiful. Just as the least adequate child in a family can become more impaired when he becomes the object of pity and oversympathetic help from the family, so can the "lowest" segment of society be chronically impaired by the very attention designed to help. ... They automatically put the recipient[s] in a "one-down" inferior position and they either keep them there or get angry at them. (pp. 444–445)

This societal process has grave implications for both beneficiaries and victims. As I have discussed elsewhere, Whites, upper- and middle-class people, males, and heterosexuals, as beneficiaries of the societal projection process, have been able to stabilize themselves and their communities by keeping large amounts of the tension, conflict, contradiction, and confusion of the larger social system confined to the victims (the poor, people of color, gays, etc.) of the projection process and their communities (Pinderhughes, 1989). I have questioned the impact on both victims and beneficiaries of their entrapment in their roles and the consequences of these responses for their interaction with one another. I have also questioned the significance of these entrapped societal roles for the work of helpers, who are seeking to empower their clients. In cross-cultural treatment situations, practitioners who are White, male, and/or middle class or who are positioned in any other ongoing power role are thus vulnerable to perceiving and handling clients who occupy subordinate societal roles (such as people of color, women, the poor, mental patients, or those positioned in any other socially powerless roles) in a manner that is largely beneficial to the practitioners themselves. These notions give substance to the issues and themes that have emerged from my family research:

1. The nonexistence of African Americans in the consciousness of the larger society. Not existing has serious consequences. This is especially significant given the solid identity Africans had when they came here.
2. The nullification of the Black male. Even when the mother was named in birth and christening documents, the father was always omitted,

during slavery and often afterward as well. This was a systematic oblitera-tion of his existence.

3. The vulnerability of slaves to development of a fused identity as a result of the enslavement process, which encouraged them to define them-selves through identification with the master, the oppressor, the dominant one. This was an invitation to poor self-differentiation. Thus does the "non-self" imposed by slavery and by the making of a slave (Elkins, 1976) become understandable.

4. The vulnerability of African Americans to emotional cutoff due to their inability to claim the White part of their lineage and to the absence of the White fathers, which placed yet more emotional burden on the Black fami-lies. The consequence of such cutoffs was an intensification of the emotional processes within the families. (This factor was, of course, compounded by the systematic, intentional splitting up of African American families under slavery by selling family members to other White slave owners.)

5. The vulnerability of African Americans to the negative stereotypes of their masters (who perceived them as dumb, dirty, evil, sexual, etc.). They might develop a negative identity by internalizing these stereotypes or spend enormous energy trying to maintain a positive identity. They might take the role of victim, struggling to manage an extreme sense of powerlessness, or try to achieve some sense of power through manipulation, passive–aggressive or oppositional behavior, striking back, or becoming dependent (Pinder-hughes, 1989). At times, developing exaggerated stereotypical behavior—becoming superdumb, a superstud, or superaggressive—has been a way to seize the initiative and thus to overcome feelings of powerlessness.

6. The vulnerability to responding to the pain of oppression by sealing off the pain, not talking about it, not asking, not trying to understand. This leads to secrecy, which can cause serious disconnection from oneself. As Stiver (1997) has put it, "Secrecy's pathological effects can have enormous ramifications for how one develops a sense of reality, understands and trusts one's own experience, and establishes relationships."

7. The tendency for a behavior I have labeled "not knowing" to become one's essential learning style. Child psychologists are more than familiar with children whose poor school performance and learning problems are linked to their efforts to keep hidden emotionally laden, overwhelming events of loss and abuse.

Undoing the negative consequences of these entrapped societal roles is an imperative for the mental health profession. In my search to give mean-ing to the facts that I have learned about my own and my people's history, I was able to accomplish the following, which freed up enormous energy in the family and in myself personally:

1. To understand myself and my family in the context of history, as well as the present. I was able to develop a sense of continuity with the past, which made me more connected in the present. That sense of continuity brought with it a greater sense of clarity and confidence about who I am and from whence I came. My "I-ness" is now more secure and integrated. I can see my family realistically in all its complexities—strengths as well as weaknesses.

2. To label the complexities, contradictions, and gaps that, when unnamed and unidentified, have created confusion and entrapment for the family, becoming crazy-making and costly in energy. Filling gaps in information and revealing secrets have reversed the sense of disconnectedness, ignorance, and not knowing.

3. To identify the myths, misconceptions, and distortions that have reinforced both my own and others' "stuckness" in the family process and our entrapment in societal processes that maintain people in contradictory, even paradoxical positions. An example of such a position is that of so-called "elite" victims—oppressed persons who are treated as special and different from their group and who learn to seek solace in a perception of themselves as better than their fellow sufferers. I came to understand how people's responses to racism, which are used to cope with pain and shame, can create even more problems: identification with the aggressor (elitism or domination of others), skin color prejudice, denial of family pain, cutoff from the family, and keeping secrets to deny the pain.

4. To undo the emotional cutoff from my extended family that was the result of poverty, racism, and shame. In learning about the strengths of my mother's people and understanding their struggles, I could let go of the shame related to illegitimacy and poverty. In becoming more connected with them, I found that my present relationships became less burdened as well, because the intensification (fusion) of emotional processes caused by the cutoff was lessened.

As for our work as helpers, I believe that what I have learned can enhance our understanding of personal emptiness, meaninglessness, depression, family cutoff, fusion, intensified emotional processes, maladaptive beliefs—all consequences of entrapping societal roles. It can also provide a basis for developing coping strategies.

All of us—African Americans, other people of color, and Whites, too—must take responsibility for finding ways to tell our stories responsibly. We who have been victims must help others to understand the true context of our shared existence—our struggles in the entrapping roles in which we have found ourselves. We must identify our strengths and realize why we may have embraced negative stereotypes and how we have coped with our status as victims in the societal projection process. This is our story and we must tell it. As the victims of the Holocaust have shown, not only can survivors and their descendants free themselves, but perpetrators (and their descendants) can also liberate themselves when victims are allowed to tell their stories and be heard. Thus, when the stories of African Americans, descendants of those who were entrapped in slavery and its destructive aftermath, are listened to by those who have been "beneficiaries," the victims will really feel heard. And those who are beneficiaries must also tell their stories, examining how and why they may have been trapped in exploitative positions as beneficiaries, vulnerable to using the victims to relieve tension and reduce anxiety for themselves. In our work, this means that we must take responsibility for the way our personal need for the gratifying power role of helper, compounded by our aggrandized cultural group status in society, can make us doubly vulnerable to using our clients (who may well be victims in the societal process) to relieve our own anxiety or tension (Pinderhughes, 1989).

We must not let our society's pressure for cost containment, brief therapy, and partialized goals divert us from the importance of this task. Only when we deal with such connection to our context, clarifying our societal roles as well as our personal need, will we become truly effective in our helping endeavors with those who have been victimized by these roles. This includes not only African Americans but also indeed any clients we want to help toward self-empowerment. Only through bearing witness to this history and these narratives can we join our clients in their struggles to reinforce the functioning necessary for a genuine change in their victim status. Then we will really be ready to help them develop the networks and communities that will support and nourish them as families and individuals. Then and only then can the social system of which we are a part sustain them instead of undermining them.

Our country is rapidly becoming a mosaic of many cultures. Our readiness to receive them all, to honor their cultures *and* their histories, will determine whether or not our thrust toward pluralism in the 21st century will be for us all a tragedy or a triumph.

REFERENCES

Blockson, C. (1977). *Black genealogy.* Englewood Cliffs, NJ: Prentice-Hall.

Bourgeois, L. (1976). *Cabanocey: The history, customs and folklore of St. James parish.* Gretna, LA: Pelican.

Bowen, M. (1976). Theory in practice of psychotherapy. In P. Guerin (Ed.), *Family therapy: Theory and practice.* New York: Gardner Press.

Elkins, S. (1976). *Slavery: A problem in American institutional and intellectual life.* Chicago: University of Chicago Press.

Franklin, J. H. (1966). *From slavery to freedom.* New York: Knopf.

Griffin, S. (1992). *A chorus of stones: The private life of war.* New York: Doubleday.

Haley, A. (1974). *Roots.* New York: Doubleday.

Herbert, D. (1976). Introduction to Black genealogy. *Southwest Louisiana Records, 13*(2).

Laird, J. (1989). Women and stories: Restorying women's self-constructions. In M. McGoldrick, C. Anderson, & F. Walsh (Eds.), *Women in families: A framework for family therapy.* New York: Norton.

Lifton, R. (1993). *The protean self.* New York: Basic Books.

Pinderhughes, C. A. (1973). Racism and psychotherapy. In C. Willie, B. Kramer, & B. Brown (Eds.), *Racism and mental health.* Pittsburgh, PA: University of Pittsburgh Press.

Pinderhughes, E. (1978). Affiliativeness in Western Nigerian social organization: Toward an understanding of modern Black American life. *Proceedings of the Ninth Annual Conference of the National Association of Black Social Workers,* 212–221.

Pinderhughes, E. (1983). Empowerment for our clients and for ourselves. *Social Casework, 64*(6), 331–338.

Pinderhughes, E. (1989). *Understanding race, ethnicity and power.* New York: Free Press.

Pinderhughes, E. (1990). The legacy of slavery. In M. Mirkin (Ed.), *The social and political contexts of family therapy* (pp. 289–305). New York: Gardner Press.

Pinderhughes, E., Hopps, J. G., & Shankar, R. (2007). *Power to Care: Clinical practice effectiveness with "overwhelmed clients."* New York: Free Press.

Stiver, I. P. (1997). A relational approach to therapeutic impasses. In J. V. Jordan (Ed.), *Women's growth in diversity: More writings from the Stone Center* (pp. 288–310). New York: Guilford Press.

Sword's plunge introduced LaPice name to Louisiana. (1963, February). *The Times-Picayune New Orleans.*

CHAPTER 10

The Discovery
of My Multicultural Identity

Fernando López-Colón

My sense of who I am has not come easily. My beginnings were shrouded by a mysterious tragedy that occurred at the time of my birth, the details of which were withheld from me for decades. I was raised in foster care, receiving only a handful of cryptic visits from my father and completely cut off from my mother. I was given no sense of who my people were, where I came from, or even what my racial and ethnic background was. The defining struggle of my life has been to find the racial, ethnic, and cultural aspects of myself, to uncover the truth of the events that transpired at my birth, and to integrate these discoveries into my sense of who I am.

MYSTERY AND CONFUSION:
MY LIFE FROM BIRTH TO 17 YEARS

I was fortunate enough to land in the care of wonderful foster parents. "Mom" was a Swiss–German immigrant to the United States. At 19 she arrived in New York, worked as a domestic, learned to speak Brooklynese English, married, and bore a daughter. After her husband died of pneumonia, she met my foster father—a cab driver in Brooklyn who was of English heritage; he had previously been married and then divorced after the death of his only child, also a daughter. He was 15 years older than Mom.

"Dad" was a good man. He and my foster mother built the house in which we lived, in spite of the fact that he had a stiff hip and a shortened leg from polio as a child. As I was growing up, he put together bikes and built toys for me. And at Easter he painted beautiful, European-style Easter eggs. He was a wonderful father figure and shaped my character in valuable ways.

Mom and Dad entered into what became a 25-year common-law marriage, which lasted until Dad's death at the age of 72. After Mom's daughter was grown and married, they began to take care of foster children. During the 15 years that I lived with them, I had 10 foster brothers who stayed with us for varying lengths of time.

Our diverse household was the context in which I first began to wonder about my racial and ethnic identity. Although I didn't yet know that my biological parents were Puerto Rican, I was well aware that my skin, hair, and eyes were darker than anyone else's in our home. Four of my foster brothers were German; three were English; one was Scotch, one Irish, and one a Jew. The contrast made me certain that I did not belong to my foster parents the way other children belonged to their parents.

The neighborhood was also quite diverse. An extended Italian family lived next door. Three generations of Italians would gather on weekends to eat, laugh, drink wine, argue, play music, and have great family times together. I was fortunate to have these Italian neighbors, because their hearty way of life, expressiveness, and darker skin gave me a hint of who I might be. Growing up within a family in which most of the other members were of Northern European origin was an ever-present source of confusion and uncertainty.

While I was being raised under Mom and Dad's care on Long Island, my biological father was a sergeant in the U.S. Army, stationed in New York City. Although his barracks were about an hour away, he visited me only occasionally. I was confused by his visits but filled with curiosity and respect for him in his impeccable uniform. Each of his infrequent visits brought up troubling questions about who I was, to whom I belonged, and what had happened to my mother. I had never seen her.

At about the age of 5, I began to ask questions about my real mother, to which Mom and Dad had no answers. It may have been at their urging that my father visited for the particular purpose of telling me about my mother. He suggested we go for a walk around the block, possibly so we would not be overheard by my foster family. It felt like he was letting me in on a big secret. He told me that soon after I was born, my mother got a fever and died. I realized that I would never get to see her. I felt very sad on hearing this, and also smaller somehow—diminished and less complete.

Not long after that, I was visited by my father's youngest sister, her husband, and their daughter. They were very warm people and introduced themselves as my aunt, uncle, and cousin. I was thrilled to discover I had more family. Their skin, hair, and eyes were the same color as mine. Although the excitement of their visit was tinged with the fear that they had come to take me away, we enjoyed our time together immensely. Sadly, they never visited again, and those feelings were fleeting.

On another occasion, I was visited by some more dark-skinned people. An old man named Isaac, a younger man, and a boy arrived and asked to see me but did not reveal who they were. It seemed as though they must be connected to me in some way, but they wouldn't give any indication of our relationship. We talked awkwardly as Mom served them coffee and cookies in the living room. They asked to take some pictures of me, and I posed with my dog, Butch, in front of the house. They thanked us and left. The whole thing had a very strange air, and for decades it remained a mystery to me.

Meanwhile, I was enjoying school and getting along well with my peers, yet there were painful moments in elementary school that set me apart and deepened my confusion about who I was. When I was 10 years old, our music teacher decided my first name, Fernando, was too long. So he took it on himself to give me a shorter, anglicized name: "Ferd." In front of the whole class, he announced that my name would now be Ferd. I was stunned. I couldn't speak to object as my name was wrenched away from me. From then on, the other teachers, my classmates and friends, and sometimes even my foster family called me Ferd. I experienced a deep sense of loss and shame and, again, a feeling of being diminished.

Even though I had lost my Puerto Rican first name, I relished the Hispanic nature of my last name, Colón. During one of his visits, my father took great care to explain the importance of putting an accent over the last o. If I didn't, he warned, people would confuse my name with the large intestine. I consider this one of the few gifts my father gave me: He instilled in me a sense of pride about my name. And every time I accented that o, I felt a connection to him and a family lineage.

Another incident I vividly remember was being verbally abused in the sixth grade. I got into an argument with a classmate when we both wanted to sit in the same chair. We started arguing, and he ended it by calling me a "nigger." I was totally unprepared for such a thing. I never thought of myself as Black, but I knew I wasn't White. In addition to the fear and anger I felt at being hit with this loaded word, I was deeply ashamed. The incident reopened the painful and still very unresolved question of who I was. Was I Black, or White, or both?

The next defining incidents took place when I was 15. Out of the blue, my foster father suffered a massive stroke and went into a coma. We were able to care for him at home until he died, several days later. I was devastated by this loss and grieved for his death as though he were my real father. Dad had given me his love and been a guiding influence for me on many levels. I would miss him very much.

Later that same year, my father was discharged from the army. There was a lot of discussion, which I was not privy to, about whether I would go to live with him or continue to stay with my foster mother. This was a pivotal point in my life. My connection to my father was rather thin. Although he had helped me to some extent with the question of who I was, he had not been present enough for me to feel really connected to him. On the other hand, I felt profoundly connected to my foster home, where I had received love and continuity. I knew that I did not want to live with my father. I hoped he would stay nearby so that he might become more of a presence in my life, but that was not an option.

My father decided that he would return to Puerto Rico and that I would stay in the foster home, finish high school, go on to college, and live "the good life" in the United States. I felt relieved and abandoned at the same time. It was a confusing time, but one thing was clear: My father's decision meant the end of what little connection I had to him and to a sense of family.

MAKING MY WAY IN THE WORLD: MY LIFE FROM 17 TO 33 YEARS

In the fall of my junior year in college one of my friends introduced me to his cousin, a freshman named Lois. Lois was very attractive and receiving a fair amount of attention from other men on campus. So I decided I had to do something different, which was to pay her no attention at all. It worked. When she invited me to a Sadie Hawkins dance, we began a serious courtship. And at the end of that year, we married.

Our wedding was a mixed experience for me, as it brought our differing family backgrounds into sharp contrast. Lois's parents (of Scotch, Irish, French, and English descent) were there, along with her two sisters, her extended family, and an abundance of long-standing friends from childhood, high school, and college. However, no one from either my foster family or my biological family attended (so the wedding didn't really bring Lois's and my families together). Two good friends from high school and five or six recent college buddies were there for me. I felt good about becoming a part of my wife's family, but I also felt a void where my own family should have been. For me, the day was both joyful and somber.

I went on to graduate school in clinical psychology. I had considered medicine and the ministry, but the idea of being a psychologist prevailed—perhaps because it was a natural extension of my childhood experience, in which I helped my younger foster brothers grow up. In the second year of graduate school, we had our first child, a beautiful brown-complexioned baby girl. It was an astounding experience for me, not only because I became a father, but because it was the first time that I felt part of an intact, biological family unit.

Throughout my high school and college years, my father and I hardly corresponded. But through his rare letters, I accumulated bits and pieces of information about my extended families. When I was 18, I learned my mother's first name, Margarita. When I was 19, I learned that both sets of my grandparents were farmers. In response to our announcement of our daughter's birth, my father wrote that he was the 4th of 14 children, 10 of whom were still alive. I was amazed to discover that I had such a large extended family. My father also said he knew very little about my mother's family, except that she had a sister who had three children.

In 1961, Lois and I had our second child, a son. His birth prompted me to write another letter to my father, in which I also asked more questions about my mother. In response, my father reported that after my birth, my mother got sick and was returned to her family in Puerto Rico. She was cared for on her family farm until she died, a year or so later. This was not what my father had told me when I was 5 years old, and it dawned on me that my father had been lying. I gradually became intent on finding some answers. I needed to learn more about my family, meet them, and reestablish face-to-face contact with my father. So, at the age of 33, I decided that it was time to visit Puerto Rico.

THE "IDENTITY SEARCH": MY LIFE FROM 33 TO 37 YEARS

I made my first trip to Puerto Rico in 1968. Lois accompanied me, as did our children (we now had three, who were 10, 7, and 4 years old). By now I had earned my PhD in clinical psychology, obtained a university position, and begun a private practice. It had been 16 years since I had seen my father, and I felt both elation and anxiety at the prospect of our meeting again. On hearing the news of our trip, my father wrote and informed me that he had remarried and included a recent photo of himself and his new wife, Lydia. With the help of this photo, we were able to recognize each other at the airport and reintroduce ourselves to each other.

It was not a warm greeting, but the mood became more comfortable over the 3 weeks we were there. The children's natural warmth helped break the ice with my father; he even carried our youngest piggyback occasionally, a gesture of uncharacteristic playfulness. Despite my father's reserve, his family welcomed me warmly. On countless occasions, we would all pile into the car and set off to visit another aunt, uncle, or cousin. In particular,

I reconnected with the aunt and uncle who had visited me when I was 6 and began what has become a close friendship with them and their daughter, Nancy.

The trip was not the vacation we had naively hoped it would be. It was a very stressful experience for Lois, especially because of the unfamiliar and intense mode of relating that is so characteristic of Puerto Ricans. But the intensity of their interactions matched the intensity I felt in finally finding my extended family. I was one of them, and I belonged. It was exhilarating.

During one memorable visit, Lydia talked to my father and aunt in hushed tones. There seemed to be something important going on as she urged him to grant a request. Lois and I had no idea what was being said. My father looked ominously at them, then at me. Then he sighed and said, "*Sí.*" My aunt hurried to get something, and I could tell from Lydia's excitement that they had something to show me. My aunt brought out a dusty sack and laid it on the table. Carefully, she slid out its contents and produced a photograph. It was my mother and father's wedding portrait. It was the first time I had ever seen a picture of my mother. I was dumbfounded. As I pored over every detail, it dawned on me that my face bears a striking resemblance to my mother's face. Lois, Lydia, and my aunt all wept. My father stood there and said nothing.

My aunt and uncle gave me the wedding picture to take home to copy. It felt as if they were palpably giving me a missing piece of myself, and I felt very grateful. For the first time, I felt a satisfying connection to my mother. Yet the wedding picture raised still more painful and haunting questions. Where in Puerto Rico had she lived? Was her family still there? What was she like? And if she hadn't died just after my birth, as I had been told, why had she returned to Puerto Rico without me or my father? My attempts to discuss these issues with my father were difficult. He was tense, guarded, and evasive. He did reveal a few details: the name of my mother's hometown, as well as the fact that she had an uncle named Isaac and a sister named Dominga, who had three children. He insisted that they had all moved to Washington, D.C., but he didn't know their address. This made no sense to me—that my aunt, her children, and her uncle would all move to the States and stay there. It just didn't ring true. But why would my father lie? I resolved to continue searching for the truth about my mother.

By the summer of 1971, I had prepared for my second trip to Puerto Rico by brushing up on my Spanish. I decided to go alone because it would not be a vacation. Relations with my father were still somewhat tense, but an increasing bond grew between me and Lydia. Although she could speak no English and we could barely communicate, she was very sympathetic to my cause. Lydia was an orphan herself and had grown up in very difficult circumstances. I understood later that her gentle prodding behind the scenes often prompted my father to share more information with me. Probably as a result of her insistence, my father gave me two more photos of my mother. Although he had told me the name of her hometown on the earlier visit, he said when I pressed him on this occasion that he didn't know how to get there. I understood this to mean that he didn't know how to get there psychologically, and I realized I would have to go alone.

I headed to the western part of the island, toward my mother's hometown. On the way, the weather suddenly changed, and I found myself in a tropical rainstorm that forced me off the road. At first I felt blocked and frustrated. But then I thought, "No, this is it! Nothing is going to stop me from getting to my mother's hometown, *nothing*." When the rain became less intense, I drove on through the flooded roads. After a while, the Volkswagen's battery conked out, but I persevered. I was able to replace the battery with the help of two locals, a father and a son who refused to let me pay them for their labor. I sensed my luck had turned.

Before long I arrived at my mother's hometown. I had no idea where to begin looking for any of her family; I merely had her name written on a piece of paper. I remembered my father's once mentioning that my mother was a Baptist, so I decided to begin looking at the Baptist church. Unfortunately, the minister had only recently moved to town and did not recognize my mother's family name. He suggested that we go to the local hospital to see whether there were any birth or death records on file. We did but were unable to find any record of her.

Disappointed, we were about to leave when I happened to mention my great-uncle, Isaac—who was by now deceased, or so I assumed. The hospital clerk immediately recognized Isaac's name and directed us to his house. There I discovered that Isaac was still living at age 92 but was in a coma. He was being cared for by one of his adult daughters, who invited us in and chatted with us at his bedside. For some reason, I felt a sense of gratitude and a deep connection to him. Not knowing how else to express this feeling, before we left I leaned over and gave him a kiss on the forehead.

Isaac's daughter knew my mother's sister, Dominga, and gave us directions to find her. When we knocked at her door, Dominga answered. The minister started to introduce us, but Dominga's reaction interrupted him. On seeing my face, she gasped. Her hands flew to her mouth and she burst into tears, saying, "*La cara! La cara!*" ("The face! The face!"). She was seeing my mother's face in mine and realized who I must be. She and the minister exchanged words, and it seemed that yes, finally, I had found my mother's sister. All of this was happening so suddenly that it seemed almost too good to be true.

Dominga brought us into her living room and hurried to locate pictures. She found one in particular and handed it to me, shaking with excitement. In it, I saw myself at age 6 on the front steps of my foster parents' house with my dog, Butch. This was the photo that those "mysterious visitors" had taken. I was amazed. And then the story came tumbling out. The whole family had been desperate to find out what had happened to Margarita's baby. Uncle Isaac had visited me, along with her cousin Jaime and her son Frank. They reported that I was doing well in the foster home and showed the family this picture of me. Now I knew why I had felt such gratitude toward Isaac: He had been instrumental in bringing news of me to my mother's family.

After we had spent some time at Dominga's house, she took us to the family farm where she and my mother had grown up. It was now owned by another of Isaac's daughters and her husband. Excitedly Dominga introduced me to them and to their children and grandchildren. It was my first glimpse of the extended family on my mother's side, and the resemblance between these children and my own was striking. One of my second cousins was also named Fernando, and we even looked alike! Here, I felt I truly belonged—that I, too, had a place in a real, biological, blood *familia*.

At the farm, I also met Isaac's son Jaime, who had introduced my parents when he and my father were both in the army. I was thankful that his fluency in English enabled us to talk freely. He said he had felt some responsibility to check on me while he was stationed in New York during those years. "Your mother was my favorite cousin," he said. He then told me what had really happened to my mother. After my birth she had become violently ill from the anesthesia. Although she got physically better, she then became emotionally depressed and started to hallucinate. She was transferred to a state psychiatric hospital on Long Island. When her condition did not improve, Jaime appealed to the welfare department for funds and made arrangements for her to return to the family farm. She stayed with her family for 9 months but could not emerge from the severe depression. Finally, she was admitted to a psychiatric hospital in San Juan, where she remained until she died—*25 years later*. She had died in 1962, from aspirating some food.

I was curious about my father's role in this. Jaime said that on one occasion, after my mother had returned to Puerto Rico, my father sent her some money; after that, however, the family never heard from him again. It was Jaime who later arranged to visit me in the foster home with Isaac and little Frank. Jaime said that my father had only agreed to it on the condition that they would not reveal who they were, that my mother would not be mentioned, and that I would receive no information about their family. Jaime believed that my father was afraid of my mother's illness and that this was the reason he was never heard from again.

Jaime translated for Dominga, who said with tears in her eyes that my mother had always remembered me. Dominga had made the trip to San Juan to visit her every weekend, and during each visit, for 25 years, my mother had asked about me. Dominga believed that if my mother had been able to see me, her depression might have lifted.

Before I left, I called to let my father know that I was in my mother's hometown and that I would be back later that night. I thought he would be waiting up to talk to me when I returned, but he wasn't; he had gone to bed. The next day I told my father that I had found Dominga, met some of the family, and visited their farm. He did not seem pleased about this and wanted to know exactly whom I had met. I told him and conveyed their invitation for him to join me in a family reunion on the upcoming Saturday. He was quiet and didn't respond.

Despite his guardedness, I continued to seek out details of my mother's life. I visited the psychiatric facility where she was kept and succeeded in getting to review her voluminous 25-year record. Now I had the facts: names, dates, events, and family information. The record corroborated exactly what Dominga and Jaime had told me. I felt more grounded; it was beginning to sink in that I had found the truth about my mother.

On Friday night, my father said he had decided not to go with me to the reunion on Saturday. He said he couldn't face Isaac. Although I told him that Isaac was in a coma and would not be there, he said, "No. They are all mad at me for not letting them see you. It has spread like a cloud through the family. No," he said, "get me Jaime's address. Then someday, on my own time, I'll go back, look him up and get him to talk to the family and make it right." I was frustrated by my father's decision. He had abandoned my mother when she, as he said, "went crazy." He had allowed her child to be taken away from her and hidden me from her family. He had lied to me about what had happened. And, finally, he had not even kept me with him. It was clear that he and I needed to talk.

The next morning my father and I sat down together. I hoped that if I openly shared with him what I had discovered, he might be truthful, too. I began by telling him that I had discovered things about my mother that he didn't know and that I wanted to share them. I told him about her being in the psychiatric hospital until she died in 1962. His immediate reaction was anger. He felt I had been investigating him as if he were a criminal. I replied that although I could see why he might feel that way, I still had a right to know the truth about what had happened to my mother. Then he said, "I knew she was crazy. I didn't want to tell you because I didn't know how your mind would take it." When I heard this, his behavior and secrecy began to make some sense to me: He was afraid that her mental illness might affect me in some way and wanted to protect me from it as best he could. He had truly believed it would be better for me to think that she was dead, and then he had had to cut me off from her family to protect his lie. Now, finally, I had the whole truth.

I was deeply touched by the dilemma that he believed he was in, and with that knowledge I could begin to let go of my resentment and forgive him. Lydia later told me that after she and my father talked about all of these events, he wept.

I went on to spend the day with my mother's family at their farm. Before we arrived there, Dominga, Frank, and Evelyn (my cousin Frank's sister) took me to the cemetery where my mother was buried. It was an emotional experience for all of us. As we stood before her grave, my aunt and cousins wept. I had a strange feeling come over my whole being. I didn't understand what it was, but I felt a sense of resolution: I had somehow reestablished my broken tie to my mother, and not even the reality of her death could ever break it again. I felt complete, whole, and at peace. It was a very sacred moment for me.

We went on to the farm, where about 30 people came for the day—cousins, children, grandchildren, and some close friends who had known my mother in her younger years. Beer and wine flowed freely, and they all took great pleasure in introducing me to their family specialties: fried plantains, spicy rice and beans, roasted goat, and an incredible flan made with tropical fruits. We spent the whole day together, each member of the family recalling for me experiences they had had with my mother. It was their way of giving her back to me. Jaime said, "You know, Fernando—I had a feeling that one day you would come and find us. I have looked forward to this for a long time."

At one point, Dominga went into the house and found a family photograph. It was a group portrait of several families: Isaac with his children and grandchildren, Dominga and her children. Everyone in the picture was someone I had now met at this farm or heard stories about. Dominga gave me a huge, radiant smile and gestured that the picture was for me. Pressing it into my hand, she said *"Tu familia"* and then enveloped me in her arms. It was, without a doubt, a homecoming.

On experiencing the open warmth of my mother's extended family, I felt an even more complete sense of myself. I now had the fullness of the other half of my identity and could see, touch, and embrace my roots. At last I would no longer feel painfully different from other people who had close ties with their blood families. I would now be able to answer the once painful questions about my family background without shame, embarrassment, or confusion.

I feel like a whole person. I have a strong sense of being fully here, of having finally arrived. I am a living member of a blood family that extends into the past and future, over innumerable generations. I now know where my place is in the chain of humanity. (See Figure 10.1 for my genogram.)

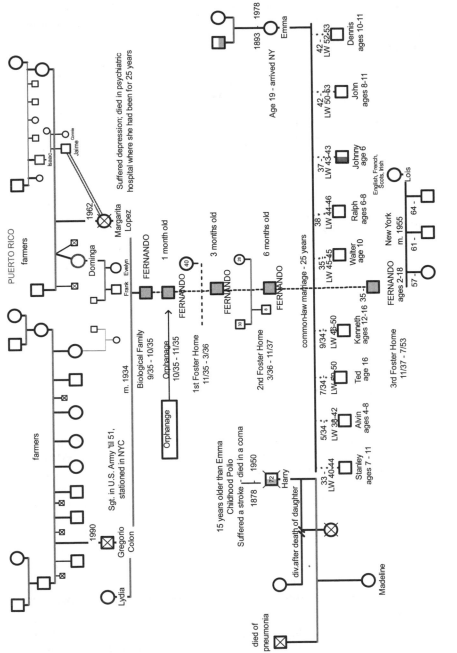

FIGURE 10.1. Genogram for Fernando López-Colón.

CHAPTER 11

Our Iranian–African American Interracial Family

Jayne Mahboubi
Nasim Mahboubi

Interracial marriage challenges the racial definitions of our society. As David Douglas puts it:

> My parents' marriage forced their families to confront their own racism. Their union brought into being children whose very existence called into question the concept of race. Their marriage served as a silent example to countless younger couples who in increasing numbers are crossing the line that separates Black from White in this country. Their marriage and others like it help to move our society beyond the limitations of Black and White. They are powerful beacons of hope for a promising future. (Douglas & Douglas, 2002, p. 342)

We hope that the story of our interracial family will, by identifying strengths, supports, and healthy perceptions of mixed-race families, contrast with the theories of pathology and social deviance used by dominant society to explain multiracial families. And we hope that our story will encourage others to do as David Douglas suggests and move beyond the polarized definitions of race in which our society has become so negatively mired. We illustrate our family's life cycle to highlight common threads with other families while identifying key elements that are unique to our family and perhaps other multiracial families. By sharing our story in this context, we hope to contribute to the subsequent normalization of mixed families. We speak in our separate voices when describing our individual experiences and as "we" when we try to convey joint experiences or thinking.

INTRODUCTIONS

I, Jayne Mahboubi (JM), am in my late 50s and was born in Atlanta, Georgia, to a middle-class family. I was identified racially as *colored* on my birth certificate, *Negro* throughout the 1950s, *Black* in the 1960s, *Afro-American* in the 1970s, and *African American* from the 1980s to the present. I always identified monoculturally. I have been married to Ahmad Mahboubi, an Iranian immigrant, since 1979. We have one daughter, Nasim. We live in the Atlanta area, where I am a psychotherapist specializing in family therapy and addictions.

Ahmad Mahboubi is in his late 50s. He was born in the north of Iran to parents who were tea farmers in a rural village. After never having had to identify himself racially, Ahmad was classified as *White—non-European* on his arrival to the United States. During a short residence in East Africa (Tanzania, Zambia, and Kenya), he identified himself by his nationality rather than his race, not being familiar with the system of racial identification. He currently identifies himself as Iranian. He is living in religious exile from Iran and has not returned home since the Iranian revolution in 1979. He is the owner of an electronics manufacturing company.

I, Nasim Mahboubi (NM), am in my early 20s and was born in East Ridge, Tennessee. I have identified as *biracial, biethnic,* and *bicultural* since third grade, when I was formally introduced to the concept of racial classification while attempting to complete the biological data section of a state-administered academic exam. I have just graduated from American University in Washington, D.C., where I studied international development and peace and conflict studies. I am currently working at the Baha'i World Centre in Haifa, Israel.

JAYNE'S PERSPECTIVE

Our relationship as a couple began in Atlanta, Georgia, in the late 1970s, when I was beginning my master's degree in social work at the University of Georgia. Ahmad had recently arrived to pursue his engineering degree at the Georgia Institute of Technology. We met at a Baha'i gathering and began our brief but intense courtship in 1979. The question of whether to marry was more challenging for me as a Southern-raised, self-proclaimed

Black revolutionary of the 1960s who fought for racial equality and was definitely distrustful of White Americans. I was not sure about my stance toward Middle Eastern foreigners due to a lack of experience with them. I found myself at a crossroads in my beliefs about racial equality and whether I could imagine myself in a lifelong relationship with someone so culturally and racially different. I was in a graduate program that purported to be knowledgeable about marital and family issues, so I consulted my professors about my dilemma. I was told not to enter into a marriage with a man from the Middle East, where women are treated as chattel. My dean told me that I was viewed as a self-assured, independent Black woman who would probably not be compatible with an Iranian man. It was unclear to me whom they expected I might couple with, but it seemed that it would certainly not be an Iranian. It was 1979, the height of the Iranian hostage crisis and of newly brewing negative sentiments about people from that area of the world. Fortunately, I pressed on toward marriage.

Breaking the news to our families of origin posed another challenge. In the Baha'i faith, parents must give their consent for marriage. Ahmad's family in Iran, never having seen me, gave their blessings and consent, purely based on their trust in his choice. My Southern Black parents were not so sure they wanted a White person, let alone a foreigner, in our family. They were also concerned about my future in such a marriage. Gaining their consent was not going to be easy. My mother, born in 1911, had lived all her life in the South and had traveled minimally within the United States and never abroad. She was being asked to consent to the marriage of her youngest daughter to an immigrant from halfway around the world. My father, born in 1908, though more traveled than my mother, was nevertheless firmly rooted in his African American community and did not venture far from it. I found myself asking for their blessings to bring someone very different into our family. They were not having it. My mother, who I thought knew nothing of Iran, watched the nightly news, on which she had repeatedly seen 10,000 Iranians in Tehran Square yelling, "Death to America!"—the same clip the news programmers used to illustrate the Iranian political attitude toward America.

To his credit, Ahmad was understanding of my parents' position, and we agreed that we would not marry until they were comfortable with our union. We were in agreement that for us the blessings of our parents were important for our marriage to be successful. We would give them time to get to know him. After 9 months they consented, and we were married. There was a growing negative sentiment about Iran in this country, and at the time we were living in South Georgia, an area known for its long-standing disgust for interracial relationships. As a young couple, we experienced many incidents, both covert and overt, which clearly reflected public disapproval, but we persevered. Most of the incidents reflected people's shock at the mere sight of us together. Once a car almost ran into a pole when they were looking at us walking together holding hands. On another occasion when we entered a busy restaurant together, the entire restaurant went quiet until we were seated. We learned to take pleasure in these events and would demonstrate our awareness of the situation by some small gesture, such as taking a bow before being seated.

Ahmad and I went through the typical struggles of adjustment from single to married life, which entailed negotiating nearly everything: Who would cook? Who would clean, and why? I thought of myself as a liberated woman and on some level bought into the stereotype that all Middle Eastern men were domineering of women and expected them to become their servants after marriage, and I wasn't having it. Although in our case the negative stereotypes of Middle Eastern men proved untrue, we had many discussions to dismantle the prejudices that I had. But even more significant for us was learning how to merge two strong cultures into something we could both feel comfortable living with, without feeling negatively compromised. This was not easy for me because, although alluring, Iranian culture also felt engulfing to me. I had never before remembered thinking so consciously about my culture, except in the 1960s when I was involved in the Black Power movement. I was shaped by the ideologies of Stokely Carmichael, Malcolm X, and others in my transformation from Negro to Black. This shocked my parents, who were more aligned with the thinking of Martin Luther King, Jr., and Mahatma Gandhi. All of the work I did during the 1960s assisted in my development of a strong, comfortable Black identity, something difficult to develop in a country in which people of color were not valued. Similarly, Ahmad was comfortable with his cultural identity even in the early 1980s, when it seemed that all Iranian people were being touted as terrorists and anti-American. With both of us equally strong culturally, the challenge was to merge the two into one household. We had to make room in our relationship to understand our racial and cultural struggles and how they affected our marriage. I wanted to preserve some of his culture in our home, especially as he was in religious exile from Iran, but also to preserve my own. We eventually found ways to do this. I think a key was our respect for each other's culture. I have made a point of learning as much as I could about Persian culture. Ahmad has done the same for African American culture. Much of this learning happened before we were married and continues even now. This was a result of our desire to know each other but also stemmed from our belief system that promoted unity in diversity as an honored tenet for living.

One of the unifying points of our marriage was that we were both members of the Baha'i faith. Each of us became aware of and attracted to Baha'i before we met each other in Atlanta. I was introduced to the principles of Baha'i in 1968 in Nashville, Tennessee, and Ahmad in Tehran, Iran, in 1973 on opposite ends of the globe. I became affiliated with the faith in 1974 in Atlanta and Ahmad did so in Hamadan, Iran, in 1974.

The essential message of the Baha'i faith is that of unity. Baha'is believe that there is only one God, one human race, and they work toward creating a global society. Baha'is believe that some of the fundamental principles needed for such a unified, global society are the elimination of all forms of prejudice, full equality between the sexes, recognition of the essential oneness of the world's major religions, the elimination of extremes of poverty and wealth, universal education, the harmony of science and religion, a sustainable balance between nature and technology (Bábá'i International Community, 2007).

Our shared belief system has helped us to navigate our married life and continues to nurture and support us. Baha'is have believed since their beginning in 1863 that interracial marriage is the fulfillment of the principle of abolishing racial prejudice. This principle has also afforded us the support of an entire international community that subscribes to these principles, allowing us to create a relatively seamless harmony of our races and cultures.

Ahmad and I have lived in a Black neighborhood in which he experienced prejudice from our neighbors. We have also been viewed as a little strange by his culture, since out-marriage among Iranians is not common.

The introduction of children into a mixed-race family complicates the hurdles with which families must contend. Outsiders questioned our union, and often asked "What about the children?" posed in a way that suggested we were selfish. "Won't your children be stigmatized and 'mixed up' because of your choices?" We realized our children would face discrimination based on their mixed-race heritage and on the prejudice against race mixing in this country. We were clear in our belief that they would be strong in all ways due to their heritage and that it was our responsibility to transmit strength to them. During the stillbirth of our first child, a son, Amir, we even experienced prejudice from my doctor, who was overheard saying, "That's the way these people are"—suggesting that something defective about our union had led to the stillbirth. The loss, however, strengthened the bond between us as a family and transformed our tragedy into a sacred experience. Though my family had eventually given consent for our marriage, they had actually been doubtful that it would last. However, when they saw Ahmad attending to my critical condition while I was in the hospital after the loss of our child, they were convinced of his devotion and commitment to our marriage and to me. They were finally convinced that our marriage was more than a pathway for Ahmad to obtain a green card. After this initial ordeal, we were blessed to have our daughter, Nasim. Early on we grappled with how she should identify racially. Ahmad and I had both accepted monoracial identities all our lives without much question. Because of her physical characteristics, we thought it would make sense for her to identify as Black, as this is how others would perceive her. But we were determined to teach her to value all parts of her racial/cultural self, especially those things others would likely devalue. She was African American and Iranian, two groups who are perceived as less valuable than the dominant race and culture in America. We settled on telling her she was Black for all practical purposes. Later, when she was older, she had to educate us about how she wanted to identify.

NASIM'S PERSPECTIVE

While recounting life experiences and collecting personal data for this chapter, I shed many tears and held back many more, some for reasons still unclear to me, some for the pain and others for the pride surrounding my racial and cultural identification. Reliving experiences that were both marginalizing and noteworthy in my journey toward self-identification has indeed brought many emotions to the surface that had previously been repressed in an attempt to be "normal."

My first lessons in race are clearer to my parents than to me, although several blurry occasions do stand out involving playmates mentioning either that they didn't want to play with me because I was different or that their parents didn't allow them to play with people like me. These instances were almost always associated with my Blackness. As I began school, roll calls became instant markers that I was different, not only because I was Black but also because my name was Nasim Mahboubi. Humiliation was inevitable the first week of each school year, as well as with each announcement of my birthday or other recognition of me in schoolwide assemblies. On those days I was made to explain "what I was," easing the anxiety not only of classmates but also of teachers and administrators who were so eager to place me in a box. Throughout my childhood, both of my parents made sure that I was exposed to positive expressions of Black culture. I never attended school in my district because of my parents' insistence on my being exposed to positive Black role models that would be harder to find in our small Atlanta suburb. They made the decision to move to Atlanta so that I would be able to know my extended Black family, something I would not have the opportunity to do with my Iranian family, who are all still living in Iran. My parents did not divide the teaching of their respective cultures to me. They taught me aspects of each culture. Their respect for and knowledge of both cultures, as well as their respective struggles both individually and as a couple, have been strengths for our family. In fact, it was my mother who taught me Persian cooking and Persian dance, and it was often my father to whom I communicated my frustrations with racist interactions I faced.

During my adolescence I learned to compartmentalize my cultural identity. I attended a primarily White, Christian, private school, where there were a handful of Black students and even fewer Middle Eastern students. The students of color sat together at the lunch table, an adaptive strategy on our part. It was during my middle and high school years that I bore the heaviest brunt of racism and, as a result, came subconsciously to identify as Black. I dated Black boys, listened to hip-hop music, and played down my Persian ethnicity so as not to jeopardize my spot in the "Black clique"— until September 11, 2001. At that moment, my Persian identity came flooding back to me all at once. I immediately feared for my father's safety and hoped that the horror stories of White terrorists threatening to kidnap my father during the 1979 Iranian hostage crisis and again during the Gulf War were not reoccurring. It was during those few weeks that I was reminded that I was not American ... enough.

While I still identified with radical notions of racial equality, wrapped my hair in solidarity with Afrocentric movements, and refused to participate in the Black history plays that featured only the Black students dancing and singing year after year, high school and college provided the opportunity for me to learn to decompartmentalize my heritage. Learning to let others struggle with the categories they wanted to place me in was an important lesson I learned during these years. I could go from identifying with a militant Nikki Giovanni poem to sharing stories of Tahirih, an Iranian feminist from the late 1800s, in the same class period, forcing the professors to do their own research.

College has been the first time I have made friends and felt completely comfortable owning both sides of myself every day, all day, no matter what. I sometimes find it interesting that a Persian friend can make a racist comment, forgetting that I am Black, or a Black friend can make an anti-Middle Easterner comment, forgetting about that part of my identity. I attribute this to their putting me into a box for their own comfort that does not necessarily correspond with the definitions I have chosen for myself. Instead of brushing such comments off, I remind them that I am a member of the race at the brunt of the comment. This is not only freeing for me but also educative for my friends, reminding them that two distinct ethnicities/races can live harmoniously inside of one person. Throughout my college career I have met many other mixed-race students who have shared similar paths to self-identification. Such friendships, especially among bicultural students, have helped me feel a sense of belonging that I have been unable to find in exclusively Black or Persian groups.

I attribute my newfound comfort in embracing both races and cultures inside of me to the reunion between my Iranian extended and nuclear families. We had never met each other, and my father had lived in exile for 30 years, so my Persian heritage, though very present in some ways, seemed intangible. Iran has been no more than bedtime stories and fragrant dishes. Our family reunion in Dubai, besides having tremendous personal meaning for me, made my Persian identity more complete and more legitimate. Because my features do not immediately identify me as Persian and I do not speak the language fluently, my acceptance in the Persian community has always been based on my novelty rather than my birthright. But the question of my acceptance became quickly irrelevant once I experienced such a warm welcome into my Iranian family.

WHERE WE ARE NOW

Ahmad and I (JM) are currently in our 28th year of marriage, and we are entering the sixth decade of our lives. Much has changed in our country over the years since our relationship began and much has not. ... We have had four presidents, not one of whom has been either a person of color or a woman; mixed-race children now have their own magazine; and mixed-race couples are much more common in the movies, as well as in real life, than ever before. The number of mixed marriages in our country has quadrupled. We have learned many things from our experience as a multiracial/multicultural family. It is essential to foster an atmosphere of openness in which racial and cultural differences can be discussed with seriousness and with humor. Ahmad and I have learned a lot about not taking ourselves too seriously. One example comes to mind that occurred when I was asked to speak on race unity and social justice in a small Georgia town, with all its Southern charm and prejudiced history. The local chapter of the Ku Klux Klan, dressed in full regalia, was challenging the event. As I spoke from the podium, I glanced out and saw Ahmad pointing to a Klansman who was standing next to him and saying to our mixed-race toddler, "clown." I knew Ahmad had never seen a Klansman in his dress and assumed he was a clown. Deep inside I had a horrible fear about the possible danger and rage that the mere sight of my daughter would raise in this Klansman. I don't remember much about the points I made during my presentation, so anxious was I to rush over to get my daughter and Ahmad. Later we had a great laugh and discussion.

We attempted to foster conversations about race and culture with Nasim. It began with helping her develop a pride in her name, Nasim, meaning in Persian "gentle breeze," and Mahboubi, meaning in Arabic "beloved." Hence her name is "beloved gentle breeze." When she was very young we made an attempt to expose her to all types of cultures in which she would not feel "other" due to her racial and cultural mix—Persian, African American, as well as many others. She was born in a very monoracial/monocultural town, and we were concerned that her self-concept be validated. So we moved to a more diverse city where we would not be viewed as quite so different. We decided to move to allow her differentness to be appreciated and accepted more readily. As adults we felt better able to handle the adversity resulting from our differentness, but we needed to protect her as much as possible while she was developing a healthy sense of herself. We consulted with parents of other mixed-race children and exposed her as much as possible to others like her. There were books specifically with mixed-race characters, hard to come by in the mid-1980s, and crayons with flesh colors close to hers for coloring images of herself.

When she reached school age, it was necessary to think about where she would be exposed to role models who validated her and were a part of her race and culture. In the South there were schools that had no Black teachers but lots of Black children, which was unacceptable for our family, so we had to search for schools with both. We were able to find community that supported our uniqueness and many times mirrored it. We were friends with other mixed-race couples who had children, as well as friends who were supportive of and excited about interracial marriage. As this chapter is being written, Nasim is graduating college and leaving home to work in an international community in Israel, where more than 70 cultures are represented. We are moving into the empty-nest phase of our relationship and looking forward to what will happen next with us as a family. Will we ever travel to Iran? Will we ever see a Black president? What will our "golden" years bring? We will stay tuned.

Looking back, we are happy that we were able to transcend the racial and cultural borders that society often lays out for people of superficial intimacy (such as "my best friend is Black or I dated a Black person once" to suggest one's acceptance of someone who is considered different) as opposed to the experience of people of extreme differentness becoming family, in which kinship transcends bonds of race and culture and connects us with bonds of love. As we have attempted to present to you some of our individual experiences as an interracial family, what we want most to communicate is that the composite of those experiences is what it took for the creation of a unified, secure, healthy identity that could not be pathologized by researchers, storytellers, or anyone. For only we ultimately can self-define, identify, value, and contribute our strengths to move our society forward.

REFERENCES

Báhá'i International Community. (2007, July 8). *The Baha'is—What is the Baha'i faith?* Available at *bahai.org/faq/facts/bahai_faith*.

Childs, E. C. (2005). *Navigating interracial borders: Black–White couples and their social worlds.* New Brunswick, NJ: Rutgers University Press.

Douglas, D., & Douglas, B. (2002). *Marriage beyond Black and White: An interracial family portrait.* Wilmette, IL: Baha'i Publishing Trust.

Root, M. P. P. (1992). *Racially mixed people in America.* Newbury Park, CA: Sage

Root, M. P. P. (1996). *The multiracial experience: Racial borders as a new frontier.* Thousand Oaks, CA: Sage.

CHAPTER 12

Voluntary Childlessness and Motherhood
Afterthoughts

Marlene F. Watson

I have borne thirteen children, and seen them most all sold off to slavery, and when I cried out with my mother's grief, none but Jesus heard me! And ain't I a woman?
—Sojourner Truth

Imagine growing up in the 1970s when women and Blacks were marching for equal rights and the freedom to choose their own destinies. For a young Black woman—albeit naive—it was like traveling through a city in which all the traffic lights were clearly green, telling me to go. I bought the hype, believing that I had the freedom to make the same choices as my White counterpart. I had what bell hooks (2000) described as a romantic notion of personal freedom. I had not yet learned to examine systems of power, privilege, and oppression. Nor had I begun to understand the planned invisibility of the interrelatedness of race, gender, and class oppression in society's power game.

THE FACE OF INDIVIDUALISM

The cover-up for society's White supremacist, capitalist, patriarchal class structure is "rugged individualism." Anyone, woman or man, White or a person of color, willing to work hard can achieve the American dream and be a valued member of society—this is the bill of goods we are sold. But we are not all equally valued, afforded the same opportunities to work hard and to make hard work pay off, and, for sure, not all of us enjoy White privilege (Wildman & Davis, 2005). For example, would I, as a hardworking professional single Black mother, be applauded for my rugged individualism? I do not think so. Rather, I would be labeled with the one-size-fits-all negative single-Black-mother identity given to all Black women.

THE SIGNIFICANCE OF CHOICE

Some young, White women were choosing to have out-of-wedlock children or no children at all. It was the age of the sexual revolution and feminism. By the way, most of us had feminism, or "women's lib" as it was popularly known, wrong. It was not about being equal with men, because not all men are equal. And it was not just about burning bras, choosing not to become mothers, or creating a hierarchy of womanhood based on work at home or away from home. It was about exposing and ending sexist oppression as one of society's concealed philosophical power structures (bell hooks, 2000).

But what did this newfound freedom really mean for me? The decision whether or not to become a single mother by choice was a loaded gun for me. Forced breeding in slavery made Black women single mothers. Forced mating of Black girls and women with multiple men in slavery made Black women promiscuous. Disallowed Black marriage and the removal of men from family life in slavery made Black women super-Black women. Cultural and societal messages told me that I could not depend on a Black man and that single Black mother-headed families were pathological. Family shame about out-of-wedlock children and family beliefs that children keep women from succeeding and trapped in bad marriages frightened me. Personal signature themes (Aponte, 2003, personal communication) around competence and control held me hostage.

Without thinking critically about what it meant or about the role of racism and oppression in my decision, I simply vowed not to have children. Recently, while I was getting a pedicure, a young Black technician announced to me that she did not want children and planned to have her tubes tied. Leading up to this announcement was her description of "relationship troubles" with her boyfriend, whom she said was not ready for commitment. Immediately, I felt a deep visceral reaction in the pit of my stomach. I was looking back on myself 20-something years ago. Significantly, I was also seeing the deliberate dismantling of the Black family in slavery and the manipulation of today's Black men and women into runaway brides and grooms. "Ain't I a woman?" came into my mind, with the corollary thought, "Ain't he a man?" The defeminization of Black women and the stripping of Black men of their masculinity in slavery make us doubtful.

FEAR AND DECISION MAKING

I wanted control of my future, a future that I thought I could best control by staying "child free." But what I really wanted was control of my fears: the fear of raising children in a racist society and the fear of being a single Black mother, a dreaded fate that appeared certain for many Black women. Over 50, unmarried, and childless, it is safe to say that I avoided being branded a single Black mother. But still I paid a price. Living with the loss of motherhood, an afterthought in my voluntary childlessness, is another afterthought, the powerful organizing role of race in my decision.

For most women of all races, the future is undeniably and intimately tied to their children. Having children is what still defines women in many corners of our society. But as an educated Black woman with limited prospects for marriage, it was hard for me to hear the call of motherhood without hearing society's negative valuation of single Black mothers.

THE CRISIS OF BLACK MOTHERHOOD

Looking back, my story began when slave women were forced to become breeders and slave men were forced to become studs for the purpose of producing human cargo—slave children. Today, after many heart-wrenching confrontations with the woman in the mirror, I know that race was the shadow lurking in the back of my mind, making me afraid to have children. Yes, it was fear that drove me away from having children and toward living with the loss of motherhood, of giving birth to my own child. It was not until I attended a workshop given by Lee Mun Wah, director of the film, *Color of Fear*, at one of the American Family Therapy Academy's (AFTA) annual conferences that my growing awareness of the role of race in my voluntary childlessness was confirmed. He asked all the people of color who saw race as a factor in their decision to have children to stand. Standing, looking around at the number of my peers acknowledging publicly that race was significant in their decision to have (or not to have) children opened the door to my feeling entitled to mourn the loss of motherhood.

My not having children was about more than my not wanting the hassle of diapers, breast-feeding, day care, and the tug-of-war between mommy and career. It was about much, much more. It was about how society defined me as a Black woman, how society would define my Black child, and the state of Black marriage amidst the ruins of the Black family from slavery.

On the surface, motherhood was a choice. Way back in the deep recesses of my psyche, I felt the struggle. I experienced motherhood as a soul crisis. Thus it is with a great deal of empathy that I remember slave women who were forced to become mothers, then forced to live with the loss of motherhood because their children were sold away from them. For me, at least on the surface, motherhood was optional, but in the unconscious mind, I felt the slave woman's and my own difficult inner journey to motherhood and childlessness.

High on feminism, the civil rights movement, and my supermodern boyfriend, who repeated over and over that he did not want children, I posted guards—rationalization, intellectualization, and denial—at the gates of the prison I was creating for myself. Erecting walls built of psychological defenses, I hid out rather than confronting the nagging feelings I had about motherhood. Like the slave woman who must have agonized over motherhood because giving birth was sentencing her child to a life possibly worse than death, I later (when I was 38, brokenhearted, and without any prospect of marriage with someone whom I thought was a suitable mate) agonized over having a child out of wedlock and sentencing both myself and my child to being another Black statistic. Unlike the slave woman, I thought I had a real choice. Still, the slave mother and I were soul sisters. We were both Black women—targets in a racist society.

Visions of myself pregnant and unmarried surrounded by my White peers at work every day and my fatherless child were overwhelmingly unpleasant enough to make me forget about thoughts of becoming a single mother. If only I could have visited the Wizard of Oz and asked for courage. Where was my fairy godmother?

Although African American children have been highly valued because of the loss of children and millions of Black people in slavery, little attention has been given to the crisis of motherhood that may exist for some African American women because of slavery, oppression, and internalized racism. Here I hope to give voice to the slave mother and to myself, honoring the loss of motherhood and uncovering the painful history of Black women. Concomitantly, I hope to end the silence of women living without children, whether by accident or design. Our stories need not remain in the closet, and we need not slip quietly into the disgraced corner of family life where we shield ourselves with silence.

ON BEING DIFFERENT

When I was growing up, any child born out of wedlock was considered a bastard. Because my mother and father were not married, I had to live with the social stigma and shame of being a bastard child. My mother was from an intact family, and I distinctly remember my grandmother's admonition, "Don't have children unless you are married."

My childhood sensitivity to society's view of unwed Black mothers and their bastard children rolled with me into adulthood. Despite the change from "bastard child" to "love child" during the hippie culture, imprinted in my mind were the statistics hailing Black women as promiscuous unmarried mothers on welfare. Unmarried White mothers were portrayed as educated, rationally thinking individuals making a conscious decision about children and marriage.

Fooling myself, not allowing the unconscious to become conscious, I painted over the Black woman with my professional degrees and education, claiming that marriage and children were not important to me and that I was an educated woman making a rational decision about motherhood and marriage, like the White women who were saying no to children. Restless and dissatisfied with something (I now know that that something was marriage and children) about my life that I could not name, I headed back to school (school has always been a good hiding place for me, but when I think of the other alternatives used by some to mask emotional conflicts, I count my blessings) to become Doctor Watson, not single Black mom, at the age of 32.

Now mind you, I thought I knew myself very well. I did already have two degrees in psychology, and I thought they were the "proof in the pudding," as my mother was so fond of saying when she questioned something. With my degrees in psychology as proof, I did not bother to ask myself relevant questions about my decision not to have children. I was also the oldest of five children, so I had been around enough babies to know motherhood up close. Or so I thought. It would be some years before I began to long for motherhood and to grieve the loss of never having my own child or grandchild.

THE SECRET LIFE OF A BLACK WOMAN

"First comes love, then comes marriage, and then comes the baby carriage" was a childhood hand game I played. It all seemed so simple back then ... love, followed by marriage and ultimately motherhood. Love came at 15, and it endured over a period of years. Unfortunately, it failed to provide a pathway to marriage and motherhood, as the jingle from my favorite childhood hand game had led me to believe. For years, I secretly thought of marrying and living the lifestyle of a married, professional Black couple with children.

Dreaming of wedding bells but not remembering my dreams in waking life, I did not hear the sound of wedding bells or my biological clock ticking.

Finally, at age 38, I heard them both in waking life and decided to step back onto the sleeping path. Afraid of confronting my secret desires, I put my "S" (Super Black Woman—the armor of Black women) on and wore it proudly to fend off my insecurities.

Nonetheless, the call of motherhood was getting louder, but without marriage I pretended not to hear it. I was absolute about not being an unmarried Black mother, and the odds of finding a husband as a 30-something highly educated professional Black woman were not in my favor. Fear and choice were not just opposite sides of the same coin; they were inseparable, leaving me in a twisted emotional knot.

As college students, my boyfriend and I declared that we did not want children. He even went so far as to say that he thought pregnant women looked disgusting. Sadly, it was him I was thinking of when I tried to have my tubes tied at the age of 25. (Perhaps more out of patriarchy than concern for me as a young Black woman, the White male doctor said, "No, wait until you're older.") Lying to myself, I thought it was what I wanted. Now I know that it was the politics of motherhood and the long-range impact of power, privilege, and oppression in our daily lives.

My boyfriend was busy playing the field and had no intention of making a commitment to me. Lying to myself, my ready response to all the people who asked me about marriage was: "It isn't a big deal because I'm not having children." Truthfully, I dreamed of being a bride from the moment my grandmother gave me a 3-foot doll dressed elegantly in a white lace wedding dress with all the trimmings for Christmas when I was 6 years old. (Having a better understanding of how my mind works, I have to ask myself if I want to be a bride or a wife when I think of marriage these days; the two are not necessarily the same.) The beautiful bride doll with all the trimmings was White, blonde, and blue-eyed. Without anyone ever speaking a word, I was getting the message that brides were White, not Black. This message would be reinforced at multiple levels and in multiple ways: media, research, the incarceration rate for Black males, and the number of single Black women.

UNMARRIED AND CHILDLESS

Not to marry is a loss for Black women. Loss of motherhood because of the loss of marriage is compounded loss for Black women. However, the loss of marriage and/or the compounded loss of marriage and motherhood for Black women are ignored, reframed, minimized, and pathologized. Moreover, these losses have been completely removed from the context of slavery and oppression. Again, distorted notions of individualism suggest that Black men and women are not suitable mates and therefore do not merit marriage. (I would love to talk to Secretary of State Condoleeza Rice as Black woman to Black woman about being never married and childless.)

CHILDLESSNESS AND THE FEMININE IDENTITY

Motherhood as the foremost marker of fulfilled womanhood is fundamental to women's lives and experiences. Hence childlessness, whether involuntary or voluntary, has tremendous implications for millions of women. Because of society's traditionally held belief that a woman's duty is to be a mother, it stands to reason that motherhood or the absence of motherhood may shape a woman's sense of self. For some women, childlessness is a profound crisis of feminine identity, particularly in cases of infertility or the unavailability of marriageable men. Sadly, the experience of childlessness is often one about which women are silenced.

The social and psychological consequences of women's decisions concerning childlessness may not receive much attention, and therefore women are likely to shoulder the burden of such decisions alone. Because motherhood is socially idealized as the saintly pursuit of selflessness and optimal womanhood, the woman living without children may be looked on suspiciously and with diminished value, especially if her childlessness is not the result of infertility. Even when childlessness is involuntary due to infertility, the expectation of motherhood may still exist because of medical advances in treating infertility. Structural barriers to treatment, appropriateness and/ or risk of treatment, and treatment inequities due to racism and homophobia tend not to be considered. Thus women living with involuntary childlessness may not escape the social stigma of childlessness because motherhood may be seen as attainable by any woman wanting it badly enough (McQuillan, Greil, White, & Jacob, 2003).

Internalizing childlessness, some women may react to perceived resentment of their unworthy freedom by overemphasizing male qualities of achievement and autonomy. But as women we need to embrace individual expressions of womanhood without feeling as if we have to give up our feminine identity. With increasing childlessness, whether by chance, choice, or the myth of choice, it becomes not only important but also necessary for women to achieve fulfilled womanhood outside of biological motherhood. Moreover, women and men must work toward eliminating sexist oppression through motherhood by acknowledging that all women need to have a sense of their own individuality for optimum personal growth. Similarly, we must end oppressive divisions and distinctions between mothers and nonmothers by focusing on motherhood as a kinship or relational structure that nourishes and sustains people.

RETHINKING MOTHERHOOD

Childlessness seems to threaten the patriarchal social order and to defy individualistic assumptions of womanhood and family. Collectivist cultures such as my own African American culture promote "other mothering." Thus I have experienced the intimacy of being an "other mother" with my niece and nephews. However, the historical and cultural losses inherent in my voluntary childlessness remain largely unrecognized by both African American and dominant White culture. As such, social support does not exist within which I might grieve the loss of biological motherhood. Losses associated with abortion and voluntary childlessness become unspeakable for women because we do not have the socially recognized right to grieve based on often simplistic and politically motivated views of women's actions.

It is important to note that not all voluntarily childless women need or want to grieve the loss of biological motherhood. Research has found that prolonged psychological distress is linked to involuntary childlessness and not to voluntary childlessness (McQuillan et al., 2003). But society in general and women in particular could benefit from greater appreciation of the complexity of women's identities. Expanding the definition of motherhood to include social mothering or other mothering might lead not only to a much more inclusive definition of family but also to a more positive identity for all women. Additionally, it might lead to a greater sense of social responsibility in all of us—women and men.

CONCLUSION

Conventional values emphasizing biological motherhood tend to create a hierarchy of womanhood without attending to issues of racism, sexism, classism, homophobia, and other structural inequities in society. The motherhood ideal at the core of women's identities lacks appreciation for individual differences and expressions of womanhood. Stigmatized single Black motherhood and the loss of Black marriage as an aspect of Black women's history may account for voluntary childlessness and accompanying feelings of motherhood loss in some Black women.

Significantly, the definition of involuntary childlessness should be broadened to include childlessness due to the absence of marriage or a male partner. Likewise, the definition of mothering should move beyond giving birth to include social mothering (McQuillan et al., 2003). Of particular importance, parenthood as the central basis of the female identity for all women should be rethought, given women's diversity, fertility, and social circumstances.

Child or childless, Black or other, "Ain't I a woman?"

REFERENCES

hooks, b. (2000). Feminism: A movement to end sexist oppression. In M. Adams, W. J. Blumenfeld, R. Castaneda, H. W. Hackman, M. L. Peters, & X. Zuniga (Eds.), *Readings for diversity and social justice: An anthology on racism, anti-Semitism, heterosexism, ableism, and classism* (pp. 238–240). New York: Routledge.

McQuillan, J., Greil, A., White, L., & Jacob, C. (2003). Frustrated fertility: Infertility and psychological distress among women. *Journal of Marriage and Family, 65*(4), 1007–1018.

Wildman, S. M., & Davis, A. D. (2005). Making systems of privilege visible. In P. Rothenberg (Ed.), *White privilege: Essential readings on the other side of racism* (2nd ed., pp. 95–101). New York: Worth.

CHAPTER 13

Grieving in Network and Community
Bearing Witness to the Loss of Our Son

Jodie Kliman
David Trimble

The sudden death of our 19-year-old son, Jacob Kliman-Trimble, challenged us to go on after losing so much of what had given our lives meaning. Commitments to social justice and spirituality that Jacob (mostly) embodied in his short and complicated life shaped our decision to share our ongoing connection to him with our communities and helped us to survive.

To describe how and why we have tried to share the blessings of Jacob's life with others, we must share some of his life. We grieve and make meaning of our lives by bearing witness to the radiance and the tragedy of Jacob's life, seeking to spare others his ending and to ensure the memory of our beloved child in all his richness.

At his bar mitzvah, Jacob, who loved family and friends of different races, beliefs, and sexual orientations, argued with Biblical prohibitions against planting mixed seeds or wearing garments of mixed fibers (Leviticus 19:19). He had a passionate sense of justice, a loving, compassionate heart, and an infectious enthusiasm for enjoyment, sweet mischief, and play.

But Jacob struggled mightily in his short life. He had learning disabilities and attended specialized school programs. He was hospitalized with a manic psychosis at 16. When he was 17, his birth mother, Delana, who had lost contact after placing Jacob in our arms, wrote to say that she was dying.

She died days before we flew to Texas. Our families shared grief over Delana and joy over the reunion, adopting each other. We then learned of Delana's bipolar disorder and her substance abuse during her pregnancy with Jacob.

Delana's death devastated Jacob, despite her family's loving embrace. His substance abuse and mood disorder spiraled out of control. His family's, therapists', and teachers' increasingly desperate efforts failed to contain him. Conflict escalated. Yet, even when his rage and despair were at their worst, even when he cried that he hated us and that we had never loved him, he kept showing us that he loved us and knew we loved him. When we tried to talk about his despair, he railed against our "acting like therapists, not parents." But after his death, friends told us that Jacob was the one who had listened to their problems, "like a therapist." He worried about us. He wanted our happiness and hated to make us cry. His frequent outbursts of lovingness and laughter renewed our hopes and sustained all who loved him.

After a second hospitalization at 18, Jacob refused treatment and dropped out of school. Relatives, friends, birth kin, our family therapist, and school helpers supported our anguished refusal to feed or shelter him while he destroyed himself. We had long feared for his life, but never so profoundly or helplessly. We could no longer protect him. Over several months, Jacob returned home and to recovery, relapsed, refused treatment, and lost his home twice more. A drug dealer put a gun to his neck the day his friends graduated high school. That day, he entered detox. He asked for a Christian Bible and began reading deeply. He had already rejected his mother Jodie's Judaism and was, like his father David before him, on a spiritual search. Although his leaving Judaism hurt us, we saw that belief in Jesus was his best hope for sobriety and gave our blessing.

Jacob moved to a short-term drug treatment facility, where he told us that he had committed to sobriety because he knew that substances would soon kill him and that the stress could kill us prematurely. He apologized, from the bottom of his heart, for having blamed us for his substance abuse and other hurtful behaviors. On a day pass, we bought a silver cross he wanted for a chain Jodie had given him years earlier. The healing between us had begun.

Knowing he needed long-term treatment, Jacob decided to go to Heartland Christian Ministries, an evangelical recovery program that put him to work and gave him a modest living. It seemed to be the passionately Christian community he sought. At Heartland, Jacob learned to stay sober, work hard, and repair and drive farm trucks. His deep faith in God helped him resist his addictions, sustaining him through doubt and distress. Jacob loved working up to 60 hours a week as a diesel mechanic and was rightly proud of his talent. After years of struggle and avoidance at school, he heard his mechanics supervisor say that he was his best student ever.

Heartland was a mixed blessing. Although Jacob had agreed to stay a year, he asked to come home and finish high school after 7 months. He was distressed over the program's rigidity, homophobia, and racism. We had witnessed his pastor's alarmingly rageful judgments and anxiously relented— with conditions. Jacob agreed to our conditions, put down $6,000 he had earned on a Pontiac GTO, and asked us to cover payments until graduation. We agreed, despite concerns over the GTO's speed, to show our support for his recovery. Cars were Jacob's greatest joy, and he knew he would lose both it and his money if he reneged on his commitment to sobriety.

He returned 7 months' sober, determined to make a life for himself. He planned to finish high school and go to college for certification in mechanics, so he could do what he loved and did magnificently. The day he died, he told a close friend that he wanted to teach young people mechanics at his own shop.

Jacob's return brought us all profound redemption. No longer obscured by substances, his sweet spirit shone forth. The loving relationships we had enjoyed before were restored. For the first time in years, Jacob believed in himself. Without those 7 healing weeks before he died or our shared healing in his programs, we cannot imagine having any vestige of peace now.

His friends later reported that Jacob had begun experimenting with "having a beer" days before he died. We had seen subtle mood and attitude shifts and challenged him, but we had no evidence to justify taking his car keys. The night he died, Jacob drank seven beers and some rum. His friends later described him as "real hyper." We understand this to mean he had a manic episode. Ryan, who survived the crash, said that Jacob had "wanted to see how fast he could take the engine." He reached 147 miles per hour before losing control and crashing. Jacob's seat belt tore, his door fell off, and he fell out; the car rolled over and crushed his torso. For a few minutes, Jacob called out Ryan's name, then breathed his last in silence. Ryan saw him make peace with his God as he passed from this life. Despite our Jewish beliefs, it comforts us that Jacob had time to ask Jesus for forgiveness and believed he had gained entry to heaven.

When Jacob died, our family, Jacob's friends, and our interwoven personal, professional, and spiritual communities gathered to share and hold our grief. Word spread among friends and colleagues at the American Family Therapy Academy, the Massachusetts School of Professional Psychology, the Center for Multicultural Training in Psychology, and the Boston Institute for Culturally Accountable Practices. Colleagues and friends from hundreds of miles away joined our local communities at the funeral and shiva (the Jewish custom of gathering at mourners' homes), organized by members of our Temple Sinai congregation, relatives, and local and long-distance friends and colleagues. For weeks after Jacob died, members of our community shopped, cleaned, and cooked for us, checking in regularly.

Far more than our involvements with our personal and professional communities, Jacob's loving spirit and ability to weave together diverse networks brought over 500 people to his funeral. Dozens of childhood friends left college to attend; although many people were away for school vacation, at least half the mourners were classmates and teachers. The night before the funeral, the young woman Jacob had been seeing delivered a letter about how much Jacob had talked about us, loved us, knew we loved him, and been grateful that we had given him the chance to redeem his life. She told us of the sweet and tender time they spent hours before alcohol and mania wrenched him away.

Just as our community mobilized to help us, we had to reach out to Jacob's and our networks. We needed others to help us bear witness to who he was and to the lessons of his short and precious life. We needed the comfort of continuing to parent in some way and knew that Jacob would want us to care for his friends, as he had. We worried about many of Jacob's more recent friends, who lived high-risk lives, struggling with substance abuse and self-destructive decisions. Two friends had died because of these problems in recent years; both deaths had set off cascades of self-destructive behavior among their friends.

Seeking to prevent a new cascade, we found purpose and meaning in writing funeral words addressed to Jacob's high-risk friends. As our rabbi, Andrew Vogel, read our words, together we began extending the blessings of Jacob's life. Jacob had lived values of caring, concern, and connection, with vital energy and a loving heart. He overcame huge obstacles to redeem his life, although he stumbled at the end. We believed that both his redemption and his last act of lethal impulsivity offered crucial lessons to his peers. We challenged them to make their own lives a blessing, through honoring Jacob and learning the lessons he re-learned too late, in his dying moments. The strength to write and share our anguished pleas for learning and healing came in part from *tikkun olam*, the Jewish spiritual commandment to heal a broken world, person by person and as a whole. Broken ourselves, we realized that only in community could we survive this worst of blows.

Our need to reach out to Jacob's friends was shaped by our political and Jewish collectivism and by our network therapy mentors, Ross and Joan Speck and Carolyn Attneave, who had taught us to heal by assembling large groups of people who had not adequately grieved. We were inspired by courageous bereaved parents who preceded us on this terrible journey. Mamie Till dared to open her son Emmett's casket for the world to see her child's battered body and say no to racial violence; she dedicated her life to that cause. Israelis and Palestinians in the Bereaved Parents Circle, having lost their own children, commit themselves to preventing more violent deaths on either side. By embracing their suffering, they nurture compassion for themselves and others (Hardy, 2006). We can never achieve what such parents have done, but it comforts us to take small steps down their paths of healing.

Jacob's love for his friends and our memories of his recruiting us to help some of them also moved us to reach out. When Jacob's girlfriend ran away from home in ninth grade, he remembered that Jodie's late best friend had run away as a teenager. He asked her spirit to guide his girlfriend to our house, where, indeed, she arrived for help. This young woman, steadfastly present for us now, has dedicated her college work and sobriety to Jacob's memory. Jacob appreciated the gifts our beloved dead have to offer us, which helps us appreciate and share the gifts we still derive from his short life.

Jewish mourning traditions call for open grieving and lifelong remembrance and prayer to honor our dead. Our congregation, Jewish relatives, and Jews in our network generously witnessed our public grief and remembrance. Friends who said they had not sufficiently grieved their loved ones told us that our public invitation to grieve together helped them. *Kaddish*, the mourner's prayer, can be said only with at least 10 people—we had not understood this wise requirement before our grief needed loving witnesses.

Our immediate and extended families incorporate many cultural traditions. While raising Jacob as a Jew, we also accommodated the secular Christianity of David's older children, Ransom and Jessica. The year Jacob became Christian, David was converting to Judaism, and Jessica became a Kadampa Buddhist. As Jacob struggled for sobriety and direction at Heartland, David drew on his Christian heritage and Jewish learning to help make Jacob's Christian faith work for him. Jacob's identification with his birth family (particularly his birth mother, who had reclaimed her life on being born again a few years before dying) influenced his conversion. When we adopted Jacob, his birth family claimed English, German, and Dutch ancestry, but our older children found African ancestry in Jacob's beautiful nose. Jacob always considered himself multiracial because of his adoptive siblings' multiracial heritage. At our reunion, Jacob's Texas relatives told him of their probable African descent and his Cherokee great-great-grandfather. He was thrilled to strengthen his cultural links to Ransom and Jessica's Nipmuc, Narragansett, and African ancestors and proudly identified (some of) his birth kin as "antiracist rednecks."

Days after the Jewish funeral, we held a Christian memorial service at Jacob's church, honoring Jacob's religious choice. We read our new words, in our Jewish voices, to a smaller, largely Christian group, with a greater concentration of Jacob's higher-risk friends. In conducting this sorrowful network assembly (Speck & Attneave, 1973), we sought to amplify the spiritual message of Jacob's life, evoking the joy of his playful and loving presence and cautioning his friends about taking risks before living long enough to grasp the fragility of life. David emotionally recounted Jacob's death, which Ryan had described to us days earlier in a numbed and traumatized voice. Hearing David retell his story in agonizing detail, Ryan finally wept deeply as Jodie held him. It gave Jodie comfort to hold this sobbing boy in her arms when she could no longer soothe or protect her own child. It soothed David to help Ryan grieve. David felt the presence of Jaakko Seikkula, who wrote of traumatic experience stored in the body being "vaporized into words" (Seikkula & Trimble, 2005, p. 468). Earlier, Kaethe Weingarten, the most mindful of witnesses (Weingarten, 2000), helped us recognize how we had made Jacob's funeral into a healing network assembly. Through the Witnessing Project (*www.witnessingproject.org/archives.html*), she has made our funeral and memorial words available to anyone who might benefit from them.

Our family therapist, David Treadway, school counselors, and teachers had stayed with us throughout Jacob's difficult years, and they grieve with us now. They witnessed Jacob's struggles over loving us and rejecting us and himself and over depending on us but wanting to be free. David Treadway had previously helped us recognize how our terror of making dangerous mistakes with our vulnerable child sometimes led us to treat each other's different responses to him as threats to Jacob's life. With Jacob gone, so, alas, is the urgency of disagreeing about how to keep him alive. After Jacob's death, our therapist helped us stay in deep, respectful connection in the face of our sometimes divergent ways of grieving and making spiritual sense of Jacob's life and death.

When Ryan told us about Jacob's death, he said that he should have been the one who died, that Jacob was the better person. We insisted that Ryan live, telling him that Jacob could not have lived with having killed him and that Ryan's bearing witness to Jacob's passing was vital to our bearing the loss. David told Ryan to "bring me your children"—an injunction to live a long and full life. The next night, after Jacob's funeral, Ryan and his girlfriend, Silvana, conceived Venezia, sooner than we had hoped. One day after the Jewish ritual of unveiling Jacob's gravestone, this beautiful girl, for whom we have become informal grandparents, was born—a needed reminder that life insists on continuing. Her parents say she is a gift from Jacob. Having lost our grandchildren with Jacob, we cherish Venezia and other babies born to Jacob's friends.

Jacob was beloved at school despite his troubled history. Students and staff were drawn to his warmth, humor, intense relatedness, passionate concern for others, and dazzling smile. Jacob's friends lived in the projects, owned summer homes, were peer counselors, substance abusers, high school dropouts, athletes, and winners of academic scholarships. He was an intensely loyal friend. For his memorial service, one childhood friend composed a love song for Jacob. Another spoke tearfully of Jacob's life-long devotion despite this boy's social awkwardness and isolation, testifying that Jacob's friendship had kept him alive. The mother of his dearest grade school friend, remembering Jacob as the one person her son cried with in sixth grade when she had cancer, gave Jodie the beautiful beach glass "calm stone" that Jacob had given her when she was getting chemo. We hold it for soothing reminders of his loving heart and all the lives he touched.

Jacob's loving heart continues to touch his network. Ryan and Silvana have committed to sobriety since losing Jacob and hearing our words. Another friend had skipped school for weeks before Jacob's death; he returned the day Jacob died to grieve. He gives credit to hearing our funeral and memorial words for his staying in school. He and other dropouts are now in college. At the funeral and memorial, Jodie shared Jacob's repeated early childhood question, "Why are we here?" Of all her answers, Jacob was most satisfied with the simplest: "to help other people." After the memorial, a friend of Jacob's told Jodie that she had asked Jacob the same question 2 years earlier, from the depths of addiction, "more dead than alive." Jacob had offered his favorite answer and with it, hope to go on. We recently hosted a baby shower for this now sober and healthy college student.

Jacob's friends, their parents, and our colleagues have reported additional stories of young people redirecting their lives out of grief and love for Jacob and respect for our messages. A memorial scholarship in his name is now awarded annually to students who have done the most to turn their lives around. We were proud that Jacob was known as a peacemaker among his peers. In his memory, David has joined the Board of Artsbridge, a project to engage Palestinian and Israeli youth in dialogue about difficult issues through training in the arts and forming relationships among future leaders who we hope will collaborate to build a just peace between their peoples. Jodie has been working to bring mental health professionals and community workers together in a series of peace psychology conferences at the Massachusetts School of Professional Psychology.

Since we lost Jacob, many people have touched us with their compassion. At times, some have told us they admire how honestly we share Jacob's story and reach out to others despite our grief. These words do not comfort, as they do not bear witness to our experience. Our actions do not reflect exceptional generosity. They are what we must do to survive. To go on, we must have our son in our lives. Because he died so young, we never had the joy of seeing him recover from his relapse or become the loving spouse and father and gifted mechanic he would have been. We keep him present for us in part through his living relationships with others and by introducing new people to him. This writing has been arduous, reopening fresh torrents of grief, yet we trust that, as you read our words, you will join the communities who hold our Jacob in their hearts and thereby help us to hold our sorrow.

Two years into our mourning, we always feel profound sadness, and often terrible emptiness and despair. Yet our networks continue to hold us throughout unpredictable outbursts of grief, and we comfort each other daily. We rely on our certainty that our lives and Jacob's life and spirit are held in webs beyond the material and interpersonal networks of our communities, that there are meanings beyond our comprehension in the patterns of our lives, and that Jacob's spirit and our own remain connected through the oneness of the universe. It is not enough, but it must do.

REFERENCES

Hardy, K. V. (2006). *Embracing suffering, legacies, life notes, and the self of the therapist*. Paper presented at the annual conference of the Multicultural Family Institute, Sayreville, NJ.

Seikkula, J., & Trimble, D. (2005). Healing elements of dialogue: Therapeutic conversation as an act of love. *Family Process, 44*(4), 463–477.

Speck, R. V., & Attneave, C. L. (1973). *Family networks*. New York: Pantheon.

Weingarten, K. (2000). Witnessing, wonder, and hope. *Family Process, 39*, 389–402.

CHAPTER 14

Going Home

**One Orphan's Journey
from Chicago to Poland and Back**

John Folwarski

Although the phrase "illegitimate Polish Catholic orphan" is not exactly a Jungian archetype, it certainly was an abiding label for the personal and ethnic heritage that informed my world from the time I was 4 years old. Even after I earned advanced degrees, became a college professor and later a therapist, and raised two children (now college graduates), the negative associations of these words, like flashbacks, often invade and render unreal whatever is going on in my life.

In recent years this label has been taking on a much more manageable shape. Eileen Simpson (1987) described the difficulties of interviewing adults who had grown up in orphanages. Many "were as furtive about their past as if they had been in reform schools, and were unable to rid themselves of the feeling that they were somehow responsible for having been institutionalized. Others were afraid of being discriminated against professionally or patronized socially" (p. 146). Becoming nonfurtive about my own past has been a journey.

MY FAMILY BACKGROUND

I have pieced together most of what I know about my original family through arduous research over the past 35 years. I now know that my maternal grandfather's name was Jan Folwarski, that he was a painter for a Chicago railroad, and that he died in the flu epidemic of 1918. His wife, Julianna Gasior, washed floors to support the family after his death and through the Depression. They had seven children (I had thought there were only four). Their death certificates listed Austria as the country of origin, and only a few years ago I discovered that they came from Nowa Wies' and Harklova Wies', small villages in the Austrian-occupied section of Poland. The four children who were around when I was born were my mother, Mary (Marianna); her two older brothers, Stanley (Stanislaw) and Frank (Franciszek); and her younger sister, Louise (Ludwika).

When I was 34, I got hold of my records from the Chicago Family Court, which told me the following: When my mother was 20, she had a relationship with a man named Tom Bieschke and became pregnant; he denied paternity. The family was poor and ashamed and petitioned the court to place her in a mental institution. I was left in the hospital until 6 months later, when the family was notified that I could stay no longer; so they took me home, receiving $6.90 biweekly from the Bureau of Family Welfare for my care. Just before my fourth birthday, my grandmother died. The social worker interviewed the family, and my mother told her that they had no jobs and no money, that my uncle Stanley was abusive, and that my grandmother's dying wish was for me to be placed. My mother was diagnosed "feebleminded," committed to a state hospital, and sterilized, and I was sent to St. Hedwig's Orphanage. A social worker's review for the court a few years later stated that she was surprised that no one had visited me except to bring my clothes and toys, believing that I would be better off that way. I did not leave St. Hedwig's until I was 17.

ST. HEDWIG'S ORPHANAGE

Our orphanage was Polish Catholic: the priests, the nuns, and the children. From its opening in 1911 to its closing in 1959, more than 7,000 children were cared for there. We gave money to support the Polish cause in World War II and dutifully thought of the "starving children in Poland" when we wasted food.

A sense of ethnicity, however, was not primary. The world was divided in our minds between Catholic and Protestant, as well as between orphans (us) and "city guys" (everyone else). We envied "new guys," kids who came to us well past kindergarten age, who had a lot more information about the world outside the gates and who were not yet numbed by the rules of total obedience to authority that had become our way of survival.

The orphanage became our family. Actual parents were grouped for us under the heading of "visitors," allowed to visit twice a month. The nuns wielded day-by-day parenting power, though the final authority lay with Monsignor Rusch. The various benefits and abuses of that power—the rules, roles, and relationships that developed—are part of our individual and collective memory.

Although those at the orphanage became our closest relatives, I'm not certain it ever became my home. I recall that, as an 11-year-old returning from Confession, I was suddenly seized with an overwhelming terror that the buildings could fall apart and crush me. It was like an awful nightmare that has recurred throughout my life. I would have defined "home" as a place where, when you ask questions, somebody actually responds. Later, given what is perhaps a universal feeling of children in orphanages that there is never enough to eat, I came to define "home" as a place with a refrigerator that you are entitled to open and take whatever you want without asking.

THE CATHOLIC CHURCH

Underpinning and overriding everything else in the orphanage was the towering figure of the Catholic Church, Polish style. In that setting, something like martyrdom was a well-nourished daydream, a crowning goal of life if one were worthy and courageous, as real a wish as wanting to be a fireman, a pilot, or a cop. Devotionals about the lives of Polish saints and martyrs, supported by daily rewards for wanting to be a good Catholic, shaped our most basic beliefs and our value system.

Of course, this is not uniquely Polish. Catholicism has its own life and detail in other ethnic Catholic cultures. Perhaps the uniqueness of Polish Catholicism lies in its historically greater fusion between ethnicity and religion. Polish immigrants, in particular, have depended on the Church to a far greater degree than have most other Catholic immigrant groups. After all, Poland had disappeared from the map of Europe for 125 years! Identity rested with connection to the Church. Poles came to an America already dominated by Irish clergy. Poles' need to preserve their identity even led at one point to a full-blown schism and the formation of the Polish National Catholic Church. Fears of the loss of Polish identity worked their way into Polish family life in many ways. In the orphanage, these fears intensified. The isolated nature of the institution as Polish religious family highlighted its fragility. There was little connection with the major culture, which in this case was viewed as a "benefactor" whose daily donations earned our gratitude. The absence of contact with other Chicago cultural neighborhoods, however, nourished our acceptance of the nuns' convictions that the secular city and the Protestant world were also powerful threatening forces: it was no accident, we were told, that "Pulaski" Road was changed to "Crawford" Avenue. The institution's goal was to preserve and protect our faith and our Polish heritage.

For our time there, the Church was the family. All the patterns that govern family systems also governed the orphanage family, except that nuns were the mothers and priests were the fathers—certainly a peculiar psychic connection.

LATER CONTACTS WITH MY PARENTS

In the seventh grade I learned that my mother had been released from Dixon State Hospital. For many years afterward, I felt guilty for not wanting her to be out. What I knew consciously was that I would lose my status as a "pure orphan" (kids who had no "visitors"); I was also painfully aware that I did not know her and did not know what to say. Mainly, I had some notion that she was "crazy" and that I would be called "the kid with the crazy mother." When she first visited, she had bandages on her legs that I thought covered scars from shock treatments (images from the movie *The Snake Pit*), and I feared for years, in addition to everything else, that I had "insane blood." Of course, I never told this to anyone. I did awkwardly tried to make conversation with my mother. I once asked her who my father was, and she said he was a sailor who died in the war. I never asked about him again, nor about any of the other relatives. Years later, I was told that my mother had been in a fight in a kitchen where she was working; she had left, and no one had heard from her since. After many years of searching, I found out in 1988 through the Social Security Administration that she had died in a nursing home in Chicago in 1987. When I later visited the nursing home, one woman, who had been on the staff while my mother was there, told me she had never mentioned she had a son. That bothered me a lot. I felt somehow responsible for her dying in an institution.

In the late 1960s, I sought out my biological father. I found him in a suburb of Chicago and got him to agree to see me. I had all the pertinent facts from the court records. He told me he was married and had six children, none of whom were home at that moment. He looked like me; he showed me a picture of his eldest son, who also looked like me. In response to my story, he said, "I don't remember no girl named Mary." He then told me that he himself was adopted and that he "knew a lot about this stuff." He would be glad to gather family information for me—"but, of course, it would take a little dough." I did not go back to look for him until 1994 when, regretfully, I could not find him.

RECONNECTING WITH THE ORPHANGE
AND THE FAMILY NEIGHBORHOOD

In 1994 I was ready to take my 17-year-old son, David, on his first trip to Chicago. We went with two fellow Hedwigians, Tom Suchomski and Joey

Popera, to old St. Hedwig's. We traded memories of a frequent nighttime ritual: We would get into bed after saying our night prayers; the nun would say good-night in Polish, and we would respond. Then darkness and silence would reign, and one was free to say, "Ah, now I can think anything I want!" And we did. On occasion the lights would suddenly flash back on: Someone had talked! Then we would have to kneel with our arms in the air (the way Moses prayed) and keep them up until the talker confessed.

The only year I failed to carry out this ritual was the one year in the sixth grade when the reigning nun took me into her cell late each night and sent me back very early in the morning. I have wrestled with the meaning of that troublesome secret relationship for 50 years, viewing her secretly as my "Evangeline," because our relationship started one night in the dark game room as she showed us slides of that great poem and gently touched my forehead. Despite much effort, I was never successful at "blaming" her. Recently, I have become aware that her first touches had promised to replace what I had lost by coming to the orphanage. I think I am ready to stop waiting for Evangeline to return.

During my 1994 visit an elderly man suggested I go to St. Adalbert's Cemetery to find the Polish people who used to live in the surrounding area. I did. Almost all the Felician nuns who raised us are buried there, all with the same style and size of tombstone. In the middle is the tombstone of Monsignor Francis S. Rusch, at least 20 times as large. The "family" is together.

RECONNECTING WITH MY POLISHNESS

For myself, I cannot differentiate how much of which element (illegitimacy, being a de facto orphan, religion, being institutionalized) explains the abiding sense of not belonging that I always felt. I do know that my being Polish is a key factor as well. Polish Americans, like orphans, have been members of a socially definable but disenfranchised class, with its sense of humiliation crystallized in Polish jokes and its deeper feelings of shame relegated for the most part to the realm of denial. Reconnecting with my Polishness, however, enlarged for me my sense of home and family. This included a new sense of the Felician nuns. In the United States, the Felicians "were recruited from immigrant peasant families most of whom were strangers to life in industrial cities and strangers to the high Polish culture of the upper classes" (Radzialowski, 1975, p. 22). In the early part of the 20th century, many Polish women faced a deck stacked against them: They were Polish, they were Catholic, and they were women. The order offered "social mobility ... education, position, social status, travel" (Radzialowski, 1975, p. 22), not to mention family approval for their choice of "a vocation." Joining a religious order provided them with safety, purpose, and status. Re-visioning those caretakers as real young women with a real history helps locate me outside the emotionally charged vulnerability of our mutual life at St. Hedwig's; it ameliorates my sense of the nuns' absolute authority and of the hypnotic magic of religion.

MY LAST RELATIVE: THE END OF MY SEARCH FOR MY AUNT

I continued to search for my family. My last remaining relative was Aunt Louise. I first attempted to contact her by sending a letter through the Social Security Administration, but I never knew whether she got it or whether they really sent it. In December 1994, I wrote another letter, but this time a kind Social Security clerk slipped me the information that my aunt had changed her name (as many Poles did), to Louise Gerry Fowler. I pictured her as a distraught Polish bag lady somewhere in Chicago, so I had the clever idea of enclosing a check for $100, figuring that at least I could trace the check. I wrote what I thought was a moving letter to get her to want to see me.

Months went by with no response, and the check was never cashed. In the summer of 1995 I made another trip to Chicago, examining records at the library, the Polish Genealogical Society archives, voting records, and so on. The very day I returned home to New Jersey, I was stunned by a call from a Maryknoll priest in San Francisco, who told me that Louise G. Fowler had died and that he was the executor of her estate. He got my name from the county administrator's office. My letter and check were found in her safety deposit box. She had died in a hospital, where she would not tell anyone anything personal about herself. When the doctor needed author-ity to pull life supports, the administrator went through her apartment and found a copy of a will she had made in 1965 (when she was turning 50), naming the Maryknoll Fathers as inheritors and executors. In her safety deposit box they found my letter to her. When I told the priest who I was, he said, "Are you a blood nephew?" and assured me that she would have a good Catholic funeral. I said I would fly out that night. By the time I got there, he had hired the law firm that wrote the will to represent the Mary-knoll order. The priest was out of town, and there was no one to talk to. I felt as if I were 4 years old and the walls were tumbling down. The hospital told me where the funeral was to be held.

I went to the wake. No one else was there. I met the priest and the pallbearers at the church. My head was spinning. I had never fully decided what I thought about ethnic burial practices. However, on this occasion I gave deep thanks for wakes. There is no way I can adequately describe the importance to me of finding her actual body—looking at her, touching her, and in particular stroking her beautifully manicured, red-polished fingernails. I remarked on these to the funeral director. He, of course, had no way of knowing what all this meant to me, so he responded professionally, "Thanks ... they weren't like that when we got them." Despite the emptiness of the occasion, touching my aunt's body made be feel for the first time like a fully three-dimensional person, almost "at home."

Soon after the service, the priest sent me a letter congratulating me on being a "fine, Christian gentleman." In the letter, the priest continued with appreciation of my accomplishments, considering that I "was a child of shame and disgrace"—words written with no apparent awareness of their meaning nor discomfort that they were still a part of his emotional and doctrinal vocabulary. I was not pleased. I sent another letter to him and to his superior, asking them to consider our family history and award some small portion of my aunt's estate ($416,902.09) to my family or my children. That letter was never answered.

In piecing together the events of my aunt's life, I made contact with a social worker who had played a large part in convincing her to go to the hospital during her last illness and who was the only one I talked to who was privy to one of her personal statements. She told me that my aunt had once told her in confidence that she was from Chicago, that her sister was once raped and had a little boy whom the family had put in an orphanage, and that this "broke her heart." That was important. It makes me terribly sad to think that she and I missed out on a connection because of her anxiety that I might blame her for having abandoned me as a child—the furthest thing from my mind.

NO LONGER AN ORPHAN IN HISTORY

They say, "Nothing can change until it first becomes what it is." An essential ingredient in dealing with unresolved mourning is to feel the loss, in overcoming denial to feel the pain, and in dealing with rage to feel the helplessness. As inheritor of the title "illegitimate abandoned orphan," I have needed to feel and accept all three and move on. A common theme in my orphanage days was "going home." Certainly for me, and perhaps for many other orphans, reconnecting with our ethnic roots is a way to go home, to be legitimate, to be grounded in history.

In the absence of real bodies, living or dead, information can be the furniture of home. Biographies need earthly details, and it is difficult to be a connected self with a disconnected history. Although information itself cannot, of course, protect orphans from the "exquisite vulnerability" that makes them "go numbly where they are told" (Simpson, 1987, p. 157), it can help provide them with a safe way to re-form their lives and to diminish the numbing hold of a time when that vulnerability made them open to being preyed on by needy caretakers, ambitious benefactors, and other real predators (such as Al, the brother of one of our nuns, who seduced a host of young boys, grooming them with gifts and rides in his car). Of great help to me was finding positive information in early records. Later successes in life are far from unimportant, but in my experience they do not have the identity-affirming power of lines in the Chicago Family Court records such as "The little boy was clever and adorable," or "The family said that nothing could persuade them to give him up" (R. Gordon, personal communication, Summer, 1968).

I do not view my Polish reconnection as a substitute for a family that might have been but, rather, as a discovery of the fuller, and heretofore unknown, corporeality of the actual ocean of life from which I sprang. It is not as good as finding a village of relatives happy to see me or finding my real live aunt. Still, it's close!

THE LAST TEN YEARS

One of the unfortunate consequences of abandonment is the precarious, if not surrealistic, quality of all subsequent attachments. Although that aura never quite vanishes, its power can indeed be greatly subdued, allowing for normal resilience and fairly comfortable risk taking. Perhaps one way we can recoup at least a bit of our momentum is to reestablish connections to past, present, and future. It is difficult to overstate the importance of these rediscoveries of my family's experience. Someone once said that a good story is one that is "able to hold children from play and old men from the fireside." Stories about members of my Hedwigian family certainly do that for me. This history can surround and nourish my sense of identity, helping me feel safe and rooted through Chicago all the way back to Poland, modulating what has been called "the loneliness of the long-distance ethnic" (Gladsky, 1992, p. 249).

Eva Hoffman (1989, p. 5), remembering her departure from Poland in 1959 that soon launched her into a successful writing career in the United States, says she felt "pushed out of the safe enclosures of Eden." Her wording is worth quoting here:

> Many years later, at a stylish party in New York, I met a woman who had told me that she had had an enchanted childhood. Her father was a highly positioned diplomat in an Asian country, and she had lived surrounded by sumptuous elegance, the courtesy of servants, and the delicate advances of older men. No wonder, she said, that when this part of her life came to an end, at age

thirteen, she felt she had been exiled from paradise, and had been searching
for it ever since.

No wonder. *But the wonder is what you can make a paradise out of.* I told
her that I grew up in a lumpen apartment in Cracow, squeezed into three rudimentary rooms with four other people, surrounded by squabbles, dark political
rumblings, memories of wartime suffering, and daily struggle of existence. And
yet, when it came time to leave, I, too, felt I was being pushed out of the happy,
safe enclosures of Eden.

I am aware of the syndrome that institutionalization produces on its
long-term inmates.

Freed prisoners who want to go back to prison are not too dissimilar to
long-term institutionalized orphans. The prison or orphanage becomes safe
and familiar when the world is too threatening. Rewriting your history as a
reinvention of yourself can be invaluable, but rewriting a narrative from the
unearthed real stories of real siblings that you really knew in real time, all
of whom really knew you, is another story indeed. What is often rewritten
is the internalized script, the inner dialogue that can go on forever trying to
right itself. Of course that *is* important. However, it is surprisingly easy to
forget that the *actual history* matters, surprisingly easy to forgo the option
of finding those actual people.

I have the good fortune to have had at least 200 siblings. In 1998, I
attended a St. Helwig's alumni reunion and began regular contact with a
number of old classmates and a few of the nuns from our era. In addition
to the great satisfaction of filling in the blanks about siblings unheard from
in half a century, there is emotional substance to the biographical detail discovered. Each reconnecting contact is a way of going home again, enriching
memory and solidifying identity, re-viewing the orphanage as a family to
which I belong, not as one to which I had been banished. It would be difficult to overestimate the pleasure of finding out about my siblings:

Joe Arendaczyk ran away and lived in a large Motorola carton, which
he had set up in the big bushes along the gate that separated the
orphanage from St. Adalbert's Cemetery. He lived on the "free"
crabapple trees in the cemetery and on money he made by stealing
wreaths in Cemetery #1 and selling them to ladies entering Cemetery #2 off Newark Avenue.
Albin Zukowski joined the air force and taught at West Point until he
retired.
Eugene K., who was abused by the same nun I was, "became an alcoholic" and later shot himself.
Sister Teresilla, the music nun and the absolute favorite of the kids, had
herself been one of the original orphans at St. Hedwig's. No wonder
she was so special.

It turned out that it was *not* our fault that the nun on the girls' side fell out of the window to her death when she was washing our windows. Many of the nuns later agreed that she would probably have fallen out even if we had been good.

Mr. Paul, the carpenter, did not just disappear. Father Elmer got rid of him for "disobedience" in making tops and giving them to the kids for free without asking permission.

Sister Felicia and Sister Laudina had a fistfight in Laudina's cell one night.

It is *not* a mortal sin to beat a nun at checkers.

I had pictures of my classmates Wally Prim and Billy Zelasko that their families did not have, and they were thrilled beyond belief to receive them.

Robert Friedman sent me pictures his aunt and mother had taken on visiting Sundays, including one of me in fifth grade with a broken collarbone.

John Biel had managed to get a video made in the 1940s containing many movies of our processions, events, and outings.

One autumn day when Eugene Cesarz was leaving St. Hedwigs, he popped into class, raised his right arm dramatically, and said "In a little while you shall see me ... then again a little while and you shall not ... for I go to my Father."

We used to caddy for Father Elmer Wojtanowski every summer. Our pay was a root beer float (a "black cow"). For the last five summers since the reunion, a few of us have gone there to play golf. Ritualistically, we treat ourselves to the same pleasure.

Frances Nowobilska, who married our classmate Robert Yesokietous, came to the orphanage because her father had shot her mother; her mother had previously told the parish priest that if she died he should give her children to Father Rusch at St. Hedwig's so they could be raised as good Catholics.

At our reunion "disclosure" dinner, I had looked forward to telling my "siblings" all about our sixth-grade nun taking me in at night, not sure what to expect as their reaction. I had kept that secret for various reasons, not the least of which was fear of their rejection. Somehow when I told the story I expected to hear the first four notes of Beethoven's Fifth Symphony in the background. Instead, Mike Mieszala said, "Hell, we knew that. We used to wait every night for her to take you in, because we knew that once her light went out, she would never come back, and we could do what we wanted: talk, raid the Spizarnia [food pantry], walk around, and whatever." When I reminded them I was the smallest kid in the class and that I wondered why she chose me, Joey Popera said matter-of-factly, "Maybe she liked little boys." The laughter that followed was disarmingly refreshing, and this unexpected new perspective has remained the definitive take on that episode.

Sometime prior to the reunion I had written to Sister Angelita, who I thought could validate my feelings regarding my experience in sixth grade. She wrote back saying that I was so needy back then that I must have imagined it all.

At the reunion we visited the graves of the nuns, and I noticed that someone had placed flowers on the grave of Sister Laudina, the one who had abused me. Later we visited the nursing home where several of the surviving nuns still lived. I was touched to see Sister Armella and Sister Aquinatta, whom I had always liked. I decided to talk with them about my experience with Sister Laudina and ask whether they knew anything about it, wondering how they might respond. They said they knew nothing and seemed to become very uncomfortable, as though they wanted to end the visit. They did not acknowledge the reality of what I had told them, but they also did not deny it.

About 3 months later Sister Armella wrote me an extremely detailed letter about the nuns' lives. It was as much an acknowledgment and letter of accountability as one could write who did not know the particulars of a situation, and it was a great gift. She wrote about some of the difficulties of the nuns had who worked there, isolated from their families and from the larger community. She stated that she was "glad there were no more orphanages." We continued to correspond, and later she wrote me that the nuns had played basketball after we were asleep at night! I had already made my peace with Sister Laudina's abuse, but the generosity of Sister Armella was a great gift I would never have received had I not dared to approach the topic. I am glad I did. Sister Aquinatta continues to send me good wishes in the form of novenas and special prayers, another indirect but nonetheless real validation.

I suspect that for many orphans who search out their roots, dead ends and disappointments are more common than "miracle endings." Nevertheless, next to spiritual transcendence, exploring one's actual and ethnic history is a safety deposit box full of treasures—an earthly "home" and a way toward becoming more fully the person you are. Simpson makes some profound connections between our country as a nation of immigrants and the concept of orphanhood: "The United States, which has been called the home of the persecuted and the dispossessed, has been since its founding an asylum for emotional orphans" (1987, p. 221). She notes that many who have assimilated by changing their names and forgoing their roots "have no way of estimating their spiritual loss" (p. 225). For me, despite some heavy negative associations with my Catholic experience, I like the basic idea that we all started out in paradise and that part of the explanation for the universal anxiety of humankind is that none of us is at home; we are all orphans, cut off from our original household.

We have a new granddaughter, a 2-year-old charmer named Karina. She is now at "home" in New Jersey with her parents (our son David and his Armenian wife, Sona). Sona has roots and family in Israel, Lebanon, and Jordan, my wife Helen in Syria and Connecticut.

God forbid Karina should ever be displaced or suffer the loss of us all. If she did, her journey home would surely be multicultural. The focus of her emotional fervor would depend, naturally, not only on our diversity but on the actual people we are and the actual experience she has had of us, our relatives, and our friends.

The focus of this article, of course, comes out of my own life experience, which includes not only a sudden disruption of continuity by placement at St. Hedwig's, but also a rich infusion of Polish culture by nuns and priests similarly displaced for other reasons. It is the sudden total loss of home and connection that prompted my comparing myself with prisoners and groups displaced by war or forced repatriation. Years later it was rewarding to discover in Polish history much that gave texture and meaning to what before had seemed to be an uncommonly isolated experience. "Going Home" for me thus included reclaiming the orphanage, the family that sent me there, and the culture from which both parenting caretakers descended, uprooting an understandable but nonetheless strange longtime wish to not recognize any of them.

Going home would be, of course, different for us all. For many without major discontinuities, some of the focus here may not seem as relevant, but then again the wish to return home is kindled for most of us, I believe, by a need to recapture youth, redeem time, and recover losses, the common thread being the need to belong.

REFERENCES

Gladsky, T. (1992). *Princes, peasants and other Polish selves: Ethnicity in American literature*. Amherst: University of Massachusetts Press.

Hoffman, E. (1989). *Lost in translation*. New York: Penguin Books

Radzialowski, T. (1975). Reflections on the history of the Felicians in America. *Polish American Studies, 32*(1), 19–28.

Rathnow-Killips, R. M. (Ed.). (1994). *The Hedwigian II* (Vol. 13, No. 1). Blanchardville, WI: The Women and Men of St. Hedwig's Alumni Association.

Simpson, E. (1987). *Orphans: Real and imaginary*. New York: New American Library.

CHAPTER 15

Legacies of White Privilege

Lisa Berndt

I want to share with you a letter I wrote to the great-grandfather of my great-grandfather, a man introduced to me in family lore and genealogy books as General Griffith Rutherford. I wrote it in response to an invitation to stand with Native American and African American colleagues and offer a piece on European American accountability at a conference on "healing the wounds of history" (White & Denborough, 2005, pp. 53–57). It was certainly a healing experience for me to have a chance to address in very personal yet public way the dis-ease of White privilege. It also provided me with an unexpected joy—the opportunity to embark on a frank and loving relationship with ancestors I had been reluctant to trust.

My first sense of this dis-ease that goes with privilege came when, as a child, I noticed that the city swimming pool in Waco, Texas, where I visited my grandparents, was a lot older and more run-down than the sparkling new pool where I played in my mostly White subdivision in suburban northern Virginia. My grandmother assured me that I would not want to swim in the "Nigra pool." It was not said directly, but I got the message that our pool was nicer because "we" were better. The myth of racial superiority was right there ready to fit into my childhood meaning system about who's in, who' out, who's safe who's not, who's us, who's them, who deserves what and why. At the same time, I learned, you are not supposed to talk about it, and you are certainly not supposed to say "Nigra." I felt deeply embarrassed to have the skin color I had but glad to have a nice pool to swim in.

I came of age in the 1960s and '70s. At dinner we would watch as startling images flickered forth from the small Sony black-and-white TV: images of fire hoses and dogs turned on dark-skinned people, guns turned on students, body counts, leaders gunned down. I could tell the world was shifting, that history was happening around me. It seemed that the good guys were no longer the good guys, and there was a sense of excitement and threat, but I had no vocabulary to make sense of what I was seeing.

Meanwhile, the movements I had glimpsed on the TV screen were changing the culture and making the "wounds of history" much more visible to the mainstream folks like me. They were movements that offered liberation not just to people of color but to White people as well. In the 1980s and '90s, I was trying to be a good therapist and listen to people's experience in the context of their experience, and when I did that I kept finding that racism was right there. Because of those movements, there was now a vocabulary available for understanding that experience. Taking leadership from people who had been marginalized gave me access to analyses of power that helped me put words to the vague uneasiness I had been feeling all along.

It was a jolt to be confronted about my privilege and its effects, but it was a helpful jolt. I found it refreshing when people cut through the haze and told the truth. And the truth was that racism was permeating even the well-intentioned profession I had chosen and that I had better stop to learn more about it before I continued to perpetuate it. This led to joining with other activists to address the racist practices and assumptions in our field and our community, and this led to relationships in which I heard more from people of color about their everyday experience. This, in turn, informed me about how my privilege works. Learning the history of racism in this country led me to understand my own family history and to see how the protections my family has enjoyed were put in place and at whose expense.

I still did not know what to do with the shame and despondency that accompanied these discoveries. In my urge to change things quickly (perhaps to relieve my own discomfort), I wanted to distance myself from my ancestors and to condemn them, just as I wanted to shun White people who did not feel the same urgency I did. But anti-racist allies encouraged me to lean into the discomfort rather than recoil from it. They encouraged me to approach my ancestors with interest and openheartedness, along with a sober awareness of the toll their actions took on others. This letter is an attempt to do that.

I want to acknowledge the delicacy of bringing these relationships into public view. I am talking about real people's lives. When I speak of White privilege and class privilege, I am also calling forth the stories of those whose lives and hopes and loves were wrested away through the workings of that privilege. Those stories are not mine to tell, but my story and that of my

ancestors intersect with theirs. I speak of great pain, great loss inflicted by
my people on native people and African American people—pains and losses
that reverberate to the present. I ask that you hold all of our generations
tenderly as you read this letter.[1]

Dear Sir,

*I began writing this letter as an opportunity to stand together with
others I love and respect to weave our histories together: Native American,
African American, European American. I wonder what you think of all
this, being invited to this magnificent place (Spelman College in Atlanta)
so full of ancestors and ancestors-to-be, all with stories to tell. To me this
is important, vital, healing, this acknowledgement of what and who has
come before.*

*To me, being together here today is about breathing into our place in
history—yours, and mine, and our people's, and all people's—and honestly
coming to terms with what this means. It was my grandfather who first
introduced me to you, General, shortly before he died. He, Grandmother,
and I would sit around the kitchen table and reminisce. We would talk
about connections and disconnections and missed connections among our
loved ones. We talked about the memories we loved best and some of the
disappointments we shared. Grandmother would always prepare a ham,
because she thought I loved ham, and make that blueberry and Jell-O
salad I couldn't get enough of. Granddad would talk about his brothers
who had passed on, his mother, and his father, Lester, who supposedly had
gambled away what was left of the Rutherford land.*

*In my family and in my culture, there have always been patches of
silence, like fog, or like ice. We all knew: You don't go in there. It felt like
shame, but I'm not sure what to call it. Because of those patches of silence,
it was never really clear where we came from or what awful thing somebody had done that nobody was talking about. The ice started to crack
when I learned that my grandparents had been married at a Ku Klux Klan
meeting. I came to realize that what was left of Great-Granddad Lester's
prestige derived from his leadership of the Klan around Paris, Texas, in the
1920s. I was horrified to discover this and to find out more about what life
was like for African Americans in North Texas at that time, but it helped
make sense of things.*

*There are many patches of silence that I would like to traverse. So
much fog to see through, so much ice I want to thaw. It is in this spirit
that I am trying to know you better, General. Because your story and mine
and Lester's and my granddad's aren't separate. I don't know much more
about you than fragments of recorded history allow. I know that you and
your parents left Ireland for the North American colonies when you were
an infant in 1721 and that your parents died on that voyage. I wonder*

*what that was like for you. I know that cousins took you in and saw
to your education in New Jersey. For you, it meant safe arms to receive
you at the end of your voyage. Looking back from here, it is clear that a
certain life, certain opportunities, rose to greet you from the moment you
arrived. In fact, those connections with nation-builders were probably
already made when your parents decided to come to this land.*

*I know that you worked as a surveyor though Virginia and into
North Carolina, where you made your home. I know you married Mary
Elizabeth, had eight children, and took part in community-building and
government-forming. I know you were elected to the colonial legislature in
North Carolina, that you voted for the Declaration of Independence, and
that you loved to show your grandchildren the snuffbox George Washington had given you on a visit to your home. These are stories that connect me to the history I learned in school, and I felt pride and belonging
and ownership when my grandfather shared them with me. I also know
that you joined the colonial army and that by 1776 you were a brigadier
general, fighting the British and Indians. I was grieved, and horrified, to
read that you led forces that burned 30 Cherokee villages—a campaign
that "opened the way" for the Treaty of Long Island and the ceding of all
Indian land east of the Blue Ridge Mountains. I believe you were rewarded
for this action with large amounts of land.*

*I know that you moved in circles of power that set you up in the
world of plantation finance—the economy founded on slavery—and
that your lifestyle and much of your legacy was supported by the forced
labor of African people. Because of who was in charge, these events were
documented in written history. So my acquaintance with you has derived
from the parts you played in events that promoted the development of one
nation, the United States of America, and that had disastrous effects on
other nations—Indian nations and African nations. This is what I know of
you. I wish I knew more.*

*Although I was raised in a military family, there is so much about
your life and actions that I don't understand. What did you think you were
doing when you set fire to those villages? What made it possible for you
to do these things? Did you use words like "collateral damage"? Did you
have moments of doubt? Did the voices of the women and children stay
with you? They have stayed with me.*

*And how did these actions shape our family's future? What are the
legacies that we carry? I believe they are mixed legacies. There is no doubting the layers upon layers of privilege that we accumulated as we reaped
the benefits of White supremacy and White dominance. Generations of
our family have also taken pride when they have looked at maps of North
Carolina or Tennessee and seen our family name. There is a triumphal version of our family history that glories in your achievements.*

But there are also the legacies of shame. Of silence. Of the half-truths and untruths that have propped up our privilege through the years. It is very uncomfortable, queasy, disorienting, standing on stolen land, profiting from violence and stolen labor, living a fraudulent birthright. I believe it has kept us from talking to each other in life-giving ways.

General, I would like very much to know what you think about how history remembers you. How else might you have wanted to be remembered? How did those close to you experience you? What kind of friend, neighbor, husband, and father were you? I know a little about your grandson, Newt: that he struggled with alcohol and died young. I know that you lost your eldest son in battle. How did Mary Elizabeth feel about that loss? Your long absences? Your imprisonment by the British? Your campaigns against the Cherokee? What did you tell her about what you did while you were away?

My father left for Vietnam in 1968, when I was 11. He wrote cheerful letters about the weather and told us the tourist version when he came back. But he came back different—quieter, more angry, withdrawn. He told me much later that one of his jobs as a legal officer was to prosecute AWOL (absent without leave) soldiers. Often he would counsel them to stay with their assignment. The son of an old friend heeded such counsel and was killed. This incident haunts my father to this day. Even more haunting, he says, was the way the Vietnamese were treated in their own land. He said he could never feel at ease as an American again.

Does anything haunt you? I wonder. There is much about our past that haunts me, that fills me with sorrow. I think of those Cherokee villages. I think of the enslaved Africans on those plantations, the men and women and children terrorized by Klan violence, the villagers and boy soldiers in Vietnam. I think about the links between all these and our lives, General, and a profound sadness and remorse arise. It is a remorse that shapes many of my actions.

How can we begin to atone for those lives so exploited, ravaged, and stolen? For the ongoing effects of systems and practices and actions and policies that paved the way for some and blocked that way for others— that treated some as God's gift and others as invisible or worse? We know that denying the truth doesn't work. So what if we tried it differently? It seems we could operate from a different sort of strength.

What if we took up the opportunity to learn more about, to listen deeply to, the experiences of those whose lives and livelihoods were devastated in the creation and maintenance of this nation? What if we set out to reclaim the humanity we lost in trying to rob others of theirs? What if we dedicated ourselves to learning how racism was and is constructed and to working in schools, courts, hospitals, financial institutions, governments, arts, neighborhoods, and relationships to take it apart? Perhaps these are legacies we can leave for my generation's great-grandchildren, steps toward a world in which the shared ownership of history—past, present, and future—is acknowledged and valued.

General, contacting you in this way, and learning the histories of others whose lives our people have affected, gives me perspective and, somehow, hope as well. I wonder whether this might be an important process for you, too. Someone asked me once, "Don't you think our ancestors keep learning, too?" I like this idea a lot. Maybe honesty lets us keep learning from each other. One thing I do know is that I don't have to figure this all out myself. This isn't just about you or me or my family. This is about all of us, and perhaps together we will figure out how to talk about it and where to go from here.

I have a longing to know you and to be known by you. It's a longing that speaks to my sadness at my grandparents' passing with so much left unsaid between us. It is a longing that speaks to my hope that we don't have to separate from each other, that we don't have to forget where we have come from. My longing to know you is linked to my hope that people from different nations, across generations, might be able to come together to face what has happened in this land and to this land, and what this has meant for all of us.

General, I'm not aware of traditions in my culture for contacting you, for even having this conversation, for talking with you about your assumptions and mine. I wonder what questions you would have for me, and I look forward to ongoing conversations. But I have been told that, in other people's traditions, for me to speak here today involves speaking on behalf of my ancestors.

And so I'd like to close by saying, to you, with you: It's time for you and me and all in between to come forward with the pieces of history from which we've tried so hard to protect each other and ourselves. We deserve to know, so we can begin to take responsibility, to participate in repairing what we can and taking a respectful place in what is to come.

Yours sincerely,
The great-granddaughter of your great-grandson,
Lisa Kathleen Rutherford Berndt

I continue to correspond with the general and his progeny in letters; I talk to him and others on long walks and bring them along on trips to museums, as I continue to learn about history as experienced by those who have been marginalized. I write and speak to many generations of grandmothers, whose answers never fail to soothe and fortify me. It helps me greatly to take racism personally. I believe that this sense of being in touch with my ancestors and their struggles and their limitations and the consequences of their actions—on their descendents and the descendents of those they harmed—can bring more life to my life and more compassion to my relationships with myself and with others. It challenges the old "who's in, who's out" thinking that can contaminate even my anti-racist work.

When I see a news item or talk to a child experiencing rage at how he is alienated at school, I feel the reverberations of the lives and laws that came before. When I am in professional meetings or "case" conferences, I feel the ancestors of all of us present, and it affects how I think and speak. Meanwhile, as this reciprocal relationship with my family of long ago continues to deepen and expand, so does my relationship with my living elders, and this is a gift beyond measure.

Privilege is like a spell. Its thrall is seductive and powerful. It depends for its power on silence and comfort, and it exploits our desire for belonging by leading us to exclude. Because one of the privileges of privilege is the option to ignore it, I try to live in a way that keeps racism and its effects in my awareness every day. Learning about racism—its effects, its construction, and its history—breaks the spell. And when the spell is broken, connection becomes possible. We can take up responsible membership in the human race. For me, learning about racism is about learning to use privilege in partnership with those denied it (Waldegrave, Tamasese, Tuhaka, & Campbell, 2003). It's about healing the uneasiness, the deep loneliness of being cut off from the past and from each other, so that we can have a strong foundation for joining community and taking collective action.

NOTE

1. This letter was originally published in White and Denborough (2005, pp. 87–92). Copyright 2005 by Dulwich Centre Publications. Reprinted by permission. Available at *www.dulwichcentre.com.au*.

REFERENCES

Waldegrave, K. T., Tamasese, K., Tuhaka, F., & Campbell, W. (2003). *Just therapy—A journey*. Adelaide, South Australia: Dulwich Centre Publications.
White, C., & Denborough, D. (2005). *A community of ideas: Behind the scenes*. Adelaide, South Australia: Dulwich Centre Publications.

CHAPTER 16

Transforming a Racist Legacy

John J. Lawless

I began first grade in 1971, and the city in which I lived was in the midst of a busing controversy, similar to others across the nation. This controversy was invisible to me and my brothers, yet we were active participants in it. At the end of the first day of school, a group of White children stopped playing games to throw rocks at the school bus while yelling "niggers stay home." This is a very vivid memory of my youth because I was one of those White boys throwing the rocks.

This is representative of how my cultural knowledge was generally experienced as a child. I grew up in a working-class family in Utica, a medium-sized city in upstate New York. My mother and father, who had both grown up there, worked hard to provide emotional and material support for my brothers and me. We lived in a two-family house that my parents owned on a street with many families like us: two-parent, working-class, White, and mostly Catholic. I played primarily with other White Irish German working-class children from families like my own. My intersecting privileges were supported and celebrated across many experiences. Some of these experiences were cultural traditions (e.g., Irish Weddings), and I remember them fondly. At other times these cultural experiences encouraged, supported, and praised acts of oppression (e.g., throwing stones at Black children on a bus). These cultural experiences strengthened my prejudices by exposing me to what are acceptable forms of cultural expression, ideas about who could or could not participate and how one could behave.

What follows are a few experiences in my cultural development that "stalk" me about my racial upbringing. These experiences are always present, poking and prodding me to be accountable to myself, to challenge other people with privilege, to remain committed to dismantling a cultural legacy of oppression, and to create a cultural legacy celebrating the complexity of culture (Brayboy, 2007). But first, let me briefly contextualize the city I grew up in.

Utica was ethnically and racially diverse. Yet this diversity was constrained by boundaries as to where one could live, shop, and work. And although there was some blurring of the boundaries between European ethnicities, the boundaries across racial lines were significantly less flexible. Prior to the 1940s, the African Americans had made up 5% of the city's population. But then the African American population began to increase dramatically due to Southern Black migrant farmworkers and laborers looking for an opportunity to escape the oppressiveness of the South (DeAmicis, 2002). During this same period, political power began to shift from the Irish American population to the Italian American population, while World War I and II dampened the participation of German Americans in community activities (Bean, 2002). Thus, issues of diminishing political power of the Irish and the shame of the Germans during the childhood of my parents, coupled with the increase of a racially different population, created a context in which racism flourished.

Although the stone throwing lasted only 1 day, the context was set for racial tension to thrive. Young Black boys and girls were seen as outsiders to "our" school in the 1970s, much as their parents and grandparents had been in the early 1940s. To diminish the racial tension, playground games were created that pitted Black students against White students. These were games to demonstrate cultural loyalty. When these games could not contain our racial tension, physical violence erupted. I can remember this violence being supported by my father, who would ask me if I beat up any niggers that day. This question taught me that physical violence toward Blacks was acceptable.

Whereas my father supported my racist behavior, my mother supported possibilities that would eventually chip away at my racist attitudes. In particular, she supported my friendship with an African American boy, Dave, one of my closest friends in early elementary school. To have a Black friend contradicted cultural norms. There was a discrepancy between my overt racist behaviors and the intimacy of this relationship, which I did not fully realize until Dave moved away. I can remember the deep sorrow I felt when he left. This sorrow exposed the contradiction for me. How could I feel sadness for an African American friend yet engage in racist behaviors? Racism permeated my social environment. I heard racial slurs when people of color were not around. I witnessed prejudiced treatment of Black children by teachers and school administrators. It was everywhere: at school, in the community, and in my family.

For a significant part of my childhood, I actively participated in these overt racist behaviors. My racism changed when I started high school. In high school I was exposed to a larger community with more diversity, not only in terms of race and ethnicity but also in terms of attitudes. I had friends with whom I could make racist comments without any challenges. At the same time I was developing friendships with White people who did not approve of me making racist remarks. This became especially clear when I was a freshman in high school. One night, while having dinner at a friend's house, I called a classmate a nigger. Immediately I knew something was not right. The room became quiet, and my friend's father and mother challenged my language. They asked me why I thought it was acceptable to use that word in their house. They challenged me to think about the effect of my words and how they represent me to the world. The challenge was not meant to shame me but to engage me in a conversation and to make me think about my racist attitudes. It was the first time that my racism was highlighted in a way that I could have a conversation about it.

Whereas this conversation helped me to think of myself, it was a relationship with a coworker that first brought institutional racism to my awareness. During high school I developed a close relationship with Jim, a young African American man with whom I worked in a hospital cafeteria. We often discussed our goals but never the issue of race until we started to talk about college. Both of us did well in school, engaged in extracurricular activities, and had good SAT scores. As we discussed college, Jim expressed concern that college might not be possible for him. He said he was the first person in the family going to college, and he had anxiety about how he would pay for it and fears that his race might hinder his application. I had assumed his situation was the same as mine. I never thought about possible differences. As we talked about college and life beyond it, I began to understand for the first time the powerful role race played in shaping opportunities regardless of a person's qualities.

While these experiences in the outside world helped to shape my awareness, two events in my family of origin years after high school profoundly influenced my movement away from racism. I grew up with two brothers, my fraternal twin, Robert, and another brother, Patrick, 2 years younger. Robert and I were very close and supportive of each other, though we were very different. He was quiet and introspective whereas I was energetic and willing to share my opinions. I was in the middle of everything, whereas he preferred to stay on the sidelines. This was also reflected in our roles in racial fights. I would be more aggressive, and he would prefer to hang out. He would get involved in my fights to protect me but rarely instigated a cross-racial fight. This was true throughout our schooling.

After high school I went away for college while Robert stayed home to attend a local college. At age 20, he was diagnosed with a cerebral aneurysm, and he died of it 3 years later. After an Irish Catholic funeral, our community returned to our house to remember my brother's life. That day many friends, community leaders, and extended family members came together to support my family while celebrating my brother's life. One of the most moving moments of the day was when the African American boys with whom Robert and I fought as children came to the house to pay their respects. Although the racial tension between us had diminished significantly since high school, they were coming into a neighborhood and a house in which racism lived and was still present. I was amazed at their courage to come to our house and grateful to see that my family welcomed all of these young men into our home. On that day, the color of *their* skin did not matter. This became a significant moment in changing racism in my life and for my family. The generosity of these young men in coming into my racist home to pay their respects to my brother strengthened my resolve to change the racism around me, including in my family.

After my brother's death, I made a commitment to examine my racial privilege. I was able to hear people confront me about my overt forms of racism, but more important, I was willing to listen to people to confront me about my racial microaggressions. And I wanted this same process to occur in my relationship with my mother and father. For more than 10 years following the death of my brother, I was unable to articulate how racism in our family affected my relationships with them. When an opportunity arose to discuss my anger, sadness, and shame around racism, I would remain silent or rant and rave at my parents. Both were equally ineffective. I would challenge my father around his racist language, but these confrontations always ended in the same way. When he dismissed my thoughts and feelings, I would get angrier, and finally I would disconnect myself from him. And in this process, my mother would remain silent or ask us to "just let it go." We did not discuss how racism affected my development and, more important, our relationships. My anger, sadness, and shame about how racism shaped my life did not have a voice. My inability to state my position and my parents' inability to hear my emotions altered the closeness of our relationship. This changed 11 years after my brother's death, when my first son, Connor, was born. Soon after Connor was born, my father made a racist slur in front of him. Rather than engaging him in the usual way (i.e., silence or anger), I tried to talk to him about how his racist statements affected me. I told him I wanted this legacy of racism to stop with me. At first he denied my concerns, but I informed him calmly that he would not see his grandson if he could not contain his racism. He then began to talk with me about issues of racism. The conversation was not long, but it was very meaningful. We were able to discuss his childhood and his confusion over my concern. Although he minimized his racism and could not understand my conviction, he was able to briefly acknowledge my concerns. That was 9 years ago, and although I do not know what my father says when I am not around, I have not heard him make a single racial slur around my children since that discussion.

As my voice in my family became stronger concerning racism and racial privilege, I have struggled with the difficult task of using my voice with my friends and peers and in larger systems. Could I challenge my White male peers regarding racial privilege and still remain connected to them? Was I willing to actively confront acts of oppression when this action could disconnect me from my friends? Would it seem disloyal? These questions were scary for me. The strong cultural value of loyalty meant that you did not raise issues that could disrupt trust. My fear of finding myself isolated was very strong. To overcome this fear, I took small chances. I challenged old friends over issues of racial privilege. I found that some of my close friends were unable to hear my concerns and challenges. This resulted in me losing some long-time friendships. Yet other friends were able to hear my challenges, leading to positive changes in our relationships. We would talk about our lives in ways that we had not done before. I also developed new friendships that were supportive of my journey. As a result, I began to develop a stronger social network that supported me when I challenged issues of power, privilege, and oppression while confronting my assumptions. These small steps led to larger steps by which I could challenge my colleagues, community, and larger systems such as the family therapy organizations to which I belonged.

And although my risks with my friends and colleagues have strengthened my voice, I still wrestle with those oppressive remnants of my cultural history. The throwing of the rocks, the violence on the playground, and the racial slurs are vivid memories that I wish I could forget, yet these same memories help to remind me to actively and overtly give witness to injustices in my personal and professional life. I struggle with a profound sense of personal discord as I think of these aspects of myself. I want to minimize or deny the violence I participated in. I want to think of myself as a good person, and these racist behaviors do not fit that definition. It would be easier to fix my gaze on those actions that were exceptions to my racism and to demonstrate that I am not a racist. I have struggled with this process in writing this chapter, yet I know my denial moves me away from the reality of that time. As a child, I was indoctrinated into this invisible web of racism, and in my later years as a youth, I became aware of my racism, and it was a source of pride. Although I was able to create cross-racial friendships during my childhood and high school years, they were not the norm. I have engaged in overt acts of racism, as well microaggressions against people of color. Thus the question remains, How can I change? One of my mentors always says, "Challenge yourself, challenge personal and professional friends, and become an ally around issues of social justice." Through these challenges I can rebel against my racist history and speak more openly about my racism. By conveying how my racism has hurt others and myself, I can create a new cultural legacy for myself, my family, and my community.

REFERENCES

Bean, P. A. (2002). "Deutschtum" on the Mohawk: Utica's German-American community. In J. S. Pula (Ed.), *Ethnic Utica* (pp. 77–100). Utica: Utica College.

Brayboy, B. M. J. (2007, January). *The quality of knowing and learning: Indigenous epistemologies and qualitative research*. Keynote address at the 20th annual Qualitative Interest Group Interdisciplinary Qualitative Studies Conference, Athens, GA.

DeAmicis, J. (2002). The search for community: Utica's African-Americans. In J. S. Pula (Ed.), *Ethnic Utica* (pp. 7–36). Utica: Utica College.

CHAPTER 17

The Semitism Schism

Jewish–Palestinian Legacies
in a Family Therapy Training Context

Linda Stone Fish

As a trainer in family therapy with a focus on social justice and self of the therapist, I am careful to make sure that I am responsible with my privilege and power. As a Caucasian who has benefited and continues to benefit from White privilege, I am constantly on alert for ways that I interact with students that may unintentionally perpetuate oppressive practices. As a heterosexual female, I am hypervigilant with my language and keenly attuned to the signs of marginalization of those fearful to voice their gender and sexual preferences. And as an adult who had the privilege of financial security as a child, I am forever reminding myself that many of my students are financially burdened and how important it is to give my all to training because they and their families have sacrificed so much so that they may train as family therapists. Of course, I am not perfect, but I take my work very seriously.

Until Laura entered our training program, I believed that I was, although a work in progress, pretty good at understanding, as much as one can understand another, how it feels to be marginalized. I am Jewish. While being White and financially secure, I grew up in the shadows of the Holocaust. Most of my family were lucky enough to get out of Eastern Europe before the Nazi invasion, and they worked tirelessly for the creation of the state of Israel so that we would have a homeland and a refuge for the misplaced Jews of the world who had nowhere else to go.

I have a framed letter on my wall at home written to my grandfather, from Chaim Weizmann, the first president of Israel, typed on December 5, 1947. He wrote the following:

My dear Judge Stone:

I heard to my deep regret that you are not well and laid up in the hospital as the result of the strain which you went through during the sessions of the UNO. I feel very deeply with you because I realize what it means to work incessantly for a cause and find oneself in a tense condition for a long time. But it is now over and I am sure you have the satisfaction of knowing that your great work was not in vain, and this I am sure will help you get better in the shortest possible time. It is certainly my ardent wish and I send you my cordial greetings. I know that you don't need my thanks, you did it like all of us for the sake of the cause.

The cause, of course, was the state of Israel.

With great pride, I grew up, and with an omnipresent reminder that *they* did not really like *us* so we had better stick together. I grew up in a large extended family in a Jewish neighborhood in the suburbs of Boston. Because I grew up in an environment in which I did not interact with many non-Jewish people until I went to high school, my first conscious experiences of oppression did not occur until I was a full-fledged adult. For my first year of college, I went to a small school in the Midwest and was placed with, perhaps, the only other Jewish girl at the college as a roommate. I transferred my second year to a larger college and was placed with three girls, two of whom were Jewish. Because Jews make up less than 3% of the population, I have to assume that someone in the room and board offices thought that Jewish college students would appreciate being placed together. It was not until I was a doctoral student, however, that I came face-to-face with a view of myself as the detested, vilified, and/or not-seen *other*.

The many experiences of anti-Semitism I have experienced since I was a doctoral student have made me a stronger Jew. Before them, I was Jewish-identified by chance. After them, I became Jewish-identified by choice. When people I care about, whom I have lovely relationships with, say hateful things about my beliefs, my religion, and my people, I have a couple of choices. I can cut off from them and risk losing my integrity as a person and as a family therapist, or I can learn about myself in relationship. I choose to look at the anti-Semitic remarks and ask myself what I believe about the Jewish religion and about Jews. This procedure has helped me develop a stronger devotion to Judaism and a more complex understanding of myself. This understanding helps me stay connected to all types of people. I experience the violent rage that makes me want to harm another, which helps me understand the perpetrator of violence. I experience the devastating hollowness of the unseen and the writhing hurt of the victimized, which helps me understand the oppressed.

Because of these experiences and their impact on me as a therapist, I helped create the Syracuse University (SU) Marriage and Family Therapy (MFT) Program training model, with an emphasis on training therapists and scholars to challenge themselves through fostering relationships with others who hold various and diverse worldviews. By working toward the creation of an environment of respect, honesty, and integrity, the program served to increase cultural sensitivity, heighten students' awareness of self in relation to others, and generate an understanding of the role played by context in issues presented in therapy. The training model was based on the epistemological multicultural perspective articulated by Hardy and Laszloffy (2002, 2005). I have also written about the development of individuals in therapeutic contexts that mirror this model (Stone Fish, 2000) and use it in my work with sexual minority youths who come out to their families while still living at home (Stone Fish & Harvey, 2005). I briefly describe how the model worked in a training context.

The MFT faculty members worked toward creating a therapeutic environment within academia that privileged honest, open, and intimate dialogue while remaining forever mindful that faculty are responsible for grading, evaluating, and training students. As part of this context, the entire faculty met with each student individually in the first year of the student's training program to discuss her or his progress toward her or his degree and, equally as important, her or his progress toward the ability to use herself or himself in relational therapy sessions to help create honest, open, intimate, and difficult dialogues. Another venue used toward creating these environments is a doctoral retreat that occurs once a semester, an evening and daylong meeting with all the faculty and all the doctoral students.

Difficult dialogues are specific exchanges in which the possibility for increased intimacy and increased relational skill is present. Difficult dialogues tend to be characterized by anxiety, fear, excitement, anger, hurt, and wonder (Stone Fish & Harvey, 2005). They are uncomfortable conversations in which the intent is for people to challenge themselves and those with whom they are having these conversations to face and embrace their different positions while staying in relationship. Difficult dialogues are particularly challenging for all participants because each is required to express beliefs and opinions that they may never have expressed before, to themselves or to others, while staying connected to and sometimes even nurturing the very people who are activating these uncomfortable beliefs. Our training model fostered the idea that learning to handle differences in ways that humanize those different from you is an advanced relational skill that evolves out of sustained difficult dialogues, so we were perpetually encouraging them to happen.

I helped facilitate the dialogues between students and between students and faculty when issues came up in which a student was hurt by an inadvertent and/or conscious violation or oppressive practice. So, for example, when a fundamentalist Christian student was challenged by a lesbian whom he was trying to befriend, I helped them work on their relationship, while gently and persistently helping him hold himself accountable for the power imbalance in their relationship and the ways in which his position violated her very being. This was the easy part—holding someone else accountable for the ways in which they are hurtful. More difficult, as any entitled person knows, is holding *yourself* accountable when you have done something hurtful or when you have benefited from the hurtful things that happened before you. Even more difficult is holding yourself accountable when you do not believe you are! This is where Laura comes in.

Laura was a master's student in our program at a time when I was chairing the department, but that is not the only relationship that we had. She and I also had children who went to school together. Her oldest son and my oldest son, both seniors in high school at the time, were in many of the same classes together, though not friends. I knew of her son and therefore of Laura because he was a talented musician and a well-respected member of the school community. Both of our sons also periodically wrote commentaries for the school newspaper, though I had never read any that her son wrote, being interested only in my son's commentaries and quite proud of his talent in articulating his point of view. One of those points of view was pro-Israel at a time, a few years back, when the Middle East conflict was heating up and in the news.

Laura contacted me before applying to the program, and we went to lunch. She told me she was interested in applying, and we spent the time talking about the program and getting to know one another through stories about our families and the similarities and differences between us. I remember distinctly leaving the meeting with intense and strong positive feelings for Laura, thinking that she was wise, warm, and intuitive. I also remember thinking that our lives intersected in so many ways and that she was my polar opposite. I lead with my head, she with her heart; my four children work around my schedule, she worked around her four children's schedule; she spoke poetically and I was blunt, and the list went on. She eventually applied to the program, and I was enthusiastic about her entering.

THE DIFFICULT DIALOGUE

In a retreat a few years ago, when a crisis was occurring between Israeli soldiers and Palestinian civilians, a faculty member voiced his outrage at the injustice he witnessed on TV as he watched the Israeli soldiers armed with guns and the Palestinian civilians armed only with rocks. I froze and then said, with the rage of generations behind me, "Don't go there. This is really dangerous territory. The media is biased, Israel is misunderstood, everyone hates the Jews, and this is just another example of anti-Semitism." My strong and intense protective response came from some primordial place in me, and I thought to myself, Linda, you'd better take a look at that rage before you alienate others and cut off more conversation. For the time being, however, I effectively cut off all conversation and we moved on. Or so I thought.

The next week, the entire faculty was meeting with master's students in individual interviews to assess their clinical readiness. Laura was one of those master's students. When she applied to the program, she informed us that her father was Palestinian and that he, though now a U.S. citizen, was publicly speaking and teaching about the Palestinian–Israeli conflict. She periodically talked about her Palestinian heritage in class, and I was eager to hear more about it as I learned more about her, although I taught her only in a class on family therapy theory that did not leave room for much discussion or family-of-origin conversations. I thought her Palestinian heritage was just that, a heritage that was something that came before her, that was in her past; not considering the current climate of hostility toward Arabs and Arab Americans.

The clinical readiness interview began with Laura, and she asked, quite bravely, whether she could talk with me about concerns that she had. She said that she did not feel safe talking about these concerns alone and wanted the support of the faculty. She then went on to share that she was concerned that about the discrepancy between what she perceived as an intolerant and prejudicial commentary from my son about the Palestinians, and what was being taught so vigorously in the program. The largeness of the discrepancy was confusing to her and created fear about what the implications might be for her and in the broader context of prejudicial politics. She referred to my son's commentary in the school newspaper as violently anti-Palestinian and said that her son had written a rejoinder and that my son had expressed hostility toward him for the rejoinder. She had asked for funding from the department, and when she mentioned this to her brother, he had reminded her that she would never get funding from a Jew nor from an institution that was so heavily run by Jews. Her brother had expressed, and she shared the same concern for her son when he applied and was rejected from two Ivy League colleges after writing a fervent essay about the Palestinians and human rights violations. She was articulate and passionate, and I was completely dumbfounded.

I listened carefully to what she was saying and did my best to hold her tenderly with my words as she spoke. At the same time, I was balancing my intense internal reaction to that which she was saying. This is the "difficult" in the difficult dialogue—that is, balancing new and profound information about oneself while remaining lovingly engaged and accountable in relationship. My internal reaction, at first, was shock and certainly some considerable defensiveness: Everyone blames the Jews, we're such an easy target, we are only trying to stay alive, and how about all the injustices that the Arab world perpetuates against Israel, and so forth and so on. But then, as I stayed focused on listening intently to what Laura was saying about herself and her experience of me, it was like having the wind knocked out of me. I saw and experienced her truth for the very first time: that I, my offspring, and my ancestors in our hypervigilant necessity to defend ourselves, had violated her ancestors, herself, and her offspring. And then it hit me that maybe, just maybe, I had never addressed the complexity of the stories I was told and continued to tell. It was always in front of me, but I had not let it in.

I expressed tremendous appreciation for her courage and shared what an honor it was for me to bear witness to her pain. I apologized. My apology came from a place of utmost compassion for her position. My strong Jewish identity, my Zionism, and the pride with which I educated my children about our heritage and their great-grandfather's legacy had clearly violated Laura's and Laura's children's sense of safety and fairness. My wounds from anti-Semitism and my hypervigilant protectiveness of Israel prevented me from recognizing the way my power and privilege inadvertently infuriated and silenced Laura. I believe this apology allowed Laura to feel heard and protected, and we moved on. I, however, have not been the same.

After this meeting, Laura gave me a book that her father had written that detailed the loss of his homeland at the time that my grandparents were fighting for theirs. The book was painful for me to read, and I had to put it down a number of times, but read it I did. I felt the same passion from her father that I used to feel when hearing my grandfather and my Hebrew School teachers speak about Israel. Before Laura, I had not been taught, nor had I sought to learn, some of the consequences of my grandfather's fight toward justice and a respite from the death of so many of my relatives.

Before Laura, I had not considered the parallels of racism, discrimination, and struggle that is her and her family's experience. It is only in the last couple of years that Arabic has even been a language you could find in a college course book. Her father's first language was Arabic, though, growing up in middle class, White, suburban America, it was not until Laura was in her teens that her father began to bring some of his heritage into the fabric of his children's upbringing. Before Laura, I had been merely a neutral bystander in the current climate of discrimination against those of Arab descent in the United States.

"The hottest places in hell are reserved for those who in times of great moral crisis maintain their neutrality" is a Dante quote that greets my family and me as we walk in the door to our home. The inherent dilemma, which I still struggle with today, is how to fight for what we believe is just in a time of great moral crisis without violating others' justice. Hardy and Laszloffy (2002) eloquently detail the psychological response to oppression. Horizontal violence is a response to oppression in which marginalized groups use violence against their own or other marginalized groups. How do I teach my children to be proud, Jewish-identified citizens of the world, hypervigilantly fighting against their own self-hatred, which may occur from subtle anti-Semitism that they experience, while also teaching them to be just with others?

To prevent maintaining a sense of neutrality in times of great moral crisis, we must enter difficult dialogues with people whose worldviews, historical legacies, and current life situations are different from ours. Healing begins through difficult dialogues in which we are vulnerable enough to learn something significant both about ourselves and about the other. Successful dialogues are those in which hierarchy, power, and privilege are acknowledged and those who hold privileged positions in these dialogues hold themselves accountable. This accountability is one in which our compassion for ourselves and others leads not toward shame or pity but toward understanding and knowledge. There are no simple solutions, but we must be willing to enter into the process with open minds, open hearts, compassion, and character.

REFERENCES

Hardy, K. V., & Laszloffy, T. A. (2002). Couple therapy using a multicultural perspective. In A. S. Gurman & N. Jacobson (Eds.), *Clinical handbook of couple therapy* (pp. 569–593). New York: Guilford Press.

Hardy, K. V., & Laszloffy, T. A. (2005). *Teens who hurt: Clinical interventions to break the cycle of adolescent violence.* New York: Guilford Press.

Stone Fish, L. (2000). Hierarchical relationship development: Parents and children. *Journal of Marital and Family Therapy, 26*(4), 501–510.

Stone Fish, L., & Harvey, R. C. (2005). *Nurturing queer youth: Family therapy transformed.* New York: Norton.

CHAPTER 18

My Evolving Identity
from Arab to Palestinian to Muslim

Nuha Abudabbeh

This chapter describes my Palestinian American Muslim identity. It is an effort to help others understand the complexity of families from backgrounds like mine and the complex interplay of our historical experiences on our specific experience in the United States, especially since September 11, 2001. I will discuss Islam from a personal perspective, sharing my experience as a therapist who went through a number of the changes that many other Muslims have gone through.

Islam is a way of life, practiced in as many diverse ways as there are Muslims and different Arab countries. My family is no exception. My parents began life in an untraditional way. They waived having a wedding and donated whatever they would have spent on a wedding to those fighting to preserve Palestine intact. Even more unusual, their parents did not oppose them. In addition, my mother, who was highly sought after, chose my father from a number of very wealthy suitors. Her choice was based on his education, not his wealth. He was the only suitor who was a graduate of a prestigious university in the United States. This way of thinking, although truly in keeping with Muslim spirit of favoring education over wealth, and forgoing a traditional wedding ceremony (more of a European tradition) was not the practice followed by most of those around them. My parents were not representative of the Muslims of their time. However, they were married in an era (1936) in which Western cultural norms were practiced in a variety of forms. Those who dared to create their own fusion of these cultures (Arab, Palestinian, and Muslim, with a "dash" of Western) were often admired by others. Today any individualistic interpretation of Islam or its fusion with any other cultural norms would probably be met with severe punishment. Islam is expressed differently depending on the history of each of the countries in which it is practiced, its geography and composition. Muslims are guided by the Quran (the holy book for Muslims), as well as the *hadith* (the sayings of Mohammed). Both of these remain open to different interpretations *(tafsir)* by different scholars *(ulama)*. This practice also contributes toward distinct differences among Muslims in their interpretation of Islam. Two distinctly different interpretations are represented by the Sunnis and the Shiites. In addition, differences in adherence to Islamic teachings are manifested according to how conservative the Muslim or the Muslim country is. This contrast is evident when comparing Islam as practiced in Saudi Arabia, the strictest form of Sunni Islam (Wahabism), with that of Tunisia (where some laws, especially pertaining to women, have been changed).

Any therapist working with Arabs will witness these differences in their clientele. Over the past 30 years of my professional career, I have witnessed these differences among my Arab patients. The secular Muslims have very different expectations of their children and wives than do religious Muslims. I have seen a Muslim dressed in black, covered from head to toe *(burka)*, accompanied by her similarly dressed 13-year-old, and a Muslim in a miniskirt; a Muslim male who would not shake hands, and a Muslim who saw no contradiction with Islam in embracing a female therapist; Muslims who interrupted a session to pray, and those who never prayed.

I was born in Palestine before the creation of Israel. I left when I was 1 month old because my family relocated to Turkey. Having completed his studies in horticulture in California in 1932, my father was one of the pioneers in that field in the entire Middle East. On hearing of his expertise, Kamal Ataturk, the president of Turkey, asked my father to consult with his government. My father had chosen this field because his family had owned citrus groves in Jaffa, Palestine. He and his family were always politically active and paid a heavy price for their political involvement during the tumultuous period in Palestine, which motivated the move to Turkey, where he could provide a more peaceful life for his family. He was the youngest of his brothers, two of whom were killed tragically. The rest of the family was overly protective and encouraged him to leave Palestine when an opportunity came. This left his eldest brother to continue to look out for the family and to manage their citrus groves. My father, who had studied to help manage the family property, was never given an opportunity to accomplish that dream because he could never return to Palestine, which became Israel and inaccessible to Palestinians after 1948. He spent the entirety of his life as a "foreigner" in every country in which he lived and even died in a "foreign" country without ever seeing Palestine again.

The move to Turkey, where my parents spent 18 years, was the beginning of a never-ending dialogue between them as to whether to apply for citizenship or not. This pivotal discussion revolved around the issue of having to give up hope of returning to Palestine. Although my parents were never able to settle that argument satisfactorily, it was the beginning of my own journey spiritually and physically, which forced me to constantly reexamine my own "identity" and where I might make my living to avoid the anguish that my parents had experienced throughout my early life.

In Turkey I was an Arab living as a transplant from a different country with a family that identified as Arabs and Palestinians and as non-Turks. Our status as non-Turks drew us to establish relationships with other non-Turks—Italians, French, and Lebanese. In elementary school, classes began with one student reciting allegiance, declaring that we were Turks. Each morning a different student led the school with this statement, which the other students had to repeat. When my turn came, I, at age 7, refused to utter the words. The incident was received with perplexity and led to a meeting with my family. It was gratifying when my mother showed her support of my allegiance to my Arab Palestinian identity, explaining to the principal that it was only natural that I would not make statements that did not reflect who I was. As Turkey was a secular country, Islam was exercised only at home and in a very social and informal way. Besides teaching me that I was a Muslim, my mother focused on teaching me Arabic and rudimentary information about Islam. My life in Turkey was only the beginning of my being in touch with non-practicing Muslims, as well as with other nationalities. My Muslim identity was reinforced each summer when we visited my grandparents in Palestine, who were practicing Muslims. Thus I began to form a Muslim identity, in keeping with one of the most important teachings of Islam: to be a part of a larger world in which a Muslim can live in harmony with others regardless of their non-Muslim identity or non-Muslim lifestyle.

In keeping with my parents' reinforcement of my Arab and Palestinian identity, they made two attempts to place me in a boarding school in Palestine. The first was in a German Catholic school in Palestine. This was interrupted by the 1948 war following the establishment of the State of Israel. This placement lasted less than a year, and its end result, as far as I can remember, was that I lost the most precious baby dolls I had ever possessed.

The second attempt was a placement at a Quaker school, where I was once more challenged as far as my Arab and/or Palestinian identity was concerned, because my Arabic was "homegrown" and had a distinct Turkish accent. A mixed message was conveyed during my stay at this school. On the one hand, I was welcomed as the descendent of a learned Muslim man who was so progressive that he had written some of the hymns we sang on Sunday. On the other hand, despite the teachers' making a fuss about my great-grandfather, the students continued to call me the "Turkish girl." Though my Muslim identity was never challenged, my Arab identity was. I took it on myself to begin fasting for the month of Ramadan, although I had never done so at home. Not only did I fast, but I also organized a number of other Muslim girls to fast with me.

The challenge to my identity, Palestinian as well as Muslim, continued to play a central role in my adjustment to college. The American University in Beirut, Lebanon, was secular. However, being a Palestinian during that period in Lebanon's history was disadvantageous. As Palestinian families had moved into Lebanon, the Lebanese had become more committed to their own identity, fearing the imbalance brought about by the influx of dispossessed Palestinians, especially those who were Muslims. This created a potential for disequilibrium in the politics of Lebanon, in which religion played a significant role. The country had always sought to create a balance between the multiple religious groups, which included Shiites, Sunnis, Maronite Christians, Druze, and Protestants. One of the fears parents had was the possibility of romantic liaisons between their children and others of different faiths. Many students developed relationships that were eventually doomed because of parental disapproval. Some of these relationships actually ended in the tragedy of a homicide or suicide because of the family disapproval. This was the beginning of my coming to terms with the limitations imposed on me as a Muslim girl. It was clear that regardless of how open my family was, the idea of marrying a non-Muslim was a hurdle I would have to deal with at one point or another.

My Muslim identity was reinforced on my return to Palestine (now occupied by Jordan) to teach science at a teacher's training institute, where I resided in a boarding school. This first assignment put me again in an environment that fostered my Muslim identity while allowing me to continue to remain close to non-Muslims. Although the students were from Palestinian refugee camps, the teachers were mostly Christian Palestinians. During this year of teaching I took up praying the five prayers per day, in addition to fasting during Ramadan. My students were all practicing Muslims and were from very poor families from Palestinian refugee camps. I knew that I had to provide an appropriate role model for them. This was the first of many efforts to adapt to or possibly please others in whatever environment I found myself.

After 1 year of teaching, I decided this was not my calling. I headed back to Lebanon to complete my studies, vacillating between medicine and psychology. But switching from medicine to psychology was no small decision and was regarded unfavorably by my family. Even the American student counselor attempted to dissuade me from choosing psychology, saying, "Why would an Arab girl want to become a psychologist? Arabs need teachers, not psychologists." Resenting the counselor's "colonial" attitude that she knew best, I disregarded her advice and pursued psychology.

My first job with my master's in psychology was in Tripoli, Libya, where my parents had relocated. I became director of a new center for impoverished families, partially funded by the United Nations Educational, Scientific, and Cultural Organization (UNESCO), offering multiple services, including child guidance. I also taught psychology to U.S. airmen stationed on one of the biggest air force bases through a University of Maryland program. In contrast to my Lebanese experience, my life in Libya was remarkably positive. Through the confirmation of my identity as both a Muslim and a Palestinian by non-Palestinian Arabs, I formed a more comfortable attachment to my Muslim identity. In contrast to my having to look as "western" as possible and un-Muslim as possible in Lebanon (miniskirts, bikinis), in Libya I gladly covered my arms and gave up my high-couture Italian clothes. This seemed a small sacrifice in return for the immense affection and love I received from the Libyans. It was the embracing and validation I had always yearned for. What was appealing about this Muslim experience, which I found true among other North Africans as well, was their flexible interpretation of Islam. This interpretation, which allowed women to marry outside their religion if the man converted to Islam, seemed progressive and in keeping with what I thought was a more sensible interpretation of Islam. It fit the way Islam had been presented to me in my family. But the comfortable niche I found in Libya did not take me away totally from my non-Muslim attachments. Through my teaching at the American base I continued to explore my growing American side, which was highly associated with a work ethic and yearning for higher education and intellectual stimulation. The two sides, the Muslim and the secular, continued to flourish without any conflict once I was exposed to Islam as practiced by North Africans.

In pursuit of higher education, I left North Africa with a heavy heart mixed with the excitement of finally making it to the United States, where my father had completed his studies. Attending graduate school at an all-White university without the flavor of foreign students required a whole new set of coping mechanisms. Blissfully ignorant of the intense anti-Palestinian sentiment on and off campus, I simply acted Palestinian, Arab, and Muslim, in that order. My advisor, who suggested that I dress like the rest of the students, triggered one of my first recollections of nonbelonging. This must have been a "subtle" hint that I already looked and acted different without having to dress differently. If I experienced discrimination during my college years, it was too subtle for me to notice. Throughout my graduate experience, only three students showed me hospitality.

My career following my PhD repeated two experiences I had had earlier in Libya. One was totally American: I worked for the government and seemed always to be an outsider, accorded no respect for my religion or acceptance of my ethnic background. The other was my work with private patients, which was with people of multiple ethnicities but primarily of Arab descent, work that seemed to go in waves as I went from seeing second-generation Arab Americans and other ethnic groups affiliated with them to seeing recent Muslim and Arab immigrants to the United States. Before 9/11, Muslims presented with a variety of issues, including conflict between their practice of Islam and the challenges facing their children in a non-Muslim world. My own experiences as a Muslim woman both prior and subsequent to arrival in the United States enabled me to offer appropriate interventions.

From the late 1960s until 9/11, being Palestinian and being non-Caucasian seemed to go hand in hand. The Muslim identity seemed to be a natural part of that combination. It was an identity I carried without fanfare or fear. It was simply part of who I was. The main impact of 9/11 for me was to enhance my identification with some Muslims and to distance me from others. I was painfully aware of the potential backlash: surveillance by the government and other possible retributions by either the government or individual persons. I was painfully aware of the burden of carrying two identities that were targets in my adopted country. As time has passed since 9/11, I seem to have moved closer to my secular Islamic identity regarding required rituals while becoming more strongly attached to my Muslim identity in relation to other Muslims. It is so much a part of who I am to identify with the underprivileged and mistreated that the more my adopted country targeted Islam, the more I had to lift my head high to declare my Islamic identity.

I always manifested my Islam by practicing some of the requirements, and I never experienced any alienation and/or exclusion from others for being Muslim. I do not attribute this to looking different from the others or adhering to a dress code that separated me from others. In contrast to my inclusion as a Muslim, I have definitely experienced exclusion as a Palestinian and an Arab. This varied in different settings. In fact, my Palestinian identity was a badge of honor in certain countries, as well as among certain groups in the United States.

In the post-9/11 period, I find myself where my father found himself so many times—with an intense need to belong and have a "home." I discover that I am indeed homeless. I have to reassess my "outsider" and "other" identity in a country I had come to call "home." Unlike my father, I had never lived in one country that I came to identify as home. I accept that where I have lived for the majority of my life has to qualify as my home. I am entirely grateful to a heritage that has prepared me to undertake the task not only of living with the challenge of nonbelonging but also of converting that into a strength. Having witnessed my family's ability not only to make friends but also to establish strong ties with those around them regardless of their ethnicity, or religion, I was able to find something I could cherish in others regardless of their class, color, ethnicity or religion. I have been blessed with parents, grandparents, aunts, and uncles who all taught me by example that living with others was a privilege and a source of strength as you reach out and incorporate what they have to offer into a more comprehensive perception of the world.

The Arab world has gone through a significant transformation in the past few generations. A transformation that began with a reaction to repression by Western powers was fueled further by the creation of the State of Israel, which went beyond colonization in an act of usurpation of land and the demolition of the whole nation called Palestine. This historical experience became the pivotal event that symbolized the erosion of the self under defeat and a significant shift in the realities of the Arab being. The implanting of a country based on one religion created a great deal of upheaval for many Arabs who lived through that era. It affected different countries in different ways, and it influenced a noticeable transformation in the interpretation of Islam and its practices. This transformation was influenced also by the search for identity in response to colonization by more than one Western power. After an initial identification with the colonizer (a whole generation that became enamored of Western cultural norms), these norms were rejected. This rejection led to gradual change from a secular Arab Muslim identity to a more pronounced and committed Muslim identity. The Arab sense of humiliation and shame was the catalyst that spurred dramatic change and transformation among Arabs. It is not surprising that religion became the balm to cure all hurts. Islam provided crucial human basic needs, such as a sense of belonging and a clear structure, and filled a vacuum created by the failure of Western cultural norms to meet these needs.

The 9/11 tragedy widened the chasm between the Western cultures and the Muslim world. Somehow the whole world of Islam was transformed from a culture of its own complexities to a culture and/or religion of defiance of the West. The defiance was sporadically expressed in violence that was alien to the history of Islam and to its teachings. Such expressions as "suicide bombing" and "jihad" suddenly emerged as part of the Western media lexicon. The word "jihad" took a menacing meaning and seemed to have very little connection to its original meaning. This distortion seemed to be relatively easy to impart.

The history of Islam had been consistently described in the West as being spread by the sword. Unbeknownst to most Westerners, the word "jihad" is not meant to prod Muslims to use the sword against the infidel. "Jihad," in fact, stands for a deeper, more psychologically oriented concept meaning '"struggle" toward submission. Another concept that has been distorted during the anti-Muslim frenzy is that of suicide bombing (the willingness of Muslim young men to kill themselves). A very shallow interpretation was readily available, as it became attached to both monetary gains and brainwashing. Islam forbids suicide but not martyrdom. The suicide bombers are considers martyrs because their act is committed for a cause they believe in. Within their cultural norms, they do not differ from the Japanese kamikaze warriors during World War II who were willing to die to defend their country. The Japanese act has not been scrutinized with the same vigor or negativity as have Muslim suicide bombings.

I have had to find my own Palestinian, Arab, and Muslim therapist self within this new world of contradictions. I have evolved with what my patients brought into the sessions. I had to frame this evolvement within the shortcomings of not belonging to any one of these identities. I have, however, found peace in adhering to values that have kept me focused on my own mission in life. Driven by a history of injustice, I have found solace in facilitating a better life for those I have treated.

TEACHINGS OF ISLAM RELEVANT TO WORKING WITH FAMILIES

Islam goes beyond guiding a Muslim in prayer and religious requirements. It gives specific rules and regulations to govern how Muslims are expected to lead their lives, treat spouses and members of the family, and legislate every other issue in life (social, economic, and political). It is a religion grounded in everyday practical needs, including satisfying a partner's sexual needs, providing guidance on how to deal with a woman and how to satisfy a man's sexual drive. Some of the suggested legislation regarding women and sex that was brought about by Islam was considered revolutionary at a time when women were buried alive. Beyond these progressive steps taken in the seventh century, not too many changes have been implemented in Muslim societies since, and thus what may have been revolutionary then is presently archaic.

The Arabic language, literature, and the hadith are full of *aquaa*l (sayings) rich with guidelines that address every aspect of life and could supplement the therapeutic process. In addition to the sayings, examples from the prophet's life can be a guide. For example, the fact that men and women did mingle in the days of the prophet can be used to direct a family in dealing with expectations of females in the family. Any report of abuse or violence should be challenged as against Islamic law. To encourage striving toward independence, the saying that implies a decision to count both on destiny and on one's own effort could be cited: A newly converted Muslim left his camel outside without tying it, counting on God to take care of it. On returning to fetch the camel, it had naturally strayed away. The prophet's response was: "You can factor in God's will only after he sees that you have done your part. You should have had the wisdom to tie up your camel before you expected God to do his part of protecting your camel or you from harm."

As interpretation of the Quran is highly subjective, it can be used in counseling by giving interpretations that can facilitate resolving both parental and marital relationship problems. Early Muslim history is replete with stories about the prophet, as well as his disciples, that demonstrate coexistence with both Jewish and Christian people in harmony by following the teachings of the Quran and the hadith. They are also role models for patience (God is patient with those who are patient) and kindness (God treats well those who treat others well). These examples can assist in providing culturally appropriate interventions. But, of course, the therapist must be cautious in exploring any patient's Islamic convictions.

Although space does not allow much explanation, I offer a few hints regarding Muslim customs:

- Some Muslim men will not shake hands. A greeting of "Salaam Mu Alikum" is exercised by all Muslims in encountering one another even if they do not know one another, and it is a fine response.
- Anticipate the possibility of Muslim clients having to pray while in your office. This may mean providing a prayer rug and also being able to inform them where the sun sets, so that they know in which direction to pray.
- It may help to allow a parent and/or a partner to attend an interview, especially when clients are deciding whether the therapist is the right person for their family member.
- Take into consideration the special holidays and/or hours of fasting in scheduling appointments.
- Discuss with clients their feelings about being treated by a non-Muslim or a secular Muslim.
- A male therapist having to see a female patient should accommodate Muslim customs by allowing a male relative of the female to be present in the session if needed.

What is remarkable is that Islam emphasizes the role of reason and education. This significant part of the Islamic teachings could contribute to our therapeutic approach. The emphasis on reasoning could fit with a cognitive behavior therapy that has a distinct Muslim interpretation. A potential danger might be basing one's decision making on the past, but Islam has the potential to become a cognitive behavioral approach that combines education and reason. Because Islam provides distinct guidelines for behavior toward partner, children, and parents, whatever the therapist provides in therapeutic interventions has to draw from those guidelines.

CHAPTER 19

Biracial Legitimacy
Embracing Marginality

MaryAnna Domokos-Cheng Ham

QUESTIONING MY IDENTITY AND LEGITIMACY

As a child, if people asked me my name, I would at first hesitate and wonder what they meant by the question. Would they want to know the ethnic origins of my surname or what purpose my name served for me? I would then choose to answer both of these questions because of the doubts I had about my ethnic and racial legitimacy. My name reveals my ethnic and racial identity. However, throughout my childhood and adolescence I did not know my legitimate or legal name, because my mother believed it placed a stigma on both of us. My mother had me use her maiden name to conceal my father's identity from me and, more important, to hide my racial and ethnic origins.

Whatever name I choose to use, as a biracial person I approach an introduction of myself at best with awkwardness and occasionally with intense anxiety evoked by ambivalence about my self-disclosure and transparency. The dominant internal question for me is "Who am I?" How I answer this question has been influenced by increased demographic trends toward interracial marriage and multiracial births. The question raises for me a choice: Either I convey through my name that I am a biracial person, or I do not reveal my identity as a biracial person. In the United States the meaning of racial differences has been constructed by the holders of power (Root, 1996). So after I determine how I want to position myself with those in

213

power, I often use the name that allows me to join with those who have the power and that best serves my purposes. I decode my mixed racial heritage to others by constructing an identity for myself that matches their expectations and the demands of their social context. I straddle at least two worlds and have one foot in and one foot out of each one.

With a small pit of anxiety in my stomach, I say, "Hi, my name is Mary-Anna Domokos-Cheng Ham." This is my customary introduction for any professional group of people. Fifteen years ago, at my first group meeting of research fellows at East–West Center in Hawaii, the small pit became a large ball of anxiety. In the group were fellows from mainland China, Taiwan, Outer Mongolia, India, and Japan and me, a biracial person. Domokos, the first name of my surname, is my mother's Transylvanian maiden name; Cheng is my Chinese father's name; and Ham is the surname of my Anglo-American husband. On this occasion my concern with my name was that I could not be identified with any of the racial groups represented and would thus be marginal to everyone. My name could not provide an easy segue to join with others in the room. In fact, some individuals might even be offended by the apparent mixed racial origins of my names.

My mother's beliefs about her marriage and my identity were shaped by the context in which she had been raised: an immigrant community that was naive to the demands of its adopted country. The comments made about me by my teachers and fellow students were influenced by historical events at a particular the time: World War II. Thus the question "Who am I?" was confused by other questions: "Can I believe what others say about who I am?" and "Will others believe what I tell them about who I am?"

Who I am begins with the story about how my mother disclosed to me who my father was. This pivotal event was a bolt of lightning that shattered the false sense of identity my mother had constructed and illuminated a different path for my life to follow: my decisions about career; my relationship with my husband and children; my self-image; and, in general, the focus of my life.

There I was in 1957 ready to leave at 8 P.M. on a plane from California to New York, a journey that would take 12 hours. I was beginning my freshman year at an elite private college. My mother's third husband appeared excited for me. His idea was to take me, with my mother, for a farewell celebration dinner. I could not think of a better way to say good-bye. My suitcases were packed, and we drove to San Francisco for our special meal. But, once we were in my favorite restaurant, I felt my chest constrict and my throat ache. I knew I was picking up tensions between my mother and her husband. Halfway through the meal her husband said he had something to tell me: He planned to leave my mother and seek a divorce. I held back tears. I was going to lose "the Brit," the man who helped me with math problems, who played the violin while I accompanied him on the piano, and who went on long car trips with my mother and me. Then, without warning and without even a slight hint about what was coming, my mother said she had something she wanted to tell me. "I thought this would be a good time to tell you who your father was. I never wanted to tell you while the war was going on. You know there was so much prejudice against Orientals." Without emotion, my mother told me that my father, a man I never knew, was Chinese. I was surprised and defenseless. Now, whenever I recall the conversation, I remember only driving to the San Francisco airport and sitting awake all night on the plane to New York City.

I heard the words my mother said that evening, but I could not fully accept what she had said. Repeatedly I reviewed the event, which I had stored among my memories. From these memories, I slowly began to take hold of who I was. For years I wondered whether people knew I was a biracial person. If they did, I wondered whether they had intentionally led me to believe I was someone who I was not. I can never be certain of the answers to these questions. But these memories contribute to my identity.

In second grade, I often walked home with several girls in my class. They would frequently taunt me with sing-song chants, "Ching Chong China Man," and pull on my long braids. My feelings were hurt. I felt rejected, isolated, and ugly. Their actions never made sense to me. Once I asked my mother if I was really Chinese. Emphatically she said, "No, you're not Chinese. You're Hungarian and your grandparents are from Transylvania—everyone there has high cheekbones and straight black hair—that's common."

So often we are unaware of the social realities that guide our lives. In fact, our reality is based on metaphors from our early childhood experiences and from lessons learned from our families and from community institutions, such as schools and religious establishments. These metaphors are constructions from cultural norms that give meaning to particular events and transactions between groups within the larger systems of society. Groups—culture and society—regulate the meaning of reality by defining it. Skin color and facial and other physical characteristics provide examples of how society manipulates the meaning of reality. In specific situations biracial individuals have a difficult time knowing whether others are reacting to an explicit sensory experience or an intuitive fabrication of their internal state of mind. They find themselves without a clear racial reference group. In this ambiguous position they become marginalized by those who determine social reality (Root, 1996).

GAINING SELF-KNOWLEDGE THROUGH AWARENESS: MY MOTHER'S STORY

My mother's life story, her struggles with her position in the social context and history, had become mine. I am able now to recognize the power of the symbiotic relationship between my mother and me: Her emotions became mine and mine became hers. Her perceptions of her position in the social context and her response to the effects of World War II, which bombarded our daily lives, were also mine. What I believed to be historical fact was what she told me, and how she lived her life was the template I used for constructing a meaning of my own experiences. Whenever I asked myself, "Who knows and understands me?" my answer was always my mother, a person who did not feel that she belonged to mainstream society. My perceptions of myself reflected her perception of herself and me.

From the time of my birth, which coincided with the beginning of the European theater of World War II, my mother and I were together without my father. He had left my mother soon after they were "married" in Nevada, a state that forbid interracial marriage between "yellows and Whites." My mother was naively unaware of the prejudice and discrimination toward Chinese in California, where we lived. Without her Chinese husband or her caring, protective, immigrant Hungarian parents, who were living in Michigan, she had no one to interpret her situation for her: having an Asian baby at a time when Japanese Americans were being uprooted to relocation camps. My mother was unaware of exclusionary housing laws directed at Asians. She recalls how she was forced to move from apartment to apartment because "landlords would not rent to us since I had an infant who looked 'Oriental.'" When landlords did rent to her, they then asked us to move because other tenants complained about my Asian appearance. Sometimes they told her not to use her husband's name, so, to be safe, she used her maiden name.

Throughout my childhood my mother and I were unaware of the factors contributing to our social position. We did not know we were caught "in a racist discourse constructed around a 'boundary dispute'" (Bhabha, 1991). Neither of us understood what created the power differential between Chinese and Caucasians. We experienced the disorder, confusion, and pain that an unresolved dispute about the boundaries for legitimacy brought. Only in my adult life could I understand how the historical context of California during World War II was a social drama that brought turmoil to the existing social structure. This contributed to our inability to negotiate the invisible boundaries of legitimacy.

The history of U.S. laws regulating the legitimacy of biracial relationships played a pivotal role in my mother's confusion about being in a biracial relationship and her eventual wish to conceal from me the race of my father. Antimiscegenation laws began prior to the Revolutionary War. In 1661 Maryland passed a law to prohibit marriage between Blacks and Whites. California in 1880 instituted a prohibition against marriage between Whites and Negroes, mulattos, and Mongolians (a term that mainly applied to Chinese at that time). Again, California in 1909 passed a law to add Japanese to its list of races forbidden to marry Whites, and yet again California in 1945 passed a law to add Malays to this list (Sickels, 1972; Sollors, 2000). In 1967 the Supreme Court ruled, in the case of *Loving v. Virginia*, that Virginia's antimiscegenation law was unconstitutional (The Oyez Project, 1967). Even after this pivotal Supreme Court ruling, biracial couples continued to experience the effects of the political, social, and economic exclusion that had existed for over two centuries. It was not until 2000 that the last antimiscegenation law (in Alabama) was repealed.

When my mother was 80 years old, she gave me an essay she had written describing what it was like for her to live in California during World War II with an Asian-looking baby and no husband. She knew how it felt to be biracial. My existence, my physical being, had become part of her identity. And my identity was influenced by her understanding of who I was as a biracial infant. Reading her essay and reflecting about what I might have felt in her place deepened my understanding of her plight, as well as of myself.

SELF-INTEGRATION: EMBRACING MARGINALITY

I knew myself as a biracial person from different sources: my mother, my schoolmates, and my teachers. Their truths contributed to the construction of my identity. However, these sources offered only limited visions or partial truths, which I now believe were influenced by a racial ecology, a context comprising economic, societal, and political dimensions (Root, 1992). As a child I accepted partial truths to understand my identity. Yet, whenever I had to define who I was, both to myself and to others, I was caught in a crisis of representation (Clifford, 1986). If I was to deepen my own self-definition, I had to elaborate on partial truths to broaden the space in which truths could be known and represented (Anderson, 1997). My childhood memories are examples of the discovery I made: that truth is constructed in the eye of the beholder and can only be known as a partial truth (Root, 1992). My partial truths were representations of reality as they evolved over time. To define myself as an integrated person, I needed to hold two or three pictures of myself simultaneously, from the past, the present, and the future.

An opportunity to hold two or three pictures of myself at the same time came about when I was doing research with a Chinese anthropologist at the East–West Center, a think tank for integrating ideas from Eastern and Western cultures. At the end of my first week, an anthropologist colleague from Inner Mongolia invited me to attend a lecture with him. He thought I might be interested because the lecturer, his friend, a professor of musicology from Beijing University, was going to talk about the similarities between Transylvanian–Hungarian (Magyar) and Inner Mongolian (Chinese) folk music. As we walked into the hall the lecturer immediately came over and said, "You must be Transylvanian and Chinese—I can tell." What I learned that night was that the rhythms and structure of the music from both cultures were similar. More important, I learned that I had a space in the universe. I could acknowledge myself—and feel more acutely a sense of pride and respect for myself.

This experience offered me a unique opportunity to see myself as an integrated entity, a whole, fully accessible person who was not a patch-work of discrete, identifiable components. From the musicologist I sensed inclusion and legitimacy, an explicit gesture of acceptance. Racial and eth-nic legitimacy can be expressed in different ways: from full acceptance of mixed-race people without erasing the differences of a multiracial experi-ence to full acceptance of a specific community without making an issue of a person's multiracial heritage—for example, "passing" as monoracial (Nakashima, 1996). As a biracial person who had always been marginal to the social normalcy of the dominant, I felt that night that I had found acceptance as person with multiracial experiences.

Without clear boundaries and well-defined rules for gaining legitimacy and thus acceptance by the dominant culture, it is no wonder my mother was unable to acknowledge and define my identity to others and to me. She could not pass on to me a legacy of Chinese tradition because she had only a limited experience of the culture. She showed me notebooks of her attempts to learn calligraphy and the Chinese language. However, without my father as transmitter of the culture, she knew she would be unable to teach me what I needed to become culturally Chinese. Her only attempts to convey the meaning of Chinese to me were through a Chinese friend who often took care of me. My mother felt that she was not able to do more, and so she covered up her limitations by concealing from me the legacy of a culture she did not understand. Instead, she declared that I was solely from her own Hungarian–Transylvanian immigrant heritage.

DECONSTRUCTING MARGINALIZATION

Even though as a child I joined my mother and told others I was Hungarian, I now clearly characterize myself as biracial and in a position of marginality. However, when I describe my societal location as marginal, I then need to clarify the societal positions of centrality and periphery. Similar to my child-hood experiences with the invisible boundaries of legitimacy, for many adult years I never seemed to know how to locate myself in the societal center. What I did know was that the center had undeniable power over the entire structure of our society (Ferguson, 1991). I struggled not to be relegated to a peripheral societal position. Regardless of how I wanted to be known and how my mother attempted to construct societal centrality for me, both she and I allowed ourselves to be defined by an entity we did not understand and could not always recognize.

Once I learned my father's identity, I felt that I had the burden of being in a position outside the societal center, yet I discovered the privileges and responsibilities of societal marginality. My position between the center and the periphery makes me particularly vigilant to the precarious coexistence between two powerful and competing forces. Balanced between the dominant culture and its outcasts, I have gained empathic understanding of both. I believe that my responsibility is to use my understanding of multiple perspectives to be a cultural broker. My responsibility is to create a bridge through empathic communication (Ham, 1989a, 1989b). Both personally and professionally I am often a translator between those in the center and those at the periphery. My interpretations are informed by my residing in the margin between the center and the periphery, so that I can observe both domains.

To be in Hawaii at the East–West Center was for me more than a privilege. I experienced for the first time the feeling of being in the center. I learned that the State of Hawaii has a significant biracial population: 21.4% of the Hawaiian population, in contrast to 3.6% of the overall U.S. population (U.S. Census Bureau, 2003). Immediately I found that I "fit in" with others who were like me. Hawaii gave me the opportunity to experience my own identity in a way I never had before. Whenever I was in any public place, such as a grocery store, restaurant, or just walking down the street, I saw other *hapa haoles*, a Hawaiian term designating someone of Asian or Pacific Island origin mixed with European heritage (Root, 1996). One afternoon at the library I noticed that the young man who was checking out my book had blond hair and green eyes with epicanthic folds, a dominant characteristic of Asian eyes. I found myself starring at him to the point at which I thought I was embarrassing him. He then said with a slight laugh, "See, I look just like you." As I left the library, I reflected about the exchange and concluded that in Hawaii we both were legitimate members of a marginal domain: not members from the dominant culture or societal center yet not delegated to the periphery of the societal center.

A WORLD IN TRANSITION: AN OPPORTUNITY FOR BIRACIAL LEGITIMACY

I can only assume that change does not lead to an end point but is a continuous process of grappling with multiple realities. From a position of fear of and anger toward the dominant social context, a position I had learned from my mother, I have chosen, instead, to move toward a position of advocacy for social justice. Commitment to my clients' welfare, fairness in my treatment of students, and collaborative interactions with my colleagues are all qualities essential for respectful relationships that are the basis of social justice.

Because of my struggles with multiple identities, I am aware of the difficulties others have in shaping and reshaping their social identities. The changing demographics of the population in the United States seriously challenge the validity of personal truth and undermine the credibility of knowledge that the powerful and privileged claim. Perhaps the self-understanding of biracial people can enhance society's understanding of intra- and inter-group relations, identity, and resilience (Root, 1992). As part of the transitional process within world politics, the status of the biracial person finds legitimacy. Our society cannot ignore statistics. The U.S. Census Bureau reported in 1992 that the number of biracial babies is increasing at a faster rate than the number of monoracial babies, with the number of multiracial babies increasing more than 260% since the early 1970s in contrast to the 15% increase in monoracial babies during the same period of time (Root, 1996; U.S. Census Bureau, 1992). Biracial and multiracial people are now poised in our society to undertake the role of cultural brokers by using their multiple perspectives to create bridges where empathic communication can take place.

REFERENCES

Anderson, H. (1997). *Conversation, language, and possibilities: A postmodern approach to therapy*. New York: Basic Books.

Bhabha, H. K. (1991). The other question: Difference, discrimination and the discourse of colonialism. In R. Ferguson, M. Gever, T. T. Minh-ha, & C. West (Eds.), *Out there* (pp. 71–87). Cambridge, MA: MIT Press.

Clifford, J. (1986). Introduction: Partial truths. In J. Clifford & G. E. Marcus (Eds.), *Writing culture: The poetics and politics of ethnography* (pp. 1–26). Berkeley: University of California Press.

Ferguson, R. (1991). Introduction: Invisible center. In R. Ferguson, M. Gever, T. T. Minh-ha, & C. West (Eds.), *Out there* (pp. 9–18). Cambridge, MA: MIT Press.

Ham, M. D. (1989a). Introduction: Constructing a bridge between different world views. *Journal of Strategic and Systemic Family Therapies, 8*, 1–2.

Ham, M. D. (1989b). Empathic understanding: A skill for "joining" with immigrant families. *Journal of Strategic and Systemic Family Therapies, 8*, 36–40.

Nakashima, C. (1996). Voices from the movement: Approaches to multiraciality. In M. P. P. Root (Ed.), *The multiracial experience: Racial borders as the new frontier* (pp. 79–97). Thousand Oaks, CA: Sage.

The Oyez Project, Loving v. Virginia, 3388 U.S.1 (1967). Retrieved March 18, 2008, from *www.oyez.org/cases/1960–1969/1966/1966_395*.

Root, M. P. P. (Ed.). (1992). *Racially mixed people in America*. Newbury Park, CA: Sage.

Root, M. P. P. (Ed.). (1996). *The multiracial experience: Racial borders as the new frontier.* Thousand Oaks, CA: Sage.

Sickels, R. J. (1972). *Race, marriage, and the law.* Albuquerque: University of New Mexico Press.

Sollors, W. (Ed.). (2000). *Interracialism: Black–White marriage in American history, literature, and law.* New York: Oxford University Press.

U.S. Census Bureau. (1992, March). Marital status and living arrangements. *Current Population Reports* (series P-20: Population characteristics, No. 468). Washington, DC: U.S. Government Printing Office.

U.S. Census Bureau. (2003, July). State and county QuickFacts. Retrieved August 23, 2003, from *quickfacts.census.gov/qfd/states/15000.html.*

PART III

Racial Identity and Racism

Implications for Therapy

CHAPTER 20

The Dynamics of a Pro-Racist Ideology

Implications for Family Therapists

Kenneth V. Hardy
Tracey A. Laszloffy

We are simultaneously delighted and chagrined to write this chapter. We had naively hoped against all odds that when the subsequent editions of this book were written that there would be little need for a discussion of racism, particularly as we conceptualize it. Privately, and perhaps much too optimistically, we had hoped that the increased emphases devoted to race and racism via the "diversity," "multiculturalism," and "anti-racism" movements of the past decade would have eliminated the need for a discussion of a pro-racist ideology. In many ways, these movements may have unwittingly increased the need to bring the dynamics of the pro-racist ideology into much sharper focus. It appears that the more we, as a society, become cognizant of race, the more cautious we become. We walk on metaphorical eggshells while our awkwardness and ineptitude in addressing race-related issues clash sharply with our underlying belief systems. This dynamic has provided fertile territory for the nurturance and perpetuation of a pro-racist ideology. Consider the following examples, all of which occurred in the past year, ironically while we were collecting our thoughts regarding the rewriting of this chapter.

The Case of the Nappy-Headed Hos

Nationally syndicated talk radio shock disc jockey Don Imus ignited a heated discussion regarding race and free speech that sent reverberations throughout the United States and abroad. After a basketball game in which the talented women's basketball team from Rutgers University in New Jersey was playing for the NCAA College Championship, Imus referred to several of the African American players during his broadcast as "nappy-headed hos" (slang for "whores"). Both Imus and his ardent supporters claimed that no harm was done nor intended. They posited that because hip-hop recording artists, most of whom are African American, typically use similar descriptions to refer to Black women, the outrage at his remark was essentially misguided, exaggerated, and unjustifiably accusatory. A large number of African Americans were not only outraged but genuinely offended by the remark. Many Blacks considered his comment racially offensive and inflammatory. Imus, amid major protests by civil rights groups, radio and television Network executives, and their corporate sponsors, was eventually terminated from his radio show.

In some ways, the case of the "nappy-headed hos" mirrored the dynamics of another racially inflammatory outburst involving a celebrity.

The Case of Niggers, Pitchforks, and Slavery

Accomplished actor and comedian Michael Richards was recorded during one of his stand-up comedy routines responding to two Black male hecklers from his audience with a belligerent racial rant. Referring to the men as "niggers," Richards told them: "Shut up! Fifty years ago we'd have you upside down with a fucking fork up your ass." Richards, a White male like Imus, also claimed that he meant no harm. Unlike Imus, Richards indicated that he was baffled by his aggressive racial rant and "didn't know where those comments came from." He decided to go to both therapy and cultural sensitivity training in his quest to find answers.

The Case of "He Ain't Ugly and Dumb Like da Others"

United States Senator and Democratic presidential candidate Joseph Biden of Delaware also made the national news with a questionable and controversial racial comment. When asked by an interviewer what he thought of fellow senator and Democratic presidential opponent Barack Obama, an African American, Biden stated, "I mean, you got the first mainstream African American who is articulate and bright and clean and a nice-looking guy. ... I mean, that's a storybook, man." Following an outcry from the African American community, Biden corrected his statement and stated that his words had been misconstrued.

We have highlighted the aforementioned vignettes because they are the embodiment of a pro-racist ideology. Although we used the examples of national personalities, the underlying dynamic is so pervasive that it affects all of us. We believed Richards when he stated that he didn't know where the comments came from, yet *we* knew. They came from inside of him, as they did in the cases of Imus and Biden and as they do with most of us. These specific attitudes, beliefs, and behaviors are the by-products of a pro-racist ideology, a point we return to later in this chapter.

DEFINING OUR TERMS

The controversy surrounding Imus, Richards, and Biden reminded us once again of one of our most compelling realizations regarding race and racism. Throughout many of our interactions in conducting workshops as well during personal interactions, it has been our experience that no matter how egregious the racial infraction, most people do not consider themselves to be racists; they think of themselves as "good people." They do not believe that race should be a basis for determining the types of opportunities or treatment that are afforded to individuals or groups. Because of their commitment to this premise, these individuals assume that their ideology and behavior reflect this ideal. And yet, despite the fact that many people are committed abstractly to racial justice, in concrete ways they lack racial sensitivity.

We define "racial sensitivity" as the ability to recognize the ways in which race and racism shape reality. It also involves using oneself to actively challenge attitudes, behaviors, and conditions that create or reinforce racial injustices. A salient dimension of achieving racial sensitivity involves identifying and resisting the pro-racist ideology that is an integral dimension of U.S. society. We define "pro-racist ideology" as a generalized belief that espouses and supports the superiority of Whites. This ideology reinforces the racial status quo whereby Whites are assumed to be more valuable than people of color (Laszloffy & Hardy, 2000). A pro-racist ideology also supports a system of opportunities and rewards that consistently privileges Whites while oppressing and subjugating people of color.[1]

Support of a pro-racist ideology may manifest itself in comments or actions, as illustrated by the three vignettes we used in the beginning of this chapter. Or it can also be manifested through the tolerance of existing conditions that are inherently racist. Thus, when an individual tolerates a racist circumstance by not challenging it, her or his inaction unwittingly supports a pro-racist ideology. We believe that the more one challenges a pro-racist ideology, the more racially sensitive one is, and vice versa. We struggle with this phenomenon in our own lives. It seems that each day we encounter a comment or condition that appears to support a pro-racist ideology. As a result, we are faced continually with the dilemma of how to respond. It is exhausting and threatening to raise constant challenges to a pro-racist ideology. Because this type of vigilance can easily irritate and alienate others, such a stance is hard to maintain. One of the ways we remain focused on and committed to challenging a pro-racist ideology is by agreeing to hold one another accountable. In this way, our relationship provides a check-and-balance system that enables us to continue speaking out against manifestations of a pro-racist ideology, even when it seems easier or more expedient not to do so.

Another significant observation we have made is that many people are uncomfortable discussing race and racism. Their discomfort often results in the adherence to the myth that race is not important and that it is possible for one to be "color-blind." This myth seems to persist despite an abundance of evidence suggesting that virtually everyone sees color and that our society is racially stratified in such a way as to favor Whites and disadvantage people of color.

We believe that one of the reasons it is difficult to acknowledge seeing color is the fear that *seeing* will automatically be equated with *discriminating* against another on the basis of color. Many people, Whites especially, live with the fear that they will be accused of being racists. Because many of these same people believe themselves to be "good people" who are committed to racial justice, they find it difficult to acknowledge anything that might lead to the accusation that they are racist.

To circumvent the fear that is often associated with admitting that one sees color, we first emphasize that we do not assume that either seeing color or admitting that one sees color is the same as discriminating against someone on the basis of color. For example, in our relationship we often discuss our racial differences. Obviously, by doing so we are acknowledging that we see color. However, this acknowledgment has never been tantamount to either of us thinking about or treating each other in a derogatory or inequitable manner. We have been able to embrace our identities and explore our differences without attaching differential values to these things.

Second, we draw a distinction between the terms "pro-racist ideology" and "racist." We prefer to refer to individuals as supporting a pro-racist ideology rather than identifying them as racists. The term "racist" is a totalizing label that does not afford an individual the opportunity to be anything other than a racist. In contrast, stating that someone has acted in a way that supports a pro-racist ideology does not unalterably condemn the totality of that person's character. It leaves open the possibility that the individual can alter her or his behavior accordingly and thereby still be a "good person." We observed this dynamic regarding Imus, Richards, and Biden. In each case, many supporters of all races rallied around each man to provide testimonials attesting to his good character, moral stature, and commitment to issues of diversity. In essence, each of the men had well-documented records of being a "good person."

THE UNINTENTIONAL NATURE OF PRO-RACIST IDEOLOGY

The notion that it is possible for individuals to say they believe in racial justice while acting in a way that supports a pro-racist ideology may seem contradictory. Yet we have found that an overwhelming number of pro-racist attitudes and actions are unintentional; that is, they occur outside the awareness of the perpetrator (Ridley, 1995). Therefore, it becomes possible to support racial justice verbally and ideologically while being simultaneously unaware of the ways in which one's attitudes and behaviors perpetuate a pro-racist ideology. The following example shows how a well-intentioned school principal was able to commit a racial insensitivity and therefore support a pro-racist ideology without having any awareness of his actions.

A school had initiated a consultation with us because its personnel wished to address a number of racial inequalities that had been observed in the system. Although almost all of the teachers and staff members were White, the student population was 50% African American. During the many months that we worked with the school, the principal, who was White, demonstrated unrelenting support for all of the many difficult initiatives we had undertaken in our efforts to address racial inequalities and insensitivities throughout the school system. He undoubtedly was personally committed to promoting a racially tolerant and just climate in the school. Through our many interactions, we developed unwavering faith that he believed in the importance of eradicating racism. Moreover, it was clear that he worked hard in his interactions to act in a way that supported his commitment, both personally and professionally. This brief background information provides an important context for understanding the events that transpired on the first day of the new school year during a school–parent orientation meeting.

During the orientation, the principal assumed his position at the microphone and began to talk with parents and teachers who were gathered. He spoke warmly about the school community and described how he saw it as an extended family. He then acknowledged that there were newcomers to "the family" whom he wished to identify so that they could be welcomed officially. He gradually worked his way around the room, pointing out new faces and extending welcoming words to new parents and teachers. Finally he acknowledged an individual who happened to be an African American male (one of the few in the room). He smiled at him warmly and then introduced him by saying, "This is one of our new parents, Mr. Adams. His son Tyler just started here in the first grade."

After a brief pause, a teacher jumped forward and said, "Oh, this isn't Tyler's dad. This is Mr. Johnson." Mr. Johnson, as it turned out, was a teacher's aide who had been working in the school for the past 4 months. There was a moment of tense quiet, and then the principal laughed nervously and said, "Oh, of course I know you, Mr. Johnson . . . yes, you are a great worker."

At one level the principal's mistake did not appear to have anything at all to do with race, and yet on another level, it had everything to do with race. In this example, the principal's behavior, albeit unintentional, lacked racial sensitivity and reinforced a pro-racist ideology. Confusing an African American staff person, after 4 months of service, with a new parent seemed to reflect the common stereotype that "all Black people look alike." The potential insult inherent in the situation was compounded by its irony. The principal had just finished talking about what a close-knit "family" the school was, and yet he was not able to differentiate between a staff member who had been a member of this "family" for 4 months and a new parent. Essentially, the staff person was invisible to the principal. He had no more awareness of him than he had of a virtual stranger. This invisibility was consistent with the devaluation and marginalization that Black people endure on a daily basis within a pro-racist society (Ellison, 1952; Franklin, 1993).

In the context of our own relationship, we have experienced the unintentional expression of a pro-racist ideology repeatedly. It is rare that we receive acknowledgment that our relationship is built on mutual trust, shared values, open communication, and a willingness to struggle with our differences. Instead, it is often judged according to old slavery-based narratives. During slavery the complex interaction between race and gender gave birth to a number of damaging stereotypes, some of which still persist today. One of the most common of these was that Black men regarded White women as idealized objects of beauty and status, whereas White women viewed Black men as brutish, mindless heathens who would revere and worship them blindly. This stereotype reduced the complexity of human experience to an absurd and grossly twisted depiction of Black men and White women. Both were objectified by this construction, which merely served to reinforce the power and domination of White men over Black men, White women, and also Black women, who were no less marred by this construction.

The attributions and assumptions that cloud our relationship in the minds of others reveal the ways in which this slavery-based narrative festers in the unconscious and informs perceptions of reality outside most people's awareness. Those who make these racially based attributions do not usually perceive themselves as acting in a manner that is reinforcing a pro-racist ideology. Intentions aside, however, it appears that our relationship evokes a slavery-based narrative from some of our friends, colleagues, and onlookers. This construction denigrates the basis of our relationship and the complexity of our humanness, and it also serves to maintain White male supremacy.

As the targets of discrimination and prejudice, people of color incur the bulk of the burden of a pro-racist ideology. However, all individuals within society suffer from this ideology's inevitable erosion of the foundation that supports the establishment and maintenance of viable relationships. Such an ideology breeds hatred, mistrust, and callousness. It strips individuals and groups of the essentials of their humanity and thereby compromises the health of all relationships at every level.

In family therapy, in which the promotion of healthy relationships is central, the damaging effects of a pro-racist ideology are especially poignant. Relationships constitute the centerpiece of family therapy. Therapists must first establish effective relationships with their clients before therapy can occur. In addition, despite variations in style and theoretical framework, all family therapists strive to help their clients forge more healthy and meaningful relationships with each other. Unfortunately, however, when a pro-racist ideology remains unrecognized and/or unchallenged by therapists, it can infiltrate the therapeutic process in subtle but disruptive ways, thereby undermining the efficacy of the treatment process. The following example provides an illustration of this point.

> The therapist, who was White, asked the client, who was African American, about her family of origin. During the conversation the therapist learned that the client had several younger siblings. Both she and her siblings were well educated and had established successful careers. The therapist responded to this information as follows: "Your parents must be very proud of you and your brothers and sisters, especially because I imagine it must have been difficult for a poor family to provide their children with all the resources and opportunities that supported your many accomplishments."
>
> The therapist made several other comments while the client sat silently. After several minutes had passed, the client interrupted the therapist by stating, "I just have to comment on something that's bothering me. A few minutes ago, you made a statement about my family being poor while I was growing up. Why did you assume that? I never made any references to my family's economic situation. If I had, then I would have mentioned that we were financially well off."

On what basis did the therapist conclude that the client's family was poor while she was growing up? Is it possible that the therapist had unconsciously evoked the classic stereotype that all African American people are poor? More important, did the client believe that this was the explanation for the therapist's assumption?

The therapist in this example had good intentions. She was committed to racial justice and believed she was racially sensitive. However, her unconscious association between Blacks and poverty was an expression of pro-racist socialization that manifested itself outside her conscious awareness. Once she was confronted with her act of racial insensitivity, she was mortified and deeply embarrassed. She had never meant to offend or denigrate the client, and yet, despite her best intentions, she had committed an act of racial insensitivity.

In this particular case, the client commented on the offense; this made it possible for the therapist and client to engage in a racially candid discussion and thereby to salvage their relationship. However, because of the defensiveness and criticism that racially candid comments tend to engender in mixed-race settings, many people of color learn early in life to censor such remarks while in the presence of White people. Therefore, although the client in this vignette risked confronting the therapist, it is more likely that clients in similar situations will remain silent.

Unfortunately, when acts of racial insensitivity remain unacknowledged in therapy, they tend to compromise the therapeutic relationship. If the therapist's act of racial insensitivity had remained unacknowledged, ultimately it would have sabotaged therapy. Moreover, because the racial dimensions of the case would have been outside of the therapist's awareness, she could easily have found a way to "blame" the client for being resistant rather than recognizing the role she herself had played in undermining the relationship. This case highlights how the dynamics of a pro-racist ideology can infiltrate the therapeutic process.

Because of the toll that a pro-racist ideology takes on relationships of all types, it represents a serious impediment to the treatment process—one that therapists must assume an active role in confronting and resisting. We have found that because many individuals are unaware of the existence and effects of a pro-racist ideology, the process of effectively challenging it is extremely difficult, both in and out of therapy. After all, one cannot actively resist a phenomenon to which one is oblivious.

Efforts to highlight the ways in which individuals may unwittingly support a pro-racist ideology often invite tremendous defensiveness and anxiety. Certainly this is understandable in light of the fact that such insight deeply challenges individuals' preferred views of themselves (Eton & Lund, 1996). Hence, when the external feedback persons receive about themselves contradicts their internal representation of themselves, a form of dissonance is created. This is especially poignant with regard to racial issues, because race is such a volatile topic in our society.

Helping individuals to begin to see and eventually resist the ways in which they may unintentionally support a pro-racist ideology is a painful and difficult process. If it is not pursued in a thoughtful and gentle manner, it can have the opposite effect. It can stifle those whose intentions and motivation would otherwise make them prime candidates for racial sensitivity. Furthermore, when the promotion of racial sensitivity is pursued too abruptly or harshly, it can generate levels of anxiety and defensiveness that can short-circuit the process of changing racial attitudes.

We live in a society in which a pro-racist ideology is both pervasive and damaging. Unfortunately, many individuals are not consciously aware of this ideology and the ways in which it informs their lives. As a result, they are limited in their capacity to mount an effective resistance against it and its effects. As therapists who believe in the importance of promoting healthy and viable relationships between and among individuals and society, we are especially committed to the process of encouraging awareness of and active resistance against a pro-racist ideology.

STEPS TOWARD GREATER RACIAL SENSITIVITY: IMPLICATIONS FOR THERAPY

The following provides a map with which therapists can begin to enhance their racial sensitivity by learning how to defy a pro-racist ideology in their lives and thereby in therapy. Our approach challenges a traditional "cookbook" approach of teaching therapists the "1, 2, 3's" of how to be more racially sensitive in therapy. We do not believe there is a simple formula or a "knapsack" of techniques that one can employ. Rather, we envision this as a process that is rooted in how one lives on a daily basis. Because we believe that the line between therapy and everyday life is blurred, we find it impossible for therapists to separate who they are outside therapy from who they are inside therapy. Thus the process of becoming racially sensitive begins with the way each therapist lives his or her life (Hardy & Laszloffy, 1992). Once change occurs at this level, it is our belief that these changes will be manifested automatically within the therapy process.

Becoming Aware That Race Matters

Before one can commit to challenging a pro-racist ideology, it is necessary to acknowledge first that race matters. Despite the romantic myth that "race does not matter because we are all human," race remains a major marker of reality in all realms of our society.

Recognizing the Existence of a Pro-Racist Ideology

After one acknowledges that society is organized around the concept of race, it then becomes necessary to recognize the ways in which race is used to structure vast and deeply entrenched inequalities between groups of people. Thus the issue is not simply that people perceive racial differences but that there exists an ideology that attaches differential values and rewards to these differences. As a result, all of us live in a society in which a pro-racist ideology results in the privileging of Whites and the oppression of people of color. It is virtually impossible to become active in resisting a pro-racist ideology until one is capable of identifying and acknowledging its existence.

Enhancing Cross-Racial Experience

Once one understands that race is a central societal organizing principle and that it shapes society through the lens of a pro-racist ideology, the next step toward racial sensitivity is increasing one's cross-racial exposure. It is only through consistent and direct contact with racially diverse people that one is challenged to learn more about oneself as a racial being—which is the next step.

Exploring One's Own Racial Identity

Interrogating oneself about one's racial identity is salient. Individuals need to ask themselves such questions as "What does it mean to be [whatever my racial identity is]?" and "What implications does this have for my relationships with others who are racially similar and different?" To take myself (T. A. L.) as an example, part of examining my identity as a White person has meant facing the implications of my Whiteness, even when I do not intend such implications. An example that stands out for me occurred in a class when I challenged Sarah (an African American female) about a point she made regarding a particular family therapy theory. I expressed a lot of criticism, and she made it clear that she felt that I was implying she was stupid. Eventually she acknowledged that our interaction had racial overtones for her. She was not free to interpret our interaction without considering that I was White and she was Black. She could never rule out the possibility that my criticism might have been informed by a pro-racist ideology whereby I had treated her disrespectfully on the basis of race.

This incident was quite difficult for me because I had to come to terms with the fact that two divergent realities were simultaneously true. On the one hand, I knew in my heart that my criticism and my style of interaction were not racially motivated. But on the other hand, from Sarah's perspective it *was* racial, and that reality was as true as my own. I had to find a way to embrace both truths. I had to be clear to myself about the basis for my interaction with Sarah. However, regardless of my intentions, I had to understand and take responsibility for the implications of my racial identity and behavior.

When therapists understand and can take responsibility for themselves racially, this understanding is an important therapeutic tool. Similarly, when therapists have limited knowledge of and access to themselves racially, we regard this limitation as one of the greatest impediments to the delivery of effective therapy. The degree to which therapists understand themselves racially provides the foundation for taking the next difficult step of confronting the ways in which they may collude with a pro-racist ideology.

Challenging Pro-Racist Ideology First in Oneself and Then in Others

All individuals are socialized in a pro-racist society; therefore, to some degree, we all internalize some pieces of this ideology. As a result, the question is not "Do I manifest a pro-racist ideology?" but rather "*How* do I manifest a pro-racist ideology?" A common misconception is that it is only White people who can support a pro-racist ideology. All people are socialized in a society that espouses this ideology, and thus all people are vulnerable to absorbing and reflecting its principles. For instance, it is not only White people who have colluded with a pro-racist ideology by reducing our own relationship to slavery-based stereotypes.

In addition, I (K. V. H.) have had to confront the ways in which a pro-racist ideology has made it difficult for me to accept other people of color who are not as racially conscious as I wish they were. As a result, I often want to disconnect from and punish them out of my frustration. But in my better moments, I realize that doing so would only reinforce the system I am committed to changing. Therefore, rather than rejecting or lashing out against those with whom I struggle, first I confront myself and try to understand the source of my frustration. With time, I begin to realize that we are struggling in different ways with the same demons. This insight enables me to reach out and use myself as a basis for connecting with and eventually challenging those with whom I struggle. Taking the initiative to confront ourselves first helps to position us to challenge others in a similar way.

Persisting in Spite of Criticism or Rejection

Challenging a pro-racist ideology can be difficult because of the volatility associated with the subject of race. Moreover, such challenges often generate discomfort in others, who may not have come to terms with the existence of a pro-racist ideology and/or with the role they have in perpetuating it. However, for those who have been diligent about exploring their racial identity and probing their relationship with a pro-racist ideology, it is possible to retain the clarity of vision and inner emotional resolve to persist in spite of others' reactivity and criticism.

A BRIEF PERSONAL NOTE ABOUT US

In our relationship we have had to confront criticism, innuendo, and racially laden attributions on a regular basis. As an African American male and a White female, we have struggled with and grown through our efforts to forge a professional partnership dedicated to promoting racial justice, both in the world at large and specifically within the context of family therapy. Our differences traverse the spectrum of diversity (i.e., race, gender, religion, age, professional status). And yet, despite these differences, we have worked together most successfully for well over a decade. We believe that one of the critical factors associated with our success has been our relentless commitment to addressing and confronting the ways in which both our similarities and differences shape our relationship. Through this process we have learned a great deal about our racial identities and ourselves, particularly with regard to the dynamics of race and racism. Our process of racial exploration has almost never been easy, but it has always been insightful and beneficial.

CONCLUSION

In this chapter, we have discussed how a pro-racist ideology can be sustained through seemingly benign and unintentional actions (or inactions). We have also endeavored to illuminate the connection that exists between how one lives one's life on a daily basis and what occurs in therapy. Our hope is that we, as therapists, will better appreciate the ways in which even the best intentioned among us can unintentionally support a pro-racist ideology. Therefore, all of us need to undertake the difficult and sometimes painful task of confronting a pro-racist ideology in ourselves and in each other, whatever our racial identity, both within and outside of therapy. Only through this deliberate and consistent process can we begin to chisel away at the racial barriers that keep us divided.

NOTE

1. hooks (1989) uses the term "White supremacy" in a similar way.

REFERENCES

Ellison, R. (1952). *Invisible man*. New York: Random House.

Eton, J. B., & Lund, T. W. (1996). The 1990s: An emphasis on meaning. In J. B. Eron & T. W. Lund (Eds.), *Narrative solutions in brief therapy* (pp. 30–38). New York: Guilford Press.

Franklin, A. J. (1993). The invisibility syndrome. *Family Therapy Networker, 17*(4), 32–39.

Hardy, K. V., & Laszloffy, T. A. (1992). Training racially sensitive family therapists: Context, content and contact. *Families in Society, 76*(6), 364–370.

hooks, b. (1989). *Talking back: Thinking feminist, thinking Black*. Boston: South End Press.

Laszloffy, T. A., & Hardy, K. V. (2000). Uncommon strategies for a common problem: Addressing racism in family therapy. *Family Process, 39*, 35–50.

Ridley, C. R. (1995). *Overcoming intentional racism in counseling and therapy*. London: Sage.

CHAPTER 21

White Privilege and Male Privilege

A Personal Account of Coming to See Correspondences through Work in Women's Studies

Peggy McIntosh

Through work to bring materials from Women's Studies into the rest of the curriculum, I have often noticed men's unwillingness to grant that they are over-privileged, even though they may grant that women are disadvantaged. They may say they will work to improve women's status, in the society, the university, or the curriculum, but they can't or won't support the idea of lessening men's. Denials which amount to taboos surround the subject of advantages which men gain from women's disadvantages. These denials protect male privilege from being fully acknowledged, lessened, or ended.

Thinking through unacknowledged male privilege as a phenomenon, I realized that since hierarchies in our society are interlocking, there was most likely a phenomenon of white privilege which was similarly denied and protected. As a white person, I realized I had been taught about racism as something which puts others at a disadvantage, but had been taught not to see one of its corollary aspects, white privilege, which puts me at an advantage.

I think whites are carefully taught not to recognize white privilege, as males are taught not to recognize male privilege. So I have begun in an untutored way to ask what it is like to have white privilege. This paper is a partial record of my personal observations, and not a scholarly analysis. It is based on my daily experiences within my particular circumstances.

I have come to see white privilege as an invisible package of unearned assets which I can count on cashing in each day, but about which I "meant" to remain oblivious. White privilege is like an invisible weightless knapsack of special provisions, maps, passports, codebooks, visas, clothes, tools, and blank checks.

Since I have had trouble facing white privilege, and describing its results in my life, I saw parallels here with men's reluctance to acknowledge male privilege. Only rarely will a man go beyond acknowledging that women are disadvantaged to acknowledging that men have unearned advantage, or that unearned privilege has not been good for men's development as human beings, or for society's development, or that privilege systems might ever be challenged and *changed*.

I will review here several types or layers of denial which I see at work protecting, and preventing awareness about, entrenched male privilege. Then I will draw parallels, from my own experience, with the denials which veil the facts of white privilege. Finally I will list 46 ordinary and daily ways in which I experience having white privilege, within my life situation and its particular social and political frameworks.

Writing this paper has been difficult, despite warm receptions for the talks on which it is based, for describing white privilege makes one newly accountable. As we in Women's Studies work to reveal male privilege and ask men to give up some of their power, so one who writes about having white privilege must ask, "Having described it, what will I do to lessen or end it?"

The denial of men's overprivileged state takes many forms in discussions of curriculum change work. Some claim that men must be central in the curriculum because they have done most of what is important or distinctive in life or in civilization. Some recognize sexism in the curriculum but deny that it makes male students seem unduly important in life. Others agree that certain individual thinkers are blindly male oriented but deny that there is any systemic tendency in disciplinary frameworks or epistemology to over-empower men as a group. Those men who do grant that male privilege takes institutionalized and embedded forms are still likely to deny that male hegemony has opened doors for them personally. Virtually all men deny that male overreward alone can explain men's centrality in all the inner sanctums of our most powerful institutions. Moreover, those few who will acknowledge that male privilege systems have over-empowered them usually end up doubting that we could dismantle these privilege systems. They may say they will work to improve women's status, in the society or in the university, but they can't or won't support the idea of lessening men's. In curricular terms this is the point at which they say that they regret they cannot use any of the interesting new scholarship on women because the syllabus is full. When the talk turns to giving men less cultural room, even the most thoughtful and fair-minded of the men I know well tend to reflect or fall back on conservative assumptions about the inevitability of present gender relations and distributions of power, calling on precedent or socio-biology and psychobiology to demonstrate that male domination is natural and follows inevitably from evolutionary pressures. Others resort to arguments from "experience" or religion or social responsibility or wishing and dreaming.

After I realized the extent to which men work from a base of unacknowledged privilege, I understood that much of their oppressiveness was unconscious. Then I remembered the frequent charges from women of color that white women whom they encounter are oppressive. I began to understand why we are justly seen as oppressive, even when we don't see ourselves that way. At the very least, obliviousness of one's privileged state can make a person or group irritating to be with. I began to count the ways in which I enjoy unearned skin privilege and have been conditioned into oblivion about its existence, unable to see that it put me "ahead" in any way, or put my people ahead, overrewarding us and yet also paradoxically damaging us, or that it could or should be changed.

My schooling gave me no training in seeing myself as an oppressor, as an unfairly advantaged person, or as a participant in a damaged culture. I was taught to see myself as an individual whose moral state depends on her individual moral will. At school, we were not taught about slavery in any depth; we were not taught to see slaveholders as damaged people. Slaves were seen as the only group at risk of being dehumanized. My schooling followed the pattern my colleague Elizabeth Minich has pointed out: whites are taught to think of their lives as morally neutral, normative, and average, and also ideal, so that when we work to benefit others, this is seen as work which will allow "them" to be more like "us." I think many of us know how obnoxious this attitude can be in men.

After frustration with men who would not recognize male privilege, I decided to try to work on myself at least by identifying some of the daily effects of white privilege in my life. It is crude work, at this stage, but I will give here a list of special circumstances and conditions I experienced, which I did not earn but which I have been made to feel are mine by birth, by citizenship, and by virtue of being a conscientious law abiding "normal" person of good will. I have chosen those conditions which I think in my case attach somewhat more to skin-color privilege than to class, religion, ethnic status, or geographical location, though of course all these factors are intricately intertwined. As far as I can see, my African American co-workers, friends, and acquaintances with whom I come into daily or frequent contact in this particular time, place, and line of work cannot count on most of these conditions.

1. I can if I wish arrange to be in the company of people of my race most of the time.
2. I can avoid spending time with people whom I was trained to mistrust and who have learned to mistrust my kind or me.
3. If I should need to move, I can be pretty sure of renting or purchasing housing in an area which I can afford and in which I would want to live.
4. I can be pretty sure that my neighbors in such a location will be neutral or pleasant to me.
5. I can go shopping alone most of the time, pretty well assured that I will not be followed or harassed.
6. I can turn on the television or open to the front page of the paper and see people of my race widely represented.
7. When I am told about our national heritage or about "civilization," I am shown that people of my color made it what it is.
8. I can be sure that my children will be given curricular materials that testify to the existence of their race.
9. If I want to, I can be pretty sure of finding a publisher for this piece on white privilege.
10. I can be pretty sure of having my voice heard in a group in which I am the only member of my race.
11. I can be casual about whether or not to listen to another woman's voice in a group in which she is the only member of her race.
12. I can go into a music shop and count on finding the music of my race represented, into a supermarket and find the staple foods which fit with my cultural traditions, into a hairdresser's shop and find someone who can cut my hair.
13. Whether I use checks, credit cards, or cash, I can count on my skin color not to work against the appearance of financial reliability.
14. I can arrange to protect my children most of the time from people who might not like them.
15. I do not have to educate my children to be aware of systemic racism for their own daily physical protection.
16. I can be pretty sure that my children's teachers and employers will

tolerate them if they fit school and workplace norms; my chief worries about them do not concern others' attitudes toward their race.

17. I can talk with my mouth full and not have people put this down to my color.

18. I can swear, or dress in second hand clothing, or not answer letters, without having people attribute these choices to the bad morals, the poverty, or the illiteracy of my race.

19. I can speak in public to a powerful male group without putting my race on trial.

20. I can do well in a challenging situation without being called a credit to my race.

21. I am never asked to speak for all the people of my racial group.

22. I can remain oblivious of the language and customs of persons of color who constitute the world's majority without feeling in my culture any penalty for such oblivion.

23. I can criticize our government and talk about how much I fear its politics and behavior without being seen as a cultural outsider.

24. I can be pretty sure that if I ask to talk to "the person in charge," I will be facing a person of my race.

25. If a traffic cop pulls me over or if the IRS audits my tax return, I can be sure I haven't been singled out because of my race.

26. I can easily buy posters, postcards, picture books, greeting cards, dolls, toys, and children's magazines featuring people of my race.

27. I can go home from most meetings of organizations I belong to feeling somewhat tied in, rather than isolated, out-of-place, out-numbered, unheard, held at a distance, or feared.

28. I can be pretty sure that an argument with a colleague of another race is more likely to jeopardize her chances for advancement than to jeopardize mine.

29. I can be pretty sure that if I argue for the promotion of a person of another race, or a program centering on race, this is not likely to cost us heavily within my present setting, even if my colleagues disagree with me.

30. If I declare there is a racial issue at hand, or there isn't a racial issue at hand, my race will lend me more credibility for either position than a person of color will have.

31. I can choose to ignore developments in minority writing and minority activist programs, or disparage them, or learn from them, but in any case, I can find ways to be more or less protected from negative consequences of any of these choices.

32. My culture gives me little fear about ignoring the perspectives and powers of people of other races.

33. I am not made acutely aware that my shape, bearing, or body odor will be taken as a reflection on my race.

34. I can worry about racism without being seen as self-interested or self-seeking.

35. If my day, week, or year is going badly, I need not ask of each negative episode or situation whether it has racial overtones.

36. I can be pretty sure of finding people who would be willing to talk with me and advise me about my next steps, professionally.

37. I can think over many options, social, political, imaginative, or professional, without asking whether a person of my race would be accepted or allowed to do what I want to do.

38. I can be late to a meeting without having the lateness reflected on my race.

39. I can take a job with an affirmative action employer without having co-workers on the job suspect that I got it because of race.

40. I can choose public accommodation without fearing that people of my race cannot get in or will be mistreated in the places I have chosen.

41. I can be sure that if I need legal or medical help, my race will not work against me.

42. I can arrange my activities so that I will never have to experience feelings of rejection owing to my race.

43. If I have low credibility as a leader, I can be sure that my race is not the problem.

44. I can easily find academic courses and institutions which give attention only to people of my race.

45. I can expect figurative language and imagery in all of the arts to testify to experiences of my race.

46. I can choose blemish cover or bandages in "flesh" color and have them more or less match my skin.

I repeatedly forgot each of the realizations on this list until I wrote it down. For me white privilege has turned out to be an elusive and fugitive subject. The pressure to avoid it is great, for in facing it I must give up the myth of meritocracy. If these things are true, this is not such a free country; one's life is not what one makes it; many doors open for certain people through no virtues of their own. These perceptions mean also that my moral condition is not what I had been led to believe. The appearance of being a good citizen rather than a troublemaker comes in large part from having all sorts of doors open automatically because of my color.

A further paralysis of nerve comes from literary silence protecting privilege. My clearest memories of finding such analysis are in Lillian Smith's unparalleled *Killers of the Dream* and Margaret Andersen's review of Karen and Mamie Fields' *Lemon Swamp*. Smith, for example, wrote about walking toward black children on the street and knowing they would step into the gutter; Andersen contrasted the pleasure which she, as a white child, took on summer driving trips to the south with Karen Fields' memories of driving in a closed car stocked with all necessities lest, in stopping, her black family should suffer "insult, or worse." Adrienne Rich also recognizes and writes about daily experiences of privilege, but in my observation, white women's writing in this area is far more often on systemic racism than on our daily lives as light-skinned women.

In unpacking this invisible knapsack of white privilege, I have listed conditions of daily experience which I once took for granted, as neutral, normal, and universally available to everybody, just as I once thought of a male-focused curriculum as the neutral or accurate account which can speak for all. Nor did I think of any of these perquisites as bad for the holder. I now think that we need a more finely differentiated taxonomy of privilege, for some of these varieties are only what one would want for everyone in a just society, and others give license to be ignorant, oblivious, arrogant, and destructive. Before proposing some more finely-tuned categorization, I will make some observations about the general effects of these conditions on my life and expectations.

In this potpourri of examples, some privileges make me feel at home in the world. Others allow me to escape penalties or dangers which others suffer. Through some, I escape fear, anxiety, or a sense of not being welcome or not being real. Some keep me from having to hide, to be in disguise, to feel sick or crazy, to negotiate each transaction from the position of being an outsider or, within my group, a person who is suspected of having too close links with a dominant culture. Most keep me from having to be angry.

I see a pattern running through the matrix of white privilege, a pattern of assumptions which were passed on to me as a white person. There was one main piece of cultural turf; it was my own turf, and I was among those who could control the turf. I could measure up to the cultural standards and take advantage of many options I saw around me to make what the culture would call a success of my life. *My skin color was an asset for any move I was educated to want to make.* I could think of myself as belonging in major ways, and of making social systems work for me. I could freely disparage, fear, neglect, or be oblivious to anything outside of the dominant cultural forms. Being of the main culture, I could also criticize it fairly freely. My life was reflected back to me frequently enough so that I felt, without regard to my race, if not to my sex, like one of the real people.

Whether through the curriculum or in the newspaper, the television, the economic system, or the general look of people in the streets, we received daily signals and indications that my people counted, and that others either didn't exist or must be trying, not very successfully, to be like people of my race. We were given cultural permission not to hear voices of people of other races, or a tepid cultural tolerance for hearing or acting on such voices. I was also raised not to suffer seriously from anything which darker-skinned people might say about my group, "protected," though perhaps I should more accurately say prohibited, through the habits of my economic class and social group, from living in racially mixed groups or being reflective about interactions between people of differing races.

In proportion as my racial group was being made confident, comfortable, and oblivious, other groups were likely being made unconfident, uncomfortable, and alienated. Whiteness protected me from many kinds of hostility, distress, and violence, which I was being subtly trained to visit in turn upon people of color.

For this reason, the word "privilege" now seems to me misleading. Its connotations are too positive to fit the conditions and behaviors which "privilege systems" produce. We usually think of privilege as being a favored state, whether earned or conferred by birth or luck. School graduates are reminded they are privileged and urged to use their (enviable) assets well. The word "privilege" carries the connotation of being something everyone must want. Yet some of the conditions I have described here work to systematically overempower certain groups. Such privilege simply confers dominance because of one's race or sex. The kind of privilege which gives license to some people to be, at best, thoughtless and, at worst, murderous should not continue to be referred to as a desirable attribute. Such "privilege" may be widely desired without being in any way beneficial to the whole society.

Moreover, though "privilege" may confer power, it does not confer moral strength. Those who do not depend on conferred dominance have traits and qualities which may never develop in those who do. Just as Women's Studies courses indicate that women survive their political circumstances to lead lives which hold the human race together, so "underprivileged" people of color who are the world's majority have survived their oppression and lived survivors' lives from which the white global minority can and must learn. In some groups, those dominated have actually become strong through not having all of these unearned advantages, and this gives them a great deal to teach others. Members of so-called privileged groups can seem foolish, ridiculous, infantile, or dangerous by contrast.

I want, then, to distinguish between earned strength and unearned power conferred systematically. Power from unearned privilege can look like strength when it is in fact permission to escape or dominate. But not all of the privileges on my list are inevitably damaging. Some, like the expectation that neighbors will be decent to you, or that your race will not count against you in court, should be the norm in a just society. Others, like the privilege to ignore less powerful people, distort the humanity of the holders as well as the ignorant groups. Still others, like finding one's staple foods everywhere, may be a function of being a member of a numerical majority in the population. Others have to do with not having to labor under pervasive negative stereotyping and mythology.

We might at least start by distinguishing between positive advantages which we can work to spread, and negative types of advantages which unless rejected will always reinforce our present hierarchies. For example, the feeling that one belongs within the human circle, as Native Americans say, should not be seen as privilege for a few. It is, let us say, an entitlement which none of us should have to earn; ideally it is an unearned entitlement. At present, since only a few have it, it is an unearned advantage for them. The negative "privilege" which gave me cultural permission not to take darker-skinned Others seriously can be seen as arbitrarily conferred dominance and should not be desirable for anyone. This paper results from a process of coming to see that some of the power which I originally saw as attendant on being a human being in the United States consisted in unearned advantage and conferred dominance, as well as other kinds of special circumstances not universally taken for granted.

In writing this paper I have realized that white identity and status (as well as class identity and status) give me considerable power to choose whether to broach this subject and its trouble. I can pretty well decide whether to disappear and avoid and not listen and escape the dislike I may engender in other people through this essay, or interrupt, take over, dominate, preach, direct, criticize, or control to some extent what goes on in reaction to it. Being white, I am given considerable power to escape many kinds of danger or penalty as well as to choose which risks I want to take.

There is an analogy here, once again, with Women's Studies. Our male colleagues do not have a great deal to lose in supporting Women's Studies, but they do not have a great deal to lose if they oppose it either. They simply have the power to decide whether to commit themselves to more equitable distributions of power. They will probably feel few penalties whatever choice they make; they do not seem, in any obvious short-term sense, the ones at risk, though they and we all are at risk because of the behaviors which have been rewarded in them.

I have met very few men who are truly distressed about systemic, unearned male advantage and conferred dominance. And so one question for me and others like me is whether we will be like them, or whether we will get truly distressed, even outraged, about unearned race advantage and conferred dominance and if so, what we will do to lessen them. In any case, we need to do more work in identifying how they actually affect our daily lives. We need more down to earth writing by people about these taboo subjects. We need more understanding of the ways in which white "privilege" damages white people, for these are not the same ways in which it damages the victimized. Skewed white psyches are an inseparable part of the picture, though I do not want to confuse the kinds of damage done to the holders of special assets and to those who suffer the deficits. Many, perhaps most, of our white students in the United States think that racism doesn't affect them because they are not people of color; they do not see "whiteness" as a racial identity. Many men likewise think that Women's Studies does not bear on their own existences because they are not female; they do not see themselves as having gendered identities. Insisting on the universal effects of "privilege" systems, then, becomes one of our chief tasks, and being more explicit about the particular effects in particular contexts is another. Men need to join us in this work.

In addition, since race and sex are not the only advantaging systems at work, we need similarly to examine the daily experience of having age advantage, or physical ability, or advantage related to nationality, religion, or sexual orientation. Prof. Marnie Evans suggested to me that in many ways the list I made also applies directly to heterosexual privilege. This is a still more taboo subject than race and privilege; the daily ways in which heterosexual privilege makes married persons comfortable or powerful, providing supports, assets, approvals, and rewards to those who live or expect to live in heterosexual pairs. Unpacking that content is still more difficult, owing to the deeper imbeddedness of heterosexual advantage and dominance, and stricter taboos surrounding these.

But to start such an analysis I would put this observation from my own experience: The fact that I live under the same roof with a man triggers all kinds of societal assumptions about my worth, politics, life, and values, and triggers a host of unearned advantages and powers. After recasting many elements from the original list I would add further observations like these:

1. My children do not have to answer questions about why I live with my partner (my husband).
2. I have no difficulty finding neighborhoods where people approve of our household.
3. My children are given texts and classes which implicitly support our kind of family unit, and do not turn them against my choice of domestic partnership.
4. I can travel alone or with my husband without expecting embarrassment or hostility in those who deal with us.
5. Most people I meet will see my marital arrangements as an asset to my life or as a favorable comment on my likeability, my competence, or my mental health.
6. I can talk about the social events of a weekend without fearing most listeners' reactions.

7. I will feel welcomed and "normal" in the usual walks of public life, institutional and social.
8. In many contexts, I am seen as "all right" in daily work on women because I do not live chiefly with women.

Difficulties and dangers surrounding the task of finding parallels are many. Since racism, sexism, and heterosexism are not the same, the advantaging associated with them should not be seen as the same. In addition, it is hard to disentangle aspects of unearned advantage which rest more on social class, economic class, race, religion, sex and ethnic identity than on other factors. Still, all of the oppressions are interlocking, as the Combahee River Collective Statement of 1977 continues to remind us eloquently.

One factor seems clear about all of the interlocking oppressions. They take both active forms which we can see and embedded forms which as a member of the dominant group one is taught not to see. In my class and place, I did not see myself as a racist because I was taught to recognize racism only in individual acts of meanness by members of my group, never in invisible systems conferring unsought racial dominance on my group from birth. Likewise, we are taught to think that sexism or heterosexism is carried on only through individual acts of discrimination, meanness, or cruelty toward women, gays, and lesbians, rather than in invisible systems conferring unsought dominance on certain groups. Disapproving of the systems won't be enough to change them. I was taught to think that racism could end if white individuals changed their attitudes; many men think sexism can be ended by individual changes in daily behavior toward women. But a man's sex provides advantage for him whether or not he approves of the way in which dominance has been conferred on his group. A "white" skin in the United States opens many doors for whites whether or not we approve of the way dominance has been conferred on us. Individual acts can palliate, but cannot end, these problems. To redesign social systems we need first to acknowledge their colossal unseen dimensions. The silences and denials surrounding privilege are the key political tool here. They keep the thinking about equality or equity incomplete, protecting unearned advantage and conferred dominance by making these taboo subjects. Most talk by whites about equal opportunity seems to me now to be about equal opportunity to try to get into a position of dominance while denying that systems of dominance exist.

It seems to me that obliviousness about white advantage, like obliviousness about male advantage, is kept strongly inculturated in the United States so as to maintain the myth of meritocracy, the myth that democratic choice is equally available to all. Keeping most people unaware that freedom of confident action is there for just a small number of people props up those in power, and serves to keep power in the hands of the same groups that have most of it already.

Though systemic change takes many decades, there are pressing questions for me and I imagine for some others like me if we raise our daily consciousness on the perquisites of being light-skinned. What will we do with such knowledge? As we know from watching men, it is an open question whether we will choose to use unearned advantage to weaken hidden systems of advantage, and whether we will use any of our arbitrarily-awarded power to try to reconstruct power systems on a broader base.

REFERENCES

Andersen, Margaret. (1984, November). Race and the social sciences: Teaching and learning discussion. *Radical Teacher*, pp. 17–20.

Combahee River Collective. (1982). A Black feminist statement. In Gloria T. Hull, Patricia Bell Scott, & Barbara Smith (Eds.), *All the women are White, All the Blacks are men, But some of us are brave: Black women's studies*. New York: The Feminist Press. (Original statement dated 1977)

Smith, Lillian. (1949). *Killers of the dream*. New York: Norton.

CHAPTER 22

Dismantling White Male Privilege within Family Therapy

Ken Dolan-Del Vecchio

Denials which amount to taboos surround the subject of
advantages which men gain from women's disadvantages.
These denials protect male privilege from being fully
acknowledged, lessened or ended. ... I think White males
are carefully taught not to recognize male privilege.
                    —PEGGY MCINTOSH (1988, p. 1)

If you do not understand White supremacy (racism)—
what it is, and how it works—everything else that you
understand will only confuse you.
                    —NEELY FULLER, JR. (1969, p. A)

Most texts on the practice of family therapy, like most everything that has
been published in the United States and other Western nations, are written
by, about, and primarily for White people. This chapter focuses on White
privilege itself and, more specifically, on the profoundly significant ways in
which our work with families is shaped by the social processes underlying
the privileges that we who are White and male take largely for granted.

As a White man, I must legitimize my words on the subject of race and
gender privilege by first noting that my awareness of this subject and all of
my thinking about it have arisen through my connections to people who
are racially and sexually different from me. I am grateful for the patience

and tolerance demonstrated by Monica McGoldrick, Nydia Garcia-Preto, Roberto Font, Theresa Messineo, Rosemary Woods, and other mentors who helped me begin to move away from complicity with White male supremacist culture.

DOMINANT VALUES AND FAMILY THERAPY

Proponents of traditional theories that have privileged intrapsychic processes, those who believe in the medical model (DSM-IV; American Psychiatric Association, 1994), and, more recently, promoters of solution-focused and narrative therapies argue that their approaches offer "neutrality" or "objectivity." In reality, however, this means that the values informing these approaches do not conflict substantially with widely held values and ideas regarding the optimal structure for family life and the meanings ascribed to life's difficulties.

Bill O'Hanlon and Michele Weiner-Davis's (2003) *In Search of Solutions: A New Direction in Psychotherapy* presents a therapeutic model that rarely questions dominant values. Emphasizing positive connotation and adaptive rather than transformative change, this model overlooks, and thereby reinforces, oppressive social realities.

> So for example, a father who intervenes and interferes when the mother is disciplining her son might be told, "I am struck with your willingness to protect your wife's relationship with your son. When you step in as you do, you prevent her from being the 'bad guy' and take that responsibility on yourself. You must be fairly selfless in this regard." (p. 105)

This positive reframing of the man's behavior reinforces sexism by praising him for undermining his wife's parental authority.

Salvador Minuchin, Michael P. Nichols, and Wai-Yung Lee (2007), in *Assessing Families and Couples: From Symptom to System*, proceed in much the same manner. In the case that follows, Minuchin consults with a White heterosexual couple and their two sons, 11-year-old Spencer and 6-year-old Tyler. The couple presents the disruptive behavior of their older son as the identified problem. Minuchin reports the following therapeutic conversation:

> ALFRED: Yes, I'm more the culprit. I sometimes contradict her when she tries to impose discipline. But I work late, and when I come home I want to be with my children and she wants them to go to bed.
>
> JOAN: But first you play golf, and then you come late and want to play with the children.

ALFRED: So if I have a good time at golf, I shouldn't have time with my children?

JOAN: But I'm with them all the time, and I need some time alone.

The focus on Spencer is sidelined, and the parents' competitiveness becomes central. I'm impressed by the intensity with which they play the game of Who is the Better Parent, and by the possible consequences of this disturbing sport, in which the children, in effect, become the ball.

DR. MINUCHIN: (*to Joan*) Do you think he exploits you?

I've deliberately chosen a strong term. That allows the spouses to reject the exaggeration while going on to explore the conflict.

JOAN: Exploit? No, certainly he doesn't exploit me. (p. 39)

Where Minuchin identifies "the game of Who is the Better Parent," I see instead the patriarchal gender drama that frees a husband to play during his after-work hours while his wife remains tied to endless family service. After finishing his playtime outdoors, this husband feels entitled to undermine his wife's parental authority and his two sons' sleep schedule in order to enjoy additional playtime with the children. Note Minuchin's question to Joan, "Do you think he exploits you?" and the italicized explanation that follows. Minuchin sees this gender drama as well but chooses to manipulate Joan into discounting as an "exaggeration" any attention to her exploitation.

Not only does this husband exploit his wife, but in all likelihood this exploitation provides a model for his son's disruptive behavior. Minuchin, however, trivializes the interplay of gender and power at the center of this family's difficulties.

Later within the same case discussion Minuchin seeks to convince us of his neutrality: "Notice that my comment was neither an interpretation nor a directive. I simply described what happened" (p. 39). His actions show, however, that he confuses neutrality with support for patriarchal gender patterns.

A therapist who assumes a "neutral" stance pretends that each partner in a couple relationship has equal power (i.e., that the relationship developed outside of any larger historical and relational context). As the preceding examples illustrate, such a therapist actually endorses the oppressive social patterns, including sexism, racism, and homophobia, that contribute to the structure of all relationships in our society (Almeida, Dolan-Del Vecchio, & Parker, 2007; Comas-Díaz, 1991; Dolan-Del Vecchio, 2008; Dolan-Del Vecchio & Lockard, 2004; Hall & Greene, 1994; Hardy, 1996; Hernandez, Almeida, & Dolan-Del Vecchio, 2005; Laird & Green, 1995;

McGoldrick, 1987; McGoldrick, 1998; McGoldrick, Anderson, & Walsh, 1991; Pewewardy, 2004; Tamasese & Waldegrave, 1993).

MY PHILOSOPHY AND VALUES

I believe that a therapy that heals families is also a therapy directed by necessity toward healing communities and ultimately toward healing civilization—such is the completeness and inescapability of our connections to one another. The 20th century saw collective struggles against ancient practices of domination unfold in every realm of life and in every corner of the globe. Ours is an era in which colonizers are finally being dislodged, in which slavery is finally being outlawed, and in which women are finally being made citizens in many (though still not all) places on the globe. With the unfolding of the labor movement, with middle-class White women's movement for parity with White men, with movements for social justice for men of color, and with lesbian and gay rights movements in our own country, the times have borne witness to collective struggles against a multitude of institutional structures of domination.

The outset of the 21st century finds a renewed struggle to maintain these gains, as the United States government unleashes war in the Middle East, leaves poverty-stricken people of color unprotected in the path of Hurricane Katrina, and passes legislation empowering the president to label any citizen an "enemy combatant" and thus strip him or her of the legal protections guaranteed other Americans.

At the same time that structures of domination are being challenged, the dominant (White heterosexist male) discourse has produced no widely accepted notions of power aside from that of power as "domination over." Consequently, we White men tend readily to imagine that if other groups are gaining economic and political power, then we must be losing it (Lerner, 1995). As middle-class White women gained unprecedented political and economic power during the final three decades of the 20th century, the most visible response from middle-class White men was not profeminist initiatives that celebrated these gains. Instead, backlashes proliferated. "Fathers' rights" groups flourished, driven by men's growing fear that legal protections for divorced mothers, children, and domestic violence survivors could only undermine the rights of men. Recognizing that manhood could no longer be reliably measured by the right to subordinate women, White men consumed the writing of Robert Bly and Joseph Campbell. They also rushed to join sweat lodges and drumming circles—all in a desperate gambit to reclaim the "mythopoetic" essence of masculinity.

Today, the "family values" crusade argues that gay marriage somehow threatens the "institution of marriage." These crusaders vilify alternative family structures in an effort to enforce the traditional, male-dominated–female-serviced family model as the only valid option.

Within the "power as domination" paradigm, wherein any visible difference ignites a battle for supremacy, there is no place for "both–and"—no place for respectful and collaborative bridging across differences. As Audre Lorde (1984) put it:

> We have all been programmed to respond to the human differences between us with fear and loathing and to handle that difference in one of three ways: ignore it, and if that is not possible, copy it if we think it is dominant, or destroy it if we think it is subordinate. But we have no patterns for relating across our human differences as equals. (p. 115)

Our civilization can no longer afford conceptualizations and practices of power built on these "us or them" polarities, however, because of our unavoidable proximity to one another. We live in a world in which miraculous advances in communications, travel, and information processing bring us together in ways previously unimaginable. In a civilization in which difference, since the dawn of recorded history, has metant domination (Eisler, 1987), we are challenged to find new paradigms for connection if any of us are to survive and prosper. We have entered an era in which—because the paradigm of dominance hierarchy will no longer hold, because of the new smallness of our world and our undeniable connections to one another, and because of our identification as healers—psychotherapy and struggles to end domination are joined.

THERAPY BASED IN LIBERATION CONSCIOUSNESS

Therapy based in liberation consciousness works to dismantle the hierarchy of power underlying White male heterosexual privilege (Almedia, Dolan-Del Vecchino, & Parker, 2007; Dolan-Del Vecchio, 2008; Dolan-Del Vecchio & Lockard, 2004). Two case illustrations follow.

Josh, a White man of Eastern European Jewish heritage in his early 20s, was in a dilemma. Several months previously, during a 4-month period of time in which he and Susan, his White, Jewish fiancée, had broken up and were not seeing each other, he impregnated a woman named Linda. Josh then ended the relationship with Linda and reconciled with Susan. With the support of advice from friends, his parents, and his brother, Josh kept Linda's pregnancy secret from Susan in an effort to "protect her" (see Figure 22.1). The baby was born 4 days before his initial consultation with me. Josh first told Susan about the child on the day of delivery. He was now considering terminating the relationship with Susan because he felt her emotional response to the news of his newborn daughter was excessive and unpredictable. "Hey,

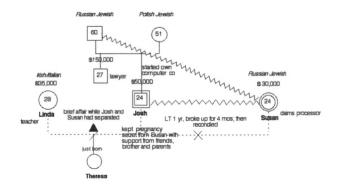

FIGURE 22.1. Josh and Susan's family: Placing parenting over patriarchy.

I told her what's going on! Besides, the whole scenario's under control—I don't want anything to do with the kid, but I will pay child support … there's nothing to worry about … so I don't know what she's so freaked out about! Besides, I'm trying to start a new business, and that's where I really have to put my energy, not into this bullshit!" He presented this story in a tone I use too frequently myself—a style of voice common to us White men. It's a tone that suggests a solid belief in the correctness of our singular vision. I have heard Monica McGoldrick describe the voice of White male privilege as the voice of a person who presumes to "hold the truth of the universe within."

Josh believed that the issue he and Susan needed to address was their "communication problem," related mostly to Susan's excessive emotionality and difficulty understanding him with accuracy. He seemed to assume that my role would be to help Susan calm down, listen to reason, and help him "keep his eye on the ball" with his new business.

My hypothesis, however, centered on Josh's decisions to keep Linda's pregnancy a secret from Susan and to invalidate her concerns and responses when she learned about the birth of his daughter. I saw Josh's entitlement and his emotional blindness as connected to our shared socialization into White manhood within this culture. Raising consciousness regarding patterns of socialization, I believe, shifts some life decisions from "inevitable and unavoidable" to the realm of deliberation and choice. For Josh, this would mean an exploration of the cultural and familial processes that convinced him to resign from most emotional connections with other human beings, to disavow his accountability to his woman partner and to his child, and to instead sacrifice his humanity to the ravenous masculine deities of work and financial success.

I began to ask Josh an array of questions designed to spark in him some awareness of how his current dilemma, including his vision of fathering and other relational responsibilities, along with his overall pattern of relational decision making, was connected to White heterosexist male socialization:

> "Where do you imagine you got the idea that it is reasonable for a man to try to 'protect' his woman partner from unpleasant or difficult realities that concern both of them? Would you consider it respectful to 'protect' a male friend or business partner in the same way? What rules within our society contribute to your belief that you have no responsibility at all to 'protect' the mother of your child and that financial support is an adequate contribution to the life of your newborn daughter? How would you imagine your average man would feel and respond if his fiancée concealed the fact of her child's existence? What are we White men taught regarding our primary responsibilities toward our children, and how do you imagine that the teaching women get on this topic is different? How do you imagine this teaching and the pressures connected to it might be different in a family of color, where the prospects for men making big money are more remote due to institutional racism? What do you imagine, from your infant daughter's point of view, are the most important things her father can give her?"

The work included family-of-origin sessions with Josh's parents and couple and individual sessions with his fiancée. After much directed questioning, Josh's father voiced a willingness to support Josh's developing more than a monetary connection with this child if he so desired. The father was also guided toward reevaluating his view of Susan, whom he saw as demanding, childish, and unsupportive of Josh. I wondered whether he would be so negating of his child's partner's life and needs if this were his daughter and her partner was Josh. I also wondered whether he would so readily disavow his new grandchild if it were a grandson instead of a granddaughter. Josh's mother saw these issues in a more balanced way, but her voice was constricted by the presence of three males in her family.

In order to gain a fuller understanding of the relationship while also orienting Susan's attention to the often hidden or taken-for-granted dimensions that form the foundation of heterosexual partnerships, I began to work with the couple by seeing Susan individually for a survey of power and control dimensions. Predictably, she related that Josh demonstrated a number of controlling patterns within the relationship, including characterizing Susan's emotionality as craziness while presenting a void of emotionality himself; regularly intimidating her by using a loud, belligerent voice; and consistently assuming that he would be the one to define shared realities. He demanded that his compartmentalized experience of relationships—a hallmark of male socialization—be the standard. For example, if Susan asked Josh a question about the status of the legal process regarding custody, he might angrily shut her down and then a half hour later feel baffled by Susan's irritability toward him when he invited her out to dinner. He might tell this story, starting with asking her to go out to dinner, as evidence of Susan's bizarre moodiness and unwillingness to "open up to" him. Tying this kind of pattern together for Josh and asking him to take responsibility for his control and intimidation became a part of the work of therapy.

Family therapy based in liberation consciousness rebalances the traditional practice of blaming women through a process of inquiry regarding men's relational patterns and male socialization across multiple systems levels. Steven, a 17-year-old White male of Italian heritage, was brought to see me because of withdrawn behavior at home, punctuated by moments of explosive verbal and sometimes physical outbursts toward his mother (see Figure 22.2). Donna and Al, Steven's parents, both believed that the core problem was between Steven and his mother. Many family therapists would be inclined to agree, hypothesizing perhaps that this "overly involved" mother was "enmeshed" with her son and that his violence toward her was an attempt to gain the space necessary for proper male development.

In my formulation, however, this family's problem (as well as their idea of the problem) reflected the overly responsible role in which heterosexual women are typically cast by the parental irresponsibility of their male partners, as well as the ambivalence with which our society teaches us to view closeness between a mother and a son (and, more particularly, the assumption of authority by a mother over her teenage son). Donna's position as the target of Steven's rage was probably more the result of her acceptance of parental responsibility than it was of anything as pathological as "enmeshment," and both her overresponsibility and Steven's rage and isolation were connected to Al's underresponsibility and distance. My hypothesis was aligned closely with the thinking Olga Silverstein presents in *The Courage*

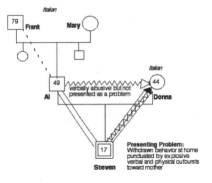

FIGURE 22.2. Steven's family: Expanding, masculinity to include respect for women and emotional connection among men.

to Raise Good Men (Silverstein & Rashbaum, 1994). This book provides an essential reexamination of mother–son relationships within (White) families.

Steven and I talked about what it takes to be respected as a man within high school culture. We talked about how power as physicality and as control over oneself and others is the standard and stoicism and anger are the allowed emotions. We talked about the risks of being labeled a "fag" or a "girl" if a young man's actions differ from these prescriptions. We explored the implications of being labeled "feminine" or "homosexual" (i.e., how females and homosexuals are devalued). From there, we moved into an exploration of how Steven had seen the men in his family deal with conflict. He mentioned his father's abusiveness toward both himself and his mother.

A private conversation with Donna revealed Al's long history of abusiveness. Although he had never been physically violent, Al had regularly abused and intimidated Donna by loudly screaming insults and foul names at her. After these explosive episodes, Al would sometimes not speak to Donna for days. Because Donna assured me that she felt absolutely safe with my revealing the content of our conversation to Al, I opened a dialogue with him about his abusive actions. Al said that he was ready to do "whatever will help my son." In order to make his communication deliberate, comprehensive, and clear, Al was coached on writing a letter to Steven in which he apologized for his emotional abusiveness and distance in a way that claimed full responsibility for his behavior. Within this letter, he acknowledged that his abusive actions toward Steven's mother were the model for Steven's own abusiveness toward her.

The therapy with this family included an exploration of multigenerational legacies. During a meeting with Al and his father, Frank, we discussed how traditional White working-class family structures at the time of Al's childhood had contributed to Frank's absence from his son's life and how norms of male stoicism had contributed to Frank's never acknowledging with his son the losses connected to that distance. We discussed the emotional and functional burden this structure had placed on Al's mother, Mary. Al was helped to see how the needs unmet by his father contributed to his demanding posture within his own marriage. Frank and Al readily agreed when they were encouraged to invite Steven into their conversation by taking him out to dinner and sharing much of what they had discussed.

CONCLUSION

Years of indoctrination into a relatively powerful and relatively blind place within the social order were challenged for me when I entered family therapy training under the supervision of Monica McGoldrick. My experience since then convinces me every day that if we White men are to understand and intervene in a truly respectful and constructive fashion with families, we must engage in training relationships with women, people of color, and people who are gay and lesbian (if one is heterosexual), in which we can experience a strong measure of accountability. Only if this occurs—only if we relinquish center stage and claim wholeheartedly the role of students relative to teachers whose gender, race, and sexual orientation locates them where they experience the impact of White male supremacy—will we remain reasonably conscious of the social realities that structure all of our lives, both publicly and privately. I believe, moreover, that the continuance of these kinds of connections throughout our professional careers is warranted, as the world is only too ready to reappoint those of us who are White and male to the position of unquestioned experts—and we, unfortunately, are too ready to accept these appointments.

REFERENCES

Almedia, R., Dolan-Del Vecchio, K., & Parker, L. (2007). *Transformation Family Therapy: Just families in a just society*. Boston: Pearson, Allyn & Bacon.

American Psychiatric Association. (1994). *Diagnostic and statistical manual of mental disorders* (4th ed.). Washington, DC: Author.

Comas-Díaz, L. (1991). Feminism and diversity in psychology: The case of women of color. *Psychology of Women Quarterly, 15,* 597–609.

Dolan-Del Vecchio, K. (2008). *Making love, playing power: Men, women, and the rewards of intimate justice*. New York: Soft Skull Press.

Dolan-Del Vecchio, K., & Lockard, J. (2004). Resistance to colonialism as the heart of family therapy practice. *Journal of Feminist Family Therapy, 16*(2), 43–66.

Eisler, R. (1987). *The chalice and the blade: Our history, our future*. New York: Harper & Row.

Fuller, N., Jr. (1969). *The united independent compensatory code/system/concept: A textbook/workbook for thought, speech, and/or action for victims of racism (white supremacy)*. Available at *Amazon.com*.

Hall, R. L., & Greene, B. (1994). Cultural competence in feminist family therapy: An ethical mandate. *Journal of Feminist Family Therapy, 6*(3), 5–28.

Hardy, K. V. (1996). The theoretical myth of sameness: A critical issue in family therapy training and treatment. In G. W. Saba, B. M. Karrer, & K.V. Hardy (Eds.), *Minorities and family therapy* (pp. 17–34). Binghamton, NY: Haworth Press.

Hernandez, P., Almeida, R., & Dolan-Del Vecchio, K. (2005). Critical consciousness, accountability, and empowerment: Key processes for helping families heal. *Family Process, 44*(1), 105–119.

Laird, J., & Green, R.-J. (1995). Lesbians and gays in families: The last invisible minority. *Journal of Feminist Family Therapy, 7*(3–4).

Lerner, M. (1995). *The assault on psychotherapy*. Keynote address presented at the Family Therapy Networker Symposium, Washington, DC.

Lorde, A. (1984). *Sister outsider.* Freedom, CA: Crossing Press.

McGoldrick, M. (1987). On reaching mid-career without a wife. *The Family Therapy Networker, 11*(3), 32–39.

McGoldrick, M. (Ed.). (1998). *Re-visioning family therapy: Race, culture, and gender in clinical practice.* New York: Guilford Press.

McGoldrick, M., Anderson, C. M., & Walsh, F. (Eds.). (1991). *Women in families: A framework for family therapy.* New York: Norton.

McIntosh, P. (1988). *White privilege and male privilege: A personal account of coming to see correspondences through work in women's studies* (Working Paper No. 189). Wellesley, MA: Wellesley College Center for Research on Women.

Minuchin, S., Nichols, M. P., & Lee, W.-Y. (2007). *Assessing families and couples: From symptom to system.* Boston: Pearson Allyn & Bacon.

O'Hanlon, B., & Weiner-Davis, M. (2003). *In search of solutions: A new direction in psychotherapy* (Rev. ed.). New York: Norton.

Pewewardy, N. (2004). The political is personal: The essential obligation of white feminist family therapists to deconstruct white privilege. *Journal of Feminist Family Therapy, 16*(1), 53–67.

Silverstein, O., & Rashbaum, B. (1994). *The courage to raise good men.* New York: Penguin Books.

Tamasese, K., & Waldegrave, C. (1993). Cultural and gender accountability in the "just therapy" approach. *Journal of Feminist Family Therapy, 5*(2), 29–45.

CHAPTER 23

Latinas in the United States

Bridging Two Worlds

Nydia Garcia-Preto

They stand on a bridge between two worlds, rejecting and loving, frightened and hopeful, screaming and praying, taking steps back and forth, learning to choose how much to change and how much to stay the same. They are learning to take care of themselves.

Latinas in the United States represent many different countries, races, cultures, and socioeconomic groups. Their adjustment to U.S. society varies, depending on why they come, the support systems they have here, their race, their level of education, and their fluency in English (Garcia-Preto, 2005; Vasquez, 2004). The stage of life they are in when they arrive is very significant, as is the place where they settle. The experience of a 15-year-old *mestiza* who settles in Washington, D.C., with her parents after experiencing the trauma of war in El Salvador will be very different from that of a 34-year-old Black Dominican arriving with her 2-year-old son to live with her 40-year-old cousin who is raising four children by herself in the Bronx. However, regardless of our social location, certain values are transferred down to us if we grow up in homes in which our parents hold some allegiance to their Latin culture. Most of us are caught in cultural paradoxes as we struggle to shape our identities from early in life onward (Comas-Díaz, 2004; Garcia-Preto, 1994; Boyd-Franklin & Garcia-Preto, 2004; Gil & Vazquez, 1996). It is a lifelong process!

The process by which Latinas adapt to mainstream American culture is always in flux, as new immigrants arrive and older generations dream of returning home. For most of us it is a process of selective adaptation, becoming American only to the extent that it feels safe. Sometimes while making our lives here, we lose our language and connection to the land and history that gave our ancestors essence. White skin and European looks, or Black skin and African features, make it easier to pass for "American," but always with a feeling of apprehension—of being found out and seen as impostors, second-class "Americans." Having children with a blond-haired, blue-eyed person of European ancestry may guarantee our children's passing, but it is more likely that the Indian and African genes of our ancestors will make our children beautifully tanned, almond-eyed Latinos. It is through our children's search for identity that we often find our roots and revel in the glory of our history, the pride of our people.

This chapter is about Latinas as we find our place in the United States, make our lives, and live our dreams. Walking a tightrope, balancing at the edge of a cliff, we often live between two worlds. I do not want to disregard the importance of men in our lives, but my focus here will be on stories about mothers and daughters—distant and close, rejecting and loving, learning from each other to fight, to dream, and to die—that portray our struggles, pain, and liberation as we move through the life cycle negotiating cultural conflicts at different stages. Some of us hold on tightly to our Latin roots, afraid that if we step into the "American" world, we will fall into a precipice and lose ourselves. Others leap into the new world, rejecting the past and hoping to find a better place with more options. The therapeutic interventions I offer are intended to help Latinas build bridges that connect the two worlds and to provide a safe place from which to choose what to keep from the old culture and what to take from the new. They provide perspective about the sociopolitical context in which Latinas live and the ways in which prejudice and racism affect their lives. The goal is to encourage transformation and liberation of the spirit by validating personal strengths, maintaining family connections, and creating a sense of community and support.

GOOD LITTLE GIRLS

Traditionally Latinas have been raised primarily by their mothers, with the help of other women in the family, to be respectful and to behave in ways that are considered feminine. The expectation has been to raise "good little girls" who grow up to be "good women." In this country, where Latinas are often without the support of other women in their families, meeting this expectation can be difficult.

When I work with Latinas, I often hear them scream and yell at their daughters, "Stop acting like a boy. Don't climb on the couch like that—sit down with your legs crossed. Now, be respectful to *la señora* when she speaks to you. Don't interrupt until she speaks to you." It all sounds so familiar. I remember being punished as a little girl for climbing trees and acting like a tomboy and not being able to talk back to my mother because that was disrespectful. I have said to myself, and have heard other Latinas say, "I'm not raising my daughter that way." I don't want my daughter to worry about *el que diran* (what people will say). Yet there is a part of me that is taken aback by the strong emotions my daughter expresses and worry that people might view her as loud, aggressive, and competitive, qualities that do not fit the "good little girl" picture. In my office, I gently put a stop to the mothers' yelling and screaming and begin to address the care and love that mothers and daughters feel for each other.

Parents usually tend to place more restrictions on Latinas as they get older, and sometimes the limits and expectations they impose may seem unreasonable to teachers and counselors at school. For example, 10-year-old Estela was referred to me by a school counselor because she kept complaining bitterly to her teachers that her parents refused to let her play sports and about the strict rules at home. My first meeting was with Estela and her mother, because her father was unable to attend the session. As I engaged them, it became clear that Dolores, a 34-year-old Colombian, was trying very hard to raise her daughter in the best way she knew. As most Latinas do, she had the primary caretaking responsibility for her children and was accountable to her husband for Estela's behavior. Antonio, a 36-year-old Ecuadorian, was strict and did not like Estela to go out of the house after school. After clarifying with them why the school had made the referral to me, I asked Dolores for permission to encourage Estela to talk about her unhappiness.

We listened to Estela's complaints about not being allowed to play sports or visit friends after school, and then Dolores explained that she didn't think playing sports was feminine and that she worried that her daughter would get hurt. She and Antonio wanted Estela to grow up to be a good, respectable young woman and thought that girls who played sports were rough and wild. I asked Dolores if she had ever been to the after-school games or seen her daughter play. She hadn't. I told her that from what I have seen in this country, girls who play sports are usually good students and develop positive attitudes about themselves that keep them from getting into trouble. I suggested that if she and her husband met with the teacher and counselor who referred them to me, they could all develop a better understanding of each other's concerns about Estela. I added that it would also give the parents a chance to ask questions about the sports program for girls. Apparently Estela had athletic talent, and the gym teacher was encouraging her to play and develop those skills. I offered to help arrange the meeting if they chose to do it.

Encouraging Dolores to ask Estela questions about why she liked playing sports, and which sport she liked better began to make it easier for mother and daughter to talk to each other. I could see the proud smile on Dolores's face as she listened to her daughter's enthusiasm when she spoke about basketball and softball. Not only were they able to talk about sports, but also the conversation expanded to friends, family, and different perceptions about how girls should act. The meeting with the teacher and counselor did take place; although Antonio was not able to attend, Dolores, with my help, asked questions about the sports program and was proud when she heard about Estela's athletic skills. The teacher and counselor also told her that usually girls who play sports stay out of trouble, because they have less time to hang around and get bored. The meeting at school, my introducing information about girls and sports in U.S. culture, and my facilitation of conversations between mother and daughter about their differences had the effect of transforming for Dolores the meaning of "good girl." A new dimension was added, which included some of the values that mainstream American culture offer to women. Estela was able to find a place for herself, while still remaining respectful of and close to her parents, which for Latinas is a source of validation and security.

WHERE HAVE ALL THE VIRGINS GONE?

Most Latinas go into high gear to guard their daughters' virginity, especially as they reach adolescence. It is as if we hear a call to respond to an ancient cultural myth about women and virginity that ensures women safe futures in the hands of honorable men, but only if they are virgins. This myth emanates from the double standard about gender roles in patriarchal societies (such as those in Latin America and in the Caribbean), which limits the sexual freedom of women and gives men authority over them (Stevens, 1973; Comas-Díaz, 1991; Garcia-Preto, 2005; Gil & Vazquez, 1996). It is also reinforced by the Catholic religion. Although the double standard also applies to women in the United States, they tend to experience greater sexual freedom than Latinas do in their countries of origin. The difference often creates cultural dilemmas for Latinas living in this country, especially during adolescence, and at a time in history when adolescents seem to be engaging in sex earlier and earlier. A study by Grunbaum et al. (2001) found that in the United States, by the time adolescents reach the 10th grade, 45.6% of students have had sex. And, although there is a strong cultural component to parental fears about their daughters becoming pregnant, in 2000 Latinas in this country had the highest birth rate (94 per 1,000 women ages 15 to 19).

By comparison the teen birth rate among African Americans was 79; among Native Americans 68; among non-Hispanic Whites, 33; and among Asian Americans, 22 (Ventura, Mosher, Curtin, Abma, & Henshaw, 2001).

Generally in the United States, adolescent girls are given freedom to go out with girlfriends, sleep at their houses, talk with boys, and go on dates without chaperones. In contrast, in Latin American cultures, girls tend to be supervised more closely when they go out with friends; dating does not take place until much later; and it is not unusual for siblings or adult relatives to be present on dates. The responsibility for protecting a girl's virginity and keeping her reputation unmarred falls primarily on mothers. The extent to which Latino families hold on to these values in their countries of origin depends on their level of education, their social status, and whether they lived in rural or urban areas. In this country these values are affected also by the length of time families have lived here, the place in which they settle, and socioeconomic factors. The greater the cultural gap between families and the new culture, the more likely it is for conflicts to erupt between mothers and daughters during adolescence over the issue of virginity, as children tend to adapt faster than parents to a new culture. The case of Magda, a 15-year-old, brown-skinned Salvadoran who had recently arrived in this country with her parents, illustrates this point.

Magda was referred to therapy by a bilingual social worker who ran groups at school for recently arrived Latino students. After one of the group meetings, Magda spoke to the social worker about the problems she was having at home. She was feeling trapped and frightened and was thinking of hurting herself. She had lied to her mother by telling her she was going out with a girlfriend but instead had gone to meet her boyfriend. When her mother found out, she restricted Magda from going out of the house or speaking to friends on the telephone, and she threatened to send Magda back to El Salvador with an uncle if she broke these rules. Magda felt that the punishment was extreme and unfair and was angry with her mother.

Magda came to the first appointment with her mother, Rosaura, who was feeling angry, betrayed, and unable to trust her daughter, whose future she thought would be ruined unless she supervised all her outings. She worried about drugs and crime, but her worst fear was that Magda would end up as she herself had done—pregnant and "having to get married." Rosaura's parents were very strict, but, like Magda, she had sneaked out to meet a boy—Miguel, her future husband. Her parents had not approved of him or his family and had not allowed him to come to the house, but when she became pregnant at 16 they had made her get married. Rosaura was in love and wanted the baby, but as they struggled with poverty and lived through the war in their country, Miguel began to drink heavily and to distance himself emotionally. She wanted Magda to have a different life, which was why she had pushed to come to this country, in hope of a better future.

As she talked about her past in therapy, Rosaura stated clearly that she did not want to repeat the mistakes her parents had made. She had tried to compromise by allowing the boy to visit Magda at home, even though she felt uneasy about not knowing his family. However, he could visit only when she was present, and Magda could not go out with him unless she had a chaperone. Magda understood that her mother was trying to meet her halfway, but she was embarrassed to tell the boy. Many of the Latinas she had met at school had been in this country longer and were allowed to go out with boys without chaperones. She envied their freedom and felt embarrassed by her mother's rules. As treatment progressed, Rosaura began to see more clearly that regardless of how hard she tried to protect Magda's virginity, her daughter was in control of her own sexuality. Instead of repeating her parents' mistakes by imposing rules that she herself had broken, she began to use her life experience as a resource to teach Magda how to value herself as a woman. We talked about the fallacy in the "virginity myth" and agreed that in reality women cannot rely on men to "take care of them."

Choosing what to keep from their old culture and what to take from the new culture became a therapeutic theme. Magda began to appreciate her mother's strengths as a woman, as she listened to Rosaura talk about her present goals with regard to Miguel, who had become more and more peripheral in their lives. His drinking had continued to increase in this country, where he felt alienated and powerless. He blamed Rosaura for pushing him to come here and was verbally abusive toward both her and Magda. Rosaura was considering a separation, but she needed financial stability before making a decision. We dealt with issues of safety at home and debated possible strategies for getting Miguel into treatment.

Listening to Rosaura speak about possible options for her own life encouraged Magda to talk about her concerns, dreams, and goals for the future. Whereas guarding Magda's virginity had formerly been Rosaura's main goal as a mother, in therapy she became her daughter's ally, planning together for a future in which they could both be independent. Introducing information—such as the fact that many young Latinas in the United States are at risk for unintended pregnancy and sexually transmitted infections, including HIV, because of the challenges posed by changing cultural norms, discrimination, poverty, and limited access to health care (Villarruel, 1998)—served to give some validity to Rosaura's fear and to put it in context. They could be loyal and respectful toward each other without losing the emotional connection that gave them strength or feeling bound by the patriarchal legacies that keep women obedient and dependent on men and that sexualize their sense of self-worth. Virgins and martyrs go hand in hand in Latino cultures, and their glorification perpetuates male dominance and female oppression (Vega & Filippi, 1988).

WALKING A FINE LINE: LATINAS LIVING INDEPENDENTLY

Traditionally, most Latinas have been expected to live with their parents until they marry and to leave home only as brides dressed in white. Going away to college may be another acceptable way to leave home, but usually they are encouraged to go to school close to home. Moving out to live alone in an apartment is hard to explain to relatives, friends, and neighbors and puts a woman's reputation at risk. Having a good reputation has been necessary for a woman to have a good marriage and to be acknowledged in the community as a *doña* (a woman who is deserving of respect). Sex before marriage, especially with more than one man; expressing pleasure about having sex; or living alone places women precariously on the edge of losing their good reputations and being labeled as *putas* (whores). For Latinas the cultural message has been that sex is for procreation, not for pleasure. The line between *putas* and *doñas* is very fine (Stevens, 1973; Espin, 2004; Garcia-Preto, 1990; Gil & Vazquez, 1996).

Claudia, a 24-year-old Cuban, came into treatment at the suggestion of her friend Cristina, a 27-year-old Argentinian I had previously seen in therapy. Claudia worked as a store clerk and lived at home with her parents. Recently she had begun to experience anxiety attacks and was having difficulty leaving the house to go to work or to go out with friends. Cristina thought that the problems Claudia was having at home were probably the cause. While I was taking a genogram (McGoldrick, Petry, & Gerson, 2007) and asking about the situation at home, Claudia said:

> "I don't mind living at home. My parents don't stop me from going out, and I can't afford to live alone. Anyway, I would be too scared to live by myself, and my parents' fear would be so great that they would die from a heart attack! They are constantly worrying and advising me about friends and the men I meet. Cristina lives with another friend and would like me to join them, but my parents don't approve of her because she goes out with all kinds of men, and people talk."

Finding the right man had become a primary goal for Claudia, who felt that the only way she could leave home was through marriage. Her parents' approval was very important, and the man's acceptance of her obligation toward them was essential. Her parents had come to the United States in the 1970s and had problems adjusting and making a living. Now in their early 60s, they were thinking about retirement. They still held on to many of the traditional values that were part of their culture and expected Claudia to be respectful and loyal; they were protective of her reputation. She was the youngest of three children and the only daughter. The two older brothers were married and living busy lives with their families in nearby towns, which kept them less involved with their parents. Their absence increased Claudia's sense of obligation toward her parents, fitting with the cultural expectation in Latino families that women are the caretakers. It is not uncommon for Latinas who assume or are assigned this type of caretaking role to remain single (Hines, Garcia-Preto, McGoldrick, Almeida, & Weltman, 1992).

In therapy, Claudia began to define more clearly her own values, attitudes, and beliefs about life, people, relationships, and sexuality. She spoke about her personal dreams and ambitions and recognized that in order to feel freer to make decisions about her life, she needed to have greater financial independence. Her anxiety lessened, and with Cristina's help she enrolled in some college courses, which helped her gain confidence. The clearer she became about her personal goals, the less bound she felt by cultural expectations that limited her potential. For instance, she realized that she could be close to her parents and show them respect without losing her individuality or choice to exercise her rights as an adult woman. She felt more entitled to spend weekends away from home with friends and to keep some of her relationships with men private without feeling that she was being disloyal to her parents. The parents' fears didn't go away, but because Claudia felt more competent and confident herself, she was less frightened about moving on with her life. Unlike Cristina, who loved the freedom and anonymity she had in this country, Claudia had ties to the Latino community and wanted to keep these connections. She still wanted to share her life with a good man and to have her own family; however, she realized that making these the primary goals in her life had placed her in a powerless and helpless position, with little option for making decisions that promoted her well-being.

BREAKING ALL THE RULES: LATINA LESBIANS

Latinas who "come out" as lesbians break all the rules. They are openly challenging a culture in which women have limited options, especially if they don't marry a man and have children. They struggle against beliefs that link women's femininity to the Virgin Mary, mother of God. To want a woman and to make love to a woman mean assuming a position of power in a culture in which men dominate and are free to express their sexuality in ways for which women would be condemned. Latina lesbians are perceived not only as rejecting the essence of being female but also as usurping male power; thus they are a double threat to the culture.

When Ana, a 26-year-old Puerto Rican lawyer who was a closeted lesbian, spoke in therapy about her terror of coming out to her mother, I understood the spiritual desolation a Latina can feel for breaking the rules her mother lives by.

"Just the thought of telling my mother that I'm a lesbian makes me panic. She wouldn't be able to deal with it at all. I would lose my family. My mother believes that homosexuality is a sin, and it would kill her to know that I am choosing this lifestyle. One of my sisters knows, but she thinks that if the right man came along I would get over it. I want to move in with Vicky and not have to lie about our relationship to my family, but the fear of losing them is paralyzing. Sometimes I think God is punishing me."

Ana anticipated that her mother would be shocked, devastated, and furious at her for bringing dishonor to the family. She could hear her mother say, "How can you be so disrespectful to dare tell me such a thing? You were put on this earth to be a woman, to have children, to be a good mother and wife. You are going against God. How dare you disgrace this family?" The fear of both losing her family and of being punished by God kept her in the closet.

For Latinas, being lesbian means that they go against two moral prohibitions that the culture imposes, especially on women: sexuality and homosexuality. They fear rejection by their mothers, the culture, and the community, often hiding and denying who they are while feeling damaged and unacceptable (Anzaldua, 2007). I could hear Ana's fear and sadness as she envisioned her mother's horror; I was reminded of how, 37 years after her death, I still catch myself imagining the dismay of my dead mother's spirit at how I live my own life. I used the metaphor of the bridge to help Ana find a way to stay connected to her mother in Puerto Rico and the parts of the Latino world that still nurtured her, while also validating her life in this world. I was exhilarated when Ana was able to write a letter in which she came out to her mother, while also expressing her love and inviting her mother to visit. Although there was fear in her eyes, there was also the glow of liberation.

Cherrie Moraga, in her book *The Last Generation* (1993), talks about the active role that lesbians have played in the area of Chicana liberation (e.g., their work on sexual abuse, domestic violence, immigrant rights, indigenous women's issues, health care, etc.). Because of the marginalization and rejection that they often experience in both their families and their culture, lesbians are in a special position to address areas that need change in both contexts. Chicana lesbian writers such as Moraga and Anzaldua (Anzaldua, 2007; Anzaldua & Moraga, 2002; Moraga, 1993) have been among the first to explore how homophobia, gender roles, and sexuality are learned and expressed in Chicano culture. They have been pioneers in establishing a Chicana feminist perspective, which has influenced not only lesbians but also heterosexual women who have been socialized in Latin American cultures. Their poetry and prose have given voice to the struggles that many

Latina lesbians face when they try to integrate cultural values into their lives that deny their being. I have found sharing their work with lesbian clients helpful in promoting transformation and liberation in their lives.

MOTHERHOOD

Motherhood is probably the most important goal in life for Latinas, and the acclaim they receive when their first child is born is a great reinforcer, especially if the baby is a boy. Motherhood has been romanticized in Latino literature and music, and the associations made between mothers and the Virgin Mary has an explicitly religious quality. Having children both raises the status of women in society and is a rite of passage into adulthood, which confirms both the masculinity of the father and the femininity of the mother (Garcia-Preto, 1990; Gil & Vazquez, 1996). Becoming a mother, however, also implies that a woman must sacrifice herself for the children. This emphasis on motherhood and self-sacrifice creates dilemmas for women who cannot have children, who choose not to have them, whose children are taken away, or who have them but also work and have lives outside the home. Can they be respected and valued as women by their families and friends if they do not have children? And what price do they pay if they do have children but must take jobs in order to survive?

Working outside the home is a necessity for many Latinas in this country, but it forces them to fulfill conflicting role expectations. According to official statistics, in 2004, 55.6% of Hispanic women in the United States were employed (U.S. Census Bureau, 2004). Not being able to stay home to raise and protect their children places such women in a dilemma, especially when other women in the extended family are unable to offer support with child care. Mutual aid in the extended family has been a cultural pattern that provides support and flexibility for women, but for Latinas in this country it may not be an option. Often they have no female relatives here, and if they do, the other women may be too overwhelmed themselves to provide support. According to the culture, a good mother does not put her children at risk by leaving them with "strangers" (i.e., anyone outside the family). When confronted with conflicting role expectations, they are likely to choose their role as mothers, even when it causes problems for them at work.

Celia, a 34-year-old Dominican "Lati-Negra" (Comas-Díaz, 1994), was referred to therapy by an employee assistance program counselor. She worked at a factory, and her frequent absences from work had become a problem. Even when she did make it to work, she seemed preoccupied; her level of productivity had diminished to the extent that she was on the verge of losing her job. Celia had recently arrived with her 2-year-old son to live with a cousin. Unmarried, poor, and with little education, she came to the United States looking for a better life and future. Once here, however, she had to experience not only the shock of a new culture and language but also the prejudice and racism of a society that rejects Blacks.

Her 40-year-old cousin, Mercedes, had come to this country almost 20 years ago, shortly after her marriage; she was now divorced and struggling financially to raise four children on her own in a neighborhood plagued with crime, drugs, prostitution, and AIDS. She provided Celia with a place to stay and helped her find a factory job. However, because she was emotionally drained by her children's various problems, she had quickly felt the burden of two more people depending on her. Celia had started to work, and Mercedes was temporarily taking care of her son, but she knew that she needed to find a place to live and permanent child care. Her anxiety had escalated with the pressure of knowing that she would have to "fly solo" (Anderson, Dimidjian, & Stewart, 1995) in this new world sooner than she had expected.

In therapy, Celia talked about feeling guilty and fearful whenever she left her son. She wanted to be a good mother, and the thought of leaving him with strangers or in a day-care center frightened her. Even now that Mercedes was caring for him, she found leaving him intolerable, a feeling that was exacerbated by her son's fearful crying whenever she went to work. However, she needed to work in order to make a life in this country, and missing work to stay home with him was jeopardizing her job. She was regretting her decision to come to this country and considered the possibility of returning or of sending her son to Santo Domingo to stay with her mother. Framing her son's behavior as a normal reaction to separation at that stage of child development reduced some of her fear and guilt. Feeling less anxious about leaving her son, she began to look for child care; through a woman at work, she learned about a day-care center in the neighborhood where other Latinas took their children.

Taking her son to the day-care center helped Celia to connect with other women and to feel less isolated and dependent on Mercedes. Initially, she had expected from her cousin the type of support that Latinas have traditionally provided for each other in their extended families, and she felt resentful and disappointed when Mercedes began to set limits. Inviting Mercedes to a therapy session helped strengthen their connection as they reviewed their family history in the Dominican Republic, their failed relationships with men, and their reasons for migrating. They laughed and cried while telling family stories, especially those that Mercedes remembered about Celia's childhood. Listening to her cousin speak about the problems she was having with her 18-year-old son, who lived at home and was addicted to heroin, and with her 16-year-old daughter, who had just returned home pregnant after running away with an abusive, alcoholic 20-year-old man, helped Celia understand why Mercedes needed to set limits.

Framing Celia's problems within a social context that is racist and prejudiced against Latinas, especially when their skin color is dark, helped her put into words some of the feelings of oppression she was experiencing at work. She had felt the looks, and even though she didn't understand English, people's tone and attitude when they spoke to her felt demeaning. Although Mercedes was trying to sponsor her, she was not yet a legal resident; this fact added to Celia's anxiety, especially at work, but also whenever she had to seek medical care for herself or her son. Through our discussion, she stopped feeling personally responsible for the racist attitudes of people at work. Encouraging Celia to expand her network of connections helped her to learn about safe places where she could go for health care and to find information about getting her immigration papers in order. As she got more in touch with her strengths, her work performance improved, and she was able to offer more support to Mercedes, who no longer experienced her as a burden. She felt less pressured to move out right away and less anxious about her son, who seemed to be adjusting well at the day-care center. Although she still missed him, she no longer felt neglectful when she went to work. Instead, she felt that she was being a good mother by earning enough money to pay for good child care and to save for their own place. Motherhood continued to be the most important role for Celia, but it was no longer her only goal or identity. Taking care of herself and taking charge of her life became goals that enabled her to be both a responsible woman and a caring mother.

ANSWERING THE CALL: LATINAS CARING FOR RELATIVES

Answering the call to take care of old, poor, or frail parents or other relatives is deeply rooted in the soul and imprinted in the heart of Latinas; it is another rite of passage that defines womanhood. Not being able to meet that obligation stirs up incredible guilt for most of us and raises questions about our womanhood. My mother died at 48, and I, as the oldest granddaughter, felt the responsibility of taking care of her mother, who lived until she was 93. The problem was that she lived in Puerto Rico and I in the United States, and changing residence for either one of us would have been impossible. For some of her neighbors and relatives, however, the solution was clear: I should move back to the island. My grandmother had come to live with us in the States when my mother was still alive, and it had not worked. She didn't like the winters or the isolation of living in the suburbs. My mother couldn't stand the constant complaints and felt criticized. Fed up with their arguing, and feeling called on to serve as a mediator, I couldn't wait to go far enough away to graduate school that commuting wouldn't be an option. To my parents, leaving home to go to college was an acceptable alternative to leaving home as a bride dressed in white.

Grandmother—fragile in health but strong in spirit—decided to return to the island, where she could keep the doors and windows open for neighbors to stop and chat and could walk to the corner store without asking someone to go and talk for her because she didn't know the language. Sad and feeling like a failure, my mother worried about her mother's health but understood that not everyone can adjust to living in this country (where neighbors stay in their homes, barely saying hello as they climb in and out of their cars or do their chores in the yard). Shortly after this my mother died. It was now my turn to worry about my grandmother and to feel disloyal whenever I would get a call from a relative to come visit because her health was declining. She held on for 10 years after my mother's death, and I traveled back and forth to the island—always feeling shame in my heart that I wasn't meeting my obligation but knowing in my mind that I was doing as much as I could and still live my life.

CONCLUSION

Cultures do not remain static; they are always in flux. For us Latinas in the United States, a new reality evolves as we integrate two cultures. My personal knowledge of what it means to live between two worlds is a major part of what I offer Latina clients. It is what enables them to trust me with their struggles and to look to me for guidance. Even after living here for decades, some Latinas and Latinos are still struggling with cultural shock. My job is to help them understand, often for the first time, the cultural journey they are still embarked on. What I offer beyond my skill as a therapist, my sociopolitical awareness, and my own experience of immigration is my optimism. Although it is never easy, I know it is possible to shuttle between these two worlds. I am able to share the metaphor of the bridge as a safe place to understand the world in which they grew up and the possibilities of the new world they have entered. When I help people construct the bridges they need for this journey between cultures, my own bridge becomes sturdier and wider (Garcia-Preto, 1994).

REFERENCES

Anderson, C., Dimidjian, S., & Stewart, S. (1995). *Flying solo*. New York: Norton.
Anzaldua, G. (2007). *Borderlands*, la frontera: *The new* Mestiza. San Francisco: Aunt Lute.

Anzaldua, G., & Moraga, C. (Eds.). (2002). *This bridge called my back: Writings by radical women of color.* New York: Kitchen Table—Women of Color Press.

Boyd-Franklin, N., & Garcia-Preto, N. (2004). Family therapy: The case of African American and Hispanic women. In L. Comas-Díaz & B. Greene (Eds.), *Women of color: Integrating ethnic and gender identities in psychotherapy* (pp. 239–286). New York: Guilford Press.

Comas-Díaz, L. (1991). Feminism and diversity in psychology: The case of women of color. *Psychology of Women Quarterly, 15,* 597–609.

Comas-Díaz, L. (1994). Lati-Negra. *Journal of Feminist Family Therapy, 5*(3–4), 35–74.

Comas-Díaz, L. (2004). Integrative approach. In L. Comas-Díaz & B. Greene (Eds.), *Women of color: Integrating ethnic and gender identities in psychotherapy* (pp. 287–318). New York: Guilford Press.

Espin, O. M. (2004). Feminist approaches. In L. Comas-Díaz & B. Greene (Eds.), *Women of color: Integrating ethnic and gender identities in psychotherapy* (pp. 265–286). New York: Guilford Press.

Garcia-Preto, N. (1990). Hispanic *mothers. Journal of Feminist Family Therapy, 2*(2), 15–21.

Garcia-Preto, N. (1994). On the bridge. *Family Therapy Networker, 18*(4), 35–37.

Garcia-Preto, N. (2005). Latinos: An overview. In M. McGoldrick, J. Giordano, & J. K. Pearce (Eds.), *Ethnicity and family therapy* (2nd ed., pp. 141–154). New York: Guilford Press.

Gil, R. M., & Vazquez, C. I. (1996). *The Maria paradox.* New York: Putnam.

Grunbaum, J. A., Kann, L., & Kitchen, S. A. (2002) . Youth risk behavior surveillance— United States, 2001. Morbidity and Mortality Weekly Report Surveillance Summaries, 51(SS–40), 1–64.

Hines, P. M., Garcia-Preto, N., McGoldrick, M., Almeida, R., & Weltman, S. (1992). Intergenerational relationships across cultures. *Families in Society: The Journal of Contemporary Human Services, 23,* 323–328.

McGoldrick, M., Petry, S., & Gerson, R. (2007). *Genograms in family assessment.* New York: Norton.

Moraga, C. (1993). *The last generation: Prose and poetry.* Boston: South End Press.

Stevens, E. D. (1973). *Marianismo:* The other face *of Machismo* in Latin America. In A. De Castello (Ed.), *Female and male in Latin America* (pp. 90–101). Pittsburgh, PA: University of Pittsburgh Press.

U.S. Census Bureau. (2004, March). *Current Population Survey: The Hispanic population in the United States [Data tables].* Washington, DC: Author.

Vasquez, M. J. T. (2004). Latinas. In L. Comas-Díaz & B. Greene (Eds.), *Women of color: Integrating ethnic and gender identities in psychotherapy* (pp. 114–160). New York: Guilford Press.

Vega, A. L., & Filippi, C. L. (1988). *Virgenes y martires.* Rio Piedras, Puerto Rico: Editorial Antillana.

Ventura, S. J., Mosher, W. D., Curtin, S. C., Abma, J. C., & Henshaw, S. (2001). Trends in pregnancy rates for the United States, 1976–97: An update. *National Vital Statistics Reports 2001, 49*(4), 1–9.

Villarruel, A. M. (1998). Cultural influences on the sexual attitudes, beliefs and norms of young Latina adolescents. *Journal of the Society of Pediatric Nurses, 8*(3), 69–81.

CHAPTER 24

Therapy with Mixed-Race Families

Tracey A. Laszloffy

The system of power in the United States depends on the notion that human beings can be discretely placed within mutually distinctive racial groups. Access to social power, resources, and opportunities is distributed on the basis of these groups. Hence maintaining the "separation" of races is essential to preserving this system of power. If the boundaries that define racial groups were to become blurred and ambiguous, it would become increasingly difficult and eventually impossible to discern who belonged to the dominant and who belonged to the subjugated groups. Hence interracial relationships and mixed-race people pose a threat to the boundaries that divide the dominant group from subjugated groups (Nakashima, 1992).

In the United States, the threat posed by "mixing" between members of socially distinct racial groups has resulted in strict social and legal prohibitions designed to discourage and even punish interracial unions and to deny and devalue mixed-race people. For example, the *law of hypodescendence* tries to deny the existence of mixed-race identity by forcibly assigning those with mixed-race parentage to the racial group of the parent with the least racial social status (Davis, 1991). Similarly, the *one-drop rule* (Davis, 1991) denies mixed-race heritage by asserting that anyone with even a drop of Black blood was to identify as Black. In those instances in which mixed-race identity has been recognized, it almost always has been in the most devaluing manner. The stereotype of the tragic mulatto who is maladjusted, confused, and inferior has been prominent for centuries. Consequently, mixed-race people have been the marginal among the marginal throughout U.S. history.

Luckily, the tides have started to shift. The 1967 Supreme Court decision that banned antimiscegenation laws as unconstitutional paved the way for significant changes in society's attitudes toward and treatment of interracial couples and mixed-race people (Root, 1996). In every decade since 1970 the number of interracial marriages has doubled, and the mixed-race birthrate has quadrupled (Eddings, 1997). Although these shifts in social climate are significant, nonetheless we continue to live in a society that clings to the notion that monoracial groups exist and that seeks to preserve the boundaries that have been constructed to divide people racially. It is within this context that mixed-race families must find ways to value and affirm themselves and that mixed-race people must understand, define, assert, and continuously negotiate their racial identity.

RE-VISIONING THERAPY WITH MIXED-RACE FAMILIES[1]

Within family therapy, the body of knowledge devoted to addressing issues of race in general and the specific needs of mixed-race families is limited. A vital aspect of re-visioning family therapy with mixed-race families must focus on therapists' developing a requisite level of knowledge, skill, and comfort with regard to racial issues. Although marriage and family therapy training programs are required to address race in the curriculum, a wide gap often exists between meeting the minimal standards and actually helping students acquire the awareness and sensitivity necessary to effectively address race-related issues in therapy. Consequently, therapists—White therapists in particular—often lack sufficient racial awareness and sensitivity, thereby compromising their ability to accurately identify and work with race in therapy.

Most clinical training problems adequately promote awareness, but it is much more challenging to also promote sensitivity. And yet those therapists who are best prepared to address racial issues in therapy are those who possess both. In the spirit of re-visioning family therapy with mixed-race families, salient attention must be focused on helping therapists to develop both racial awareness and sensitivity. For a more comprehensive discussion of how to accomplish this, the reader is referred to Hardy and Laszloffy (1992, 1998) and Laszloffy and Hardy (2000).

DILEMMAS AND CHALLENGES
FACING MIXED-RACE FAMILIES

Mixed-race families experience all of the same crises and stressors as those who are monorace, plus all of the unique dilemmas and challenges associated with living in a racially polarized and divisive society. Perhaps the most basic issue that mixed-race people grapple with is how to identify racially and how to manage the myriad dynamics and dilemmas associated with racial identification. Because no legitimate social space exists in the United States with regard to mixed-race identity, individuals must either deny their mixed racial roots by identifying with only a single race or create an identity that is not recognized or validated by the broader society. Hence the quintessential quandary facing mixed-race people revolves around identity issues, namely, having to choose between denying their multiracial heritage or facing the devaluation that comes from claiming it.

Family Dynamics and Children's Racial Identity Development

The challenges of trying to define and assert a clear racial identity as a mixed-race person are often exacerbated by family dynamics that complicate how children think and feel about themselves racially. Because of the emotional weight that family relationships carry and because parents and families are the primary socializing force in children's lives, their influence on children's racial identity development cannot be overstated (Gibbs, Gibbs, & Nahme, 1998). There are three dynamics in particular that can undermine or compromise children's racial identity development in mixed-race families.

Messages Sent about Race

Parents and other family members communicate numerous messages to children about race and the various racial groups that constitute their heritage. Inevitably, racial identity development is influenced by these messages. Of particular importance is children's exposure to negative or devaluing messages about any of the groups that they have membership in, because this compromises their ability to embrace and successfully integrate these aspects of themselves into their self-concept. Even more challenging than receiving consistently devaluing messages is receiving mixed messages about race from parents and families. Contradictory messages are confusing for children because it is unclear which messages they should follow. Often, parents send an explicit message to their children that all races are equal, while simultaneously behaving in ways that communicate a contradictory implicit message that some racial groups are more valuable than others. When this occurs, children are left with the daunting task of having to discern which message to follow.

There are different ways in which parents and other family members can convey racial messages. The most obvious is through the comments they make. Racial messages also are conveyed through lifestyle choices. Where parents choose to live, who they socialize with, where they work, and what they do for entertainment all communicate messages about race. Finally, racial messages are conveyed by the level of comfort that adults manifest around people of different races. The extent to which parents and other family members manifest either a sense of comfort, ease, and openness or a sense of awkwardness, anxiety, or irritation toward members of a particular racial group sends specific messages about race that influence children's racial identity development.

Parental Racial Loyalty Binds

When parents have destructive conflict, it creates the perception that sides must be taken, and children often get trapped in loyalty binds. Although loyalty binds occur in many families and are tied to a broad range of issues, within mixed-race families, there is a potential for loyalty binds to become racialized, either explicitly or implicitly, and this can affect children's racial identity development.

> Sue is Filipino and Jason is African American. They divorced when their daughter, Millie, was 10 and their son, Jon, was 8. Their divorce was highly conflictual and bitter, and both parents often spoke negatively of the other in front of their children. In therapy, both children expressed tension and anxiety, feeling torn between their parents. They each made it clear they loved their parents and were worried about the repercussions of doing anything that either parent would perceive as taking the other's side.
>
> To complicate matters, the loyalty bind the children were trapped in also had racial dimensions, because each parent construed the children's racial identification as a loyalty issue. For example, Millie told the therapist that on one occasion her mother became angry when she heard her listening to rap music. Sue perceived Millie's behavior as evidence that she was racially identifying with her Blackness and therefore with her father, which she saw as disloyal to her.
>
> Similarly, Millie told her therapist how her father had become irritable with her when she confessed to him that she wanted to learn more about Filipino culture. His response suggested that he saw his daughter's interest as an expression of alignment with her mother and hence as being disloyal to him. In this family, as is so common, the children were trapped between their parents' conflicts, fearful of doing anything that the other would perceive as disloyalty. Moreover, these loyalty conflicts had become racialized. As a result, the loyalty bind the children were caught in was affecting their freedom to explore and embrace their respective racial heritages. This case illustrates how racial loyalty conflicts in mixed-race families can complicate children's process of racial identification.

External Racism

Because race is always an issue in society, all mixed-race families encounter racism to some degree. Especially when children reach school age, interactions with teachers and other children increase the probability that they will encounter racism. Depending on the specific nature of an incident, encounters with racism can stimulate feelings of confusion, anger, anxiety, uncertainty, shame, and conflict. Although it is important for parents and families to take an active role in preparing children to face and manage inevitable encounters with racism, not all families are poised to do so. Some families are buried in denial about the realities of racism, preferring to live under the premise that the world is how they want it to be, rather than accepting how the world really is. Other families recognize the presence of racism but lack the skills or comfort to address it directly, hence they, too, lean toward avoiding the topic altogether. Unfortunately, not addressing the realties of racism is unhelpful for children. Because racism is an unavoidable part of life in the United States, parents and families have a responsibility to educate and prepare children for what lies in the world beyond their front door.

One factor that tends to compromise how well parents are able to prepare their children to expect, understand, and manage encounters with racism is one of the parents being White. This is especially likely to be the case if parents are no longer a couple and the White parent has primary custody. Most White people have a limited practical understanding of racism. The ultimate privilege of Whiteness is not having to be aware of one's Whiteness or aware of the benefits it affords (McIntosh, 1998). Conversely, most people of color cannot escape being aware of their racial identities or the many biases and barriers associated with who they are racially. Because of the differential experiences and perceptions of the world that are rooted in different racial locations, it is not uncommon within mixed-race families with one White parent for that parent to struggle with understanding their children's racial experience. Additionally, because White parents are less likely to possess the experience, knowledge, and skills to manage encounters with racism, they are less likely to know how to offer support and guidance to their children. This limitation takes on greater weight in families in which the couple unit is not intact and the White parent is the custodial parent.

A common assumption is that a White person who is or was in an interracial relationship and has mixed-race children will automatically possess racial awareness and sensitivity. Interestingly, this is often not the case. In some cases, a White parent may have grown up with limited cross-racial contact and, even after partnering with a person of different race, may continue to live a lifestyle that affords minimal contact with people of color. When a White parent has a limited appreciation for his or her children's context as people of color, children suffer the loss that comes from not having a parent who can truly validate their race-related experiences and offer useful guidance and direction.

IMPLICATIONS FOR THERAPY

Race shapes all human interactions, and therefore it shapes the lives of all families and the process of therapy at all times. Consequently, the importance of the therapist's level of racial awareness and sensitivity cannot be overemphasized. The information provided here to help therapists understand and address the dynamics and issues that specifically confront mixed-race families is of limited value if therapists have not worked with themselves to develop racial self-awareness and sensitivity. Although this applies to therapists of all races, it is especially critical for White therapists. By virtue of our racial privilege, it is especially hard for us as White therapists to see, recognize, and know how to attend to the often subtle ways that race shapes not only clients' lives but also the very process of therapy itself. As mentioned earlier in this chapter, re-visioning therapy with mixed-race families begins with therapists looking within to probe and examine their racial identities and how these identities shape their experiences, values, beliefs, and biases. Only when therapists have worked enough with themselves to achieve racial awareness and sensitivity can they turn their attention to working with mixed-race families in therapy.

Assessment

For mixed-race families, racially based challenges and concerns may or may not be related to the presenting problem(s) that bring them to therapy. In instances in which race is a factor, clients may not readily be aware of or willing to deal with race directly. Therefore, therapists must be mindful of the significance of race and open to exploring how race may be related to the presenting issues and the process of therapy. To assess whether race is related to clients' presenting issues, it is helpful for therapists to broadly inquire about racial issues using questions such as the following.

- Tell me how you have negotiated your respective racial differences.
- What role does race play in shaping your family relationships?
- I know we live in a racially divided society, one that makes it hard for people to relate cross-racially. What effect has the broader context had on your family and how you negotiate race between you?
- How often do you discuss race or racial issues? When race is a topic for discussion, how does the conversation typically play out?

The way that clients respond to these or other open-ended questions offers vital clues about how and in what ways race may (or may not) be related to their presenting issues or dynamics. In addition to listening to what clients say, therapists should also pay close attention to the following:

- Do these questions seem to be new or to be something they've thought about a lot?
- What emotional reactions do questions appear to arouse (ease, anxiety, reactivity)?
- How similar or dissimilar are individual responses?
- Does one partner or family member defer more to another in answering?
- Are their responses specific or generalized and clichéd?
- What themes characterize their responses?
- What things do they reveal about early learnings/experiences with race?
- How much overall awareness does each seem to have about race?
- To what degree do they perpetuate or challenge racial stereotypes (e.g., the devaluation of Blackness and overvaluation of Whiteness)?

Listening to and observing how clients respond to open-ended questions about race will reveal many things, including whether or not race is an issue requiring some attention. Observing how people behave, in addition to what they say, is essential to assessing whether there are race-related family dynamics that may be affecting children's racial identification and therefore warrant attention.

Intervention Strategies

Should therapists determine that there are racially based dynamics, dilemmas, and challenges that warrant attention, a variety of intervention strategies can be used in therapy.

Confronting Devaluing or Mixed Racial Messages

Often, when parents convey devaluing or mixed racial messages, they do so unintentionally and out of ignorance. However, lack of intention does not change the problematic consequence of expressing racially devaluing or contradictory messages. It is important, therefore, for therapists to be attuned to seeing and addressing such messages. Sometimes, merely calling clients' attention to their disparaging remarks or actions is all that is needed to bring about a shift. In other cases therapists may need to spend considerable time helping clients understand how and why a given comment or behavior is insensitive or offensive. Once this is finally grasped, further attention may need to be devoted to helping clients explore and then challenge the underlying assumptions, values, and experiences that contribute to such comments and behaviors. As an alternative to calling clients out directly about the messages conveyed by their content statements, lifestyle choices, or nonverbal vibes, it is recommended that "curiosity" be employed. Being curious is a way of helping clients to make explicit for themselves the messages they are sending and their consequences.

Freeing Children from Racialized Loyalty Binds

In families in which there are divisive tensions and conflicts between the parents, therapists should observe whether and how these things may have contributed to racial loyalty binds for children, with corresponding implications for children's racial identification. When parental conflicts ensnare children in racial loyalty binds, it is necessary to begin by drawing parents' attention to the ways in which they have created a situation in which their children feel torn between them or have sided with one against the other. Some psychoeducation may be necessary to educate parents about how destructive these kinds of dynamics are for children. Additionally, specific attention should be focused on helping parents understand the racial dimensions of the loyalty binds. Once parents are aware of how their children have been triangulated into their conflicts and how the racialized dynamics are affecting them, therapists should coach parents until they are able to communicate clear, explicit messages to their children that acknowledge the loyalty binds and that give kids explicit permission to have their own relationships with each parent and with all parts of their racial identity.

> In the case of Sue and Jason, Sue in particular had a very difficult time accepting that she was compelling her children to "take her side" and that the pressure she was applying encompassed racial issues as well. In fact, until both parents saw a videotaped clip of their daughter Millie describing the conflicts she felt, neither Sue nor Jason truly understood or accepted what he or she was doing. At that point, the therapist worked with both parents concerning how they would talk to their children. It was important to do this long before bringing the family together. After much coaching, the therapist brought the family together and directed each parent to tell their children some version of the following:
>
> > "Whatever issues are between your dad/mom and me don't involve you. We have our disagreements, but it's okay for you to love us both. We won't feel like you are choosing one of us over the other.

> You love us both, and it's okay for you to relate to both of us. We want you to be proud to be both Black and Filipino."

Freeing children from racial loyalty binds is more complicated when parents are aware of the pressure they are applying and are convinced that doing so is the best thing for their children. In these situations therapists should align themselves with the parents' devotion and commitment to protecting their children and acting on behalf of their best interests. Additionally, therapists should educate parents about the psychosocial damage that pressure such as this can have on children, explaining that healthy development is fostered when children are provided with diverse perspectives about race and the freedom to make their own choices.

Fostering Strategies for Resisting Racism

When parents fail to teach their children about the realities of racism and to prepare them to manage and respond to such situations, this failure often is tied to a deeper underlying dynamic that involves a reticence to address race openly. Hence for therapists the task is often one of actively teaching families to have open, direct "race talk" that is challenging but not destructive. Facilitating racial dialogues in therapy is a way of teaching families that they can safely discuss race openly and honestly. As it becomes easier and more comfortable for families to address racial issues directly, therapists can then support parents in talking with their kids about how to determine whether someone has acted in a racially insensitive or denigrating way and, if they have, to explore how that might make them feel. Attention also should focus on discussing how kids can respond if they are faced with a racially offensive situation. Therapists can work with families to hone their ability to make distinctions about times when they should push back and confront racism and when it is best to pull back and opt to let something slide. There is no formula that can be applied to determine which direction is the best to follow in any given situation. The best course of action is often dictated by the disposition of the people involved, as well as a host of contextual variables. Some clients benefit from establishing a set of guidelines, such as developing a cost–benefit analysis that they can apply to help determine when to push back and when not to.

As previously mentioned, one factor that tends to undermine parents' abilities and willingness to deal directly with racism is one parent being White. For many White parents, the nature of their Whiteness is such that they lack the kind of life experience that fosters an understanding of how to effectively address racial obstacles their children may encounter. Hence, to assist parents in helping their children develop strategies for resisting racism, it often is necessary to spend some time with White parents in particular promoting racial awareness and sensitivity. One way of accomplishing this is by assigning RASE (racial awareness and sensitivity enhancement) homework.

RASE homework consists of contracting with clients to engage in experiences or conduct research that will expose them to the realities of race and racism in this society. To promote awareness, (White) parents can be assigned a "research project" that will educate them about how racial inequalities organize society. For example, they might be asked to research the racial identities of the members of different governmental bodies, the leaders of major corporations, the owners of professional sporting franchises, and so forth. Such exercises promote awareness, which is a necessary first step; however, it is necessary to go beyond this by also encouraging sensitivity. The only way this can happen is by creating lived experiences that foster a visceral, sensory, emotional appreciation for another person's experience. For example, (White) parents might be assigned to attend a social, religious, political, or civic event at which most of the attendees are of a racial group that is not their own. As part of their experience, clients would have to reflect on what happened while they were there, what they understood and did not understand, how they chose to participate, and how it felt to be in a marginal position. Processing their experiences in therapy and their answers to these questions provides an excellent opportunity to help clients enhance their appreciation for how race shapes social interactions and how it feels to be in a marginal position.

SUMMARY

In the United States, mixed-race people must either deny their multiracial identity by identifying with only a single race or create an identity that is not recognized or validated by the broader society. Consequently, the core issue facing mixed-race people is how to identify racially and manage the assortment of dynamics, dilemmas, and challenges associated with racial identification in a society that denies and devalues multiracial identity. This chapter examined several family dynamics that commonly undermine or compromise how mixed-race children explore, define, assert, and negotiate their racial identities. Strategies for intervention were presented, including how to support parents in teaching their children how to understand and manage encounters with racism.

NOTE

1. Usually the term "mixed race" includes families in which both parents are monorace but of different racial backgrounds, as well as families in which one or both parents

are of mixed race. In this chapter, use of the term "mixed-race families" refers to the latter definition.

REFERENCES

Davis, F. J. (1991). *Who is Black?: One nation's definition*. University Park: Pennsylvania State University Press.

Eddings, J. (1997). Counting a "new" type of American. *U.S. World and News Reports, 123*, 22–23.

Gibbs, J. T., Gibbs, H., & Nahme, L. (1998). *Children of color: Psychological interventions with culturally diverse youth*. San Francisco: Jossey-Bass.

Hardy, K. V., & Laszloffy, T. A. (1992). Training racially sensitive family therapists: Context, content and contact. *Families in Society, 76*(6), 364–370.

Hardy, K. V., & Laszloffy, T. A. (1998). The dynamics of a pro-racist ideology: Implications for family therapists. In M. McGoldrick (Ed.), *Re-visioning family therapy: Race, culture, and gender in clinical practice* (pp. 118–128). New York: Guilford Press.

Laszloffy, T. A., & Hardy, K. V. (2000). Uncommon strategies for a common problem: Addressing racism in family therapy. *Family Process, 39*, 35–50.

McIntosh, P. (1998). White privilege: Unpacking the invisible knapsack. In M. M. McGoldrick (Ed.), *Re-visioning family therapy: Race, culture, and gender in clinical practice* (pp. 147–152). New York: Guilford Press.

Nakashima, C. L. (1992). An invisible monster: The creation and denial of mixed-race people in America. In M. P. P. Root (Ed.), *Racially mixed people in America* (pp. 162–178). Newbury Park, CA: Sage.

Root, M. P. P. (Ed.). (1996). *Multiracial experience: Racial borders as the new frontier*. Thousand Oaks, CA: Sage.

PART IV

Implications for Clinical Practice

CHAPTER 25

Working with LGBT Families

Elijah C. Nealy

When lesbians and gay men describe their childhoods and early adolescences, they are often characterized by a profound sense of difference. Many gay men have a sense of their sexual orientation by the age of 5–6 years; lesbians often by 12–13 years. Much like immigrants in a new country, lesbians and gay men find themselves surrounded by a heterosexual history and culture that is not their own. The rituals (courtship, engagement, bachelor parties, wedding showers, marriage) and the relationships (heterosexual male–female), the language (boyfriend–girlfriend, husband–wife) all seem disconnected from their experience of themselves. From an early age, they often know that their lives and choices (children, careers, partners, religion) will play out differently from the paths of those around them.

Unlike ethnic immigrants, their own families are also different, a dynamic that creates an even more profound sense of being a stranger in a foreign land. Lesbian, gay, bisexual, and transgender (LGBT) individuals cannot rely on their families to "teach" them how to manage or respond to harassment and discrimination. In fact, homophobia and transphobia often exist within the family, so young people find themselves dealing with harassment, discrimination, and/or invisibility at school, on the streets, and at home.

Whereas many immigrants can choose to live in or near their own ethnic communities, queer people for many generations have had no visible community. They have been relegated to "gay ghettos" such as the Castro in San Francisco or Greenwich Village in New York City or to gay bars and clubs that are typically hidden from mainstream heterosexual society. Even today, despite such mecca as San Francisco and New York City, this subaltern world continues, with young lesbians, gay boys, and gender-different youths typically finding themselves separated from others who are like them as they grow up and come of age.

This dynamic of isolation can be pervasive, profound, and all-encompassing. Lesbian and gay people find themselves isolated from their own gay culture, from mainstream heterosexual society and culture, from their families of origin because of their differences, from mentors and role models with whom they can relate, and from peers and friends who resemble themselves and their emerging identities (Garnets & D'Augelli, 1994).

This feeling of being different is very quickly followed by an awareness that this difference is somehow wrong, shameful, and not to be spoken aloud. Historically, LGBT identity has been variously labeled a crime, a sin, a psychiatric illness, a developmental aberration, and a result of dysfunctional family dynamics. Homosexuality was a diagnostic category in the DSM till 1973; gender identity disorder remains in the DSM-IV today.

In addition, from early on LGBT persons are surrounded by immense loss—growing up without visible role models and without connections to queer history and queer culture, growing up not even knowing that they have a history and a culture. How many young European American LGBT persons grew up hearing about the queer courage and creativity of Leonardo da Vinci or Joan of Arc? How many young gay African Americans grew up hearing about the work of Bayard Rustin or the wisdom of Audre Lorde? How many queer Jews and Christians grew up hearing the scripture stories of Ruth and Naomi or Jonathan and David as their love stories?

COMING OUT

In the face of these dynamics, the coming-out process poses numerous challenges. Coming out is a continual process, one that is never over. Thus it is an ongoing stressor throughout the life cycle (Johnson & Colucci, 1999). Coming out also occurs on multiple levels: to oneself, to other LGBT folks, to family, friends, coworkers, professionals, and neighbors. Although coming out is generally considered healthy, disclosure to parents is often the most stressful experience an LGBT person faces (LaSala, 2000).

The experiences of LGBT persons as they come out to their families are many. Robert, a 40-year-old African American gay man, living with HIV for 17 years, remains disconnected from his family of origin because they refuse to accept him for who he is. CJ, a Latina lesbian, raised two girls with her partner of 20 years and just last year spent Christmas together with her partner instead of going home to her family of origin alone, because her partner is not welcome there. Esther, a 20-something Jewish bisexual woman, spent undergraduate school in a relationship with a woman that was closeted not only from her family but even from her closest college friends; 5 years later, she is still dealing with the trauma of going through a divorce in isolation. Pauline, a 65-year-old African American woman, spent Thanksgiving as usual with her extended family; for the first time, she talked openly about a 15-year relationship with a woman that had recently ended, and then she found herself not invited back for Christmas.

There are particular challenges for LGBT couples who may be at different places along the coming-out continuum; for example, one partner may be out with his or her family of origin but the other is not out; one may be comfortable attending LGBT events, the other may not. The same can be true for couples whose families are at different points along the coming-out continuum, leaving LGBT individuals sometimes forced to choose between partner and family.

Even in 2008, when LGBT people speak the truth about their lives and loves, it can lead to harassment and discrimination, loss of family connections, loss of friends and coworkers, loss of jobs or custody of children, or loss of ethnic community connections. Recent studies tell us that 97% of students in public high schools report regularly hearing homophobic remarks from peers; 39% of LGBT youths report being physically harassed (pushed, shoved, etc.); and 17% report being physically assaulted (punched, kicked, injured with a weapon, etc.) because of their sexual orientation or gender identity. Being home is not necessarily a safer place. Some one-third of LGBT youths report abuse from family members as a result of their sexual orientations and/or gender identities (Massachusetts Youth Risk Behavior Survey, 2005; Vermont Youth Risk Behavior Survey, 1999). In senseless acts of violence, young gay men such as Matthew Shepherd and Rashawn Brazell still lose their lives for living their truth. National estimates tell us that an average of 20 transgender people are victimized by a hate crime every month. One or two, such as Brandon Teena and Gwen Araujo, are murdered simply for being who they are (Gay Data, 2006).

Yet despite these challenges, most LGBT people exhibit tremendous strength and courage as they navigate the coming-out process. Tyrone's story reflects this courage.

> The LGBT Community Center, where I work, is housed in a large old public school building. Six thousand people come and go each week, attending some 300 cultural, professional, educational, spiritual, and recreational groups and 90 different 12-step meetings. A few months back, I encountered the mother of a 16-year-old African American young man who announced that she had just called the police to get her son out of our program so she could take him home with her immediately. She was incredibly angry about his being at the LGBT Center, asserting that he was far too young to know he was gay.

As I attempted to engage her, I learned that her son had come out to her the day before by slipping a note in between some school permission slips. He had written that he was gay and that he was coming to after-school programming at the Center. She talked about being a single parent, about how close she and her son were, and how she couldn't understand why he had never talked to her about this if he really was gay. As the police arrived, I continued to work with her, trying to explain the challenges of coming out for teenagers and what her son might need from her at this moment in his life.

When Tyrone emerged, his mother began yelling at him, insisting there was no way he could be gay. A few minutes later, she laid down an ultimatum, demanding that he return the house keys and find somewhere else to live if he refused to come home with her that moment. Tyrone courageously responded, saying that he knew he was gay and that he knew this was not going to change. He went on to say that he loved her but that she would have to accept the truth of who he was. Then Tyrone announced that he was going to finish his group and handed her the house keys. The mother and I talked awhile longer as the police looked on. In a moment of real parental strength and love, she gave me the house keys to return to Tyrone, and we arranged for an older cousin (who happened to be an "out" lesbian) to meet him and go home with him that evening. A few weeks ago, I ran into Tyrone in the lobby of the Center and asked him how it was going at home. He told me of the improving conversations with his mother and proudly showed me a gold medallion she had just given him that said "Number 1 Son." (For further resources on work with LGBT adolescents, see Mallon, 2000, and Stone Fish & Harvey, 2005).

Tyrone's story and the stories of many others remind us of the truth of the tremendous loss that LGBT people sometimes carry about—their spiritual, emotional, and sometimes literal disconnections with family; the truth about the pain that LGBT people of color often encounter as they struggle to embrace the complexities of their multiple identities; the trauma that queer youths experience day in and day out being harassed and bullied in schools and on playgrounds. Yet these same stories also reflect tremendous strength, courage, and resilience.

LGBT PARENTS

The 2000 Census reported that at least one out of three lesbian couples and one out of five gay male couples are raising children nationwide (Bennett & Gates, 2004). Recent research consistently indicates that children raised in LGBT-headed families are just as healthy and well-adjusted as their counterparts raised by heterosexual parents, despite persistent myths and stereotypes to the contrary. In fact, most research indicates that the sexual orientation or gender identity of the parent is far less significant than is the quality of the connections between parent and child (American Psychological Association, 2007; Patterson, 2006).

LGBT persons form families in many different ways. Some individuals draw on reproductive technologies such as donor insemination or surrogacy. Others become foster parents or adopt children. Some individuals and couples have children from a previous heterosexual relationship (Mallon, 2004; National Gay and Lesbian Task Force [NGLTF], 2007). Queer relationships often experience a lack of socially recognized and affirmed rituals or rites of passage. Many times affirmation from families of origin and community institutions is withheld. These realities form both stressor and strength as LGBT couples are forced to create their own life-affirming rituals with their children, kinship families, and families of choice.

Queer couples still experience many barriers to creating and sustaining families. LGBT parents and their children frequently experience prejudice and discrimination because of their sexual orientation or gender identity. When this prejudice is manifested by judges, legislators, and medical and mental health professionals, LGBT couples often find themselves faced with loss of custody or visitation rights and prohibitions on adoption.

In most states, LGBT families confront a consistent and pervasive lack of legal validation and recognition. In the few states that offer civil unions (or even marriage, in Massachusetts), LGBT couples and families still have absolutely no access to the more than 1,100 federal protections that come with marriage. In fact, in most states, LGBT couples are not even guaranteed the right to establish a joint legal relationship to the children they are raising together.

The impact of this lack of legal recognition is most evident in three arenas. First, because same-sex partners are not recognized as spouses, LGBT couples with children are far less likely to have access to health insurance than are their heterosexual counterparts. Second, when an LGBT parent dies, the surviving partner and children are not entitled to the deceased parent's Social Security benefits. The economic impact of this loss can be staggering for many LGBT families. Third, an analysis of federal income taxes indicates that because of their inability to file joint tax returns, a same-sex couple in which one parent stays at home with the children pays more in federal income taxes than a married heterosexual couple in a similar situation (Bennett & Gates, 2004).

MULTIPLE LAYERS OF STIGMA

Sometimes LGBT persons of color are pulled between their ethnic communities and LGBT communities and consequently experience a profound intersection of oppressions. As one Mexican American lesbian put it, "If you're barely surviving, and then you're going to take the risk of losing the respect, and the love, and the sense of place that you have with your own family, you have nothing. ... So, why add more stigma to yourself? Why take one more horrible risk to be further disenfranchised from society?" (Trujillo, 1991). In fact, coming out as historically defined can be viewed as a modern White Western cultural phenomenon that is often framed and experienced very differently in queer communities of color and in more postmodern contexts (Laird, 2003).

Cultural differences concerning safety, coming out, and physical and sexual expression can also vary across queer cultures. In one relationship between a White gay man and an African American gay man, the White gay man didn't understand why his partner wouldn't hold hands with him or be affectionate in public. The White partner felt rejected and interpreted his partner's reluctance to express affection publicly to mean that he was ashamed of the relationship or of his partner, that he was still closeted and not proud of himself. In reality, the varying degrees of public affection were not so much about intimacy and/or rejection but very much about race, ethnicity, and safety. The White gay man inherently felt safer on the streets than did his African American partner.

In another situation, a Latino lesbian was very physically affectionate and wanted lots of hugging and holding from her Asian American partner, who was far less comfortable with physical affection. It was easy for the Latino partner to experience this as rejection when it was really about cultural differences in various queer communities.

GENDER IDENTITY

One's gender is composed of several different elements. All three—sex, gender role, and gender identity—contribute to our understanding of our gender.

- *Sex* refers to biological, anatomical, or organic sexual markers such as vagina, ovaries, eggs, estrogen levels, and menstruation for females and penis, testis, sperm, and testosterone levels for males. We tend to think of these as very clear distinctions, yet the truth is more fluid. Variations in our sex include chromosomal variations, changing hormonal levels as we age, biological changes due to illness (such as hysterectomy, mastectomy), and the varied anatomical differences faced by intersex individuals who are born with characteristics of both sexes.
- *Gender role* is defined as the social and perceived expectations of gendered acts or expressions; for example, expectations that boys

play with trucks and girls play with dolls, that boys wear pants and girls wear skirts, and that boys date girls and girls date boys.

- *Gender identity* involves our *self*-conception of our gender; it concerns how I see myself, how I feel about myself and my gender identity, and it may or may not have an organic component.

All of us have grown up with very strong Western cultural notions about gender identity and gender expression. These ideas affect how we see ourselves and those around us. These expectations tell us that there are only two types of normal (i.e., acceptable) humans: heterosexual females with typical "feminine" characteristics and heterosexual males with typical "masculine" characteristics.

"Transgender" is the term most often used to describe people who transcend typical gender paradigms. It is an umbrella term used to describe the many different gender communities such as bigendered, butch queen, cross dresser, drag king, drag queen, femme queen, female-to-male, male-to-female, preop(erative), postop, nonop, transsexual, trans-woman, trans-man, or, in Native American culture, two-spirit.

Although gender has typically been thought of as a binary construct, it can be better understood as a continuum. Individuals of transgender experience who live in the "in-between places" may challenge our notions of gender normalcy, and, as a result, people who are gender different are stigmatized by the dominant culture. The binary-gender assumption renders transgender persons as "other" and "queer," defining them as gender transgressors and subjecting them to ostracism, hatred, physical and sexual assaults, self-hatred, suppression of their true selves, and even murder.

TRANSGENDER COUPLES

Trans-couples may consist of two transgender individuals or one trans-identified person and their non-trans-identified partner. In light of all our cultural baggage and binary notions, trans-couples are forced to develop extraordinary strengths and concomitantly face enormous stressors on many fronts.

Coming out for trans-persons is similar but not identical to the process for LGB persons. It begins with an increasing awareness that one is different, the sense that how I see myself in terms of gender and how others perceive me does not match up. In these early stages, trans-individuals often find themselves forced to compartmentalize their lives, to hide the true parts of themselves, to remain closeted at all costs. LGB persons sometimes have the ability to "pass" (be perceived as straight), but trans-identified individuals rarely have that privilege. Coming out for trans-individuals calls forth tremendous personal resources. Maintaining one's own sense of identity in the face of invisibility, oppression, and discrimination profoundly challenges trans-persons' inner strength and determination.

The transitioning process itself brings its own stresses and emerging strengths. Think for a minute about the challenges of shifting identities— an individual born a biological female who lives as a lesbian for 40 years and then transitions as a trans-man, or a birth-identified male transitioning to a trans-woman, dealing with loss of identity and privilege. Many times these transitions lead to disconnections from the trans-person's own family and from their family of origin due to ignorance and lack of acceptance. Trans-couples can find themselves disconnected from family affirmation and supports. There are no rituals or rites of passage to mark one's gender transition and its impact on their relationships. Major challenges for most trans-couples include dealing with in-laws and extended family members. If the trans-couple has children, fear about how their children will adjust to one parent's gender transition is often a major concern and one that requires significant support.

Trans-people often experience multiple disconnections from community. For example, a lesbian transitioning to become a trans-man may be forced to disconnect from the lesbian community; a heterosexual woman who becomes involved with a trans-partner may often find herself disconnected from "straight" community; trans-people of color experience even greater disconnections, often feeling cut off from their racial/ethnic communities or forced to choose between their ethnic communities and the trans-communities with which they have begun to form connections.

For couples in which both partners are trans-identified, differences between partners may lead to particular stressors—for example, if one person is able to pass, that is, has the ability to be perceived and identified as a non-trans-person, and the other partner is visibly trans and not able to pass. Finances and sex are always hot relationship issues. These can be exacerbated for trans-couples if one partner's visible trans-identity creates difficulty obtaining employment or if the couple has differing levels of comfort with their own and each other's bodies. Another source of struggle can occur if one partner is able to have gender-confirming surgery and the other is not or chooses not to do so.

When only one partner is transitioning, couples often experience a destabilization of their relationship (Malpas, 2006). The gender transition can raise questions about sex and sexuality, sexual orientation, and intimacy. For example, a heterosexual woman married to a male-to-female transsexual may find herself questioning whether her partner's transition "makes her a lesbian" now that she is no longer in a relationship with a man but with another woman. Physical changes due to hormone therapy and gender-confirming surgery can create new challenges for couples. Sometimes couples discover that although they continue to have a strong partner bond, they may have difficulty with sexual attraction and intimacy. Even when physical changes result in positive experiences for the individual and the partner, the transition itself, for a time, destabilizes the center of intimacy. Throughout this process, the couple needs support to reconnect, internalize the changes, and recenter their relationship. Although it might seem obvious that the individual who is transitioning needs resources and support, it is important to remember that trans-partners also need support and recognition. They may have an intellectual knowledge of the transition process but find that theoretical knowledge very different from the actual experience of transitioning in the couple's relationship.

WHAT DO LGBT COUPLES AND FAMILIES NEED?

In the face of these varied challenges and the experience of persistent discrimination and lack of validation, LGBT couples and families need particular things from their family therapists and other mental health providers. Some of these include:

- Nurturing, fully accepting, nondiscriminatory providers.
- Therapists who are sensitive to the diversity and variety of relationships in the LGBT community.
- Therapists who are willing to acknowledge their own cultural knowledge gaps and do something about them rather than expecting the family to educate them—for example, read books, attend workshops and trainings, and attend LGBT events.
- Therapists who are willing to stand with them as LGBT allies, who recognize what Virginia Mollenkott (2001, p. 74) meant when she reminded us that "because gender roles are by no means equitable, binary gender assumptions and roles are devastating to all of us— 'masculine' men, 'feminine' women, and those somewhere in the middle" (p.).
- Therapists who acknowledge gender identity disorder for what it is—a stigmatizing, pathologizing diagnosis by the traditional mental health system that seeks to control and dictate the lives of gender-different persons.
- Therapists committed to working with partners, children, parents, and siblings of LGBT individuals and couples so that LGBT persons are no longer forced to choose between their families and their lives.

Even more, as LGBT families are challenged to speak the truth of their lives, we need our allies to speak the truth as well. In the midst of a homophobic and transphobic culture, in the midst of an incredibly silencing and oppressive political climate, we need non-LGBT allies to speak the truth about our presence in your lives as friends, colleagues, neighbors, and family. We need our allies to speak the truth about your love for us and your acceptance of our lives and our loves. We need you to speak the truth to fellow citizens and legislators about the more than 1,100 federal rights we are currently denied because of our inability to marry. We need you to consistently ask questions about sexual orientation and gender identity in your clinical work and in your research. We need you to speak truth to the families with whom you work, challenging them to confront their own stereotypes and prejudices so they can embrace the wholeness of their LGBT family members. Only then can we together build a world that is safe and just and affirming for all families.

REFERENCES

American Psychological Association. (2007). *Lesbian and gay parenting.* Retrieved April 27, 2007, from *www.apa.org/pi/lgbc/publications/lgpsummary.html.*

Bennett, L., & Gates, G. (2004). *The cost of marriage inequality to children and their same-sex parents.* Washington, DC: Human Rights Campaign Foundation.

Garnets, L., & D'Augelli, A. (1994). Empowering lesbian and gay communities: A call for collaboration with community psychologists. *American Journal of Community Psychology, 22*(4), 447–470. Retrieved November 22, 2004, from ProQuest database.

Gay Data. (2006). *Research studies on lesbian, gay, bisexual and transgender persons.* Retrieved November 15, 2006, from *www.gaydata.org/02_Data_Sources/ds007_ YRBS/Massachusetts/ds007_YRBS_MA.html.*

Johnson, T., & Colucci, P. (1999). Lesbians, gay men, and the family life cycle. In B. Carter & M. McGoldrick (Eds.), *The expanded family life cycle: Individual, family, and social perspectives* (pp. 346–361). Boston: Allyn & Bacon.

Laird, J. (2003). Lesbian and gay families. In F. Walsh (Ed.), *Normal family processes: Growing diversity and complexity.* New York: Guilford Press.

LaSala, M. (2000). Lesbians, gay men, and their parents: Family therapy for the coming-out crisis. *Family Process, 39*(1), 67–81.

Mallon, G. (2000). *Social services with transgender youth.* Binghamton, NY: Haworth.

Mallon, G. (2004). *Gay men choosing parenthood.* New York: Columbia University.

Malpas, J. (2006). From otherness to alliance: Transgender couples in therapy. *Journal of GLBT Family Studies, 2*(3/4), 183–206.

Massachusetts Youth Risk Behavior Survey. (2005). Retrieved February 7, 2007, from www.outproud.org/article_myrbs.html.

National Gay and Lesbian Task Force. (2007). *Parenting and family.* Retrieved April 27, 2007, from *www.thetaskforce.org.*

Mollenkott, V. R. (2001). *Omnigender: A trans-religious approach.* Cleveland: The Pilgrim Press.

Patterson, C. (2006) Children of lesbian and gay parents. *Current Directions in Psychological Science, 15*(5), 241–244.

Stone Fish, L. S., & Harvey, R. (2005). *Nurturing queer youth: Family therapy transformed*. New York: Norton.

Trujillo, C. M. (1991). *Chicana lesbians: The girls our mothers warned us about*. Berkeley, CA: Third Woman Press.

Vermont Youth Risk Behavior Survey. (1995). Retrieved February 7, 2007, from *www.outproud.org/article_vyrbs.html*.

CHAPTER 26

Gay and Lesbian Couples
Successful Coping with Minority Stress

Robert-Jay Green

In this chapter, I focus on three interrelated sources of minority stress for same-sex couples: (1) anti-gay prejudice; (2) lack of a legal/normative template for same-sex relationships; and (3) less social support for the couple relationship. In addition, I describe typical problems and effective therapeutic interventions related to each of these risk factors.

ANTI-GAY PREJUDICE

The overarching difference in the lives of same-sex versus heterosexual couples is that the former must continually cope with the special risks of claiming a socially stigmatized identity. For example, it was only in 2003 that the U.S. Supreme Court ruled that consensual homosexual acts in private no longer constituted criminal behavior. Even at the time of this writing (May, 2008), it still is entirely legal in 31 states and in the U.S. military for an employer to fire or to refuse to hire or promote someone simply because they are lesbian or gay. More subtle forms of prejudicial attitudes and discrimination are prevalent in various religious denominations and local communities in the United States.

Although same-sex couples do not encounter intolerance at every turn, they experience enough of it personally, vicariously (by identification with other lesbian and gay victims of discrimination), and through antigay political initiatives to remain constantly vigilant for its occurrence (Meyer, 2003). It is impossible for a lesbian or gay person to grow up in this society without internalizing some negative attitudes and fears about homosexual feelings and the dangers of discrimination.

Most relevant to the formation of couple relationships, the difficulty accepting one's homosexuality (termed "internalized homophobia") and/or the fear of negative social and economic consequences of coming out still discourage many lesbian and gay people from forming lasting couple bonds. In many local contexts in the United States and throughout most of Africa, Asia, Latin America, and the Middle East, it remains much safer to remain closeted and to restrict one's sexual/romantic encounters to brief interludes than to increase one's visibility by living in a shared residence with one's committed same-sex partner and being seen together repeatedly. To reach the latter level of "outness," lesbian and gay partners must have successfully challenged in their own minds the negative views they were taught about homosexuality and overcome their fears of being seriously harmed by discrimination.

Successfully countering internalized anti-gay attitudes requires attributing them to societal ignorance, prejudice, fear, and the human tendency to conform to dominant norms. It also requires exposure to and social support from other lesbian and gay people whose behavior counteracts negative stereotypes about homosexuality.

In a sense, all of the techniques discussed in this chapter can help clients cope with external or internalized anti-gay prejudice. However, I present some very specific strategies here. In this aspect of the work, therapists make use of feminist, gay-affirmative, multicultural, and narrative family systems therapy principles.

The two central ideas in applying feminist theories of therapy to same-sex couples are the notions of cultural *resistance* and *subversion* (Brown, 1994). In terms of cultural resistance, therapists must start with an awareness that by loving someone of the same sex, lesbians and gay men are violating the most basic gender norms of the society. The therapist collaborates with clients in an exploration of all the oppressive social influences in their lives, influences that pressure them not to engage in same-sex love and to regard their capacity for same-sex love as bad, sinful, mentally disturbed, inferior, and so forth. This includes a careful deconstruction of all the various messages they have received about homosexuality in their families, in school, in their neighborhoods, in their religious institutions, through the media, and more generally from members of their specific racial/ethnic groups both as they were growing up and currently.

Most important, the therapist should counter these oppressive messages, neutralizing society's condemnation of same-sex love and framing homosexuality as a normal human variation, not reinforcing its denigration by the larger society. The therapist thus serves as a "culture broker," validating lesbian and gay relationships simply by viewing the partners as a legitimate couple and affording them equal care and respect.

In some couple therapy cases, partners are at markedly different levels of accepting their sexual orientations or may face different levels of acceptance at work or in their families. These discrepancies may create couple conflicts over whether and when to be "out" in their communities. Individual therapy may be indicated for the partner who suffers from a great deal more internalized homophobia than the other, especially if he or she seems ashamed to explore these aspects of self in the presence of the partner.

In addition to the work of deconstructing internalized homophobia in the sessions, therapists should encourage clients to engage in various forms of participation in lesbian–gay community organizations, including political activism if it fits their sensibilities (i.e., the cultural "subversion" aspect of feminist therapies). These acts of lesbian–gay community participation are a form of challenging the heteronormative status quo in society, implicitly naming society's homophobia (rather than the self) as the problem that needs to be eliminated.

Depending on the kind of discrimination same-sex partners face, helping them cope successfully and resiliently with anti-gay prejudice may require (1) working actively for change in one's current social environment; (2) changing to a different social environment (literally relocating geographically or quitting one's job to escape an intransigent or dangerously homophobic situation); (3) reattributing the cause of one's distress to different factors (e.g., attributing one's distress to external prejudice and ignorance rather than to personal inadequacy); or (4) recognizing that some discriminatory situations cannot be changed and then focusing on other areas in one's life.

LACK OF A NORMATIVE AND LEGAL TEMPLATE FOR COUPLEHOOD

In contrast to heterosexual couples, for whom there is a traditionally prescribed way of being a couple with explicit and implicit rules, there is no prescribed way of being a same-sex couple. For example, some of the socially prescribed rules of heterosexual marriage include expectations of monogamy, sharing responsibility for each other's aging relatives, combining financial assets, dividing instrumental/expressive and household roles somewhat along gender lines, relocating for one another's career advancement, and taking care of one another in times of serious disability. Because most same-sex partners in the United States cannot get married (except for residents of Massachusetts and, as of this writing, California), it is much less clear whether or at what turning point these same kinds of couple expectations might apply to their relationships. Elsewhere, I have termed this kind of uncertainty *relational ambiguity* (Green & Mitchell, 2008), and it tends to play a central role in same-sex couple relationships, especially in the early years of couple formation.

For example, committed heterosexual couples (typically within 1 to 3 years of starting to date) take a wedding vow to stay together "in sickness and in health till death do us part." This vow to take care of each other is also a promise to family members, friends, and other witnesses, including in most cases to "God as a witness."

By contrast, it is unclear when or whether most same-sex partners can have the same expectations of their relationship. Do same-sex partners implicitly make this vow when they move in together? After being together for 2 years or 10 years? Can there be equivalent vow making for same-sex couples when they cannot get legally married in all but two states (Massachusetts and California), and even then not in the eyes of the federal government? Is a vow made in private the same psychologically as one made in public? Is a promise made in a public "commitment ceremony" that is not recognized by the state and/or federal government the same as a promise made against the backdrop of legally enforceable marriage laws?

Lacking a preordained prescription for what being a same-sex couple means, lesbian and gay partners must develop their own basic parameters for themselves as a couple. Inevitably, they will rely to some extent on earlier observations of successful and unsuccessful heterosexual marriages. However, the same-sex composition of the couple and the unusual position of lesbians and gays in society throws into doubt how relevant these heterosexual models might be. At the very least, same-sex partners cannot conform to sex-typed gender roles without encountering the special problems that ensue when both partners enact the same gender role in the relationship (e.g., "emotional fusion" in lesbian relationships or competitive conflict or emotional distance in gay male relationships) (Greenan & Tunnell, 2002).

Furthermore, the greater variety of relationship arrangements that are acceptable within the gay community (e.g., many such couples never live together, and others have nonmonogamous relationships by agreement; shorter relationships are normative; fewer are raising children) leaves open the possibility that the lesbian or gay couple's commitment could be quite different from that of most married couples. This acceptance of nontraditional couple arrangements of all sorts seems to thrust each same-sex couple into a longer period of uncertainty and negotiation regarding its definition of personal couplehood.

The advent of domestic partnerships and/or civil unions in 10 states and of legal marriage in Massachusetts and California may help reduce the relational ambiguity for couples who attain these legalized statuses. However, at the present time, 42 other states have passed "defense of marriage acts" (declaring that those states will not honor same-sex marriages performed elsewhere). Twenty-six of those states also have passed constitutional amendments defining marriage as being only between a man and women, rendering courts in those states unable to consider the constitutionality of same-sex marriage prohibitions. Thus for the vast majority of same-sex couples, no legal status exists for their relationships. Even in states with civil unions or with marriage in Massachusetts and California, none of the *federal* benefits of marriage are available to same-sex couples (e.g., Social Security benefits for surviving spouses). Also at present, California is facing a November, 2008 ballot initiative that would alter the state constitution so that it would prohibit same-sex marraiges in the future, despite the recent California Supreme Court ruling allowing same-sex marriage.

As a result, many same-sex couples, their families, and their state governments seem to be experiencing heightened ambiguity, caught somewhere between the idea that gays and lesbians are criminal outlaws (as was literally true prior to 2003 in many parts of the United States) and viewing them as potential in-laws (as is becoming true with the recent arrival of same-sex marriage in California, Massachusetts, Canada, Spain, South Africa, and elsewhere). Even partners within a couple may be at differing points between these polar views of what it means to be a same-sex couple because of the rapid social changes in the past 5 years.

There are no easy ways to resolve these ambiguities in same-sex couple relationships. Nor should their resolution necessarily look like heterosexual marriages, in which many of these uncertainties are settled by law and tradition. In general, however, a couple tends to function best when they have clear agreements about their commitment and boundaries and when the couple's relationship is given higher priority than any other relationships (in terms of emotional involvement, caregiving, honesty, time, and influence over major decisions). Asking the following kinds of questions and arriving at clear answers can be helpful to many same-sex couples in reducing relational ambiguity:

1. How do you define being "a couple" (what does it mean to you that you are a "couple")?
2. What has been your history as a couple?
3. How did your becoming a couple affect your relationships with other family members, friends, the lesbian and gay community, and the straight community?
4. What are the rules in your relationship regarding monogamy versus sex outside the relationship? What are the rules in terms of safer sex

practices with each other and/or with others (being very explicit in terms of exact sexual practices to prevent HIV transmission)?

5. What are your agreements with one another about monthly finances, current or future debts, pooling versus separation of financial resources, ownership of joint property, and other financial planning matters?

6. Who does what tasks in the relationship and the household, and how is this division or sharing of tasks decided? Are you satisfied with the current division or sharing of these tasks?

7. What do you see as your obligations to one another in terms of caring for one another in illness, injury, or disability?

8. Are you viewing this as a lifetime commitment? If so, have you prepared legal health care power of attorney documents and wills to protect one another's interests in case of serious illness or death?

For couples who view their relationships as entailing a lifetime commitment, therapists should strongly encourage drawing up appropriate legal documents, especially health care power of attorney and wills or trusts (see Clifford, Hertz, & Doskow, 2007, for examples). If it is in keeping with their sensibilities, couples can be encouraged to have a commitment ceremony and a formal exchange of vows covering some of these issues.

Any intervention that helps the partners clarify expectations and agreements in contested areas or in areas that have never been discussed (such as finances or monogamy) will help reduce relational ambiguity. This, in turn, will increase partners' feelings of secure attachment and belief in the permanence of their union, anchoring their relationship in tangible definitions of what it means that they are a couple.

LESS SOCIAL SUPPORT FOR THE COUPLE RELATIONSHIP

Unlike members of racial, ethnic, and religious minority groups, children who are lesbian and gay rarely have parents who share their same sexual minority status. Being different from other family members in this way has profound consequences for the development of almost every lesbian and gay person. For example, because heterosexual parents have never suffered sexual orientation discrimination themselves, even the most well-meaning among them is not able to offer the kind of insight and socialization experiences that would buffer their child against anti-gay prejudice and its internalization.

By contrast, when children and parents mutually identify as members of the same minority group (e.g., African Americans, Jews, Muslims), the children are explicitly taught—and parents implicitly model—ways to counter society's prejudice against their group. Typically, such parents and children are involved together in community institutions (religious or social) that are instrumental in supporting the child's development of a positive minority identity, and parents take a protective stance toward their children's experiences of oppression.

However, parents of lesbian and gay children are typically unaware of their child's minority status and therefore unlikely to seek out community groups that would support the development of a positive lesbian or gay identity. In fact, rather than protecting their child against prejudice, parents often show subtle or not-so-subtle signs of anti-gay prejudice themselves. Instead of being on the same side as their child against the external dangers, the parents' own anti-gay attitudes and behavior may be the greatest external danger of all.

Large numbers of lesbian and gay adults in the United States, especially members of conservative religious families or of immigrant families with traditional values, still remain closeted from one or both parents who are perceived as homophobic (more frequently fathers). In terms of couple relationships, this secrecy requires either distancing from family of origin members lest the secret be revealed or forgoing couple commitments in order to stay connected with family of origin.

Although most parents do not completely reject their lesbian or gay children after the disclosure, the level of acceptance offspring receive is highly variable and usually somewhat qualified (Savin-Williams, 2001). As a result, same-sex couples frequently turn to their lesbian and gay friends for greater levels of mutual support and identification. Ideally, these friendships are woven together into a so-called family of choice (an interconnected system of emotional and instrumental support over time; Green & Mitchell, 2008).

In general, same-sex couples tend to have less interconnected social networks than heterosexual couples. The tendency toward social segregation of the straight and gay worlds generally—and between the straight and gay segments of an individual's social network—usually requires that same-sex couples have to expend more deliberate effort to create an integrated social support system that has family-like qualities. The ideal would be to integrate family members, lesbian and gay friends, and heterosexual friends into a cohesive support system.

In assessing family-of-origin support, the following kinds of questions have proven useful:

1. When did you first become aware that you might be lesbian or gay?
2. How do you think this "differentness" may have affected your relationships with family members as you were growing up?
3. If you have *not* come out to certain family members, what factors led to this decision? Are there any ways in which your remaining

closeted with your family is affecting your couple relationship positively or negatively?

4. If you have come out to certain family members, describe the process, including what preceded, what happened during, and what has followed the disclosure up to the present time?

5. If you have introduced your partner to your family-of-origin members, how have they treated your partner up until now? How have you responded to their treatment of your partner and of the two of you as a couple?

Although a full discussion of family-of-origin interventions is beyond the scope of this chapter, the first step in any effort to elicit more family support involves helping the lesbian or gay person work through any residual internalized homophobia (as described earlier). When the adult child can accept his or her own sexual orientation and choice of partner, dealing with the family is emotionally much easier, and clients can then cope with familial homophobia more dispassionately and assertively, with planning and with fewer setbacks to the couple's functioning.

Therapeutic interventions with families of origin can include: Bowen-type coaching assignments in which the client takes steps toward differentiation of self in the family of origin without the therapist present (Iasenza, Colucci, & Rothberg, 1996); conjoint family therapy sessions with all family-of-origin members together in the therapist's office; or a combination of both methods. Therapists should be cautious about doing any coaching assignments or conjoint sessions with family of origin until the lesbian or gay person has reached a reasonably sustainable level of self-acceptance.

In helping couples build a "family of choice," therapists should encourage couples to take a very proactive, deliberate stance toward the goal of developing an ongoing social support system consisting of about 8–10 individuals or couples. There are two basic steps the couple has to take in building a personal support system: first, developing or maintaining a reciprocally supportive relationship with each individual who would be a member of the couple's support system; and, second, "knitting" these individuals together into an integrated system of support. The best strategy is for the partners to become very active in a well-established organization together, attend its events regularly in order to become familiar fixtures in the organization, and take on positions of leadership or active committee involvement that require repeated interaction with the same people frequently and over months or years. In smaller or rural communities with fewer lesbian–gay organizations, the Internet may be the best venues for starting friendship networks.

The great advantage of meeting new people through existing lesbian–gay organizations is that those organizations already will have some degree of "groupness" to them, so that the couple may be able to become an integral part of an already existing social support system. Therapists who work with lesbian–gay couples should therefore be knowledgeable about relevant organizations in their communities.

If the couple's closest relationships arose at different times from different settings, more effort has to go into weaving these disparate relationships into a more cohesive unit. The only way to increase the cohesiveness of a fragmented support system is for the couple to actively, frequently, and persistently take the lead in physically bringing together the disconnected individuals or subgroups. It generally takes about 1 to 2 years to knit a disconnected collection of about 8–10 individual relationships into a functional social support system with family-like properties (a family of choice), but couples invariably find the effort worthwhile.

CONCLUSION

The therapy framework described here is summarized in Table 26.1. As a caveat to everything in this chapter, I wish to emphasize that these generalizations do not apply uniformly to all same-sex couples in therapy, many of whom enter treatment for problems that are unrelated to lesbian–gay minority stress. Also, because of space limitations, this chapter could not cover specialized therapeutic issues for same-sex couples of color, interracial couples, or couples in which one or both members are bisexual or transgender (for these topics, see especially Firestein, 2007; Laird & Green, 1996; and Lev, 2004). These same-sex couples often are subject to much higher levels of antigay discrimination from their families and their communities and usually experience significantly more difficulty integrating their social networks into a coherent whole.

In all cases, therapists should keep in mind that the most important prerequisite for helping same-sex couples is the therapist's personal comfort with love and sexuality between two women or two men. Therapists who are not comfortable with such love and sexuality may inadvertently increase lesbian and gay clients' minority stress and exacerbate their problems. Working with same-sex couples requires familiarity with lesbian and gay culture, genuine personal ease ("comfort in your bones") when dealing with lesbian or gay partners' emotions for one another, and an ability to ask and talk about homosexual sex in explicit terms with couples who are having sexual difficulties (American Psychological Association, 2000). Although readings are valuable, attitudinal learning is just as important. Given that mental health graduate programs provide minimal preparation, I recommend that therapists seek at least one expert consultation (in person or by telephone) about every same-sex couple they treat until they feel competent to provide culturally attuned care.

TABLE 26.1. Gay and Lesbian Couples: Successful Coping with Minority Stress

Risk factors	Potential couple problems	Therapeutic or preventive interventions	Outcome goals resilience
Antigay prejudice in the community and larger society	1. Internalized homophobia—fear and ambivalence about committing to a same-sex couple relationship	1. Externalizing the homophobia—viewing societal ignorance and prejudice (not homosexuality) as a problem	1. Self-acceptance of lesbian/gay identity; comfort in committing to a same-sex couple relationship
	2. Partner conflicts over how "out" the couple will be with family, at work, and in the community	2. Negotiating any "outness" conflicts between partners based on realistic constraints or dangers	2. Maximizing involvement in social contexts in which the couple can be out
Lack of normative and legal template for same-sex couplehood	1. Relational ambiguity (unclear couple commitment, boundaries, expectations, and obligations)	1. Exploration and collaboration about what being a couple means to them (roles, boundaries, mutual obligations)	1. Commitment clarity (operating as a team, primary commitment to each other, longer term planning ability, secure attachment in current relationship)
	2. Insecure attachment in current relationship	2. Creating legal documents	
Lack of social support for the couple relationship	1. Social isolation 2. Lack of couple identity in a defined community 3. Inability to get emotional support, advice, and instrumental help from a support system	1. Coaching to build "families of choice" (cohesive social support networks with interconnections among network members)	1. Embedded couple identity and community of care (social network density, reciprocity of support, higher levels of emotional and instrumental support)

REFERENCES

American Psychological Association. (2000). Guidelines for psychotherapy with lesbian, gay, and bisexual clients. *American Psychologist, 55,* 1440–1451.

Brown, L. S. (1994). *Subversive dialogues: Theory in feminist therapy.* New York: Basic Books.

Clifford, D., Hertz, F., & Doskow, E. (2007). *A legal guide for lesbian and gay couples* (14th ed.). Berkeley, CA: Nolo Press.

Firestein, B. (Ed.). (2007). *Becoming visible: Counseling bisexuals across the lifespan.* New York: Columbia University Press.

Green, R.-J., & Mitchell, V. (2008). Gay and lesbian couples in therapy: Minority stress, relational ambiguity, and families of choice. In A. S. Gurman (Ed.), *Clinical handbook of couple therapy* (4th ed., pp. 662–680). New York: Guilford Press.

Greenan, D., & Tunnell, G. (2002). *Couple therapy with gay men.* New York: Guilford Press.

Iasenza, S., Colucci, P. L., & Rothberg, B. (1996). Coming out and the mother–daughter bond: Two case examples. In J. Laird & R.-J. Green (Eds.), *Lesbians and gays in couples and families: A handbook for therapists* (pp. 123–136). San Francisco: Jossey-Bass.

Laird, J., & Green, R.-J. (Eds.). (1996). *Lesbians and gays in couples and families: A handbook for therapists.* San Francisco: Jossey-Bass.

Lev, A. I. (2004). *Transgender emergence: Therapeutic guidelines for working with gender-variant people and their families.* Binghamton, NY: Haworth Press.

Meyer, I. H. (2003). Prejudice, social stress, and mental health in lesbian, gay, and bisexual populations: Conceptual issues and research evidence. *Psychological Bulletin, 129,* 674–697.

Savin-Williams, R. C. (2001). *Mom, dad, I'm gay: How families negotiate coming out.* Washington, DC: American Psychological Association.

CHAPTER 27

Working with Immigrant and Refugee Families

Marsha Pravder Mirkin
Hugo Kamya

OUR STORIES

My (H. K.) immigrant experience embodies several identities. I was born in Uganda at a time when the country was vested in the political colonial patronage of Britain. Postcolonial Uganda witnessed tyrannical brutal regimes that forced many to flee their homeland in search of safety. The brutal rule of Idi Amin led me to flee Uganda to Kenya, where I pursued a University education. My family had been targeted by the government simply because my father belonged to one of the ethnic groups that had opposed the government policies.

I traveled at night, hitching rides from strangers and walking on foot as I crossed into Kenya with very few belongings. The journey across the border would not allow me to carry much for fear of detection and because of the uncertainty that lay ahead.

I remember sitting in a minibus with at least 13 or 14 fellow travelers. None of us said a word to each other. Although it was clear we were all escaping Uganda, none dared to mention our final destination or why we

---

The order of authorship does not reflect level of contribution as both authors contributed equally to this chapter.

were traveling at that time. We sat motionless, staring into the space that lay ahead of us. As we carefully unwrapped notes of paper currency that we were carrying with us to pay the driver, we dared not mention that we were crossing the border into Kenya. I still vividly remember sitting nervously in that minivan without daring even to make eye contact with another passenger. Everyone was suspect. No one could be trusted. As much as I wanted to connect with someone on that bumpy ride I had to maintain a distance that assured me no one else would ask me questions or recognize my nervousness. Our distance from each other, tightly squeezed in such a tight space so close to each other, felt like a necessary protection.

At various roadblocks, soldiers would pull us out of the vehicle and yell at us in Swahili, a language none of us spoke but that many of us identified with intimidation and brutality. Our fate depended on the whims of the soldier who manned a checkpoint. Some people would be hauled out of the vehicles, interrogated, pushed around, and eventually released back to the vehicle before it took off. Others were not as lucky. Guns were pointed at them. They were hit with gun butts and threatened with barrels pointed at their heads. The name on one's identification card often sealed one's fate. If you belonged to a tribe that was not in favor of the government, you were a prime suspect.

We all lived in fear, trying to escape the intimidation and uncertainty that came with these wars. We also lived in fear and distrust of each other including people we thought were our neighbors. Sometimes we knew who our enemy was; sometimes we did not have a clue. Indeed, my life was engulfed in anger as I sought to construct who the oppressor was.

My journey to flee my country brought me to Uganda's neighbor, Kenya. There I began to put my life together. I breathed a sigh of relief because I had just escaped the marauding soldiers of a dictatorial regime, but I was immediately plunged into something new and unfamiliar. I could not speak Swahili, the commonly used language in Kenya. Besides, I had a knee-jerk reaction to learning the language as it quickly reminded me of the turmoil in Uganda. Being male, I became suspect again in Kenya. The first people I encountered wondered whether I had been a collaborator with the regime in Uganda.

Survival was paramount. I needed to make it. I needed to be strong. I needed to let my host country embrace me even as I knew very well that they detested me. I needed to balance a range of emotions to survive. I could not find work nor present papers that qualified me for any work. I did not have any. Employers knew well what was going on in Uganda, but they needed to "protect" themselves from the "bad guys."

As I found my footing in Kenya, I began to reevaluate my life. I did menial jobs. I looked forward with hope that things would change in Uganda.

I began school as soon as I could secure my academic records. There were a lot of people who needed to be convinced that I was who I said I was. As the war raged in Uganda, it became harder to stay in Kenya. Many Ugandans again were suspects. We were all suspects. With more people escaping Uganda, Kenya put Ugandans under surveillance. One such program was the so-called "*Kipandilisho*," a Swahili term that referred to being "documented." All Ugandans had to carry a large 4 × 6 identity card that had to be stamped regularly to authenticate their legal status.

Leaving Kenya and traveling to the United States brought with it mixed feelings. On the one hand, there was excitement to come to a country that was previously presented to me as embracing diversity. But on the other, the move brought to the surface old images and feelings of alienation. I needed to assert myself, to prove myself every step along the way. Many things I took for granted did not matter. I found myself in a place where I needed to name who I was.

I was reliving the trauma I was leaving behind. It colored my perception of my new home. I met several people whose stories were different from my story but who nonetheless suffered from the effects of general exposure to the devastation of wars. I spoke a language that I thought was English, but my pronunciation raised eyebrows as people often made comments about my accent.

There is nothing that could have taught me (M. P. M.) more about the strength and resilience of refugees and immigrants than hearing Hugo's story and hearing it from such a compassionate, smart, empathic clinician. Even though I am the child of an immigrant mother and the grandchild of four immigrant grandparents, it is only recently that I began to look at the cultural and bicultural experience that defined my family and shaped my childhood. Unlike Hugo, I was born in the United States, and I am Caucasian. My experience in the United States is very different from Hugo's. Although my family had little money, I was born into White privilege and I never had to struggle to learn the language spoken around me or figure out how to share the nuance of my language with someone who did not understand the words. I did not have to leave people I loved in different countries or wonder when or whether I could visit again. I did not have to worry about what someone would think of me because of my accent or whether I would be able to become a citizen, and I did not have to tolerate insults based on my skin color or immigration status. But my mother and grandparents did, and I am the recipient and now molder of the intergenerational transmission of their experience. With time, my family entered the world of White privilege, but not before experiencing the trauma of leaving family behind in other countries and of coping with the deaths of family members who had not been able to flee; of being laughed at for their accents; taunted and discriminated against for their religious beliefs; misunderstood in their values; kept out of colleges and jobs because of their religion. Yet the family and immigrant community provided them with support, comfort and hope, helping them to develop strengths that the broader community would overlook. The legacies passed on to me were complicated, a mixture of hope and fear along with a deeply ingrained mandate to work for social justice. My mother and her parents escaped Polish pogroms before the *Shoah* (Holocaust). She was in the United States while her brother, his wife, their children, and all her aunts and uncles were murdered in the Shoah. My mother left school to join an organization whose mission was to save European Jewry and later to resettle refugees. I was born into this transgenerational story, and I see myself as an ally to my colleagues and clients who are immigrants. My hope is that my voice can support my colleagues and clients and that through writing we can challenge the larger system and support the strengths that immigrant families bring with them and develop throughout this process.

Our stories echo many other stories of refugees who have been driven from their homes and have settled in the United States, often under very harsh circumstances. For some, the journey to the United States has involved a transnational migratory pattern. Some of these refugees have lived in at least one other country before securing entry into the United States. Most refugees are escaping wars and internal conflicts in their home countries. Most are young, with no professional skills except those that would give them access to low-paid service-sector jobs. They are in poor health and often live in substandard housing. They are underemployed, subjected to racism, and may suffer mental health problems including anxiety and clinical depression (Arthur, 2000). Many refugees, however, do make it. The struggles they encounter before coming to the United States often increase their resilience in the face of the problems they encounter here.

Often, immigrant families do not present problems related to the immigrant experience. Instead, the presenting problems may focus on a child's misbehavior or a spouse's estrangement. Often, family members are blaming each other or being blamed by outsiders for problems in the family. Rarely do people look at the impact on the family of the premigration, migration, and postmigration experiences or the larger societal response to immigrants. Yet, a shift in the story can help individuals and families transform themselves and their relationships. It is critical to generate an understanding that includes these contexts of immigrant/refugee experience. All too often, therapy supports the pathologizing, disempowering stories rather than focusing on strength and resilience and exploring how the challenges of migration affect refugees and immigrants.

THE THERAPIST'S POSITION

To do this work, we as therapists must be able to bear witness and to send the message that we can tolerate hearing the story. We need to be humble: We cannot possibly know as much about the culture of origin as the families who see us do. We need to listen carefully to their stories and learn as much as we can about their migration history, loss and trauma, "culture shock," strength, and resilience. We need to challenge ourselves to see and hear the larger context—including, for example, race, gender and class—as we listen to the family's experience. We need to be able to take a proactive stance to connect families with the resources they need, whether that means a culturally compatible church, an advocate within the school system, or social services.

As we hear their stories, we need to pay attention to both the relational costs and gains of immigration and listen for the place of disconnection as well as places of healing and strength. We need to become aware of the "cultural fit" between the family and therapist, as well as between the immigrant and U.S. society (Breunlin, Schwartz, & MacKune-Karrer, 1992; McGoldrick & Giordano, 1996; Mirkin, 1993). We do not know in advance where this road toward biculturality will lead; each family's journey is unique, and different aspects and degrees of the old and new come together in their journey toward biculturality. Indeed, even this biculturality has complex facets to it. It is always dynamic and evolving (Laird, 2000).

For those of us who are entrenched in the dominant culture, our cultural imperatives are invisible to us. We need to challenge ourselves to see what we have not seen, especially when our cultural beliefs and values clash with those of immigrant families.

THE PREMIGRATION EXPERIENCE: TERROR AND MULTIPLE LOSSES

First, we need to look at the degree of trauma experienced in pre-migration: the terror and multiple losses that were experienced by many immigrant families (Alvarez, 1995; Breunlin et al., 1992; Hernandez & Inclan, 1993; Lee, 1990; Llerena-Quinn & Mirkin, 2005). Why and how did the family leave the old country? What happened to them before they left? Who was left behind and why? This preemigration experience encompasses not just the events prior to the immigrants' departure but also the remote history and context for these immigrants. The vestiges of colonialism with its suppression and oppression continue to haunt many immigrants.

Engaging in this work means being able to bear witness to the trauma experienced by many families pre- and postmigration. Can we hear our colleagues or clients who, like Hugo, escaped from a traumatic situation, migrating through another traumatic experience, and arriving finally in a country to face yet other traumatic situations?

Consider the case of Mot, a 19-year-old child I (H. K.) have worked with for several years. Mot was forced to leave his home at the age of 10 because of the civil war that was raging in his country, Sudan. He trekked from Sudan to Kenya, where he lived in a refugee camp. He had many traumatic experiences, which included seeing fellow marchers die from drowning and being told to kill a girl who had tried to escape. He described long journeys and crossing many rivers:

> "Sometimes, we crossed the same river two or three times to escape being noticed by the enemy. We kept running. We did not know who we were running away from. We could not trust anyone. It was very scary. Some of the children belonged to the enemy, and they reported us. We were too scared to sleep at night. We wondered what would happen to us."

In my work with Mot, I have increasingly become aware of how much he fears the dark. Daylight does not bring any comfort or consolation. He is constantly hypervigilant. Any slight change in the routine overwhelms him. His suspicion of others has become a coping strategy for him. Recently, he has begun to talk about losses in his life. But some of these losses have also reawakened the terrors of his past.

Even when a family does not emigrate to escape from terror, it is important to gather the pre-emigration information. This includes as broad a picture as possible of the culture of origin, and what each family member values from the culture. If family members disagreed about whether to migrate, it is important to hear how or by whom the decision was made and the repercussions within the family of the differing opinions. Also, even when a family arrives intact, they have still experienced the loss of friends, the familiar culture, the familiar neighborhood, schools, and way of life. It is important to pay attention to those losses, even if they feel less gripping and traumatic to us as therapists than do the accounts of terrorized immigrants. Indeed, one client has told me (H. K.) that what he misses most is the shared history with his family members whom he left behind (Kamya, 2005b). He misses growing up together with his siblings, sharing in the jokes and games with them.

Many families do not arrive intact. Suarez-Orozco, Todorova, and Louie (2002) report that 85% of children are separated from at least one parent during the immigration process and that 49% were separated from both parents. They report that children who immigrate separately from their parents show more symptoms of depression. For many of these children, irritability, anger, rage, and aggressive behaviors can mask the depression.

When mothers immigrate first in an effort to support families back home, many become *domésticas*, household workers receiving very limited pay (Hondagneu-Sotelo & Avila, 1997). When children and mothers are reunited in the United States after years of living apart, the adjustment can be very difficult for both the child and the mother (Llerena-Quinn & Mirkin, 2005). The mother has spent years dreaming of the reunion, working hard under often difficult and low-paying conditions to make it possible for the child to receive the opportunities she could not herself receive. Over the years of living without the parent, the child has developed other strong bonds with caretakers who are often grandmothers, aunts, or larger extended family. The child has friends, a familiar language, comforting foods, and a way of life that is suddenly disrupted by migration and the child finds him- or herself with an unfamiliar parent in an unfamiliar country speaking an unfamiliar language. The adjustment is often difficult, but it can be contextualized not as a parent–child conflict particular to a family but as a normal response to loss and to life cycle transitions that are out of sync.

Nannies who care for other people's children are caught in a painful contradiction of raising other people's children while being unable to raise their own. One Ugandan woman described to me (H. K.) the struggle she feels:

> "Much as I would like to hold and cuddle my daughter who lives many miles away ... I cannot ... and I miss my daughter ... but I must continue to hold my employer's kid because I need the job and because she reminds me of my own daughter."

Such experiences underscore not only the emotional turmoil immigrants experience but also the hard daily choices they have to make. The losses arising out of the pre migration experience often characterize key aspects of the post migration experience that require clinicians' attention.

THE POSTMIGRATION EXPERIENCE

Cultural Bereavement

Cultural bereavement is central to the lives of refugees and immigrants. They continually seek to make meaning of their lives, especially as they negotiate the numerous losses of migration. Any meaningful clinical intervention must take this into account. This profound sense of loss is often exacerbated by stressors in the United States. Most immigrants are continually asking themselves who they are in an attempt to restore cultural meaning in their lives. Immediate resettlement issues are key to building these cultural meanings. At times, practitioners mistakenly seek to delve into the trauma when refugees are not prepared to engage in such conversations.

Class and Race

Central to the experience of many immigrants of color is the degree of racism and shortage of opportunities in their new country. Many immigrants have experienced overwhelming forms of alienation in their home countries, in the countries through which they migrate, and finally in the United States, where one of the most pernicious forms of alienation many experience is the racism that pervades American culture (Hardy & Laszloffy, 1994). The discrimination that immigrants experience grows out of the history of oppression and racism in the United States. They lack power in most areas of their lives. For African immigrants who come as professionals and then decide to stay, over 76% have doctoral or master's degrees (Apraku, 1991). Most come to the United States as highly skilled professionals, but many are unable to secure jobs in their area of skill or profession. This population sometimes ends up doing low-status jobs for which they are overqualified (Kamya, 2005a). For them the promises of the American dream are far from realized. Downward mobility is a painful reality for most Africans (Kamya, 2005a; Arthur, 2000). A taxi driver trained as an architect struggled with the knowledge that he could not do his respected and valued job in this country. A woman who advertised her housecleaning services had been a psychologist in her country of origin. Both recognized that their accents, race, difficulty with English, negative stereotypes about their countries of origin, and licensing requirements made employers discriminate against them. These changes of status are often as traumatic as changes in financial circumstances.

Most of the professional African immigrants who find commensurate work confine themselves to educational and economic activities. The zeal for education appears to drive their interest. They may sometimes pursue another degree as they seek to compete in the American enterprise. This group will combine student life, professional life and work life. Writing about African immigrants in the United States, Arthur (2000) notes that Africans' engagement in American life is carefully restricted to educational and economic activities that promote survival. Education, especially in the American context, becomes the avenue to upward mobility and economic advancement. Clinicians working with immigrants need to be conversant with the "push" and "pull" factors that often lead immigrants to leave their countries (Kamya, 2005a; Apraku, 1991).

There are others who are confined to nonprofessional or blue-collar jobs (Arthur, 2000). They often have limited opportunities with no health benefits and may be exploited by employers. They become worker bees, often taking on more than one job to survive. Nanny work is very common for women, who work long hours outside the home. Although they may make substantial income, their earnings barely cover basic expenses, leaving little "extra" for health maintenance. Indeed, personal medical care usually gets little attention, often to their detriment, and they may see doctors only in emergencies.

Health

Immigration is associated with a decline in health for Latinos (Hummer & Rogers, 2004) including depression among children separated from their families (Suarez-Orozco et al., 2002), and depression and stress for Jamaican college students as they acculturate (Buddington, 2002); second generation Mexican-American mothers have babies with lower birth weights (Guendelman, Gould, Hudes, & Eskanazi, 1990; Rumbaut & Weeks, 1996). A recent disturbing correlation emerged between immigrant status and vulnerability to schizophrenia (Cantor-Grae & Selton, 2005) with the risk for developing schizophrenia increasing significantly as one moves from first to second generation. At highest risk for schizophrenia were immigrants coming from developing countries and from countries where the majority of the population is Black (rather than White or labeled "not White or Black.") Cantor-Grae and Selton (2005) believe that "social defeat," or the never-ending stress and marginalization of being an outsider, can contribute to vulnerability to schizophrenia. Therapists may become advocates for health care parity and assist immigrant families in navigating an often impenetrable health care system. Therapy becomes more than "talk"—case management and advocacy play a role as well.

Further, cultures have vastly different definitions of and attitudes about illness that play out most dramatically for the immigrant generation. For a dramatic discussion of cultural clashes and health, we recommend Anne Fadiman's (1997) *The spirit catches you and you fall down.*

CULTURE OF ORIGIN, ACCULTURATION, AND BICULTURALITY

A primary issue for immigrant families is the level of difference in values between the culture of origin and the dominant culture of the United States. Therapists from the dominant culture may assume that the norms they grew up with are universal, though this is far from the case. The clash of cultures may threaten a family's existence.

> Several years ago, I (M. P. M.) consulted with a therapist who worked with a Cape Verdean family referred because the parents reportedly beat their children. The parents responded that corporal punishment was regarded as useful discipline in their village. If they hadn't reacted to their children in this way, they would think of themselves as negligent parents. They felt demeaned, disempowered, and confused by DSS intervention. In that case, it was helpful to look at corporal punishment not in terms of right and wrong, but in terms of United States law. We explained that this is a law based on ideas of raising children that are different from their beliefs and that may not make sense to them. Yet it is the law. We wondered aloud how we could be resources as the adults developed other ways of being responsible parents that would not cause law enforcement agencies to intervene.
>
> With another client from Nigeria that I (H. K.) worked with to address issues of discipline that had led to DSS intervention in his family life, I spent time exploring cultural understanding of discipline. This Nigerian man talked about his own upbringing. He began to show more comfort as he told stories that reminded him about how he was raised. After several meetings, he was able to lament the loss of his home culture not so much concerning discipline as concerning his hopes and dreams. Therapists must join immigrants as they grieve their losses.

When our clients share ideas that are different from our own, and they also come from a culture that is unfamiliar to us, we often attribute their belief systems to their culture of origin. But sometimes clients have had trouble in their culture of origin as well, and it is useful to find out whether a family's values and behaviors are representative of their culture of origin or whether they are idiosyncratic within that culture.

We also need to understand who is considered part of the helping system in the culture of origin. In the United States, mental health professionals are sought for healing while people from other cultures might look for healers from a range of religious leaders and elders. Who are their healers? What types of healers are avoided? Who do we and the family then include in our treatment team? Very often, religious figures play a much larger part in the client's dealing with problems than mental health providers have assumed. Questions about religious beliefs and whom the family wants included in the therapy from the religious community might be helpful. These "go-betweens" (Kamya, 2005b) are often consulted, especially at key moments in people's lives.

Intrafamilial Cultural Differences

There are times when couples seek treatment because of conflict between them that could be better understood as differences in the lifestyle and values between their cultures of origin (Kliman, 1994).

> A couple came into therapy because the woman felt that the man was "too needy" and was placing excessive demands on her, whereas he felt hurt and angry at what he called her unresponsiveness. As we explored his immigration history, we began to understand that he had lived in a tribal village where at least 20 family members were available for consultation and collaboration on issues as they arose. The discussion and advice seeking that was valued by his culture of origin was now focused on this one relationship. His wife, whose ancestors came from Germany, viewed her husband's behavior as "needy" rather than engaged and collaborative. By clarifying and respecting the values of both cultures, the therapy focused not on his "neediness" but on seeking out a larger, culturally syntonic support system and placing cultural values at the center of the marital conversation.

Parent–Child Struggles

A common cause of parent–child struggles concerns rates of acculturation (Montalvo & Gutierrez, 1990; Szapocznik, Rio, Perez, & Kurtines, 1986). For example, in some families, parents may try to maintain the values of the culture of origin, whereas children often learn English more rapidly and have greater exposure to the norms of the new culture through school and friendship. Without knowing English or the dominant customs of the United States, parents may depend on children to navigate the new living situation, which can result in the child's belief that her parents are not as competent and skilled as her friends. Parent–child struggles may intensify as the child tries to act like her peers and parents see these behaviors as turning against the family and its values. Further, as parents count on their children for tasks the adults used to do, the roles may be reversed, which is particularly problematic for families from cultures with clearly delineated hierarchies.

Using a process they call Biculturality Effectiveness Training, Szapocznik and his colleagues (1986) define the conflict not as between generations but as between cultures. All family members are then asked to specify what they value about the culture with which they are less identified, thus valuing both cultures and redefining the conflict in a way that makes resolution possible.

It is important also to recognize that what the dominant U.S. culture calls "enmeshment" may be a healthy family constellation in another culture.

For example, adolescence in some Latino cultures can be a time of bringing the young women into the women's circle, allowing them to be included in adult conversation (Llerena-Quinn & Mirkin, 2005). This "bringing in" rather than supporting separation can be mistaken by U.S.-born therapists for unhealthy enmeshment rather than understood as culturally syntonic mature connection.

CASE EXAMPLE

A therapist asked for a consultation, reporting that she was having difficulty working with a truant teenager and her mother. She said the mother was never home to supervise the children and refused the suggestions she made. I (M. P. M.) learned that Mrs. Benito, 14-year-old Ana, and two younger brothers had immigrated from Mexico 2 years earlier, not long after her husband's accidental death. The paternal grandmother had been living in the United States for the previous 5 years. Mrs. Benito found a small apartment and her mother-in-law began to live with them. Ana was responsible for caring for her siblings and grandmother after school, while her mother worked, and on the evenings that her mother went to school. About a year later, Ana became truant, staying out very late without informing her mother where she was going. The school referred the family for therapy.

The therapist met with Ana and her mother and recommended that Mrs. Benito give up one of her two jobs and her evening courses so that she could be more available. She suggested that Ana was a parentified child and that the caretaking burden be lifted from her. The therapist was looking at the family through a White, middle-class, Northwest European lens whereas Mrs. Benito's world was a very different one, and Ana was straddling both. I attempted to enter the mother's world, where daughters were expected to assume major household responsibilities at early ages. She did not understand why this was so problematic for Ana. Mrs. Benito knew she needed her jobs and courses to make a difference in her life and in the lives of her children. Yet, the experts told her to give these up. She felt doomed. At the same time, Ana was in public school, where she more quickly acculturated and yet remained loyal to her family and her sense of duty and responsibility. When she stopped going to school, she maintained her household tasks but also stayed out late to do what she thought American girls did.

The therapist made recommendations based on unchallenged assumptions and a traditional model of family therapy. She tried to restore the hierarchy, develop boundaries between parenting and sibling subsystems, and noted Mrs. Benito's "resistance." She ignored the grandmother and placed the entire burden of the family on the mother. Instead, a culturally sensitive therapy would acknowledge the pull between the old and the new and understand the struggle as a cultural clash, with an acknowledgment that the family is searching for a way of life that incorporates both cultures.

We then looked at the isolation experienced by a family who had lost so much. We connected mother and grandmother with a culturally familiar church so that they could begin to feel "part of" and not "separate from." From this community, Mrs. Benito received some of the help she needed so that neither she nor her children were forced to do the impossible. Ana contributed to the household by being responsible twice a week for an informal church member-based babysitting cooperative. On the other days, other families would watch Mrs. Benito's younger children which left Ana free from major household tasks, on those days.

We did not accept the ageist exclusion of the grandmother. Although she could no longer contribute to household tasks, it was clear that she was very central to the family as the banner carrier for tradition and a clear voice about child rearing.

Most important, we validated and respected their struggle, the major changes in their lives, and their attempts to cope while maintaining family integrity. The emphasis was on relationship (mourning their loss, affirming existing relationships, and developing new ones), restorying (not accepting the story that Mrs. Benito was resistant, Ana was rebellious, and the grandmother was insignificant, but rather developing a story that focused on strength, relationship, and resilience), and expanding the context (so that the immigration experience and the need to counter personal and cultural isolation are the foreground).

POLITICS, CRITICAL ISSUES, AND NASCENT TRENDS

The lives of most immigrants have been profoundly influenced by the political relationship between their home countries and the United States. The politics of African countries, for example, often have a negative effect on how African immigrants are perceived in America. Immigrants may have come out of complicated war and conflict situations that they cannot explain or understand (Kamya, 2005b), yet they are often asked to act as spokespersons for their home countries. Indeed, for many their trauma may have shut them off from the day-to-day politics of their home countries. The recent war on terror that has targeted al Qaeda has highlighted Osama bin Laden as the mastermind behind various terror tactics. In working with unaccompanied minors from Sudan, I (H. K.) have heard these young men's concern that they have become targets of ridicule and contempt from their peers simply because Osama is said to have lived in Sudan at one time.

Many of them report not having had any knowledge of his terror group before coming to this country but now feeling they have to explain not only to U.S. Homeland Security but also to their peers that they had no ties to this terror group. At times, they feel targeted for conditions and events over which they have no influence. Holding open discussions about these issues in family therapy may alienate an immigrant family. If they have supported groups that are no longer favored by the United States, they may experience any discussion about their home country as a threat to their existence. Indeed, they may seek to provide a "party line" as a way of saving face. Family therapists must listen attentively to the emerging stories, including unpopular viewpoints that immigrant families may hold.

A second critical issue is the impact of U.S. laws and their enforcement on both documented and undocumented immigrants, many of whom are feeling unsafe, unwanted, and targeted. The recent raid on a New Bedford, Massachusetts factory that employed undocumented immigrants was described by Senator Ted Kennedy (2007) in a press release:

> This is the haphazard way DHS [Department of Homeland Security] handles the problem of illegal immigration. They have said that they had planned this raid for months, but had made no provision to house the workers they arrested. Instead, the workers were rounded up and immediately transported by DHS to Texas and other states, far from their families, without even an opportunity to say goodbye. The DHS knew that many of these workers had children at home, but they did not do nearly enough to protect them. As a result, children came back to empty homes; at least one nursing baby went to the hospital with dehydration; and hundreds cried themselves to sleep, wondering where their loved ones were and why they had disappeared.

The trauma of arrest and family separation is a nightmare under any circumstances, but for some immigrants this may be a replication of previous trauma in their countries of origin. Immigration reform is on the political table right now, and family therapists need to be aware of how the political and legal spheres affect the psychological lives of families. Advocacy may therefore become part of our work as family therapists.

SUMMARY

Working with immigrant and refugee families challenges us to move beyond the cultural norms and imperatives that we take for granted, to allow in the strength, resilience, and richness of families of other cultures. We need to understand the immigrant experience in its broadest context, which includes the premigration life of the family, the experience of the migration, and the benefits and obstacles that families face in the United States. This involves exploring experiences of loss and trauma, and it also means being able to look at discriminatory policies, racism, classism, and xenophobia, which cause pain to so many immigrant families. It is a privilege to accompany immigrant families along that road.

ACKNOWLEDGMENTS

We would like to thank Dr. Roxana Llerena-Quinn whose insights helped to shape this chapter, and Lasell College students Mabel Valenzuela and Merryl Raubeson for their insights and research.

REFERENCES

Alvarez, M. (1995). *The experience of migration: A relational approach in therapy* (Work in Progress No. 71). Wellesley, MA: Wellesley College, The Stone Center.

Apraku, K. (1991). *African émigrés in the United States.* New York: Praeger.

Arthur, J. A. (2000). *Invisible sojourners: African immigrant diaspora in the United States.* Westport, CT: Praeger.

Breunlin, D. C., Schwartz, R. C., & MacKune-Karrer, B. (1992). *Metaframeworks: Transcending the models of family therapy.* New York: Jossey-Bass.

Buddington, S. A. (2002). Acculturation, psychological adjustment (stress, depression, self-esteem), and the academic achievement of Jamaican immigrant college students. *International Social Work, 45*(4), 447–464.

Cantor-Grae, E., & Selton, J. (2005). Schizophrenia and migration: A meta-analysis and review. *American Journal of Psychiatry, 162,* 12–24.

Fadiman, A. (1997). *The spirit catches you and you fall down.* New York: Noonday Press.

Guendelman, S., Gould, J., Hudes, M., & Eskanazi, B. (1990). Generational difference in perinatal health among the Mexican-American population: Findings from HHANES 1982–84. *American Journal of Public Health* (Suppl.), *80*(12), 61–65.

Hardy, K. V., & Laszloffy, T. A. (1994). Deconstructing race in family therapy. In R. Almeida (Ed.), *Expansions of feminist theory through diversity* (pp. 5–33). Binghamton, NY: Haworth.

Hernandez, M., & Inclan, J. (1993). A conceptual framework for therapy with ethnic minority families. In *AFTA resource packet: Honoring and working with diversity in family therapy.* Washington, DC: American Family Therapy Academy.

Hondagneu-Sotelo, P., & Avila, E. (1997). "I'm here but I'm there": The meanings of Latina transnational motherhood. *Gender and Society, 11*(5), 548–571.

Hummer, R. A., & Rogers, R. G. (2004). Nativity, duration of residence, and the health of Hispanic adults in the United States. *International Migration Review, 38*(1), 184–212.

Kamya, H. (2005a). African immigrant families. In M. McGoldrick, J. Giordano, & N. Garcia-Preto (Eds.), *Ethnicity and family therapy* (3rd ed., pp. 101–116). New York: Guilford Press.

Kamya, H. (2005b, Summer). The impact of war on children and families: Their stories, my own stories. In J. Kliman (Ed.), *Touched by war zones, near and far: Oscillations of despair and hope* (AFTA Monograph Series, Vol. 1, No. 1). Washington, DC: American Family Therapy Academy.

Kennedy, E. (2007). New Bedford immigration raid press release. Retrieved June 2, 2007, from *http://kennedy.senate.gov/newsroom/press_release.cfm?id=0D94582B-45BC-4CA8-9D01-4F0673E06EB5*.

Kliman, J. (1994). The interweaving of gender, class, and race in family therapy. In M. P. Mirkin (Ed.), *Women in context: Toward a feminist reconstruction of psychotherapy.* New York: Guilford Press.

Laird, J. (2000). Theorizing culture: Narrative ideas and practice principles. *Journal of Feminist Family Therapy, 11*(4), 99–114.

Lee, E. (1990). Family therapy with Southeast Asian families. In M. P. Mirkin (Ed.), *The social and political contexts of family therapy* (pp. 331–354). Needham, MA: Allyn & Bacon.

Llerena-Quinn, R., & Mirkin, M. P. (2005). Immigrant mothers: Mothering in the borderlands. In M. P. Mirkin, B. F. Okun, & K. L. Suyemoto (Eds.), *Psychotherapy with women: Exploring diverse contexts and identities* (pp. 87–110). New York: Guilford Press.

McGoldrick, M., & Giordano, J. (1996). Overview: Ethnicity and family therapy. In M. McGoldrick, J. Giordano, & J. Pearce (Eds.), *Ethnicity and family therapy* (2nd ed., pp. 1–27). New York: Guilford Press.

Mirkin, M. P. (1993). Some thoughts about cultural diversity. In *AFTA resource packet: Honoring and working with diversity in family therapy.* Washington, DC: American Family Therapy Academy.

Montalvo, B., & Gutierrez, M. (1990). Unevenness of cultural transition: Nine assumptions for work with ethnic minority families. In G. Saba, B. MacKune-Karrer, & K. Hardy (Eds.), *Minorities and family therapy.* New York: Haworth Press.

Rumbaut, R. G., & Weeks, J. R. (1996). Unraveling a public health enigma: Why do immigrants experience superior perinatal health outcomes? *Research in the Sociology of Health Care, 13*(B), 337–391.

Szapocznik, J., Rio, A., Perez, Z. A., & Kurtines, W. (1986). Bicultural effectiveness training: An experimental test of an intervention modality for families experiencing intergenerational–intercultural conflict. *Hispanic Journal of Behavioral Sciences, 8*(4), 303–330.

Suarez-Orozco, C., Todorova, I. L. G., & Louie, J. (2002). Making up for lost time: The experience of separation and reunification among immigrant families. *Family Process, 41*(4), 625–641.

CHAPTER 28

A Fifth-Province Approach to Intracultural Issues in an Irish Context

Marginal Illuminations[1]

Imelda Colgan McCarthy
Nollaig O'Reilly Byrne

The word in language is half someone else's. It becomes
"one's own" only when the speaker populates it with his
own intent, his own accent, when he appropriates the word,
adapting it to his own semantic and expressive intention.
—MIKHAIL BAKHTIN (1981, p. 293)

In family therapy literature, a focus on multiculturalism has enabled practitioners to develop culture-specific practices when working with persons from different ethnic groups other than those of the dominant culture (McGoldrick, 2005). The term "multiculturalism," as a societal orientation and concern, points to an emerging moral sensibility of the public in diverse contexts and orients citizens to a more open, pluralist, and participant society. Implicit in this concern is the recognition of the potential for the silencing of marginal groups by the politically and culturally dominant. At the level of theory, it challenges cultural stereotypes and attributions of otherness and difference as "a view from nowhere" and relocates the latter view as a colonizing posture. Therefore, as a requirement of justice, the value aspirations and needs specific to a particular cultural group are accorded moral recognition within a multicultural stance. However, a multicultural-ism that proliferates an endless fallout of stories without acknowledging their interplay with the dominant cultural narratives with which they coex-ist will ultimately fail in its moral quest.

For the purpose of this chapter, we are using an intracultural account to elaborate the particular story of one family who live on the margins of Irish society. Like other welfare recipients, the members of this family are eminently vulnerable to state interventions.

COMMUNITY DEVELOPMENT AND THE EMERGENCE OF A FIFTH PROVINCE APPROACH

In an attempt to redress this top-down stance of state services, commu-nity development and other associated projects, politically and spiritually informed by narratives of justice, speak to the possibility of an authentic cul-tural partnership with marginalized groups. Campbell, Tamasese, and Wal-degrave (1998) of the Just Therapy group in New Zealand refer to the ethi-cal responsibility of dominant groups to enter into a decolonizing awareness and to the responsibility of practitioners as "a sacred task to bring health and welfare to the people." In their work, as in our own, the coauthoring of new stories (White & Epston, 1990) is addressed to the particular cultural experiences of the people we work with while simultaneously remembering the overarching dominant cultural narratives that constrain them.

Since the mid-1980s, we have worked under the team name of the Fifth Province Associates (FPA). During this time we have collaborated with a colleague, Sister Jo Kennedy, who has undertaken a key role in forward-ing community action–education–therapy projects in a deprived community (Kennedy, 1994). As an experienced professional, a family therapist, and a member of a religious community, she shared housing with the people in a high-density public housing project. Her presence there was a sign and a witness to the inception of noncolonizing practices addressed to the dire needs of this community. Initially, as an "outsider," she had to sustain much hostility and suspicion from the community. With time, her witness to the hardship of the day-to-day life of the people made her an acceptable com-munity member. In turn, our team was given the opportunity by Sister Jo to develop a more refined, focused political and spiritual orientation for our own practice. We have learned much from her ongoing work marked by the love implicit in commitment, creativity, and physical endurance.

Out of our many collaborative conversations with Sister Jo and her work in developing community initiatives and becoming kindred in that community, we were privileged to develop an "insider's" perspective drawn from the weave and tangle of many stories told to her, the events she has witnessed, and the advocacy she has articulated as a member of the community.

THE METAPHOR OF THE FIFTH PROVINCE

The issues of intracultural diversity and silenced voices have been concerns for us since we began to work together in 1981. The story we tell in this chapter is the story of just one particular kind of intracultural marginalization: the story of a family living in poverty. Because of the processes of marginalization that occur in our society, those who are poor are socially excluded, and the stories of their lives on the edge are often silenced. Thus, listening to these silenced accounts becomes an ethical and political act of no small significance. Out of these concerns, we adopted the metaphor of the Fifth Province (Byrne & McCarthy, 1995; Colgan, 1992; Kearney, Byrne, & McCarthy, 1989; McCarthy & Byrne, 1995; McCarthy, 1994).[2] The metaphor is taken from Celtic mythology and the work of two Irish philosophers, Richard Kearney and Mark P. Hederman (Hederman & Kearney, 1977). In the work of this team, the metaphor of the Fifth Province enables a re-viewing of the issues of power, justice, and language in relationships. In the words of the Irish president Mary Robinson, the Fifth Province is that place in each of us which is open to the other. It is in itself a metaphor for multicultural perspectives, as it refers to the possibility of holding together multiple stories and social realities in dialogue. For us, it is a province of possibilities, of imagination, and of ethics.

TOWARD AN ETHICS OF IMAGINATION

Imagining another person calls for an ethic of care. To imagine the life of another is to adopt a stance of ethical responsibility toward the other. Placing such a stance within a therapeutic domain that features issues of social justice is also a political act. Thus imagining a Fifth-Province dis-position[3] in systemic therapies is, for us, about occupying a borderline territory between one's own world and the worlds of those we are in conversation with. Richard Kearney (1996) has outlined an ethics of imagination that is underpinned by three main principles. The first is the acceptance of the other. The second principle refers to the right of all to be heard and to have the testimony to their experiences witnessed. The final principle is the imagining of future possibilities. We incorporate these principles when we utilize the Fifth Province metaphor. As a province of possibilities in language and imagination, it also becomes a province or domain of ethics. If those from marginalized groups are to be able to tell the stories of their lived experiences in a context in which normative compliances are expected, then we must also recognize that there is a danger of subjecting them to silence and co-option (Byrne & McCarthy, 1995). We hold that imposing normative expectations on marginalized clients without reference to their contexts of adversity constitutes a colonial therapeutic stance that distances us from the subjugated "other."

INTERCULTURAL MARGINALIZATION AND SYSTEMIC THERAPY

With a history of long periods of colonization behind us, we as Irish therapists wanted to honor our long oral tradition of storytelling of survival. We also imagined that life on the edges would produce stories that might not reside comfortably within many of our normative discursive frames. As such, we hold strongly that it is the responsibility of therapists from Western traditions to reflect on their own practices and theories and not expect clients to fit the norms of their professional practice. If this latter occurs, there is a danger that both the therapist and the clients will blame the client for the lack of fit. In culture-blind practices, therapists can become nonconscious oppressors in the guise of helping (Kearney et al., 1989; Byrne & McCarthy, 1995; Lorenz, 1994). Under such a regime, clients have little choice but to subjugate themselves further in order to avail themselves of help. Thus they are in danger of being complicit in their own betrayal.

STORIES AND CONVERSATIONS IN THE FIFTH PROVINCE: A FAMILY–PROFESSIONAL NETWORK

In our collaboration with Sister Jo, we have had the opportunity to have conversations with families judged by an array of professionals to be incorrigible or inaccessible to services. In family–professional network meetings in which Sister Jo's community alliance with the family provided cultural safety for the work, it was possible for families to assert their concerns and to reclaim responsibility for culturally fitting solutions. We have experienced these emergences through a process by which the family's particular account could be spoken of without fear of correction or censure. Furthermore, we as professionals, previously limited by an outsider's view, sometimes heard for the first time stories that were crucial in the family's self-understanding

The work we re-present in this chapter included a paternal grandmother, Chrissie; a separated father, Joe; a single mother, Mary; and Joe and Mary's

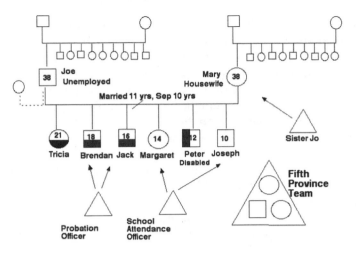

FIGURE 28.1. The family–professional network.

six children—Tricia, 21 years; Brendan, 18 years; Jack, 16 years; Margaret, 14 years; Peter, 12 years (severely mentally and physically disabled, and not present at the interviews); and Joseph, 10 years.[4] Also included were a probation officer, a school attendance officer, Sister Jo, ourselves, and our FPA colleague Philip Kearney,[5] who conducted the interviews. (Figure 28.1 illustrates the entire family–professional network.) Throughout the excerpts that follow, we highlight a Fifth-Province dis-position in which a family's tale of outrageous and harmful acts, for which state censure was never far removed, was transformed. In its place, through conversation or inquiries pitched at the extreme edges of risk, a story of struggle involving family dismemberment and death facilitated an authentic expression of this family's tragedies in their own words. In our experience, the opportunity to speak in this way creates possibilities for new and less harmful connections to emerge. The image of an injured child becomes at first the herald of guilt and later the liberating symbol of innocence.

Assembling the Family–Professional Network

Mary, Sister Jo, the school attendance officer, and the probation officer attended the first meeting with us. Mary explained that she had met with and listened to numerous professionals who advised her on the merits of controlling and supervising her children, all to no avail. Of immediate concern was the fact that Margaret and Joseph had absented themselves from school and would soon become subject to a placement in a residential school by the courts. The older children, Tricia, Brendan, and Jack, were experiencing grave difficulties with drugs and violence, and Peter attended a special school for children with serious intellectual disabilities.

Despite the inventory of difficulties as described by Mary, her status as protector of her children was not in question. The clarity of her stance as she voiced her care and love for her difficult children was the familiar story of many mothers in that community for whom Sister Jo was a resource person. By anchoring ourselves to this mother's concern, it became possible for us to imagine the possibility of speaking to the children on the mother's behalf, not by way of displacing her or inserting a societal authority. In this way it became possible to speak with and listen to the children in a way that honored their mother and did not threaten her place. This professional acknowledgment of Mary's perspective provided an area of cultural safety for the children, in which they might not be constrained from speaking to a group of listeners (client–professional system) about what most mattered to them.

We went on to suggest that the second network meeting might also include the children. Mary and Sister Jo agreed. To everybody's surprise, there was no difficulty in assembling them all, apart from Peter. Although their day-to-day lives suggested harmful activity, dispersal, and disconnection, it soon became clear that the possibility of family connection and continuity held a precious place in their lives. Using excerpts from the second meeting, we attempt to show how our inquiry, which we refer to as "questioning at the extremes," threaded together a family narrative of tragic desperation, in which forces of extinction and survival coexisted in an uncommonly close partnership. Questioning at the extremes is a mode of inquiry that directs questions toward revealing the extreme possibilities of a presented story. As an example, in this scenario, killing oneself was assumed to be the extension of drug and alcohol abuse.

A Question of "Harmful" Extremes

The word "harm" was introduced by Mary in the first session, as she expressed her ongoing concerns about her children's dangerous actions. It thus became the "motif" that proposed danger to, if not extinction of, individual family members. As Mary's central concern for her children, it guided the inquiry to a point at which the children could give an account.

PHILIP: Who is it that has taken overdoses in this family?

BRENDAN: Me and Jack.

PHILIP: Just the two of you?

BRENDAN: Yeah. Me and Jack, mostly.

PHILIP: (to Tricia) Have you taken overdoses?

TRICIA: I have.

BRENDAN: One.

JACK: Two.

TRICIA: I take a lot of tablets in the day.

PHILIP: Yeah, but have you taken deliberate overdoses?

TRICIA: Yeah. Twice.

PHILIP: Twice. You tried to kill yourself?

TRICIA: (*looking confusedly to mother*) No.

BRENDAN: No, he [Jack] is the only one who tried to kill himself.

PHILIP: He is the only one who has tried to kill himself (*Jack nods agreement.*) ... using tablets or what?

JACK: Tablets and drink.

What was surprising here was the willingness of the three older children to give first-person accounts of their involvement in acts of deliberate self-harm through drug and alcohol abuse. As is seen in this segment, the children correct a common professional assumption that overdoses refer to deliberate self-harming behaviors. Rather, there is a whole range of behaviors involving the abuse of intoxicants that is a structured feature of their community. They insisted on the distinction between intentional (Jack) and nonintentional (Tricia and Brendan) effects of self-harming behaviors.

The Risk of Suicide: A Mother and Son

PHILIP: (*to Mary*) And which of them do you think is most likely to harm themselves, through overdosing or whatever?

MARY: I think mostly Jack. He can be about the most depressed, in that ... he is inclined to ... Brendan will take tablets, but it might not be with the intention to kill himself—but he [Jack] would just keep on taking them. He has often walked over to the flats, where there are drugs around, and he was 3 days out of his mind, and I had him taken out of the flats and home.

PHILIP: So would you think that Jack is the most likely candidate for suicide?

MARY: Yeah.

PHILIP: And after Jack?

MARY: Brendan or Tricia, but I don't know if they would just take them at the moment, but not think that they are going to ... not really wanting to kill themselves.

PHILIP: Would you say that your mother might commit suicide, Brendan?

BRENDAN: If we keep on going on the way we are, she will.

PHILIP: You think so?

BRENDAN: Yeah.

PHILIP: When did you first think of that as a possibility?

BRENDAN: The last 4 or 5 months.

TRICIA: I would say my mother would have taken her life long ago if my brother wasn't the way he is today. She knows he is depending on her, you know.

PHILIP: Which brother—Peter?

TRICIA: Peter, yeah. Peter is brain-damaged, too.

PHILIP: Yeah.

TRICIA: He can't walk or anything.

PHILIP: So you think if it weren't for him, your mother would have killed herself a long time ago?

TRICIA: Ah, yes, if it weren't for him she wouldn't be here today—or neither would we, you know.

PHILIP: I see. What would have happened?

TRICIA: She would either have killed herself or left us.

PHILIP: I see, yeah.

BRENDAN: And we would be after driving her to do it.

JOSEPH: And if she had died, we would have killed ourselves.

BRENDAN: Then if she died, we would have killed ourselves, and if she went, everything would have been worse and worse and worse.

JACK: And we probably would have followed her.

PHILIP: Yeah, OK ...

JOSEPH: If she left us, there would be nothing left of the family.

The theme of suicidal risk was developed by Mary in response to Philip's question, as she made distinctions among her children and confirmed declarations they had already made. Staying within the thematic frame of suicide, Philip raised the question as to whether Brendan, as oldest son and commentator on family issues, considered his mother to be in this risk category. What followed from the children was an acutely stark and condensed reply to an extreme question. This dialogue, which had the structure of a chorus, drew on and focused the question on the shared tragic experience of the family. Of cultural interest here is the fact that these barely literate children, with poor attention skills and much intragroup aggression and conflict, could produce in language a synchrony of voices of such dramatic structure and intensity. Each response adds to the emotional charge of the family narrative drawn from their shared experience—guilt and innocence.

From the children's point of view, Mary, as mother, protector, and caretaker, was the most tragically affected by Peter's injury, and this was the thread that maintained her tenuous presence in the family. This was the story that condemned and bound the children to a guilty stance toward both their mother and Peter. In addressing this interminable self-condemnation, the team through Philip referred to it as a "spell" cast over their lives from which they must be released. To discuss their liberation from this "spell," we suggested another meeting with the adults. At Mary's suggestion, the father and paternal grandmother, Joe and Chrissie, would also be invited.

Sacrificial Losses: A Father and Son

The following excerpt of a conversation occurred in the third family–professional network meeting. As noted, Joe and Chrissie attended, as Mary had considered them to have a powerful influence on the lives of her children. As the session progressed, it emerged that Peter's accident, his disabilities, and his place in the family related not only to the children's spellbound state but also to Joe's sense of helplessness and desperation. Peter, when he was 2 years old, had fallen through a refuse chute in the government-subsidized apartment building where the family lived. He was in the company of Brendan, then 8 years old. Joe wanted to wipe away the event by killing either himself or Peter. In recognizing Peter's importance to Mary, he decided to "give up everything that meant anything to me" and leave the family.

PHILIP: We talked a little the two previous times we have been here about other major events, like Peter's accident ...

JOE: That was just ... that was ... I wouldn't even go into that now, you know what I mean? (*Voice breaks.*)

PHILIP: It is too upsetting?

JOE: I think I would still be at home today if that had not happened to Peter, you know. Because I know for a fact, and she [Mary] knows as well, if I was to stay in that house for 3 days with that young fellow, I would smother him.

PHILIP: I didn't know that. (*To Mary*) Did you know that?

MARY: He came in one night, and (*to Joe*) you were drunk and I was putting Peter to bed and you came up and you did say that to me.

JOE: I had the pillow and I was going to do it, and I was crying and I said to her, "The only way I can ... "

MARY: And I nearly lost my reason. ... I have never really forgotten that, you know . . . .

JOE: I mean you are looking at a child who was perfect and running around. It was unfortunate that it had to be him that it happened to.

MARY: But he is so lovable.

JOE: Like you see kids now running around with their toys and everying. I know how wild he was, and seeing him now ... I mean that ...

PHILIP: Did you hear what Mary has just said, that he could be so lovable? Because I was very struck by your kids' talk about how important Peter is in the family.

JOE: I mean Peter is everything—I mean, if anything happened to him now, I don't know, like, but there is no way I could live with the guy, you know. I couldn't live in the same house as him. I can't even bear to look at him. Don't get me wrong—every time I go up there and I see Peter, I think of the way he was. I cannot accept what happened to him.

PHILIP: Is that the hardest thing for you to accept?

JOE: Well, you put yourself in my shoes.

PHILIP: Sure ... Well, I can't even begin to. ... You have had many things to accept, I imagine.

JOE: I just will never accept that. That is just one thing I will never accept. I was praying that he would not even come out of the hospital. Like when they told us about the damage that was done to him and everything.

MARY: Well, I wanted him back, no matter what way I got him back. I just wanted him.

JOE: We did not get Peter back.

PHILIP: And you are saying that that is the reason why you are not in the house? That is why you left?

JOE: Well, that was really the breaking point between me and her. She took a nervous breakdown. I was running to the hospital to her, I was running to the hospital in the morning, at dinnertime, and in the evening to Peter, and she was in hospital 6 or 7 months, whatever it was, and I was trying to manage the kids on my own, by myself. It was just too much. I just couldn't cope, and that was it. I ended up cracking up myself then as well.

PHILIP: What happened?

JOE: Ah, well, I took a couple of overdoses (*voice trembles*) and that myself. Then I said to myself I would be better off getting rid of him rather than getting rid of myself. And I think I would have anyway.

PHILIP: And that is still the same for you?

JOE: Oh yeah, I still feel the same way about it, yeah, even to the present day. I mean I have talked to her [Mary] of this before.

MARY: No, I never heard those points so much before, I really didn't.

PHILIP: Which ones?

MARY: About Peter, regarding him dead and that. Just one night he did it, and I thought it ... I overlooked it because I thought you were just drunk that night. You were crying and that. I think I said it to you, and I have never forgotten it.

JOE: Yeah, I know, yeah.

MARY: But I didn't think you felt that strongly. I thought it was because you were just drunk that night.

JOE: It is just like having a building, and you going away on holidays for a week and just looking, and your building is just condemned. I mean, it is the same way with Peter. I mean, Peter is going to need to be lifted around for the rest of his life. I mean, there is no way is he ever going to be able to live a life.

PHILIP: Has it anything to do with the circumstances of his accident?

JOE: How do you mean?

PHILIP: How he got injured. Or is that irrelevant? Is the fact that he is now handicapped ...

JOE: How he got injured ... and there are still an awful lot of lies being told about how Peter got injured, and I don't think anybody has been able to face up to it, even up to the present day ... exactly what happened to Peter. It has never really come out into the open, what really happened to Peter.

PHILIP: And who is most affected by that?

JOE: I don't know, to tell you the truth, I don't know.

PHILIP: I mean, is it the two of you, or is it the children, or is it ...

JOE: Oh, I mean, I know she was broken up something terrible about it. I mean, I was broken up, but what could we do?

PHILIP: What I am asking about is the circumstances of the accident. You say that has never been dealt with. Is that right?

JOE: Oh, no, it was dealt with and all that in courts and everything like that, if that is what you mean.

PHILIP: No, no, I mean in terms of the way you get on with each other as people. Who gets blamed for it?

JOE: Who gets blamed for Peter's accident?

PHILIP: Yeah.

JOE: Well, I always blame Brendan for Peter's accident, and I always will.

PHILIP: And how does that affect your relationship with Brendan?

JOE: It doesn't affect my relationship with Brendan now, because, I mean, he was only a child himself.

The Peter who was remembered—the one who didn't come back, the one condemned to "uselessness"—is an allegorical symbol of the family's historical experience of slum clearance.[6] In cleaning up eyesores, did the official culture forget its obligation to the people who, for generation after generation, gave birth, lived, and died in this place? It was as if Joe was here reminded of that abrupt transition from a home to a useless and condemned building when he thought of his injured son. However, in his telling, part of the responsibility for Peter's accident also resided within the family. It was this latter catastrophe that pushed him to further displacement. His leaving could be seen not only as a separation from his wife or on abandonment of his family but also as a sacrifice to protect Peter's life.

Philip invited an exaggerated comparison (a questioning at the extremes) between these two losses—Joe's leaving and Peter's injury—for Mary. Chrissie, by way of validation, was in no doubt about the greater loss—"the injury to her son." In this and her further statement—"because I think more of my sons than I would of my husband any day"—she cited the position of mother and child as central to "family." Following this affirmation, Mary then found a way to include herself in a story of motherhood that again included a father.

PHILIP: (to Chrissie) Which do you think was the greater loss for Mary, the injury to Peter—what happened to him—or Joe leaving?

CHRISSIE: The injury to her son.

PHILIP: Was more than her husband leaving?

CHRISSIE: Um.

PHILIP: You are very clear about that.

CHRISSIE: Um.

PHILIP: (to Mary) Do you agree?

CHRISSIE: Because I think more of my sons than I would of my husband any day.

PHILIP: Did I catch that right?

CHRISSIE: I think more of my sons than I would of my husband any day.

PHILIP: Yes, that is what I thought you said, yes. Would that be the same for you, Mary?

MARY: Yes, well, I brought them into the world, you know. He is part of both of us, really, but still I love them all. If it happened to any of them I would have still felt the same way. It wouldn't have been important.

JOE: I think I would still be in the home today if that had not happened to Peter, you know.

In a confessional autobiographical mode, Joe, Chrissie, and Mary made manifest to a group of listeners the criminal and the tragic narratives that authorized their lives. The unity of this account stands in stark contradiction to the moral sensibility of normative conventions. It draws together the "justice" exacted from father's "choices" in the family and a pathos of failure and weakness in his exclusion. His self-justificatory appeal moved between lived experience and anticipated evaluative judgments. Joe's remark, "Well, you put yourself in my shoes" and Philip's rejoinder, "Sure ... well, I can't even begin to" is an acknowledgement of the incommensurability of discourses and an authentic distance of positions between the two speakers in this instance.

The Injured and the Innocent: A Connecting Narrative between Statutory Mandates and a Family's "Guilt"

From a position of distance and the expectation of normative evaluation, the team was called on by the family's story to register a response beyond a passive and condemnatory listening. The image of Peter, everywhere evident in the family's account, as the injured and the innocent was the resonant key that opened the many-layered narrative of guilt and innocence. This was the centripetal image that held the personal and political narratives of injustice, guilt, and innocence. Peter, the unspeaking one, became the allegorical lodestone for both the professionals and the family members. His innocence pointed to possibilities for reauthoring, through which the family members and professionals might move beyond blame and counterblame and in which the innocence of the family might be glimpsed by all. We in the team began to ask of ourselves, "What is it that Peter might see when he looks at his family? What is it that Peter asks for?" He was the bearer of the most injury, and yet he did not blame or accuse. We imagined that he saw the family members as they would wish to see themselves, if they were not blighted by adversity, failure, and self-condemnation. The following was our attempt to incorporate an ethical imagining.

The Team's Message

PHILIP: (*to Joe*) The story you have told us about Peter is absolutely central. ... It seems that the family's possibilities ... in a sense stopped with Peter's accident. That the possibilities of people in this family going on to a life of happiness and fulfillment stopped because of Peter's injury and his handicap. ... It is as if when you look into his face you say something like, "I cannot enjoy my wife, my kids, my family because of what happened to you." It almost comes across that everybody in the family is under a spell. That because this child was injured and handicapped, "we are not free." In a sense, it is as if he has all the innocence ...

JOE: (*Nods.*) Yeah.

PHILIP: And everybody else has all the guilt. So that is what we now see as the spell your family is under, and that it is for you people to decide whether that is going to continue or not. Because if you don't, there is no doubt but that the outside society (*pointing to professionals*) will intervene.

JOE: Um.

PHILIP: And they will come and place your kids in care, and they will be doing it for the best reasons in the world. But somewhere in there, there is the possibility to change that for yourselves. We imagine that if we could see the world, see the family from Peter's eyes, we would see only the good side—of being taken care of, of people smiling at him, people doing things for him. I would say he would see an awful lot of good about the people in this family.

JOE: Ah, yeah, I would agree with that, all right, like if it was Peter looking out and like the way he is. Yeah, of course he would, yeah.

PHILIP: He had an extraordinary powerful influence in this family. It is as if everyone is going around under a sentence since his accident, really.

JOE: Well, that is what the priest said to us. He said it to us ... the priest in the hospital. "This is going to change your lives completely. When you walk outside the door now, after you know the news, you know how bad things are. It is going to be a completely different world out there. Even the road you walk on is going to seem different.

PHILIP: OK, well, I am saying that I believe it doesn't have to be like that always. ... It seems to me that you have made a huge sacrifice since then. You gave up a lot.

JOE: I gave up everything that meant anything to me.

PHILIP: Yeah. I think Mary gave up a lot, too.

JOE: She did, of course, yeah.

This was the team's acknowledgment that a professional stance is never "innocent" (McCarthy, 1991; Andersen, 1995). Most professional discourses are shot through with normative and professional judgments that inevitably collide with marginalized personal accounts (Byrne & McCarthy, 1995). Peter's transformation was a blight cast on the family, cutting Joe adrift and spellbinding the children in self-destructive and violent disarray. Mary's remark, "I wanted him back, no matter what way I got him," expressed a mother's valuing of a life, however disabled, as the deepest affirmation of an ethics of care. Philip addressed Joe, as the bearer of guilt.

PHILIP: Maybe you have paid whatever dues have to be paid, and maybe for your kid's sake you need to ... perhaps ... stop paying them. I don't know, it is just a thought, because otherwise the kids may think they have to go on paying them forever.

JOE: I know, yeah (*rubbing his eyes.*)

PHILIP: And that is the way they are behaving.

JOE: I know what you mean, like they feel guilty, as well.

PHILIP: Yeah, and they may think that the only way that they can be in the world is to continue to pay those dues, and they don't have to. (*Joe nods.*) Because Peter is not asking it of them.

JOE: I know that, yeah.

In this inclusive move, Joe reconnected himself with his children in their mutual but invalidating narrative of guilt and failure. These family members were the invalids beyond Mary's reach. Only Peter, standing outside condemnation, was able to recognize them and asked nothing of them except care.

CONCLUSION

To sum up the views we have expressed in this chapter, a narrative of a unique family or personal situation will remain exotic and incomprehensible if it is isolated from the larger social and cultural context that pervades it. Therefore, the contextual interplay between the larger narratives of injustice that simultaneously and tragically penetrate the lives and the personal stories of the marginalized everywhere is constantly acknowledged. It is within this multilayered, resonating interplay that meaning is extended beyond the isolated words of both clients and professionals through the actions of speaking, inquiring, exaggerating, listening, and reflecting. What emerges, we believe, within this personalized and politicized cocreation is the possibility of an authentic emotional encounter.

In the years since this series of meetings, this family continues to exhibit its archetypal shape, although its members now hold themselves somewhat more aloof from professional intervention. Sister Jo remains as a neighborly resource to members of this family and to others in the community. The probation and school attendance officers reported a dramatic decrease in tension and experienced a release from the impossible double agendas of and contradictions between social control and therapeutic support in the ensuing period.

NOTES

1. It is a feature of Celtic manuscripts such as the eighth-century *Book of Kells* that major illuminations are placed in the margins.
2. The Fifth Province may or may not have existed. There are many versions. Some say it was a province of imagination and possibility—a place that was "other" to the pragmatic concerns of the "real" world. Others cite it as a druidic place at the center of Ireland, where the four provinces met and where kings and chieftains came to receive counsel and resolve conflicts through dialogue. Today its only remaining trace is in the Irish language, in which the word for province is *coiced*, which means "fifth" (Byrne & McCarthy, 2007; McCarthy & Byrne, 2001).
3. "Dis-position" is a term used by the FPA. It is hyphenated to illustrate movement between the taking of a position and the nontaking of one by a therapist. The term was first used by Seamus Heaney in the foreword to an issue of the Irish journal *The Crane Bag*, which was edited by Irish philosophers Richard Kearney and Mark P. Hederman (Heaney, 1977, p. 7).
4. The names of all family members have been changed.
5. Philip Kearney worked with us until 1995 and collaborated in the development of the ideas and practices outlined in this chapter.
6. The area in which this family lived had originally been built as a barracks for the British Army in the previous century. During the 1960s this housing had been demolished, at which time the families were abruptly dispersed, disrupting their community identity and sense of place. Some of the original families were rehoused here in what is now an area constructed of concrete blocks, courtyards, and towers.

ACKNOWLEDGMENTS

This chapter is dedicated to Sister Jo and to the family we describe here. We also acknowledge Philip Kearney, our colleague and dear friend of many years.

REFERENCES

Andersen, T. (1995). Reflecting processes: Acts of informing and forming. In S. Friedman (Ed.), *The reflecting team in action*. New York: Guilford Press.

Bakhtin, M. (1981). *The dialogical imagination* (M. Holquist, Ed.; C. Emerson & M. Holquist Trans.). Austin: University of Texas Press.

Byrne, N. O'R., & McCarthy, I. (2007). The dialectical structure of hope and despair: A Fifth Province approach. In C. Flaskas, I. McCarthy, & S. Sheehan (Eds.), *Hope and despair in narrative and family therapy: Reflections on adversity, forgiveness and reconciliation* (pp. 36–48). Hove, UK: Routledge.

Byrne, N. O'R., & McCarthy, I. C. (1995). Abuse, risk and protection. In C. Burck & B. Speed (Eds.), *Gender and power in relationships*. London: Routledge.

Campbell, W., Tamasese, K., & Waldegrave, C. (1998). Just therapy. In M. McGoldrick (Ed.), *Re-Visioning family therapy*. New York: Guilford Press.

Colgan, F. I. (1992). *The Fifth Province model: Father–daughter incest disclosure and systemic consultation*. Unpublished doctoral dissertation, University College Dublin.

Heaney, S. (1977). Preface. *The Crane Bag, 1*(1), 6–9.

Hederman, M. P., & Kearney, R. (1977). Editorial. *The Crane Bag, 1*(1), 10–12.

Kearney, P. A., Byrne, N. O'R., & McCarthy, I. C. (1989). Just metaphors: Marginal illuminations in a colonial retreat. *Family Therapy Case Studies, 4*, 17–31.

Kearney, R. (1996). Narrative imagination: Between ethics and poetics. In R. Kearney (Ed.), *Paul Ricoeur: The Hermeneutics of Action*. London: Sage.

Kennedy, J. (1994). Living and working in a poor community. *Human Systems, 5*(3–4), 209–218.

Lorenz, W. (1994). *Social work in a changing Europe*. London: Routledge.

McCarthy, I. C. (1991). Colonial sentences and just subversions: The potential for love and abuse in therapeutic encounters. *Feedback, 3*, 3–7.

McCarthy, I. C. (1994). Abusing norms: Welfare families and a Fifth Province stance. *Human Systems, 5*(3–4), 229–239.

McCarthy, I. C., & Byrne, N. O'R. (1995). A spell in therapy: It's between meself, herself, yerself and yer two imaginary friends. In S. Friedman (Ed.), *The reflecting team in action*. New York: Guilford Press.

McCarthy, I. C., & Byrne, N. O'R. (2001). Resisting daughters: Father–daughter child sexual abuse disclosure. In A. Cleary, M. Nic Ghiolla Phadraig, & S. Quin (Eds.), *Understanding children: Vol. 2. Changing experiences and family forms* (pp. 185–204). Dublin, Ireland: Oak Tree Press.

McGoldrick, M. (2005). Irish families. In M. McGoldrick, J. Giordano, & N. Garcia-Preto (Eds.), *Ethnicity and family therapy* (3rd ed.). New York: Guilford Press.

White, M., & Epston, D. (1990). *Narrative means to therapeutic ends*. New York: Norton.

CHAPTER 29

Working with African Americans and Trauma

Lessons for Clinicians from Hurricane Katrina

Nancy Boyd-Franklin

African Americans, particularly those living in poverty, are very vulnerable in trauma situations such as natural disasters. The case example of Hurricane Katrina is used to illustrate how cultural insensitivity intensifies suffering. It is hoped that this exploration of the implications for mental health providers will facilitate the implementation of culturally competent services to African American survivors of future traumas.

HURRICANE KATRINA: DISASTER CASE EXAMPLE

There has been an ongoing debate within the mental health field as to whether racism can qualify as a cause for posttraumatic stress disorder (Franklin, Boyd-Franklin, & Kelly, 2006). For the thousands of African Americans clinging to rooftops for rescue, attempting to find safety themselves by navigating treacherous water strewn with floating bodies, and left with no food and water for days in the Superdome and the Convention Center, there is no such debate.

Hurricane Katrina stands as a vivid example of the double trauma that can occur during disaster situations for African Americans and other people of color: (1) the disaster-related traumas of loss of life, loss of home and community, physical dislocation, and separation from loved ones; and (2) a second level of trauma caused by the effects of racism and poverty.

Although individuals from all racial and socioeconomic groups were affected by Katrina, the 67% of New Orleans residents who were African American and poor (Dyson, 2006; Troutt, 2006) were disproportionately affected by the devastation of Katrina and by post-hurricane traumatic experiences (Dass-Brailsford, 2006; Dyson, 2006; Law, 2006; Troutt, 2006).

Hurricane Katrina exposed the obvious "secret" that poor Black people are the "forgotten Americans"—they live in segregated urban communities throughout this country, as was the case in New Orleans; thus they are rendered "invisible" to the larger population. Their needs are often not considered in disaster planning, including mental health service delivery.

RACE AND CLASS DYNAMICS: THE LESSONS OF KATRINA

Hurricane Katrina highlighted a long-existing racial divide in this country in terms of the perception of racism and classism. A poll that surveyed perceptions of racism and poverty was conducted by CNN and *USA Today* on September 13, 2005, approximately 2 weeks after Katrina. Sixty percent of Blacks surveyed viewed race as a factor in the slow response to Katrina victims in New Orleans, whereas only 12% of Whites gave this response (CNN, 2005; Dyson, 2006; Troutt, 2006). Survey participants were also asked about poverty. Whereas 63% of Blacks saw the poverty of the victims as a factor in the slow response to Katrina, only 21% of Whites gave this response (CNN, 2005).

The glaring racial divide on racism and classism just discussed is illustrative of the debate on the psychological impact of racism within the psychological community. For many years, the perceptions of African Americans were discounted in discussions of racism, especially in the past 30 years, during which blatant racism was replaced with a subtle variety that could be more easily denied (Franklin et al., 2006; Blitz & Pender Greene, 2006; Carter, 2007). Within the past 10 years, a growing body of research has documented the psychological trauma of perceived racism. A number of research studies (Carter, 2007; Utsey, Chae, Brown, & Kelly, 2002) have shown that racism produces psychological stress and emotional trauma. This is one of the greatest lessons that can be learned by mental health providers from Hurricane Katrina.

THE NEED FOR MENTAL HEALTH PROVIDERS TO BE ABLE TO ADDRESS THE ISSUES OF RACISM

Therapists from other racial and cultural groups must be trained to be sensitive to the fact that African American clients may experience psychological trauma due to racism. African American clients often report that therapists seem unable to understand their pain when they describe such experiences in therapy. Some have reported that their therapists have debated or dismissed their perceptions of racism (Boyd-Franklin, 2003). According to Dass-Brailsford (as cited in Law, 2006, p. 42), one of the most important lessons of Katrina is that mental health providers must "be willing to openly discuss the effects of institutional racism and the role of power and oppression" in the lives of their African American clients.

When clinicians challenge clients' subjective experiences of racism, African Americans may be hesitant to address these issues, particularly in cross-racial treatment (Boyd-Franklin, 2003). It is imperative that clinicians of all ethnic backgrounds be trained to allow African Americans to express their anger at racism in psychotherapy and counseling sessions. The Association of Black Psychologists echoed these sentiments in a publication titled *Guidelines for Providing Culturally Appropriate Services for People of African Ancestry Exposed to the Trauma of Hurricane Katrina*:

> Mental health practitioners providing services to the African American survivors of Hurricane Katrina must be willing to honestly discuss the roles of institutionalized racism (and classism) in the woefully inadequate response of the federal and state governments. The African American survivors need an outlet to vent their frustrations with governmental bureaucracy that was appallingly slow in responding to a crisis situation involving a predominately poor and Black population. (Cokley, Cooke, & Nobles, 2006).

Historic experiences with racism and oppression underlie a response termed "healthy cultural suspicion" (Boyd-Franklin, 2003) that some African American clients demonstrate toward therapists and counselors who are involved in providing cross-racial treatment. In disaster situations, especially, that legacy of mistrust can lead to profound experiences of anger and rage. Clinicians need the ability not to take their clients' responses to racism personally (Boyd-Franklin, 2003). The Association of Black Psychologists has addressed this clinical responsibility in their guidelines: "Providers of services to the African American victims [should] be sensitive to and nondefensive of the reality of historically conditioned mistrust" (Cokley et al., 2006).

CULTURAL INSENSITIVITY IN THE RESPONSE TO KATRINA

Priscilla Dass-Brailsford, initially the only person of color on a mental health team deployed by the Red Cross to Louisiana after Hurricane Katrina, had prior experience in working with trauma victims in both South Africa and Boston. She reported that the lack of cultural understanding hindered the efforts of fellow disaster responders to help poor African American survivors (Law, 2006):

> In Dass-Brailsford's view, many dominant-culture responders to Katrina meant well, but were culturally myopic about the importance of religion and extended family to evacuees. That cultural disconnect made it hard for many responders to help a desperate population.

Dass-Brailsford was one of the first psychologists to recognize the impact of race, culture, institutional racism, and classism on both the conditions preexisting the disaster and the nature of the response:

> One thing was clear: The poverty among evacuees had been building for years, as Whites fled New Orleans for better-paying jobs and safer neighborhoods. Before Katrina, the city was home to the country's largest working-poor [African American] population. After Katrina, that population was worse off than ever.
>
> The hurricane did not sweep away the social ills and other problems that many survivors faced before the storm. ... Instead, new losses heightened preexisting issues. (Dass-Brailsford, as cited in Law, 2006, pp. 41–42)

LESSONS FROM KATRINA FOR MENTAL HEALTH PROVIDERS

In addition to her recommendation that clinicians be willing to discuss racism, mentioned earlier, Dass-Brailsford (as cited in Law, 2006, p. 42) offers the following lessons for mental health providers based on her own experiences:

- Understand African Americans' worldview, language, communication style values regarding community and interpersonal relationships.
- Acknowledge the role that religion and spirituality may play in healing.
- Relief-effort coordinators [should] strive to include responders that reflect the survivors' ethnic, racial and social backgrounds.

THE NEED FOR CULTURALLY DIVERSE AND CULTURALLY SENSITIVE DISASTER RESPONDERS

Dass-Brailsford (as cited in Law, 2006) had two major concerns about the mental health providers' responses to the victims of Hurricane Katrina: (1) few were persons of color and (2) although well meaning, many were not culturally sensitive (Dass-Brailsford, as cited in Law, 2006). The need for the American Red Cross and other disaster responders (including police and fire departments, national guard, emergency medical technicians, doctors, nurses, mental health organizations, clergy) to recruit and train more African American and other ethnic minority responders is apparent, as is the need for cultural sensitivity training (Cokley et al., 2006). In addition, because faith-based organizations are among the most powerful in many Black communities (Boyd-Franklin, 2003), there is a need for disaster relief organizations to partner with faith-based organizations, particularly African American churches, that have historically been the source of help on physical, emotional, and spiritual levels. This need is discussed further later.

UNDERSTANDING OF THE EXTENDED FAMILY ISSUES IN TIMES OF DISASTER

African American families have been characterized for generations by strong kinship networks that often include immediate and extended family members such as aunts, uncles, grandparents, cousins, and so forth. In addition, non-blood relatives, such as godparents, friends, neighbors, community figures, and "church family," may also be considered family members (Boyd-Franklin, 2003; Hines & Boyd-Franklin, 2005). Family therapists have long argued for a family systems approach in addressing the needs of African American clients (Boyd-Franklin, 2003; Hines & Boyd-Franklin, 2005). A disaster such as Hurricane Katrina makes this need all the more apparent. As mental health providers, we can learn a great deal from the mistakes that were made during Hurricane Katrina to assist us in planning for the provision of services to African Americans in future disaster situations.

Many of the communities most affected by Hurricane Katrina in Louisiana, Mississippi, and Alabama were those in which poor African Americans had lived for generations. These areas had a unique "culture" all their own that the hurricane swept away, along with the lives of loved ones and their homes. Two areas profoundly damaged by Katrina and its aftermath, the Ninth Ward and the Lower Ninth Ward of New Orleans, exemplified this situation. It was common for the family home to be passed down from generation to generation, often representing the only material possession the family had. Elderly family members were often adamant about not leaving these homes, and their relatives, who could have evacuated, would not leave them behind. For those who were too poor to own cars or too elderly or disabled, evacuation was not an option.

One of the most important mental health interventions in any disaster situation is establishing a reliable system for identifying and locating family members and close friends. In African American culture, in which family members may have daily in-person or phone contact with many members of the extended family, not being able to locate key family members was traumatic. Those of us not directly affected by the hurricane can never forget the television coverage of distraught individuals begging for some news of their family members' whereabouts and their frustration at not knowing whether loved ones were dead or alive, nearby or transported to some unknown location. Particularly heartbreaking were the pleas of parents separated from their children. Attempts to reconnect separated family members to persons from the same community would have been particularly helpful in the first days and weeks after Katrina.

Elders, particularly older female relatives and friends, are often central to the "heart and soul" of the family (Boyd-Franklin, 2003; Hines & Boyd-Franklin, 2005). Because of a long tradition of kinship care provided by grandparents, aunts, and uncles in the African American community, older relatives, often with serious medical conditions, attempted to care for their grandchildren in horrendous situations without food, water, or medicine. Mental health providers often overlook the role of older men in African American families, who may also play a crucial caretaking role. Many viewers remember the agonizing recollections of a grandfather whose wife had drowned because she encouraged him to take their grandchildren first in the rescue boat.

THE CONCEPTS OF "HOME" AND "HOMEPLACE" FOR AFRICAN AMERICANS

In response to the catastrophic trauma of forcible removal from homes in Africa, horrible conditions of transportation to America, and consequent enslavement—a multigenerational cultural and racial memory kept alive through the oral tradition of storytelling—African Americans developed physical, spiritual, and emotional survival skills that fostered multigenerational resilience. One of these survival skills is the development of a "home" or "homeplace" (Burton, Winn, Stevenson, & Clark, 2004).

Although a need to feel a sense of belonging is universal among cultures, it is difficult for those who have never experienced the history of slavery, the diaspora, the Maafa, and the legacy of discrimination, segregation, and racism that have affected the lives of generations of African Americans to understand the overwhelming sense of attachment that many African Americans feel to the concept of "home" or "homeplace" (Boyd-Franklin, 2003; Burton et al., 2004).

In a world that is often a very dangerous place for Black people, "home" or "homeplace" is, as bell hooks (1990) has described it, a safe place where African Americans could "strive to be subjects, not objects, where we could be affirmed in our minds and hearts despite poverty, hardship, and deprivation, where we could restore to ourselves the dignity denied us on the outside in the public world" (p. 42). Burton et al. (2004) elaborated on this concept:

> The homeplace involves multilayered, nuanced individual and family processes that are anchored in a physical space that elicits feelings of empowerment, belonging, commitment, rootedness, ownership, safety, and renewal. Critical elements of the homeplace include social attachments and relationships characterized by distinct cultural symbols, meanings, and ritual. In the context of a defined physical space, these attachments and relationships shape individuals' and families' sense of social and cultural identity. (pp. 397–398)

Their homes, containing legacies of family history through stories and storytellers, photographs and family Bibles, may have been the only possessions of value that poor African American New Orleans residents had. Even for those who did not own their homes, their immediate neighborhood defined their lives. For many the concept of "homeplace" encompassed their communities, church homes, and the close communal network of people who made up their blood and non-blood "families"—a multigenerational web of familiarity, safety, love, and protection lost in the devastation.

Survivors who remained or returned were overwhelmed by the surreal experience of viewing the destruction and devastation that is still everywhere. It is estimated that about 80% of African Americans, particularly those who are poor, may never be able to return to their homes (Dyson, 2006; Troutt, 2006). In sharp contrast to the haste with which restoration occurred in the business district, destinations that attracted tourists, such as the French Quarter, and middle- and upper-income residential areas, the unique aspects of African American culture that defined pre-Katrina New Orleans are likely never to be recreated or replaced.

Some members of the news media questioned the reluctance or inability of many of the African American residents to evacuate in advance of Hurricane Katrina. Many ignored factors relating to poverty—that is, lack of transportation, money, credit cards, or alternative housing—and commentators were universally ignorant of the cultural importance of "homeplace." Even therapists often misunderstand the tremendous significance of "homeplace" in their treatment of African American clients (Burton et al., 2004).

As I have traveled to speak with survivors of Katrina throughout the country, I have heard from them what hooks (1990) and Burton et al. (2004) have described as a deep and painful yearning and longing for their homeplace. Social service and mental health providers too often focus their attention on the necessity of helping survivors to find new homes without acknowledging the profound sadness and "soul wound" created by the loss of their homes. People need the time to express and grieve for this profound loss. For many of the African Americans, the deaths and displacement of family and community members in the wake of the hurricane to a wide range of cities throughout the country was reminiscent of the forced uprooting experienced during slavery.

African Americans are part of a communal culture, and isolation is the most deadly of human conditions. They need the opportunity to share their family stories, special memories, and the shattering sense of loss. African Americans are storytellers—they keep the oral tradition alive. In treatment, it is important to help a person recount his or her memories of "home"and to grieve for everything and everyone that was lost (Burton et al., 2004). Many African Americans are enthusiastic recorders of all family events, whether happy or sad, so that one of the most difficult losses for families was the destruction of cherished pictures, photos, and other family memorabilia commemorating births, weddings, family reunions, deaths, funerals, and so forth.

Sometimes individual or even family therapy is not enough. For some survivors, the use of groups or multiple family groups of others from their homeplace has been very effective in the healing process. For some clients, writing or dictating their memories was very healing because it kept alive their sense of "home" and was something concrete that they could share with their children and other family members. The role of "testimony therapy" in the healing process is discussed later.

RELIGION, SPIRITUALITY, AND THE ROLE OF BLACK CHURCHES

The history of African Americans in this country has been permeated with experiences of death, loss, brutality, oppression, and racism. Religious and spiritual beliefs provide support and comfort, particularly during times of disruption, loss, and grief (Boyd-Franklin, 2003; Hines & Boyd-Franklin, 2005), and are deeply ingrained in the culture. Acknowledging spirituality as a major source of resilience and survival skills is often necessary for culturally competent disaster response with African Americans.

In psychotherapy, some African Americans will express psychological distress in spiritual terms. For example, African Americans will recite Psalm 23 from the Bible in desperate times and when facing death: "Though I walk through the valley of the shadow of death, I shall fear no evil for Thou art with me." Spiritual metaphors are also frequently used to express survival and psychological resilience. Boyd-Franklin (2003) and Mitchell and Lewter (1986) give numerous examples of spiritual metaphors that can be very helpful to clinicians.

It is very important for mental health providers to ask directly about religious and spiritual beliefs (Boyd-Franklin, 2003; Hines & Boyd-Franklin,

2005), as there is great diversity among African Americans. Various denominations of Christianity are well represented, such as Baptist, Methodist, African Methodist Episcopal (AME), Episcopalian, Roman Catholic, Presbyterian, Church of God in Christ, Jehovah's Witnesses, Seventh-Day Adventist, and more. In addition, increasing numbers embrace the Nation of Islam, other Muslim groups such as Sunni Muslim, and African religions (Boyd-Franklin, 2003; Hines & Boyd-Franklin, 2005). Mental health providers should be aware of the range of religious and spiritual beliefs among African Americans (Boyd-Franklin, 2003).

New Orleans and the rest of Louisiana have significant numbers of Black Catholics. It was not uncommon for Catholic churches in many Louisiana communities to subtly incorporate African American traditions, music, and culture into their services. African Americans, displaced to other parts of the country after the hurricane, often felt lost and isolated in Catholic churches that were predominately White. Unfortunately, many of the well-meaning social service and mental health responders did not understand the significance of this further dislocation and did not give the victims the opportunity to talk about and grieve this loss or to address it in therapy.

African American churches of all denominations often play a major role in the lives of family members and the community. Many members of African American churches have had a multigenerational history together and view each other as their "church family," who will rally to their side in times of need—bringing food and comfort to the ill and elderly and supporting a family through the tragedy of death and loss. Funerals are extremely important "rites of passage" and a deeply rooted African legacy. Funerals are so important in African American culture that they will often take place a week or more after death in order to give all of the extended family members time to travel (Boyd-Franklin, 2003). Death is often seen as a "home going" to heaven. Funerals are considered "celebrations of the life" of the deceased. The combination of sadness at the loss of the deceased family member and celebration of the journey to heaven are epitomized in the "jazz funeral," common to New Orleans and other parts of Louisiana.

The devastation experienced by African American survivors of Katrina was amplified by their inability to locate or identify departed relatives and give them a "proper" funeral. Dass-Brailsford (2006) and Law (2006) described the astounding cultural insensitivity in the aftermath of Katrina in which mental health responders were told:

> "Ignore the dead. . . . We want the living." The comment struck Dass-Brailsford as deeply insensitive to the strong kinship ties and religious values among African Americans in the Deep South. . . . "They were not prepared to ignore their dead," she said. "In fact, they could not continue living until their dead had been accounted for and respectfully put to rest." (Dass-Brailsford, as cited in Law, 2006, p. 40)

One of the most powerful interventions that mental health providers can offer in such times is to help survivors find out what has happened to their deceased relatives. For those who have a spiritual orientation, helping family members to pray for those who are lost or missing is another important intervention. After immediate survival needs have been met, providers can support the family in organizing a memorial service for family and friends of the deceased to share their memories, pray for the soul of their departed member, and begin to bring some closure to their grief and loss. Although many therapists become concerned about "boundaries" in such situations, many African American families greatly appreciate health and mental health providers who attend the wakes, funerals, and memorial services for their loved ones. This gesture can significantly deepen the therapeutic bond (Boyd-Franklin, 2003).

Davis (personal communication, 2005), an African American psychologist and trained Red Cross disaster responder, availed himself of his contacts with Black churches in Houston to aid Katrina victims who had been uprooted and transported. In marked distinction to the Red Cross, volunteers mobilized through Black churches were culturally and racially similar to the Katrina survivors. They were also very familiar with the language of spiritual metaphor and hope that so contributed to the resilience of many of the African American survivors and were often able to bring comfort to the victims who had lost so much.

One unfortunate circumstance following Hurricane Katrina was that local authorities and nonsectarian disaster responders such as the Red Cross did not reach out to African American churches in the localities to which the survivors of Katrina were sent. In fact, many churches were initially restricted from providing services at relief centers and shelters, such as the Astrodome in Houston (Davis, 2005).

One of the most important lessons of Katrina for mental health providers, therefore, is the importance of establishing partnerships with African American Churches and other faith-based organizations. This forging of partnerships can be particularly helpful when the mental health provider is from a different cultural or racial group. These partnerships should occur on an ongoing basis and not have to wait to be constructed in the wake of a disaster.

EMPOWERMENT THROUGH TESTIMONY THERAPY

"Giving testimony" is a tribute to the resilience of African American survival and a time-honored tradition in many Black churches and faith-based communities. The process relates a trajectory of a person facing a horrible, life-threatening, or destructive experience or the painful death of a loved one and then describing how "God brought them through." This process affirms the pain and loss—familiar to a group that has experienced unparalleled pain, loss, destruction, discrimination, and racism—but gives hope to all that even in the darkest hour, God will see one through.

This is a powerful spiritual and cultural tool that can be used in therapy with African Americans (Akinyela, 2007; Boyd-Franklin, 2003), particularly if it draws on the communal aspects of the African American tradition and is done in family, group or multiple family group sessions (Akinyela, 2007; Boyd-Franklin, 2003). It can be helpful even in individual treatment. For example, a therapist can say to an African American client:

> "You have a very powerful testimony. You have been through the greatest loss of your life. It got so bad that at times you doubted God and you were afraid that you could not make it through. The hurricane took your Mama, your Daddy, your home, and all that was familiar to you, but your testimony is that God has seen you through. You are a survivor. I hope that you can share your testimony some day with others because it is so powerful and filled with hope."

Of course, a therapist should use a spiritual metaphor only with African American clients who have already conveyed spiritual or religious beliefs when asked. It should never be imposed on someone who does not share those beliefs. Therapists, as human beings, instinctively want to offer comfort and hope to those who suffered unimaginable pain and loss on a traumatic and catastrophic level. We have to be willing to let our clients express their anger at God, at the government, at the disrespect and racism they experienced, at their family members who died or left them, and at us before we can help them to access the triumph of their testimony.

LEST WE FORGET

In summary, this chapter has explored the tragedy of Hurricane Katrina as an example of a disaster that has led to catastrophic trauma for countless African American survivors. It has discussed the lessons that can be learned and the implications of providing mental health services to African Americans in future trauma situations. This chapter stands in tribute to the resilience of these survivors of Hurricane Katrina, and I hope that the lessons learned will empower us as mental health providers to intervene more effectively in the future. I also hope that it empowers us to speak out against the racism, discrimination, and poverty that Katrina brought to our collective consciousness. Only then can we honor the requests of the survivors that we "never forget" (Boyd-Franklin, in press).

REFERENCES

Akinyela, M. (2007, April). *Everything is everything: Africentric approaches to healing and self-healing.* Paper presented at the Culture Conference of the Multicultural Family Institute, Highland Park, New Jersey.

Blitz, L., & Pender Greene, M. (Eds.). (2006). *Racism and racial identity: Reflections on urban practice in mental health and social services.* Binghamton, NY: Haworth Press.

Boyd-Franklin, N. (2003). *Black families in therapy: Understanding the African American experience* (2nd ed.). New York: Guilford Press.

Boyd-Franklin, N. (in press). Racism, trauma, and resilience: The psychological impact of Hurricane Katrina. In K. Wailoo, R. Anglin, & K. O'Neill (Eds.), *Katrina's imprint: Race and vulnerability in America.* New Brunswick, NJ: Rutgers University Press.

Burton, L. M., Winn, D. M., Stevenson, H., & Clark, S. L. (2004). Working with African American clients: Considering the "homeplace" in marriage and family therapy practices. *Journal of Marital and Family Therapy, 30*(4), 397–410.

Carter, R. T. (2007). Racism and psychological and emotional injury: Recognizing and assessing race-based traumatic stress. *Counseling Psychologist, 35*(1), 13–105.

CNN. (2005). *Reaction to Katrina split along racial lines.* CNN.com, September 13, 2005, *www.cnn.com/2005/12/Katrina.race.poll.index.html.*

Cokley, K., Cooke, B. G., & Nobles, W. (2006). *Guidelines for providing culturally appropriate services for people of African ancestry exposed to the trauma of Hurricane Katrina.* Available at *www.abpsi.org/special/abpsi_article1.pdf.*

Dass-Brailsford, P. (2006). Eye witness report: Ignore the dead; we want the living! Helping after the storm. Available at *www.apa.org/pi/oema/special_sectionon_Katrina_march%202006.pdf.*

Dass-Brailsford, P. (2007). *A practical approach to trauma: Empowering interventions.* Thousand Oaks, CA: Sage.

Dyson, M. E. (2006). *Come hell or high water: Hurricane Katrina and the color of disaster.* New York: Basic Books.

Franklin, A. J., Boyd-Franklin, N., & Kelly, S. (2006). Racism and invisibility: Race-related stress, emotional abuse, and psychological trauma for people of color. *Journal of Emotional Abuse, 6*(2/3), 9–30.

Hines, P. M., & Boyd-Franklin, N. (2005). African American families. In M. McGoldrick, J. Giordano, & N. Garcia-Preto (Eds.), *Ethnicity and family therapy* (3rd ed., pp. 87–100). New York: Guilford Press.

hooks, b. (1990). *Yearning: Race, gender, and cultural politics.* Boston: South End Press.

Law, B.M. (2006). The hard work of healing: Katrina's cultural lessons. *APA Monitor on Psychology, 27*(9), 40–42.

Mitchell, H., & Lewter, N. (1986). *Soul theology: The heart of American Black culture.* San Francisco: Harper and Row.

Troutt, D. D. (2006). *After the storm: Black intellectuals explore the meaning of Hurricane Katrina.* New York: New Press.

Utsey, S. O., Chae, M. H., Brown, C. F., & Kelly, D. (2002). Effect of ethnic group membership on ethnic identity, race-related, stress, and quality of life. *Cultural Diversity and Ethnic Minority Psychology, 8,* 366–377.

CHAPTER 30

Once They Come

Testimony Therapy and Healing Questions for African American Couples

Makungu M. Akinyela

AN AFRICAN-CENTERED THERAPY

In this chapter I describe a process of testimony therapy (Akinyela, 2005) for couples that engages an African American couple in a culturally sensitive manner using four healing questions in the first session. I first began developing the ideas and practices of testimony therapy in 1996. It is an African-centered therapy represented by a range of practices grounded in the culture, history, and experience of the African American community. Testimony therapy is *communitarian* in that it emphasizes the person *within* community. It is also social constructionist in its outlook, positing that people's ideas and practices are socially constructed and *culturally* mediated.

Testimony is a metaphor from the Black cultural–spiritual tradition of *testify'n*. In the Black church tradition, testify'n is a ritual in which community members are invited to "give their testimony." Testimony as a discursive therapy shares similar ideas and practices with such therapies as narrative (White & Epston, 1990; Freedman & Combs, 1996) and solution-focused therapy (Berg & Hopwood, 1992), as well as with other culturally focused therapies such as just therapy (Tamasese, Waldegrave, Tuhaka, &

Campbell, 2003). I have written elsewhere (Akinyela, 2004) that testimony is distinguished from these other discursive therapies primarily by its reliance on metaphors grounded in oral tradition and musicality rather than in literacy and written narrative metaphors. These metaphors of orality guide the therapist to focus not only on what is said in therapeutic conversations but also on how it is said, that is, the style and rhythm of a conversation and the images it evokes.

The interpretations of African American culture discussed here specifically rely on the shared cultural meanings that exist within the African American community and may or may not be applicable to the broader African diaspora. As with all therapies, the social and cultural contexts of both the therapist and the client must be considered as testimony ideas are put into practice.

Why African-Centered Therapy?

Over the past two decades there have been various critiques of the field of family therapy, such as a feminist critique (Werner-Wilson, 1997; Avis, 1986; Goodrich, Rampage, Ellman, & Halstead, 1988) and cultural critiques of the field (see McGoldrick & Hardy, Chapter 1, this volume). Perhaps most significantly, since the 1980s family therapy has been challenged by social constructionist theories of change to reconsider assumptions about how change occurs in the therapeutic process (Anderson & Goolishian, 1988; Gergen, 1998; White & Epston, 1990; Freedman & Combs, 1996).

Articles about therapy with Black people are usually written from a Eurocentric standpoint within the broader context of multiculturalism and diversity. These articles privilege helping White therapists develop *cultural competency* (Bean, Perry, & Bedell, 2002; Becker & Liddle, 2001) and rarely privilege the knowledge of Black people. Few have contested this stance in the way that feminist critique of family therapy allowed the privileging of women's knowledge and experience as central to the development of feminist family therapy. Nancy Boyd-Franklin's (2003) *Black Families in Therapy*, although not claiming an Africentric worldview, has been an important effort toward accomplishing the privileging of Black knowledge and experiences. This groundbreaking book, originally published in 1989, was for a long time the only text in family therapy written about Black people in the self-conscious voice of a Black therapist. An African-centered perspective asserts the agency of African Americans as self-determining subjects with their own resources for healing. The African-centered therapist looks to indigenous practices, metaphors, spiritualities, and understandings of mental health and wellness to set the pace for therapeutic work with families and individuals.

PRINCIPLES OF TESTIMONY THERAPY

Testimony therapy as an African-centered therapy is grounded in the oral tradition of African American people. This oral tradition is evidenced in both the spoken word and the music of African Americans. In oral cultures metaphor is a primary way that human beings communicate and discuss various experiences and concepts that are familiar in order to explain experiences and concepts that may not be familiar. Valuing the importance of orality in Black culture is a foundational principle of testimony therapy. Testify'n is the metaphor that describes both the practice and the process of therapeutic work.

Testimony and Spirituality

Testimony therapy honors the spiritual traditions of African Americans and recognizes that in the culture of Black people the dichotomous line between secular and sacred is often blurred. We understand spirituality as that experience of connectedness and relationship that is expressed in the customs, rituals, music, and traditions of Black people. Spirituality (Paris, 1995; Ephirim-Donkor, 1997) is also understood and expressed as an honoring of elders and ancestors and a respect for the collective history and past of descendants of Africans enslaved in America. Spirituality is widely expressed by Black people through belief in God and in various religious practices and traditions. I assume that a unifying theme across social contexts is the power of the spoken word, the sustaining influence of rhythm and beat, and the healing power of ritual. These themes are understood within a context of community and belonging. When this communitarian context is disrupted, people may find themselves seeking the help of a family therapist or other healer.

Nurturing Hopefulness by Identifying Victorious Moments

Hope is fundamental. Holding onto hope despite apparent circumstances of doom and gloom is an important aspect of the African American ethos. Hopefulness in the face of tragedy or crisis is a consistent theme in Black music of all genres. Hopefulness is often expressed through humor, as well as a healthy sense of irony and paradox. Testimony therapists focus on listening for *victorious moments*, which contradict the stories of defeat and powerlessness. By further curious questioning about the moment, these victorious moments are nurtured to place the doom-and-gloom story in a broader context of lived experience to provide new meanings for the testimony.

The First Session

In their work on common factors in therapy, Duncan and Miller (2000) point out that 15% of what works in all therapies is the placebo factor, or the client's sense of hopefulness for a positive outcome to therapy. Although this might seem mathematically insignificant (the therapist–client relationship is 30% of what works), the therapist's ability to identify and nurture hopefulness in both partners by the end of the first session can be critical to the couple's deciding to engage in the therapeutic relationship. When hopefulness is not nurtured and therapy is focused on the pathology and on a blow-by-blow retelling of what is wrong with the relationship, the therapist may find him- or herself caught in a quagmire of doom and gloom. The couple is left in the same place of hurt and anger as they were when they tried to solve difficulties on their own. Doom-and-gloom sessions are characterized by each client's attempting to convince the therapist of how terrible, unfair, or just evil the other partner is. These sessions are often defined by high levels of emotional turmoil, anger, character assassination, discounting of ideas, denials, and distrust. The therapist is left feeling bogged down in an emotional quagmire, and the couple sees no point in continuing therapy. Instead of ending with a sense of hopefulness, doom-and-gloom sessions leave the couple, as well as the therapist, feeling that there is little hope for the relationship.

The Four Healing Questions

The four healing questions of testimony therapy were developed as a structured conversation that can guide clients in telling their stories in ways that begin with their pain and move them toward hopeful chosen testimonies (outcomes) about their own lives. These questions are meant to encourage couples to think about their relationships in ways that are different from their usual patterns of thinking. These questions are:

1. *What happened to you?* What event, circumstance, or situation has occurred in your life to bring you to this place with me?
2. *How does what happened to you affect you today?* In other words, what does your life terrain look like since this event or experience? How are your relationships and your emotional life affected?
3. *After all that's happened to you and the effect that this has had on you, what gives you the strength to hold on?* What is the secret to your survival?
4. *What do you need to heal?* This last question helps the client to express a theory of change. This is important in that it places the cli-

ent at the center of the process and assumes that clients are experts in their own lives. The four healing questions, asked in this order, help the therapist to guide couples in organizing their experience as a story.

CASE EXAMPLE

The following story illustrates the use of the four healing questions in an initial consultation I had with Shayla and Terry, a middle-class African American couple. They sought therapy to deal with the emotional distance that had been growing between them over the past 3 years of a 10-year marriage. Shayla and Terry had a 5-year-old son who was born with a crippling illness that required 24-hour care. As a result, Shayla worked from home with a small home-based business, and Terry worked away from home in the information technology industry. The couple rarely found time for themselves and, until recently, had never been on a vacation. The consultation was initiated by Shayla following a "disastrous" vacation. She was concerned about disconnection from her husband and Terry's disregard for her feelings. Shayla had spent several months planning the vacation. She arranged for her mother to accompany them to assist with child care. Her primary complaint was that Terry did not participate in the planning and did not know where they were going until they got into the car to leave.

When African American couples such as Shayla and Terry make a decision to consult with me, I am powerfully mindful of the importance of this first session. For African American men in particular this decision is more than an individual one. It carries important cultural meaning. This decision often flies in the face of decades of cultural tradition and healthy cultural paranoia about letting other people into a family's business. Many times, for African American men to sit and discuss marital partners with a stranger is an implication of masculine weakness within a context in which there is already an assumption of the emotional inferiority of Black men. As this couple arrives at my office I realize that this first session may be my only opportunity to create an environment that feels culturally safe and familiar enough for the couple to want to continue. Couples often come to consult with me after seeing another therapist who they will complain seemed unable to understand their cultural nuances and made them feel alienated or misunderstood in the therapy.

Terry attended the first session because of worry about his wife's anger and resentment directed toward him since the vacation. He could not identify any problems in the marriage. This couple had difficulty identifying what specifically was troubling their relationship and causing it to feel gloomy. After hearing why they had come to talk with me, I decided to help the couple give their testimony by introducing the four healing questions.

THERAPIST: Well, I understand that things just don't seem right in your relationship and you are not communicating. Shayla, that's making you real unhappy, and Terry, you say you don't see any problems. But we used to have this saying in my house when I was growing up: "If mama ain't happy, ain't nobody happy!" Does that sound familiar to you?

TERRY: *(laughing)* Yeah! I guess it's about like that around our house right now.

THERAPIST: So even though you don't feel like you have any problems, it seems like you can say that since Shayla ain't happy that means you ain't happy either, is that right? (*Terry and Shayla both laugh and look at each other nodding their heads in affirmation.*)

I use this reference to the culturally familiar "If mama ain't happy, ain't nobody happy" with Terry both to open up a space of comfort and to reach an agreement with Terry and Shayla that things were indeed uncomfortable in the relationship and that it was OK to talk about it in our session. I have learned to rely on familiarity with cultural humor and metaphors to create an atmosphere of comfort and safety for African American clients who come to consult with me. As the laughter subsides, I acknowledge the difficulty in defining a specific problem with them and introduce the first healing question.

THERAPIST: I know it's kind of hard right now to put your finger on what feels bad, but many times I've found if you can just identify the last time something happened that really made you feel the way you do now, that can be a good start. You called me about a week ago to come in to talk. Tell me *what happened to you* to make you want to come to a therapist about your marriage.

SHAYLA: Well, I called you after we came back from our vacation. It just made me feel crazy! I was looking forward to that trip so much. Terry didn't think we had the money, but I found a way after saving and planning to make sure it happened. ... It's so hard taking care of our son all the time with no breaks. I found a place to go, booked the hotel, and even planned things for us to do together. I got my mother to come along with us to take care of our son. ... I was so excited. But Terry didn't seem to care one way or another. He was just along for the ride. He didn't even know where we were going! And when we finally got there he didn't seem interested in doing anything I had planned. He just sat around. We didn't talk much or anything.

TERRY: I don't really know what she's talking about. I enjoyed myself. It was real relaxing. I just thought everything didn't always have to be so perfect.

THERAPIST: So, Shayla, you were really excited about your plans for the trip. You really needed this trip after working so hard with your son day in and day out, and it sounds like you really needed for Terry to be excited about the trip, too. And, Terry, you did have a good time, but somehow even though you were having a good time, Shayla didn't know that that was happening for you. So now you're feeling miserable, Shayla, and Terry, you're feeling Shayla's tension, and finally you get back home after all this has happened. So, looking at all these events, *how has what happened to you affected your marriage today?*

SHAYLA: (*Begins to cry softly.*) We don't laugh like we used to. When we talk to each other it's hollow and superficial. . . .

TERRY: Yeah, it's like we're tiptoeing around each other. . . .

THERAPIST: Like walking on eggshells. . . . .

TERRY: Yeah. And we have not had a lot of intimacy for a while, but now we don't even go to bed together. . . .

THERAPIST: So you noticed before that your love life has been suffering, but now since you're avoiding being in the bed at the same time, there's even less chance you'll want to be intimate with each other . . . is that it?

SHAYLA: Yes, that's it, and now I don't entrust my emotions to him anymore. I'm afraid of being disappointed.

THERAPIST: Terry, have you noticed that about Shayla? Have you noticed that she does not trust her emotions with you?

TERRY: Yeah, I noticed it and it frustrates me.

THERAPIST: So one of the effects of this bad vacation that happened to you is that you are frustrated, Terry, because you notice that Shayla now withholds her emotions from you. Also, the two of you walk around each other on eggshells and you both notice that not only are you not being intimate with each other, but you are also avoiding even going to bed together, is that right? (*They both nod and say yes acknowledging this.*) And now, as you look at what happened to you and as you look at how what happened to you is affecting your marriage today, can you tell me *what gives you the strength to go on* in this marriage? (*Both Shayla and Terry look at each other and then they look away and take a few seconds to think about the question.*)

TERRY: I love my wife and I love my son. Even when things get bad, I know that. I knew that when I got married that this was a once-in-a-lifetime commitment.

SHAYLA: I love Terry, too. He is a wonderful man. He always tries to better our lives and our situation. He's always home when he is not working, and he's very responsible. When things get really bad, I pray a lot. (*Terry nods his head in agreement to this last statement and says, "Me too."*)

I take particular note of several important turns here. Often when African American couples come to therapy, there is a discourse about both African American men and African American women that shapes the conversation covertly. It is assumed that African American men are unable to express feelings of love and commitment or to act on them, and it is assumed that African American women do not respect the efforts of Black men to care for them and their children. In this exchange Terry and Shayla have overtly challenged the covert assumption. This will be powerful information to return to in future sessions. The couple's mutual reliance on their spiritual faith (a common factor of African American cultural strength) will be another important subject to return to as we work to develop an alliance between the couple in the future. I now become interested in uncovering *victorious moments* in this couple's story that contradict the doom-and-gloom story that they have been influenced by up until now. I begin this by asking the fourth question.

THERAPIST: So after what has happened to you with this disaster vacation and looking at how what happened is affecting your marriage ... the emotional distance, the walking around on eggshells ... no intimacy ... with all of that, if this marriage could be healed, *what would that healing look like*?

TERRY: That feeling of awkwardness would go away. We'd be more intimate with each other, and we'd be closer to our son. We'd talk more and laugh. We'd take some time out and go places together.

THERAPIST: What would you notice in Shayla, Terry.

TERRY: She would have energy. She'd be empowered. She'd be happy around our son and more patient. I'd know that she is with me. I'd be more calm with her.

THERAPIST: What would Shayla notice about you?

TERRY: I'd be more outgoing. I'd smile at her when we talk. I'd be more encouraging to her and pay attention to her more.

SHAYLA: If our marriage was healed, the bed would be made by Terry more and he'd take out the trash. (*They both laugh.*) We'd have more hugs when he goes to work in the morning. Our kisses would be more intimate, and he would come to bed with me at night.

THERAPIST: What would Terry notice about you?

SHAYLA: He'd notice that I have more of a sex drive and that I'm at peace. He'd notice me smiling more and I'd sing! I'd touch him in public, and I'd talk about how I admire him.

CONCLUSION

I hope you are able to hear in your imagination the rhythms created by the call and response of this conversation. Of course in print it is very linear. In real life in this conversation there is lots of cross-talk, give and take, call and response, pauses and empty spaces that are often important to the construction of metaphorical meaning in conversations between African American people. This oral tradition is rooted in African American spirituality and Black church testify'n rituals. In such a ritual a church elder may begin humming or singing a song, perhaps a familiar spiritual. After a few lines have been sung, someone might stand and wait patiently until the singing trails off. The one standing then begins to talk and tell a story. These stories in the ritual of testify'n begin with a recounting of personal or family problems experienced by the teller. As he or she tells the story, he or she is encouraged every sentence or so with a response of "amen" or "yes," or perhaps someone will affirm, "that's right." The storyteller who begins haltingly and uncertain of the direction of the story seems to gain in confidence as the responses become stronger and more frequent. A rhythm begins to build up, and the story of doom and gloom begins to transform into a recounting of how, in spite of the problem, "with the Lord's help" things have gotten better. By this point the witnesses have become full participants in the story, acknowledging their own certainty that the assessment of the good outcome is a correct one. By the end of the story, both the teller and the witnesses have woven their call and response to tell a community story. This community construction of a preferred story is a central idea guiding an understanding of testimony therapy. These are the rhythms and communitarian nuances that I worked to develop with Terry and Shayla in this first conversation.

After this initial consultation, Shayla and Terry continued in couple therapy and used their responses to the fourth question to collaborate with the therapist on shaping their preferred testimony about their marriage. Using the healing questions as a guideline for the initial conversation with the therapist helped the couple to focus on exactly what events hurt Shayla and contributed to the sense of "not communicating." The four questions can be an extremely powerful therapeutic tool. They allow clients to tell their story and explore the impact of life events in the *now*. Importantly, by directing the conversation in this way, the therapist focuses on nurturing hopefulness in the first session in order to raise the possibility that couples will desire to return for a follow-up session.

Once African American couples come to us, the first session is the most important opportunity we will have to engage them in a journey of collaborative healing. Despite ideas about the reluctance of African Americans to seek therapy, I believe that when African American people are provided with a safe, culturally familiar, and affirming therapeutic environment that is clearly in the image and interest of Black people, they will come to therapy. My intention in creating this culturally safe and inviting environment is for my own therapeutic work to play a part in the larger goal of giving voice to the African American community's self-reliant and self-determining healing practices.

REFERENCES

Akinyela, M. (2004). Meeting the trickster at the crossroads: Oral cultures and the use of metaphor in therapeutic conversations. In S. Madigan (Ed.), *Therapeutic conversations: 5. Therapy from the outside in* (pp. 111–122). Vancouver, British Columbia, Canada: Yaletown Family Therapy.

Akinyela, M. (2005). Testimony of hope: African centered praxis for therapeutic ends. *Journal of Systemic Therapy, 24*(4), 5–18.

Anderson, H., & Goolishian, H. (1988). Human systems as linguistic systems: Preliminary and evolving ideas about the implications for clinical theory. *Family Process, 27*(3–4), 371–393.

Avis, J. (1986). Feminist issues in family therapy. In F. Piercy & D. Sprenkle (Eds.), *Family therapy sourcebook* (pp. 213–242). New York: Guilford Press.

Bean, R., Perry, B., & Bedell, T. (2002). Developing culturally competent marriage and family therapists: Treatment guidelines for non-African-American therapists working with African-American families. *Journal of Marital and Family Therapy, 28*(2), 153–164.

Becker, D., & Liddle, H. (2001). Family therapy with unmarried African American mothers and their adolescents. *Family Process, 40*(4), 413–427.

Berg, I. K., & Hopwood, Y. (1992). Doing with very little: Brief treatment of the homeless substance abuser. *Journal of Independent Social Work, 5*(3–4), 109–120.

Boyd-Franklin, N. (2003). *Black families in therapy* (2nd ed.). New York: Guilford Press.

Duncan, B., & Miller, S. (2000). *The heroic client: Doing client-directed outcome-informed therapy.* San Francisco: Jossey-Bass.

Ephirim-Donkor, A. (1997). *African spirituality: On becoming ancestors.* Trenton, NJ: Africa World Press.

Freedman, J., & Combs, G. (1996). *Narrative therapy: The social construction of preferred realities.* New York: Norton.

Gergen, K. J. (1998). Constructionism and realism: How are we to go on? In I. Parks (Ed.), *Social constructionism, discourse, and realism* (pp. 147–156). Thousand Oaks, CA: Sage.

Goodrich, T., Rampage, C., Ellman, B., & Halstead, K. (1988). *Feminist family therapy: A case book*. New York: Norton.

Paris, P. (1995). *The spirituality of African peoples: The search for a common moral discourse*. Minneapolis: Fortress Press.

Tamasese, K., Waldegrave, C., Tuhaka, F., & Campbell, W. (2003). *Just therapy: A journey*. Adelaide, Australia: Dulwhich Centre.

Werner-Wilson, R. J. (1997). Is therapeutic alliance influenced by gender in marriage and family therapy? *Journal of Feminist Family Therapy, 9,* 3–16.

White, M., & Epston, D. (1990). *Narrative means to therapeutic ends*. New York: Norton.

CHAPTER 31

Climbing Up the Rough Side of the Mountain

Hope, Culture, and Therapy

Paulette Moore Hines

Recently, a young therapist questioned what (if any) impact she could possibly have on a family that had been in and out of the mental health system for 16 years. The therapist's frustration was heightened by the fact that the mother seemed less disturbed than she, the therapist, about her family's situation. She wondered, "Is this mission impossible, or have I invested in a career that makes very little real difference in the lives of the people I am trying to help? Am I helping my clients to be hopeful, or are they teaching me to be hopeless?"

These same questions prompted me to review my own experiences, both personal and professional. How could I face an aunt and cousin who had lost four children in a house fire? How could I embrace my own pain without showing despair when meeting with a mother who was desperately trying to achieve some distance from the grief she had felt since the traumatic death of one of her twin sons? She and her husband had watched and participated in an unsuccessful rescue effort as their son cried for help.

Given the social, economic, and political times in which we all live, we are repeatedly confronted with the issues of hope and hopelessness.

367

As therapists, we sometimes feel overwhelmed about the possibility that the problems our clients present can be resolved. Some clients, in contrast, appear undaunted, and we are either amazed at their survival skills or convinced that they are in denial. In other instances, our clients convey a sense of hopelessness, a dis-ease of spirit, whereas we as therapists see possibilities and struggle to help them free themselves from self-imposed limitations. A third scenario is one in which both our clients and we ourselves have a sense of helplessness.

In spite of the pull to supply our clients with the answers to their problems, neither our personal life experiences nor our professional training prepare us to envision the answers to some dilemmas. We must also confront the reality that there are some problems for which there may be no concrete resolution, either immediately or in the long term.

In the face of such circumstances, the ability genuinely to convey and encourage hope is key to retaining clients in the helping process and to motivating them to make behavioral and cognitive shifts that can enhance their functioning and improve the quality of their lives. This chapter advances the premise that every culture has means of preserving the lessons that have been learned over generations about psychological survival. Using African American culture as an example, the chapter explores the therapeutic benefit of turning to the wisdom of those who have survived circumstances that confound us and our clients, and it offers guidelines for clients in making this connection. The chapter further highlights the importance of our being able to tap readily into our own reservoirs of hope when it is lacking in our work.

BELIEFS AND WELL-BEING

There is a clear relationship between our beliefs and our emotional and behavioral functioning. Beliefs, embraced intuitively and uttered spontaneously in crisis situations, may either function as anchors during a storm or promulgate a sense of hopelessness and helplessness. Fortunately, our beliefs are acquired through life experiences, and they can be altered likewise.

Counseling and therapy are not modalities that African Americans turn to easily. When they do, few walk in and request treatment for their hopelessness. Nevertheless, there is no greater challenge to be faced by African Americans, a population challenged by generations of past and ongoing daily acts of social injustice, and by those who work with them than maintaining and encouraging, in more culturally laden terms, the will to "keep on keeping on."

CONNECTING WITH THE PAST
IN ORDER TO MOVE FORWARD

Struggle characterizes our African American history, our present, and, no doubt, our future. African Americans have historically recognized that maintaining the will to live life to its fullest and never to give up is vital to our physical, psychological, and spiritual survival, and we have proved to be masters at doing so under unimaginable circumstances. Without hope, for example, the slaves who traveled the Underground Railroad would have succumbed, and the outward symbols of racist segregation would not have been outlawed. Now in the 21st century the issue of "keeping our hope alive" remains central to the well-being and literal survival of African Americans, collectively and individually. For the majority of African Americans, freedom from the shackles of slavery has not given rise to freedom from pain and suffering.

Cornel West (1993) and others have directed increasing attention to the link between escalating social, economic, health, educational, and political problems on the one hand and the erosion of connections with cultural values and traditions on the other. African and African American tradition involves looking to our elders for the wisdom they have drawn from the research laboratories of life. Yet connecting with the oppression that our forebears experienced both during slavery and since the Civil War era brings forth conflicting wishes for many African Americans: the wish to forget the inhumanity our ancestors suffered and the wish to remember their amazing capacity not only to survive but also to transcend difficult circumstances and overwhelming odds.

Countless recognized and unsung heroes and "sheroes" were first physically enslaved and then segregated; the real victory was their audacity in believing in themselves and in maintaining a sense of dignity, self-respect, concern for one another, and hope for a better day. These were individuals who kept their spirits intact even though they were repeatedly treated as if they were dangerous or invisible. They had to struggle mightily to overcome the oppressive forces of poverty and racism. In short, the African American story is one of unrelenting struggle—people searching for a way to be happy, to function at their fullest potential, and to be free from the scars of the past and the restrictions of the present.

Lerone Bennett (1991) wrote that the voices of the past speak to us of hope, endurance, and daring. They tell us that life does not exist in the absence of connection with family and our culture. They tell us, among other things, that nothing can destroy us here if we keep the faith of our fathers and mothers and put our hands to the plow and hold on. They suggest that we can call on the story of the collective and draw strength and direction.

African American culture is distinctive in the reliance placed on oral communication to transmit beliefs, values, and traditions across generations. Proverbs and jokes; religious sermons and prayers; poetry; spirituals, the blues, and other forms of music; and stories and fables drawn from African and African American tradition are rich in wisdom about endurance and remaining spiritually healthy in spite of unrelenting oppression. Although the messages may be linked to either secular or religious sources, the themes are constant because of the strong spiritual orientation that permeates African American culture.

Folk Wisdom

Among African Americans, interest in preserving the wisdom of our elders is apparent in the recent popularity of what are known as "books of affirmation" (Riley, 1993; Vanzant, 1993; Copage, 2005). These old sayings, quotations, and proverbs drawn from African and African American experience are intended to pass on a message of empowerment. These messages have particular significance and familiarity for many African Americans. Some, such as "Stand tall, walk proud," and "Even an ant may harm an elephant," prompt us to let go of hopelessness and believe in ourselves. Others, such as "What storm is there which has no end?" and "Tough times don't last, tough people do," remind us that troubled times will come to an end. Yet others prompt us to take risks and to persevere: "If there is no struggle, there is no progress"; "When life knocks you down, land on your back, because if you can look up, you can get up"; and "You don't get there because, you get there in spite of."

Some messages connect us with our past and future, eliciting images of what has been and images of what can be. They draw attention to our interrelationship with one another through our commonalities in experience. These include the following: "Our successes have been earned while we stood on the shoulders of those who came before us"; "Reach back, give back"; "Look from whence you have come"; "Lose not courage, lose not faith, go forward." The power of these messages to energize, mobilize, and promote transformation is readily apparent both inside and outside the therapeutic process.

Spiritual Beliefs

Two-thirds of the people of the United States consider spirituality or religion to be important or very important in their lives and may prefer approaches that are sympathetic to spiritual values (Richards & Bergin, 2005). Even when they are not involved with organized religion, African Americans tend to hold biblically based beliefs, although they may not identify them as such.

Cooper-Lewter and Mitchell (1986) have outlined a number of basic beliefs in African American culture that are tied to Judeo–Christian tradition and traditional African religion. These include reminders of the power of God (e.g., "God is in charge," "God knows everything and is an all-wise protector") and of the security that a just God offers (e.g., "God is just, fair, and impartial," "God is gracious, offering unqualified love," "God regards all persons as equal"). Common religious beliefs also pertain to the sanctity of life and basic human rights (e.g., "Each person is absolutely unique and worthy of respect," "We should not surrender to the pressures of life and give up in despair," "We are all related as a family"). The values that are encouraged by these beliefs parallel those espoused in the therapeutic community: forgiveness of self and others, self-discipline, respect for self and others, courage, honesty, ability to let go of negative emotional states, and so forth (Richards & Bergin, 2005).

When African Americans call on spiritual and religious sources of inspiration, we call not only on the wisdom of our ancestors but also on the power of a higher spirit. Family stories, fables, poetic prayers, daily meditations, sermons, and such hymns and spirituals as "Let Me Tell You How to Move a Mountain" or secular songs such as "Image Me" contain messages that encourage an outlook that promotes triumph over obstacles. They proclaim that no matter how bad things seem, everyone's life is worth living. They encourage perseverance, forgiveness, not wasting one's time on vengeance, celebrating one's uniqueness, self-understanding, and unconditional love. They encourage us never to feel alone. They remind us that when we partner with the higher power, nothing can penetrate our armor. Although we may not know what the future holds, we need not be fearful. We *can* move from obstacles to possibilities. We *can* run a race with one foot, if necessary.

When we lack any clue about how to proceed, or when we run out of steam and cannot try or cannot conceive of what to do next, the implication of adopting such a perspective is clear. As Weingarten (2007) points out, hope is not just a noun but a verb; hope drives action. Solutions are more likely to be found when we actively continue to search for them.

CLINICAL IMPLICATIONS

The training of most therapists does not allow us to deal with spiritual beliefs and values easily. The anxiety associated with addressing religious beliefs is even greater, for a variety of reasons. First, unfamiliarity breeds discomfort.

Second, many therapists interpret the mandate to be "neutral" in transactions with clients to mean that they should avoid discussions about religious and spiritual beliefs and values. Some fear that they will abuse their power and influence clients toward adoption of their own viewpoints. Other therapists are closed to conversations with clients about their religious beliefs because of the ways that religion has been misused to support oppression.

Clearly, to ignore the interrelationship among mind, body, and spirit is to draw an artificial distinction that distances us from our clients. Although we can abuse our influence, the truth is that we convey messages through our omissions, as well as through what we say and do in therapy. We are probably less likely to influence changes in our clients' basic beliefs about religion than we are changes in other domains. We have also matured in our recognition that there can be healthy, as well as unhealthy, religiosity. A person's religious beliefs and values may heighten stress, provide a haven from stress, foster higher moral behavior, and/or promote personal growth and fulfillment (Spilka, Wood, Hunsberger, & Gorsuch, 2003).

Regardless of whether their belief systems are grounded in secular or religious folkways, clients will vary in their abilities to readily articulate their basic beliefs. They will also vary in the extent to which they make a conscious, active effort to access cognitions (and associated images and positive "self-talk") that can empower them when they face obstacles. Therapists can help clients to pinpoint the basic beliefs that shape their worldviews, feelings, and behaviors by tracking their statements and asking direct questions. It is important to explore the personal meanings that underlie abstract belief statements (e.g., "I believe God will make a way"), even when the language that clients use is familiar. Another key therapeutic task is to help clients understand that many of their beliefs are not based on absolutes and that they may wish to evaluate whether it is worth holding on to a given belief—or at least to their notion about how to translate that belief into action—that may have been helpful in the past but that may no longer serve them well. To the extent that it is relevant to clients' well-being and therapeutic goals, therapists should facilitate awareness of inconsistencies in beliefs, as well as inconsistencies between beliefs and behavior. The aim in these instances should be to help clients evaluate their positions, expand their perspectives, and draw their *own* conclusions about which beliefs they cling to and which they let go.

In some instances, the challenge may be to help clients develop strategies to gain inspiration to go on with their lives when they are immobilized with despair. For example, a client whose son had been killed in a gang murder became immobilized every time he had to go to court for the arraignments of the young men who were charged with his son's murder. To support his hope, I showed him and his family a film clip during therapy about a woman whose life was transformed when she found a way to forgive the gang member who had killed her son. Her story provided my client with an alternative script, which allowed him to speak to his son's killer at the hearing, to forgive him, and to go home and extinguish the candles that he had been burning for his son since his untimely death 2 years before.

In other instances, clients simply need to be encouraged to make more consistent use of the resources they have already identified and previously used, particularly in tough moments.

Working across Differences

Although many clients prefer therapists who share their beliefs and value systems, their bottom-line concern is having a place where they can talk openly without being judged. A therapist may have beliefs that are dissonant with a client's, or the therapist and client may share common beliefs that may originate from disparate sources. In either instance, it is possible for the therapist to be empathic and creative and to generate hope in therapeutic transactions. When therapists greet clients with genuine respect and an openness to learning about them, there is a greater potential for discovering commonalities of experience that transcend differences. For example, it may be difficult for therapists in the mainstream to experience the same emotion and empowerment as some clients do when listening to a spiritual; however, the same therapists can fully appreciate the notion that music, words, and images drawn from past experience can connect people, at a multisensory level, with memories of inner peace and hope and of a point in time when they felt happy, protected, and safe (for example, listening to "Twinkle, Twinkle, Little Star" or some other song cherished during childhood).

A Clinical Case Example

A poignant illustration of the application of cultural narratives in the context of family therapy and how helping people link to their past, present, and potential future is transformative (McGoldrick & Hines, 2007) is provided by the case of a client, Jerry, who complained of anger and depression after he was demoted on his job. Jerry's preoccupation with what he viewed as an act of racial discrimination had resulted in considerable tension between him and his wife, as well as with his two adolescent children. He noted that his recent experience had left him feeling deflated and hopeless that a Black man could ever be treated justly in this society. The quality of his work had declined, and he had begun to have panic attacks when driving to work each day. He felt ashamed that his finances would not allow him to quit his position; he saw himself as the only one of four children that his aging parents could depend on for support, and he was also anxious about putting away funds for his own children's college education. Jerry had begun to withdraw from everyone and had lost interest in all of his former social and cultural activities. His wife complained that he would not share his thoughts and feelings with her; Jerry viewed himself as a hypocrite in that he found himself unable to model positive functioning for his children.

During the review of Jerry's family history, he revealed that his grandfather was the person who had most significantly influenced him as a child. He recalled that one legacy passed on by his grandfather was the belief that "When one door closes, another opens." Within the context of a family session, we explored Jerry's thoughts about what his grandfather had meant when he cited this adage, as well as what Jerry had wanted to convey to his children on the numerous occasions he had repeated these same words. Jerry had shared very little with his children or his wife about his childhood. He assumed that they had little interest, but, even more, he feared he would be overwhelmed by feelings of loss. His two teenagers, who had done little to hide their reluctance to come to therapy, showed a high level of interest in the discussion about their ancestors. Jerry shared a story with his family about a time when his grandparents' farm was sold at auction following several years of bad crops and the family was forced to give up most of their acquisitions. Although the bank had granted additional time to many of his grandfather's European American neighbors, his request for an extension had been denied. For the first time in many years, Jerry allowed himself to cry as he recalled the awe and pride he felt when his grandparents looked the auctioneer and bankers in the eye and walked proudly away from the home they had built themselves. His grandfather subsequently established a small trucking business, which sustained his family through the Great Depression.

When asked what advice his grandfather would give Jerry about coping with his current situation, Jerry imagined he would say, "Another person can't ride your back, unless it's bent." Discussion followed regarding how Jerry might better align his behavior with his grandfather's prescription. Among other things, Jerry reported that he had begun to read from a book of meditations daily. Aware that Jerry gave himself little or no room to lean on others for support even in the most difficult times, the therapist asked Jerry about the nature of his prayers. Not surprisingly, Jerry had operated from a firm conviction that it was OK for him to pray for others but that it was selfish to ask for anything for himself. The therapist prescribed that Jerry begin a ritual of praying at least once a day, during which he was to ask God for help with his own problems.

Jerry and his wife discussed with the therapist their varied notions about how they would recognize God's answer to Jerry's prayers. Jerry's unresolved guilt about being away at college during the last month of his grandfather's life surfaced. His inability to forgive himself had kept him distant from his grandmother during the remaining years of her life. Jerry was becoming very conscious of the double standards that he applied in his life in that he was far more forgiving and less demanding of others than he was of himself.

The subsequent therapy continued to build on the value Jerry placed on his grandfather's wisdom and his heightened awareness that he had departed from it. He was asked (1) to project himself forward in time and to visualize himself having resolved his current dilemma by calling on the cumulative wisdom of his ancestors; and (2) to define the minimal changes necessary to shift from his present (undesirable) situation to the scenario he had visualized in which his dilemma had been resolved. With the therapist's coaching, Jerry developed a plan to visualize his grandfather coaching him prior to each planned encounter with his boss. His boss seemed to be unbalanced by Jerry's calmness and self-confidence and began to back down from the power and control games he had initiated shortly after Jerry's demotion. Jerry ultimately decided to take an early retirement package, and his wife agreed to support him in starting his own consulting firm.

Our Clients, Ourselves: Avoiding the Hopelessness Trap

As therapists, we are generally attuned to the instances in which clients assume postures of hopelessness, imposing limitations on the possibilities that they can conceive because they are unable to see beyond their beliefs, imagination, and self-definition. We are less apt to recognize the negative influence that our own hopelessness has on our clients.

Most frequently, we have a sense of when our clients are likely to terminate therapy prematurely. This circumstance may result from our failure to communicate a sense of hope regarding the challenges the clients face. As one client put it, "Why invest my time and money in coming to see someone who only leaves me feeling worse?" African American clients, in particular, are very attuned to " negative vibes" (i.e., nonverbal messages), as well as to what is or is not communicated verbally. A message of hope that is insincere is unlikely to lead to positive results.

Within the context of a typical therapy hour, we have little time to process the barrage of information that is shared by clients. There is even less time available to ponder the roots of and remedies for our own hopelessness when it surfaces. We share with our clients a need to recognize when we are so afflicted; we also share a need to slow our pace occasionally, in order to embark on a process that can help us find a means of spiritual renewal.

Ongoing self-reflection and discussion with colleagues can provide insights that will assist us as therapists in mapping a path from hopelessness to hopefulness. Questions that may prove valuable in this process follow:

1. When you feel hopeless, what are the cues?
2. Who has loved you in your life? Is there a particular person, image, thought, or story that you are likely to access to help you cope?
3. What are the cultural messages and family stories that have been passed down to you about coping with adversity?
4. How are your personal beliefs and patterns of coping similar to or different from those held by most people in your family or culture?
5. Are there situations that are rightfully construed as hopeless?
6. Are there occasions on which one may actually do harm by encouraging hope?
7. To what extent is your way of responding to adversity different from those of the clients who have proven most challenging to work with in therapy?
8. What strategies do you use to diminish burnout and revitalize yourself?
9. How do you distinguish between times that it is reasonable to continue therapy with a client and times that you should transfer the case because you feel hopeless about the potential for a positive outcome?

CONCLUSION

On occasion, our clients' well-being is tied to figuring out concrete solutions to their problems; more frequently, though, the key issue is a loss of the will that is necessary to pursue possibilities, however limited these may be. The basic premise of this chapter is that we therapists and our clients alike can find guidance regarding how to protect and heal our bruised spirits by turning to the wisdom of our ancestors, through whatever means this knowledge has been preserved. Within African American culture, proverbs, folk sayings, poetry, movies, literature, art, music, and stories drawn from African and African American tradition not only inspire but offer specific prescriptions about how to avoid and master obstacles in life. We and our clients can be empowered by reaching into and beyond ourselves and tapping our cultural legacies.

REFERENCES

Bennett, L. (1991, February). Voices of the past. *Ebony*, 120–122.

Copper-Lewter, N., & Mitchell, H. (1986). *Soul theology*. Nashville, TN: Abingdon Press.

Copage, E. (2005). *Black pearls for parents: Meditations, affirmations, and inspirations for African-American parents*. New York: Morrow.

McGoldrick, M., & Hines, P. (2007). Hope: The far side of despair. In C. Flaskas, I. McCarthy, & J. Sheehan (Eds.), *Hope and despair in narrative and family therapy* (pp. 51–62). New York: Routledge.

Richards, I. S., & Bergin, A. E. (2005). *A spiritual strategy for counseling and psychotherapy* (2nd ed.). Washington, DC: American Psychological Association.

Riley, D. (1993). *My soul looks back, 'less I forget*. New York: HarperCollins.

Spilka, B., Wood, R., Hunsberger, B., & Gorsuch, R. (2003). *The psychology of religion* (3rd ed.). New York: Guilford Press.

Vanzant, I. (1993). *Acts of faith*. New York: Simon & Schuster.

Weingarten, K. (2007). Hope in a time of global fear. In C. Flaskas, I. McCarthy, & J. Sheehan (Eds.), *Hope and despair in narrative and family therapy* (pp. 13–23). New York: Routledge.

West, C. (1993). *Race matters*. Boston: Beacon Press.

CHAPTER 32

Interracial Asian Couples
Beyond Black and White

Tazuko Shibusawa

A young Asian therapist who recently graduated from a master's program in clinical social work is employed at a community mental health clinic that serves Asian Americans. Among her first clients are Karen, a 24-year-old Taiwanese American, and Michael, a 24-year-old European American. The two met in college and have been together for 2 years. Michael initiated therapy because he wants to marry Karen, but he feels frustrated and stuck because Karen gets very anxious every time he brings up the subject. Karen says that she loves Michael but knows that her father will oppose the marriage because Michael is not Chinese. Karen has never told her father about Michael out of fear that he will disown her if he found out that she was involved with a non-Chinese man. Karen does not feel that she can go against her father's wishes and becomes anxious and paralyzed. Michael thinks that Karen needs to become more independent from her family.

The therapist understands the ways in which Karen feels caught between her family and Michael. At the same time, she believes that the ideal clinical outcome for Karen is to be able to "follow her heart." In trying to assess Karen's anxieties, the therapist begins to create a list of possible reasons that Karen is not able to stand up to her father, including her inability to individuate from her parents, her overwhelming fear of her father's anger, and her position as a parentified child. In haste, the clinician begins to focus on what she perceives to be Karen's issues. She views Karen's need to submit to her parents' expectations at the expense of her own desires as problematic. She does not take into account Karen's possible discomfort with Michael's apparent lack of concern about the way his family might react to having a non-White daughter-in-law and with the pressures of being the first person of color to marry into Michael's family. Nor does she take the time to consider what issues of Michael's were played out in his relationship with Karen. The therapist also experiences difficulty connecting with Karen. She senses that the way she asks questions makes Karen feel uncomfortable. After a few sessions the couple drops out of therapy.

I was the therapist in the preceding vignette close to 30 years ago. The growing recognition of the need for ethnic-specific mental health services for Asian Americans had led to the opening of the clinic where I was employed. The entire staff was Asian, and there was an implicit assumption that Asian clinicians knew how to work effectively with Asian clients merely because we were Asian. Although I was excited to be able to work in the Asian American community, I remember often feeling like a failure when faced with clients like Karen. On the one hand, I would hear my "internal supervisor" telling me that I should be more "clinical" with my Asian clients—why was I treading so gently, why couldn't I be more direct with my clients, why did I feel so insecure and worried about what my Asian clients thought of me, and why such a strong need for acceptance? On the other hand, my "Japanese self" would question why I was not able to be more Asian in my interactions with my clients—why was I asking questions that seemed so foreign to them, why couldn't I ask questions in a more indirect and elegant way, and why was I forcing my clients to talk about things that seemed so private to them?

It was not until many years later, when Vincenzo DiNicola, an Italian Canadian colleague and family therapist, told me about the Italian proverb "*traduttore traditore*" (translator, traitor; DiNicola, 1997) that I was able to view my conflicts in a new light. I began to realize that the dilemma that I had been experiencing was "not only personal, but political" and perhaps common to other ethnic therapists who had been trained in the Western model of psychotherapy. I was, as the proverb illustrates, betraying aspects of my Western psychotherapy training when translating concepts into the context of Asian culture, and, furthermore, I was betraying myself and my clients when trying to conceptualize our experiences within a Western framework. This sense of "betrayal" can be a heavy burden for bilingual–bicultural therapists, because working with a sense of integrity is fundamental to our relationship with clients.

Among the different therapeutic modalities (i.e., individual, couples, and families), couples therapy in which one or both partners are Asian can be the most challenging for Asian clinicians such as myself who were trained in North America. The reason is that clinical theories about functional marriages and couplehood are based on Western assumptions and values, including the notion of "falling in love" as a requisite for marriage or committed relationships. The very act of talking to a third party about intimate relationships is also an alien concept for many Asians.

In this chapter, I discuss the ways in which Western assumptions and values that are embedded in couples therapy pose challenges when working with couples with an Asian partner. I will first present background information on Asian Americans and intermarriage and then discuss some of the lessons that I have learned while working with Asian clients in the context of couples therapy.[1]

ASIAN AMERICANS: BACKGROUND

The first wave of immigrants from Asia arrived in the United States from the mid- to late 1800s and early 1900s from China, the Philippines, Korea, India, and Japan. Most of the immigrants settled in Hawaii and on the West Coast, areas that continue to have large concentrations of Asians. The youngest descendants of the first wave of immigrants are currently fourth and fifth generations. Whereas over 27 million Europeans immigrants arrived in the United States during the same period, the Asian population remained small because of various exclusionary immigration policies, which stemmed from the 1790 Naturalization Law that limited citizenship to people who were White. The exclusionary policies culminated in 1924, when virtually all immigration from Asia was banned. This ban continued into the 1940s.

The second and third waves of immigration from Asia began after the enactment of the 1965 Immigration Law, which eliminated national-origin quotas. Since then Asians have immigrated for professional opportunities, family reunification, and to seek refuge and asylum, as in the case of Southeast Asians and Tibetans (Reeves & Bennett, 2004). Currently, 70% of all Asians in the United States are foreign born, compared to the total U.S. population of 11.1% (Reeves & Bennett, 2004). As mentioned earlier, while some Asians are fourth and fifth generation, almost four-fifths of Asians in the United States speak a language other than English at home (Reeves & Bennett, 2004).

Asian Americans are one of the fastest growing ethnic groups in the United States. In fact over 40 percent of the Asian population in the United States entered the country between the years 1990 to 2000 (Reeves & Bennett, 2004). According to the U.S. 2000 census, there are close to 12 million people who identify as Asian (Reeves & Bennett, 2004). Asians in the United States are a diverse group, representing more than 43 different ethnic groups, speaking 100 different languages and dialects, and affiliated with a wide range of religions, including Buddhism, Christianity, Hinduism, Islam,

Janism, Judaism, Sikhism, and Zoroastrianism (Rastogi & Wadhwa, 2006). The six largest Asian nationalities in the United States are Chinese (23.8%), Filipino (18.3%), Asian Indian (16.2%), Korean (10.5%), Vietnamese (10.9 %), and Japanese (7.8%).

Asian Americans are also diverse in terms of socioeconomic status, educational background, and levels of acculturation. For example, although a large number of Asian Americans identify as middle class, 14% of Asian Americans live below the poverty line, a figure that is higher than that of the average U.S. population (Asian Americans/Pacific Islanders in Philanthropy, 1997). Because of the diversity within the Asian American population, addressing Asians as one ethnic group can lead to the risk of overgeneralization and stereotypes.

RACISM

The ways in which racism affects Asian Americans are often not visible to non-Asians, because when race is discussed in the United States, the focus tends to be on the Black–White dichotomy. On the one hand, Asians are upheld by Whites as a model minority for their economic and educational achievements; on the other hand, this stereotype not only ignores the needs of Asian Americans but is also used to denigrate African Americans and other ethnic groups. While touted for their achievements, Asians are simultaneously treated as "perpetual foreigners" who are unable to assimilate and, therefore, cannot be trusted (Kim, 1999). A prime example of this prejudice is seen in the case of Dr. Wen Ho Lee, the Taiwanese American nuclear scientist who was falsely accused of espionage on behalf of China (Lee & Zia, 2002). Even fourth- and fifth-generation Asians continue to be treated as if they are "foreigners," something that would never happen to the descendants of European immigrants.

Gender-based ethnic stereotypes, another dimension of racism, have different effects on Asian American men and women. Asian women are usually stereotyped as docile and submissive and desirable by the opposite sex. Asian men, on the other hand, struggle with negative stereotypes of being socially dull, "nerdy," and inept with respect to American culture (Pyke & Dang, 2003). Both heterosexual and gay Asian American men live with the pervasive stereotype of being emasculated (Eng, 1997). For example, in the following account, author David Mura (2005), a third-generation Japanese American writer, discusses the influence of stereotyped images on his development of masculinity:

> For years … each beautiful white woman had seemed a mark of my exclusion. The stereotype of Asian women is a doll-like submissiveness and a mysteri-

ous exotic sensuality, qualities which make them attractive to Caucasian men who have trouble accepting women as equals. As an Asian American male, I was placed in category of neutered sexuality. ... None of the women I saw on television, in the movies, or read about in books dreamed of a lover like me. ... (Mura, 2005, pp. 148–149)

ASIAN AMERICANS AND INTERRACIAL MARRIAGES

Interracial marriages in the United States increased significantly after the last miscegenation laws were abolished in 1967. The total number of interracial marriages in the United States soared from 1% in 1970 to nearly 6% in 2000 (Harris & Ono, 2005). The rates of interracial marriages differ according to racial groups. Although much attention has been paid to Black–White interracial marriages, Whites and Blacks have lower rates of exogamy than Latinos or Asians. According to Harris and Ono (2005),[2] who based their study on the 1990 census, close to 96% of White women, White men, and Black women and 90% of Black men are in endogamous marriages (i.e., have a spouse of the same ethnicity). In the case of Latinos and Latinas, about 80% have spouses of the same ethnicity. Asians, on the other hand, have lower rates of endogamy. Only 65% of Asian women and 78% of Asian men have Asian spouses. Furthermore, 30% of Asian women and 18% of Asian men are married to Whites.

It is thought that Asian women marry out more than men do because dominant society is more receptive of Asian women than men, because Asian women acculturate at faster rates than Asian men, and because the system of "mail order brides" applies only to women (Le, 2006). It is important to note that the rates of exogamy differ according to nativity and nationality groups among Asians. Asians who are native born (i.e., children or descendents of immigrants) are more likely to marry outside of their ethnicity than those who are immigrants. As for nationalities, among U.S.-born or -raised Asian Indian men and women, close to 70% have endogamous marriages, 20% are married to Whites, and 4% to other Asians (Le, 2006). In contrast, among U.S.-born or -raised Koreans, 63% of the men are married to Korean women, and only 40% of Korean women are married to Korean men. Twenty-four percent of Korean men are married to White women, and 48% of the women have White husbands (Le, 2006).

There has also been a recent increase in Asian interethnic marriages, especially among U.S.-born Asians. Some researchers predict that intermarriage among Asians may lead to the development of a pan-Asian ethnicity, similar to the historical marital patterns among White ethnic groups during the 20th century in which intermarriage among various European immigrant groups led to the formation of a distinct "White" group in the United States (Qian and Lichter, 2001).

Michiko and David

David and Michiko, who are in their early 40s, sought couples therapy at David's insistence. The couple have been married for 15 years and have two children, ages 12 and 10. David is European American and Michiko is Asian, originally from Japan. They moved from another state 6 months ago because of David's job transfer. David has been working for a Fortune 500 company and sought the job transfer because he considered it an opportunity to move up the corporate ladder. David states that he has been dissatisfied with their relationship for the past few years and feels that something has to be done if they are to stay together. David complains that Michiko has been overly involved with the children and does not seem to care about their relationship as a couple. Michiko appears depressed and acknowledges that she has been having difficulty adjusting to the move. Not only did she lose her friends and support system, she also lost her part-time job and has not figured out what kind of work she wants to pursue. Michiko finds attending to her children more demanding than before because her oldest daughter, in particular, has been having difficulties settling into her new school. During the intake session, David is very vocal about what he wants from Michiko—emotional and physical intimacy—and articulates his needs in a self-involved way, evoking in the therapist an image of a child having tantrums when he is not able to get what he wants. Michiko, on the other hand, is withdrawn, and seems to be at a loss with David's insistence on his desire for her to be more attentive to him.

If this couple were both White, therapists would probably take into consideration the history of the relationship, the move as a possible crisis, family life cycle stages, conflicts over intimacy, power dynamics, and each partner's goals for therapy despite differing foci based on their theoretical orientations. The therapists would not need to take into account the complex ways cultures shape the experiences of couplehood. Nor would they need to examine the ways in which their theoretical assumptions, founded on Western cultural ideas, form their assumptions about intimate relationships.

The following are some of the assumptions that are inherent in Western psychotherapy and that can limit therapists' understanding of cultural conflicts between interracial couples such as Karen and Michael or Michiko and David. When discussing culture, it is important to note that cultures are not static entities; they are always in a flux, as are individual members of these cultures. Thus it is not my intention to describe Karen and Michiko as the torch bearers of traditional Asian cultural values. However, when using Western psychotherapy with non-Western clients, it is important to consider the possibility that no matter how acculturated clients are, it is most likely that their worldviews contain constructions that differ from those of Westerners.

CENTRALITY OF THE MARITAL/COUPLE UNIT

In most Asian cultures, marriage has traditionally been viewed as a union of two families or households, rather than two individuals. Marriages were arranged to ensure the succession of the patrilineal line. In countries such as China, Korea, Japan, and Vietnam, which have been influenced by Confucianism, parent–child relationships take precedence over marital relationships. The reason is that in patriarchal societies, women are considered as outsiders who have entered the family through marriage (Chung, 1992; Koyano, 1989; Min, 1998). Also, in traditional Asian cultures, the goals and needs of the family take precedence over the needs and desires of individual members (Agbayani-Siewert, 1994; Ho, 1994; Pettys & Balgopal, 1998).

As stated earlier, when working with Karen and Michael, I had believed that the optimal outcome for Karen was to "follow her heart" and had thought that she should not sacrifice her desires for her family. My view was based on the Western notion of selfhood and ego development—that individuals need to develop the ability to make their own decisions and be in control of their own lives. I was also influenced by the Western notion that for marriages to be successful, partners need to separate psychologically from their parents (Wallerstein & Blakeslee, 1995).

I had also minimized the impact that immigration had on Karen's family. Karen grew up with the stories of the hardships that her parents had endured to come to the United States and the tremendous sacrifice that they had made to send her to college. As with many children of immigrants, Karen shouldered the expectations of actualizing her parents' dreams of life in the United States. Included in the parents' dreams were future generations of Chinese children. Whereas the need to fulfill one's parents' dreams is viewed from a Western psychological perspective as "enmeshment" or lack of individuation, family cohesion and the willingness to relinquish one's desires and aspirations for the good of the family have historically contributed to the survival of many immigrant families in the United States (Ying, Akutsu, Zhang, & Huang, 1997).

ROMANTIC LOVE AS A PRECONDITION FOR MARRIAGE

Romantic love and passionate love are conceptualized as a universal experience and viewed as a criterion for intimate relationships in Western cultures. Yet romantic love as a precondition for marriage is also a relatively new phenomenon in Western societies. It was not until the 18th century, with the separation of work and home, that emotional and sexual intimacy between spouses came to be viewed as a desirable state (Aries, 1985). Some scholars also argue that the notion of romantic love is a product of individualistic cultures and that love is experienced differently in collectivistic cultures (Beall & Sternberg, 1995). Individualistic cultures encourage people to focus on personal fulfillment, which in turn facilitates choosing partners who make them feel fulfilled. As part of the notion of having the power to shape one's destiny, people in individualistic cultures also believe that they have choices in selecting partners. In collectivistic cultures, individuals do not necessarily believe that they have individual choices. This is reinforced by the belief that it is fate that dictates one's marriage partner. For example, the Chinese concept of *yuan* (connection), which is widespread in East Asian nations, is based on the Buddhist belief that relationships are formed in life because of destiny (karma) and that individuals have little control over their destiny (Chang & Holt, 1991).

In Western culture, there is a distinction between passionate love and companionate love, in which passionate love involves emotional intensity and sexualized feelings (Noller, 1996). David and Michiko's conflicts are illustrative of the cultural differences in expectations of the nature of love in couple relationships. David looks to Michiko to fulfill his needs for closeness and is frustrated that they are no longer passionate as a couple. He views this as a loss and a sign that Michiko is no longer invested in their relationship. In traditional Asian marriages, companionate love, which is characterized by respect and trust (Noller, 1996), is valued over passionate love.

In East Asian cultures, emotional bonding between people is explained as the result of *chin*, which is a Chinese word. *Chin* is known as *jeong* in Korean and *jyo* in Japanese culture and is based on the same Chinese written character. Although it is difficult to translate *chin* into English, the word encompasses feelings, empathy, connection, tenderness, compassion, sentiment, trust, bonding, and love (Kim, Kim, & Kelly, 2006). Unlike the West, where emotions are thought to be located in the individual, *chin* denotes an intersubjectivity in which feelings are a shared experience. In Western cultures, an individual experiences, owns, and acts on the feelings of love. *Chin*, on the other hand, exists outside of people and is something that is experienced among people rather than owned. In fact, in Japanese culture, having affection for another person is characterized as "catching *jyo*," similar to the way someone would "catch" a cold.

In romantic relationships, people are expected to demonstrate their feelings of love. In the case of David and Michiko, David believes that couples need to make the time to nurture and express their intimacy. For Michiko, once there is a trusting relationship and companionship, the feelings between them do not necessarily have to be demonstrated or articulated. Her commitment to David is expressed through her role as wife and mother, not as a romantic lover. Thus, when working with couples like David and Michiko, it is important that the therapist acknowledge that the very notion of love is a social construction (Beall & Sternberg, 1995) and that the way love is constructed in Western culture is not necessarily a prerequisite for functional marriages.

CONCLUSIONS

When working with interracial couples, it is important for clinicians to examine how our theoretical assumptions about intimate relationships are shaped by Western cultural values. Unless we are aware of our own cultural lenses, it is easy to privilege one worldview over the other and to pathologize the spouse who is of another culture. Understanding another person's culture can start only with understanding the lenses through which we view the world. It is equally important to acknowledge the struggles that ethnic therapists experience in integrating their Western training and applying them to their own communities. The increase in immigrant populations has resulted in the need for bilingual–bicultural therapists. Training programs should not assume that bilingual–bicultural students can automatically translate Western concepts into their practice and be effective with their clients. The act of therapy itself is a foreign act in many cultures. Thus attention must be given to how this foreign act can be helpful and collaborative without "betraying" the client or the culture of psychotherapy.

ACKNOWLEDGMENT

I would like to express my appreciation to Dr. Irene Chung and Dr. James Runsdorf for their helpful comments.

NOTES

1. This chapter is based on my experiences with heterosexual couples, which naturally limits its scope.

2. There are a number of studies of interracial marriages in the United States, with varying rates and figures. The study by Harris and Ono (2005) was selected for this chapter because they take into account the racial composition of local marriage markets
instead of the entire racial composition of the United States.

REFERENCES

Agbayani-Siewert, P. (1994). Filipino American culture and family: Guidelines for practitioners. *Families in Society, 75*(7), 429–438.

Aries, P. (1985). Love in married life (A. Foster, Trans.). In P. Aries & A. Bejin (Eds.),
Western sexuality: Practice and precept in past and present times (pp. 130–139).
New York: Blackwell.

Asian Americans/Pacific Islanders in Philanthropy. (1997). *An invisible crisis: The educational needs of Asian Pacific American youth*. San Francisco, CA: Author.

Beall, A. E., & Sternberg, R. J. (1995). The social construction of love. *Journal of Social
and Personal Relationships, 12*(3), 417–438.

Chang, H. C., & Holt, G. R. (1991). The concept of *yuan* and Chinese interpersonal
relationships. In S. Ting-Toomey & F. Korzenny (Eds.), *Cross-cultural interpersonal
communication* (pp. 28–57). Newbury Park, CA: Sage.

Chung, D. K. (1992). Asian cultural commonalities: A comparison with mainstream
American culture. In S. Furuto, R. Biswas, D. Chung, K. Murase, & E. Ross-Seriff
(Eds.), *Social work practice with Asian Americans* (pp. 27–44). Newbury Park, CA:
Sage.

DiNicola, V. (1997). *A stranger in the family: Culture, families and therapy*. New York:
Norton.

Eng, D. L. (1997). Out here and over there: Queerness and diaspora in Asian American
studies. *Social Text, 52/53*, 31–52.

Harris, D. R., & Ono, H. (2005). How many interracial marriages would there be if all
groups were of equal size in all places? *Social Science Research, 34*, 236–251.

Ho, Y. F. (1994). Cognitive socialization in Confucian heritage cultures. In P. M. Green-
field & R. R. Cocking (Eds.), *Cross-cultural roots of minority child development*
(pp. 285–313). Hillsdale, NJ: Erlbaum.

Kim, C. J. (1999). The racial triangulation of Asian Americans. *Politics and Society,
27*(1), 105–138.

Kim, I. J., Kim, L. C., & Kelly, J. G. (2006). Developing cultural competence in working with Korean immigrant families. *Journal of Community Psychology, 34*(2),
149–165.

Koyano, W. (1989). Japanese attitudes toward the elderly: A review of research findings.
Journal of Cross-Cultural Gerontology, 4, 335–345.

Le, C. E. (2006). Interracial dating and marriage. Retrieved October 28, 2006, from
www.asian-nation.org/interracial2.shtml.

Lee, W. H., & Zia, H. (2002). *My country versus me: The first-hand account by the Los
Alamos scientist who was falsely accused of being a spy*. New York: Hyperion.

Min, P. (1998). *Change and conflicts: Korean immigrant families in New York*. New
York: Allyn & Bacon.

Mura, D. (2005). *Turning Japanese: Memoirs of a Sansei*. New York: Grove Press.

Noller, P. (1996). What is this thing called love? Defining the love that supports marriage
and family. *Personal Relationships, 3*, 97–115.

Pettys, G. L., & Balgopal, P. R. (1998). Multigenerational conflicts and new immigrants: An Indo-American experience. *Families in Society, 79*(4), 410–424.

Pyke, K., & Dang, T. (2003). "FOB" and "whitewashed": Identity and interalized racism among second generation Asian Americans. *Qualitative Sociology, 26*(2), 147–172.

Qian, Z., & Lichter, D. T. (2001). Measuring marital assimilation: Intermarriage among natives and immigrants. *Social Science Research, 30*(2), 289–312.

Rastogi, M., & Wadhwa, S. (2006). Substance abuse among Asian Indians in the United States: A consideration of cultural factors and treatment. *Substance Use and Misuse, 41*, 1239–1249.

Reeves, T. J., & Bennett, C. E. (2004). *We the people: Asians in the United States (Census 2000 Special Reports, CENSR-17)*. Retrieved October 28, 2006, from *www.census.gov/prod/2004pubs/censr-17.pdf*.

Wallerstein, J., & Blakeslee, S. (1995). *The good marriage*. Boston: Houghton Mifflin.

Ying, Y. W., Akutsu, P. D., Zhang, X., & Huang, L. N. (1997). Psychological dysfunction in Southeast Asian refugees as mediated by sense of coherence. *American Journal of Community Psychology, 25*(6), 839–859.

CHAPTER 33

Working with Families Who Are Homeless

Peter Fraenkel
Chloe Carmichael

Thelma, a 29-year-old African American single mother subsisting on welfare since the birth of her second child, has lived with her 10-year-old and 3-year-old sons for 11 months in a New York City homeless shelter. The father of her second child is in prison for a minor drug possession charge; she is no longer in touch with the father of her older son, who moved out of state and has struggled with a crack/cocaine addiction. She has a strained relationship with her mother, with whom she and her children lived in a two-bedroom Section 8 (federally subsidized) Bronx apartment for 2 years until the mother's boyfriend, often drunk or high, began "making passes" at her. When Thelma reported this to her mother, her mother became angry and jealous and asked her daughter and grandsons to leave. She added that they would have to leave anyway, because housing officials had been making unannounced inspections to determine whether families were "doubling up," as subsidized housing places strict restrictions on how many family members can live in the unit. With no viable housing offered by other extended family members and with nowhere else to go, Thelma entered the New York City shelter system. Like all families seeking shelter, she first went to the Emergency Assistance Unit (EAU), where families sleep on cots (or, when it is full, on benches or the floor) in one large room, are interviewed by a case worker to determine their eligibility for temporary housing, and, if eligible, then placed in a Tier II shelter, sometimes staying for a few days or weeks in one shelter before obtaining their final placement.

389

Two months ago, Thelma enrolled in a home health aide training program. Thelma—who completed high school at 18 and worked in various temporary secretarial positions (without health insurance or other benefits) until her youngest son was born—thought that the program would provide her with an initial experience toward her goal of returning to school and becoming a registered nurse. Her frequent contacts with emergency room personnel due to both of her sons having serious asthma had increased her interest in health care as a profession, as she felt she "could do a better job" than the physicians and nurses who treated them "as a 'case,' not as people." She carefully determined that the training program served as an approved substitute for any work experience program (WEP) assignment under the welfare policy that requires recipients to work full time for their welfare stipends. However, she had nothing in writing to that effect. Despite the challenges of obtaining child care for both of her boys in the shelter, she had completed 6 weeks of perfect attendance in the 8-week training program when her welfare case manager called and informed her that she was to report to a WEP assignment—"cleaning some building." She told the worker that she had almost completed the training program and that immediately after completion she would be placed in a job and thereby remove herself from welfare. The worker did not find the training program on the list of approved WEP substitutes and insisted that Thelma report to the building tomorrow or face immediate sanctioning (cancellation of her welfare). Thelma contacted the training program and asked them to contact welfare, which they said they would do. Thelma asked for 1 day off to straighten out the issues with welfare, but the training program regretfully informed her that even thought she'd been an excellent student, the program required perfect attendance, and they could not make an exception. If she left now, she would forfeit the entire 6 weeks and have to start again.

The next day, after Thelma elected to attend the training program, her welfare worker called to inform her that she had been sanctioned; she then took the morning off from the training program to speak to her worker in person and was told sternly that it was too late. Because the worker was backed up with other appointments, Thelma did not see her until 2 P.M. Returning to the training program the next day, she learned that her enrollment had been cancelled for missing the previous day. She then had to engage a lawyer and attend a "fair hearing" to contest the sanction. At the time of our interview with her, Thelma and her two sons remained in the shelter on minimum "safety net" welfare, with no training program, a fair hearing in 3 weeks, and no prospects of permanent housing.

Despite these enormous challenges and her obvious frustration, Thelma interacts with us in a warm, open way, with grace, dignity, and humor. She and her sons relate to one another affectionately; she gently but firmly guides the 3-year-old Jamal away from dangerous table corners in the shelter director's office. Randall, the 10-year-old, shyly

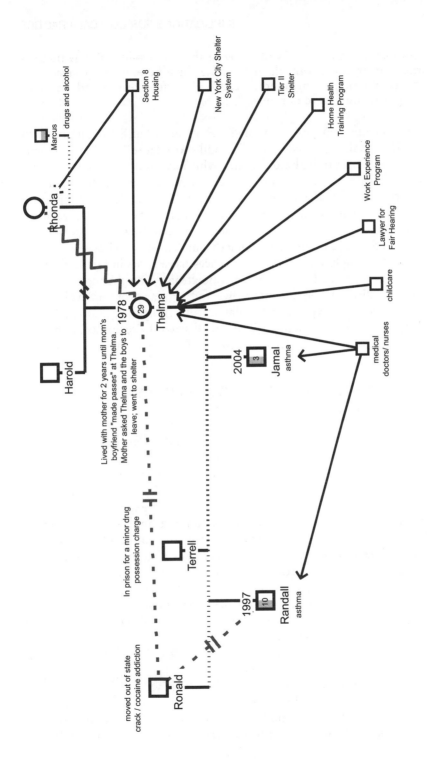

FIGURE 33.1. Ecogram showing multiple stressors for a family in a homeless shelter.

describes some challenges of living in the shelter—"can't have school friends over, don't want them to know I live here, gotta go inside the unit by 9 P.M. even in summer 'cause of curfew, feeling sad 'cause of being here and not in our own place."

This vignette captures many of the challenges faced by families who are homeless, challenges that extend beyond those faced by other economically and socially marginalized families who have housing. It exemplifies the exceptional resilience regularly evidenced by families in this situation. Drawing on a decade of experience and research in a multifamily program called Fresh Start for Families in three New York City shelters (Fraenkel, 2006a, 2006b; Fraenkel, Hameline, & Shannon, 2009), we describe a number of practices found useful in reducing the impact of homelessness on family identity. Although many of these practices have roots in family therapy, we selected and adapted them for this context based on the input received from families through detailed interviews and regular program evaluations that engage them as experts and collaborators (Fraenkel, 2006a). Before describing these specific practices, we briefly discuss the reciprocal impact of the social location of the clinician and that of families living in shelters.

MUTUAL INFLUENCE IN WORK WITH FAMILIES WHO ARE HOMELESS

Clinicians' social locations shape their work and interactions with families who are homeless. For instance, we are 2 of 10 White members of the 22-member multiracial (Black, Latino, Southeast Asian, White), multiethnic, mostly middle-class, and well-educated university- and institute-based staff conducting this program. It has been critical to expand and maintain our awareness of the challenges of understanding and interacting across these wide gaps of social location in class, race, and cultural background— not only between ourselves and the families but also in our relationships with the shelter staff members, who are mostly persons of color with less educational and social class privilege, and with persons of color on our program staff. I (P. F.)—as director of the program and the most frequent presenter of the work at conferences and in writing—have also recognized my responsibility to conduct and present this work in ways that address the impact of my social location and to be especially responsive to concerns and comments from my colleagues of color.

There are several specific practices in which we regularly engage to maintain our awareness and reduce the negative impact of our social location on this work. First, the model used to create and refine the program (Fraenkel, 2006a) focuses on creating a respectful, collaborative relationship with families and shelter staff. The therapist adopts a stance of a learner about challenges and coping from people (both families and shelter staff) who have often managed remarkably well in the face of tremendous obstacles. The therapist may offer therapeutic ideas and activities, but in a tentative manner that invites the family to evaluate the usefulness of these.

Second, we "institutionalized" regular consultations with senior colleagues of color on all aspects of the program and research by making these consultations the first principle of the collaborative family program development (CFPD) model. Third, as mentor/supervisor to my student staff, I (P. F.) have attempted, through the feelings I share and the questions I ask, to create a climate in which we allow ourselves to be deeply affected professionally and personally by our encounters with families in the shelter. We all—and in particular those of us who are White—must work to remain mindful and to counteract the ways in which race and class privilege operate, often without our awareness, to create emotional distance between ourselves and less advantaged families. "Being affected" includes experiencing and sharing in staff meetings feelings of anger, sadness, hopelessness, and uselessness; guilt about one's own privilege and ability to return to a home at the end of the work day; frustration when adult members of families do or say things that seem likely to jeopardize their status in the shelter or put them at risk of closer monitoring by child protective services, welfare, or other larger systems agencies; and the joy and sense of being privileged to witness the greatness of the human spirit and the power of family connection to prevail over injustice.

Openness to being affected also refers to our willingness to reflect on traumatic and difficult moments in our lives and families of origin, as memories may be stimulated by witnessing the trauma affecting families in shelters. For me (P. F.), this has meant recalling family legacies of immigration to escape ethnic and religious persecution, genocide, poverty, war-related trauma, mental illness, my parents' marital conflict and divorce, and fleeing my family as a teen during a particularly bad time, supporting myself and staying in a friend's roach-infested living room for my first year of college. Memories of these experiences and drawing on the positive aspects of my family life to thrive in spite of some hardship provide me with an analogue to help in understanding the experiences of families in the shelters.

For me (C. C.), working with homeless families reinforced what I already knew: that homelessness does not fit neatly into a stereotypical box. I often felt during my work with families that some initially surmised, from my White skin and polished vernacular, that I could not share their history of homelessness. However, I was homeless as a teenager. I recall banding together with other homeless people during difficult times—when it was particularly cold, when we had little food. As a result, I felt a strong sense of kinship with the families once we began talking about homelessness. Though I decided not to disclose my history to the families we worked with, my experiences helped me recognize what I shared with them, while acknowledging important differences. Rather than interfering, the more I recalled those memories during my work, the more I was able to connect with the families.

As part of creating an open dialogue across differences, it is important for clinicians to take the lead in mentioning to the family early on their awareness of the aspects of social location that afford them privilege. This can best be done in a matter-of-fact manner that does not place them center stage or inadvertently communicate a kind of self-congratulatory pride in being such culturally sensitive persons. For instance, I (P. F.) typically mention in the first contact with a family that as a White, middle-class guy who has never been in a shelter, I will rely on them to learn what it means to experience homelessness. I also invite families to tell me if I say or do something with them that suggests that I do not understand their experiences. They usually respond with nonverbal indications of relief, as well as subtle signs of feeling respected—sitting up a bit, a more open, warm, relaxed facial expression, and as they describe powerful experiences, a look while speaking of, "Do you know what I mean?" Other staff members find their moments to say something similar relative to their own social locations.

Finally, there is a kind of compassionate curiosity—asking detailed questions that show real interest in the family's experiences and admiration of their coping abilities, as well as having the ability to "hang" and have fun with families and not behave stiffly or preciously—that families have told us creates a warm, trustworthy connection that leads them to feel that we view them as people and not cases. As one older mother of two teenagers put it in a follow-up interview, "You all didn't treat us like you were workers and we were clients; you treated us like we were friends, and that's what made the difference, and let me stop here or I'll start crying."

CHALLENGES FACED BY FAMILIES WHO ARE HOMELESS

Familiarity with the mind-numbing scope of challenges faced by families who are homeless better prepares the clinician to manage the family's (and their own) sense of being overwhelmed and of hopelessness and to maintain a collaborative stance in generating coping solutions both within the family and between the family and larger systems. The literature on the impact and correlates of homelessness is vast and is presented in a wide range of journals and websites.[1] A brief review is also found in Fraenkel et al. (in press). Families who are homeless lack most of the material foundations that enable human growth—housing with adequate space, informal networks of social support and child care, safe places for children to play, affordable and reliable transportation, steady income. These and other deprivations, experienced by all economically marginalized families, are greatly exacerbated by not having a place to live.

The need to restore fundamental resources while living in a public institution results in a high level of involvement with larger systems. As Thelma's experience illustrated, the contradictory messages and ever-changing requirements of the slow-moving welfare, housing, and employment bureaucracies, the often overwhelmed and uninterested workers, and the unwelcoming physical environments of these agencies communicate a lack of respect that can be experienced as patronizing and stigmatizing as parents simultaneously seek housing, employment, child care, health care, and schools—all while managing the requirements of shelter residence and attempting to maintain a semblance of family life. As one mother put it, "I feel like I do things that finally help me get my head above water so that I can breathe, and then something else happens and I'm drowning again."

Families of color are significantly more likely to experience homelessness than are White families, suggesting that homelessness represents a profound condensation of race-, ethnicity-, language-, and class-based oppression.[2] The loss of the "homeplace" (Burton, Winn, Stevenson, & Clark, 2004) and encounters with the strict regulations of and monitoring by social service systems compounds the traumatic impact of homelessness, eliciting memories of their history of racial oppression (Boyd-Franklin, 2003).

Homeless parents are more likely to have histories of childhood physical abuse, sexual abuse, and domestic violence than are similar families with housing. Likewise, they have more physical and mental health problems and less access to health services. Some of their problems may contribute to their vulnerability to homelessness; others are exacerbated or caused by the trauma of homelessness.

Families who are homeless experience intense stigma and blame, including the myth that they are lazy or mentally ill, and homeless children are taunted and bullied in school. In our studies, teens invariably reject the notion that they are "homeless," stating that this word should be reserved for people living in the streets. Yet the alternative names they give to their circumstances still reveal their sense of stigma: Jail, Central Booking, the Dumpster, Losers' Alley. One 15-year-old boy smiled knowingly and said, "No one wants to look at it that way, but that's really what it is. Homeless—that's actually what we are. That's why we got so many other words for it."

The policies of homeless shelters—designed to preserve order, cleanliness, and security—represent a major source of stigma, at least in how they are often enforced. Curfews, restrictions on where extended family or friends may visit, the presence of security cameras throughout the shelter, unannounced inspections to assess whether parents have adequate food in the refrigerator,[3] and nighttime fire alarms—with the threat of eviction if rules are broken—can create a prison-like atmosphere. When parents are admonished by staff members in front of their children for returning even a few minutes after curfew or having a child playing too rambunctiously, the hierarchy, closeness, and respect between parent and children can be disrupted, and family members may experience an intense mix of anger, fear, shame, and powerlessness.

These moments can also be experienced as racist attacks. For instance, one 53-year-old African American father of two teenage daughters described being chastised in front of his daughters by a Black security guard who had once been homeless: "He's just trying to show me he's a Black man that made it out, and trying to make me feel like I ain't nobody and got nothin.' He wants to forget he been in the same situation." Similarly, a Latina mother reported that one of the African American caseworkers seemed much more effective in finding services for Black families than for Latino/Latina families. Whether these perceptions are accurate or not, families in shelters often experience interactions as disrespectful and stigmatizing.

The effect on families of such shelter interactions may compound the already challenging adaptations they need to make in roles and responsibilities. Teens and even children may be pressed by necessity into taking family caretaking roles for which they are unprepared.

In sum, stigma compounds the material deprivations and administrative hassles families experience in reestablishing themselves in the community. It amplifies their stress and degrades their sense of family identity, leading them occasionally to outbursts or "misbehavior," missed appointments, or temporary refusal to obey rules due to being overwhelmed, to fear, and to demoralization, all of which may be viewed by social service staff as confirming negative evaluations of the family, resulting in further stigmatizing interactions.

Conflict with extended family often plays a part in a family becoming homeless. A large percentage of families who become homeless (especially teens or young women with young children) have either been living with their parents or "doubling up" with families after an eviction or other loss of home. The resulting disruptions of connections to extended family (e.g., cutoffs) are painful emotionally, but also contribute practical difficulties, such as a loss of child care or simply having fewer people to rely on.

The cutoffs from partners and extended family that so often accompany homelessness may be particularly problematic and stigmatizing for families of color because it violates cultural norms of high levels of connectedness and support (Boyd-Franklin, 2003; Falicov, 1998). The well-meaning, culturally sensitive family therapist might suppose that repairing these cutoffs would be a crucial early step in work with homeless families to reestablish themselves outside the shelter. However, families in shelters are typically reluctant to reconnect with their extended families *until* they have reestablished themselves in housing and employment, as they do not want to reconnect from a "one-down" position of need and dependence.

COLLABORATIVE AND EMPOWERING PRACTICES

Importance of a Collaborative Stance

If there is one main recommendation to the family therapist working with families who are homeless, it is to adopt and maintain the collaborative, resilience-oriented stance (Walsh, 1998) of an "appreciative ally" (Madsen, 2007). The "multistressed" nature of their lives can lead the clinician also to feel overwhelmed and to respond by attempting quickly to "take charge." However, to do so may inadvertently suggest to the family that the clinician views them as irresponsible or incompetent. Indeed, working with families who are homeless—like working with families who have experienced other relational traumas, such as domestic violence and incest (Sheinberg & Fraenkel, 2001)—requires the clinician to *slow* the pace, at least initially, to establish a "rehumanizing" relationship, one in which families' strengths can reemerge from under the weight of their challenges and problem narratives. Above all, families in this situation need an opportunity to experience themselves as reempowered, competent, thoughtful, caring, and worthwhile.

Usefulness of Shelter-Based Multiple-Family Group Programs

The specific practices described in this chapter were created in the context of the Fresh Start multiple-family group program. Working with families in such groups allows them to hear directly from one another that they are not alone in their struggles. It also allows them to hear each others' coping strategies and to help each other, which is central to regaining a sense of competence and value. This process helps to create "microcommunities" of support and care within the shelter that extend beyond the group. It is also an efficient way to reach many families at once, an important consideration given that a family's length of stay in the shelter is unpredictable and that they may be placed in permanent housing too far away to continue with the present clinician. In addition, through the collaboration with shelter administrators and other staff, such a program serves to transform the shelter from primarily a context of supervision and constraint into a community of care (Fraenkel, 2006a, 2006b).

Witnessing the Story of Becoming Homeless and Eliciting Stories of Strength

Prior to a family's joining a Fresh Start group, we interview them in depth about challenging experiences, resources and coping strategies, and ask them to advise us about what they would most desire in a support program that would meet their needs. It is important to make time for the family to tell their story of challenge and coping and to reflect on what kind of assistance they want from the therapist. This will likely be the first time that the family has had an opportunity to tell their story and have their experience empathically witnessed, as other contacts with social service providers tend to be rushed and task oriented. As the family is likely to focus readily on the details of the events that led to their becoming homeless and on their negative experiences in the shelter, the therapist needs initially to be the "holder of curiosity" about resilience and coping. To encourage families to shift the balance between accounts of challenges and accounts of coping, it is important to ask for details about coping.

Externalizing Homelessness

We invite families to give a name to the impact of homelessness on their lives and then to notice over the ensuing weeks the steps they take to minimize its impact. As with externalizing other problems, this practice appears to help families separate their fundamental identity from their current conditions and stressors, creating more space to expand on descriptions and activities that reassert their preferred identity and putting the experience of homelessness "in its place."

Family Play and Creative Activities

As Gil (1991) has long noted, family play and arts activities can stimulate family creativity, communication, and cooperation, allowing the family to "tell their story" in a different way. The following activities from our group program can be adapted to individual family therapy.

Challenge and Coping Mobiles and Collages

Give the family five or more blue-colored cards with holes punched on the top line. Ask them to write one challenge on each card. Challenges can be drawn from previous discussions, although this activity typically leads families to identify additional ones. Then on another five or more green cards, ask them to write a coping approach to match each challenge. Next, ask the family to hang all the challenge cards on one piece of string and the coping cards on another piece. Attaching the two strings to opposite ends of a dowel or clothes hanger allows the family to create a mobile. This concrete, visual display of the balance between challenges and coping can lead to a range of different discussions. For instance, they may note the need to create additional coping approaches, celebrating their resourcefulness.

Some families may prefer to create a collage with the challenge and coping cards using markers, crayons, and magazine pictures.

Work and Housing Genogram

Families can construct a genogram that focuses on the education, employment, and housing of immediate and extended family members. In contrast to common descriptors in the social service world of these families as "locked in generations of grinding poverty," families almost invariably have work histories that provide a source of pride and sense of possibility and reduce the impact of internalized racism and classism.

Family and Work Goals Time Line

As a way to help families regain a sense of a more promising future, we have them complete a time line extending from the present into the future. We provide a sample that shows a line for the whole family and a line for each person, so that their goals can all be represented and they can see how these goals fit together. The family chooses how far into the future to project the time line—just until next month, up to next year, the next 5 years, or further.

Letters to (or from) the Future

With the same goal of expanding the family's sense of future, we invite them to write a letter to or from themselves in the future. Included in the letter is what everyone in the family will be doing in work and school, how everyone will feel about him- or herself, each other, and the family as a whole, where they will live, what kinds of things they will own, what kinds of activities they will do for fun and enjoyment as a family, and anything else they hope for in the future. Families are also invited to express appreciation to themselves for having gone through the current struggles toward that future.

SUMMARY

Working with families who are homeless is a powerful experience that requires the therapist to be fully present—as a responsive listener and witness to pain and as an admiring fan and advocate for their prevailing, as a conduit of the wisdom of therapeutic practices, and as a human being who also suffers.

NOTES

1. Three excellent websites are the National Center on Family Homelessness (*www.familyhomelessness.org*), the National Alliance to End Homelessness (*www.endhomelessness.org*), and the National Center for Children in Poverty (*www.nccp.org*). Those interested in the references for any of the specific findings mentioned in this chapter may contact the first author.
2. Ninety percent of homeless persons in New York City—but only 53% of the city's population—are Black or Latino. One in every 10 Black children and 1 in every 20 Latino children resided in a shelter over a 5-year period (Coalition for the Homeless, 2005: *www.coalitionforthehomeless.org/advocacy/research.html#basic_facts.*).
3. One mother reported that she kept a few steaks frozen in the freezer because, "Even though we're Muslim and vegetarian, if the security guards check the fridge and don't see meat, they ask me why I don't have meat in the fridge for the children."

REFERENCES

Boyd-Franklin, N. (2003). *Black families in therapy: Understanding the African American experience* (2nd ed.). New York: Guilford Press.

Burton, L., Winn, D., Stevenson, H., & Clark, S. L. (2004). Working with African American clients: Considering the "homeplace" in marriage and family therapy practices. *Journal of Marital and Family Therapy, 30*, 397–410.

Falicov, C. J. (1998). *Latino families in therapy: A guide to multicultural practice.* New York: Guilford Press.

Fraenkel, P. (2006a). Engaging families as experts: Collaborative family program development. *Family Process, 45*, 237–257.

Fraenkel, P. (2006b). Fresh Start for Families: A collaboratively-built community-based program for families that are homeless. *AFTA Monographs, 1*, 14–19.

Fraenkel, P., Hameline, T., & Shannon, M. (in press). Narrative and collaborative practices in work with families that are homeless. *Journal of Marital and Family Therapy, 35*.

Gil, E. (1991). *The healing power of play.* New York: Guilford Press.

Madsen, W. C. (2007). *Collaborative therapy with multi-stressed families* (2nd ed.). New York: Guilford Press.

Sheinberg, M., & Fraenkel, P. (2001). *The relational trauma of incest: A family-based approach to treatment.* New York: Guilford Press.

Walsh, F. (1998). *Strengthening family resilience.* New York: Guilford Press.

CHAPTER 34

Coyote Returns

A Reconciliation between History and Hope

Robin LaDue

Hear me my chiefs. I am tired, my heart is sick and sad.
From where the sun now stands, I will fight no more forever.
—CHIEF JOSEPH, NEZ PERCE (1985)

"Klahowya! Welcome, my friends, to our circle of stories. Please, sit and warm yourself by the fire for we have much to speak of tonight and our time is limited. Listen, for the jays are calling and that means visitors are coming. Listen, my friends, for the fire and the river have stories to tell. Join us in this place of darkness and light, of heat and cool. Welcome, my friends! Come and tell us your story."

With these words, my auntie opened my naming ceremony, the first one held for a member of the LaDue family in four generations. I cannot build a fire for you or hold the door open to a sweat lodge for you. But I can ask for your patience in the telling of the story to come. I can say "Mahsie Mahsie" for your kindness and express my hope in the sharing of knowledge. So, my friends, I welcome you to join me on a journey, a journey of my life and of my people.

I would like to share stories with you; some of loss and grief and some of hope and reconciliation. I would like to speak with you of historical trauma and current survival. I would like to share with you my story, of my people and of my hopes for the future. I would like to speak with you of the horse people, the cedar trees, and the blood that runs through my veins and the traditions that are bred into my bones. I would like to speak of the sweat lodge, of the medicine wheel, of the things I rarely speak of, for, in my middle age, I find I do not have much to say; my words are almost all used up. But, bear with me for a few moments and I will tell you a story, the ending of which is not known. ...

JULY 20, 2002

I sat that July day in a metal grandstand in the sun watching the dancers as the men in their flamboyant costumes with feathers and bells, leggings and fans stomped and pranced onto the grassy field. The women came forward in their stately manner, their feet moving in time to the drumbeat. Their headdresses, belts, and shawls were in matching shades of color ranging from the purist blue to the deepest black. The little ones, dressed in everything from elaborate costumes to shorts and tennis shoes, wove in and among the adults. The smell of alder cooked salmon and Indian tacos filled the air. As I sat there that day, three figures in long red T-shirts, shorts, and sandals danced into view. It had only been 9 days since my second heart procedure, and I was feeling grateful and scared, as it was my first day out in the sun and among life after 18 months of hospitals, cardioversions, and heart procedures on two sides of the country.

My eyes followed the three small figures, one with long curly dark hair and dark eyes, one with reddish hair, green eyes, and freckles, and the third with light brown hair and dark brown eyes. It was the first, last, and only time I would see my 5-, 7-, and 9-year-old nieces dance in the grand entry at the huge SeaFair Intertribal Pow-wow in Seattle. I sat there on that hot July afternoon, and nothing could have been more healing and more heartbreaking than watching those beautiful girls dance. Five generations of LaDues had passed, and with those generations had passed the Cowlitz and Taidnapem land, our language, our culture, and our tribal and band identities.

My birth name is Robin Annette LaDue, but my given name, bestowed on me by the only remaining traditional elder in my family, my aunt Lucile LaDue, is Tek Tek e'lus s'leday. The spelling is not accurate, as my English-language typewriter cannot catch the fluidity of spelling inherent in the Lushootseed language, the language that is written and is close to the Salish/ Sahaptin dialects once spoken by the Taidnapem people. I am one of the few Taidnapem people left, and, officially, I am enrolled with the Cowlitz tribe, although, as my deceased father declared in his adamant way: "We are Taidnapem and the government cannot tell a Taidnapem from a Cowlitz or a Yakima, but we can!"

In this chapter, it is my intent to discuss, very briefly, the far-reaching consequences of Indian policy, occupation, and other antecedents of historical trauma. This is, basically, my own story and the story of my family. It is all too common in Indian country, but it is also as unique as any of our stories.

The concept of historical trauma is certainly not one limited to the Native people of this land. Intergenerational passing of the consequences of trauma are well known in the children of Holocaust survivors, whether it be the children of the parents who lived through the horror of Nazi Germany and the Polish concentration camps, the children of our own concentration camps of World War II, the horror of Rwanda and the former Yugoslavia, or the ongoing genocide and racism of the United States government in Iraq and against the Native people of this country. It should not escape anyone's notice that a "plank" of the platform of the Washington State Republican Party called for the complete abrogation of tribal sovereignty as recently as 2000. It is an interesting notion that a political party can call for the termination of a people, but that is the truth of the history of the United States and, of course, a primary causal agent of historical trauma.

Termination, a euphemism for genocide, has been and continues to be a formal policy of the United States government, always for economic gain and for the control of natural resources. The mental health issues prevalent in Native communities today can be traced directly to the formal termination policies and the laws passed by the federal government as it relates to Native people. It would take and has taken thousands of books and articles to detail the tragic history of the Native people of North America, but it would also be remiss not to present, albeit in a highly limited manner, what issues face Native people as we move well into the 21st century.

NATIVE AMERICAN MENTAL HEALTH ISSUES

The primary issue facing Native people today is no different than it has been for the past 515 years: survival. Native people, now far more present in urban than rural areas of this country, face the long-term consequences of historical trauma. The antecedents of current mental health issues can be separated into the following categories:

- loss of land
- loss of population
- loss of language
- loss of traditions (e.g., hunting, fishing, spiritual practices, clothing)
- loss of Identity

The mental health effects of historical trauma include, but are not limited to, the following:

- posttraumatic stress disorder
- anxiety
- alcoholism
- depression
- suicide
- sexual abuse
- physical abuse

Each one of the antecedents listed strips away the connections of a community, of families, and of individuals' connection to their history. Let's start with the loss of land. The loss of land and, thus, of cohesiveness weakened my tribe as a whole, but it did not weaken the passion for the return of our recognition and the return of our land. Despite the crushing blow of losing our land, our general council, made up of any enrolled Cowlitz, met twice a year, and the tribal council met on a regular basis. These people, for a variety of individual reasons, held the torch for the survival of our tribe. My grief is that my father, the man who called his children "stick Indians," the literal translation of the word "Taidnapem," died 10 years before the Cowlitz tribe was once more considered resurrected and restored from extinction.

But, it should be remembered that extinction took many forms. By the time many of the treaties were written, the horrible epidemics of the early 1800s had swept through the country, decimating the Native people—by 90% in some tribes. Stop for a moment and consider that figure: 90%, 90%. What would that mean in the United States today? A loss of 90% of the current U.S. population would leave only 3,000,000 people in this vast land. The people who were gone would include teachers, ministers, engineers, elders, physicians, dentists, road workers, nurses, people from every walk of life. The children and the elders would be the ones most likely to die, but, in actuality, with a mortality rate of 90%, few would be left. Culture, communities, and families would be destroyed, at the worst, and disrupted, at best. This was the case for thousands of Native people living in the Northwest as a consequence of the epidemics of the 1800s. Left in their place were those who had survived but at a terrible cost. And lest one believe that this was damage enough, more was to come.

Children are the heart and soul of any family, community, and society. Protect the children, and the community is protected. Sacrifice the children, and the costs to families and communities are incalculable. The assault on Native children, those who survived the epidemics, now came from a new source, the boarding schools, frequently run by "Christian" churches but, in actuality, bastions of abuse, death, and cultural genocide.

Native children were removed, often forcibly, from the care of their parents and sent hundreds of miles away to these schools. As Carolyn Marr so eloquently wrote, "School administrators worked constantly to keep the students at school and to eradicate all vestiges of their tribal cultures." Such vestiges included language, dress, and spiritual practices. The trauma of being torn from one's family and being beaten, sexually abused, screamed at, and degraded constantly is one lived by thousands of Native people and is another contributor to historical and individual trauma.

The consequences of termination and assimilation policies, described by Metcalf in her 1976 article on Navajo schoolgirls, included a loss of traditional child-rearing practices. The consequences of the trauma of the boarding schools and all inherent practices still live in the destruction of Native families. These consequences are documented as including alcoholism, incest, violence, early death, and depression. In a survey of the population of prisons, it is noted that Native people, who make up a minuscule proportion of the population of the United States, are grossly overrepresented. The negative consequences of incest, domestic violence, and depression are well known.

Alcoholism, as is widely reported, is a scourge in Native communities. It was introduced hundreds of years ago and, in myth and fact, was often used to "ease the skids" in terms of "negotiations" and signing away of rights. It was also used as a self-medication for trauma and against the horrible grief of being dispossessed and of countless losses. In reviewing the causes of death among Native people, cirrhosis and suicide ranked numbers 6 and 8, but alcohol is a contributing factor to the top five causes.

Alcohol use begins young in Native communities. Use among Native women contributes to the high rate of fetal alcohol spectrum disorder (FASD) prevalent in certain subgroups of this population. The presence of FASD, by definition, signals a community and individuals in distress. People born with FASD are at increased risk for behavioral, learning, and legal problems and, in many instances, at an increased risk for alcohol abuse themselves. Individuals with FASD are more likely to be sexually exploited and the girls to be young mothers. Research indicates that alcohol abuse contributes to higher levels of domestic violence and sexual abuse in families. It becomes a circular situation, with alcohol use being a consequence of trauma and then becoming a contributor to trauma.

Identity, the definition of one's self, is the heart of one's life. Although it is difficult to conceive for many people, the social and legal identity of Native people has been defined by the United States government. Identity among Native youths has often been compounded by the issue of mixed race, physical appearance, and status as enrolled or not enrolled. It should be noted that Native Americans are the only people who have a card to "prove" the origins of their blood, race, or ethnicity. As the generations have passed, Native people have intermarried with other groups, and with this intermarriage has often come further dilution and loss of culture. The use of quantum severely restricts who can and cannot be a tribal member. This is an issue that many Native people, of all ages, struggle with. Those Native people who were adopted by non-native families often lost their sense of culture, as well as family ties (Trimble & LaDue, 2004).

The problem of Native children being adopted systematically into non-native families became so severe and so widespread that the 1978 Indian Child Welfare Act was passed. This law gave jurisdiction of Native children back to the tribes and mandated a specific process by which Native children could be placed in foster care and/or adoptive homes. It should be noted that this act is not always followed, but it did slow the loss of Native children from their parents (Wabanaki Legal News, 1996).

It may appear odd or absurd to people of certain ethnicities that Native identity is a mental health issue. However, in historical context, the eradication of identity as a Native person was the sole goal of laws, policies, and the boarding schools. One of the more interesting experiences of my life came at a multicultural conference. I was discussing many of the issues presented in this chapter. I have the brown hair and green eyes of my mother's Greek blood and the high cheekbones and distinct nose of my father's Metiie and Taidnapem blood. At the end of my presentation, a lovely African American woman rose to praise me for claiming my Native heritage when it was "obvious that I could pass."

The comment was meant as a compliment, but, in actuality, it totally ignored the spiritual and historical connection I have with my Taidnapem blood. I have never felt that my identity as a Native person was an active choice; it is simply who I am. It appears difficult for certain people to understand that the embracing of one's culture and ethnicity would be something they value over being assimilated into the "greater culture." In fact, assimilation was a formal policy for Native people, and one that continues to contribute to anxiety, depression, and another generation of historical trauma.

As I stated earlier in this chapter, identity is the heart and soul of who we are. It is insulting to those of us who have struggled to maintain a tribal and traditional identity to see it worn so lightly by those who have no right. The attitude of taking from a culture without understanding the history has been present from the start of this country—again, beginning with the theft of our lands.

At the start of this section, I listed some of the consequences of historical trauma in terms of mental health issues facing Native Americans. The primary issue is posttraumatic stress disorder. Constraints limit my ability to discuss any of these issues in great detail, but it is recommended that the reader investigate the references noted at the end of this chapter.

HEALING AND HOPE

It is important to recognize that there have been steps, albeit now more than 30 years ago, to legally address the loss of self-determination, culture, religious freedom, and the custody of Native children. The major examples of such laws are listed here, and this list is not inclusive. It should be noted, however, that no significant piece of pro-Native legislation has been passed at the federal level in years.

The Self-Determination and Education Assistance Act of 1975 (Public Law 93-638) was a piece of legislation that allowed tribal entities to contract directly with the federal government, and, in far-reaching ways, it began to set the tone for much of what has occurred on a government-to-government basis for the last part of the 20th and the start of the 21st centuries.

In 1976, with the Indian Health Care Improvement Act, the serious health issues facing Natives were beginning to be acknowledged, and tribal-specific health plans were put in place. Many tribes have now elected to have their own tribal health facilities and to contract with the Indian Health Service. This places the onus of care on the tribes but also allows more autonomy.

In 1978, two critical pieces of federal legislation were passed: the Indian Religious Freedom Act and the Indian Child Welfare Act. For the first time in the history of this country, Native people were given the right to practice their Native traditions, and tribes were allowed to have jurisdiction over their children. These rights seem so obvious and appear to be so embedded in the constitution of this country that to understand that these basic human needs were denied the Native people in this country is shocking.

I will not discuss in any detail the healing practices of my people, as I am protective of them and, in all honesty, do not have permission to write or speak of them in a public forum. What I will say is that my people understood the balance needed between the physical, the spiritual, and the emotional. It is this loss of balance and the loss of the traditions that continues to lead to an imbalance and the sickening of our spirits. Given the problems so briefly touched on in this chapter, what is the answer? Is there an answer? Is there time left? Is there anyone left to change this situation? My view of the "solution" is discussed in the remainder of this chapter.

I believe that the answer is always in the land and always in the traditions, the two most precious aspects of Native life. The return of land and the resurrection of tradition have been and will be the cornerstones to the survival of Native people. I can speak of this from personal experience. When I was 40, I returned from living in New Zealand for 4 months. In the space of time I was out of the country, the Cowlitz Tribe purchased, ironically, 13.5 acres that had been stolen from us more than a century before.

In May 1995, at the age of 40, for the first time in my life I sat in a lodge on Cowlitz land, with Cowlitz and Taidnapem people, next to the Cowlitz River. The sense of joy that was present in the lodge that night and in my heart and soul has rarely been matched. I heard, for the first time, Cowlitz songs and Cowlitz words spoken in prayer. Over the years, I have sat in lodge with dozens of people. I have been able to sit with my Cowlitz and Taidnapem elders and cousins. I have felt the tears and stress of grief and life melt away in the heat and steam and darkness of that sacred place.

In September 1997, I stood in the grass on the tiny piece of land owned by my tribe. In the warmth of that late summer day, I heard my beloved auntie speak the words of greeting. I stood with friends and relations and my husband. I saw clouds race over the sky and, as the words of my auntie's greetings died away, I saw a miracle. Seven crows flew overhead; two eagles passed above us, bringing their blessings; and from the woods surrounding the lodge came the sweet call of the owl. I stood there and in the sacredness of that time, my auntie bestowed my Cowlitz name on me, Tek Tek e'lus s'leday, Owl Woman.

Over the years, at times I have lost sight of those memories, and my soul has suffered because of this. After my respiratory arrest and my 4 minutes of death, I came to doubt the Creator, and my soul wept. Yet I recall the place of death not as fear or anguish but as a realm of infinite softness, peace, and serenity. In my saner moments, I remember a night in lodge, far to the east in Montana, with twelve Sioux and Assinboine women. I recall lying in the heat of the lodge, listening to the beautiful and ancient songs of the Sioux. I rolled onto my back to catch a breath, and, as I lay there, the lodge disappeared, and I walked out into the stars and the never-ending reach of the universe. I stood in awe of the gift I had been given, and I heard a voice call me home.

I remember my Taidnapem heritage, Sceniwah, Katompkin, Frank, Roy, Charles, Robin, Tracy. We are now seven generations of LaDues. We are the horse people and the tenders of the land. I remember, from a memory in my cells, my heart, my brain, my soul, the ones who came before, and I see the ones to come. I know that in the prayers we offer and the touch of the land, in the dances and the ceremonies, there is healing. In the breath of my horse on my neck, in the hugs of my nieces, in the grace of my auntie's face, in the holding of an eagle feather and in the smell of the lodge fire, I know I am truly of the Taidnapem and Cowlitz people, and the healing of my heritage will restore my mind, heart, and soul.

I have seen this over the years, and I know that in healing our spirits we will survive. So my solution to the centuries of historical trauma and the pain and destruction it has caused is land and ceremony. As Leslie Marmon Silko (1988) in her seminal work *Ceremony* so lovingly said, if we can find the right ceremony, we can heal our souls. This I know to be true.

It is tempting at times to stop the fight, as did the great Nez Perce chief, Joseph. But doing so affirms the victory of despair over hope, of evil over good, of greed and spite over generosity. All of these wonderful gifts I have been given through the people who have touched my life: Dale and Gracie, Larry and Rona, Gerry, Monica, and Nydia, Maria and Anne, my four aunties, my uncle, and my father, and my dear, dear friends. In the presence of these people, I have found the strength to carry on and to believe in the Creator. I have found, through the love of people and in the ceremonies of lodge, naming, and dance, that despair loses and hope wins.

And so, as I move well into my sixth decade, I believe—despite the continued efforts of the government, individuals in power, and the gas and oil, fishing, timber, and farming industries to strip away rights, land, and hope—in the strength of culture and of speech. I believe that, someday, somewhere, somehow in the future, as my nieces become adults and maybe mothers, they will remember the day they danced in the sun with the drumbeat echoing in their ears and their feet moving in time with the beat, the song they heard being one with an ancient and timeless rhythm. I hope that, if and when that day comes, they will share the songs with their own children and pass on the pride of blood.

It is common to provide a dedication at the start of any work, but I am choosing to place this one at the end. To six generations of LaDues, I owe my life and the breath in my body. And so, as we come to the end of this brief journey through time and history, my dedication is to all of the Taidnapem who came before and to my beloved elders who are now gone or are finishing up their lives' journeys and to the ones just starting their lives:

Katompkin, christened Marguerite
Frank
Roy, Dove, and Wes
Betty, Jack, Barbara, Lucile, Charles, and Margaret
Sandra, Michael, Robin, Charles, Gretchen, and Terri
Traci, Sydney, Nova, Taylor, Shannon, Elijah, and Jensen

My gratitude to you all.

REFERENCES

Access Genealogy. (2004–2008). *Washington Indian Tribes*. Retrieved from *www.access-genealogy.com/native/washington/*.

Brown, D. A. (1991). *Bury my heart at Wounded Knee: An Indian history of the American West*. New York: Holt.

Centers for Disease Control and Prevention Office of Minority and Health Disparities.

(2008). *American Indian and Alaska Native populations.* Available at *http://www.cdc.gov/omhd/Populations/AIAN/AIAN.htm*

Chief Joseph Nez Perce. (1985). *I will fight no more forever.* New York: Mass Market Paperbacks. Original work published 1877.

City of Vancouver. (n.d.). *History of Vancouver: Early Northwest native people* Retrieved March 1, 2008, from *www.cityofvancouver.us/history.asp?menuid=10466&submenuid=10537&itemID=16091.*

Fitzpatrick, D. A. (2004). *We are Cowlitz.* Lanham, MD: University Press of America.

Gidley, M. (1979). *With one sky above us: Life on an Indian reservation at the turn of the century.* Seattle: University of Washington Press.

Holm, T. (1996). *Strong hearts, wounded souls: Native American veterans of the Vietnam War.* Austin: University of Texas Press.

Holm, T. (2003). *The great confusion in Indian Affairs.* Austin: University of Texas Press.

Indian Health Service. (2002). *Speaking with one voice: Reauthorization of the Indian Health Care Improvement Act.* Retrieved March 1, 2008, from *www.ihs.gov/AdminMngrResources/reauthor/index.cfm.*

LaDue, R. A. (2000). *A Native American manual for parents and caregivers of children, adolescents and adults with fetal alcohol syndrome and fetal alcohol related conditions.* Rockville, MD: Indian Health Service.

Matthiessen, P. (1991). *In the spirit of Crazy Horse.* New York: Viking.

Metcalf, A. (1976). From schoolgirl to mother: The effects of education on Navajo women. *Social Problems, 23*(5), 535–544.

Native Americans in the United States. Wikipedia *http://en.wikipedia.org/wiki/Native_Americans_in_the_United_States*

Silko, L. M. (1988). *Ceremony.* New York: Penguin.

Streissguth, A. P., LaDue, R. A., & Randels, S. P. (1986). *A manual on Indian adolescents and adults with fetal alcohol syndrome.* Seattle: University of Washington.

Trimble, J. E., & LaDue, R. A. (2004). Law and social identity and its effects on American Indian and Alaska Native youth. In K. Barret & B. George (Eds.), *Race, culture, psychology and the law* (pp. 299–308). Thousand Oaks, CA: Sage.

Walker, R. D., & LaDue, R. A. (1986). An integrative approach to American Indian mental health. In C. Wilkinson (Ed.), *Primer in ethnic psychiatry.* New York: Plenum Press.

Wabanaki Legal News. (1996). *Indian child welfare update.* Retrieved 2008 from *www.ptla.org/wabanaki/icwa.htm.*

Wilkinson, C. F. (1999). *Fire on the plateau: Conflict and endurance in the American Southwest.* Washington, DC: Island Press.

Wilkinson, C. F. (1987). *American Indians, time, and the law: Native societies in a modern constitutional democracy.* New Haven, CT: Yale University Press.

Willard, W., Thomas, R., McDanial, R., Paxson, C., & LaDue, R. A. (1982). Seminar in Native American community development: A university-based training model. In C. Geisler (Ed.), *Indian social impact assessment: Social impacts of rapid resource development on native lands.* Ann Arbor: University of Michigan Press.

PART V

Implications for Training

CHAPTER 35

Teaching White Students about Racism and Its Implications in Practice

Norma Akamatsu

This chapter focuses on a fundamental problem in teaching clinical practice across race and cultural difference: how to develop greater attunement to and facility in talking about power and the experience of inequality, especially among those in positions of privilege. As I have listened to people of color and White people talking together about race, ethnicity, and culture, the conversation frequently diverges around the phenomenon of power (hooks, 1995; Pinderhughes, 1989; Sue & Sue, 1990). Power differences are less apparent to the privileged, who can more readily accept a view of American society as classless and color blind—the myth of the "level playing field." But the unrelenting experience of inferior status, economic discrimination, marginalization, and injustice, common to many people of color and other disadvantaged groups, demarcates social disparities that can become brutally salient to some while remaining veiled to those who are protected.

Words and phrases such as "multiculturalism" and "cultural difference" often obscure the linking of "different" and "less" in our society. Yet this very inattention to the experience of inequality can nullify attempts at "cultural sensitivity" and can most certainly look like the privilege of "not having to notice"—which can arouse much anxiety and defensiveness.

McGoldrick's (1994; see also Chapter 8, this volume) account of the halting expansion of her own awareness is a candid illustration:

> Over the years, I have been mystified by the reactivity of men to [feminist] issues. ... Longtime male colleagues came up to me and said, " ... Why are you so angry at men? Did you hate your father? ... I'm not sexist. I've never mistreated a woman, so why are you blaming me for all this? Why are you saying we have the power? ... We men have problems too, you know. After all, we're not allowed to feel." (p. 42)
>
> Within the past few years, I began to be confronted with race and racism and now it was I who was on the other side of the power imbalance. Suddenly, I wanted to say to others the same things men had been saying to me: "Why are you so angry? ... I have nothing to do with racism, slavery or segregation. I've never mistreated a person of color. I would love to change things, but I don't have the power, either. White people have experienced oppression, too—let me tell you about it." (p. 42)

Romney (Romney, Tatum, & Jones, 1992), from her vantage point as an African American professor, writes:

> I am always struggling as a teacher who is a member of a targeted racial group to understand the experiences of Whites when they confront their own racism. In the last Psychology of Oppression class I taught, I shared ... that I could not fully understand why White students found it so upsetting to be called a racist. I explained that from an African-American perspective my thinking is that, of course, White people are racist. Racism is embodied in the culture. ... Both I and the students of color in class began to understand that the term racism evokes for many Whites an all-or-nothing feeling. ... (p. 103)

Working as a biracial team of anti-bias educators Ayvazian and Tatum (1996) summarize:

> Many people of color understand the power differential inherent in the three manifestations of racism: personal, cultural, and institutional. They view racism not as an individual issue but as a systemic problem. However, many White people still characterize racism as a virulent form of individual prejudice—they reduce the problem to ... "individual acts of meanness." They are unschooled in the systematic ways that racism has been institutionalized and are oblivious to the reality of privilege given automatically and invisibly to White people every single day. (p. 18)

"RACISM 101": FIRST LESSONS

Because of the embeddedness of racism in our society, White skin privilege is a camouflage for those who are not targeted and who may never perceive the need to examine such power dynamics. It is imperative to introduce specific course content describing how "invisible" disadvantages operate (see Acknowledgments at the end of the chapter).

Differentiating personal, institutional, and cultural racism is a crucial foundation and a useful starting point. In our course, these distinctions are explained and clarified in our very first class to prepare for that day's assignment: Students are sent in pairs to roam the surrounding New England town and to compile a list of 20 examples of cultural racism, defined as "any message or image prevalent in society that promotes the false but constant idea that White is the standard, ideal, normal." Computer ads, monuments, magazine covers, greeting cards, cosmetics, and baby products that portray only White people are frequently cited. Recognizing the elevation of Whiteness and eradication of peoples of color, like a rap on the head from the Zen master, suddenly awakens many White students to the pervasive ordinariness of a now-blatant cultural racism: "I was surprised at my surprise," one student proclaimed.

We also present basic information about systemic forms of contemporary racism that are more subtle than the legal segregation of the past, such as discriminatory banking and real estate practices or the corporate "glass ceilings" that limit promotion of peoples of color (see, e.g., Smiley, 2006; Tatum, 2007). We discuss racism in educational systems and the considerable impact of negative expectations, an effect long considered in our field. Psychologist Claude Steele (1992) has researched the effects of stigma:

> Terms like "prejudice" and "racism" often miss the full scope of racial devaluation in our society ... in all of us, not just in the strongly prejudiced ... even in Blacks themselves. ... Sooner or later it forces on its victims [the] painful realization ... that society is preconditioned to see the worst in them. (pp. 72–74)

Finally, we invite students to examine their own work contexts, using the Multicultural Organizational Assessment Inventory (Jackson & Holvino, 1988), which outlines seven types of organizational responses to racism. The impact of exclusionary organizations (e.g., country clubs) pales in comparison with the farreaching effects of organizations with an attitude of passive compliance: "Our doors are open, but 'they' don't apply!" An African American diversity trainer succinctly observes, "I'm less afraid of the men in white sheets than the men in blue suits" (Kenneth Jones, personal communication, June, 1996).

RACISM AS DOMINANT DISCOURSE

Many White students begin to experience an uneasy puzzlement over their previous inability to notice these pervasive systems of inequality. The framework of "dominant discourses," used by narrative therapists (e.g., Hare-Mustin, 1994; White & Epston, 1990; White, 1993), makes sense of their predicament. Pointing to the underlying values embedded within cultural norms, that which is "regular" or "commonsense" is subjected to new analysis and review. The subtle endorsement of particular arrangements of privilege and power is an especially important implication.

For example, when a Latino family therapist complains about a national family therapy conference brochure that depicts photographs of White clinicians only, a White colleague realizes with shocked dismay that she had not even noticed the omission. White (1993) emphasizes how the biases embedded within the dominant discourse are hidden by their very ordinariness, a sense of normality that functions to preclude questioning.

Pedagogical efforts follow that attempt to create a wedge of awareness that might help students "stand outside" of their accustomed views. Drawing attention to both the influence of larger social contexts and their embedded values is central to a process of deconstructive inquiry, a critical scrutiny of our own "taken-for-granted realities and practices" (White, 1993, p. 34).

PUTTING THE WORLD BACK INTO THERAPY

A family therapist proudly describes her approach to a racially and ethnically diverse caseload: "I treat them all the same." Much of our theory has shared this bias, universalizing the experience of the White middle class. By contrast, a fundamental and long-standing position of family therapists—especially those who have worked with marginalized populations—assumes the absolute necessity of taking into account and including in the therapeutic conversation the impact of wider contexts (see, e.g., Auerswald, 1968; Boyd-Franklin, 1989; Crawford, 1988; Goldner, 1985; Hardy, 2000; Waldegrave, 1990). I ask students to consider the "mental health" implications of contingencies such as the following:

- What if a family runs out of money for food by the third week of the month?
- What if a lesbian couple is raising a 14-year-old son in middle America?
- What if he earns $90,000 and she earns $25,000?
- What if she has a civil service position and he can no longer find a job in the manufacturing industries that used to employ him?
- What if they both work outside the home, yet she does 80% of the housework and child care?
- What if he is a 17-year-old Puerto Rican youth with no viable strategy for ever earning more than $15,000 a year?
- What if she is the only African American girl in her elementary school?

Finally, we consider the implications of locating the effects of these problems *within* people rather than taking broader social problems into account.[1]

WHITE IS HEALTHY: EUROCENTRIC THEORY

One student's list of cultural racism examples included these entries: "Band-Aids, Barbies, our theories." Although initially difficult to perceive, cultural biases are discerned gradually, stimulating a renewed analysis of the political impact of ideas. In this way, the implicit endorsement of Eurocentric communicational styles, nonverbal behaviors, and ways of handling emotion, as well as the focus on the heterosexual nuclear family structure, becomes apparent. (See Part I of this book; Falicov, 1995; Hardy & Laszloffy, 1994, for a fuller account of such bias.)

Recognition of such preconceptions also promotes a more critical perspective on ethnic differences (McGoldrick, Giordano, & Garcia-Preto, 2005) and disrupts a "you-have-ethnicity-and-I-don't" mentality. We move beyond a one-sided description of "them" toward a recursive dialogue in which the clinician's own cultural and professional assumptions are also called into self-awareness and questioned. Students are encouraged to consider and make explicit the links between their preferred clinical ideas and practices and some of the meaningful personal experiences and cultural contexts that have informed these choices (White, 1993). They can invite their clients to do the same. For example, the following questions engage immigrant mothers and their daughters in a conjoint deconstruction of their differing cultural premises about gender roles (Akamatsu, 1995):

- What is the traditional role for women in your culture, as you understood it, based on your particular family experience?
- What was the impact of immigration or living in the United States on the traditional role?
- What aspects of the traditional role have the women in your family followed and what have they not followed? Based on what experiences?
- Do you see yourself as similar to or different from your daughter (or mother) in this regard?

LOCAL KNOWLEDGE

The deeply entrenched tendency to disqualify the experience of targeted people requires our energetic attention and ingenuity to redress.[2] More specifically, acts of resistance can be identified and validated and the resilience required to manage oppression acknowledged: "What does your tenacity say about what you are really committed to in your life?" (see Walsh, Chapter 5, and Hines, Chapter 31, this volume; White, 1993).

Therapists and teams can constitute what Hoffman (personal communication, May, 1995) calls an "honoring community," bearing witness to both the painful realities of oppressive situations and the strengths apparent within clients, including the adaptive value of behavior that might easily be labeled problematic if the demands of the broader social context are ignored. Personal choices and the values underlying preferred actions can be highlighted and explored (Denborough, 2005; White, 2005).

Students or faculty of color can offer their personal experience or critical feedback as a way to expand others' sensitivity to an unfamiliar existential territory. However, a recurring problem is that the burden of teaching is habitually placed on the disadvantaged, exacerbating the lack of initiative taken by those in power. Furthermore, to discuss the impact of a subjugated status is an inherently distressing step that renders a person immensely vulnerable. A student of color protested, "I am tired of being 'The Experience' for White students." Ayvazian and Tatum (1996) emphasize that people of color must feel that such activity benefits *them* and that clear guidelines safeguard the conversation.[3] In the absence of such direct reports, there are many useful books, films, and videos that relate quite powerfully the experiences of targeted people.[4]

For other important reasons, it might be better to postpone face-to-face dialogue until after some work is done independently by each group. Those in the targeted group may benefit from the freedom to focus on their own needs and agendas first. For those in the dominant group, apprehending their own privilege—the benefits automatically bestowed, embraced, and relied on—can be an identity-shifting awakening, often greatly discomfiting for people of color to witness.

STANDING OUTSIDE ONESELF

Self-reflexiveness can be encouraged in those in a position of dominance, even without such dialogue. Taking the role of "emissaries," students can attempt to look through the lens of a particular marginalized group for the relevance of theory and practice. The experiences of gays, lesbians, bisexual, and transgendered people, members of specific ethnic groups, single parents, and childless couples, as well as people of color, have gained new prominence in this way. Another aspect of this reflexivity is considering how members of dominant groups may themselves be perceived—"imagining others imagining you"[5]—which can expose more of the "invisible" mantle of privilege (see also Miller & Garran, 2008). Some questions raised are:

- Considering specifically how you look, talk, dress, and so forth, what stereotypes do you think people of color might hold about you?
- How might clients of color experience a predominantly White agency?
- How might social workers of color feel in these contexts?
- What might be useful in a dialogue between a White social worker and a client of color? That is, what do you imagine needs to be heard or experienced to break the expectation of being stereotyped and to open space for authentic dialogue?

"MULTIPLEXITY"

As White students develop more awareness and knowledge, it is necessary to address possible feelings of guilt or defensiveness about the advantages they enjoy. The notion of multiple social identities is quite useful—the highly particular "combination of multiple contexts and partial cultural locations" an individual may occupy "where views and values are shaped and where power or powerlessness are experienced" (Falicov, 1995, pp. 376–377).

Theories of racial identity development for Whites and people of color are also helpful (e.g., Helms, 1990; Tatum, 1992, 1997), highlighting the relativity and context-dependent nature of our experience of our own race. Inevitable collisions can be demystified, such as the mismatch between a student of color invested in networking with other people of color and a White student eager to initiate cross-race connections.

But key to the notion of "multiplexity"[6] is the paradox that we may be disadvantaged in some contexts yet privileged in others:

> In each form of oppression, there is a dominant group (the one that receives the unearned advantage, benefit, or privilege) and a targeted group (that is denied ...). We know the litany of dominants: White people, males, Christians, heterosexuals, able-bodied people, those in their middle years and those who are middle or upper class ...
>
> We also know that everyone has multiple social identities—we are all dominant and targeted simultaneously. I am, in the very same moment, dominant as a White person and targeted as a woman. (Ayvazian, 1995, p. 17)

The underlying duality—the coexistence of one's own privileged and targeted positions—is not easy to apprehend emotionally. It requires a more complex view of identity in which these contradictory experiences form ragged layers. This demands a particular sort of "both–and" holding that relies on the ability to "contain opposites":

The [both–and] metaphor embodies an intellectual, political and psychological ideal: the attempt to recognize the value of competing and contradictory
perspectives and to tolerate the psychological experience of extreme ambivalence without splitting ideas and people into good and bad. (Goldner, 1992,
pp. 56–57)

LIVED EXPERIENCE

I have found that one of the most useful ways to approach the complicated
issue of multiple social identities is through telling my personal story as a
third-generation Japanese American. I have likened my growing up to a
checkerboard of disadvantage and privilege in which I was catapulted from
"pauper" to "prince." I was one of the poorest kids, among the very few
children of color, in an elementary school of predominantly quite well-to-
do White children. From there, I went on to Booker T. Washington Public
Junior High School 54, where I was conspicuously advantaged as one of the
most economically secure youngsters in a predominantly Black and Puerto
Rican student body with a high proportion of families supported by welfare.
I first developed consciousness of race amid the still-lingering anti-Japanese
stereotypes of World War II, came into adulthood during the Vietnam War
years of "gooks" and "dinks," and, in between, was identified as a member
of a "model minority." I tell the story of a road trip to the South in 1957 in
which my then 11-year-old brother needed to make an emergency bathroom
stop. My father pulled up to a roadside diner, and Johnny raced to the rest-
rooms in the back, only to come careening out front to the car again: "The
bathrooms have signs. One says 'White.' The other says 'Colored.' Where
am I supposed to go?" And without skipping a beat, my mother told him
firmly: "White. White. You go to the White bathroom."

This anecdote has come to symbolize my sense of participation in privilege. When I imagine how other people of color (people of other colors)
might look at me, I would guess that, despite its hazards, the social access
conceded to Asians in this society is perceived as a "relative privilege."[7]
Acknowledging the advantages that I can recognize in my life has eased
my conversations with people of other targeted groups. A student pointed
out, very importantly, how this acknowledgment simultaneously recognizes
another's disadvantage and becomes an important form of validation.

THE PROBLEM OF COMPETING "-ISMS"

As political and economic forces increasingly threaten to divide and con-
quer some of us more than others, our connections become vital and tenu-

ous. Our sense of oppression is a double-edged sword. The marginalization we have experienced, when unacknowledged, can polarize and divide us. Given a dominant discourse of "equality," these experiences are typically suppressed. We are all starved for validation. But the need for acknowledgment of the particular injustices we have endured can drive us into a symmetrical, mutually isolating competition to be heard. At the same time, these experiences, although different and unique, can provide a basis for coalition and a connecting arc/ark of mutual recognition. Over time, collectively, we will have to learn to balance our need for validation with acknowledgment of our privilege and a readiness to validate another's suffering. A defensive holding on to our sense of disadvantage is likely to be experienced as denial of another's oppression. Ironically, we may be released from our defensive posture only by another's acknowledgment of our pain.

For their final assignment, students are asked to inventory both the dominant and the targeted positions they occupy (in relation to racism, sexism, classism, heterosexism, religious oppression, "able-ism," and ageism) and to write about "what personal experiences have brought the issue of racism to life for you."[8] This assignment formalizes an ongoing process, apparent in their journals, of connecting with the emotional truth of racial oppression through their own experiences of marginalization as women, working-class people, Jews, gay, lesbian, bisexual, or transgendered people, persons with disabilities, and/or survivors of familial violence. The "both–and" process of journaling about these or other experiences, while increasing awareness of privilege, is also pivotal in the educational process. This exercise further addresses the confusion of those who enjoy a broad array of advantages. A heterosexual White male student noted his "triple dominance" with abashment. However, even amidst an accounting of his privilege, he was able to identify areas of private suffering that constituted a personally meaningful basis for empathy with racial oppression that were also important in developing his commitment as a White anti-racist activist. Acknowledgment in the form of detailed and attentive written responses to their journals by both coteachers, who constituted a small "honoring community" for the students, further supported this development.

CONCLUSION

Some months after completion of our racism class, a student's letter was published in her local newspaper, registering her distress at the mistaken arrest of an African American woman on shoplifting charges:

> There's no way around it. If you grew up in this country, you absorbed negative information about anyone who was not White. You were also fed negative

information about anyone who was gay, lesbian, bisexual, overweight, old, with a physical or mental challenge, poor, or even female. No, this is not your fault. You didn't ask to be born into this. But you were. If you're White, you might feel racism affects you, and it does; psychologically, spiritually, emotionally ... but it's not the same as the daily grinding experience for people of color, who are systematically oppressed. The responsibility to dismantle racism and every other "ism" belongs to each and every one of us.

Passionately,

Anna Gailitis

As practitioners/teachers who occupy positions of privilege and who choose to confront racism, we must stand ready to initiate dialogue about power and to demonstrate that we possess the "ears" that can hear these concerns. As we continue to learn more and talk together more openly, teaching situations and the practice of therapy offer possible new sites of awakening, connection, resistance, and coalition.

ACKNOWLEDGMENTS

I wish first to acknowledge and thank the Rev. Dr. Andrea Ayvazian for her inestimable contribution to the work discussed in this chapter. To educate myself, I joined with her to form a biracial teaching team for a required course on racism at the Smith College School for Social Work in 1995. I developed the "clinical applications" portion of a course that she originally designed. This discussion is oriented to the teaching of White students. Due to a student initiative to permit students of color to have the choice to group together, my classes consisted exclusively of White students.

I also wish to acknowledge the architect of Narrative Therapy, Michael White, whose commitment to social justice and equality was made manifest in a life's work that provided the framework for bringing political consciousness to clinical work and clarifying the values we live out in all that we do.

NOTES

1. These questions were suggested by the work of Carter (1988), Crawford (1988), Waldegrave (1990), and White and Epston (1990).
2. We have used White's "Conscious Purpose and Commitment Exercise" to provide students with a direct experience of the difference between a pathologizing description (in this case of their choice of profession) and a deconstructive inquiry that affirms their positive values, as revealed through a search of the history of personal experiences and ethical decisions that informed this choice
3. See Miller and Garran (2008) for a comprehensive review of cross-racial dialogue formats.
4. *True Colors* (Lukasiewicz & Harvey, 1991), an NBC *Primetime TV Magazine* story, is

one example. A White man and an African-American man who pose as new arrivals to a Midwestern city are secretly videotaped while searching for jobs, taxis, apartments, cars, and so forth. The chasm separating them is conveyed with stunning immediacy by the literally split-screen portrayal of their unequal experiences.

5. E. H. Auerswald introduced me to this approach in his design for a cross-cultural dialogue among diverse high school students, which I facilitated in Hawaii in 1976. His idea was to videotape discussions on ethnicity and stereotypes among homogenous groups. Tapes were then exchanged across groups for their responses, which we also videotaped and fed back to the original group.

6. This is Cornel West's word, employed during a dialogue on Black–Jewish relations with Michael Lerner, October, 1995, Mount Holyoke College, South Hadley, Massachusetts.

7. This statement is not intended to discount the reality of anti-Asian discriminatory attitudes. Chang (1995), for example, points out how the "model minority myth … renders the oppression of Asian Americans invisible."

8. Grillo and Wildman (1995) note the danger of presuming to understand one sort of oppression through personal experience with another. However, there is a subtle but significant difference between an uncritical substitution of one experience for another and the coming to life of another's experience through reference to one's own.

REFERENCES

Akamatsu, N. (1995). The defiant daughter and compliant mother: Multicultural dialogues on woman's role. *In Session: Psychotherapy in Practice, 1,* 43–55.

Auerswald, E. H. (1968). Interdisciplinary versus ecological approach. *Family Process, 7,* 202–215.

Ayvazian, A. (1995). Interrupting the cycle of oppression: The role of allies as agents of change. *Smith College School for Social Work Journal, 13,* 17–20.

Ayvazian, A., & Tatum, B. (1996, January–February). Can we talk? *Sojourners,* 16–19.

Boyd-Franklin, N. (1989). *Black families in therapy: A multisystems approach.* New York: Guilford Press.

Carter, B. (1988). The person who has the fold makes the rules. In M. Walters, B. Carter, P. Papp, & O. Silverstein (Eds.), *The invisible web: Gender patterns in family relationships.* New York: Guilford Press.

Chang, R. (1995). Toward an Asian American legal scholarship. In R. Delgado (Ed.), *Critical race theory: The cutting edge.* Philadelphia: Temple University Press.

Crawford, S. (1988). Cultural context as a factor in the expansion of therapeutic conversation with lesbian families. *Journal of Strategic and Systemic Therapies, 7*(3), 2–10.

Denborough, D. (2005). A framework for receiving and documenting testimonies of trauma. *International Journal of Narrative Therapy and Community Work,* Nos. 3 & 4, 34–42.

Falicov, C. (1995). Training to think culturally: A multidimensional comparative framework. *Family Process, 34*(4), 373–388.

Goldner, V. (1985). Feminism and family therapy. *Family Process, 24,* 31–47.

Goldner, V. (1992). Making room for both–and. *Family Therapy Networker, 16,* 54–61.

Grillo, T., & Wildman, S. (1995). Obscuring the importance of race: The implication of making comparisons between racism and sexism (or other -isms). In R. Delgado

(Ed.), *Critical race theory: The cutting edge* (pp. 564–572). Philadelphia: Temple University Press.

Hardy, K. (2000). African American experience and the healing of relationships. In D. Denborough (Ed.), *Family therapy: Exploring the field's past, present and possible futures*. Adelaide, Australia: Dulwich Centre.

Hardy, K., & Laszloffy, T. (1994). Deconstructing race in family therapy. In R. Almeida (Ed.), *Expansions of feminist family theory through diversity* (pp. 5–33) New York: Haworth Press.

Hare-Mustin, R. (1994). Discourses in the mirrored room: A postmodern analysis of therapy. *Family Process, 33*(1), 19–35.

Helms, J. (Ed.). (1990). *Black and white racial identity: Theory, research and practice*. Westport, CT: Greenwood Press.

hooks, b. (1995). *Killing rage/ending racism*. New York: Holt.

Jackson, B., & Holvino, E. (1988, April). Developing multicultural organizations. *Journal of Applied Behavioral Science and Religion*, 14–19.

Lukasiewicz, M., & Harvey, E. (Producers). (1991). *True colors* [Video]. (Available from MTI/Film & Video, 420 Academy Dr., Northbrook, IL 60062)

McGoldrick, M. (1994). The ache for home. *Family Therapy Networker, 18*, 38–45.

McGoldrick, M., Giordano, J., & Garcia-Preto, N. (Eds.). (2005). *Ethnicity and family therapy* (3rd ed.). New York: Guilford Press.

Miller, J., & Garran A. M. (2008). *Racism in the United States: Implications for the helping professions*. Belmont, CA: Thompson Brooks/Cole.

Pinderhughes, E. (1989). *Understanding race, ethnicity and power: The key to efficacy in clinical practice*. New York: Free Press.

Romney, P., Tatum, B., & Jones, J. (1992). Feminist strategies for teaching about oppression: The importance of process. *Women's Studies Quarterly, 20*(1 & 2), 95–110.

Smiley, T. (Ed.). (2006). *The covenant with Black America*. Chicago: Third World Press.

Steele, C. (1992, April). Race and the schooling of black Americans. *Atlantic Monthly*, pp. 68–78.

Sue, D. W., & Sue, D. (1990). *Counseling the culturally different: Theory and practice*. New York: Wiley.

Tatum, B. (1992). Talking about race, learning about racism: The application of racial identity development theory in the classroom. *Harvard Educational Review, 62*(1), 1–23.

Tatum, B. (1997). *Why are all the Black kids sitting together in the cafeteria?: And other conversations about race*. New York: Basic Books.

Tatum, B. (2007). *Can we talk about race?: And other conversations in an era of school resegregation*. New York: Beacon Press.

Waldegrave, C. (1990). Just therapy: Social justice in family therapy. *Dulwich Centre Newsletter, 1*(62), 1–23.

White, M. (1993). Deconstruction and therapy. In S. Gilligan & R. Price (Eds.), *Therapeutic conversations*. New York: Norton.

White, M. (2005). Children, trauma and subordinate storyline development. *The International Journal of Narrative Therapy and Community Work*, Nos. 3 & 4, 10–21.

White, M., & Epston, D. (1990). *Narrative means to therapeutic ends*. New York: Norton.

CHAPTER 36

Visioning Social Justice

Narratives of Diversity, Social Location, and Personal Compassion

Matthew R. Mock

Our stories are not always composed by us, but come to us in powerful ways from others. If, as children, family members describe us in a particular way, these family stories often remain the same no matter how we change. What others believe about us, what we learn in school, in the media and from the reactions of strangers, define our stories.

In searching for alternative narratives about ourselves, we are often drawn to stories about others. Listening to these stories may offer us new possibilities, but if our new life stories are to fully emerge, we must also challenge the underlying myths and prejudices that limit us.

—ELLEN PULLEYBLANK COFFEY "The Variable Tales of Life" (2007)

It is my deep belief and experience that there are some core perspectives that form the foundation of learning about diversity and family therapy. Families are not only diverse in and of themselves, but they also certainly exist in multicultural contexts. Issues of race, culture, class, gender, sexual orientation, ability, spirituality, religion, geographic location, immigration status, and their interrelated social dynamics are critical aspects of family lives. Cultural competence, multicultural psychology, multiculturalism, ethnic identity, cross-cultural communication, and disparities in mental health care are all topics that inform our approaches to working with families.

Practitioners in the mental health field have shown increased attention to incorporating culture and diversity in their work. The practice of family therapy is undergoing dynamic changes to make cultural context part of the frame in which problems are understood and from which solutions emerge. As working with families, in part, means strengthening relationships, it is essential that family therapists understand some of the immense challenges, complexities, and difficulties that families confront and that weaken bonds. The social contexts in which we each live are a central issue. The therapist's own social location in working with families must be understood to appreciate not only what the family is experiencing but also the roles of the therapist and of relationships in helping to heal some of the divides or problematic patterns.

A steady stream of publications has come from practitioners with long-standing experience and credibility in working with multicultural communities. These materials provide essential information for working with ethnically diverse families and their communities (see, e.g., McGoldrick, Giordano, & Garcia-Preto, 2005; Lee, 1997; Boyd-Franklin, 2003; Duran & Ivey, 2006; Falicov, 1998; Root, 1992; Ridley, 1995; Green, 1998; McGoldrick, 1998). There are also other resources. For practitioners who think systemically, the cultural genogram (see McGoldrick, Gerson, & Shellenberger, 1999; Hardy & Laszloffy, 1995) is an essential tool for assessment of family patterns and historically contextualizing kinship networks in terms of race, culture, class, gender, faith, family process, and migration histories. Others therapists who work more individually may use an outline for cultural formulation to frame an assessment process leading to clinical diagnosis (see American Psychiatric Association, 2000). These invaluable tools help shape our understanding and appreciation of cultural diversity in all clinical situations.

McGoldrick, Giordano, and Garcia-Preto (2005) describe how their training programs for family therapists and other clinicians proceed from the personal to the theoretical to clinical implications. Beyond the influences of ethnicity and culture and explorations of the hierarchies of gender, social class, sexual orientation, race, religion, and different abilities, therapists or those in training understand that cultural dimensions are not individual issues but part of complex dynamics that are socially structured within a particular sociopolitical context.

In order to utilize any sources of information on cultural diversity, practitioners must begin by understanding the dynamics of their *culture* and *social location*. An individual's *social location* means the groups that he or she belongs to because of his or her position in society and history. It also refers to the relative standing between the groups. How we are defined and treated based on our race, culture, gender, sexual orientation, religion, geographic location, and different abilities frames our social location within a specific context. Our identity, including our identity within our families, is heavily influenced by the social rules, roles, power, and privilege (or lack of) conferred on us by the larger society around us.

There must also be an appreciation of *intersectionality*; that is, an individual's exposure to the multiple, simultaneous, and interactive effects of different types of social organization and his or her experiences related to prejudice and power or societal oppression. Our social locations may be framed under an all-encompassing conceptual umbrella, with one group being dominant or privileged over another that is targeted with less power or marginalized. Figure 36.1 depicts one model (Roberts, 1993) this overarching umbrella of multiple societal oppressions.

Several notable writers, researchers, scholars, and practitioners of family therapy have written about the role that power, especially unequal power, has played in identity development, relationships, family dynamics, and equality among communities. Tatum (1997) likens cultural racism to "smog" from which we are all unprotected. Additional "-isms," such as classism, heterosexism, or ageism, may be viewed as other pollutants in the air we breathe and water we drink. Although we were not the original creators of this pollution, we may inadvertently perpetuate them through acts of omission or commission. Everyone is exposed to these societal pollutants. Some breathe or drink them in gulps daily. For others exposure is more subtle as they carry on their daily lives. All of us—young or old, gay or straight, rich or poor—are affected.

OVERVIEW OF MY TRAINING COURSE: DIVERSITY, CULTURAL COMPETENCE, SOCIAL LOCATION, AND SOCIAL JUSTICE

There continues to be a growing need to address power, privilege, and the social location of therapists and trainees in work with their clients. Social equity, social justice, understanding disparities, and taking stands against violence in all forms—including oppression—are all core to the content and process of what I teach. Cultural competence means that clinicians have attitudes, knowledge, and skills that enable them to work effectively in cross-cultural situations (Cross, Bazron, Dennis, & Isaacs, 1989).

Differing from other competencies, cultural competence in our work with families is not an end destination but a continuous journey. After all, as is the case with all "-isms," including racism, getting "sick" may not have been our fault, but getting "well" might very well be one of our primary responsibilities as practitioners. I share my own view that cultural

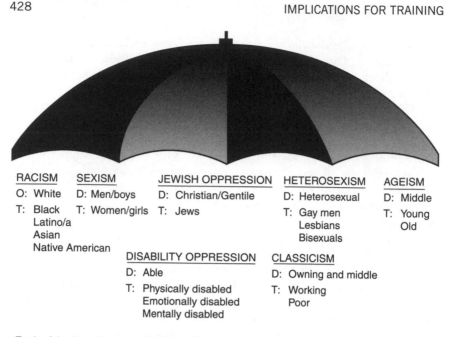

RACISM	SEXISM	JEWISH OPPRESSION	HETEROSEXISM	AGEISM
O: White	D: Men/boys	D: Christian/Gentile	D: Heterosexual	D: Middle
T: Black	T: Women/girls	T: Jews	T: Gay men	T: Young
Latino/a			Lesbians	Old
Asian			Bisexuals	
Native American				

DISABILITY OPPRESSION	CLASSICISM
D: Able	D: Owning and middle
T: Physically disabled	T: Working
Emotionally disabled	Poor
Mentally disabled	

Each of the "isms" is a manifestation of the larger system of oppression, which is the systematic subjugation of one relatively less powerful social group (targets = T) by another relatively more powerful social group (dominants = D). This system is sanctioned by cultural beliefs and institutional practices, the results of which benefit one group at the expense of the other:

Oppression + Prejudice + Power

Each form of oppression shares the characteristics of stereotypes: a differential between empowered and disempowered groups, occurring on multiple levels (individual, cultural, institutional), and being learned through a system of socialization.

FIGURE 36.1. The umbrella model of oppression. Each of the "isms" is a manifestation of the larger systems of oppression, which is the systematic subjugation of one relatively less powerful social group (targets = T) by another relatively more powerful social group (dominants = D). This system is sanctioned by cultural beliefs and institutional practices, the results of which benefit one group at the expense of the other. Oppression = Prejudice + Power. Each form of oppression shares the characteristics of stereotypes, a differential between empowered and disempowered groups. Occurring on multiple levels (individual, cultural, institutional), and being learned through a system of socialization. From American Family Therapy Academy (1993). Copyright 2003 by the American Family Therapy Academy. Reprinted by permission.

competence might be best framed as having the *ability and power to not know* absolutely everything about another person's cultural history as it has impacted their social interactions, individual and family identity, and having a comfortable clinical stance that embodies this perspective (Mock, 2003). For practitioners, *cultural humility* (Tervalon & Murray-Garcia, 1998) and *personal compassion* (Mock, 2005) mean lifelong commitments to self-reflection and evaluation, to self-critique and to redressing power imbalances, even in our relationships with families and clients. These are our contributions to social justice. In order to work with families, we must understand ourselves.

On a personal level, I tell my audience or trainees that if we have done our work well together, we will have elevated passion to learn more. With great appreciation for others' works on race and racism (see Carter, 1995; Jones, 1997), power (see Pinderhughes, 1989; Creighton & Kivel, 1992; Akamatsu, 1998), and multiple oppressions (see Anderson & Middleton, 2005; Hardy & Laszloffy, 1995), I offer a practical approach that I have found effective. My approach is not a panacea by any means. I provide some viewpoints, facilitate our storytelling, and share some cultural histories that may help inform our clinical perspectives. The following comes from what I have learned as a professor, administrator, and practitioner for more than 25 years.

CHALLENGES OF TEACHING ABOUT SOCIAL LOCATION

Many potential pitfalls exist in recognizing our social location among others. Discussions can become polarized, and there are inherent risks of feeling exposed, judged, or singled out as an oppressor or as someone marginalized. We must be cognizant that these responses may be replications of cutoffs, of traumatic experiences, of ignorance, of internalized prejudices, or of the cycle of oppression itself.

One White, male intern described his prior learning in this way:

> "As a student, we have to take this course on diversity. It is important, of course. But I disagree with how it was taught. While I feel I have tried to understand my White privilege, I felt I was beaten up in the course and made to feel bad. I agree that as a White male, I have unearned special privileges others do not have. I do not agree that I have to pay the price for others. In some ways the class did not open up my eyes but shut me down and had me walk away with a bitter taste. I will never go through that again."

Similarly, another therapist felt this way:

"It [a course addressing racism and psychotherapy] was like being thrown into the deep end of a pool without knowing how to swim. Some of us have been practicing therapy for a while. Others were interns about to enter the field. In the course, each of us had to fend for ourselves, knowing that we were in deep water. It was hard because I believe in our hearts we all want things to be better. That's why many of us are in the field! Rather than invigorating us, the leader left us exhausted and almost paralyzed."

Even students of color who represent diversity have voiced prior negative experience in their learning, as reflected in the following statements:

"As a Black female, I was looking forward to the course on cultural diversity. But the conversations we had only created more divides. I felt that each of us had to choose sides, with people of color on one and White or rich on the other. This was with some of my own colleagues with whom I had built a relationship. In some ways the course did more damage. I know some people who are still not talking or are afraid to out of frustration that they will just be misunderstood again. I was disappointed because it only made people more uptight and divided."

"To be quite honest, I go to the diversity classes thinking that either I have to defend myself, or at least be on my guard. If not that, then one set of stereotypes will be replaced by another. As a biracial Latina lesbian who grew up poor but now doing okay financially, it just doesn't fit. I grew up with a pretty liberal background among educators. We go through training in family therapy because we want to help, to make a difference. I have seen people share their family background, then regret it. We know we have to be competent to practice. The diversity classes I have taken give the message we are all incompetent unless we match the client. How realistic is that? Don't get me wrong. The course wasn't a waste of time; it just didn't move us forward."

For such critical conversations and understanding of our social locations to occur, I feel it is essential that everyone feels engaged and that there is a focus on possibilities.

SETTING A CONTEXT FOR LEARNING

When I was growing up, the middle child of seven children, we started dinner only when all nine of us were at the table, and we were given permission to leave only after the last person was done. This was how we managed scarcity of food and also how we avoided being pulled away from family togetherness. No matter what, we were always to be mindful of each other and to make and maintain a place at the table for each other. Similarly, in order to learn about social location and our own place in the socially constructed world of inequities, it is important to have a safe context in which to learn together. I beseech my audiences to think about the time and place that we interact in as being like "a living room." In the living room, it is comfortable, perhaps cozy at times, but at all times everyone has a place and a voice, and we acknowledge that each person's presence is respected and valued.

LEARNING AGREEMENTS AND CRITICAL STANCES IN SHARING PERSONAL NARRATIVES

Unlike in other conversations, the emotional charge of talking about "-isms" can lead to serious cutoffs and shutting down among participants. Structured, facilitated training sessions with authentic dialogue based on learning agreements can take participants to a level they have not thought possible to reach before (Herzig, 2006; Mock, 2005; Herzig & Chasin, 2006). To set up a safe and enduring context for learning through personal narratives, I provide a list of learning agreements to attendees to help us have honest, authentic conversations about our social locations. Some essential learning agreements for attendees follow:

• *Speak from an "I" place.* Do not speak for someone else. That would be taking away his or her voice. Relate what you experience, hear through your filter, sorting and sifting to make meaning.

• *Be fully present.* In these times of "call me, fax me, text me," it is a challenge to be present at all levels—mind, body, spirit, heart, and soul. Try to put out all distractions. Avoid crosstalk and side conversations that divide attention.

• *Experience, speak, and hear with mindfulness.* Listen, speak, and experience others respectfully. Be aware of the "space" you occupy and "share the air." Mindfulness means being deeply aware of what is going on within us as we experience powerful interactions.

• *Honor confidentiality.* Given that we will speak with candor and share opinions and insights, it is important that what is said stays in the room. There is to be no disclosing of others' individual stories or calling another person out. What we learn can be shared generally.

• *Enter into dialogues rather than debates.* By entering into dialogues, we can safely share time and commitments to work between ourselves rather than in direct opposition to one another. There is no intended "winner" or "loser"; no one is "right" or "wrong." By having dialogues, we are working to have meaningful, thoughtful interchange.

• *Each reserves the right to pass.* A person's thoughts can remain his or her own until he or she is ready. We each enter conversations differently, some more reflexively, some reflectively. A response every time is not mandatory.

• *Try to provide amnesty, forgiveness, for each other.* Sometimes, we all say uninformed or less than fully informed things. In order to move forward to address disparities in treatment and social injustices, we must be aware of what has happened that has been wrong, unfair, or dysfunctional for relationships. We are not intended ignorance or misinformation, we may act in ways that cause pain to others. In order to correct this, there is a need to seek understanding, forgive, strive for reparations, and remain in a respectful relationship.

• *Strive to be authentic and compassionate.* In order to share our stories honestly, we must be authentic among ourselves. Rather than struggling to remain "politically correct" in the face of others, striving to be "personally compassionate" (Mock, 2005) can be transformative.

• *Cultural competence is about our own sense of cultural humility.* It is not just about what we know but also about what we do not know. We can never truly know another person, her or his experiences, lives, and legacies, unless we are open to acknowledging what we do not know.

• *Enjoy the benefit of discovery.* Openness to new perspectives and experiences creates new possibilities and can bridge impasses and create new ways of being with each other.

I ask all of the attendees whether they need any clarification of the preceding learning agreements, whether there is a need for additional ones (which we will negotiate), and finally, whether each of us can agree to adhere to them. As facilitator, I model these agreements and assist the group to embody them.

NARRATIVES AS PERSONAL STORIES, AS SIMPLE "GIFTS" OF CONNECTION

In order to open family therapy students and other future professionals to new perspectives, I find engaging participants in the sharing of personal narratives through a structured process to be very positive and to have a strong impact. I frame the telling of narratives by the amount of time each person is to share and carefully listen and diversify their pairing by different characteristics (e.g., height, shade of skin, hair color). Participants are facilitated to meet in dyads often with others with whom they have had little or no interaction previously. This part of discovery moves people out of their usual comfort zones. The seeming simplicity of the story sharing in dyads connects participants and forms ways to be in connection. I have them consider the view that personal stories or narratives are precious gifts, ones that we value and do not give away to others, as to do so would be disrespectful.

Some of the structured partner sharing I have participants engage in is framed through the lenses of different topics of inquiry. One way in which I immediately engage and facilitate the group is the sharing of personal stories, with related questions, that may focus on some of the following:

1. Their names. Specifically, share your family name of origin as far back as you can trace it, as many of us are "strangers" from different places with different languages and different pronunciation, spellings, and cultural meanings of our names.

2. Someone who is a hero, male or female, to you. This could be someone whom you know, someone actually in your life, or someone who is mythical or historical, someone we only read about whom we may not have the fortune to meet. Why are they heroes to you? How do they influence your life, and what you are hoping to do as a therapist?

3. A "cultural transitional object." A "cultural transitional object" is something that connects us to our culture, something that has significant meaning and importance and may even engender some emotional response and connection.

4. A time when you or your family sought help or care from others. Were there cultural healing practices, beliefs, or rituals that you and your family engaged in when you were growing up? What might your ancestors have done to seek care for illness or maintain wellness for the family?

5. A grand celebration for an important life transition. Who would be there? What would be some of the foods, rituals, processes that would be a part of your celebration? Many of us like to think we live in a "global village." How is that reflected in your gathering?

6. As a young child, your own first awareness of difference. In vivid detail, as though you were put into that exact situation once more, recount the words, sounds, smells, colors, and all of the visceral surroundings of the event. What was the source of the difference? How did you feel about that understanding of human difference? How did people close to you respond? Would you have wanted someone to do something differently? How has your reaction to that event and interaction changed?

As we debrief, we ask questions about new learning and what created new perspectives. The process usually connects the audience. Everyone has stories of rich fabrics and hues that create commonalities. They enjoy the interweaving of discovery, of interconnectedness, despite their different worldviews and life experiences. There is confirmation that each of us has a culture. They will often share stories about cultural objects, rituals, or people that have great meaning to them that they have not shared with others.

What oftentimes challenges them the most are stories of their "first awareness of difference." Having come together and finding common ground through preceding dialogues, this exercise strikingly addresses social differences. The vast majority of the time, the experiences of difference are less than positive or outright negative. They will tell painful stories of racism. They will also reflect on what they experience as differences created by gender, class, abilities, size, education, rural versus urban residence, or immigration status.

CONVERGENCES AND DIVERGENCES OF OUR SHARED NARRATIVES

In order to understand the human condition, to have compassion and empathy, all of which are core to our work, it is essential that we understand what makes us similar and what makes us different. We have similarities of relatedness and human connection. We also have differences in life experiences framed in a cultural worldview. We have commonalities of identity, such as nationality. There also exist profound differences that are often socially constructed and maintained.

We experience differences in social standing by race, culture, class, gender, sexual orientation, age, faith, abilities, geographic location, education, and so forth. It is now common for family therapists and human service providers to have been sensitized to understand the importance of their social location, especially in working with children and families. Concepts of privilege, marginalization, dominant groups, and target groups may be intellectually understood. However, what I often find lacking is how this social standing, especially in relationship to the families and communities that we work with, has specific relevance to our work. In one setting in which I teach, it is mandatory that graduate psychology students take an initial class on racial awareness. As discussed earlier, some White students walk away feeling singled out and guilty for past historical injustices. Students "of color" may feel outraged that they come from histories of inequality. In the many years that I have taught courses, I hear students speak of feeling wounded or disconnected. The point is, while being more aware of privilege and power differences, these adult learners—some who may work with families—sometimes will feel more closed down and pained rather than more equipped to deal with social justice and equality as an essential part of their work. These students may be aware of their relative power or lack of it; they sometimes are less aware of owning it and what to do about it to be effective healers.

As practitioners contextualize the challenges or problems faced by individuals as part of a family system, they are more often able to identify specific life stressors, such as traumas, losses, accidents, or life changes. It is less frequent for therapists to identify sources of oppression as psychosocial or socioenvironmental problems, even when given the opportunity in the course of a DSM diagnosis on Axis IV (American Psychiatric Association, 2000). The Multicultural Family Institute of New Jersey (MFINJ) provides a visual framework of the context for assessing problems (Figure 36.2). I share this rich resource with my trainees. Visually they are made aware that it is easier to talk about the "horizontal stressors" than the "vertical stressors," specifically the "-isms," such as racism, sexism, classism, and heterosexism.

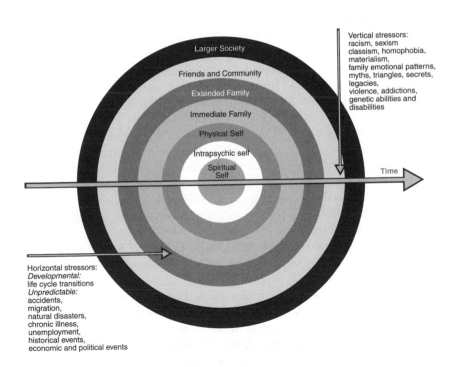

FIGURE 36.2. Context for assessing problems. Copyright by the Multicultural Family Institute of New Jersey. Reprinted by permission.

WITNESSING REFLECTIVE NARRATIVES
ON SOCIAL LOCATION AND INJUSTICE

It is important that we use multiple methods for this significant learning about our social location. Although it is beyond the scope of this chapter to provide details on all of the methods I incorporate, I want to give examples of some film and video materials that I have found effective. With each film listing, I provide a brief description of why I find them powerful.

- *Silent Beats* recreates a scenario of three racially different individuals, culminating in a showdown with potentially violent outcomes.
- *The Way Home* provides powerful, authentic dialogue from diverse women about their day-to-day experiences of social difference.
- *All Orientals Look the Same* viscerally captures audiences in the perniciousness of stereotypes in faces and words, in this case for Asian Americans.
- *Stories of Healing the Soul Wound* reminds us of the legacies of painful histories, in this case of Native Americans, and how they still persist in individual lives.
- *Mambo Mouth* provides humorous yet stinging insights into the undocumented immigrant experience, specifically of Latinos. The film makes the audience aware of how myopic and forgetful people are about their own family and national histories.
- *The Psychological Residuals of Slavery* documents an unjust, shameful time in American history with insights as to how African Americans continue to be affected by this history and manifestations of it.
- *Crash* depicts the volatile intersection of multiethnic individuals, urban race relations, and struggles to overcome fears of differences.
- *The Joy Luck Club* contains scenarios representing generational and acculturation differences and communication clashes.
- *Pursuit of Happyness* provides portrayals of class, opportunity, and social standing differences.
- *The Kiss* provides ways in which we can rise up despite the mistreatment of others by stepping out of our comfort zones to ally with others, in this case a gay man.
- *Listening to Children* provides a poignant narrative of the experience of 6-year-old Ruby Bridges during desegregation in New Orleans. Her insights about compassion amid hate invigorate others to strive for social justice.
- *The Split Horn* demonstrates the healing of a Hmong family through cultural rituals and the power of possibility when we do not impose our own views but value the traditions of others.

The preceding are samplings of the media materials I consider using while teaching about social location. I find these to be very useful strategically, as they allow participants to step back and critique, rather than being privately exposed. The materials also evoke the range of emotional reactions that help engage trainees.

MOVING FORWARD FROM OUR SOCIAL LOCATION TO SOCIAL JUSTICE

In order to help trainees find sticking points in addressing social injustice, I try to establish points of difference and examine particularly sensitive areas. It is important to talk not just about hypothetical situations but also about actual reality and what actions we can take as interveners, as family therapists.

The dialogues that individuals have had about their social locations and experiences of oppression or witnessing oppression are always powerful. They engender fear, pain, and sadness on the one hand, and anger, rage, and outrage on the other. It is important not to stop here but to move to possibilities for future commitment and action.

I often group attendees by threes to share a narrative based on the following questions:

> Think of a time when you were mistreated, treated as less than or less than equal to someone else. ...
>> Who was there?
>> What happened?
>> What would you have wanted to happen?
> Think of a time when you observed someone else being mistreated, treated as less than or less than equal. ...
>> What happened?
>> What did you do?
>> What would you have wanted to do? [It is important to make this dialogue safe and acceptable as we cannot take actions in all situations]

After debriefing on these narratives, I work with my trainees to identify commonalities of experience. We work together to identify all of the aspects of these experiences that would make a positive difference during or after these insidious events. We identify characteristics of allies, those who would stand up if needed, that would break the cycle of oppression in that moment. There is unanimous agreement that each and every one of us can be an ally personally and professionally, including in our work with families.

COMMENTS ABOUT THE USE OF ONESELF

At particular junctures of our mutual learning experience, I often model storytelling for my participants. It is my belief that, if we cannot perform some of the very things we ask of others, change is more difficult and less authentic. As a Chinese American family therapist who grew up in a "resource-stretched context," I share some of my own stories about growing up in a predominantly White, middle-class community in Los Angeles. My fellow learners inevitably become more engaged in the learning process, often feeling safer to tell their own stories to others using the learning agreements I have set forth.

Sometimes, at a particular juncture toward the end of the class, I work with the class by sharing a story of a social situation that appeared to be an incident of discrimination. I tell the story of an Asian American man similar to myself who seemed to be mistreated in a department store. As he tried to make a purchase in the store, he was regarded by the salesperson as though he were not there. When she did attend to him, she interacted with him with suspicion. After he protested, she put the problem back on him, demeaning him by speaking slowly, as though English were not his first language (although it was) and insisting he not cause trouble. I ask attendees to consider why they might decide whether it was an act of discrimination (i.e., due to race, class, communication differences) or not, giving potential alternative explanations (the man had been rude previous to the incident; a warning had been out that a man fitting his description had been a problem earlier; etc.). Together we try to construct the potential story and deconstruct it in order to consider how we might have intervened. In the end, I tell them that I was the Asian American man. They may act with surprise, dismay, or even shock. Most come away from the story with understanding of how pervasive and insidious mistreatment through social inequities and power differentials can be. Rather than being culturally competent, they experience what it is to appreciate cultural humility and personal compassion.

MAKING FINAL COMMITMENTS
AND ISSUES OF ACCOUNTABILITY

It is my belief that making a commitment as a family therapist or human service provider to social justice in everyday practice is among the hardest work that we do. I am also realistic about the fact that, although the aforementioned trainings can seem transformational in the immediate moment, they may not be in the long term. Attendees often give me feedback that they feel more hopeful, invigorated, and more connected in their commitments to make a difference toward equity in their work with families. Although I sincerely commend them for their genuine hard work, I also challenge them about the reality we face: that, as we go back to day-to-day life, the social forces that underlie inequities will creep back in and even undermine their newly constructed commitments to social justice.

As an illustration of this, sometimes I will ask trainees to address a letter to themselves. I have each write a note that lists what specific commitments they will make to social justice as family therapists. The commitments must be framed as specific acts, such as "I will point out incidences of sexism as they arise" or "When my families use derisive language, I will inquire about their meaning" or "When I witness acts that contribute to cycles of mistreatment, I will stand up and interrupt them." I then take these commitments and put them in self-addressed envelopes. Well after my teaching session is over, I put them in the mail. I have had students tell me how powerful their response is on receiving their own letters. They will reconsider their own accountability and, how hard it is to maintain. Some will also tell me how liberating it was that they had actually followed through on their commitments.

In becoming therapists, we can learn the theories, mechanics, and components of interventions based in theory. What we actually do with what we learn is the art of therapy. Similarly, the way I use narratives to teach about social justice is not simple or linear; it is a complex art with potentially beautiful results.

REFERENCES

Akamatsu, N. N. (1998). The talking oppression blues: Including the experience of power/powerlessness in the teaching of "cultural sensitivity." In M. McGoldrick (Ed.), *Re-visioning family therapy: Race, culture, and gender in clinical practice* (pp. 129–143). New York: Guilford Press.

American Psychiatric Association. (2000). *Diagnostic and statistical manual of mental disorders* (4th ed., text rev.). Washington, DC: Author.

Anderson, S. K., & Middleton, V. A. (2005). *Explorations in privilege, oppression, and diversity*. Belmont, CA: Brooks/Cole.

Boyd-Franklin, N. (2003). *Black families in therapy: A multisystems approach*. New York: Guilford Press.

Carter, R. (1995). *The influence of race and racial identity in psychotherapy: Toward a racially inclusive model*. New York: Wiley.

Coffey, E. (2007, May 29). The variable tales of life [Letter to the editor]. *New York Times*, p. D3.

Creighton, A., & Kivel, P. (1992). *Helping teens stop violence*. Alameda, CA: Hunter House.

Cross, T., Bazron, B. J., Dennis, K. W., & Isaacs, M. R. (1989). *Towards a culturally competent system of care: Vol. 1. A monograph on effective services for minority children who are severely emotionally disturbed.* Washington, DC: Georgetown University, National Technical Assistance Center for Children's Mental Health.

Duran, E., & Ivey, A. (2006). *Healing the soul wound: Counseling with American Indians and other native peoples.* New York: Teachers College Press.

Falicov, C. J. (1998). *Latino families in therapy: A guide to multicultural practice.* New York: Guilford Press.

Green, R.-J. (1998). Training programs: Guidelines for multicultural transformation. In M. McGoldrick (Ed.), *Re-visioning family therapy: Race, culture, and gender in clinical practice* (pp. 111–117). New York: Guilford Press.

Hardy, K., & Laszloffy, T. A. (1995). The cultural genogram: Key to training culturally competent family therapists. *Journal of Marital and Family Therapy, 21*(3), 227–237.

Herzig, M. (with Chanin, M.). (2006). *Constructive conversations about the Israeli–Palestinian conflict: A guide for convening and facilitating dialogue in Jewish communities in the US.* Watertown, MA: Public Conversations Project Press.

Herzig, M., & Chasin, L. (2006). *Fostering dialogue across divides: A nuts and bolts guide from the Public Conversations Project.* Watertown, MA: Public Conversations Project Press.

Jones, J. (1997). *Prejudice and racism.* New York: McGraw-Hill.

Lee, E. (Ed.). (1997). *Working with Asian Americans: A guide for clinicians.* New York: Guilford Press.

McGoldrick, M. (Ed.). (1998). *Re-visioning family therapy: Race, culture, and gender in clinical practice.* New York: Guilford Press.

McGoldrick, M., Gerson, R., & Shellenberger, S. (1999). *Genograms: Assessments and intervention.* New York: Norton.

McGoldrick, M., Giordano, J., & Garcia-Preto, N. (Eds.). (2005). *Ethnicity and family therapy* (3rd ed.). New York: Guilford Press.

Mock, M. (2003). Cultural sensitivity, relevance, and competence in school mental health. In M. Weist, S. Evans, & N. Lever (Eds.), *Handbook of school mental health: Advancing practice and research* (pp. 349–362). New York: Kluwer Academic/Plenum.

Mock, M. (2005). Personal compassion and alliance building. In S. Anderson & V. Middleton (Eds.), *Explorations in privilege, oppression and diversity* (pp. 155–163). Belmont, CA: Brooks Cole.

Pinderhughes, E. (1989). *Understanding race, ethnicity, and power.* New York: Free Press.

Ridley, C. (1995). *Overcoming unintentional racism in counseling and therapy: A practitioner's guide to intentional intervention.* Thousand Oaks, CA: Sage.

Roberts, J. (Ed.). (1993). *Honoring and working with diversity in family therapy.* Washington, DC: American Family Therapy Academy.

Root, M. P. P. (Ed.). (1992). *Racially mixed people in America.* Thousand Oaks, CA: Sage.

Tatum, B. (1997). *"Why are all the Black kids sitting together in the cafeteria?": And other conversations about race.* New York: Basic Books.

Tervalon, M., & Murray-Garcia, J. (1998). Cultural humility versus cultural competence: A critical distinction in defining physician training outcomes in multicultural education. *Journal of Health Care for the Poor and Underserved, 9*(2), 117–125.

FILMS MENTIONED IN THE TEXT AND REFERENCED IN MY WORK

All Orientals look the same (1986; director: Valerie Soe).
Crash (2004; director: Paul Haggis).
The Joy Luck Club (1993; director: Wayne Wang).
The kiss (1992; director: Phillip Kan Gotanda).
Listening to children (1995; director: Buddy Squires).
Mambo Mouth (1982; director: Thomas Schlamme).
The psychological residuals of slavery (1995; director: Kenneth V. Hardy).
Pursuit of happyness (2007; director: Gabriele Muccino).
Silent beats (2005; director: Jon M. Chu).
The split horn: Life of a Hmong shaman in America (2001; director: Taggart Siegel).
Stories of healing the soul wound (2005; director: Donna Schindler).
The way home (2002; director: Shakti Butler).

CHAPTER 37

Re-Visioning Training

Kenneth V. Hardy
Monica McGoldrick

Although literature on ethnicity has burgeoned in the past 25 years, integration of material on ethnicity in mental health professional training remains a "special issue," ignored for the most part in research, taught at the periphery of psychotherapy training and rarely written about or recognized as crucial by or for therapists of European origin (Green, 1998a, 1998b). Many family therapists are still trained without reference to the insidious role that hierarchies related to culture, class, race, and gender play in the United States. We are taught concepts of human development, psychopathology, and family functioning from the totally skewed patriarchal, classist framework of the dominant white[1] groups in our society. We are taught that you can learn about "men's issues" and not mean issues of African American men, because their experiences are never referred to. In general, when we have talked about couple therapy, solution-focused therapy, sex therapy, the family life cycle, or dual-career families, we have been referring only to white heterosexual families. For awareness of diversity to become truly integrated into our work will require a transformation of our field that has barely begun (Green, 1998a, 1998b).

As we put the finishing touches on this volume, we are just a few days removed from one of the largest civil rights demonstrations of several decades. Thousands of people, albeit disproportionately Black, descended on the small town of Jena, Louisiana, to protest the harsh sentencing and refusal of bail to an African American teenager accused of beating up a white youth. Many have noted that the detainment of the Black youth in the Southern jail and the protests that it has precipitated are reminiscent of race relations of 40 years ago in the South. The parallels have encouraged some to ask out loud, "How little have things really changed since 1967, if these types of injustices still persist?"

We raise the issue here not to spearhead a discussion about the inequitable treatment that Blacks and other disenfranchised groups still receive in the judicial system, but rather to comment on how incredibly difficult it is to undo and redo deeply entrenched practices. This is the sociopolitical context in which family therapy is embedded. If we are not careful, we are all at risk of replicating the patterns of the broader social order. We all become capable of creating training programs, clinics, and other institutions that are Jena-like in how they conduct normal everyday business.

We must change our training so that discussion of culture becomes part of *all* conversations about theory, practice, and research in our field. In the first edition of this book, Robert-Jay Green (1998a) predicted that "race will become a major nucleus around which new developments in the theory of family therapy will emerge" (p. 95). He predicted also that "the study of therapist–client interracial differentness will help illuminate the more general process of negotiating differentness between therapist and client" (p. 95), beyond just the difference of race, stimulating "studies of how other therapist–client differences affect treatment process and outcome" (p. 95). He thought "the study of race and family functioning will not be simply another peripheral vein, but rather a chamber at the very heart of family therapy" (p. 95). Unfortunately, we are still facing the major theoretical task laid out by Green: "to weave together multicultural theory (including factors of race, gender, ethnicity, social class, physical ability, sexual orientation ...)," religion, and life cycle stage, "and traditional family systems theory into a coherent whole" (p. 95). Green put forth a very tall order—that:

> This new "Multicultural Family Systems Theory" must link the individual, family, and cultural perspectives in a manageable way; it must be flexible enough to encompass all of sociocultural diversity and practical enough to be applied in the new health care delivery and other treatment contexts. (p. 95)

Unfortunately, even a decade later, we remain a long way from Green's recommendations, and diversity does not yet characterize our profession. Unfortunately, whiteness more aptly defines and characterizes the practice of our profession. "Whiteness" is a political descriptor of those who have unearned privilege in relation to others in the society. It is a characterization that exists because racism exists. We cannot continue to train white therapists to work primarily with white families. Most family therapy training gives minimal lip service to cultural issues. Probably not even 5% of the faculty of most family therapy training programs and courses are people of color, as are less than 10% of family therapists and psychologists. Yet more than 35% of the U.S. population, and a much higher percentage of the families in need of psychological help, are ethnic minorities. As Hall and Greene (1994) pointed out in their call for training in cultural competence as an ethical mandate of our times:

> The mental health professions [are] representative of the cultural norms and values of the dominant culture. Both African American and white therapists have been trained in institutions representative of the dominant culture's values, which for the most part embrace and support rather than explore or challenge the status quo. (pp. 24–25)

Racism is perhaps the most pernicious element of our culture and the hardest to deal with because of the extremely high level of segregation of our society. The forces for racial segregation are so powerful that, unless we make strong and deliberate efforts to nurture diversity, they will prevail. Whites have tended to keep themselves unaware of racism. It is not a category in our diagnostic manuals and has been invisible in our developmental theories and in our psychotherapy. We cannot assume that racism will disappear just by our being "good people" or by leaving it to people of color to deal with. It is time for all of us to stop perpetuating the problems of racism by actively addressing cultural issues in every level of our training programs.

We must change our training to incorporate cultural understandings and play our part in becoming accountable for racism. Unwittingly, our training programs have been part of the problem, reproducing the racist, sexist, and heterosexist structures of the wider society. We cannot make revisions just by modifying our reading lists. We must radically change our programs and provide concrete guidelines for transforming our training to overcome society's blinders in theory and practice. We must be deliberate in figuring out what we have to do to stop participating in the delivery of mental health care that is so full of disparities for people of color in our society.

CULTURE AND THE ORIGINATORS OF OUR FIELD

Many of the originators of family therapy, all of whom were white, had interest in cultural issues. Gregory Bateson, one of the prime movers of early family research, was a cultural anthropologist. Many others demonstrated a clear interest in cultural issues. Dick Auerswald always emphasized an ecological approach. John Weakland studied anthropology and brought it into his clinical insights. Paul Watzlawick, a linguist before he became a family therapist, provided many cultural insights from his experiences living in multiple cultures. Salvador Minuchin focused for years on work with the poor. Murray Bowen added a societal dimension to his original family theory. John Spiegel, whose work was the most overt in promoting a focus on culture, incorporated an anthropological framework at the very core of his clinical thinking. Al Scheflen and Ray Birdwhistle's work directly related to cultural dimensions of family communication that came out of Birdwhistle's earlier studies of Native tribes of Canada. Carolyn Attneave and Ross Speck's network therapy developed directly out of Carolyn's knowledge and wisdom about her Native American roots. Harry Aponte, a Puerto Rican therapist, has for years focused on spirituality and ecological clinical thinking. Braulio Montalvo, also Puerto Rican, was one of the originators of the structural approach, with Minuchin and others. Carlos Sluzki, an early member of the Palo Alto group from Argentina, always attended to issues of culture. Fritz Midelfort, one of the most creative but least appreciated early developers of family therapy, placed culture at the very center of his understanding of families. Kitty LaPerriere also always spoke from a multicultural perspective. There were also such pioneers as Elaine Pinderhughes, Nancy Boyd-Franklin, and Celia Falicov, who have specifically addressed cultural issues for decades. Our own endeavors were part of the second generation's efforts to put culture on the map as a core issue in family therapy.

But over the years, the powerful insights of many of the creative originators of family therapy were lost in cultureless descriptions, which meant primarily white descriptions of theory, practice, and research and, more recently, "evidence-based" practice. Training and therapy paid little attention to issues of diversity in marital and family therapy, which has generally been taught without much regard for the culture of the therapist or of the client. More articles relating to culture were published in the early days of family therapy than have been in more recent times (Green, 1998a). Often, even when culture was referred to, it was marginalized, as in my own work (M. M.), when we wrote of the "life cycle," we meant the white middle-class heterosexual life cycle, and then we wrote separately about the life cycle of multiproblem poor families of color or lesbian, gay, bisexual, and transgender (LGBT) families. The fields of sex therapy, couple therapy, and family therapy generally operated exclusively with theories of and for white couples and families. Psychotherapy is still conducted in general by, for, and about white people, with cultural issues marginalized as specific subcategories of the general focus. Research makes little reference to the culture of the sample, and there is no acknowledgment that the culture of the sample should always be a primary focus of research discussion.

We believe that the only ethical stance for our field to take is one that incorporates cultural understandings into the core of theory, practice, and research. We have lost a tremendous amount of human wisdom by not allow-

TABLE 37.1. Bill of Rights for Culturally Mixed People

I have the right ...
Not to justify my existence in this world.
Not to keep the races separate within me.
Not to justify my ethnic legitimacy.
Not to be responsible for people's discomfort with my physical ambiguity.
To identify myself differently than strangers expect me to identify.
To identify myself differently than how my parents identify me.
To identify myself differently than my brothers and sisters.
To identify myself differently in different situations.
To create a vocabulary to communicate about being multiracial.
To change my identity over my lifetime—and more than once.
To have loyalties and identify with more than one group of people.
To freely choose whom I befriend and love.

Note. Copyright 1992 by Maria P. P. Root. Reprinted by permission.

ing cultures beyond the dominant group to contribute to our knowledge or play a role in our theorizing, research, and practice. Furthermore, those at the margins may have particularly important insights for the dominant society. Maria Root's Bill of Rights for Racially Mixed People (Table 37.1), is good for all of us, because we all have multiple cultural identities. And no one should have to suppress parts of himself or herself in order to "pass" for normal according to the dominant culture's standards or categories.

THE COLOR OF THE FIELD

Although most family training programs indicate that they try to recruit students of color, many fail to do so. Faculty of color in training programs remain few and far between—less than 5%—with African Americans especially rare in full-time faculty positions. McDowell, Fang, Brownlee, Young, and Khanna (2002) reported that more than 80% of students in family training programs were of European ancestry. Long, Sprenkle, Dyson, King, and Richardson (2003) found that less than 5% of faculty and supervisors in American Association for Marriage and Family Therapy (AAMFT) approved family training programs were people of color and that these programs were not doing well at recruiting or admitting ethnic minority students. Lee, Nichols, Nichols, and Odom (2004) reported that there has been virtually no increase in the 2% African American supervisors in the past 25 years. The clinical membership of AAMFT is racially homogeneous and white, despite whatever efforts have been made to address this issue. Kyle Killian and I (K. V. H.; 1998) did a study of AAMFT conference content from 1980 through 1996 and found that only two people from minority cultures had served as keynote speakers at general sessions over a 19-year period.

BASIC ASSUMPTIONS
OF A RE-VISIONED FAMILY THERAPY FIELD

Our underlying openness to those who are culturally different is the key to expanding our cultural understanding. We learn about culture primarily not by learning the "facts" of another's culture but rather by changing our own attitudes about difference. In our view, the most important part of a multicultural family systems theory involves a therapist coming to understand his or her own identity and social location. Just as clinicians must sort out the relationships in their own families of origin, developing cultural competence requires first of all coming to terms with their own cultural identities. One goal would be for therapists no longer to be "triggered" by culturally based characteristics that they may have regarded negatively nor to hold to the view that their own cultural values are more "right" or "true" than those of others. Cultural self-awareness opens therapists to understanding values that differ from their own, so that they need neither convert others to their view nor give up their own values. The best cultural training for family therapists, particularly those from dominant groups, is to become aware of the cultural values of the dominant culture—or perhaps to experience what it would be like not to be part of the dominant culture.

We suggest the following assumptions as a starting point for a re-visioning of our field:

• Contextual factors such as class, race, sexual orientation, and gender are *always* relevant to discussions of theory, practice, training, and research.

• Who we are as clinicians, trainers, or researchers shapes how we see the world, and the meanings we attach to the world are powerfully shaped by the nuances of culture. Both therapist's and client's ethnicity, race, gender, class, and religious and political backgrounds influence how they will interact and view problems unless we have evidence that suggests that these factors are insignificant.

• Having a positive awareness of one's cultural heritage, just like a positive connection to one's family of origin, contributes to one's sense of mental health and well-being.

• Negative feelings or lack of awareness of one's cultural heritage are probably reflective of cutoffs, oppression, or traumatic experiences that have led to suppression of history.

• Knowing our history—personal, familial, cultural, and professional—strengthens our understanding of ourselves and our world.

• No one can ever fully understand another's culture, but curiosity, humility, and awareness of one's own cultural values and of history contribute to the ability to relate to others.

• Clients from marginalized cultures have probably internalized society's prejudices about them, and those from dominant cultural groups have probably internalized assumptions about their own superiority and right to be privileged within our society.

• Respectful clinical work involves helping clients clarify their identities in relation to their families, communities, cultural history, and relationship difficulties while also adapting to changing circumstances as they move through life.

• Clinical intervention is not neutral but requires moving toward social justice.

• Our work requires accountability for moving not just our clients but our field toward social justice, to eliminate disparities in services to all families in our society, and to make sure our field builds its professional and intellectual structure on an equitable basis.

• Becoming an effective professional requires developing the ability to work collaboratively across professional boundaries with all who serve families: psychologists, counselors, social workers, nurses, marriage and family therapists, physicians, lawyers, educators, and any others whose business involves the well-being and resilience of families.

• At the heart of the re-visioning of family therapy is our belief that we are all connected: oppressor and oppressed, rich and poor, gay and straight. The space between therapist and client is seldom as great as we have been trained to believe. Therapists are never blank slates.

SETTING UP A CONTEXT
FOR CULTURAL COMPETENCE TRAINING

The re-visioning of family therapy will inspire therapists to be unrelentingly curious not just about the influence of their families of origin on their work but also about the influences of gender, race, religion, and class. It will be an accepted understanding of training that clinical interactions are always cross-cultural interactions between the therapist's self, context, and heritage and those of the client. Cultural paradigms are useful to the extent that they help us challenge our long-held beliefs about "the way things are." But we cannot learn about culture in cookbook fashion, through memorizing recipes for relating to other groups. Information we learn about cultural differences will, hopefully, expand our respect, curiosity, and humility regarding cultural differences.

Our experience has taught us repeatedly that theoretical discussions about the importance of culture are practically useless in training. We best appreciate the relativity of values through specifics that connect with our lived experience of group differences. Thus it makes sense in training to fit any illustration of a cultural trait into the context of historical and cultural experiences in which that value or behavior evolved.

When beginning cultural training, it is extremely important to set up a context that allows generalizing about cultural differences. Of course, all generalizations represent only partial truths. We begin by personal sharing, conveying the fact that everyone has grown up influenced by ethnicity, class, race, religion, gender, and sexual orientation. We discuss the problem of stereotyping, or becoming stuck in overgeneralizations, and the problem of not generalizing, which prevents culture from being discussed at all.

We have found that to organize training only around "minority" ethnicities, as has so often been done, is not helpful. Such training perpetuates the marginalization of groups that are already at the periphery because it continues the myth that theories developed by Europeans and white Americans are the norm from which all other cultures deviate. Instead, training entails considerable deconstruction of "Western" ways of thought to challenge the dominant psychological structures as an essential part of freeing people to become more culturally competent.

Common pitfalls in discussions of these issues include being so inclusive that the discussion marginalizes racism in the "oppression Olympics," a competition among the multiplicity of cultural "-isms," in which proposals for inclusiveness become so extensive that the institutionalized racism that is destroying our society is overshadowed by discussion of other inequalities.

A second pitfall is that discussion will become polarized. As Beverly Tatum has noted in another context, those who have focused on racial identity development have done little to address gender, whereas feminist theorists have often done little to address race (Tatum, 1997). Discussions of diversity may polarize "Black–white" issues, leaving others feeling that their issues have no place. Sexism, anti-Semitism, and homophobia are pushed into the background as people argue over which oppression is the worst or most important.

We believe it is essential to focus specifically on racism and whiteness if we are to embark on accountable and ethical practice and to educate white people about the pervasiveness of microaggressions in every aspect of our theory, training, research, and practice (Sue et al., 2007). However, we still find it hard to raise some issues in the context of others. The question of how to sensitively address sexism with a couple who are themselves both victims of racism is complicated. The question of how to address negativity toward homosexuality within African American and other racially oppressed communities is equally challenging. Hall and Greene (1994) have addressed the ethical imperative of attending to the complexities surrounding issues of feminism, racism, and homophobia in relation to African American families:

> The African American woman may perceive that feminists and the feminist movement underestimate the integral role of cultural traditions and racism in her life. In a parallel experience, many African American males equate feminism with lesbianism, anti-male and white perspectives. It is imperative that feminist

family therapists examine how much of the negative perception of therapy and feminist family therapy within the African American community is based on realistic experiences as opposed to sexist attitudes and misconceptions. ... The ethical inclusion of cultural pluralism, a cultural context for therapy, as well as the examination of the influence of white privilege in feminist family therapy is essential in the provision of appropriate and meaningful treatment. (pp. 6–7)

We need to keep a multidimensional perspective, which can highlight the evil of institutionalized racism while not making less of other forms of oppression. We have to hold African American and other racially oppressed men accountable to women and at the same time understand the particular oppression they have been subjected to for generations. While moving against sexism, we have to hold white feminists accountable for their privilege and "unintentional" racism.

We must also respectfully hold white men accountable for their privilege, entitlement, and obliviousness to their role in perpetuating the current system. Their lack of consciousness is part of the structure of our society, which functions in such a way that the oppressed always know much more about the dominant groups than the dominant groups know about them, as their survival depends on this understanding.

This means that, just as we must ask white men to take responsibility for learning to be uncomfortable with organizational structures that are dominated by white men, those of us who are white must learn to become uncomfortable in all segregated situations, governmental, corporate, geographic, and intellectual—for instance, reading books about feminism or homosexuality that pertain only to white people. We must become so uncomfortable that we are moved to do something about it. Our failure to act, even when done innocently and benignly, serves to preserve the prevailing order.

Furthermore, those of us who are people of color must resist the temptation of using what Lorde (1990) aptly referred to as the "master's tools" when confronting oppression associated with gender, class, and sexual orientation. As a people who have experienced the unrelenting chokeholds of oppression and marginalization, we must use the lessons learned from our own subjugation to forge a deeper and more compassionate understanding of how the dynamics of oppression malign our lives. We must cease to participate in interactions that perpetuate polarizing notions about "who is Black/Latino enough and who isn't." We must also, with empathy and an unshakable sense of resolve, welcome our LGBT brothers and sisters. We must make certain that we do not perpetuate dichotomous assertions that one is *either* a member of the LGBT community *or* a person of color, a feminist *or* a person of color, implying that membership in one negates the other. This type of complex thinking and action is at the core of re-visioning family therapy.

GUIDELINES FOR TRAINING PROGRAMS

Mission

Programs and organizations must convey overtly in their mission statements and in their organizational policies their dedication to diversity and to a multicultural perspective. Including diversity in the stated mission of the organization establishes it as a core value that will be a major focus in future planning.

Organizational Structure

Organizational transformation to cultural competence requires conscious efforts on the part of the leadership to get all members of the faculty and staff on board to support the change. To succeed, the structure of the organization must reflect the core values that it espouses. In other words, if an organization is committed to diversity, its organizational structure should be diverse from top to bottom.

Leadership must deal with the inevitable faculty resistance to such a transformation process. With leadership consistency, the resistance can be overcome, and faculty will accept, if not all move toward, the change process. Faculty members will fear that requiring cultural "competence" on issues they do not feel sure of will mean that they may be judged incompetent. It is important that the leadership efforts toward transformation are done more with a carrot than a stick. It works better to offer incentives to faculty members to undergo extra training to increase their cultural competence or to undertake to teach a course that incorporates multicultural insights than to threaten faculty members if their course outlines do not reflect multicultural perspectives.

Collaboration is the quickest way to move toward greater cultural competence of staff members. When people work as a team, they are less likely to feel threatened and more likely to think creatively and increase their confidence. Isolating faculty members and trying to bring about change through memos and requirements rather than inspiring them with a shared vision is unlikely to work.

Recruitment, Retention, and Mentoring of Faculty

Strategies for the recruitment of new faculty and staff members should be informed by the organization's mission to ensure diversity and to promote cultural competency. The commitment to diversity must be an integral part of the organization's recruitment strategy rather than an afterthought.

Once a diverse faculty is achieved, it is important for the organization not to rest on its laurels. Creating a milieu that provides sanctuary for faculty members of color and other marginalized faculty members must be actively and consciously pursued by the organization. Faculty members from marginalized backgrounds will not stay in systems in which they have become GEMM family therapists and trainers (see Hardy, Chapter 38, this volume).

Establishing formal and informal networks to mentor both faculty and trainees of color and those from other nondominant social locations is imperative. Active mentoring programs help to enhance the retention rates of faculty members and students of color, as well as the participation of other marginalized individuals.

Recruitment, Retention, and Mentoring of Students

The recruitment and retention of a culturally diverse student population is essential to the re-visioning of family therapy. Having a diverse student population is critical to developing a sense of cultural competency. When organizations are diverse, they enable students to experience what they are learning about theoretically in the didactic portions of their training.

As with faculty, it is not enough to recruit diverse students without also devoting equal attention to efforts to retain them. Changing the culture of institutions is central to retaining a diverse student body. When the student body is significantly diversified, it is not enough for an organization to continue business as usual. Every domain of the organization must be carefully scrutinized culturally to make sure that the ideology of the organization is compatible with the needs of students from a wide range of backgrounds.

Providing ongoing mentoring to students of color that focus on their didactic and clinical needs is important but insufficient if it does not also devote attention to their cultural needs as well. Mentoring from a multicultural perspective helps students and trainees of color to deal with the inevitable and inherent struggles of learning and practicing family therapy in a field that is often oblivious to the dynamics of oppression.

CURRICULUM

Diversity and issues germane to cultural competence and social justice should be integrated throughout the curriculum. When we have succeeded in this integration, family therapy theory will take into account at its core the experiences of marginalized families. Thus more critical dialogue regarding what and who constitutes a family will become a centerpiece of theorizing efforts. Family therapy training will contextualize and critique theory based on race, class, gender, religion, and sexual orientation. Widely accepted paradigms such as the family life cycle will explicitly take into account how human development is affected by broader social conditions such as poverty, sexual orientation, and so forth. Family therapy theory will incorporate contextual variables. All clinical course content will take into account the cultural context of theory, practice, and research, so it will no longer be acceptable to relegate issues of culture and social justice to isolated courses taught by minority faculty members or to special sections of textbooks on couple or family therapy theory and practice. Rather than relying on single specialized courses devoted to designated areas of diversity, program curricula will focus on the intersection of various issues. Accordingly, trainees will be encouraged to think "relationally" while thinking culturally. "Evidence-based practice" will be required to consider "evidence" as a culture-bound phenomenon and to consider the cultural context within which research on diverse populations becomes meaningful or feasible, no longer just requiring numbers sanctioned by the dominant culture as "evidence."

SPECIFICS OF TRAINING

We believe that it is incumbent on programs to use training tools and methods that honor different modes of learning, as well as the experiences of students from diverse backgrounds. Using exercises and training approaches that assist students in assessing themselves in terms of their social context is important. Training students to use genograms to map clients not just to observe family patterns but also to understand the broader cultural dimensions of the client's context is essential to training. Training approaches need to be broadened to highlight the significance of race, class, gender, and sexual orientation within the context of family-of-origin experiences. In addition, training on human development must incorporate changing definitions of families through the life cycle. Human development and life cycle approaches built around marriage and children unwittingly marginalize the growing number of individuals who either choose not to marry or who are legally forbidden to do so. Also, those who either cannot or choose not to have children are also left out of traditional developmental conceptualizations of the "normal" family life cycle.

Cultural Sharing

We generally begin training with cultural sharing to convey from the outset that all clinical interactions require building cultural bridges from different perspectives and to engage students in exploring their cultural backgrounds. We ask students in a training group to introduce themselves by: (1) describing themselves ethnically, (2) describing who in their family influenced their sense of ethnic identity, (3) discussing which groups other than their own they think they understand best, and (4) discussing how they think their own family members would react to being referred for therapy for a psychological problem. At times we use exercises that enable trainees to have miniconversations with others in their training group to discuss cultural issues such as:

- Describe something you like most about your cultural background and something you find hardest to deal with.
- Describe how your family was "gendered"—that is, what were the rules for gender behavior, and who in your family did not conform to its gender stereotypes?
- What is your class background, and what changes have you or others in your family made because of education, marriage, money, or status?
- Describe a time when you felt "other" in a group and how you and others dealt with this "otherness."
- Describe what you were taught growing up about race and how your consciousness about this may have changed over time.

We ask trainees to think first about how their own group and perhaps that of their spouse or of close friends differ in responses to pain, in attitudes about doctors, and in their beliefs about suffering. Do they prefer a formal or informal style in dealing with helpers? Authorities? Strangers? Do they tend to feel positive about their bodies, about work, about physical, sexual, psychological, or spiritual intimacy, or about children expressing their feelings? Then we try to help them broaden this understanding to other groups through readings, film, and conversations that illustrate other ways of viewing the same phenomena.

Using Cultural Genograms

We have found genograms to be central in training clinicians to incorporate a cultural focus in their work. We routinely ask students to present their cultural genograms to their colleagues as an initial way of thinking about the intersection of family-of-origin issues and the threads of race, class, gender, ethnicity, and sexual orientation with which they are interwoven (Hardy & Laszloffy, 1995; McGoldrick, Gerson, & Petry, 2008).

The very nature of the cultural genogram requires the trainee to think concurrently about family and culture. Doing a genogram reminds each trainee that we all have culture—everyone is located somewhere on the dimensions race, class, gender, religion, and sexual orientation. Gradually trainees begin to realize that these cultural dimensions have meanings, both inside and outside the family, that become what we refer to as "major life organizing principles" (Hardy & Laszloffy, 1999). As trainees are encouraged to explore the context of their families and cultural backgrounds, they enhance their sense of cultural competency by (1) gaining a better understanding of the ways cultural and family patterns are inextricably tied together; (2) developing a more comprehensive view of themselves and others as cultural beings; (3) developing and refining their ability to engage in "context talk," that is, to discuss culture openly and nondefensively.

Social Location Exercise

As training evolves, we discuss the implications of people's social location, which becomes a core part of our assessment of each case, both for the therapist and for the client. A power analysis of cultural, racial, class, religious, and gender politics becomes a core part of all training, so that clinicians can see how power affects all clinical interactions (McGoldrick, Almeida, Bibb, Moore Hines, Hudak, & Garcia Preto, 1999).

The training usually proceeds from the personal to the theoretical to the clinical implications. I (M. M.) frequently use an exercise in which trainees discuss their own social locations and how they have shifted over the course of their own and their families' cultural journey in the United States through time. I do this by actually putting on the floor a hierarchical listing of social locations by class (from upper class, those who live on inherited wealth, to the poor, who may grow up without even the hope of employment), with subhierarchies for gender, race, and sexual orientation. Trainers model identification of their social location, and then trainees take turns moving along this hierarchy on the floor as they describe their personal and family evolution. As they do this, they explore the influence of ethnicity and religion on the hierarchies of class, race, gender, and sexual orientation. They show also how education, migration, employment, finances, health, and marital status have influenced their positions. This exercise helps trainees understand that cultural dimensions are not individual issues but are socially structured within the sociopolitical context.

An Expanded Life Cycle Framework

In our view, an expanded and inclusive perspective on human development is an essential framework within which to incorporate for students any conceptualization of human problems. Students need to have a framework for understanding clients' lives in terms of their evolution from the past (oppression, survival, migration, resilience) and into the future. Acknowledging family resources or lack of resources in intergenerational and community structure is essential for helping them make sense of their problems and facilitating their access to their strengths to resolve problems in a context in which many traditional resources may be lacking.

MANAGING DIFFICULT DIALOGUES

We have found that certain problems typically develop in cultural discussion at every level of any organizational hierarchy—among faculty, staff, clients, support staff, and administration. But encouraging difficult dialogues is the only way to promote the re-visioning of our field. We offer the following guidelines for leaders in managing dialogues about culture:

1. Familiarize a group with the dynamics of power, privilege, and oppression early in the conversation and convey that in terms of social location all of us have privilege on certain dimensions and oppression on others.

2. Share guidelines that may help trainees notice how these power dynamics work so that people can monitor themselves. They can notice their own inclination to shift discussion from a dimension on which they have privilege to one on which they are oppressed.

3. People tend to think much more easily about their own oppression than about their own privilege. Thus, for example, white people are likely to move quickly from acknowledgment of racism and white supremacy to other dimensions on which they have experienced trauma or oppression. This has the effect of short-circuiting discussion of racism. As other differences are discussed, racism tends to become submerged and sidelined. The more privilege we have, the harder it is to think about how our own actions have affected others with less privilege or to understand the rage of powerlessness. We take our privilege for granted—our right to safety; to acknowledgment; to being heard, treated fairly, and taken care of; our right to take up available time, space, and resources; and so on.

4. We believe that "staying at the table" is everything, and we make great efforts to clarify the idea that if we are to succeed in moving conversations about race and other oppression forward, staying in the conversation is the primary requirement. We try to emphasize that the conversations may get sticky, uncomfortable, or intense and that we will all make mistakes as we go along. But hanging with the conversation is everything—not letting the issues get resubmerged, which always leads to cutoff, war, destruction, and ultimately death.

5. We consider it essential to keep a multidimensional perspective that highlights the overwhelming reality of institutionalized racism, while also including other forms of oppression.

6. Discussion may become polarized particularly around the Black experience of white racism, leaving other people of color feeling invisible or excluded. People become lost in arguments over which oppression is the worst or most important. This typically leads to the withdrawal of those who feel their issues of oppression are marginalized in such a dialogue.

GUIDELINES FOR UNDERSTANDING PRIVILEGE AND OPPRESSION

Sara Winter (1977) long ago addressed her reactivity to discussions of racism:

> When someone pushes racism into my awareness, I feel **guilty** (that I could be doing so much more); **angry** (I don't like to feel like I'm wrong); **defensive** (I already have two Black friends . . . I worry more about racism than most whites

do—isn't that enough); **turned off** (I have other priorities in my life—with guilt about that throught); **helpless** (the problem is so big—what can I do?). I HATE TO FEEL THIS WAY. That is why I minimize race issues and let them fade from my awareness whenever possible.

Her reaction is the kind of response we want to address with guidelines to help white people stay at the table and become more conscious of the structure of their reactions. We thus offer the following list of common responses to discussions of racism. We lay out these guidelines in training to help participants monitor their own reactions and increase their awareness of and sensitivity to others.

Common White Responses to Attempts to Discuss Racism

• Distinguishing themselves from those with power and privilege by emphasizing their other oppressions: They refer to their great-grandfather, who was Cherokee, or to their own history of oppression as Irish, Jewish, gay, poor, disabled, or from abusive or mentally ill families. They say, "We experience oppression ourselves. Why focus only on racism?"

• Shifting discussion to the internalized racism of people of color against themselves or of one group against another: the issue of skin color within African American families, conflicts between Latinos or Koreans and African Americans, and so forth.

• Resisting group categories, saying: "We're just human beings"; "We do not think of people by color, culture, or class, but as unique human beings"; "You're creating the problem by forcing us into categories. It's stereotyping. I don't identify as white. It's not fair to force me into this categorization. It's reverse racism. How can you blame a whole race for a few individuals? My ancestors weren't even here during slavery. It's not fair for you to blame me for these problems."

• Saying they feel "unsafe" in an atmosphere of "political correctness," which makes them feel they are walking on eggshells. This focuses discussion on their discomfort, implicitly blaming those who are attempting to discuss oppression for making them uncomfortable. Such assertions make it impossible to have a discussion about their privilege.

• Refocusing discussion on their feelings of shame. By this they assume a talking position and keep the focus on themselves, implicitly asking others to listen or take care of their pain about their racist behavior.

• Disqualifying the issue or the one who raises it, by saying things like:

"Why do people always have to bring up the past? Slavery ended 140 years ago."

"People of color get so angry when they talk about these issues that it's

impossible to talk with them. I don't want to talk until they can deal with these issues in a more appropriate, less angry way."
"They never point out the clinical implications of these issues."

- Reacting with confused silence: "I'm certainly not a racist. I can't think of anything to say on this topic."
- Claiming to acknowledge racism, while going back to individual thinking when assessing the behavior of a person of color. Not getting excited about Rodney King or Amadu Diallo but being appalled about O. J. Simpson.

Common Responses of People of Color to Discussion of Racism

- "It's too painful and overwhelming. I feel so weary always having to lead whites in these discussions, and they never get it anyway."
- "Racism makes me feel so much rage. I hate to get into it. I have to choose my battles. Why should I go into it here?"
- "When I was a child, we could not even eat next to a white person or use their drinking fountain. And they still don't get it."
- "I wish I knew how to protect my children from racism. I worry how I will handle it the first time my child comes home having experienced a racist insult."

What White People Need to Do in Response to People of Color Discussing Their Experiences of Racism

- Resist the temptation to equalize the experience with a description of their own suffering.
- Resist refocusing the conversation on their good intentions.
- Listen and believe: Resist any response that could negate the experience that is being described. The only reasonable position for people of privilege to take is to "listen and believe" (Hardy, 2006).

CONCLUSION

To re-vision family therapy, training programs will need to use their privilege and social justice commitment to help dismantle well-established, deeply entrenched "this is the way we've always done it" approaches to clinical education that perpetuate the status quo. At the very least, we hope that training programs will take an active role in becoming more accountable for effecting cultural changes. They will need to increase the inclusion and representation of members of traditionally oppressed groups throughout the training program. If this is not immediately possible through the recruitment of trainees, faculty members, and supervisors from these groups, then it is imperative for the program to design special programs to increase visibility, exposure, and inclusion. Racist patterns are most likely to be replicated when only one member of a traditionally oppressed group is present. Whites are more likely to learn about oppression and privilege in a group in which a significant percentage ("a critical mass") are people of color, a context that rarely occurs for white people. If such perspectives are not adequately represented within an institution, seeking consultation outside one's organization for other perspectives is an important act of accountability. People of color must be represented in the hierarchy of institutions and programs. The most culturally competent structure has people of color at every level of the hierarchy. If that is not possible, consultation to the upper levels of the hierarchy from an outside group with experience dealing with racism and partnerships at other levels with consultants of color can help the organization move in this direction as well. It helps to have at least three perspectives present in any discussion to minimize polarization. Discussion becomes more meaningful when three or more perspectives are discussed together, at least until there is general acceptance of the importance of culture in clinical discussion. This is especially important because of our society's tendency to polarize: Black–white, male–female, gay–straight, rich–poor. It is always valuable to create a context in which overlapping and ambiguous differences cannot easily be resolved, because that fits better with the complexities of human experience. Presenting several groups also tends to help students see the pattern rather than the exception. Thus, although all Dominicans may not be alike, they may have certain similarities when compared with Haitians, Russians, or Greeks.

Both bringing attention to and discussing issues of race, class, and sexual orientation, as well as other experiences involving marginalization, must be regularly and consistently initiated by members of the dominant group and the hierarchy as a matter of principle. It has been our experience that conversations addressing any form of injustice have often been the responsibility of the marginalized person, while members of the majority group sit in silence, seeking safety and fearing reprisal. We all need to keep taking steps to find ways to contain opposites, contradictions and ambiguities— not oversimplifying the issues but also not obfuscating the prejudices and oppression that are defining and destroying us.

NOTE

1. In this chapter we have capitalized "Black" and lower-cased "white" in spite of the convention to do the reverse, because it seems to us that "Black" is a word which at least

to some extent was chosen by African Americans to refer to themselves, while "white" does not deserve the "specialness" of capitalization as an honor to the distinction.

REFERENCES

Green, R. J. (1998a). Race and the field of family therapy. In M. McGoldrick (Ed.), *Re-visioning family therapy* (pp. 93–110). New York: Guilford Press.

Green, R. J. (1998b). Training programs: Guidelines for multicultural transformation. In M. McGoldrick (Ed.), *Re-visioning family therapy* (pp. 111–117). New York: Guilford Press.

Hall, R. L., & Greene, B. (1994). Cultural competence in feminist family therapy: An ethical mandate. *Journal of Feminist Family Therapy, 6*(3), 5–28.

Hardy, K. V., & Laszloffy, T. A. (1995). The cultural genogram: A key to training culturally competent family therapists. *Journal of Marital and Family Therapy, 21*(3), 227–237.

Killian, K., & Hardy, K. V. (1998). Commitment to minority inclusion: A study of AAMFT conference program content and members' perceptions. *Journal of Marital and Family Therapy, 24,* 207–223.

Lee, R. E., Nichols, D. P., Nichols, W. C., & Odom, T. (2004). Trends in family therapy supervision: The past 25 years and into the future. *Journal of Marital and Family Therapy, 30,* 61–69.

Long, J., Sprenkle, D., Dyson, O., King, E., & Richardson, B. (2003). *Talking the talk and walking the walk.* Presentation at the meeting of the American Association for Marriage and Family Therapy, Long Beach, CA.

Lorde, A. (1990). *Sister outsider.* Berkeley, CA: The Crossing Press.

McDowell, T., Fang, S., Brownlee, K., Gomes Young, C., & Khanna, A. (2002). Transforming an MFT Program: A model for enhancing diversity. *Journal of Marital and Family Therapy, 28*(2), 179–191.

McDowell, T., & Jeris, L. (2004). Talking about race using critical race theory: Recent trends in the JMFT. *Journal of Marial and Family Therapy, 30,* 81–94.

McGoldrick, M., Almeida, R., Bibb, A., Moore Hines, P. M., Hudak, J., Garcia Preto, N., et al. (1999). Efforts to develop an equitable family training program. *Journal of Marital and Family Therapy.*

McGoldrick, M., Gerson, R., & Petry, S. (2008). *Genograms: Assessment and intervention* (3rd ed.). New York: Norton.

Root, M. P. P. (Ed.). (1992). In M. P. P. Root (Ed.), *Racially mixed people in America.* Thousand Oaks, CA: Sage.

Root, M. P. P. (1996). A bill of rights for racially mixed people. In M. P. P. Root (Ed.), *The multiracial experience: Racial borders as the new frontier* (pp. 3–14). Thousand Oaks, CA: Sage.

Sue, D. W., Capodilupo, C. M., Nadal, K. L., & Torino, G. C. (2007). Racial microaggressions and the power to define reality. *American Psychologist, 63,* 277–279.

Sue, D. W., Capodilupo, C. M., Torino, G. C., Bucceri, J. M., Holder, A. M. B., Nadal, K. L., et al. (2007). Racial Microaggressions in everyday life: Implications for clinical practice. *American Psychologist, 62,* 271–286.

Tatum, B. D. (1997). *Why are all the Black kids sitting together in the cafeteria and other conversations about race* (1st ed.). New York: Basic Books.

Winter, S. (1977). Rooting out racism. *Issues in Radical Therapy, 17,* 24–30.

CHAPTER 38

On Becoming a GEMM Therapist
Work Harder, Be Smarter, and *Never* Discuss Race

Kenneth V. Hardy

All of my formal education since high school has been at predominantly White institutions in which White middle-class values have subtly and profoundly shaped virtually all areas of the experiences. My training as a therapist technically began with my undergraduate degree at Penn State, followed by a master's degree at Michigan State and a doctoral degree at Florida State. I also completed two different postdoctoral training experiences at internationally acclaimed family therapy training institutes at the Mental Research Institute in Palo Alto and the Family Institute of Washington, DC. In addition to my formal education, I have had the privilege of receiving invaluable informal education and training while serving as a faculty member and clinical educator at three different American Association of Marriage and Family Therapy (AAMFT)-accredited graduate programs, as well as serving on the faculty of an internationally renowned freestanding family therapy institute. Prior to my experiences in academia, I spent close to 10 years serving as the executive director of the AAMFT Commission on Accreditation for Marriage and Family Therapy Education, which also contributed substantially to my professional development. All of these rich and varied experiences in the field taught me a great deal about what it truly takes to become a good, well-trained family therapist. It also sharpened my sensitivity to the myriad invisible, generally unacknowledged hardships and obstacles that aspiring therapists of color must endure and ultimately overcome to "make it."

The lessons that I learned in the field have affirmed what both my great-grandmother, Anna, and my parents often admonished me about during my youth. They warned over and over again that our society operates with two sets of rules, one for Whites and one for everyone else. They reminded me repeatedly: "As a Black you have to be twice as good and work twice as hard to be accepted by Whites." As a young naïve boy, I had only a cursory understanding of what they were really trying to teach me. In their efforts to prepare me for life in an unjust world that often destroys the dreams and ambitions of people of color, they emphasized the importance of hard work and striving beyond the bounds of what was expected. In those days, I thought "working harder and being twice as good" referred to concrete tasks. For example, if a school assignment required reading 10 books, I knew intuitively to complete 15, and to do it in an exemplary way. At the time, this was my only conception of what it meant to work harder and be twice as good.

Many argue that as the number of people of color who openly inter-act with Whites in contexts once considered off limits "for minorities" has increased exponentially, things have changed. When I question this change, I am constantly asked, "What about Oprah, Condoleezza Rice, Colin Powell, and Barack Obama?" The assertion is that things are different now, there is equal opportunity, that those who earn it, get it without regard to race, class, creed, or color. The prevailing belief is that there are no more litmus tests that Blacks and other people of color have to meet in order to be fully embraced by a society that claims to appreciate differences but that appears to be hopelessly attracted to sameness. In some ways our society is more open and accepting of people of color than was the case during my parents' and grandparents' eras. There are no "for Whites only" signs or physical barricades impeding the entrance of Blacks and other people of color through the doors of institutions of higher learning. There are no angry, hate-filled mobs shouting racial epithets and insisting that the "monkeys," "coons," or "nigras" go to their own schools, necessitating protection by the police or National Guard. Things have changed. Our (new) world is one of equal opportunity, in which justice is indivisible, and where *anybody* can be whatever he or she wants to be ... if he or she works hard enough! This mindset permeates much of society, and it is certainly prevalent in the field of family therapy. Yet many family therapy trainees of color find it difficult to comprehend why they seem to have so many hidden race-related struggles in their liberal, self-proclaimed culturally competent, culturally inclusive programs that espouse a commitment to social justice. If students of color struggle in an atmosphere that advocates social justice, it must be their problem! This brings me back to the concept of "working harder and being twice as good." I believe many trainees of color struggle in their training because they have difficulty negotiating the invisible criteria that are stipulated for them only. Trainees of color cannot simply train to become ordinary, run-of-the-mill family therapists. They have to become good, effective, mainstream, minority family therapists, what I refer to as *GEMM family therapists*—and believe me, becoming a GEMM therapist is hard work. It means that they must work harder and strive to be twice as good as their White counterparts. The work that is required is much more insidious and emotionally draining than anything I ever imagined from the early training of my parents and grandmother.

Becoming a GEMM is not a requirement only in the field of therapy. Most predominantly White organizations appear highly interested in recruiting, hiring, and retaining people of color who are either GEMMs or who show great promise or willingness to become them. Graduate schools and training institutes are no different. Because people of color have very little influence in shaping the culture of most predominantly White institutions, becoming a GEMM is essential for survival in virtually all major institutions of our society.

My experience suggests, and I think most White family therapy faculty members, supervisors, and trainees would attest, that if you must have a racially diverse program, it is much more comfortable and safer when there are GEMM therapists involved. As noted earlier, GEMMs are actually in demand in most predominantly White organizations. Although there may be some hazards involved in becoming a GEMM therapist, there are also tangible and measurable rewards. For example, most family therapy associations and training programs usually consider procuring at least one GEMM therapist among their highest organizational priorities—usually in the name of diversity, multiculturalism, and/or social justice.

Thus every trainee of color needs to know the rules for becoming a good effective mainstream minority therapist. He or she must approach the process of becoming a GEMM therapist as if his or her lives and viability in the field depended on it—and, in many instances, unfortunately, it does. It is imperative for trainees of color to understand that, as aspiring family therapists, they have to work harder. As trainees of color, they can ill afford to focus on *just* learning the rudiments of family therapy theory, completing clinical hours, mastering therapy, or excelling academically and intellectually. They must also do the hard work of meeting the field's expectation to become a GEMM therapist.

I offer the following tips to assist trainees of color in their efforts to survive in both a field and a society that claim to value diversity while remaining overwhelmingly committed to homogeneity.

1. *Never discuss race.* Remaining mute regarding race and racial issues is extremely important. Discussing race might reveal that you are hypersensitive about skin color or that you have unresolved racial issues that warrant resolution. If you must discuss race during a moment of weakness, use acceptable code words such as "minority," "ethnicity," "cultural diversity," or "others" to deemphasize race. Discussing race makes everyone tense and should be avoided, even if it makes matters worse for you personally.

2. *Accept that the field is color blind.* Avoid the mistake of believing that your skin color is as visible in your training program or in the field as it is in society. You must trust unquestionably that your fellow students and mentors see you as just another student—another human being—and that skin color is not an issue. The fact that all questions and cases regarding people of color are directed to the therapist of color is no reason to believe that skin color is the organizing principle. Please remember that having minority clients assigned to you and not to your White counterparts has *nothing* to do with race or skin color. Ignore questions by your White classmates regarding why all of the trainees of color interact together and just remember that these coincidences do not negate the fact that the field is color blind.

3. *Smile!* No matter how many racial slights or microaggressions you have to endure, stay pleasant, smile, and remain mannerly and polite. Having a "bad" attitude can stifle your progress. It is imperative that you smile at all times. When you feel isolated and alienated, smile; when you feel humiliated, when you feel misunderstood, when you feel the sting of discrimination, and even when Whites warmly tell you that they don't see you as Black, Asian, Latino, or Native American or never thought of you as a person of color—swallow the insult and *smile.* As a GEMM therapist, it is essential to maintain and exhibit a good, positive, GEMM-like attitude no matter what. Remember, there is no room in the field or in society for the inexplicably angry, belligerent, enraged person of color with an attitude problem. As a person of color, your *attitude* dictates your *altitude*!

4. *Become comfortable with invisibility.* Understand that your opinions and feelings count only when they are validated by a nonminority. Never seek recognition, especially from nonminorities; such arrogance is considered needy, narcissistic, and very un-GEMM-like. Any discomfort you experience accepting your invisibility may be misinterpreted as a lack of gratitude or appreciation for the opportunities you have been granted. Just keep smiling, stay pleasant, make no references to race, and remember that *gratitude* also will dictate your *latitude* in the field.

5. *Keep the faith.* No matter how compelling the evidence "appears," you must not yield to your racially based impulses or instincts that might lead you to draw erroneous and ill-advised conclusions about racial unfairness. Forget and/or ignore all socialization you received racially that has

heightened your ("hyper") sensitivity to racism. No matter what it seems like, no matter how blatantly obvious it appears to you and others like you, remember that racism does not exist in the field. Thus racism cannot ever constitute a legitimate reason for "innocent" acts that coincidentally involve exclusion, oppression, and discrimination. Understand that attempting to use racism as an excuse is merely a poor attempt to disguise your deeply rooted intrapsychic conflicts. No matter how strange or inexplicable the coincidences are that privilege Whites and malign people of color, you must maintain faith in the goodwill of White people.

6. *Become comfortable with cultural schizophrenia.* Refine your skills in racial identity bifurcation! The integration of self is antithetical to the rules of achieving the status of a GEMM therapist in the field. Instead, learn how to divide your complex, multicultural self into two definable selves (Hardy, 1993): (a) the self that has to function and survive in a field ideologically dedicated to diversity but experientially allergic to it (the *institutional self*); and (b) the self who has to continue to function and survive within your "culture of origin" (*cultural self*). Having the ability to maintain rather rigid boundaries between your institutional and cultural selves is an important skill to possess. To be successful, remember that the cultural self can never be exposed in the institutional context; to do so would be detrimental to your upward mobility and professional acceptance in the field. Most programs and the field, in general, find it off-putting and difficult to work with people of color who are too "ethnic," "too pro-Black, pro-Latino, or pro-Asian." Don't forget that whatever anxiety, sense of alienation, or marginalization you experience as a result of having to compromise your sense of self to participate in two worlds that you will realistically never completely and comfortably fit into will be regarded as *your* issue. Possessing the ability, poise, and composure to manage these critical self-of-the-therapist issues with no apparent difficulty is exactly what GEMM therapists are expected to do.

7. *Embrace the sameness–difference dilemma.* You must learn to live with the implicit contradictory messages of our field that encourage differences but reward sameness (Hardy, 1989). After all, the hallmark of being "mainstream" is to become a stockholder in the value system, ideology, and everyday practices that are mandated by the field. Again, my best advice to you is to keep smiling and stay polite, nonreactive, and grateful when you are constantly reminded of the sameness–difference dilemma. Acting oblivious to this catch-22 will help obscure the inherent contradiction in programs that espouse a commitment to diversity and work assiduously to find "qualified minorities," only to subtly and systematically strip them of their unique differences through a process of benign institutional whitewashing. This dilemma is further reinforced by the pedagogical approaches of many training programs, which strongly advocate paying attention to

differences within families but tend to blur and ignore differences among families. Unfortunately, trainees and families of color all get lumped into broad undifferentiated categories, such as "Asians," "Latinos," "Hispanics," and "Blacks," without even minimal regard for potential within-group differences.

8. *Support the profession.* Join the major family therapy organizations, but never question why minorities are underrepresented. To question the profession's conscience or commitment to inclusive practices would prevent you from becoming a GEMM therapist and possibly earn you the label of pushy, aggressive, hostile, emotional, or abrasive. Remain polite, keep smiling with a positive attitude, and keep the faith when noble, racially neutral explanations are provided as to why there have been a dearth of elected and appointed leaders of color in the field, very few minority keynote speakers at annual meetings, and no editors of color of the major family therapy journals or people of color serving on the governance of the major organizations that represent the field. It is vital that you relentlessly support the profession even when it *appears* that it doesn't see or support you.

9. *Remember, genograms don't lie.* Remain understanding, unemotional, and free of defensiveness when fellow, nonminority students probe for the markers of pathology that are associated with families of color, and maintain your composure when racial and ethnic jokes are told during the sharing of your genogram. Demonstrating an ability to "bounce back" from tough questions is the ultimate litmus test for measuring one's ability to become a GEMM family therapist. Use as your role model the African American doctoral student who retained her composure when asked during a genogram discussion, "So is it true that illegitimacy is the ultimate pathology in Black families?" Or the Korean student who remained self-contained during a genogram presentation as she described the death of an older brother in a car accident, only to be asked by a White classmate, "Is it really true that Asians have difficulty seeing while driving because their eyes are half closed?" Before responding too sensitively, a GEMM therapist should act as if questions such as these (no matter how bigoted) are legitimate because they "derive" from the genogram material presented—even though they obviously do not.

10. *Accept responsibility for minority families.* Accept the mandate that responsibility for providing effective treatment to families of color is your responsibility. Do not expect your nonminority colleagues to assume the burden of learning about minorities to enhance *their* clinical skills with this population. Developing a "multicultural perspective" is *your* responsibility. Be prepared to become an expert in treating minorities, whether you want to or not, whether you have the proper training or not. As a potential GEMM therapist, your clinical expertise is chosen for you, and it is impor-

tant that you embrace the "truth" that treating minorities is *your* expertise and *your* responsibility.

11. *Learn the correct language to use with minority families.* Learn to use terms such as "resistant," "recalcitrant," and "hard-to-engage," and use them liberally when working with poor and minority families. These terms will be particularly useful in helping you to prove that you "belong" and that you can be "objective." Frequent use of these terms is also a powerful indicator that you have taken your developing expertise in treating minority families very seriously.

12. *Learn to develop a situational systemic worldview.* Learn to think "systems" only in terms of focusing on interactions, feedback loops, and the importance of context. But when working with minorities, you must ignore these concepts. Thinking too systemically could force you to challenge many traditionally held beliefs regarding therapy with minorities. Thinking "too systemically" could be hazardous to becoming a GEMM therapist. Instead, develop a situational systemic epistemology (SSE). Failure to develop this may result in your inappropriately questioning the linearity of resistance, the "objectivity" of the DSM, and other widespread concepts about dysfunctionality as they relate to working with minorities. It may coax you into blurting out that racism and oppression seem germane to the problems experienced by minorities.

13. *Work harder, be smarter, and focus on abolishing* your *racial hang-ups.* Paramount to learning theory and acquiring clinical skills, you must work on your "issues," particularly your racial hang-ups. For example, never criticize the common practice of identifying only racial minority clients by their race in clinical notes. You should feel proud and special, rather than curious and insulted, that case notes almost always describe racial minorities by race but seldom describe Whites similarly.

14. *Strengthen the development of a minority psyche.* You must feign "sameness" by minimizing your racial differences to reify the "melting pot reality" while simultaneously possessing a "minority psyche." This is a difficult task, requiring a pretense that you are a nonminority person, while always having to act as a minority person. Be assertive, but do so skillfully from a subordinate position. You must mask your racial pain by being a nonreactive, level-headed "team player." Acknowledge racial attacks, insults, and microaggressions only among your friends; *never* appear in a public situation to "take it personally." Minorities who attempt to assert themselves from an egalitarian position are often (mis)construed as aggressive. Minorities who are advocates for minorities are often (mis)construed as racist anti-White or anti-majority. Racial pride and integrity are often (mis)construed as arrogance and rigidity. And by all means, watch your passion! Any expression of your affect, especially your passion, will be inter-

preted as anger and will compromise the safety that your White colleagues and mentors feel entitled to without exception.

15. *Develop comfort with being judged by others' standards.* The dominant group, who know too little about minorities to treat them, view themselves as knowledgeable enough to criticize them and you in your efforts to work with them. But don't act as if you notice this. Don't let judgments that you are "too hostile," "too passive," "too abrasive," "too sensitive," "too emotional," or "too loud" dampen your spirits. Patience, tolerance, and adaptability are core components of the minority psyche. Practice embracing unfounded judgments graciously, politely, and nonreactively, and remain perpetually open to the recommendations that Whites have about how you can improve your racially based shortcomings.

Becoming a GEMM therapist requires a total commitment to each of the tips noted. Never complain that the tips are contradictory or nearly impossible for you to accomplish sanely. Master these tips without becoming symptomatic and without residual affect. As a GEMM family therapist, this is all that is expected of you—no small task by anyone's standards.

POSTSCRIPT

Our society both in and outside the world of family therapy has changed appreciably since the days that my parents were students. Yet there is still much work for each of us to do. I believe the lessons from my great-grandmother and my parents are still true even today. In many respects, trainees of color still must work harder, be smarter, and be twice as good to make it. Perhaps what has changed is the nature of the work. Although I presented these tips in a sardonic manner with a tinge of levity, they are not funny … and none of this is a joke. We simply must change our way. It is my heartfelt hope that the re-visioning of family therapy will ignite a revolution that will radically change how we prepare the next generation of trainees of color to become family therapists. Only then will each of us—Black, White, Asian, Latino, and Native American—be able to declare proudly the long-awaited and much-deserved death of the GEMM therapist.

REFERENCES

Hardy, K. V. (1989). The theoretical myth of sameness: A critical issue in family therapy training and treatment. *Journal of Psychotherapy and the Family, 6*(1–2), 17–33.

Hardy, K. V. (1993, July). War of the worlds. *Family Therapy Networker,* 50–57.

Index